THE S. MARK TAPER FOUNDATION

IMPRINT IN JEWISH STUDIES

BY THIS ENDOWMENT

THE S. MARK TAPER FOUNDATION SUPPORTS

THE APPRECIATION AND UNDERSTANDING

OF THE RICHNESS AND DIVERSITY OF

JEWISH LIFE AND CULTURE

Beyond the Pale

STUDIES ON THE HISTORY OF SOCIETY AND CULTURE

Victoria E. Bonnell and Lynn Hunt, Editors

Beyond the Pale

The Jewish Encounter with Late Imperial Russia

Benjamin Nathans

UNIVERSITY OF CALIFORNIA PRESS
Berkeley   Los Angeles   London

University of California Press
Berkeley and Los Angeles, California

University of California Press, Ltd.
London, England

© 2002 by the Regents of the University of California

Library of Congress Cataloging-in-Publication Data

Nathans, Benjamin.
    Beyond the pale : the Jewish encounter with late imperial Russia /
Benjamin Nathans.
        p.   cm.—(Studies on the history of society and culture ; 45)
    Includes bibliographical references (p.) and index.
    ISBN 0–520–20830–7(Cloth : alk. paper)
    1. Jews—Russia—History—19th century.   2. Jews—Russia—
Saint Petersburg—History—20th century.   3. Jews—Cultural
assimilations—Russia.   4. Russia—Ethnic relations.   I. Title.
II. Series.

DS135.R9 .N38   2001
947'.004924—dc21   2001003513

Manufactured in the United States of America

11   10   09   08   07   06   05   04   03   02
10   9   8   7   6   5   4   3   2   1

The paper used in this publication meets the minimum requirements of ANSI/NISO Z39.48–1992 (R 1997) (*Permanence of Paper*).♾

To my mother
Joanne Gomberg Nathans
and to the memory of my father
Daniel Nathans (1928–1999)
my greatest teachers

CONTENTS

MAPS, ILLUSTRATIONS, AND TABLES

ix

TABLES

ACKNOWLEDGMENTS

The long list of people to whom I owe a debt of gratitude in connection with this book begins with my parents, Daniel and Joanne Nathans. They nurtured in me, among other things, a thirst for ideas and a love of language that have sustained me to this day. Although my father did not live to see this book appear in print, I hope that something of his grand spirit of inquiry lives in its pages.

Along with my parents, many friends and colleagues generously gave me the benefit of their comments on drafts of part or all of the book. They include Richard Brody, Richard Cohen, Lois Dubin, Ben Eklof, ChaeRan Freeze, Christoph Gassenschmidt, Daniel Gordon, Herbert Kaplan, Samuel Kassow, John Klier, Helene Moglen, Seth Moglen, Susan Morrissey, my brother Eli Nathans, Alexander Orbach, Derek Penslar, Janet Rabinowitch, Moses Rischin, the late Hans Rogger, David Sorkin, Shaul Stampfer, Michael Stanislawski, Richard Stites, Robert Weinberg, the late Richard Webster, Amir Weiner, Reginald Zelnik, and Steven Zipperstein. For their advice on the subject of my research as well as on the fine art of working in former Soviet archives, I am indebted to I. A. Al´tman, G. M. Deych, D. A. El´iashevich, Gregory Freeze, G. I. Ippolitova, V. E. Kel´ner, John Klier, and S. I. Varekhova, as well as to staff members at the various archives listed in the bibliography. Librarians at the University of California at Berkeley, Harvard University, the New York Public Library, Indiana University, the YIVO Institute for Jewish Research, the Hoover Institution, and the University of Pennsylvania all provided vital assistance. Katia Guth-Dreyfus of Basel, great-granddaughter of Horace Gintsburg, was an important source of information about her ancestors, generously making unpublished family memoirs available to me. Harriet F. Sigal of New York similarly provided me with unpublished family memoirs concerning Shaul Ginzburg and other figures in the late imperial

Russian-Jewish intelligentsia. To both I am profoundly grateful. Michael Blacher, Robert Geraci, Susan Morrissey, Steven Rappaport, and Theodore Weeks identified or helped procure important archival documents for my research.

The idea for this project was born during my first year in graduate school at Berkeley, in a seminar taught by Reggie Zelnik. Reggie's qualities as mentor, reader, and adviser—and, it should be added, as *mentsh*—are already legendary, and I count the chance to have studied with him as one of the great pieces of good fortune in my life. His steady encouragement, his good humor, and above all his consistently illuminating comments on my work made Reggie as close to an ideal reader as one could hope for. He has set an inspiring example of what it means to be a scholar and teacher. I would also like to thank Robert Alter and the late Amos Funkenstein, who along with Reggie Zelnik served as members of my dissertation committee at Berkeley and whose work I deeply admire. The esteemed ethnographer and historian Nataliia Vasilievna Iukhneva generously served as my adviser during an invaluable year of research in Russia.

I am grateful to my former colleagues in the History and Literature Program at Harvard University and at Indiana University in Bloomington for their generous friendship and support. In Philadelphia I am similarly lucky to be surrounded by colleagues who have made the University of Pennsylvania an extraordinary intellectual home. At Indiana and at Penn I benefited from the help of a number of research assistants: Lindsey Barton, Dina Danon, Tamar Kaplan, Michele Katz, David Khantsis, Greg Klein, Dana Ohren, Lynn Sargeant, Matt Thornton, and Anya Vodopyanov. In a category all her own is Deborah Broadnax of Penn's History Department, whose diligence and good spirits are a constant wonder.

At the University of California Press, Stanley Holwitz, Mary Severance, Laura Pasquale, and Barbara Salazar did everything to ensure that *Beyond the Pale* moved beyond the manuscript. My thanks also to Victoria Bonnell and Lynn Hunt for including my book in their distinguished series.

To my wife, Nancy Silverman, I owe the greatest debt of all. It was she who lived through the creation of this book, keeping a steady hand through the highs and lows of the entire project. Her love and companionship made bearable the otherwise intolerable solitude that writing a book requires. Our children, Gabriel, Ilana, and Dora, have been a constant delight and distraction. One day, I suspect, they will come to understand what their father was doing in the faraway city that Gabriel called "Pete Seegersburg."

Finally, I thank the following institutions for their generous financial support: the Social Science Research Council, the International Research and Exchanges Board, and the National Council for Eurasian and East European Research, all of which are supported in part with funds provided by the U.S. Department of State (Title VIII Program) and/or the National Endowment for the Humanities; the Andrew W. Mellon Foundation; the American Council of Learned Societies; the U.S. Department of Education (Fulbright-Hays program); the Memorial Foundation for Jewish Culture; the Lucius N. Littauer Foundation; the University of California at Berkeley; Indiana University, including its Russian and East European Institute; and the University of Pennsylvania Research Foundation. None of these institutions is responsible for the views expressed in this book.

ABBREVIATIONS

GARF (formerly TsGAOR)	Gosudarstvennyi arkhiv rossiiskoi federatsii, Moscow
PSZ	*Polnoe sobranie zakonov rossiiskoi imperii*
RGIA (formerly TsGIA SSSR)	Rossiiskii gosudarstvennyi istoricheskii arkhiv, St. Petersburg
RNB (formerly GPB)	Rossiiskaia natsional´naia biblioteka, otdel rukopisei, St. Petersburg
SPb-FIV-RAN (formerly LOIV AN-SSSR)	Sankt-Peterburgskii Filial Instituta Vostokovedeniia Rossiiskoi Akademii Nauk, St. Petersburg
TsGIA-SPb (formerly TsGIAL)	Tsentral´nyi gosudarstvennyi istoricheskii arkhiv goroda Sankt-Peterburga, St. Petersburg
YIVO	YIVO Institute for Jewish Research, New York, Tcherikover Archive, Horace Guenzburg [Gintsburg] Papers

Introduction

The Russian–Jewish Encounter

Take me back with you, history has left me out.
. . . I have no business being your future.
CYNTHIA OZICK, *"Envy; or, Yiddish in America"*

"When I was a little girl, the world was divided into two parts; namely, Polotzk, the place where I lived, and a strange land called Russia. All the little girls I knew lived in Polotzk, with their fathers and mothers and friends. Russia was the place where one's father went on business. It was so far off, and so many bad things happened there, that one's mother and grandmother and grown-up aunts cried at the railroad station, and one was expected to be sad and quiet for the rest of the day, when the father departed for Russia." So begins "Within the Pale," Chapter 1 of Mashke (later Mary) Antin's celebrated autobiography, *The Promised Land*. With time, Antin learned that Polotzk had much in common with the nearby town of Vitebsk, that Vitebsk was in turn linked to the city of Vilna, and that all three were parts of a larger whole known as the Pale of Permanent Jewish Settlement, which defined the boundaries of Jewish residence in the empire of the tsars and, in her mind, the invisible line separating Jews and Gentiles. And yet, Antin recalled, "How I wanted to see Russia!"[1]

Beyond the Pale is about the crossing of visible and invisible boundaries in the Russian Empire during the nineteenth and early twentieth centuries. Its subject is the encounter between Jews and Russians, the dynamics of Jewish integration into Russian society, and the various roles played in this process by individuals, social groups, and the imperial state.

We are accustomed to thinking of Jews in imperial Russia as the least integrated of all the European Jewish communities, as quintessential outsiders and scapegoats for a regime that eventually collapsed in 1917 under the weight of its own backwardness. It is a view powerfully reinforced by the mem-

---

1. Mary Antin, *The Promised Land* (New York, 1997), pp. 5–7. Antin's memoir was first published in 1912.

ories of more than two million emigrants fleeing pogroms and poverty, canonized in the paintings of Marc Chagall and the popular stories of Yiddish writers such as Sholem Aleichem.[2] More often than not, we picture nineteenth-century Russian Jews as residents of hermetically Jewish shtetls, small hamlets saturated with tradition and authenticity, where people and livestock freely mingled. Those who broke out of this world seemed to face the stark choice of revolution or exodus: either join the struggle to overthrow the oppressive regime of the Romanovs or abandon Russia and the Old World altogether, to settle in the New World or in the ancient homeland, the land of Israel.

After the Revolution of 1917 perceptions dramatically reversed, as Jews suddenly appeared as consummate insiders in the young Soviet state. They were extraordinarily visible in the upper echelons of the Communist Party, the Red Army, and the Cheka (the security apparatus that eventually became the KGB), achieving a level of integration within institutions of state power unmatched in any country at any time before or since (apart, of course, from ancient and modern Israel). In fact, Jewish visibility in the young Soviet state was even broader. In the 1920s and 1930s, Jews were a much-noted presence across virtually the entire white-collar sector of Soviet society, as journalists, physicians, scientists, academics, writers, engineers, economists, NEPmen, entertainers, and more.[3]

How are we to make sense of these disparate impressions, stemming from two adjacent historical periods that together barely encompass a single human life span? Was the Russian Revolution responsible for transforming the Jews, overnight as it were, from quintessential outsiders to consummate insiders? One cannot escape the problem merely by pointing out that "outsiders" and "insiders" refer to different subgroups within the Jewish population, or, as a Soviet-era comedian once put it, that "the Trotskys make the revolution and the Bronshteins pay for it" (Bronshtein being Trotsky's original surname). Instead, the goal of my book is to demonstrate that Jewish integration into Russian society began long before the Revolution of 1917, that its origins lie not so much in revolutionary rupture as in the particular strategies of reform practiced by both the Old Regime and new Jewish elites, and that its profound consequences—for Russians as well as Jews—were already apparent well before the Bolsheviks changed the course of Russian history.

The Russian–Jewish encounter is an essential part of the story of how and

---

2. On popular images of prerevolutionary Russian Jewry see Steven J. Zipperstein, *Imagining Russian Jewry: Memory, History, Identity* (Seattle, 1999).

3. Salo W. Baron, *The Russian Jew under Tsars and Soviets* (New York, 1987), pp. 213–18. "NEPmen" refers to capitalist middlemen whom the Bolsheviks reluctantly allowed to operate under the New Economic Policy (NEP) in the 1920s.

why the largest Jewish community in the world began its complex passage to modernity not in any of the various new worlds—the Soviet Union, the United States, or the Jewish settlements in Palestine—but in the old, under an old regime, and in the peculiar circumstances of a relatively backward but dynamic empire. The Russian–Jewish encounter was in fact emblematic of Russia's imperial dilemma, an abiding concern not just for the tsarist state, straining to maintain its grip on a kalaidoscopically diverse country, but for society as well, and more precisely for the civil society that was emerging, hesitantly, under the last three tsars.

Although the encounter between Russians and Jews formally began with St. Petersburg's annexation of eastern Poland at the end of the eighteenth century, as a result of which the Romanovs unintentionally acquired some half a million Jewish subjects, this event marked the beginning only of tsarist *administration* of the Jews. As they had done previously in the Polish Commonwealth, the Jews continued for a time to maintain a relatively high degree of communal autonomy, living as a distinct estate among Poles, Ukrainians, Belorussians, and Lithuanians, in what was now the western borderland of the Russian Empire. Not until the middle of the nineteenth century, in the wake of growing centrifugal pressures within the Jewish world as well as significant shifts in official policy, did Jews in noticeable numbers begin to speak and read Russian, to migrate to the empire's Russian heartland, and to seek out a place in Russia's social order. Only in the 1860s did the now familiar term "Russian Jew" (*russkii evrei*) gain popular currency.[4]

During the last three decades of the nineteenth century, social and geographic mobility among significant portions of the Jewish population transformed the Jews' relationship to Russian society and the imperial state. Jews became an unmistakable feature of Russia's fin-de-siècle social landscape and of public and official discourse about social change. In the words of a leading study of Russia as a multinational empire, "By the end of the nineteenth century, the Jewish Question stood at the center of discussion [about nationality], and the Jews became the most important object . . . of nationalities policy."[5]

Russia, of course, was hardly the only country in Europe where the so-called Jewish Question took on extraordinary public prominence. On the contrary, during the "long nineteenth century" (1789–1917), which was also

---

4. The earliest usage of the term I have been able to find occurred in an 1856 petition to the government from Evzel Gintsburg and other Jewish merchants; see RGIA, f. 1269, op. 1, d. 61, l. 4. By 1860 the term "Russian Jews" was part of the masthead of the Odessa newspaper *Razsvet*.

5. Andreas Kappeler, *Rußland als Vielvölkerreich: Entstehung, Geschichte, Zerfall* (Munich, 1992), p. 220.

the century of Jewish emancipation, the Jews became, and came to be perceived as, *the* pan-European minority.[6] For this reason, and because of the primacy of Europe in the minds of nineteenth-century Russians, Russian Jews, and the historians who study them, the dominant framework for the study of Jews in tsarist Russia has been the contrasting historical experience of Jewish communities west of the Russian Empire. Like Europe itself, Ashkenaz (the broad swathe of territory inhabited by Yiddish-speaking Jews, extending from Amsterdam to Zhitomir) has typically been conceptualized as containing two divergent zones, west and east. "West" refers to the large but relatively thinly populated (by Jews, that is) space between the Atlantic coast and the eastern border of Prussia; "east" refers to the far more concentrated Jewish communities of Poland, Austrian Galicia, and the Russian Pale of Settlement.

In simple demographic terms—absolute numbers and relative concentration—Jews in late nineteenth-century Russia vastly overshadowed their counterparts in Western Europe. The approximately 5.2 million Jews counted in 1897 in Russia's first empire-wide census easily outnumbered the rest of European Jewry (roughly 3.5 million) and positively dwarfed the Jewish populations of individual countries such as Germany (in 1900, 555,000 including Alsace-Lorraine), France (115,000), and Great Britain (200,000 including Northern Ireland). Only Austria-Hungary, with some 2 million Jews, came close.[7]

When these figures are considered as a percentage of the total population of the respective countries, the differences look somewhat less dramatic: West European Jews generally accounted for between 0.5 and 2 percent, while those in the Russian Empire accounted for just over 4 percent. But tsarist legislation restricting Jewish residence ensured that in the Pale their proportion of the population was closer to 12 percent. And since Jews were more likely than non-Jews to live in towns and cities rather than villages, on the local level they frequently constituted a large minority, and in towns such as Berdichev and Bialystok an absolute majority.[8] Even in the context of the empire as a whole, moreover, the 5.2 million Jews counted in 1897 were the fifth largest ethnic group (following, in descending order, Russians, Ukrainians, Poles, and Belorussians) among the more than one hundred ethnic

6. The term "Jewish Question" first appeared precisely in the sense of a Europe-wide social-political issue in Jean Czynski's pamphlet *Question des Juifs polonais, envisagée comme question européenne* (Paris, 1833). See Jacob Toury, "'The Jewish Question': A Semantic Approach," *Leo Baeck Institute Year Book* 11 (1966): 90.

7. See "Population," in *Encyclopedia Judaica* (Jerusalem, 1972), 13: 889–92.

8. Boris Brutskus, *Statistika evreiskogo naseleniia: Raspredelenie po territorii, demograficheskie i kul'turnye priznaki evreiskogo naseleniia po dannym perepisi 1897 g.* (St. Petersburg, 1909).

groups in the Russian Empire. They thus constituted the largest non-Slavic as well as the largest non-Christian ethnic group.[9]

Across the nineteenth century, the Jews' physical concentration in the Pale sustained, and was sustained by, a distinctive way of life considerably more removed from that of the surrounding population than was then the case with Jews in Western Europe. Russian Jewry possessed its own languages (Yiddish and Hebrew), forms of dress, characteristic economic pursuits (commercial, financial, or artisanal, as opposed to agricultural), and a dense network of religious, educational, legal, and charitable institutions whose task it was to sustain tradition as well as to secure the basic needs of the poor. These factors, together with the persistence of officially sanctioned legal discrimination, helped preserve Judaism not only as a religion but as a distinct social order.

To say that in the early nineteenth century Russian Jewry formed something like a society unto itself, however, is not to deny the presence in that society of significant divisions and tensions. The Hasidic schism, the last Jewish mass movement to derive wholly from indigenous sources, profoundly divided communities across the Pale, and occasionally led to conflicts that culminated in appeals to Gentile authorities for intervention.[10] By creating what was virtually an alternative rabbinate—indeed, by recasting the nature of rabbinic authority itself—Hasidism weakened the grip of the traditional oligarchy of wealth and learning. But the Hasidim did not seek intercourse with the non-Jewish world for its own sake. Nor, by and large, did their Jewish opponents, the *mitnagdim* (literally, "those who oppose [Hasidism]"). By contrast, the small clusters of *maskilim* (partisans of the Jewish Enlightenment, or *Haskalah*) that began to appear at the end of the eighteenth century in Shklov, Vilna, and elsewhere were positively eager to work with Gentile authorities in the cause of Jewish reform. Their faith in the good intentions of "enlightened" secular rulers made such an arrangement desirable; their small numbers and extreme isolation within Russian Jewry made it appear necessary. During the nineteenth century, Russian Jewry was not simply a reser-

---

9. Jews outnumbered Estonians, Latvians, and Lithuanians combined (4.1 million), Tatars (3.7 million), Kazaks (3.1 million), Georgians (1.4 million), and Armenians (1.2 million). While the empire's Muslims totaled some 14 million, they were divided into numerous ethnic and linguistic groups (e.g., Tatars, Kazaks, Bashkirs, Uzbeks). See Henning Bauer, Andreas Kappeler, and Brigitte Roth, eds., *Die Nationalitäten des Russischen Reiches in der Volkszählung von 1897*, vol. 2: *Ausgewählte Daten* (Stuttgart, 1991), pp. 77–78.

10. G. M. Deich, ed., *Tsarskoe pravitel'stvo i khasidskoe dvizhenie v Rossii: Arkhivnye dokumenty* (N.p., 1994). On the decline of the Jews' internal mechanisms of government during the first half of the nineteenth century, see Eli Lederhendler, *The Road to Modern Jewish Politics: Political Tradition and Political Reconstruction in the Jewish Community of Tsarist Russia* (New York, 1989), esp. pp. 11–57.

voir of tradition but a cauldron of intramural conflicts whose effects were to have a vital impact on the Russian–Jewish encounter.

On the whole, the story of modern Jewish communities in the western half of Europe has been organized around the dissolution of traditional Jewish autonomy and the effects of the resulting contact with European societies and cultures, usually encapsulated under the theme of "emancipation and assimilation" or "the encounter with modernity."[11] In the historiography concerning the Jews of imperial Russia, by contrast, these themes have found only limited resonance. With a topheavy, authoritarian regime and an overwhelmingly peasant society, imperial Russia appeared to offer an unlikely environment for emancipation or assimilation, or for that matter modernity. As a result, historians of Russian Jewry have focused largely on the turn *away* from the Western model: on Jewish participation in various efforts to topple the tsarist regime and fashion a radically egalitarian society; to reconstitute Jewish autonomy in new, secular forms; or to defend and reinvigorate Judaism in its distinctly East European form.[12]

The Western model of the Jewish passage to modernity has often woven together what were originally two distinct strands: the external drama of revolutionary emancipation by the National Assembly in Paris and the internal drama of the Haskalah and religious reform, centered in Berlin.[13] In this respect it bears a certain resemblance to Marx's model of capitalist society, which blended in an equally contrived manner the economy of industrial Britain with the politics of bourgeois France. And as in the case of Marxism, the disentangling of historically distinct strands of Jewish experience has begun to yield a strikingly new picture. In recent years, historians have stepped back from the mesmerizing events in Paris and Berlin in order to explore the more nuanced horizons of Jewish experience elsewhere in Europe.[14] Just as the French Revolution is no longer regarded as the paradigmatic path for the transition from Old to New Regime, so revolutionary emancipation, with its undertones of rupture and discontinuity, can no longer be taken as the norm for European Jewry as a whole. Nor can the ideologies of assimilation

11. For a recent and explicitly comparative survey of Jewish emancipation, see Pierre Birnbaum and Ira Katznelson, eds., *Paths of Emancipation: Jews, States, and Citizenship* (Princeton, 1995).

12. Two important exceptions to this trend are Louis Greenberg, *The Jews in Russia: The Struggle for Emancipation* (1944; rpt. New Haven, 1976), and more recently Michael Stanislawski, *For Whom Do I Toil? Judah Leib Gordon and the Crisis of Russian Jewry* (New York, 1988).

13. Jonathan Frankel, "Assimilation and the Jews in Nineteenth-Century Europe: Towards a New historiography?" in Frankel and Steven Zipperstein, eds., *Assimilation and Community: The Jews in Nineteenth-Century Europe* (Cambridge, 1992), p. 10.

14. The best and most recent example is Lois C. Dubin, *The Port Jews of Habsburg Trieste: Absolutist Politics and Enlightenment Culture* (Stanford, 1999). See also the essays collected in Jacob Katz, ed., *Toward Modernity: The European Jewish Model* (New Brunswick, 1987).

and religious reform that emerged in the wake of the Haskalah, which now appears far less revolutionary in its origins than it did to historians a generation ago. If their new status as citizens (or as secularly educated subjects) induced some European Jews to abandon traditional modes of group solidarity, many others responded by adopting new, voluntary forms of collective cohesion and identity.

Historians of Russian Jewry, to be sure, have scarcely needed to liberate themselves from the Paris–Berlin axis of modern Jewish history. Russian Jews were cast very early—already in the nineteenth century, in fact—as outsiders not just in Russia but in the pan-European saga of Jewish emancipation. If the Jews of imperial Russia have been situated within the European trajectory at all, it has been in the preemancipation stage of that trajectory, an analogy vividly impressed upon the minds of contemporaries by the persistence in Russia of such "medieval" practices as residential restrictions, expulsions, accusations of ritual murder, and popular violence against Jews.

But the "otherness" of Russian Jewry has consisted of far more than the enduring disabilities imposed by an allegedly archaic regime and the preservation of a traditional way of life. It is a commonplace of Jewish (especially Zionist) historiography that the modern Jewish revolution, the Jewish counterpart to the classic national revolutions of modern European history, found its epicenter precisely in the Russian Empire, and in no small measure as a result of the "medieval" depredations that Jews faced there. Excluded from what appeared to be European Jewry's Faustian bargain of emancipation in return for assimilation—so the argument runs—substantial numbers of Russian Jews were driven to pursue a different modernity. Their inspiration lay in the idea of reestablishing political sovereignty in the ancient Jewish homeland, or of building a social democracy in Russia in which a secular Jewish communal life could flourish, or in the countless crisscrossings of these two principal forces, nationalism and socialism. And all this decades before Russia's own revolutionary transformation in 1917.

Historians such as Jonathan Frankel and David Vital have placed this distinctive trajectory at the heart of their rich and influential works on Russian Jewry.[15] In contrast to their Western counterparts, Frankel has written, Russian Jews moved "directly from a preliberal to a postliberal state of development, from medieval community to projects for national revival, from a religious to a social and secular messianism."[16] The spark that allegedly fired this dramatic leap across historical epochs was the explosion of anti-Jewish

---

15. Jonathan Frankel, *Prophecy and Politics: Socialism, Nationalism, and the Russian Jews, 1862–1917* (New York, 1981); idem, "The Crisis of 1881–82 as a Turning Point in Modern Jewish History," in David Berger, ed., *The Legacy of Jewish Migration: 1881 and Its Impact* (New York, 1983), pp. 9–22; David Vital, *The Origins of Zionism* (Oxford, 1975).

16. Frankel, *Prophecy and Politics*, p. 2.

violence that swept across much of the Pale after the assassination of Tsar Alexander II in March 1881. Although a handful of intellectuals had previously articulated the idea of rejecting emancipation and assimilation in favor of autonomous national renewal, the Russian setting in general and the pogroms of 1881–82 in particular produced a crisis that transformed the idea into mass movements.

Crisis, in fact, has long been the central motif and the leading explanatory mechanism in the historiography of East European Jewry.[17] Like the examiner's question of naming a period in British history when the middle class was not rising, the historiography of East European Jewry, taken as a whole, leaves one wondering when the Jews were not in a state of crisis. Crisis has been invoked as both a cause and an effect of messianic movements, Hasidism, the Haskalah, and the mass political movements of the late nineteenth century. "Crises" of the "traditional Jewish community" have been located in the mid–seventeenth century (in the wake of the Chmielnicki massacres), the mid–eighteenth century (a result of the Hasidic schism, the Haidamak uprising, and/or the decline of the Polish monarchy), the early nineteenth century (with the extension of compulsory military service to Jews in the Russian Empire and the subsequent abolition of communal executive authority by the tsarist government), in the 1880s (after the wave of pogroms), during the First World War (due to massive expulsions of Jews from Russia's western borderlands), the early Soviet years (a product of revolution, pogroms, and rapid assimilation), and finally—and most emphatically—in the Holocaust. The shtetl, it would seem, has died a thousand deaths.

The reluctance to conceive of any path away from tradition other than that which leads through crisis threatens unwittingly to return the historiography of Russian and East European Jewry back to what the historian Salo Baron famously disparaged as the "lachrymose conception of Jewish history."[18] To be sure, Jews did face certain profound crises, and the perception of crisis cannot be discounted as a historical force in its own right. As Frankel has argued, moreover, crises can also serve as diagnostic instruments, moments when "forces normally dormant explod[e] into view."[19] But crises, like revolutions, are surely not the only moments of truth or the only forms

17. On crisis and decline as forms of historical explanation, see Randolph Starn, "Historians and Crisis," *Past & Present*, 52 (August 1971): 3–22, and idem, "Meaning-Levels in the Theme of Historical Decline," *History and Theory* 14 (1975): 1–31.

18. Salo Baron, "Ghetto and Emancipation," *Menorah Journal* 14 (June 1928): 526. The most influential statement of the crisis paradigm in modern Jewish history remains Jacob Katz, *Tradition and Crisis: Jewish Society at the End of the Middle Ages* (New York, 1961), reissued in 1993 in a new translation from the original Hebrew.

19. Jonathan Frankel, *The Damascus Affair: "Ritual Murder," Politics, and the Jews in 1840* (Cambridge, 1997), p. 2.

of historical change. We should be skeptical of their ready-made dramatic structure and the alarming frequency with which they are invoked.

According to what one might call the crisis paradigm, the pogroms of 1881–82 were the catalyst of modern Jewish politics in prerevolutionary Russia, a decisive turning point in Russian-Jewish history and indeed modern Jewish history as a whole.[20] But there have been important qualifications and amendments to this view. Studies have shown that the breakdown of medieval forms of community among Russian Jews began nearly a century before 1881, and was driven as much by intramural religious and social tensions as by external force.[21] Others have noted the emergence of Jewish radicalism (and substantial emigration) before the pogroms, or have stressed the enduring role of religious rather than secular messianism in the formation of Zionist movements, before as well as after 1881.[22] And still others have questioned the role of ideology per se in the transformation of Russian-Jewish life, apart from the intelligentsia, proposing instead that a largely pragmatic process of acculturation or "embourgeoisement" was an equally powerful current.[23]

Taken together, these responses do more than just complicate the periodization of the Russian–Jewish encounter. I believe they unsettle the entire notion of a revolutionary "leaping of phases" among Russian Jews, even one that has been nuanced so as to distinguish it (as both Frankel and Vital are careful to do) from the classic European revolutions involving machineries of state power and mass violence. I believe they point to a kind of Tocquevillian reenvisioning that seeks not to deny the profound upheaval that occurred in Russian Jewry (just as Tocqueville never denied that a revolution occurred in France in 1789) but rather to reveal the subtler forms of change as well as continuities that bridge the moment of crisis.

The debate over the nature of the Jewish passage to modernity and the relevance of the Russian setting for that passage form the point of departure

20. Frankel makes the case for "this one year, May 1881 to May 1882 . . . as of unique importance in modern Jewish history [and] in many ways a form of revolution." See Frankel, "Crisis of 1881–82," p. 9. Similarly, Vital (*Origins of Zionism*, p. 59) asserts that "the lasting consequence of the events of 1881–84 was . . . to destroy for all except an insignificant minority any real hope that Russia would move, however slowly, towards more liberal rule and towards the legal emancipation of the Jews in particular."

21. Lederhendler, *Road to Modern Jewish Politics;* Michael Stanislawski, *Tsar Nicholas I and the Jews: The Transformation of Jewish Society in Russia, 1825–1855* (Philadelphia, 1983).

22. See, for example, Y. Kaniel, *Hemshekh u-tmurah: Ha-yishuv ha-yashan ve-hayishuv he-hadash be-tkufat ha-ʿaliyah ha-shniyah* (Jerusalem, 1981), and A. Morgenstern, *Meshihiut ve-yishuv erets-yisrael be-mahatsit ha-rishonah shel ha-meʾah ha-19* (Jerusalem, 1985). For a summary of reservations regarding the notion of 1881–82 as a defining moment, see Stanislawski, *For Whom Do I Toil?* pp. 146–47.

23. See Stanislawksi, *For Whom Do I Toil?* pp. 4–6; Steven Zipperstein, *The Jews of Odessa: A Cultural History, 1794–1881* (Stanford, 1986), pp. 3–11.

for the present book. I contend that an emphasis on crisis and revolutionary rupture has obscured an important dimension of Russian Jewry's experience that lies well within the orbit of European Jewry. For despite relatively
unfavorable conditions, the historical trajectory of Russian Jewry was profoundly shaped by aspirations for civic emancipation and social integration.
These aspirations separated what Frankel labels the "medieval" and the
"postliberal" currents of Russian-Jewish life, and in fact competed simultaneously with both. Indeed, the postliberal movements that arose among Jews
in fin-de-siècle Russia cannot be fully understood without reference to their
explicit self-distancing from the hopes and perils of integration.

A corollary of my claim that aspirations for emancipation and integration
played an important role in Jewish life in late imperial Russia is the notion
that the Russian context, and the Jewish encounter with that context, gave
a specific texture to those aspirations and the attempts to realize them.[24] The
significance of the Russian setting for Jewish development (and for Russian-
Jewish relations), I will argue, went far beyond the official denial of legal
equality on the one hand and the lure of revolutionary politics on the other.
By the middle of the nineteenth century, Russia had begun to develop its
own distinctly "combined and uneven" forms of modernity, spurred on by
an absolutist state that periodically displayed an extraordinary zeal for radically reshaping society. As a result, during the half-century before the revolution of 1917, the Russian Empire was the scene of tremendous ferment.
Within the inherited social grid of legally defined estates and religious confessions there emerged new groups whose coherence was grounded in education, occupation, and class. A handful of cities became modern me-
tropolises even as they retained many features of preindustrial life. And an
embryonic civil society, whose most characteristic element was not a bourgeois middle class but a remarkably diverse intelligentsia, created the framework for new kinds of contacts across lines of nationality and religion. This
is the context of accelerating change and social dislocation in which I have
attempted to situate the Jewish encounter with Russia.

Three factors help account for the prevailing tendency to sidestep the problems of emancipation and integration in Russian-Jewish history. First, until
rather recently, Jewish integrationists in imperial Russia have been seen

---

24. With some reluctance, I employ the widely used scholarly term "late imperial Russia"
to designate the period between the emancipation of the serfs in 1861 and the Revolution of
1917. My reluctance stems from the dual anachronism built into the term: first, contemporaries
certainly did not know that tsarism was entering its final years, and second, the imperial phase
of Russia's history did not end in 1917 but was revived, against all odds and with significant
changes, under Bolshevik rule.

through the prism of their contemporary caricatures as Uncle Toms, tainted by association with the Old Regime (Jewish as well as Russian) and by their reliance on "archaic" forms of influence such as wealth and personal intercession. The "assimilationist" epithet, borrowed from contemporary Jewish polemics, has allowed historians to all but dismiss those who wanted and expected Russia, and Russia's Jews, to follow the European path. Few of the individuals to whom this label was applied, however, accepted or used it. In fact, the charge of assimilationism was frequently hurled by those who themselves had once subscribed to the goals of emancipation and integration, only to repudiate them in favor of more radical solutions. Countless figures in the Zionist and Jewish labor movements "returned" to the Jewish people in one form or another.[25] By definition, to return one must first leave, and leaving usually involved an initial faith in the possibility or necessity of integration. In branding their opponents "assimilationists," therefore, representatives of the radical Jewish movements were often engaged in an ongoing act of purging themselves of their own former identities. Traces of this ritual frequently made their way into the memoir literature, and from there have entered into the historiography.

The recent reorientation in the study of European Jewry offers a useful analytic distinction that helps move the debate beyond the categories established by the historical actors. For the purposes of this study, *assimilation* should be understood as a process culminating in the disappearance of a given group as a recognizably distinct element within a larger society. By contrast, *acculturation* signifies a form of adaptation to the surrounding society that alters rather than erases the criteria of difference, especially in the realm of culture and identity. *Integration* is the counterpart of acculturation (though the two do not necessarily go hand in hand) in the social realm—whether institutional (e.g., schooling), geographic (patterns of residential settlement), or economic (occupational profile).[26] A further distinction can be drawn be-

---

25. One thinks of individuals such as Moshe Leib Lilienblum, the would-be cosmopolitan turned Zionist and author of the influential autobiography *Hatte'ot Ne'urim* (Sins of Youth, 1876); Leon Pinsker, a major figure in the Society for the Spread of Enlightenment among the Jews of Russia before he wrote the famous pamphlet *Autoemancipation!* (1882) and helped found the Hibbat Tsiyon (Love of Zion) movement; Simon Dubnov, the great historian who began as an integrationist par excellence before turning to Jewish nationalism and the doctrine of autonomism; Vladimir Medem, baptized by his Jewish parents and educated in Russian schools, only to become a leader of the Bund; the writer and ethnographer Shlomo Rapoport, better known as Ansky, a *narodnik* (populist) consumed by the plight of the Russian peasantry who eventually returned to the Jewish national cause.

26. Fruitful applications of this distinction in modern Jewish history can be found in Todd Endelman, *The Jews of Georgian England, 1714–1830: Tradition and Change in a Liberal Society* (Philadelphia, 1979); Marsha Rozenblit, *The Jews of Vienna, 1867–1914: Assimilation and Identity* (Albany, 1983); and the essays collected in Frankel and Zipperstein, *Assimilation and Community*.

tween these three phenomena as historical *processes,* on the one hand, and their function as articulated *programs,* on the other. All of which is to say that peering beneath the "assimilationist" label represents an important first step in the historical reconstruction of the dynamics of acculturation and integration in late imperial Russia.

A second cause of the relatively scant attention given to integration among Russian Jews lies in Russia's own revolutionary "leaping of phases"—from Old Regime autocracy to socialist partocracy—which appeared to skip over precisely the kind of liberal-bourgeois society to which the emancipationist project aspired. It is as if, having scarcely registered its unanticipated victory on March 20, 1917 (when the Provisional Government in Petrograd banned all legal distinctions based on religion or nationality), the idea of European-style civic emancipation in Russia was rendered an anachronism by a Bolshevik policy that, initially at least, recognized the Jews as a national minority with specified "national rights." While Jews as individuals displayed a remarkable level of integration in the early years of the Soviet state, the Bolshevik version of national rights placed severe restrictions on their communal, cultural, and especially religious life. By the 1930s, moreover, as Soviet nationalities policy began to favor territorially defined ethnic groups, Jewish integration in sectors such as higher education, the armed forces, and the Party was subtly but unmistakably reversed.

Yet another cause of the relative neglect by historians of the integrationist current in prerevolutionary Russian Jewry is the fact that the radical movements that are alleged to have superseded it produced important institutional and archival legacies outside the Soviet Union, while the integrationists did not.[27] As the historian Steven Zipperstein has noted, "What tended to enter

---

27. Most significant, perhaps, was the loss or destruction during the Russian Revolution of the personal archives of Baron Horace Gintsburg, the unofficial leader of the integrationist current within Russian-Jewish society; Adolf Landau, the leading Jewish publisher of the late imperial period; and Genrikh Sliozberg, legal counsel to Gintsburg and a key spokesman for integration. Descriptions of these collections and their demise can be found in, inter alia, Shaul Ginzburg, "Di familiye Baron Gintsburg: Drey doros shtadlonos, tsedokeh un haskoleh," in his *Historishe verk,* 3 vols. (New York, 1937), 2: 142–43; idem, *Amolike Peterburg: Forshungn un zikhroynes vegn yidishn lebn in der rezidents-shtot fun tsarishn Rusland* (New York, 1944), pp. 53, 97; Genrikh Sliozberg, "Baron G. O. Gintsburg i pravovoe polozhenie evreev," *Perezhitoe* 2 (1910): 99, 103, 114; idem, *Dela minuvshikh dnei: Zapiski russkogo evreia,* 3 vols. (Paris, 1933), 1: 2, 254. Selected documents from these collections, usually duplicates of the originals, have survived in archives in the former Soviet Union, the United States, and Israel. Another example of the loss of an institutional legacy is the Society for the Spread of Enlightenment among the Jews of Russia, founded in 1863 (see Chapter 5). On the eve of World War I, the first volume of a planned two-volume history of the society appeared, covering its activities up to 1880. Volume 2, which would have dealt with subsequent decades, during which the society expanded enormously and virtually reinvented itself as a grass-roots organization, never appeared. The only published primary documents concerning the society's history relate to the period before 1890. After its

the historical record was often the product of the most ideologically coherent groups."[28] Though suppressed by the Bolsheviks, the General Union of Jewish Workers of Poland, Lithuania, and Russia (better known in its Yiddish version as the Bund) survived and flourished in interwar Poland and other newly independent states that were formerly part of the Pale of Settlement. The same applies to several of the Zionist parties, with the crucial addition of their base in Palestine, where a small but determined cohort ultimately realized the dream of creating a sovereign Jewish state. Such legacies—in addition to their significance even before 1917—have secured the socialist and nationalist movements the lion's share of historians' attention.

Despite their dramatically contrasting fates, the Russian and Jewish revolutions share at least one important quality: to paraphrase François Furet, both are now over.[29] For historians of late imperial Russia, the Soviet Union is no longer the "long run" it once was. It is rather a single, albeit extraordinary, chapter in the history of the peoples of the Russian Empire. The closing of that chapter in 1991 and the transition to a postcommunist era have opened up not only a new world of previously inaccessible historical documents but new questions about Russia's past. The collapse of communism and the breakup of the multinational Soviet state have restored a healthy sense of contingency to the Bolshevik Revolution, and thereby renewed interest in nonrevolutionary as well as non-Russian elements in the empire of the tsars.

In a very different manner, but at roughly the same time, the Jewish world has begun to consider whether it too has entered a post-Zionist—which is to say postrevolutionary—era, due not to the collapse of the Zionist project but to its essential fulfillment. Like its Russian counterpart, the "modern Jewish revolution" is passing into history, and therefore is coming under a new, less teleological scrutiny. That scrutiny, I believe, must include a reexamination of the experiment with Jewish integration in late imperial Russia, whose ambiguous results helped shape modern Jewish as well as modern Russian history.

While this book is principally about the encounter of Jews and Russians, it is also, inevitably, about our encounter with the past. As such, it employs the paradoxical procedures I believe such an encounter requires. The his-

---

liquidation under Stalin in 1929, the society's archive was off limits to scholars until 1989. See E. Tcherikover, *Istoriia Obshchestva dlia rasprostraneniia prosveshcheniia mezhdu evreiami v Rossii, 1863–1913* (St. Petersburg, 1913), and Y. L. Rosenthal, *Toldot hevrat marbe haskalah be-'erets rusiyah*, 2 vols. (Petersburg, 1885–90).

28. Zipperstein, *Imagining Russian Jewry*, p. 48.

29. François Furet, "The Revolution Is Over," in his *Interpreting the French Revolution* (Cambridge, 1981).

torian's craft, its power to evoke and illuminate the past, begins with reconstructing the contexts within which historical subjects lived—or, as Richard Stites succinctly stated, it involves "knowing what they knew."[30] In the case of many of the people who appear in this book, simply knowing what they knew turns out to be a considerable challenge. Precisely because they were crossers of linguistic and cultural boundaries in a highly diverse empire, precisely because they were engaged in an encounter with Russia even as Russia itself was engaged in a prolonged and rich encounter with Europe, Russian Jews who moved literally or figuratively beyond the Pale typically drew upon an astonishing array of Jewish, Russian, and European influences.

But the reconstruction of historical subjects and their subjectivities involves a second, rather different task. This is the challenge of not knowing what they did not know, of recapturing specific forms of ignorance, especially as regards outcomes of events, processes, and aspirations. This peculiar requirement of temporary feigned ignorance, or what one might call the willing suspension of hindsight, surely distinguishes historical knowledge from all other branches of learning. In the case of relations between Jews and Russians, hindsight casts exceptionally stark shadows. The pogroms, deportations, and revolutionary upheavals of 1903–21; the Holocaust (whose central staging ground was the former western borderlands of the Russian Empire, including the Pale of Settlement); the founding of the State of Israel (led overwhelmingly by Jews who had fled from the Russian Empire); the resurgence of anti-Semitism in the postwar Soviet Union; the collapse of the USSR and the resulting massive Russian-Jewish emigration at the end of the twentieth century—all these events, directly or indirectly, have reinforced the assumption that civic emancipation and social integration of Russia's Jews simply were not meant to be. I begin with a different assumption, namely, that none of these events, however decisive, deserves a monopoly over the way we interpret the history that preceded them.

Finally, the historical enterprise as I understand it requires a third mode of engagement with the past which in fact amounts to a kind of disengagement. This is the process of detaching oneself from the historical actors, their categories and claims, interpretations and obsessions, and arriving at one's own analysis of causation and meaning. In this mode, information that was invisible (because latent) or unknowable (because based on subsequent developments) to one's subjects is freely exploited for the insights it can release. Without abandoning the attempt to enter the lives of one's subjects by knowing what they knew and not knowing what they did not know, in the end a good historian retains the freedom to choose and apply analytic cat-

---

30. Richard Stites, *Russian Popular Culture: Entertainment and Society since 1900* (Cambridge, 1992), p. 7.

egories and forms of explanation that are wholly independent of the sources. Perhaps "in the end" is misleading, since I regard the various modes of relating to the past not as discrete, sequential stages of research but as an endlessly recurring set of vantage points from which to engage the historical record. They reflect, perhaps, the ceaseless contest between the desire to draw near to the human beings who populate the past and the sense of unbridgeable distance from them. In this creative tension between familiarity and strangeness, I believe, lies the source of historical understanding.

Among its various agendas, *Beyond the Pale* seeks to contribute to the effort to "bring the empire back in," that is, to understand prerevolutionary Russia not as a nation-state in the making or as a collection of separate national histories but as an imperial state and an imperial society.[31] The national state was remote from the experience of most of the ethnic groups inhabiting the territory of the Russian Empire, Russians and Jews included. Bringing the empire back in, however, constitutes a formidable task, not only because of the range of linguistic and other skills required but as a problem of historical narration. It is a truism of recent scholarship that nations are imagined, invented, and constructed, and yet this insight has scarcely weakened the tenacity with which the historical mode of thought clings to the category of the national. If one moves beyond the writing of separate histories of the many national and ethnic groups subject to the Romanov dynasty (the "one people after another" approach) and beyond the history of imperial management from the perspective of Moscow and St. Petersburg—as crucial as these are—then who or what should be the subject of one's story?

I cannot claim to have solved the riddle of how to tell the story of an empire in a way that does justice to the parts as well as the whole. Nor do I claim that the experience of Jews in the Russian Empire is a representative part that can stand for other parts. The diversity of peoples who inhabited the Russian Empire is simply too great to permit the fate of any single group to be taken as paradigmatic. But by casting my approach in the form of an encounter, or rather as a series of encounters in diverse social arenas, I hope to demonstrate that interethnic relations, while conditioned by the high politics of imperial management, developed their own specific dynamics, with profound consequences for the individuals and groups involved, as well as for the empire as a whole.

31. As Mark von Hagen has observed, "empires and multinational states generally have remained relatively undertheorized." See his "Writing the History of Russia as Empire: The Perspective of Federalism," in Catherine Evtuhov, Boris Gasparov, Alexander Ospovat, and Mark von Hagen, eds., *Kazan, Moscow, St. Petersburg: Multiple Faces of the Russian Empire* (Moscow, 1997), p. 394.

Contact among peoples and civilizations, of course, is a constantly recurring theme in human history. Russians' development over the past ten centuries is unthinkable without sustained encounters with Byzantine, Mongol, and European civilizations. How much more so for the Jews, most of whose history has unfolded in the context of prolonged sojourns within ancient Near Eastern, Greco-Roman, Islamic, and Christian societies and of the existential struggle to resist absorption by them. The task of reconstructing such encounters has often been complicated by the retrospective urge to downplay or altogether deny foreign influence. In the modern era it has been further complicated by the seemingly obligatory yet elusive category of national identity, that deceptively self-evident form of group affiliation. Nations, as Anthony Smith has observed, are among those human constructs that, "so easily recognizable from a distance, seem to dissolve before our eyes the closer we come and the more we attempt to pin them down."[32]

Precisely because of their protean quality, precisely because they are formed and maintained to a great extent *ex negativo*, in opposition to others, ethnic and national identities are often best approached by viewing them in the act of mutual encounter. To be sure, the notion of a Jewish "encounter" with Russia also runs the risk of vagueness, given that contacts took place over a long period of time, in a wide variety of settings, and across the entire spectrum of human experience, from the politics of imperial management to everyday exchanges between individuals to the realm of the literary imagination. In order to make the Russian–Jewish encounter more tangible and more analytically coherent, therefore, I have structured this book according to a particular strategy. Each of the book's four parts examines a different institutional or social arena—the tsarist government, the city of St. Petersburg, institutions of higher education, the legal profession—in an attempt to reconstruct in a variety of settings the dynamics of Jewish integration in Russia. What is usually referred to as "integration" into a "society" tends in practice to take the more limited and specific form of identification with particular units of that society. This was certainly the case in a segmented, imperial system such as tsarist Russia, where populations were governed according to dynastic, estate, and confessional principles, and where contacts among ethnic and religious groups occurred within specific social arenas, whether corporative entities such as estates and professions, institutions such as schools and universities, or urban centers. Since it takes several of these arenas as case studies, *Beyond the Pale* offers a series of thematic probes along the border of the Russian–Jewish encounter, rather than a strictly chronological narrative history. A brief overview of the book may therefore be helpful.

Part I, "The Problem of Emancipation under the Old Regime," sets the

---

32. Anthony Smith, *The Ethnic Origins of Nations* (New York, 1987), p. 2.

framework for the entire book by looking at the attempt to adapt European-style Jewish emancipation to a Russian setting during the middle of the nineteenth century. It highlights the extent to which new Jewish elites, led by the wealthy Evzel Gintsburg and his entourage, helped shape a policy of what I call "selective integration," whereby certain categories of "useful" Jews were granted the rights and privileges of their Gentile counterparts according to social estate, including the right to permanent residence outside the Pale of Settlement. In this manner, a system of incentives was established which aimed at transforming both the internal life of Jewish communities and their external relations with the surrounding society. Part I concludes by situating selective integration in the context of Alexander II's Great Reforms, with particular attention to the social vocabulary of integration across lines of estate and ethnicity.

While this study begins with official policy and never allows the state to disappear from view, I have tried to recast the issue of Jewish integration so as to render visible its social and cultural dimensions. Part II, "The Jews of St. Petersburg," examines those privileged Jews who, taking advantage of the residential freedoms offered by the policy of selective integration, moved literally beyond the Pale, to the imperial capital, which became the site of the largest and most influential Jewish community in Russia proper. Jews elaborated their own distinctive mythology of Petersburg as a "Window on Russia," in contrast to the capital's reputation among Russians as essentially foreign. I begin by analyzing Jewish settlement patterns, estate membership, employment, family structure, gender roles, and language use in order to illuminate the form and extent of Jews' adaptation to the city's distinctive urban topography. I then turn to the struggle over the formation of Jewish communal institutions in the imperial capital, including its first synagogue. Here social and religious tensions already present among Jews in the Pale rapidly came to the surface in a series of debates over communal authority, financing, and religious practice. Part II concludes with a chapter on the role of Petersburg's Jewish elites as self-appointed leaders of Russian Jewry as a whole, including their controversial response to the pogroms of 1881–82.

Part III, "Jews, Russians, and the Imperial University," traces the experience of Jewish students (women as well as men) who enrolled in Russia's institutions of higher education, moving figuratively beyond the Pale regardless of their place of study. In no other arena did selective integration, spurred by new forms of Jewish philanthropy, produce such dramatic results. Unlike their counterparts in Central Europe, Jewish students in the Russian Empire typically found themselves in a remarkably open, egalitarian student milieu. By the 1880s, the rising number of secularly educated Jews had begun to recast the hierarchy of learning within the Jewish world, planting there the quintessentially East European divide between "intelligentsia" and "folk." Jewish students also became a lightning rod for anxieties over the growing presence of non-Russians in the empire's intelligentsia, leading in 1887 to official restrictions on the admission of Jews to secondary and postsecondary institutions. After tracing the genesis of the quotas, I examine the way they fostered the emergence of separate Jewish student organizations as the "Jewish Question" insinuated itself into the academy. Part III concludes with a collective portrait of Russian-Jewish students in the aftermath of the failed 1905 revolution, based on a series of contemporary surveys conducted at institutions of higher education in Kiev, Odessa, and Moscow.

In Part IV, "In the Court of Gentiles," the newly fashioned legal profession with its ideal of the rule of law serves as the final arena in which to observe the Russian–Jewish encounter. By the 1880s, university-trained Jewish lawyers were among the leading advocates of integration. I pay particular attention to three aspects of their work: their inauguration of the study of Russian-Jewish history in order to buttress arguments for legal emancipation; their alliance with Petersburg Jewish elites and the resulting reinvention of the political strategies of those elites; and their articulation of new forms of Russian-Jewish identity in which the national dimension of Jewish life would coexist with a juridically defined transnational Russian citizenship. Part IV also explores the role of Jewish lawyers within the legal profession itself. Arguably the best educated, best organized, and most Westernized profession, lawyers offer an important case study of the impact of Russia's imperial diversity on its embryonic civil society. I explain why the bar became a haven for Jews, and then explore the debates that culminated in 1889 in the ban on their admission. In contrast to quotas in institutions of higher education, restrictions on admission of Jews to the bar emerged from within the profession itself, reflecting broad anxieties that the social mobility unleashed by the Great Reforms—and more broadly by the process of modernization— was placing Russians at a decisive disadvantage in their own empire.

The book's conclusion places in perspective the problem of Jewish emancipation and integration in late imperial Russia by comparing it to two parallel phenomena: the experience of Jews elsewhere in Europe and the experience of other minorities in the Russian Empire. It highlights the stratifying effects on Russian Jewry of half a century of selective integration, and suggests ways in which the Russian–Jewish encounter in the decades before the Revolution of 1917 prepared the ground for the remarkable place of Jews in early Soviet society.

This book could not have been written before the collapse of the Soviet Union. For nearly the entire Soviet period, archival materials relating to the Russian–Jewish encounter—like those pertaining to nationality issues in general—were all but inaccessible to historians. To be sure, this did not prevent the production of important studies drawing on the extensive body of published primary sources available outside the USSR and the holdings of a handful of archives in the United States and Israel. Until the 1990s, however, historians could only surmise what riches lay beyond their reach in Soviet archives, based on tantalizing citations from the works of a handful of scholars from the tsarist era.[33] Now we face the opposite (though far preferable) problem: access to archival treasures so vast as to appear overwhelming.[34]

My research draws on a wide range of primary sources, archival as well as published. Among the archival materials are a large number of petitions submitted to the tsarist government by Jews of nearly every conceivable stripe, correspondence between representatives of Jewish communities and local officials, communal records (*pinkasim*), interministerial correspondence regarding Jewish issues, unpublished data gathered by the state, police surveillance reports, minutes of the meetings of various official "Jewish Committees" whose task it was to guide official policy concerning Jews, and private papers (including letters) of individual Jews and Jewish organizations.

Among the relevant published materials I have relied on the extensive body of memoirs and reminiscences relating to Jewish life in tsarist Russia, contemporary works of fiction, newspapers and journals, census data, travelers' accounts, reports of government-sponsored commissions, pamphlets, and scholarly studies produced in the late imperial period. An especially valuable resource for hard-to-find information has been the sixteen-volume *Evreiskaia entsiklopediia* (Jewish encyclopedia), published in Petersburg during the decade before the First World War. It presents an added interest insofar as many of its contributors figure in my own work.

I am acutely aware that I have been able to absorb only a fraction of the new material potentially relevant to my topic, and that I have therefore left a number of important arenas of the Russian–Jewish encounter unexplored. These include the army, the economy, and many aspects of elite and popular culture. Nor does *Beyond the Pale* treat fully the status of Jews in the Polish provinces of the Russian Empire, which were formally outside the Pale

---

33. On the historiography of Russian Jewry produced in the Russian Empire and Soviet Union between 1860 and 1930, see Benjamin Nathans, "On Russian-Jewish Historiography," in Thomas Sanders, ed., *Historiography of Imperial Russia: The Profession and Writing of History in a Multi-National State* (Armonk, N.Y., 1999), pp. 397–432.

34. For a preliminary look at some of the major collections, see the following guides: G. M. Deych, comp., *Arkhivnye dokumenty po istorii evreev v Rossii v XIX–nachale XX vv.: Putevoditel'*, ed. Benjamin Nathans (Moscow, 1994); D. A. El'iashevich, ed., *Dokumental'nye materialy po istorii evreev v arkhivakh SNG i stran Baltii* (St. Petersburg, 1994); M. S. Kupovetskii et al., eds., *Dokumenty po istorii i kul'ture evreev v arkhivakh Moskvy* (Moscow, 1997); V. Khiterer, *Dokumenty sobrannye evreiskoi istoriko-arkheograficheskoi komissiei vseukrainskoi akademii nauk* (Kiev and Jerusalem, 1999); and idem, *Evreiskie dokumenty v arkhivakh Kieva, XVI–XX vv.* (forthcoming).

of Settlement and indeed constituted, as one prerevolutionary historian put it, "another, parallel 'Pale.' "[35] With time, the combined efforts of an international community of scholars will, I hope, produce a fuller mosaic. Until then, I am mindful of John Stuart Mill's admonition that the great danger in the study of history "is not so much of embracing falsehood for truth, as of mistaking part of the truth for the whole."[36]

All dates prior to February 1918 are given according to the old (Julian) calendar in use in late imperial Russia, which was behind the Western (Gregorian) calendar by twelve days in the nineteenth century and thirteen days in the twentieth. In transliterating Russian, Yiddish, and Hebrew words I have generally followed the systems used by the Library of Congress, with the exception of certain well-known names for which other transliterations (e.g., Dostoevsky and Jabotinsky) are commonly used. Faced with the politically charged task of choosing a single English transliteration for individuals and places whose names varied according to language and context (e.g., Shimon/ Shimen/Semen), I have tried to conform to the usage prevalent in English-language scholarly literature. An exception to this principle is my dispensing with certain archaic transliterations stemming from the period when German was the dominant Western language for scholarship on the Jews (e.g., Dubnov rather than Dubnow). All translations are mine unless otherwise indicated.

35. Iulii Gessen, "Zhitel´stvo i peredvizhenie evreev po russkomu zakonodatel´stvu," in *Evreiskaia entsiklopediia: Svod znanii o evreistve i ego kul´ture v proshlom i nastoiashchem*, 16 vols. (St. Petersburg, 1906–13), 7: 592.
36. John Stuart Mill, *Mill on Bentham and Coleridge* (London, 1967), p. 105.

The Problem of Emancipation under the Old Regime

Our ideal was to make European Russians out of the Jews, if one may put it that way. We wanted to express our gratitude to Russia, which we love, by means of a corpus of honest, active, educated people, of whom there are so few in Russia!

LEV LEVANDA, *letter to M. F. De-Pulé (1868)*

Russian Jewry will justifiably consider the last one hundred years the Gintsburg century.

G. B. SLIOZBERG, *Baron G. O. Gintsburg, ego zhizn´ i deiatel´nost´ (1933)*

Chapter 1

Jews and the Imperial Social Hierarchy

At the dawn of the twentieth century, when Jewish emancipation had swept from west to east across nearly the entire European continent, Russia alone among the major European states maintained a regime of legal disabilities specifically aimed at its Jewish population.[1] Why was this so?

The first historians to investigate the issue systematically were Russian Jews in the decades before 1917 who were themselves victims of official discrimination. Their works emphasized the distinctiveness of tsarist policy toward the Jews as compared to the treatment of the empire's other ethnic and religious groups, citing specifically anti-Jewish motives among ruling elites as the prime cause. A century later, in our own time, historians have modified this position by demonstrating that Russian policy toward the Jews, at least until the end of the nineteenth century, was remarkably consistent with the aims and methods of tsarist domestic policy as a whole. Without denying the presence in the tsarist government of strongly negative attitudes toward Jews, recent studies treat the absence of civil and political rights for Jews within the context of a general absence of legal rights in Russia, and argue that Jewish emancipation as enacted in Europe across the long nineteenth century would have made little sense in a society lacking the principle of equality before the law.[2]

---

1. One other state, Romania, also maintained official discrimination against Jews until after the First World War.

2. The most important older studies of official policy toward the Jews are I. G. Orshanskii, *Evrei v Rossii: Ocherki ekonomicheskogo i obshchestvennogo byta russkikh evreev* (St. Petersburg, 1877); idem, *Russkoe zakonodatel´stvo o evreiakh* (St. Petersburg, 1877); S. M. Dubnov, *History of the Jews in Russia and Poland from the Earliest Times until the Present Day,* trans. I. Friedlander, 3 vols. (Philadelphia, 1916–26); and Iu. I. Gessen, *Istoriia evreiskogo naroda v Rossii,* 2d ed., 2 vols. (Lenin-

For all its advantages, the revisionist position, like its predecessor, still focuses on what the tsarist autocracy did not (or would not) do, rather than on what it did. Russia was not simply a lawless society, but a corporative society with different laws for different social estates. More important, this corporative structure did not merely hinder a European-style emancipation but actually shaped a specifically Russian approach to the problem of dismantling Jewish separatism and integrating the empire's Jews into the surrounding society. Elsewhere in Europe, Jewish emancipation depended on the prior dissolution of hereditary social estates, whether by revolution, as in France, or by reform, as in Prussia and other German states. In Russia, the issue of Jewish emancipation arose chronologically *later* (during the second half of the nineteenth century) but at an *earlier* stage of social evolution, when a hierarchy of culturally and juridically distinct estates was still developing, with frequent prodding by an activist regime. Both aspects of the timing were important. By the 1850s, Jewish emancipation in Europe was an unmistakable point on the horizon of the tsarist regime as well as of Russia's Jews. Russia's relative backwardness, however, together with the profound social and sectarian divisions within Russian Jewry, dramatically transformed the reception of the European example. The result was a *selective integration* designed to disperse certain "useful" groups of Jews into Russia's hierarchy of social estates. For a significant portion of the Jewish population, and for Russian society as a whole, selective integration produced dramatic effects that closely paralleled those of emancipation in Europe. As in Europe, moreover, those effects inspired unforeseen and highly diverse reactions.

RUSSIA COMES TO THE JEWS

Before we investigate whether and in what manner Jews could become citizens of the Russian Empire, it would be well to recall how they became its subjects. During Europe's late medieval and early modern eras, migration—much of it involuntary—was a nearly constant fact of Jewish life.[3] Expul-

grad, 1925–27). More recent studies that explicitly revise, in various directions, arguments made in the above works include Richard Pipes, "Catherine II and the Jews: The Origins of the Pale of Settlement," *Soviet Jewish Affairs* 5 (1975): 3–20; Stanislawski, *Tsar Nicholas I;* John Klier, *Russia Gathers Her Jews: The Origins of the "Jewish Question" in Russia, 1772–1825* (De Kalb, Ill., 1986); Hans Rogger, *Jewish Policies and Right-Wing Politics in Imperial Russia* (Berkeley, 1986); Manfred Hildermeier, "Die jüdische Frage im Zarenreich: Zum Problem der unterbliebenen Emanzipation," *Jahrbücher für Geschichte Osteuropas* 32, no. 3 (1989): 321–57; and Heinz-Dietrich Löwe, *Antisemitismus und reaktionäre Utopie: Russischer Konservatismus im Kampf gegen den Wandel von Staat und Gesellschaft, 1890–1917* (Hamburg, 1978), translated and expanded as *The Tsars and the Jews: Reform, Reaction and Anti-Semitism in Imperial Russia* (New York, 1992).

3. See Jonathan Israel's survey of European Jewry in the early modern period, *European Jewry in the Age of Mercantilism, 1550–1750* (New York, 1989).

sions, invitations to settle, and new expulsions endlessly shuffled the Jews among the cities and states of Western and Central Europe. By the beginning of the seventeenth century, the majority of Jews had moved eastward, to the economically more backward part of Europe, where rulers were interested in using them to stimulate urban and commercial life. Above all, they came to Poland and the Ottoman Empire—but not, strikingly, to Russia, from which Jews were repeatedly banned. Instead, Russia suddenly and inadvertently came to the Jews at the end of the eighteenth century, as it expanded westward, annexing large portions of Poland between 1772 and 1795.

Under Polish rule, the Jews had achieved a degree of political and social autonomy unsurpassed in the European diaspora. More than in any other country, the Jews of Poland were able to engage in the full range of practices that made Judaism a distinct social order. Not only their ritual observance but their rabbinic courts of law and system of taxation were recognized and protected by the state. In each community, a governing body known as the *kahal* gathered and apportioned Jewish taxes, policed the local Jewish population, and controlled residence and membership in the community. Moreover, a country-wide institution known as the Council of the Four Lands (referring to the four major regions of the Polish commonwealth) coordinated practices among the hundreds of Jewish communities and represented them vis-à-vis Polish rulers. Though not formally part of the hierarchy of estates that composed Polish society, in practice the Jews functioned as one of the many corporate elements in this characteristically segmented "old regime" society.

The empire that annexed eastern Poland—and with it some half a million Jews—was not such a society. The status of social estates (*soslovie*, plural *sosloviia*) in Russia was particularly complex, not least because beginning with Peter the Great, official estate categories were more prescriptive than descriptive, reflecting the state's desire to fashion from the top down a European-style social order. Only at the end of the eighteenth century, roughly simultaneous with the partitions of Poland, did noble and urban estates begin to emerge in Russia as corporate bodies with certain hereditary privileges and obligations. Even these estates were relatively porous and constantly subject to intervention by the autocratic government. By the 1820s, usage of the term *soslovie* had expanded considerably, and it was applied to social groups throughout the population, while simultaneously taking on connotations of cultural as well as legal distinctiveness.[4]

4. In this discussion I draw on Gregory Freeze, "The *Soslovie* (Estate) Paradigm and Russian Social History," *American Historical Review* 91, no. 1 (February 1986): 11–36, and on two books by Elise Kimerling Wirtschafter: *Structures of Society: Imperial Russia's "People of Various Ranks"* (De Kalb, Ill., 1994) and *Social Identity in Imperial Russia* (De Kalb, Ill., 1997).

Thus Russia began to fashion a European-style society of estates even as its neighbors in Europe were busy dismantling theirs, whether by enlightened absolutist reform from above or by revolution from below. The fact that social estates in Russia appeared relatively late, were substantially the result of state initiative, and therefore were strikingly weak vis-à-vis the monarchy was to have a decisive impact on the Russian–Jewish encounter. For it was the absence of a tradition of corporate autonomy that allowed the tsarist regime to conceive of the various social estates not as obstacles to the integration of the empire's Jews but as conduits for it.

This pattern emerged soon after the first Polish Jews became subjects of the Romanov dynasty, under Catherine the Great, whose reign (1762–96) encompassed the three successive annexations of Poland. Eager to promote the growth of towns and cities, Catherine ordered in 1786 that her newly acquired Jewish subjects be registered as urban residents, with all the privileges and obligations of the urban estates—the *meshchanstvo* (artisans and petty traders) and *kupechestvo* (merchantry).[5] This sweeping inclusion of the Jews in the existing hierarchy of social estates was unprecedented in contemporary Europe.[6] For the time being, however, it had little practical effect. The tsarist government found the kahal far too convenient for fiscal and administrative purposes to consider abolishing it, and therefore autonomous communal structures remained a dominant fact of Jewish life. Moreover, substantial numbers of Jews, employed as managers of noble lands or in other rural occupations, did not live in urban centers at all. To be sure, certain Jewish merchants and petty traders made use of their new status as Russian subjects to gain access to previously forbidden Russian markets. Protests by their Christian competitors, however, combined with Catherine's general turn away from social reform in the wake of the French Revolution, led the government to scale back the estate privileges granted to the Jews, and in particular to restrict their residence to the western and southern borderlands, away from the Russian interior.[7]

A similar pattern of liberal reform in theory followed by little net change in practice characterized the reign of Alexander I (1801–25). Indeed, under Alexander numerous non-Russian peoples such as Poles and Finns were granted unusually wide-ranging forms of communal autonomy, at least on paper.[8] Four successive (and short-lived) "Jewish Committees" were convened by Alexander in an attempt to formulate a coherent policy toward the Empire's Jewish population. Although committee members included

---

5. Gessen, *Istoriia evreiskogo naroda*, 1: 22–46.
6. Richard Pipes makes this point in "Catherine II and the Jews," but concedes that the 1786 decree "was never enforced" (p. 13).
7. Gessen, *Istoriia evreiskogo naroda*, 1: 77–80.
8. Richard Pipes, *Russia under the Old Regime* (New York, 1974), p. 250.

prominent figures such as the poet and senator G. R. Derzhavin and Prince A. A. Czartoryski, their recommendations—inspired more by the emerging debates in Western Europe on the "civic improvement" of the Jews than by Russian realities—had almost no impact.[9]

Whatever the aspirations of the tsarist state, for Jews as for most other subjects the relevant juridical categories were not (yet) those of the estates, but rather the more rudimentary poll tax registry, which governed liability to corporal punishment, military service, restrictions on travel, and the institution of "collective responsibility" (*krugovaia poruka*) within a larger group.[10] For Jews of all occupations that group remained, after the Polish partitions as before, the individual Jewish community, as represented by the kahal. Thus, during the first decades of Russian imperial rule, life for the Jews changed little—as one historian put it, "a perfect illustration of the Russian proverb 'God is in heaven, and the tsar is far away.'"[11] For Russia's ruling elites, as for Russians generally, the Jews appeared similarly remote: a small, exotic tribe at the western periphery of the empire, perpetual villains in the sacred drama of Christian theology rather than subjects of a burning social problem later known as the "Jewish Question."

After the accession to the throne of Nicholas I in 1825, however, the tsar suddenly came much closer. Like his predecessors, Nicholas sought to break down Jewish separatism and autonomy through state-sponsored "merging" (*sliianie*). Unlike them, however, he took as his medium for accomplishing this aim not the embryonic hierarchy of social estates but the army. In the first years of his reign, Nicholas extended compulsory military service to many of the groups inhabiting the formerly Polish territories, including, in 1827, the Jews. Until then, Jewish communities had enjoyed the collective privilege of paying extra taxes in lieu of sending recruits.[12] After the decree of 1827, only Jewish merchants, who accounted for less than 10 percent of the Jewish population, were allowed to buy their sons' way out of military service—a privilege enjoyed by Gentile merchants as well. The rest of the Jewish population found itself, for the first time, swept up in a policy of forced integration via the Russian army. While per capita recruitment levels were no higher for Jews than for other groups, the age at which Jewish recruits were taken was often significantly lower. In some cases, boys as young as eight were taken off to begin their twenty-five years of service to the tsar. The 1827

9. The most recent study of official policy toward Russia's Jews under Alexander I concludes that it "had little immediate effect on Jewish society itself," and that the recommendations of the Jewish Committees were "a phantom in the air." See John Klier, *Russia Gathers Her Jews*, pp. 3, 116.

10. G. Freeze, "*Soslovie* Paradigm," p. 21.

11. Klier, *Russia Gathers Her Jews*, p. 3.

12. See S. Pozner, "Armiia v Rossii," in *Evreiskaia entsiklopediia,* 3: 160.

decree had a traumatic impact not only on the thousands of young Jews who were drafted but on the Jewish communities they left behind. The fact that the macabre job of selecting recruits was placed in the hands of Jewish communities themselves deepened existing fault lines based on class, religious practice (Hasidim vs. mitnagdim), and kinship. Pressured by the government to deliver ever more and ever younger conscripts, communal authorities preyed upon poorer and more vulnerable Jews, while the wealthier and better connected, especially members of the merchant estate, were able to pay or bribe their way out of service. The result, as the historian Michael Stanislawski has shown, was a substantial erosion of intramural solidarity and of the authority of traditional Jewish elites. Self-mutilation was a well-known technique among Jews (and not only Jews) desperate to avoid military service. Parents of recent conscripts would light mourning candles, as for a deceased relative, on the assumption that they would never see their sons again, at any rate not as Jews. Contemporaries noted a substantial increase in the number of Jewish riots and attacks on kahal authorities.[13] Equally telling, the *Nikolaevskie soldaty* became the subjects of numerous folk songs, tales, and legends.[14]

Much of the Jewish trauma regarding the imposition of the draft stemmed from the fear that conscripts, especially younger ones, would be forced to submit to baptism. Indeed, in the first half of the nineteenth century, most Jews, like most tsarist officials, regarded conversion as the all but inevitable outcome of "merging." Once drafted, the fabled "cantonists" (under-age draftees), who accounted for some 50,000 of the total of approximately 70,000 Jewish recruits between 1827 and 1855, did in fact convert at significantly higher rates than the Jewish population as a whole.[15] In the eyes

13. Stanislawski, *Tsar Nicholas I,* pp. 15, 32–33, 127–33. For eyewitness accounts of the practice of self-mutilation, see Carole Malkin, ed., *The Journeys of David Toback* (New York, 1981), pp. 37, 135–36; and Mary Antin, *Promised Land,* p. 14.

14. See S. M. Ginzburg and P. S. Marek, *Evreiskie narodnye pesni* (St. Petersburg, 1901), pp. 41–54, 283–302, as well as the sources cited in S. M. Ginsburg, *Historishe verk,* 3: 1–135. The drafting of Jewish soldiers under Nicholas I became an important subject of maskilic works of "high" fiction as well; see Olga Litvak, "The Literary Response to Conscription: Individuality and Authority in the Russian-Jewish Enlightenment," Ph.D. dissertation, Columbia University, 1999. Underage Jewish soldiers occasionally made their way into works by prominent Russian authors as well, including Nikolai Leskov's short story "Vladychnyi sud" and Alexander Herzen's memoirs, *Byloe i dumy.*

15. For recruitment figures, see Stanislawski, *Tsar Nicholas I,* p. 25. Stanislawski acknowledges that the number of Jewish conscripts who converted "cannot be determined with any precision." His estimate that "at least half" of the cantonists converted, however, strikes me as too high. The annual empire-wide conversion figures compiled by the St. Vladimir Brotherhood in Kiev—of questionable accuracy as well—give a lower proportion. They are reproduced in Mikhail Agursky, "Conversions of Jews to Christianity in Russia," *Soviet Jewish Affairs* 20, nos. 2–3 (1990): 77.

of the government, however, conversion levels among Jewish soldiers were disappointingly low. Unlike Old Believers and other Russian sectarians, concluded one official memorandum in 1855, "Jews do not abandon their religion during army service, in spite of the benefits offered to them for doing so." If the goal of the military draft was to promote the merging of Jews into the surrounding population, the memorandum went on to say, its effect was precisely the opposite.[16] Even among those who did convert, baptism was less a matter of professional ambition, let alone conviction, than of sheer survival under extraordinarily hostile conditions.

Thus while the military draft weakened internal Jewish authority, it did little to draw Jews into Russian imperial institutions, despite the coerced conversion of minors. Moreover, like their formal incorporation into the urban estates under Catherine, the formal integration of Jews into Nicholas I's army was quickly compromised by laws distinguishing Jewish from non-Jewish soldiers. Less than two years after the 1827 decree on conscription, Jews were restricted from certain army units, and beginning in 1832 they were subject to separate, more stringent and subjective criteria for promotion, which required that they "distinguish themselves in combat with the enemy."[17] Even more important, by 1835 Nicholas had officially established the Pale of Permanent Jewish Settlement, thereby formalizing the restrictions on Jewish residence first enacted by his grandmother Catherine. Although Jewish soldiers often served in the Empire's interior, in areas otherwise off limits to Jews, upon completion of military service they were required to return immediately to the Pale.

The difficulty of fulfilling Jewish religious commandments during military service, the specter of baptism, the denial of the normal rewards for loyal service—all these ensured that Nicholas's vision of the army, as a kind of correctional institution designed to discipline and homogenize large portions of the empire's population, failed to draw the Jews into the main currents of Russian life. To be sure, the tens of thousands of cantonists who served up to twenty-five years in the imperial army became the first cohort of Russian Jews effectively, if involuntarily, to leave the Jewish fold. But we currently know little about the actual experience of Jewish soldiers, apart from a handful of individuals, or about those who survived as veterans.[18] Their experience outside the Jewish world has been largely eclipsed by the legends they inspired within it.

16. RGIA, f. 1269, op. 1, d. 136, l. 12.

17. *Evreiskaia entsiklopediia*, 3: 162.

18. On Russian-Jewish soldiers, see Michael Stanislawski, *Psalms for the Tsar: A Minute-Book of a Psalms-Society in the Russian Army, 1864–1867* (New York, 1988), and Yohanan Petrovsky-Shtern, "Jews in the Russian Army: Through the Military to Modernity," Ph.D. dissertation, Brandeis University, 2001.

Map 1. Russian Poland and the Pale of Jewish Settlement

KISELEV AND THE "JEWISH COMMITTEE"

In matters relating to the Jews, as in so many of his other projects, Nicholas's imagination began and ended in the army barracks. The same cannot be said, however, of a handful of his senior officials who, while carrying out the policy of military recruitment, began to construct another approach to ending Jewish autonomy and isolation, an approach that would be realized only after Nicholas's death, during the era of Great Reforms. Indeed, these officials were prominent members of that small cohort of "enlightened bureaucrats" who played an important role in the preparation of the Great Reforms themselves, including the most far-reaching reform, the abolition of serfdom in 1861. They were "enlightened" in the specific historical sense of using the power of the state to increase the productivity of the population by rationalizing, centralizing, and standardizing legal norms.[19]

It was Count P. D. Kiselev, Nicholas's minister of state domains, chief of staff for peasant affairs, and the driving force behind official inquiries into the gradual abolition of serfdom, who was responsible for the establishment in 1840 of a committee to reevaluate the status of the empire's Jews. Kiselev had seen Western Europe as an officer in the Russian army's campaign against Napoleon, and had also known—but not cooperated with—leading Decembrists, liberal-minded members of elite army regiments who had attempted to stage a revolt in St. Petersburg in 1825. More to the point, he had studied the condition of Jews in Western Europe with an eye to managing Russia's own Jewish population.[20] The Committee's other members included officials such as Count S. S. Uvarov, the Minister of Public Enlightenment, and Count A. G. Stroganov, the acting Minister of Internal Affairs, both of whom were among the more forward-thinking of Nicholas' bureaucrats.[21] Since the partitions of Poland, four so-called Jewish Committees had been convened. None had lasted more than a few years or had any significant practical impact.[22] Kiselev's Committee for the Determination of Measures for the Fundamental Transformation of the Jews in Russia, by contrast, carried out its work over the course of nearly two and a half decades (1840–63), surviving well past the death of Nicholas I. In fact, none of the many tsarist committees and commissions on the Jews before or after lasted anywhere near as long, or included such high-ranking members. The im-

---

19. See W. Bruce Lincoln, *In the Vanguard of Reform: Russia's Enlightened Bureaucrats, 1825–1861* (De Kalb, Ill., 1982).

20. Stanislawski, *Tsar Nicholas I,* p. 45.

21. For characterizations of these officials, see Lincoln, *In the Vanguard of Reform.*

22. The committees were convened in 1802–4, 1806–7, 1809–12, and 1823–25. See Iulii Gessen, "Evreiskie komitety," in *Evreiskaia entsiklopediia,* 7: 441–44, and Klier, *Russia Gathers Her Jews,* pp. 120–32, 148–50, 162–67, 181.

Figure 1. Count Pavel Dmitrievich Kiselev (1788–1872).

pact of Kiselev's Jewish Committee was to be greater than that of any other such body, virtually setting the terms for Jewish integration until the collapse of the old regime.[23]

To understand what was purportedly "fundamental" about the committee's approach, we must turn to its founding document, a memorandum by Kiselev from 1840 that outlines the Jews' current condition and the means

23. The committee's voluminous files are located in RGIA, f. 1269. Although the committee did not have formal executive authority with regard to policy respecting the Jews—which, like all other areas of official policy, was ultimately subject to the will of the tsar—its recommendations, especially under Alexander II, were nearly always translated into law. With high-level members such as the ministers of finance, internal affairs, and public enlightenment, the committee generally succeeded in coordinating Jewish policy across the various ministries—in contrast to committees later in the century, when, as Heinz-Dietrich Löwe has shown, official Jewish policy became entangled in a rivalry between the ministries of finance and internal affairs. See Löwe, *Antisemitismus und reaktionäre Utopie.*

to be used for their "transformation."[24] Thirteen years after the decision to include Jews in the military draft, Kiselev noted that the number of Jews who served, and thereby were exposed to the moral and physical discipline of army life, was relatively small, while "the main body [of Jews] has remained alien to any changes whatsoever," their separation from Russia's "civilian societies" unchanged.[25] Despite the government's efforts, he argued, the Jews could not be absorbed into the Russian social order without first being morally and culturally transformed. Citing the example of Jews in Prussia and employing the rhetoric of earlier European debates on the "improvement" of the Jews, Kiselev shifted attention to the ways in which education— initially through special primary schools for Jewish children, compulsory and closely supervised by the state, but ultimately through attendance at Russian schools—could fashion a new generation free of the "fanaticism" and "prejudices" of their parents. "The estrangement of the Jews from the civil order, and their moral vices," Kiselev declared, "do not represent some sort of particular or arbitrary deficiency of their character, but rather became firmly established through [their] religious delusions," principally those of the Talmud.[26] If what appeared to the Russian government as the Jews' undesirable qualities—fanaticism, separatism, aversion to physical labor, lack of scruples—were not innate, then it followed that they were subject to planned alteration. Whereas Catherine's policies toward the Jews had been influenced by Enlightenment ideals of juridical and fiscal uniformity, Kiselev in effect applied the Enlightenment notion of a malleable and perfectible human nature in order to turn official policy in the direction of education.

Since Jewish vices, in Kiselev's view, stemmed directly from religious beliefs, it would also be necessary to act upon the Jewish "clerical estate"; that is, the rabbinate. This too was a borrowed notion, common among European regimes before the full legal emancipation of their Jewish populations. Citing the Parisian Sanhedrin—the grand assembly of Jewish rabbis and lay notables convened by Napoleon in 1807—and the subsequent establishment of consistories to ensure that rabbinical training and practice were consistent with French law, Kiselev noted approvingly that "the Jewish clergy [in France] has been turned into an instrument of the government in the execution of its policies."[27]

For Jewish schools and the rabbinate to be effective instruments of official policy in Russia, it would be necessary to abolish the kahal as a quasi-governmental institution among Jews, whatever the short-term inconve-

24. Kiselev's memorandum, "Ob ustroistve evreiskogo naroda v Rossii," was published (together with a commentary by S. M. Dubnov) in *Voskhod*, 1901, no. 4, pp. 25–40, and no. 5, pp. 3–21.

25. Ibid., p. 32. For use of the term "civilian societies" (*grazhdanskie obshchestva*), see Chapter 2.

26. Ibid., p. 3.

27. Ibid., p. 39.

niences of doing so.[28] Jewish fiscal and administrative matters would then be transferred to the city councils in the towns where Jews were registered. But unlike Catherine's automatic and therefore purely formal registration of Jews as either merchants or town dwellers (the two urban estates), Kiselev proposed instead a rudimentary but real reclassification known as the *razbor*. According to this plan, only Jews who actually had fixed residences in towns and actually worked as artisans, as merchants, or in other "useful" trades would be registered in the corresponding estates. The rest, the "useless" majority, who lived in rural areas or with no stable address, would be given five years to qualify as town dwellers, merchants, or members of the agricultural estate (*zemledel´cheskoe soslovie*); that is, farmers. Failing that, they would be drafted at twice (subsequently, at Nicholas's behest, at five times) the level of other Jews.[29]

Kiselev's memorandum set the Jewish Committee's agenda for the next decade. The kahals as the executive organs of individual Jewish communities were formally abolished in 1844 (though not the corporate status of the Jews themselves); the new classification scheme was introduced in 1846; the first state schools exclusively for Jews, as well as two state-sponsored seminaries for the training of rabbis, appeared in 1847, offering their students a coveted exemption from military service; a "Rabbinical Commission" modeled on the Sanhedrin met for the first time in 1852.[30]

But this chronology tells us little about what was actually occurring on the ground. Many kahals continued de facto to function well after 1844, though in more clandestine fashion. And kahal or no kahal, Jewish communities continued to deliver taxes and conscripts, as the state required of them.[31] Kise-

28. Kiselev (ibid., p. 6) showed full awareness of the fiction whereby the Jews, despite their formal status as members of the urban estates, continued de facto to pay their taxes through the kahal, though for reasons that are unclear he claimed that Jews were not subject to the principle of collective responsibility through the kahal. Iulii Gessen, in his entry on the poll tax in *Evreiskaia entsiklopediia*, 12: 638, refutes this view.

29. Kiselev, "Ob ustroistve evreiskogo naroda," pp. 7–8.

30. By the end of Nicholas's reign, roughly seventy Jewish schools had been established for Jewish children throughout the Pale of Settlement; see Stanislawski, *Tsar Nicholas I*, p. 98. On the history of the "official rabbis," see Azriel Shochat, *Mosad "ha-rabanut mi-ta'am" be-rusiyah* (Haifa, 1975). Stanislawski (*Tsar Nicholas I*, p. 44) writes that Kiselev "came to the conclusion that repressive measures could not solve the Jewish problem in Russia" and that his prescription was therefore "revolutionary." In fact, Kiselev argued ("Ob ustroistve evreiskogo naroda," p. 37) that repressive or what he called "police" methods were "insufficient" to transform the Jews. But he in no way repudiated the harsh conditions of the draft, and his proposal amounted to maintaining the status quo for military service by "useful" Jews, while drastically tightening the screws on the "useless." Seen in this light, his turn to education and control through the rabbinate appear less revolutionary than simply innovative.

31. Azriel Shochat, "Ha-hanhagah be-kehilot rusiyah im bitul ha-kahal," *Tsiyon* 42, nos. 3–4 (1977): 143–233.

lev's reclassification scheme, as the Jewish Committee subsequently observed, proved difficult to implement because the government lacked reliable data even on population, much less occupation and residence.[32] The
Rabbinical Commission came and went without noticeable effect, and since
Jewish communities continued their age-old practice of selecting their own
rabbis, the several dozen graduates of the government rabbinical seminaries were shunned and for the time being without influence.[33]

The state-sponsored primary schools for Jews merit a brief discussion of
their own, since they provoked considerable debate among contemporaries.
Before as well as after the creation of the state schools, the majority of Jewish boys in the Russian Empire attended traditional primary schools, *heders,*
in which learning to read and memorize ancient texts in unfamiliar languages
was combined, with greater or lesser success, with a kind of day care.[34] While
in principle Jews had had free access to Russian schools since 1804, by mid-
century relatively few had actually enrolled.[35] Beginning in the 1820s, maskilim in Odessa, Vilna, Uman, Riga, and Kishinev had founded their own,
avowedly progressive primary schools, but many were short lived. Those that
survived were but a drop in the ocean of traditional learning that was constantly replenished by the heders.[36]

By the 1840s it had become clear to Count Uvarov, the minister of enlightenment, that neither public schools nor the army—the classic instruments of ethnic integration in modern societies—had succeeded in drawing Jews out of their isolation. The nearly one hundred schools specifically

32. At meetings of the Jewish Committee in 1858 and 1859, Minister of Internal Affairs
S. S. Lanskoi reported that despite repeated attempts to classify Jews according to the *razbor,* local authorities had been unable to collect the necessary data. Moreover, most local officials were
against the policy, claiming that "an entire police force" would be required just to enforce it.
The committee also noted that in contrast to what it called the "Belgian" method of gathering
demographic information—conducting the census on a single day throughout the country—
"our census . . . is of exclusively financial significance," and was therefore ill suited to questions
involving occupation and residence. See RGIA, f. 1269, op. 1, d. 137, ll. 69, 128.

33. On the lack of influence of the first and second rabbinic commissions (convened in
1852 and 1857, respectively), see ChaeRan Freeze, "Making and Unmaking the Jewish Family: Marriage and Divorce in Imperial Russia, 1850–1914," Ph.D. dissertation, Brandeis University, 1997, pp. 133–43, and Lederhendler, *Road to Modern Jewish Politics,* p. 73. On graduates of the state rabbinical seminaries, see C. Freeze, "Making and Unmaking the Jewish Family,"
pp. 170–72, and Shochat, *Mosad "ha-rabanut mi-ta'am."*

34. For an analysis of the content and function of education in the heder, see Shaul Stampfer,
"Heder Study, Knowledge of Torah, and the Maintenance of Social Stratification in Traditional
East European Jewish Society," *Studies in Jewish Education* 3 (1988): 271–89.

35. In some cases, Jews were denied admission in spite of the law. The Jews enrolled in Russian schools in the Pale before 1841 numbered in the hundreds; in Poland the number may
have been considerably higher. See Iulii Gessen, "Prosveshcheniie v Rossii," *Evreiskaia entsiklopediia,* 13: 46.

36. Ibid., col. 45.

for Jews established by Uvarov throughout the Pale in the late 1840s and 1850s were thus a response to these twin failures. Unlike most of the government's actions toward the Jewish population, they stand out as an anomaly within the broader contours of official policy at the time. As a general matter, Nicholas I was deeply suspicious of education, and deliberately retarded its spread during the three decades of his reign.[37] The introduction of state-sponsored, tuition-free Jewish schools not only departed from this pattern but did so with support from the state treasury—support long denied to church schools.[38] In fact, apart from a similar network of state-sponsored schools for Muslims in Central Asia, established in the 1870s, the schools designed specifically for Jewish pupils were without parallel among the empire's minority groups.[39] Furthermore, by including the Hebrew Bible (though emphatically not the Talmud) in their curriculum, the schools broke with the government's normal policy of noninterference in religious education outside the domain of the Russian Orthodox Church.

It was this latter feature, combined with the deep-rooted Jewish suspicion of Gentile institutions generally, that severely limited the schools' impact, and this despite the fact that enrollment brought exemption from the much-feared military draft. Kiselev's Jewish Committee had hoped that of an estimated 85,000 school-age Jewish boys, roughly 20,000 would enroll in the official Jewish schools.[40] Instead, the committee determined in 1858 that, just over a decade after the schools' founding, a total of 3,538 boys had enrolled (with fewer than half estimated to have graduated).[41] Whatever the heder's reputation for pedagogical chaos, the picture of the government's Jewish schools that emerged from official inspection reports was hardly better. Annual dropout rates ranged from 42 to 83 percent, and in an effort to recover lost enrollment, new students were typically admitted throughout the school year. Incoming students knew little or no Russian (the usual language of instruction, along with German), and textbooks were in desperately short supply.[42] While prominent maskilim such as Kalman Shulman, Avra-

37. Patrick Alston, *Education and the State in Tsarist Russia* (Stanford, 1969), pp. 34–36.

38. While it is true that the government instituted a special tax on Sabbath candles to pay for the Jewish schools, official records indicate that proceeds from the tax never covered the entire cost of the schools. Parish schools run by the various Christian denominations relied exclusively on church funds.

39. Henning Bauer, Andreas Kappeler, and Brigitte Roth, eds., *Die Nationalitäten des Russischen Reiches in der Volkszählung von 1897*, 2 vols. (Stuttgart, 1991), 1: 358.

40. A. Georgievskii, *Doklad po voprosu o merakh otnositel´no obrazovaniia evreev* (St. Petersburg, 1886), p. 54.

41. RGIA, f. 1269, op. 1, d. 138, l. 129.

42. The dropout rates are for the 1871–72 academic year; see *Ukaz Ministru narodnogo prosveshcheniia: Polozhenie o evreiskikh nachal´nykh uchilishchakh* (St. Petersburg, n.d.), p. 41. On year-round admissions, ignorance of Russian, and textbook supplies, see F. Postel´s, *Otchet chlena*

ham Mapu, Yehudah Leib Gordon, and Emanuel Levin found much-needed employment and camaraderie as teachers in the schools, the schools' graduates have left barely a trace in the historical record. Within the Jewish population, to be sure, the schools' supporters (of whom there were few) as well as opponents (of whom there were many) tended to regard them as part of an emerging alliance between the Russian state and the maskilim, who appeared poised to step into the vacuum left by the deterioration of Jewish communal authority. In reality, however, the schools' impact was far more modest.[43]

The same may be said of the other officially sanctioned device to merge Jews into the Russian social order, namely, settlement in agricultural colonies. Ever since the end of the eighteenth century, when Catherine the Great won the northern littoral of the Black Sea from the Ottoman Turks and renamed it New Russia, the tsarist government had eagerly sought to colonize the area with its own subjects, regardless of ethnicity. New Russia, in fact, became the one major territory beyond the traditional area of Jewish settlement in prepartition Poland to be included in the final delineation of the Pale of Settlement in 1835. Despite the enthusiasm for turning Jews to agricultural labor on the part of both the government and various maskilim, however, state-sponsored Jewish agricultural colonies in New Russia failed to attract more than several hundred families.[44] Only the exemption from military service under Nicholas I boosted, temporarily, Jewish enrollment in the colonies. The tsarist regime's profound reluctance to increase contact between Jews and peasants constantly eroded official support for the project, despite the fact that Jews were settled in separate colonies. By the 1860s, moreover, the population of New Russia had expanded so dramatically that colonists were no longer needed, and in any event the majority of Jews who moved there had settled in cities such as Odessa and Elizavetgrad, rather than in rural areas.

Thus for the time being, the most significant aspect of the Russian–Jewish encounter continued to be the compulsory military service imposed on Jewish communities across the Pale, with its devastating impact on communal solidarity. The strains produced under these circumstances only intensified in the wake of the panic unleashed in Russian government circles by the European revolutions of 1848. In 1851 Nicholas sharply raised the draft quo-

soveta Ministerstva narodnogo prosveshcheniia Postel'sa po obozreniiu evreiskikh uchilishch (St. Petersburg, 1865), pp. 32–33.

43. Stanislawski, *Tsar Nicholas I*, pp. 97–109. Stanislawski's revisionist argument that the government schools for Jews made an "essential contribution to the institutionalization and consolidation of the Haskalah" (p. 108) has been substantially qualified by Lederhendler (*Road to Modern Jewish Politics*, pp. 111–12, 201nn2–3).

44. *Evreiskaia entsiklopediia*, 7: 754–57.

tas for Jews, to ten recruits per thousand members of a given community, thereby matching the levels set for certain social groups that had previously been singled out by the government for punishment.[45] So alarmed was the government, in fact, that the new quotas ignored the distinctions between "useful" and "useless" Jews articulated in Kiselev's reclassification scheme. In so doing, Nicholas acted against the fundamental principle around which official policy had previously been organized, namely, that of treating groups within the Jewish population differentially, according to their formal estate affiliation, in order to merge them into the corresponding estates of the surrounding population.

This aberration did not escape those "useful" Jews who had benefited, or at least avoided worse treatment, under the formal division of the Jewish population according to the Russian hierarchy of estates. In 1854 the Jewish Committee received a petition from a dozen Jewish merchants and "honored citizens" (an official title bestowed on highly successful entrepreneurs, exempting the bearer from the poll tax, corporal punishment, and other burdens placed on estates ranking below the nobility), protesting against the recent shift in recruitment practices. Before we examine the contents of the petition and its reception by the committee, however, let us take a closer look at its authors.

THE EMERGENCE OF NEW JEWISH SPOKESMEN

Across the first half of the nineteenth century, internal sectarian conflict and the withdrawal of external recognition of the kahal by the state (processes that had begun during the period of Polish rule), combined with the unprecedented burden imposed by Nicholas's military draft, had progressively weakened the grip of traditional Jewish communal institutions. As the historian Eli Lederhendler has shown, the kahal's exclusive right to represent a given Jewish community to the secular powers had been a critical source of authority internally, with respect to the community itself.[46] Once that monopoly was broken—that is, once the Russian state constricted the competence of the kahal and simultaneously began to accept input from other, internally unsanctioned sources—a contest for authority was unleashed within the Jewish world that would define much of Russian-Jewish history for the next century.

---

45. Stanislawski, *Tsar Nicholas I*, p. 184. These previously penalized groups included the so-called *grazhdane* and *odnodvortsy*.

46. Lederhendler has ingeniously suggested that if the monopoly on the legitimate use of violence is the defining characteristic of the state (Max Weber's definition), then the kahal's monopoly on legitimate *recourse* to the state is the defining characteristic of premodern Jewish politics. See his *Road to Modern Jewish Politics*, pp. 3–13.

A number of distinct groups took part in that contest. Because historians (myself included) have a professional weakness for those who preserve their thoughts in writing, much attention has been paid to two of the relevant groups, the rabbinate and above all the maskilim. The long inaccessibility of Soviet archives only reinforced this instinct, since it left historians heavily reliant on published sources.[47] Now that relevant archival sources are available, we can begin to restore a third group to the contest, one whose primary vocation involved not words and books but money and commerce. As significant as the Hasidim, maskilim, and their opponents were within Jewish society, relations between that society and the Russian state were to be decisively shaped by a new cohort of wealthy young merchants. More than any other group in the Jewish world, this new elite was able, by virtue of its utility to the state, to imprint its own priorities—many of them influenced by the Haskalah, to be sure—on the estate-based approach of the tsarist regime.

As the economic historian Arcadius Kahan once noted, ideological and emotional ambivalence (if not outright hostility) on the part of scholars of East European Jewry with respect to Jewish capital has rendered the Jewish bourgeoisie "*terra incognita* for both the historian and the economist."[48] While the process of social and cultural "embourgeoisement" has found a place in recent studies, a satisfactory economic history of the Jewish bourgeoisie itself has yet to be written.[49] At a minimum, Kahan suggested, the picture of unmitigated economic decline that has dominated the historiography of nineteenth-century Russian Jewry, especially in the period after the emancipation of the serfs, does not apply to the rapidly growing entrepreneurial class.[50] Here only a brief summary of what is known about the origins of the Jewish merchant elite in the mid–nineteenth century will be given, as a preface to the more substantial analysis of the impact of that elite.

The emergence of wealthy Jewish entrepreneurs was an inadvertent effect of Nicholas I's economic policies. True, Jews had long been active in trade and commerce, and Catherine's provision for qualified Jews to be reg-

---

47. As Michael Stanislawski (*Tsar Nicholas I,* pp. 134–37) has pointed out, however, rabbis in Russia during the first three-quarters of the nineteenth century left a far thinner documentary trail than did their counterparts elsewhere in Europe, even in earlier centuries.

48. Arcadius Kahan, *Essays in Jewish Social and Economic History* (Chicago, 1986), p. 18. This posthumous collection of essays and sketches represents an outline of Kahan's planned but never completed study of Russian-Jewish economic history.

49. For studies that employ the idea of embourgeoisement, see Zipperstein, *Jews of Odessa,* and Stanislawski, *For Whom Do I Toil?* and *Tsar Nicholas I,* the latter of which includes an excellent overview (pp. 170–82) of Jewish economic trends in the second quarter of the nineteenth century. For a candid account of one historian's enduring preference for Jewish intellectuals over the bourgeoisie, see Zipperstein, *Imagining Russian Jewry,* chap. 3, "Remapping Odessa."

50. Kahan, *Essays,* chap. 3, "Notes on Jewish Entrepreneurship in Tsarist Russia."

istered in the merchant estate showed that the government took their activities seriously. Indeed, by 1830 the approximately 5,000 Jewish merchants registered in the Pale made up the majority of the merchant estate in that territory.[51] By the middle of the century, some 27,000 Jewish merchants constituted nearly three-quarters of the merchantry within the Pale, and in provinces such as Volhynia, Grodno, and Podolia their proportion was higher still. Even in the first merchant guild—the wealthiest and most prestigious—Jews were the dominant presence in the empire's western borderlands.[52]

It was Nicholas I's decision to centralize Russia's tax-gathering system, in particular the taxes on the sale of alcohol, that inadvertently opened up a lucrative new arena for Jewish merchants.[53] Throughout the nineteenth century (as for much of the twentieth), taxes on the production and sale of alcohol constituted a sizable proportion, usually about one-third, of the Russian state's annual revenues.[54] Within the Pale, Jews commonly played an important part in the generation of this revenue in their capacity as distillers and tavern keepers hired by individual landowners to supply peasants with a steady flow of vodka. When Nicholas I centralized the system of leasing licenses for the liquor trade, Jewish merchants were among those eligible to become *otkupshchiki*, or tax farmers. A decree of 1848, moreover, made it possible for the wealthiest Jewish liquor-tax farmers to work outside the Pale, thereby opening up to them the vast markets of the Russian interior. By this means, individuals such as Evzel (Joseph) Gintsburg of Kamenets-Podol´sk, Vul´f Gorodetskii of Kherson, and Avram Varshavskii of Poltava gained extraordinary wealth while still (and in some cases not yet) in their thirties. "Tax farmer" was becoming virtually a synonym among Jews for "wealthy man."[55] Moreover, tax farmers' wealth derived almost entirely from business with Gentiles, and therefore provided unprecedented contact with Russians and Russian officialdom as well as economic independence from Jewish communal authorities.[56] Nor were they alone: according to various accounts, roughly 8,000 Jews "lived and made fortunes under the lucrative protection" of the tax farmers, as employees and contractors.[57] Gintsburg, one of the

---

51. Alfred Rieber, *Merchants and Entrepreneurs in Imperial Russia* (Chapel Hill, 1982), p. 57.

52. Ibid., pp. 58–59.

53. Shaul Ginzburg, "Di familiye Baron Gintsburg: Drey doros shtadlonos, tsedokeh un haskoleh," in his *Historishe verk*, 2: 122.

54. David Christian, *'Living Water': Vodka and Russian Society on the Eve of Emancipation* (Oxford, 1990), p. 6.

55. Orshanskii, *Evrei v Rossii*, p. 9.

56. N. N., "Iz vpechatlenii minuvshogo veka: Vospominaniia srednogo cheloveka," *Evreiskaia Starina* 6, no. 2 (1914): 241.

57. The figure of 8,000 is from Ginzburg, *Historishe verk*, 2: 122; the quotation can be found in Orshanskii, *Evrei v Rossii*, p. 9.

Figure 2. Baron Evzel Gintsburg (1812–1878).

most successful of the first-guild merchants, was rumored to employ nearly 100 contractors and, through them, thousands of collectors, supervisors, and administrators.[58] For his extraordinary services to the state treasury, he was made a "hereditary honored citizen" in 1849 at the age of thirty-six, the highest civilian honor short of ennoblement.[59]

Surviving accounts of the new merchant elite by Jewish contemporaries

58. Ginzburg, *Historishe verk,* 2: 122. Similar impressions are also recorded by the less reliable S. L. Tsitron, *Shtadlonim: Interesante yidishe tipn fun noentn avar* (Warsaw, 1926), p. 335.

59. B. V. Anan´ich, *Bankirskie doma v Rossii, 1860–1914 gg.: Ocherki istorii chastnogo predprinimatel´stva* (Leningrad, 1991), p. 37.

tend to be distinctly negative. Many suspected the *otkupshchiki* (or *aktsizniki* [excisers], as they were sometimes known after the introduction of an excise tax on the sale of liquor) of excessive worldliness in dress and behavior culminating in deliberate violations of religious law. According to one account, they were "the most powerful and independent flouters of custom."[60] As a popular folk song put it:

> And young tax farmers
> Are very frivolous:
> Their chins are bare [i.e., shaven]
> And they ride on horses,
> Go about in galoshes,
> And eat without having [ritually] washed.
> They go into taverns
> . . . .
> Drink tea,
> And woe to their wives.[61]

"These freshly baked aristocrats would ride about in carriages," recalled an eyewitness, "cultivating their relations with generals and provincial governors"; only those connections prevented their being stoned for flouting Jewish law.[62] Reuven Kulisher, another contemporary, concluded that the Russian Haskalah had now come to be personified by a Jew perched on a liquor barrel, sausage in hand.[63]

---

60. Vladimir Osipovich Garkavi [Harkavi], *Otryvki vospominaniia* (St. Petersburg, 1913), p. 6.

61. In Yiddish:

> Un aktsizne yunge layt
> Zaynen zeyer farshayt
> Golen di berdelakh
> Un foren oyf ferdelakh,
> Geyen in kaloshn
> Un esn ungevashn.
> Zey geyen in di traktirn
> . . . .
> Trinken tey,
> Un der vayb iz vind un vey.

Ginzburg and Marek, *Evreiskie narodnye pesni*, p. 54. I have combined what are listed as two variants of the same song, from the Grodno and Vitebsk provinces. The eighth line is missing in the original. A similar version of this song appears in Pauline Wengeroff, *Memoiren einer Grossmutter: Bilder aus der Kulturgeschichte der Juden Russlands im 19. Jahrhundert*, 3d ed. (Berlin, 1922), 2: 137.

62. N. N., "Iz vpechatlenii minuvshogo veka: Vospominaniia srednogo cheloveka," *Evreiskaia Starina* 6, no. 2 (1914): 240–42.

63. Zipperstein, *Jews of Odessa*, p. 19. Russian tax farmers appear to have had a similarly negative reputation among the general population. Kulisher's image may in fact be an adaptation

The sparse available evidence concerning the lives of Jewish merchants makes it difficult to evaluate observers' accusations of religious indifference, which in some cases may have disguised less spectacular (e.g., economic) grievances. Such accusations have insinuated themselves into much of the secondary literature concerning Russian-Jewish history, where the nouveaux riches' alleged lack of solidarity with the Jewish masses is taken as a sign of national indifference.[64] Yet at least one prominent case for which there is substantial documentation—that of the Gintsburg family—yields a far more nuanced picture. Evzel Gintsburg and several of his descendants devoted much of their fortunes to philanthropy on behalf of Jewish causes, were well-informed sponsors of Hebrew culture in the spirit of the Haskalah, and became active spokesmen on behalf of the empire's Jews. Prominent maskilim such as Metatyahu Mapu and Mordechai Sukhostaver were employed as tutors, secretaries, and librarians in their household. Evzel Gintsburg used the occasion of his last will and testament to declare his faith in "the One God, the religion of our fathers," as well as his "devotion to tsar and fatherland." Children and grandchildren who repudiated these loyalties by abandoning Judaism or permanently emigrating from Russia faced the loss of their inheritance.[65] Indeed, in his will Gintsburg had already disowned his eldest son, Zalkind (Alexander), because of his "dissolute lifestyle," turning instead to another son, Horace (Goratsii/Naftali-Herz), as rightful heir and successor.[66] Horace (1833–1909), who would eventually become far more famous than his father in both Jewish and Russian society, was described by those who knew him well as a man of the world who nonetheless kept the Sabbath

---

of a contemporary Russian caricature ("The Hook on Which to Catch a Russian") showing a tax farmer perched on a liquor barrel, dangling bottles of vodka before a group of customers. See Christian, *'Living Water,'* pp. 171–73. Christian makes the case that the wealthiest Russian tax farmers enjoyed a degree of influence vis-à-vis the tsarist government, but only as regards their own careers.

64. Examples of this stance in the works of the first generation of historians of Russian Jewry can be found in Pavel Marek, *Ocherki po istorii prosveshcheniia evreev v Rossii: Dva vospitaniia* (Moscow, 1909); Dubnov, *History of the Jews in Russia and Poland,* 2: 159; Iu. Gessen, "Popytka emansipatsii evreev v Rossii (po neizdannym materialam)," *Perezhitoe* 1 (1909): 157–58. For more recent versions, see Frankel, *Prophecy and Politics,* pp. 51–65, 74–81, and Vital, *Origins of Zionism,* pp. 45, 72–76, 103.

65. RGIA, f. 1532, op. 1, d. 1771, l. 42; "Mémoire du baron Alexandre de Gunzburg," unpublished typescript, p. 9.

66. RGIA, f. 1532, op. 1, d. 1771, l. 10. In this respect as in many others, Horace Gintsburg followed his father's example. After the family's ennoblement in 1871 by the grand duke of Hessen-Darmstadt, whose interests they had represented at the court of the tsars, Horace Gintsburg stipulated that inheritance of the title of baron was to be denied to descendants who abandoned either Judaism or Russia. G. B. Sliozberg, *Baron G. O. Gintsburg, ego zhizn' i deiatel'nost'* (Paris, 1933), p. 33. Sliozberg served as secretary to Horace Gintsburg for fifteen years.

and observed the laws of kashrut.[67] The great Hebrew poet Yehudah Leib Gordon once dedicated a collection of poems to Horace Gintsburg with the words "And I found in you what I was not expecting / A maskil who loves his people."[68] The Gintsburgs cannot stand for all Jewish tax farmers, most of whom were not nearly as active in Jewish communal affairs. Further research on the nascent Russian-Jewish bourgeoisie, however, is likely to reveal a higher degree of attachment to Jewish society than was implied by contemporary Jewish critics.[69]

67. Ginzburg, *Historishe verk,* 2: 140; Sliozberg, *Baron G. O. Gintsburg,* pp. 53–57. In his capacity as secretary of the Society for the Spread of Enlightenment among the Jews, Shaul Ginzburg had frequent dealings with Horace Gintsburg.

68. Quoted in Ginzburg, *Historishe verk,* 2: 132.

69. See the suggestion along these lines in Kahan, *Essays,* p. 88.

Chapter 2

The Genesis of Selective Integration

Evzel Gintsburg headed the list of twelve Jewish merchants of the first guild, from various provinces, who petitioned the Jewish Committee in 1854 in protest against the new draft quotas. Although as merchants they had the right to buy their sons' way out of the draft, the increased quotas inevitably resulted in greater numbers of undelivered Jewish conscripts, which in turn increased the monetary penalties imposed on each Jewish community as a whole (including merchants).[1] The petitioners, however, were not writing in the name of Jewish communities as a whole, as had frequently been the practice with previous Jewish petitions. On the contrary:

> Belonging to the highest ranks of the Jewish merchantry in Russia, and ourselves shunning the prejudices of the mob, we would consider a petition on behalf of the parasites within our nation a betrayal of you and of the best interests of our people had we not ascertained that, in fact, the raising of conscription quotas for all Jews without distinction will only increase the number of proletarians to a terrifying degree, rather than free our communities of burdensome and harmful members. If, on the other hand, only idlers were subject to the increased quotas, then all well-intentioned Jews of sufficient means, themselves horrified at the growth of such a class of people, would greet not only the present measure but all other government measures designed to keep them [the idlers] in check with genuine gratitude, and without suspicion of religious bias.[2]

1. See Iulii Gessen, "Podatnoe oblozhenie," *Evreiskaia entsiklopediia,* 12: 639, where he notes that despite their formal immunity from conscription, Jewish merchants were de facto liable for the fines incurred by the Jewish communities in which they lived, since, according to a decree of 1831, "Jewish merchants and meshchane, by virtue of the teachings of their faith, constitute one society."

2. YIVO, RG 89, folder 755, doc. 3, p. 5. A Yiddish translation of portions of this petition was published in E. Tcherikover, ed., *Historishe Shriftn* (Warsaw, 1929), 1: 779–88. In official doc-

If Kiselev's reclassification scheme were ignored, the petitioners argued, the new quotas would reduce the incentives for Jews to engage in "useful" labor. The drafting of Jews who were gainfully employed would condemn their families to the ranks of "idlers." Unemployed Jews, lacking a stable residence, would escape notice altogether. In fact, the new quotas were "physically impossible" to fulfill, and the failure to do so, though no fault of the Jews, would increase suspicion against them on the part of the government and the population at large, who already regarded Jews as inveterate draft dodgers. This development could only work against the government's own goal of "merging" the Jews, and threatened to exercise "a dangerous influence on their mutual day-to-day relations" with their Christian neighbors.[3]

The Jewish Committee, under pressure from the tsar to increase overall levels of conscription, offered only a partial concession to the merchants' request. Conscription quotas for "useful" Jews would henceforth be set at half those for the "useless," but still higher than those for non-Jews of the same estate.[4]

Nicholas's death in February 1855, however, suddenly shifted the force field surrounding the committee's deliberations. At their next meeting, less than two months later, Kiselev and his colleagues returned to the Jewish merchants' petition, and in the process took stock of the committee's fifteen years of work. Judged by the government's own aims—the merging of the Jews with the "native" population and their turn to "useful" activity—official policy had not only failed but backfired. According to a report by Adjutant General A. A. Suvorov, Jewish draftees were often too young, too sickly, or too cowardly to be of any military value. They failed, as we have seen, to convert to Russian Orthodoxy in substantial numbers. And in marked contrast to Jewish loyalty to the Russian government during the Napoleonic invasion of 1812 and the Polish rebellion of 1831, Suvorov claimed, Jewish soldiers were now often suspected of sedition, and had allegedly been sighted on British ships in the Black Sea during the Crimean War, in which Russia was currently suffering a humiliating defeat.[5]

The committee recognized, too, that the enormous pressure to provide

---

uments, "parasites" (*tuneiadtsy*) and "idlers" (*prazdnoshataiushchiesia*) were standard expressions for Jews deemed "useless" under Kiselev's reclassification scheme (the razbor). This suggests that Gintsburg et al. were familiar with such documents.

3. YIVO, RG 89, folder 755, doc. 3, pp. 3–5.

4. RGIA, f. 1269, op. 1, d. 136, l. 17.

5. Ibid., ll. 14–15, 127–29. Governor General D. G. Bibikov of the Vilna, Kovno, Minsk, and Grodno provinces, the area with the densest Jewish population in the empire, confirmed the Jews' reputation for loyalty in 1812 and 1831. Gintsburg, too, mentioned Jewish loyalty (in 1812 and 1831) in the 1854 petition discussed above; see YIVO, RG 89, folder 755, doc. 3, pp. 5–8. The charge against Jews of spying for the British was taken so seriously that in May 1856 Alexander II ordered all Jewish sailors to be transferred to land units. See *Evreiskaia entsiklopediia*, 3:162. On Russian Jews during the Napoleonic invasion and the Polish rebellion of 1831,

draftees had only exacerbated what it regarded as the fanaticism and low moral level of Jewish life, frequently leading to kidnapping and "commerce in human beings."[6] More important, however, was the effect of the draft on Jewish taxes. As Gintsburg had pointed out in a separate petition of January 1855 to Minister of Finance P. F. Brok (a member of the Jewish Committee), monetary penalties for failure to deliver conscripts had so strained Jewish communities across the Pale that the total amount of unpaid revenues from Jews had ballooned from under 300,000 rubles in 1827, on the eve of the Jews' conscription, to roughly 8 million in 1854—an increase of more than twentyfold.[7] And the increase had come despite the halving of the Jewish poll tax in 1844, which returned it to the level set for non-Jews. According to the committee's roughly similar calculations, unpaid Jewish taxes had amounted to approximately 500,000 rubles in 1827 and had increased fifteenfold by 1853, to a total of just over 8 million rubles. Military commanders agreed that the presence of Jews in the army was hardly worth such a price—or any price.[8]

In light of the negative consequences of Nicholas's conscription policy for the Russian state as well as for the Jews, the Jewish Committee urged the new tsar, Nicholas's son Alexander II, to abolish the drafting of minors immediately. He did so at his inaugural ceremony in August 1856, together with a host of other concessions to various groups previously singled out for especially harsh treatment.[9] In addition, following the position taken by the Jewish petitioners, the committee agreed to reinstate the stratified conscription quotas established by Kiselev's reclassification scheme.[10]

But now Kiselev went even further. In a memorandum to the new tsar he wrote:

> Since the founding of this committee, I have received and continue to receive a large number of entreaties and even proposals from provincial governors con-

---

see S. M. Ginzburg, *Otechestvennaia voina 1812 goda i russkie evrei* (St. Petersburg, 1912), and S. Mstislavskii [S. M. Dubnov], "Evrei v pol'skom vostanii 1831 goda," *Evreiskaia Starina* 2 (1910): 61–80, 235–52.

6. See the minutes of the meeting of July 6, 1856, in RGIA, f. 1269, op. 1, d. 136, ll. 120–23. Jewish kidnappers of Jewish boys, popularly known by the Yiddish term *khappers*, became a staple of Jewish folklore.

7. YIVO, RG 89, folder 755, doc. 4, p. 2.

8. RGIA, f. 1269, op. 1, d. 136, ll. 17, 127–29. The committee noted (l. 6) that until 1845, data on taxes owed by Jews and Russians were not recorded separately; this may account for the discrepancy between the committee's figures for 1827 and those given by Gintsburg. For a province-by-province breakdown of unpaid Jewish taxes in 1845 and 1853, see Gessen, *Istoriia evreiskogo naroda*, 2: 117.

9. Greenberg, *The Jews in Russia*, 1: 73; W. E. Mosse, *Alexander II and the Modernization of Russia* (New York, 1962), p. 37.

10. RGIA, f. 1269, op. 1, d. 136, l. 22.

cerning the fact that legislative acts regarding the Jews, together with various temporary [administrative] measures, contain many internal contradictions, as well as restrictions that impede the attainment of HIS MAJESTY's goal of merging the Jews with the general population.[11]

The contradictions Kiselev had in mind were of two kinds: those involving regional variations in the law or its application and those that resulted from the treatment of Jews as members of two estates simultaneously—the "Jewish" estate and one of the various social/occupational estates. For example, despite the fact that since 1804 Jews had been formally permitted to attend Russian educational institutions, Kiselev found that in certain areas of the Pale they were being kept out of local gymnasiums by "private decree." Similar "private decrees" had also prevented the hiring of Jews with advanced medical degrees by the state, even within the Pale. In many cities and towns, what Kiselev termed the "medieval" practice of designating certain streets and quarters for Jewish residence still held sway, and Jews voted as a separate bloc in municipal elections, notwithstanding their formal membership in the various urban estates.[12]

Initially, Kiselev's solution consisted of proposing a review of all regulations regarding the Jews to ensure "their agreement with the general aim of merging that nation with the native population, insofar as the Jews' moral condition may permit this." But in a second draft he grew bolder: he called upon the government to "gradually bring existing regulations on the Jews into agreement with the general laws for other subjects of the Empire." Rather than seeking merely to ensure that legislation on the Jews was consistent with the ill-defined policy of "merging," Kiselev now aimed to eliminate discrepancies between Jewish legislation and the rest of the legal corpus—a position that appeared to amount in all but name to legal emancipation. Repeatedly cited in subsequent years by the Jewish Committee as well as by various branches of the bureaucracy, these two formulas became the point of departure for official Jewish policy in the Reform era.[13]

In practice, Kiselev's formulas proved exceptionally elastic. The insistence on "gradual" progress that would not outpace the Jews' "moral condition" left the time frame wide open. In his 1840 memorandum, for example, Kiselev had noted that his plans for transforming the Jews "could not be fulfilled

---

11. Ibid., l. 53.

12. Ibid., ll. 53–67. Such inconsistencies within tsarist legislation, and between legislation and administrative decrees, were endemic in prereform Russia (nor did they disappear after the Great Reforms) and were by no means limited to Jewish affairs.

13. For a sample of instances in which the first formula is cited, see ibid., ll. 53, 102; d. 137, l. 1; d. 138, l. 25. For the second formula, see d. 116, l. 21; d. 138, ll. 123, 148; d. 139, ll. 74, 175.

in a short period of time; at least, one must not count on the present generation."[14] Uvarov told the visiting British-Jewish philanthropist Sir Moses Montefiore in 1846 that "it would take a long time—perhaps a century—before any difference would be perceptible" in the Jews' condition.[15] The emphasis on gradualness in Jewish reform is a useful reminder that tsarist officials saw little risk in a deliberately slow approach to reform generally. The abolition of serfdom, too, was designed with the assumption of decades of social stability, during which serfs would emerge incrementally from their position of near-slavery. "Emancipated" state peasants, for example, were placed on an exacting schedule of redemption payments to the tsarist government which was meant to extend to the 1930s.[16] As Alexander II's government pursued wide-ranging social reform in Russia, therefore, the central debate within the Jewish Committee was not so much whether as how quickly to "bring existing regulations on the Jews into agreement with the general laws for other subjects of the Empire."

In addition to the vagaries of timing, the formulas articulated by Kiselev gave little sense of the specific content of policy on the Jews. At the time, and arguably until the old regime's collapse in 1917, there were no "general laws for other subjects of the Empire," but rather a congeries of separate regulations and privileges for the empire's various estates. In reality, then, the doctrine of legal uniformity between Jews and other subjects could imply parity at best within the various estates and social groups. The Jewish Committee more than once confirmed this interpretation by paraphrasing Kiselev's instruction as the granting to Jews of "the general rights of other subjects, according to occupation [*po zaniatiiam*]," or the "equalization of the Jews in [their] rights with other estates [*s prochimi sosloviiami*]."[17] Seen in this light, the "new" program bore a distinct resemblance to the pre-Nicholaevan goal of absorbing Jews into various levels of the social hierarchy.

14. Kiselev, "Ob ustroistve evreiskogo naroda," p. 7.

15. Sir Moses Montefiore and Lady Judith Cohen Montefiore, *The Diaries of Sir Moses and Lady Montefiore*, ed. Louis Loewe, 2 vols. in 1 (1890; facs. London, 1983), 1: 332

16. Geroid Robinson, *Rural Russia under the Old Regime: A History of the Landlord-Peasant World and a Prologue to the Peasant Revolution of 1917* (Berkeley, 1967), p. 90. It should be noted that proponents of Jewish integration in eighteenth-century Europe assumed a similar time frame; the German reformer C. W. Dohm, for example, estimated that the "civil improvement" of the Jews would take "a few generations." See Jacob Katz, "The Term 'Jewish Emancipation': Its Origins and Historical Impact," in his *Emancipation and Assimilation: Studies in Modern Jewish History* (Westmead, 1972), p. 34n. The difference, of course, is that in Dohm's time, in contrast to Kiselev's, there were no examples of Jewish emancipation to serve as evidence or as a spur to action. Even at the beginning of the twentieth century, Russia's leading political figure, Sergei Witte, once estimated that Jewish emancipation would require decades, if not centuries. See Rogger, *Jewish Policies and Right-Wing Politics*, pp. 85ff.

17. RGIA, f. 1269, op. 1, d. 138, ll. 124, 238.

THE WHEAT AND THE CHAFF

But this time the results were notably different. The centrifugal pressures of military conscription, increasing economic stratification, sectarian strife, and secular learning had all contributed to the emergence of groups within Russian Jewry that were eager for broader rights. It was not simply that the merchant elite sought to cut themselves off from the Jewish masses. In fact, Gintsburg and others had begun to position themselves as unofficial spokesmen for Russian Jewry, and more than any other element within the Jewish world, they were successful in gaining the ear of the tsarist government. Inspired by the proliferating examples of Jewish emancipation in Western and Central Europe, the merchants presented the Jewish Committee with a concrete plan—based on aspirations for their own advancement as well as for the transformation of Jewish society—to put into practice the long-standing but still vague notion of "merging" Jews into the various estates.

After their partially successful protest against uniform levels of conscription among Jews, Gintsburg and eighteen merchants again petitioned the Jewish Committee in July 1856. Evidently attuned to the new, more liberal political climate in the wake of Nicholas's death, they urged that the principle of differentiating between "the wheat and the chaff" be extended from the realm of burdens (the draft) to that of incentives.[18] In contrast to the maskilim, who were fond of using the "wheat and chaff" metaphor for distinguishing among the accumulated layers of Jewish tradition, the merchant petitioners sought to apply the term to the Jews themselves. If the Jews' transformation had hitherto been disappointingly slow, they asserted, the inertia was due "exclusively to the absence of measures designed to distinguish the most worthy from the unworthy." The petition continued:

> If the young generation, raised in the spirit and under the supervision of the government; if the higher merchantry, having for many years poured its life, its activity, and its wealth into the areas [where Jews reside]; if honest artisans, obtaining their bread by the sweat of their brow—[if these groups] will be granted greater rights by the government, thus distinguishing them from those who have given no particular evidence of their good intentions, usefulness, and love of work: then the entire [Jewish] people, seeing the chosen few as objects of the government's fairness and goodwill and, so to speak, as models of that which, according to the government's wishes, Jews ought

18. Ibid., d. 61, l. 5. This document was published by Iulii Gessen as part of his article "Popytka emansipatsii evreev v Rossii," *Perezhitoe* 1 (1909): 153–57. Dubnov, in his review of Gessen's article, noted that the names of the petitioners had been left out, possibly to avoid embarrassment to the Gintsburg family, which was still one of the most prominent among Russian Jews and active in sponsoring various scholarly and cultural endeavors. See S. M. Dubnov, "Bibliografiia," *Evreiskaia Starina* 1, no. 2 (1909): 294.

to become—the entire people will joyfully strive to attain the goal set by the government.[19]

Specifically, the petitioners proposed that four groups within the Jewish population be granted broader rights. Graduates of Russian institutions of higher education were automatically to receive the title of "honored citizen" (and thus be able to settle outside the Pale); merchants of the first two guilds in good standing for ten years were to receive "the same rights as other subjects," including the right to reside throughout the empire; the same was to apply to retired soldiers; and "the best among the artisans" were to be allowed to practice their crafts, but not settle permanently, outside the Pale.

With these tangible rewards dangled before them, the petitioners declared, parents would eagerly send their sons to Russian schools. Jewish "capitalists" (meaning primarily tax farmers and moneylenders) would flock to the higher merchant guilds, thereby increasing the state's revenues and strengthening trade and commerce. And Jewish artisans, instead of suffocating from excessive competition among themselves in the Pale (and stifling the growth of a Christian artisan class there), would spread out to the Russian interior, which was starved for crafts and petty industries. "Half a century ago," Gintsburg and the other signers reminded the committee, Jews elsewhere in Europe "were no higher than we, neither in education nor in morals, neither in their way of thinking nor of living—and today they are every bit the equal of the best of their Christian fellow citizens."[20] This could be Russian Jewry's future, too.

Undeniably, these and other petitions offer breathtaking evidence of the profound intramural tensions that divided Russia's Jews. Whereas one tsarist official protested that applying "the term 'useless' to tens of thousands of people is both severe and unjust," the petitioners saw fit to echo the committee's language by using terms such as "the mob," "parasites," "idlers," and "the unworthy" to describe their fellow Jews.[21] In effect, the petitioners proposed a dramatic widening of the distinctions drawn by the tsarist regime in its treatment of various groups within the Jewish population. These distinctions were even to be given visual expression: a petition from a group of maskilim proposed that "the Jews must be ordered to change their dress for the clothing commonly worn throughout the country, according to the social class to which they belong."[22]

19. RGIA, f. 1269, op. 1, d. 61, l. 4.
20. Ibid., ll. 4–6.
21. The official was M. S. Vorontsov, governor general of New Russia, quoted in Gessen, "Popytka emansipatsii evreev," pp. 147–50.
22. Quoted in Paul Mendes-Flohr and Jehuda Reinharz, comps., *The Jew in the Modern World: A Documentary History* (New York, 1995), p. 385.

Behind the merchants' plan was certainly a desire to protect their own wealth by reducing the fiscal burden of poor or "unproductive" Jews on their communities. Yet the full import of the petitions is more complex. For the active elements of the merchant elite had something far broader in mind than simply their own well-being. The granting of freedom of residence and other privileges only to "useful" Jews was meant to serve as a powerful instrument in the elite's struggle to transform the Jewish masses, and thereby to chip away at the wall separating Jews from their neighbors. As Gintsburg's secretary, the maskil Emanuel Levin, put it in a memorandum to his employer, "We must gradually prepare our co-religionists for the great epoch, make them worthy and capable of apprehending the grand blessing whose arrival, especially under the new spirit of the current government, we have good reason to hope for."[23] For decades, isolated Haskalah figures in Russia had sought to harness the power of the state to transform the Jews' internal life: their system of education, their occupational profile, their habits and mores. Rarely had they addressed the Jews' relationship with the surrounding society or argued for an elevation of their legal status, much less their civil rights. By contrast, Gintsburg and other wealthy merchants urged the government to create an elaborate system of incentives for selected categories within the Jewish population, matching their rights and privileges with those of the equivalent categories in Russian society. With time, these incentives were meant to persuade the mass of Jews simultaneously to engage in more "productive" forms of labor and overcome their isolation from the surrounding society. Thus even as the merchant elite sought to distance themselves and other "worthy" elements from the "unworthy" Jewish masses, they took on the role of spokesmen for Russian Jewry and architects of its gradual integration.

The freedom to live and work in the Russian interior, which emerged after 1855 (and remained throughout the late imperial period) as the cornerstone of Jewish appeals for expanded rights, was articulated by the merchant petitioners primarily in terms of economic benefits to the state as well as to the Jews. But other reasons were offered as well:

> The government wishes that the sharply marked traits distinguishing Jews from native Russians be smoothed out, that in all matters the Jews adopt the way of thinking and acting of the latter. But in the western territories, which alone are open to us, there is not the sort of group with which such a rapprochement of the Jews could occur. We constitute there the entire middle group in the cities and hamlets. The Christians belong to the highest noble estate or to the group of rural dwellers [i.e., peasants]. Consequently the means

23. E. B. Levin, "Zapiska ob emansipatsii evreev v Rossii," reproduced in *Evreiskaia Starina* 8, no. 3 (1915): 301.

of our rapprochement with the native population of the Empire are to be found in the Empire [i.e., the interior] itself. We humbly request that [the interior] be made more accessible to the best among us, who will bring honor to our people and who will be able to acquire from true Russians the most outstanding of their laudable qualities.[24]

Lest we be tempted to regard these words as mere flattery, a letter to Gintsburg from Emanuel Levin clarifies the point. Responding to the criticism that most "Russian" Jews could not even speak Russian, "the language of the fatherland," Levin declared, "Is there, in the actual areas where the Jews are granted permanent residence . . . a language of the fatherland, a *Muttersprache*? The bureaucrats speak and write, though poorly, in Russian, the nobility in Polish, and the middle estate does not know how to write at all, and speaks in the Ukrainian, Lithuanian, or Zhmud dialect." The positive cultural effects of the Jews' "merging" with the "native" people would therefore come about only if the latter were Great Russians, the "dominant" nationality, rather than the Ukrainians, Poles, Belorussians, and Lithuanians in whose midst the Jews were required to live.[25] Looking back in 1870, the Jewish lawyer Il´ia Orshanskii wrote that as early as the late 1850s, Jewish elites "had begun to consider themselves not merely people and citizens, but *Russian people and citizens of Russia.*"[26]

It did not matter, and perhaps even helped, that the Russian interior and its inhabitants were virtually terra incognita for the Jews. Gintsburg, for example, did not attempt to enumerate the "most outstanding of the true Russians' laudable qualities" in the petition cited above, nor did he examine the question whether a "middle estate" was to be found among ethnic Russians. If anything, the relative foreignness of the Russian provinces—of that "strange land called Russia," as Mary Antin put it—left greater room for the imagination, for seeing the Russian people as a kind of imperial ruling class and backbone of the state.[27] Throughout their diaspora, Jews had looked to

24. RGIA, f. 1269, op. 1, d. 61, ll. 5–6.
25. Levin, "Zapiska ob emansipatsii evreev," p. 305. "Zhmud" refers to a region encompassing southern Lithuania and the northern areas of Kovno province, as well as to that region's dialect, which combined elements of Lithuanian and Belorussian. See *Entsiklopedicheskii slovar´ Brokgaus-Efrona* (St. Petersburg, 1894), 12: 27. On the brief controversy in the press concerning the viability of a Ukrainian-Jewish identity, see Roman Serbyn, "The *Sion-Osnova* Controversy of 1861–1862," in Peter Potichnyi and Howard Aster, eds., *Ukrainian-Jewish Relations in Historical Perspective* (Edmonton, 1988), pp. 85–100.
26. Orshanskii, *Evrei v Rossii*, p. 180 (emphasis in original). The essay from which this quotation is taken was originally published serially in the Russian-Jewish newspaper *Den´* in 1870.
27. The views expressed by Gintsburg, Levin, and others show that Israel Bartal's insightful analysis of Jewish belletristic authors of the Reform era, who frequently represented Russian officials in glowing terms as allies of the tiny vanguard of maskilic reformers, applies equally well to the worldview of the merchant elite. See Bartal, "Ha-lo-yehudim ve-hevratam be-sifrut

Gentile elites for protection and support, and in prepartition Poland they had forged remarkably intimate bonds with the nobility and the state. Russia had been the exception to the early modern pattern of granting charters of protection (and in some cases of tolerance) to Jewish populations. Beyond their obvious economic motives, therefore, Jewish petitions for greater access to Russia proper may well have reflected a desire to replicate the historic pattern of direct relations with "native" elites.

If their lack of familiarity with Russia fired the imagination of Jews such as Gintsburg and Levin, the converse notion—that Russians lacked experience with Jews—seems to have had a similar effect. Levin, for example, argued in 1859 that popular prejudice against Jews was relatively undeveloped among ethnic Russians, in the absence of both direct contact and a Russian public sphere in which hostility could be articulated. One of the reasons for the protracted and often nasty struggle over Jewish emancipation in Great Britain and Western Europe, according to Levin, was the constitutional form of government there, in which "the passions of the parties have a freer field of action and where the will of the monarch alone is unable to contain them." "None of this exists in Russia," Levin asserted confidently, "where public opinion is still in its infancy [and] autocratic power is not constrained by any parliamentary forms." Indeed, German Jews, having recently endured a sharp increase in anti-Semitic public discourse, could only envy their counterparts in Russia. "We, by contrast," Levin insisted, "will be dealing with a fresh people not yet possessed of a well-formed public opinion, people who, not having tolerated Jews in their midst until now, have had neither the time nor the occasion to develop feelings of jealousy or hostility toward them."[28] This was, to say the least, one of the more creative applications of the idea of the "privilege of backwardness," of Russia as a young society that could learn from and avoid Europe's mistakes.[29] Yet Levin's notion did not miss the mark entirely: the tsarist autocracy's use of social estates as the medium for Jewish integration was in fact a symptom of those estates' relatively undeveloped character and their inability to resist intervention by the regime. Levin's preference for discrete, paternalist forms of Jewish influence on the state, moreover, was fully shared by the

---

ivrit ve-yidish be-mizrah eropah ben ha-shanim 1856–1914," Ph.D. dissertation, Hebrew University of Jerusalem, 1980, pp. 15–46.

28. Levin, "Zapiska ob emansipatsii evreev," p. 302.

29. Before one dismisses Levin's idea as the wishful thinking of a politically naive maskil, moreover, it would be well to recall that in later years certain Zionist figures were not immune to similar slavophile-tinged views. In his memoirs, Mordechai ben Hillel Ha-Kohen describes his strong affection for "the Russian people on account of their simplicity, their great-heartedness, for those same people whose spirit civilization has not yet corrupted": Olami, 4 vols. (Jerusalem, 1927–29), 1: 81.

Figure 3. Emanuel Levin (1820–1913): "We must gradually prepare our co-religionists for the great epoch, make them worthy and capable of apprehending the grand blessing whose arrival, especially under the new spirit of the current government, we have good reason to hope for."

merchant elite, and exercised a decisive influence on Jewish politics until the final decades of the nineteenth century.

While Gintsburg and other merchants highlighted the increased exposure to the "laudable qualities" of "true Russians" that expanded residence rights would bring, it was the economic factors cited in their petition that resonated most forcefully among members of the Jewish Committee. If Jews had formerly been banned from the Russian interior, the committee noted, this had been at a time when Russia still lacked its own manufacturing and industry, as well as a customs network, and the Jews were engaged in smuggling foreign goods. Now, however, the situation had changed. Jewish merchants could serve as useful conduits of goods from the interior to the western borderlands, and thus deflect demand there away from foreign merchandise.

The committee, however, was not yet prepared simply to open the interior to Jewish entrepreneurs. A variety of options were considered: declaring free access for trade but without residence rights; restricting Jewish commerce and residence in the interior to a small area adjacent to the Pale, bounded by railroads connecting Mogilev, Kursk, Orel, and Kharkov; granting access only to the two capitals and select annual trade fairs; or opening cities within the Pale currently off limits to most Jews, such as Kiev, Nikolaev, and Sebastopol'.[30] All these proposals, whose conservative approach was justified in the name of gradualness, had in common the traditional method of limiting the physical space—whatever its dimensions—open to Jews within the empire, rather than relying on subtler mechanisms that would restrict access to institutions or sectors of the economy.

The committee's cautious approach was reinforced by Kiselev's departure at the end of 1856 to become ambassador to France, and his replacement by the less imaginative state secretary (and later minister of internal affairs) Dmitrii N. Bludov. In addition, Alexander II perpetuated, though in less extreme form, his father's habit of acting as a brake on the committee's proposals. Thus when the committee, summarizing its deliberations for the tsar in March 1858, noted that Jewish merchants could make valuable contributions to "the progress of civic life" (*progress grazhdanstvennosti*), the tsar responded, "What sort of progress!!! I request that this word not be used in official documents."[31]

But Jewish merchants continued to press for rights equal to those of their Russian counterparts. By 1858, moreover, Gintsburg had succeeded in building an unprecedented degree of intercommunal coordination among the petitioners. During the first half of the century, Jewish petitions had tended to come from individuals or single Jewish communities, on their own behalf; only rabbis achieved coordination across communal lines, and that infrequently.[32] The 1854 appeal to the Jewish Committee from Gintsburg

---

30. RGIA, f. 1269, op. 1, d. 61, ll. 25–27; d. 137, ll. 11–13.
31. Ibid., d. 137, l. 14.
32. For examples of individual or single-community petitions, see Klier, *Russia Gathers Her Jews*, p. 84, and Stanislawski, *Tsar Nicholas I*, pp. 120–21; on rabbinical petitions see Lederhendler, *Road to Modern Jewish Politics*, pp. 68–83. Individual and single-community petitions did not decrease in the second half of the nineteenth century; if anything, the total number of Jewish petitions grew exponentially across the century. But beginning with Gintsburg, appeals from organized Jewish elites, particularly merchants, began to attract far greater attention in government circles, and at far higher levels of the bureaucracy.

and eleven other merchants had set a precedent: its authors were from various cities and towns in different provinces, and they appealed on behalf of distinct Jewish social strata (in particular, their own) throughout the Pale.[33] One may surmise that Gintsburg's intercommunal contacts emerged from his tax-farming business. As Yaʿakov Lifshitz, an aide to the prominent rabbi Isaac Elhanan Spektor and a partisan of orthodox rabbinical authority, complained in his memoirs, "[Gintsburg] ran the tax-farming business like a minigovernment. Under him were ten province chiefs who were enormously wealthy in their own right. Almost all of them conducted themselves with ostentatious, overbearing pride, and tyrannized the province, as the district chiefs did in each district."[34] In the late 1850s, Gintsburg began to distribute model petitions to Jewish merchants in cities across the Pale, who would then endorse and submit them to the Jewish Committee.[35]

Jewish merchants in Kiev weighed in with an appeal to the minister of enlightenment (a member of the Jewish Committee), combining the familiar patriotic and economic motives. Noting that the Russian government had turned to foreign Jewish capitalists in order to finance wartime expenditures and the construction of railroads,[36] the merchants proclaimed:

> Why should Russian Jews not be the sort of bulwark for their fatherland that Eskeles, Goldsmith, Hirsch, Magdelson, and the Rothschilds are for their countries? . . . If we are not terribly mistaken, the Minister of Finance can testify as to both the Jews' abilities and the great benefit which would accrue to the state from . . . equalizing the rights of the Jewish merchantry.[37]

33. The twenty signers of Gintsburg's July 1856 petition came from nearly all the fifteen provinces that constituted the Pale, from Vitebsk to Odessa. Other towns and cities represented included Minsk, Mogilev, Zhitomir, Berdichev, Poltava, Dinaburg, Ekaterinoslav, Elizavetgrad, Kherson, and Mstislav. See RGIA, f. 1269, op. 1, d. 61, l. 7.

34. Yaʿakov Halevi Lifshitz, *Zikhron Yaʿakov*, 3 vols. (Frankfurt a. M., 1924), 2: 55, quoted in Lederhendler, *Road to Modern Jewish Politics*, p. 191n77.

35. In a letter (Oct. 20, 1859) to Bludov as head of the Jewish Committee, Gintsburg noted, with more than a hint at his own importance, "I have convinced [the] Jewish communities . . . to support our opinion with special petitions on their part." See RGIA, f. 1269, op. 1, d. 3b, l. 202. In 1858 alone the Jewish Committee received nearly identical petitions from Jewish merchants in the cities of Vitebsk (28 signatories), Grodno (12), and Mogilev (13) and the provinces of Chernigov (21) and Tavrida (32). See ibid., d. 3b, ll. 151–56, 167–70, 203–4 (model petition), 221–22; d. 137, l. 181.

36. This was in fact the case, at least as far as railroads were concerned. See Alfred Rieber, "The Formation of 'La Grande Societé des Chemins de Fer Russes,'" *Jahrbücher für Geschichte Osteuropas* 21 (1973): 375–91.

37. RGIA, f. 1269, op. 1, d. 3b, l. 194. Jewish merchants were allowed to reside only in certain sections of Kiev, and strictly on a temporary basis. This petition bears no date, but it was filed with a series of petitions from 1858, so I am assuming that it was submitted in the same year. Baron Bernhard von Eskeles was a Viennese Jew who in 1816 founded the Austrian National Bank and was its director for twenty-three years; the financier Sir Isaac Goldsmith, the first British Jew to receive the title of baron, was a prominent member of the Whig party; Josef

Just as the many publications on technology and economy issued by the Russian government's ministries—publications with which the petitioners were clearly familiar—had greatly contributed to the empire's growth, so, they argued, there ought to be an official scholarly journal aimed at spreading enlightenment among the Jews from the citadels of learning in the imperial capital. Furthermore, the petitioners proposed to raise money to endow a chair in Jewish literature at the Academy of Sciences (where not a single Jew was to be found) in St. Petersburg as well as a triennial prize for the best work on Jewish or Russian-Jewish literature. "It is painful for us," they proclaimed, "to think that our four thousand years of literary culture are [regarded as] lower than the Finnish dialects, the Tibetan or Tatar languages, which can scarcely count as many lines as we have books in all branches of human knowledge, religious belief, and feeling." As if to highlight their fluency in and affinity for Russian cultural traditions, the merchants expressed their eagerness "to be useful to the Tsar and Fatherland, in the words of the great [fabulist Ivan] Krylov, if only as a single drop of honey in the great apiary of Russia."[38]

The merchants' self-distancing from the populations of the peripheries in favor of direct ties to the Great Russian center was intended to take a political cast as well. Ostensibly to avoid "burdening" the committee with "repetitious" Jewish appeals, the merchants announced that "we have decided to elect Honored Citizen G. I. Gintsburg to be a kind of representative of all lovers of enlightenment before the person of Your Excellency."[39] Evzel and Horace Gintsburg frequented St. Petersburg for business purposes and were well connected in official circles. By 1859, Evzel Gintsburg was referring to himself in a petition to the Ministry of Enlightenment as "a person who has taken on the role, if one may express it this way, of mediation between the government and the Jewish people in the matter of education."[40] In the same year, on the pages of *Ha-Magid* (The Preacher), a maskilic newspaper published in East Prussia and imported (legally) to readers in the Pale, Gintsburg was described as "the spokesman and head of our people" in Russia.[41]

The Reform era thus witnessed a significant shift in the manner and substance of influence by Jews on official Jewish policy—and this despite the

---

von Hirsch was a Bavarian Jewish banker and philanthropist who, inter alia, built the Bavarian Ostbahn railway in the 1850s. I have been unable to identify Magdelson. The Gintsburgs were connected by business and marriage ties to several of Europe's leading Jewish finanical families, including the Rothschilds, Bleichröders, and Warburgs.

38. Ibid., ll. 197–98. I. A. Krylov (1769–1844), who became famous for his homey fables, was an early architect of a distinctly Russian literary language. References to Russian literature were still extremely rare in Jewish texts of the 1850s.

39. Ibid., l. 198.

40. YIVO, RG 89, doc. 12, p. 8.

41. Quoted in Lederhendler, *Road to Modern Jewish Politics*, p. 79.

fact that no Jewish opinion was ever actively solicited by the Jewish Committee, in marked contrast to the practice of similar committees before and after.[42] In July 1858, the ministers of finance and internal affairs, both members of the committee, endorsed the idea of granting to Jewish merchants of the first guild "all the rights of the Russian merchantry," including the right to reside on a permanent basis throughout the empire and to own land. This proposal became law in 1859, making Jewish first-guild merchants the first Jews to be officially allowed—by virtue of their estate membership, rather than on an individual basis—to settle permanently in the Russian interior.[43] "One must not confuse the unenlightened and unproductive masses," noted the committee in its recommendation to Alexander II, "with that small number of Jews who, as owners of considerable capital and overseers of wide-ranging trade both at home and abroad, differ sharply from their co-religionists."[44]

The committee was determined that for the time being the number of Jews allowed in the interior would remain small indeed: by its own calculations, 108 merchants, together with their families, would qualify immediately. Members of the second and third guilds were for the time being granted only temporary residence.[45] The number of Jewish servants and employees to be brought along into the interior was precisely limited according to the form and location of their employment: more were permitted in the capitals, fewer in rural areas, reflecting the deep and abiding fear that Jews would take advantage of peasants. Furthermore, although Jewish merchants were free to register with the executive boards of merchant societies (*kupecheskie upravy*) wherever they settled, if they or their descendants lost their membership in the first guild (as a result of business failures or for other reasons), they were required to return to the Pale.[46]

---

42. For example, Jewish delegates chosen by their communities—how democratically is difficult to say—were invited to contribute their views to a Jewish Committee in 1804, to the Vilna Commission in 1869, and to the Provincial Commissions of 1881–84. The High Commission for Review of Legislation Pertaining to the Jews of Russia (1883–88), also known as the Pahlen Commission for its chairman, Minister of Justice K. I. Pahlen, solicited the views of unelected Jewish notables, including Horace Gintsburg.

43. RGIA, f. 1269, op. 1, d. 137, ll. 110–17; *PSZ*, ser. 2, no. 34248, Mar. 16, 1859.

44. RGIA, f. 1269, op. 1, d. 137, l. 117.

45. It is worth noting that Minister of Internal Affairs S. S. Lanskoi and Minister of Enlightenment A. S. Norov had originally endorsed unrestricted residence rights for *all* Jewish merchants as well as for university and gymnasium graduates and retired soldiers who had served in the interior. See ibid., d. 138, ll. 132–33. No sooner had the government granted the right of residence in the interior to Jewish merchants of the first guild than those of the second and third guilds petitioned for similar treatment. See ibid., d. 85, ll. 1–10.

46. Ibid., d. 137, ll. 110–20. Russians who lost their membership in the first merchant guild likewise sacrificed the rights associated with the merchant estate, but remained free to settle throughout the empire.

STUDENTS, SOLDIERS, AND ARTISANS

During the following several years, the rights of other select groups within the Jewish population on whose behalf the merchants had appealed—graduates of institutions of higher learning, retired soldiers, and artisans—were also expanded, though in a similarly conservative fashion. Some of these groups sent their own petitions to the Jewish Committee, with or without the explicit backing of Gintsburg and other merchants. Students, not surprisingly, led the pack. The small number of Jewish students in Russian institutions of higher education before the 1860s were concentrated at the Medical-Surgical Academy in St. Petersburg, where roughly forty Jews matriculated between 1835 and 1854.[47] Like all other students at the academy, Jews were given full scholarships in exchange for service to the state after graduation as military physicians. But a decree of 1844 by Nicholas I requiring that Jews convert before entering state service had virtually halted employment of Jewish physicians by the state.[48] Ten years later, citing the army's need for medical personnel during the Crimean War, the director of the academy appealed—unsuccessfully—on behalf of two Jewish students who wished to enter state service. In 1856, sensing a more hospitable climate, thirty-three Jewish students petitioned the Jewish Committee directly for the right to be employed by the state:

> We are so bold as to pray that our paternal government not confuse us, who were brought up in its spirit, and not in the spirit of the Talmud, with the uneducated masses. We were educated in the same institutions together with the best sons of Russia, and merged ourselves with their life. . . . The eyes of our entire young generation are directed at us, who were the first to overcome prejudice and all kinds of obstacles and deprivations, in order to follow the merciful call of the government. Our co-religionists will judge by our fate the sincerity of all measures regarding the education of [Jewish] youth. If we are cast out, it will be a victory for the fanatics and will bring our parents to despair.[49]

47. After 1881 the academy was known as the Military-Medical Academy. See "Akademiia Voenno-Meditsinskaia" in *Evreiskaia entsiklopediia*, 1: 601–2. The figure of forty students comes from Gintsburg's 1854 petition; see YIVO, RG 89, folder 755, doc. 3, p. 7.

48. Until the creation in 1844 of the office of "expert Jew" (*uchenyi evrei*)—that is, consultant on Jewish matters to government officials in St. Petersburg and the Pale—the only points of entry for Jews into the ranks of state service were the army or the medical profession. Even "expert Jews" were conceived by the government in rather partisan terms: a secret decree of 1850 mandated that they be employed to exercise "moral influence toward weakening [Jewish] fanaticism resulting from corrupt interpretations, or incorrect understanding, of true Old Testament teachings. Expert Jews are also to be used to instill in their co-religionists a belief in the usefulness of education and to eliminate their ungrounded fears concerning persecution of their faith." See RGIA, f. 1269, op. 1, d. 136, ll. 83–85.

49. Ibid., d. 19, ll. 40–41. A slightly different version, copied from an unknown source (YIVO, RG 89, folder 755, doc. 6), reads in part: "We are so bold as to pray that our paternal govern-

Together with other petitions from individual Jewish physicians seeking employment in state institutions, this appeal helped persuade the committee in 1856 to have the 1844 decree revoked.[50]

Having won back the limited right to enter state service, Jewish students— again mostly in the field of medicine—soon proceeded to broach the subject of residence outside the Pale. In 1860, acting on rumors that the Jewish Committee was considering such rights, but only for those with doctorates in medicine, Jewish students from St. Petersburg and Kiev joined forces (in a display of coordination reminiscent of that of their merchant counterparts) to appeal for residence rights for all Jews in higher education. They began boldly, declaring that only the abolition of the Pale would ultimately put an end to the Jews' estrangement.[51] To be sure, such a policy might apply at first to "a certain class of people more useful to society." But why were (secularly) educated Jews "placed below their co-religionists who were merchants of the first guild, or their contractors and employees"? Having received their diplomas from a university or institute, Jewish students "must leave those places and societies [*obshchestva*] into whose midst they have been drawn by virtue of their education, and are deprived of the right to live in cities where there are universities, libraries, and other resources necessary for their further scholarly development."[52] The hopeless situation of Jewish students af-

---

ment not confuse us, who were brought up in its spirit, and under its watchful eye, with the masses of our unhappy tribe. We were not schooled on the Talmud, we do not belong to Palestine more than to Holy Russia. We were educated in the same institutions together with her [Russia's] best sons, and merged ourselves with their life, followed the same principles, acquired the same moral habits and customs, and are happy to render to our Fatherland the same services."

50. For other petitions from physicians see RGIA, f. 1269, op. 1, d. 19, ll. 48–49, 71–72. At the request of Minister of the Interior Bibikov (a member of the Jewish Committee who feared a sudden influx of Jews into the civil service), even with the revocation of the 1844 decree, Jews were to be allowed to enter state service only within the Pale, and were to be enrolled in the Table of Ranks (with all the privileges this entailed) only on the military, not the civilian, side. These latter restrictions were lifted between 1865 and 1867. See ibid., d. 136, ll. 68–73, and Iulii Gessen, "Vysshee obrazovanie," *Evreiskaia entsiklopediia*, 5: 863.

51. RGIA, f. 1269, op. 1, d. 138, l. 163; the number of signatories of this petition is not given. This was not the first time the notion of completely abolishing the Pale had made its way into the deliberations of the Jewish Committee. In 1856, a Jewish merchant (and honored citizen) from Riga named Moisei (Moshe) Brainin appealed for residence rights in the interior for all Jews. His petition was promptly dismissed by Kiselev (ibid., d. 136, ll. 119–20). In 1858, A. G. Stroganov, governor general of New Russia and Bessarabia and a member of the Jewish Committee, submitted a memorandum arguing that "at the present time there is no need for exclusionary restrictions against the Jews." This position was fully endorsed by Lanskoi, the minister of internal affairs, but rejected by the committee as premature. The original memorandum is in RGIA, f. 821, op. 9, d. 77, ll. 73–86; Gessen published it in full in his "Popytka emansipatsii," *Perezhitoe* 1 (1909): 158–62. For the Jewish Committee's reaction, see RGIA, f. 1269, op. 1, d. 137, ll. 130–37.

52. RGIA, f. 1269, op. 1, d. 138, l. 164.

ter graduation, argued the petitioners, was the main reason for the slow spread of secular education among Jews.

The idea of extending residence rights to Jews with higher (secular) education, first broached by Gintsburg and other merchants and later seconded by Jewish students themselves, won the endorsement of the ministers of enlightenment and internal affairs, who in fact sought to extend it to cover graduates of gymnasiums and lycées. In 1861, however, the Jewish Committee as a whole, while acknowledging the proposal as "just" and "confirmed by the historical development of legislation on Jews in other states and the present condition of Jews in those states," nevertheless invoked the principle of gradualness, and ruled that for the time being, only Jews with university degrees should be granted the right to reside outside the Pale.[53] After repeated appeals by Gintsburg and various groups of Jewish students, this right would be extended in 1872 to graduates of the St. Petersburg Technological Institute and in 1879 to graduates of all institutions of higher education.[54]

In a roughly similar way, the voices of Jewish soldiers reached the Jewish Committee after initial appeals on their behalf by the merchant elite. A pair of petitions submitted in 1859 by Gintsburg and ten other merchants (now hesitantly identifying themselves as "temporary residents of Petersburg") reiterated their appeal that retired soldiers be allowed to reside throughout the empire:

> They have given the best years of their lives to the fatherland and have lived together with their Russian comrades, in a common spirit. When they retire, they are forced to depart, at an old age and usually with their families, sometimes thousands of versts, without means, to the western provinces, where they frequently find nothing, other than the graves of their relatives.[55]

The soldiers themselves, usually having served for twenty-five years after being drafted as children, often echoed the theme of estrangement from their former communities. Thus a group of former cantonists, faced with deportation to the Pale of Settlement, wrote to the committee in 1859 that "in all but faith [we] are cut off from our birthplace." If the government tolerated their presence in the Russian interior during their "faultless service to the fatherland and the throne," would it not do so now? One retired soldier's wife, Eva Leibovich, pleaded that her family be allowed to remain in St. Petersburg, where her husband had served as a plumber in a military hospital. Not unlike the students, she argued that if merchants of the first guild

---

53. *PSZ*, ser. 2, vol. 36, no. 37684, Nov. 27, 1861.

54. RGIA, f. 1269, op. 1, d. 138, ll. 132, 148–57; Gessen, "Vysshee obrazovanie," *Evreiskaia entsiklopediia*, 5: 863.

55. RGIA, f. 1269, op. 1, d. 84, ll. 5–6. A verst is a unit of length equal to roughly two-thirds of a mile.

Figure 4. A former Jewish cantonist. Gertsl Yankl
(Zvi Herts) Tsam (1835–1915), after serving in
Siberia, rose to the rank of captain. (By permission
of YIVO Institute for Jewish Research.)

enjoyed the right of residence in the capital simply by virtue of having paid
dues for guild membership, so should her husband by virtue of his quarter-
century of service to the state.[56]

Fearing what it considered an excessive Jewish presence in the interior
provinces (by this time tens of thousands of Jews had completed the full term
of military service), the Jewish Committee was reluctant to grant the soldiers'
request. Alexander II typically responded to appeals from former cantonists
with his oft-used rejoinder, "I most definitely do not agree with this."[57] But

56. Ibid., d. 137, l. 244; d. 84, ll. 11–12.
57. Ibid., d. 137, l. 246.

their pleas found a strong supporter in the minister of war, Dmitrii A. Miliutin, a nephew of Kiselev. In the course of military service, the reform-minded Miliutin argued in a report in 1861, a Jew loses all ties to his former life in the Pale, and having become "Russified," finds it extremely difficult to return to his co-religionists and "become a Jew again."

For Miliutin, however, a more important principle was also at stake. Because of the exceptionally stringent criteria for promotion of Jews in the army—criteria imposed by civilian, not military, authorities, as Miliutin was careful to point out—"whether [a Jew] serves in an outstanding and worthy manner or only fairly has no influence whatsoever on his position in the service." Denied incentives to excel, Jews formed a "caste" within the army, "less an aid than a burden to the troops." It was, in effect, an insult to military honor to deny Jewish veterans the basic right enjoyed by other veterans of choosing where to reside after retirement. "Whatever the policy concerning the continued maintenance of general restrictions for the Jews in civilian life," Miliutin continued, "they must not weigh upon [their] standing in the military." This meant, among other things, that Jews should be promoted according to the general criteria, and should enjoy "those privileges established for all who serve."[58] Although it was not until 1867 that Jewish veterans were granted open residence rights, the policy of treating them equally with other veterans set an important precedent, and together with continued appeals by the Gintsburgs, helped ensure that the general military reform of 1874 contained no restrictive clauses against Jews, indeed did not even mention Jews.[59]

Jewish artisans, the final group mentioned in Gintsburg's petition of 1856, outnumbered merchants, students, and soldiers combined, and hence the question of their residence outside the Pale was potentially of even greater significance. In the records of the Jewish Committee's proceedings, however, there is not a single petition from artisans themselves. Instead, the debate was carried on by their self-appointed merchant spokesmen, various government officials, and landowners from Russian provinces eager for artisan labor. In 1863, committees of noble landowners from the provinces of Pskov and Kursk—just outside the northern and eastern borders of the Pale, respectively—urged the ministers of finance and internal affairs to allow Jewish artisans skilled in distilling alcohol and other trades to reside on their estates. "The best distillers are almost exclusively among the Jews," reported one petition, since distilleries were "more highly developed" in the western provinces. Furthermore,

58. Ibid., d. 100, ll. 7–11.

59. In 1860, Jews who had served in the imperial *gvardeiskii korpus* had been granted the right to remain with their families in St. Petersburg. I return to the military reform of 1874 in Chapter 5.

With the abolition of serfdom, some landowners from the interior provinces have found it impossible to maintain their agricultural endeavors as well as the various sorts of manufactories on their estates. For the upkeep of their manufactories and other parts of the rural economy they have had to invite Jews from among the local residents to manage their estates, for want of others wishing to do so.[60]

Any Jewish artisans in Pskov or Kursk, of course, were there illegally, and with the Pale only a province away, their stays were probably sporadic as well.[61] Therefore the landowners wished to see Jewish residence rights broadened, a move that the minister of finance strongly endorsed because it promised to promote "one of the government's most important . . . undertakings," the lucrative tax on alcohol, and to introduce greater entrepreneurship into the interior.[62]

P. A. Valuev, a member of the Jewish Committee and since 1861 minister of internal affairs, provided graphic evidence for the potential benefits of allowing Jewish artisans into the interior. Taking two provinces roughly comparable in physical and human geography, one—Kiev—inside the Pale, the other—Kursk—just outside it, Valuev noted that in the province of Kiev there were 5,057 artisans in a total population of 1.8 million (2.8 per 1,000 population), while in Kursk, where Jews were banned, there were only 1,446 artisans in a total population of 1.7 million (0.8 per 1,000 population). Even in "one of the most developed Great Russian provinces," Iaroslavl, the proportion of artisans was similar to that of Kursk (0.9 per 1,000 population).[63]

Citing Alexander II's injunction to "gradually bring existing regulations on the Jews into agreement with the general laws for other subjects of the Empire" as well as the various petitions from Gintsburg urging broader residence rights for "the best among the artisans," the Jewish Committee endorsed the granting of permanent residence rights outside the Pale to all guild-registered artisans, a measure that became law in 1865.[64] Like other legislation allowing select groups within the Jewish population to reside in the interior, the 1865 decree strove to maintain the principle of gradualness

---

60. RGIA, f. 1269, op. 1, d. 116, l. 8.

61. It is worth noting that in its paraphrasing of the landowners' petition, forwarded to the Jewish Committee, the Ministry of Internal Affairs wrote that the landowners had had to invite "Jews," and omitted "from among the local residents": ibid., l. 11.

62. Ibid., ll. 5, 22.

63. Ibid., l. 9. Figures for all three provinces do not include the respective provincial capitals, to compensate for the fact that Jewish artisans were banned from the city of Kiev.

64. *PSZ*, ser. 2, vol. 40, no. 42264, June 28, 1865. Other reasons for this measure cited by individual members of the committee included the need to reduce the intense pressure of Jewish competition on Christian artisans in the Pale, and the hope of reducing poverty among Jewish artisans, thereby making them less vulnerable to "Polish propaganda": RGIA, f. 1269, op. 1, d. 116, l. 5.

by ensuring that the gates leading from the Pale were opened only slightly, so as to prevent what Valuev called "a rapid flood of a hitherto alien element into the midst of the population of the Empire's interior provinces."[65] Jewish artisans who wished to settle in the interior were required to present a great number of attestations from town and guild authorities. Furthermore, once outside the Pale, an artisan could practice only that craft under which he was registered, and otherwise faced the threat of expulsion (which in fact became quite common).

Despite their cautious approach to Jewish mobility and their concern with gradualness, the reforms inaugurated by the Jewish Committee created a significant breach in the walls of the Pale and therefore a powerful engine of change within Jewish society. Responding to the 1865 decree on artisans, and more generally to the recent growth of selective integration, the leading publisher of Hebrew and Yiddish weeklies, Alexander Tsederbaum, wrote with characteristic abandon that "the interior is now open to all except those who make their livelihood from air."[66] During the last third of the century, hundreds of thousands of Jews settled outside the Pale, with the largest communities centered in the Russian capitals, St. Petersburg and Moscow. In 1897, the first comprehensive census recorded some 314,000 Jews legally residing in Russia proper or in other areas of the empire (excluding Poland) beyond the territory of the Pale.[67] Moreover, a significant number of Jews—how many is impossible to say—lived outside the Pale illegally, having failed to meet the formal qualifications for unrestricted residence.

Looking back on nearly a century of tsarist administration of the Jews, an internal government study from 1886 staked out the perceived extremes of passivity and force between which official policy maneuvered:

> Having reincorporated her age-old western territories, Russia found in them a large tribe completely alien to the native population by virtue of its morals, habits, and character, its faith and language. . . . To leave this tribe in such a state of alienation would have meant to repeat the fateful mistake of the Kingdom of Poland, to preserve a significant element that was capable of weakening or even corrupting the entire state organism. To destroy it by force would have been possible for an oriental conqueror in the manner of [the Turkic warlord] Tamerlane, but not at all for a European and Christian state. Only one option remained: direct all efforts to putting an end to the alienation of the Jewish tribe and to integrating it with the country's native population.[68]

65. RGIA, f. 1269, op. 1, d. 116, l. 6.

66. Quoted in Alexander Orbach, *New Voices of Russian Jewry: A Study of the Russian-Jewish Press of Odessa in the Era of the Great Reforms, 1860–1871* (Leiden, 1980), p. 106. Tsederbaum refers to *luftmenshen*, people who floated from one odd job to another.

67. *Evreiskaia entsiklopediia*, 11: 538.

68. Georgievskii, *Doklad*, p. 238.

A weak state had allowed its Jews to preserve their corporate autonomy, and in so doing—according to this argument—made itself weaker still. An "oriental" despot would have simply wiped the Jews out. Russia, a Christian state but a strong and highly centralized one, took the middle, "European" path: dismantling the Jews' castelike isolation by encouraging their integration with the "native population."

In reality, as I have attempted to show, the European model of emancipation into a society of citizens underwent substantial modifications in the process of being adapted to Russia's archaic social order and to the profound intramural tensions among Russia's Jews. The tsarist autocracy was careful to restrict the channels of integration and to bind them to the estate structure of the "native" population. Only when official policy incorporated specific incentives proposed by new Jewish elites was an effective framework born, one that harnessed the ambition of transforming Jewish society to the goal of increasing the Jews' usefulness to the state. Certainly, Jewish opinions were not the only ones taken up for discussion by the Jewish Committee. Governors general from provinces in the Pale submitted their own reports, offering diverse views on Jewish reform, and committee members brought to the table the viewpoints of a wide range of ministries and departments. But more often than not, it was Jewish merchants' petitions that set the committee's specific agendas and provided the closest thing to a blueprint for its final recommendations.

How are we to account for the influence in government circles of the views of Gintsburg and other wealthy merchants? Undoubtedly, part of the answer lies in the simple fact that such Jews provided hefty revenues to the state treasury. The importance of tax-farming and other government contracts for the formation of Jewish wealth in the mid–nineteenth century highlights the extent to which the Jewish merchant elite was concentrated in a sector of the economy created and closely administered by the state, thus easing access to tsarist officialdom.[69] During the late 1850s and early 1860s, for example, Evzel Gintsburg alone gathered for the treasury an annual return of well over 3.5 million rubles from taxes on vodka, placing him in the highest echelon of the empire's tax farmers.[70]

Ordinarily, such sums might raise the possibility of a certain degree of political influence. During the first decade and a half of Alexander II's reign, however, Russia's financial condition was anything but ordinary. In order to

<hr>

69. Arcadius Kahan has suggested that the well-known Gerschenkron thesis of imperial Russia's state-driven economic growth can be fruitfully applied to Jewish economic activity as well, and specifically to the emergence of Jewish financial elites with close ties to the government. The relevant empirical research, however, has yet to be done. See Kahan, *Essays*, pp. 19, 85.

70. Stanislawski, *Tsar Nicholas I*, p. 173. On the volume of revenues among tax farmers in the year 1859, see Christian, *'Living Water,'* p. 156.

manage its huge debts from the Crimean War and to finance the construction of railroads, the government inaugurated sweeping changes in public and private finance that entailed the liquidation of state credit institutions and their rapid replacement by private joint-stock companies and banks. The exacting redemption payments imposed by the government on former serfs were just one effect of the intense fiscal pressure emanating from the sudden loss of state credit.[71] It is highly likely that such pressure also favored the rise in influence of Jewish capitalists. For at the forefront of the new system of private banks stood none other than the House of Gintsburg, established in St. Petersburg in 1859 (with branches in Kiev and Paris), and close behind were other prominent Jewish bankers, such as Avram Varshavskii (whose signature appeared on a number of the merchant petitions discussed above), Ippolit Vavel´berg, the Poliakov brothers, Jan Bliokh, and A. I. Zak.[72]

Thus in contrast to the Jewish Committee's original plan of fashioning an officially trained and salaried rabbinate as the instrument of transforming the Jews,[73] the Jewish merchant elite, with Gintsburg at its head, emerged as a self-styled mediator, attempting to direct official policy toward enticing rather than coercing the Jews into "useful" occupations. An additional sign of Jewish merchants' new influence was their complete displacement of foreign Jews as consultants to the tsars regarding the government's Jewish policy. Under Nicholas I, with Jewish communities across the Pale in disarray because of sectarian conflicts and the divisive effects of conscription, it was possible for an upstart like the twenty-five-year-old German-Jewish rabbi Max Lilienthal to be invited to the imperial capital to help the Jewish Committee design the new government schools for Jews. The British-Jewish phil-

71. See Steven Hoch, "The Banking Crisis, Peasant Reform, and Economic Development in Russia, 1857–1861," *American Historical Review* 96, no. 3 (June 1991): 795–97.

72. Anan´ich, *Bankirskie doma,* pp. 1–18; Ginzburg, *Historishe verk,* 2: 127. For Varshavskii's signature, see RGIA, f. 1269, op. 1, d. 61, l. 7. Although Jewish bankers in Russia often were related by marriage to prominent Jewish banking families in Europe, it is unclear whether these alliances significantly advanced their position in Russia. The reestablishment of institutions of state credit in the 1880s dramatically reduced the importance of private banks in the financing of Russian state debt.

73. In their capacity as rabbis, the graduates of the official rabbinical seminaries had almost no effect, since Jewish communities traditionally elected their own rabbis and invariably shunned the seminary graduates as corrupted by secular influence and ignorant of Jewish law. See Shochat, *Mosad "ha-rabanut mi-ta'am,"* and Imanuel Etkes, "Parashat ha-haskalah mi-ta'am ve-hatemurah be-ma'amad tenuat ha-haskalah be-rusiyah," *Tsiyon* 43 (1978): 264–313. Moreover, the Rabbinical Commission, which was originally meant to meet annually as a sort of supreme religious body for the Jews (see RGIA, f. 1269, op. 1, d. 136, l. 137), instead convened irregularly, in 1852, 1857, 1861, 1879, 1893, and 1909. Crippled by disputes among Hasidim, mitnagdim, and maskilim, it had virtually no impact. See Lederhendler, *Road to Modern Jewish Politics,* pp. 73–74.

anthropist Moses Montefiore also visited St. Petersburg in the 1840s to intercede with Kiselev and others on behalf of Russian Jewry.[74] Once a "native" Jewish merchant elite emerged in the late 1850s as spokesmen for Jewish interests, it would not be until official visits by Baron Maurice de Hirsch in 1891 and Theodore Herzl in 1903 that prominent foreign Jews would rival—with however meager results—the House of Gintsburg.

JEWISH REFORM AND THE GREAT REFORMS

Ultimately, of course, one cannot fully explain the remarkable role played by Gintsburg and others in shaping official policy without taking into account the broader currents of reform at the time. It was in fact a classic case of political *conjuncture:* under Alexander II, Russia embarked on what one historian has called "the greatest single piece of state-directed social engineering in modern European history before the twentieth century."[75] What remains is to explain how the attempt to integrate select categories of Jews into the Russian social hierarchy related to the broader changes introduced by the Great Reforms. How, in other words, did the Great Reforms shape the context of Russian-Jewish relations, and what does this tell us about the intersection of social reform and imperial management?

One should begin by noting the considerable overlap in personnel and dynamics between the Jewish and the Great reforms. Several key architects of the Great Reforms, such as Kiselev, Uvarov, Bludov, and Stroganov, were also members of the Jewish Committee. In both cases, planning began in the 1840s in the chancelleries of "enlightened bureaucrats" and, with the exception of the ill-fated state Jewish schools, did not bear fruit until over a decade later, after Nicholas I had passed from the scene.[76] In both cases, extragovernmental views came to play a significant role in shaping official policy. To be sure, unlike the case of peasant emancipation, in which the gov-

74. On Lilienthal, see David Philipson, *Max Lilienthal, American Rabbi: Life and Writings* (New York, 1915), and Stanislawski, *Tsar Nicholas I,* pp. 69–96; on Montefiore, see Montefiore and Montefiore, *Diaries,* 1: 330–38.

75. Terence Emmons, cited in Ben Eklof, John Bushnell, and Larissa Rakhavova, eds., *Russia's Great Reforms, 1855–1881* (Bloomington, 1994), p. vii.

76. One area of contrast between Jewish and other reforms lay in the use of statistics. When it came to planning the abolition of serfdom, tsarist bureaucrats gathered and organized an impressive mass of statistical data on peasant population, land use, and other matters (see Lincoln, *In the Vanguard of Reform,* pp. 44–45, 102–3, and idem, *The Great Reforms: Autocracy, Bureaucracy, and the Politics of Change in Imperial Russia* [De Kalb, Ill., 1990], p. 65). Members of the Jewish Committee, by contrast, rued their relative lack of quantitative data, itself a reflection of the Jews' continuing separateness from many of the mechanisms of state power. See, e.g., RGIA, f. 1269, op. 1, d. 137, ll. 69–73.

ernment convened committees of provincial landowners to help plan legislation, the Jewish Committee never solicited opinions from those on the receiving end of its endeavors. As we have seen, however, the new Jewish elites
presented their views anyway, and as a result created something like a dialogue, however lopsided, with the regime.[77] In fact, just as the preparation
for the emancipation of the serfs catalyzed a kind of public opinion within
the landowning estate, so the Jewish Committee's deliberations stimulated
debates among Jews concerning their future in a reformed Russia.[78] These
debates emerged above all in Jewish newspapers—in Hebrew, Russian, and
Yiddish—that sprang to life during the Reform period. Between 1860 and
1862, no fewer than six Jewish periodicals were born, several of them subsidized by Evzel Gintsburg.[79]

Jewish commentators of the Reform era tended to discuss official reforms
strictly as a function of the personal qualities of Tsar Alexander II—his
courage, his foresight, his merciful feelings toward the Jews.[80] In their accounts, the Jewish Committee's tangled deliberations and the frequent petitions sent by Jewish groups—not to mention the tsar's generally hostile attitude toward change—were passed over in silence or ignorance. Moreover,
it was an axiom of the Jewish press that expanded rights for Jews were closely
linked to broader reforms in various arenas of Russian life. In the words of
Joachim Tarnopol, who co-founded and then became an editor of the Odessa
weekly *Razsvet* (The Dawn), the first Russian-language Jewish newspaper:

> Our reigning Emperor, . . . having devoted his attention to the solution of the
> great problems . . . of a large and unhappy class among his subjects [i.e., the

77. The dialogue between landowners and the Editing Commission (the official body responsible for drafting the emancipation legislation) was also notably lopsided. The historian
Daniel Field has characterized it as "a dialogue between the chickens and the cook": *The End
of Serfdom: Nobility and Bureaucracy in Russia, 1855–1861* (Cambridge, Mass., 1976), p. 316.

78. Terence Emmons, *The Russian Landed Gentry and the Peasant Emancipation of 1861* (Cambridge, Mass., 1968), pp. 263, 309.

79. Three weekly newspa   ˜rs appeared in 1860: *Razsvet* (The Dawn), *Ha-Karmel* (Carmel),
and *Ha-Melits* (The Mediato.). 1.   ollowing year the Russian-language *Sion* (Zion) succeeded
Razsvet, and in 1862 there appeared *Ha-Tsefirah* (The Dawn) and the Yiddish *Kol Mevasser* (Voice
of the Messenger). Efforts to publish those newspapers—as well as others that never saw the
light of day—began in 1856; see RGIA, f. 821, op. 8, dd. 255, 256, 258. Several prior attempts
by Jews to publish newspapers in the Russian Empire had come to nought, with the exception
of the short-lived Yiddish weekly *Beobokhter an der Weikhsel*, published in Warsaw in 1823. A number of mid-nineteenth-century Hebrew periodicals published in Austria and Prussia were imported legally to subscribers in the Pale. On the Reform-era Jewish press, see John Klier, *Imperial Russia's Jewish Question, 1855–1881* (Cambridge, 1995), pp. 66–122; Orbach, *New Voices of
Russian Jewry;* Yehuda Slutsky, *Ha-itonut ha-yehudit-rusit ba-me'ah ha-tesha-'esre* (Jerusalem, 1970),
pp. 9–55; S. L. [Israel] Tsinberg, *Istoriia evreiskoi pechati v Rossii v sviazi s obshchestvennymi techeniiami* (St. Petersburg, 1915).

80. Orbach, *New Voices of Russian Jewry,* p. 89.

serfs], has, in his great fairness, taken into consideration at the same time the state of our brothers. The orders and decrees promulgated in our regard reveal the firm intentions of the supreme authority to gradually improve our civil standing, in the manner of other civilized states. The emancipation of the Russian Jews will logically be the corollary of the enfranchisement of a much larger and more deprived class.[81]

Similar analogies, between the emancipation of Jews and the abolition of serfdom, or between Russian Jews and Jewish communities of other European countries, were drawn by Alexander Tsederbaum, by many other Jewish writers of the period, and occasionally by liberal Russian newspapers and journals.[82]

The Great Reforms themselves suggested a more complex picture of the Jews' eventual place in a reformed Russia. The decree abolishing serfdom in 1861, for example, set specific constraints on the sale of land to Jews. The creation in 1864 of *zemstva*—organs of rural self-government—excluded the western borderlands for fear of electoral domination by Poles and Jews, while the reform of urban self-government in 1870 maintained previously established limits on Jewish suffrage and officeholding in towns and cities. None of the Great Reforms disturbed the existing restrictions on Jewish residence. On the whole, however, the range of legal discrimination inscribed in the various reforms was far narrower than in previous legislation. Most striking were the judicial and university reforms of 1864 and the military reform of 1874, in which the otherwise common phrase "except for Jews" (*krome evreev*) hardly appeared at all.

In the long run, though, the presence or absence of anti-Jewish clauses in the various Great Reforms was less important for the Russian–Jewish encounter than the way the reforms recast the Russian social hierarchy into which Jews were to be dispersed. Whatever their function as ideal types, in practice, integration and emancipation do not release their subjects on to an even social terrain, a neutral society of individuals whose affiliations are purely voluntary. That is, regardless of where they occur, emancipation and integration inevitably involve not only the lifting of old legal or social constraints but the passage into a new (and usually subtler) social hierarchy. This

81. The passage comes from a letter (in French) sent by Tarnopol in February 1860 to the Alliance Israélite Universelle in Paris, announcing the appearance of *Razsvet*. It is among the documents published by Moshe Perlmann in "Notes on *Razsvet*, 1860–61," *Proceedings of the American Academy for Jewish Research* 33 (1965): 35–36. Tarnopol uses the French *émancipation* with regard to the Jews and *affranchisement* with regard to the serfs.

82. See Orbach, *New Voices of Russian Jewry*, p. 81; I. Sosis, "Obshchestvennye nastroeniia 'epokhi velikikh reform,'" *Evreiskaia Starina* 6 (1914): 21–41, 182–97, 341–64; Wengeroff, *Memoiren einer Grossmutter*, 2: 133. On Russian liberals see Klier, *Imperial Russia's Jewish Question*, pp. 66–67.

was certainly the case for those "useful" Jews targeted by the Jewish Committee, who were fated to encounter a Russia caught up in the contradictory developments unleashed by the Great Reforms. On the one hand, the reforms stimulated the growth of cities, the division of labor, higher education, the professions, public opinion—in a word, the basic ingredients of a civil society. The urban middle estates, historically weak in Russia, became more open and fluid, as the state turned to taxation rather than birth as the key determinant of legal status.[83] In this respect, the Great Reforms helped pave the way for the entrance of Jews into the rapidly evolving middle levels of the Russian social hierarchy.

On the other hand, the reforms hardly marked an end to the *soslovie* system as such. At the top (the nobility) and bottom (the peasantry) of that system, they largely preserved the integrity of hereditary estates. The emancipation decree of 1861, for example, called for serfs "to receive in due course the full rights of free rural inhabitants," that is, not of citizens, but of members of a specific, hereditary social group. Whatever the government's intentions, moreover, by the second half of the nineteenth century the estate structure had become part of Russian social consciousness, a cultural paradigm "providing the primary means of collective identity and forming the bedrock of social stratification."[84] The forces of inertia found expression not only in imperial legislation but in the consciousness of the population at large. Late imperial Russia was thus emerging as a complex blend of old and new social forms, poised between "the immobility of caste and the dynamism of class."[85]

THE TERMS OF INTEGRATION

Just how deeply notions of group identity conditioned Jewish integration in late imperial Russia can be seen from a brief examination of contemporary social vocabulary.[86] As has often been noted, the term *soslovie* was used across

83. Manfred Hildermeier, *Bürgertum und Stadt in Russland, 1760–1870: Rechtliche Lage und soziale Struktur* (Cologne, 1986), pp. 307–22.

84. G. Freeze, "*Soslovie* (Estate) Paradigm," p. 26.

85. Rieber, *Merchants and Entrepreneurs*, p. 416.

86. My analysis of social vocabulary is inspired by the study of the history of concepts (*Begriffsgeschichte*) as pioneered by Reinhart Koselleck and others. While *Begriffsgeschichte* is just beginning to be applied systematically to Russian as well as Jewish history, I have benefited from several fruitful examples: G. Freeze, "Soslovie (Estate) Paradigm"; Abbott Gleason, "The Terms of Russian Social History," in Edith Clowes et al., eds., *Between Tsar and People: Educated Society and the Quest for Public Identity in Late Imperial Russia* (Princeton, 1991); Wirtschafter, *Structures of Society* and *Social Identity in Imperial Russia;* Boris Ivanovich Kolonitskii, "'Democracy' in the Political Consciousness of the February Revolution," *Slavic Review* 57, no. 1 (Spring 1998): 95–107; Catriona Kelly and David Shepherd, eds., *Constructing Russian Culture in the Age of*

the nineteenth century to describe both the standard horizontal (occupational) estates and individual ethnic and religious minorities, including the Jews. A Jewish merchant, for example, was simultaneously a member of the merchant *soslovie* and the Jewish *soslovie*, a rather confusing classification scheme suggesting the conflation of ethnicity (or religion) and occupation—which on the local level was in fact often the case. Indeed, the language of estate in Russia was notoriously elastic, not to say chaotic. The meaning of *soslovie* could be stretched to fit almost any imaginable constellation: thus an 1863 petition from Christians in the city of Berdichev, protesting alleged Jewish ballot fixing in a recent election, referred to the aggrieved party as the "Christian estate," while an official document from 1865 referred to Jewish artisans as an "estate" distinct from both artisans at large and the "Jewish estate" as a whole.[87] Adding to the confusion, Jews were also referred to—and described themselves when using Russian—not only as an estate but as a social rank (*sostoianie*), a people (*narod*), a tribe (*plemia*), a society (*obshchestvo*), a confession (*veroispovedannost´*), and, less frequently, a nation (*natsiia*). By law Jews were also classified as aliens (*inorodtsy*), an intermediate category between natives (*prirodnye*) and foreigners (*inostrantsy*), even while Judaism, like all non-Christian religions, was considered a foreign faith (*inostrannoe ispovedanie*).

This baroque lexicon and the analytic disorder that characterized Russian social vocabulary across the late imperial period make it exceedingly difficult to establish direct connections between categories and the realities they were meant to signify. But other, more indirect approaches can be illuminating. Let us return to the Jewish merchant who served as an example in the preceding paragraph. He was known as a "Jew-merchant" (*evrei-kupets*) or a "merchant from the Jews" (*kupets iz evreev*), reflecting the ubiquitous contemporary practice of describing multiple identities through a string of nouns (Jew-artisan, Jew-student, etc.), rather than differentiating one aspect of identity in the form of an adjective (e.g., "Jewish merchant"). Like the language of estate, this practice reflected and reinforced an implied equivalence between social and ethnic categories.

Revolution, 1881–1940 (New York, 1998); Alex Bein, "Notes on the Semantics of the Jewish Problem with Special Reference to Germany," *Leo Baeck Institute Year Book* 9 (1964): 3–40; Jacob Toury, "'The Jewish Question': A Semantic Approach," *Leo Baeck Institute Year Book* 11 (1966): 85–106; Katz, "Term 'Jewish Emancipation'"; Reinhard Rürup, "Emanzipation—Anmerkungen zur Begriffsgeschichte," in his *Emanzipation und Antisemitismus: Studien zur "Judenfrage" der bürgerlichen Gesellschaft* (Göttingen, 1975), pp. 159–66; and three works by John Klier: "The Concept of 'Jewish Emancipation' in a Russian Context," in Olga Crisp and Linda Edmondson, eds., *Civil Rights in Imperial Russia* (Oxford, 1989), pp. 121–44; "*Zhid*: The Biography of a Russian Pejorative," *Slavonic and East European Review* 60, no. 1 (January 1982): 1–15; and *Imperial Russia's Jewish Question*, pp. 66–83.

87. RGIA, f. 1287, op. 38, d. 328, ll. 1–12; f. 1269, op. 1, d. 116, l. 5.

In a roughly analogous way, our tendency to distinguish between "the Jewish community" and "Russian society" (with its implied contrast between organic Gemeinschaft and depersonalized Gesellschaft) found no precise counterpart in the vocabulary of late imperial Russia. Jews were regarded as constituting a society (*obshchestvo*) no less and no more than did Russians, reflecting the fact that the term "society" still referred primarily to social subgroups rather than to an entire population. In fact, Jewish as well as Russian contemporaries commonly referred to the "Jewish societies" of the Pale (*evreiskie obshchestva,* usually translated as "Jewish communities"), and similarly referred to occupational or estate-based groups as "societies." Just as none of the contemporary meanings of "society" encompassed all the social levels within the ethnic Russian population, so none bridged the empire's many ethnic and religious divides. Even the term *grazhdanskoe obshchestvo* (civil society), which initially signified the civilian (as opposed to military) wing of the state's service hierarchy, wavered between singular (implicitly universal or at least national) and plural (particularist) forms. Contemporary sources speak of integrating the Jews into "civil society" but also, and just as frequently, into "civil societies," meaning the various estates. Indeed, the Jews themselves were often described as a civil society among Russia's many civil societies.[88] In this regard Russian particularism differed little from that of other old regimes and estate-based societies, which typically dealt in liberties (*Freiheiten*), not liberty, and in equalities (*Gleichheiten*) rather than equality.[89]

Bearing in mind the welter of categories describing Jews and other groups in late imperial Russia, we should not be surprised to find a similar complexity in the vocabulary describing the process of integration. Contemporary debates relied heavily on two terms, neither of which lends itself to precise translation: *sliianie* (fusion or merging) and *sblizhenie* (drawing near or rapprochement). As John Klier has demonstrated, the two were virtually interchangeable, especially the elasticity, not to say vagueness, in the way they were applied. Contemporary usage of both terms made it clear that the Jews—and not the other party—were supposed to be transformed as either a prerequisite or a result of the process. Beyond this, however, there was no consensus as to the nature and extent of that transformation, or what role the state should play in it.[90] Furthermore, like the language of group affiliation, the use of "merging" and "rapprochement" was not limited to the Jewish case or even to ethnic difference as such. Reformers who desired a softening of social stratification among Russians also spoke of "rapprochement" among the various estates, or between the intelligentsia and the

---

88. YIVO, RG 89, folder 756, doc. 62, pp. 7–8.

89. See the excellent discussion in Lois C. Dubin, *The Port Jews of Habsburg Trieste: Absolutist Politics and Enlightenment Culture* (Stanford, 1999), p. 218.

90. Klier, *Imperial Russia's Jewish Question,* pp. 66–83.

masses. At least one Jewish writer called for the "rapprochement" of different classes within Russian Jewry.[91]

Given the importance of the European model of Jewish emancipation for the "enlightened bureaucrats" in the Jewish Committee as well as for the Jewish elites who petitioned them; given the official policy of gradually equalizing the legal rights of Jews with those of the surrounding population; and given that the results of this process—as I shall argue in the chapters that follow—in many respects resembled those of emancipation in Europe, does it make sense to view the Jewish reforms of Alexander II as part of a gradual march toward Jewish emancipation in all but name? Here, too, the name—that is, the terminology—is telling. While the central issue in historians' debates about official Jewish policies in late imperial Russia has been the failure to enact emancipation, it is worth noting that the term "emancipation" (*emansipatsiia*) was very rarely used in official discourse. It does not appear even once in the voluminous protocols of the Jewish Committee.[92] Its absence may be due in part to the word's relative novelty (in Russian).[93] In official circles the preference remained throughout the late imperial period for formulas such as "bringing existing regulations on the Jews into agreement with the general laws for other subjects of the Empire," "merging the Jews with civilian society," or "equalizing the Jews in their rights with those of other estates," rather than "emancipation." Similar preferences applied to characterizations of changes in the status of the serfs. Contemporaries did not speak of "emancipating" the serfs; they spoke of the "abolition of serfdom's legal code" (*otmena krepost'nogo prava*) or, more evocatively, of the serfs' "liberation" (*osvobozhdenie*). By contrast, "liberation" was hardly ever used with regard to the Jews, whether by government officials or by Jewish or Russian commentators.[94]

91. A. E. Landau, *Den'*, Aug.1, 1870, p. 525.

92. The earliest instances of the word I have been able to find in documents of official provenance, published as well as archival, are in responses by two governors general to a petition submitted by Evzel Gintsburg in 1862. In both cases, the officials were either paraphrasing or responding to Gintsburg's own use of the term. See RGIA, f. 821, op. 9, d. 77, ll. 69–72, 204.

93. Neither the *Slovar' akademii rossiiskoi* (St. Petersburg, 1806–22) nor the *Slovar' tserkovnoslavianskogo i russkogo iazyka* (St. Petersburg, 1847) lists *emansipatsiia*. The omission is not due simply to the word's foreign origin; both, for example, list *parlament*. The earliest dictionary listing of *emansipatsiia* I have been able to find is in the second edition of Dal''s *Tolkovyi slovar' zhivogo velikorusskogo iazyka* (St. Petersburg, 1880–82).

94. A similar division of semantic labor between "liberation" and "emancipation" typically occurred in Yiddish: *befrayung fun di poyerim* vs. *yidishe emansipatsiya*. See, e.g., Ginzburg, *Historishe verk*, 2: 125–27. Exactly the same division obtained in German; see Reinhart Koselleck and Karl Martin Grass, "Emanzipation," in Werner Conze et al., eds., *Geschichtliche Grundbegriffe*, vol. 7 (Stuttgart, 1975), p. 176. The single Russian exception to this pattern that I have found occurs in a report composed in 1882 by the Jewish lawyer-activist Menashe Morgolis, who refers to the "territorial liberation [*osvobozhdenie*] of the Jews" from the confines of the Pale. See TsGIA-SPb, f. 422, op. 2, d. 1, l. 73.

Maskilic writers, however, were not shy about using "emancipation" with regard to the Jews, and did so in two distinct ways. The first was in descriptions of official policy, thereby conveying their expectation that Russia was destined to replicate the recent progress of Jewish emancipation in the West. To be sure, even in the hands of its Jewish proponents the term retained, until the 1860s, a certain foreign tinge, and occasionally required the help of an explicit definition. Thus Evzel Gintsburg's secretary, Emanuel Levin, referred in a memorandum of 1859 to "the attainment of *emancipation,* that is, full equalization in civil and political rights with Russians."[95] Beginning in the 1860s the word appeared regularly in Gintsburg's petitions to the government, as well as in the Jewish press, particularly in articles concerning Jews in Western Europe.[96]

Among the Jewish writers who were its primary users, the term "emancipation" had a second meaning as well, signifying reform within Jewish society or the individual Jewish self, that is, the abandonment of ostensibly outmoded customs and beliefs and the turn to productive labor. Thus Joachim Tarnopol wrote in 1858 of the "self-emancipation" that was occurring among Russian Jews, while a decade later the Jewish weekly *Den´* (The Day) described Odessa as "a center of Jewish self-emancipation" (*samo-emantsipatsiia evreev).*[97] Drawing on the ideology of the Haskalah, "self-emancipation" in this sense was understood not as an alternative to legal emancipation but as its inner counterpart. This second meaning was eclipsed only when the Zionist movement adopted "self-emancipation" as a battle cry for Jews to fashion their own civil and political rights by reestablishing collective political sovereignty.[98] In its original sense, however, "self-emancipation" pre-

95. Levin, "Zapiska ob emansipatsii evreev," p. 300 (emphasis in original). It bears noting that German writers as late as the 1840s referred to *Emanzipation* as a foreign term. See Katz, "Term 'Jewish Emancipation,'" p. 44. The word first gained currency in Great Britain in the 1820s.

96. For examples of the term *emansipatsiia* applied to Russian Jewry in Gintsburg's petitions, see RGIA, f. 821, op. 9, d. 77, l. 13, and d. 100, l. 432. For usage in the Jewish press, see Klier, "Concept of 'Jewish Emancipation,'" p. 123. The most frequent usage of "emancipation" with regard to Russian Jewry occurred in the articles of Il´ia Orshanskii. The more typical propensity of Jewish commentators to use *emansipatsiia* with regard to European but not Russian Jews may have had to do with state censorship policy. In 1860, the government censor ruled that all articles dealing with the "granting to the Jews of civil rights on an equal level with all other estates of the Russian Empire" would have to be approved before publication. See RGIA, f. 1269, op. 1, d. 108, ll. 6–8, and d. 138, ll. 238–42; and John Klier, "1855–1894 Censorship of the Press in Russia and the Jewish Question," *Jewish Social Studies* 48, nos. 3–4 (1986): 257–68.

97. I. Tarnopol, *Opyt sovremennoi i osmotritel´noi reformy v oblasti iudaizma v Rossii* (Odessa, 1868), p. x; *Den´,* Jan. 30, 1870, p. 66. Tarnopol composed his work a decade before it was published.

98. The Zionist meaning of the term was inaugurated in Lev Pinsker's path-breaking pamphlet, *Autoemanzipation! Mahnruf an seine Stammesgenossen von einem russischen Juden* (Berlin, 1882). In his largely unsympathetic review of Pinsker's essay, the Russian-Jewish historian

cisely captured what Gintsburg and others hoped would be the internal effect of the incentives offered by the Jewish Committee to "useful" Jews.

The problem of using the term "emancipation" in a Russian setting—at the time as well as retrospectively—has to do with more than simply its foreign origin. By the mid–nineteenth century, "emancipation" had become a political slogan in the hands of European liberal movements, "the central concept for . . . the dissolution of the hierarchy of social estates."[99] The historical specificity of Jewish emancipation in Europe lies in the way it rose on the larger tide of anticorporative sentiment. Indeed, from their inception in Germany in the 1780s, debates in Western and Central Europe about Jewish emancipation were linked to larger universal projects for dismantling (whether from above or from below) the privileges and burdens associated with hereditary estates—including Jewish corporate autonomy.[100] Perhaps the clearest expression of the anticorporative agenda driving proponents of Jewish emancipation in Europe can be found in Clermont-Tonnerre's memorable words to the French National Assembly in 1789: "We must refuse everything to the Jews as a nation and accord everything to Jews as individuals. We must withdraw recognition from their judges; they should have only our judges. . . . They should not be allowed to form in the state either a political body or an order. They must be citizens individually. . . . If they do not want to be citizens, they should say so, and then, we should banish them."[101]

It was precisely the broader anticorporative agenda that was absent from debates about Jews in Reform-era Russia, and which would not arise until the emergence of a European-style liberal movement in the decade before the First World War.[102] Whatever the ambiguous impact of the Great Reforms

Simon Dubnov focused precisely on the competing meanings of the term "self-emancipation." See Dubnov, "Kakaia samo-emansipatsiia nuzhna evreiam," *Voskhod*, no. 3 (July/August 1883).

99. Koselleck and Grass, "Emanzipation," p. 176. Significantly, in Germany it was "emancipation" that became the slogan of broad movements for reform during the Vormärz, while in late imperial Russia "liberation" performed a similar function (e.g., Plekhanov's *Gruppa osvobozhdeniia truda* and the turn-of-the-century *Osvoboditel'noe dvizhenie*).

100. Katz, "Term 'Jewish Emancipation,'" p. 33.

101. Quoted in Lynn Hunt, ed. and trans., *The French Revolution and Human Rights: A Brief Documentary History* (Boston, 1996), p. 88.

102. Paul Miliukov, the leader of the Constitutional Democratic (Kadet) Party, offered the boldest formulation of the notion that Jewish rights were inextricably tied to the dismantling of all legally inscribed estates: "The Jewish question . . . is merely a part of the question concering our general lack of equality and the absence of general civic freedoms. The question of equal rights for Jews in Russia is a question of equal rights for all citizens in general": "Evreiskii vopros v Rossii," in L. Andreev, M. Gor´kii, and F. Sologub, eds., *Shchit: Literaturnyi sbornik*, 3d ed. (Moscow, 1915), p. 167. On Russian liberals and the "Jewish Question," see Yitshak Maor, *She'elat ha-yehudim ba-tenuah ha-liberalit ve-ha-mahapehanit be-rusiyah 1890–1914* (Jerusalem, 1964), and Michael Hamm, "Liberalism and the Jewish Question: The Progressive Bloc," *Russian Review* 31 (1972): 163–72.

on Russia's estate system, that system remained the bedrock of social control and consequently of the state-sponsored attempt to "merge" Jews into the surrounding population. Only in its policy toward Jewish autonomy (especially with respect to "integrated" Jews outside the Pale) did the tsarist regime display some of the anticorporative zeal of its Western counterparts. Even in Congress Poland, where in the early 1860s the tsarist government came closest to a European-style Jewish emancipation, the abolition of serfdom and the scaling back of aristocratic privileges—much like the granting of certain rights to Jews—were essentially tactical maneuvers designed to neutralize support for Polish independence.[103]

In order to preserve the historically specific meaning of "emancipation," I have restricted my own use of the term to areas where it is linked to a general campaign against legally inscribed estates.[104] "Integration," or more specifically "selective integration," will be used to describe the process by which the tsarist state hoped to disperse certain categories of Jews into the Russian social hierarchy. Nonetheless, it is crucial to appreciate that contemporary Russians and Jews frequently understood selective integration to mean de facto emancipation for those categories concerned, analogous to the contemporary status of Jews in Central and Western Europe. For practical purposes, the Jews of the Russian Empire would henceforth be divided into what one contemporary referred to as "free" and "unfree."[105] Like Clermont-Tonnerre, moreover, the tsarist state often understood selective integration as requiring that Jews, once having been "merged," would cease to constitute a separate estate, or even a distinct social and legal entity. This point was brought home early and with ominous clarity to a group of Jewish merchants residing in St. Petersburg, who sought permission to represent

103. The dynamics of Jewish integration in Russian Poland were in some ways distinct from those in the Pale of Settlement, and a detailed treatment of the differences lies beyond the scope of this book. Two of the leading works on the subject equate the *rawnouprawnienie* granted in 1861–62 with European-style "emancipation," but in the end both concede that significant forms of legal discrimination remained. See Artur Eisenbach, *The Emancipation of the Jews in Poland, 1780–1870* (London, 1991), p. 470, and Michael Jerry Ochs, "St. Petersburg and the Jews of Russian Poland, 1862–1905," Ph.D. dissertation, Harvard University, 1986, p. xvi. Many of the anti-Jewish statutes eliminated by the Polish reforms of 1861–62 had already been or would soon be abolished within the Pale (e.g., residential restrictions in cities and towns, participation as equals in the judicial system), and Polish Jews continued after 1862 to be subject to all the general restrictions on work and residence in the empire's interior. Furthermore, the tsarist government never established a clear relationship between legislation aimed specifically at Polish Jewry and that regarding Jews throughout the empire. My understanding of emancipation as described above precludes use of the term with respect to Russian Poland.

104. When reproducing contemporary usage, however, I do employ terms such as "emancipation," "merging," and "rapprochement."

105. Ha-Kohen, *Olami*, 1: 77.

their co-religionists at Alexander II's coronation in Moscow in 1856. An official from the royal chancellery informed them that "deputations present at the coronation of His Imperial Majesty are appointed from among the estates and orders. . . . Since Jews do not constitute a distinct estate," the official concluded, they could not be permitted to send a separate delegation. By contrast, representatives of other national minorities were invited to attend, and the colorful native costumes of Bashkirs, Cherkassy, Tatars, Armenians, Georgians, and others helped put on display the staggering breadth and diversity of the Russian Empire.[106]

What happened in Russia was thus not simply a failed attempt at a European-style emancipation. During the mid–nineteenth century, Russia was still emerging—in part under state tutelage—as a hierarchy of culturally and juridically distinct estates, and it was precisely this hierarchy that various groups within the Jewish population were encouraged to enter. It was a policy shaped by the corporative structure of Russian society itself—or the image of that society in the minds of "enlightened bureaucrats"—and reinforced by the internal tensions that divided Russian Jewry.[107] Only the combination of the relative political fluidity of the Reform era and the emergence of Jewish elites eager to enter the surrounding world as equals created the momentum necessary to begin "merging" the Jews—as Minister of Internal Affairs S. S. Lanskoi put it during a meeting of the Jewish Committee—"not just on the registry lists but in actual fact."[108] Like the Great Reforms themselves, selective integration sought to engineer a gradual, cautious social transformation, and like them it produced results far different than those expected.

106. RGIA, f. 1269, op. 1, d. 59, ll. 1–2. On the symbolic language of Alexander II's coronation, see Richard Wortman, *Scenarios of Power: Myth and Ceremony in Russian Monarchy,* (Princeton, 2000), 2: 29–37. While coronations of tsars offered particularly rich occasions for the symbolic representation of Russia's social order, lesser ceremonies also repeated the exclusion of Jews qua Jews from that order. At the dedication of a monument to Gogol in 1881 in the town of Nezhin (Chernigov province), for example, a Jewish delegation bearing the traditional Russian offering of bread and salt was turned away by the governer general on the grounds that Jews no longer constituted a distinct estate. See RGIA, f. 821, op. 9, d. 155, ll. 1–3.

107. In his analysis of what he called the "homeopathic emancipation" of the Jews in the Reform era, Dubnov condemned "the objectionable principle upon which this whole system was founded, the division of a people into categories of favorites and outcasts" (*History of the Jews,* 2: 159). Whatever the moral truth of this view, it seems strangely oblivious of the fact that, as a society of estates, Russia itself—like all old regimes—was grounded in legally inscribed inequalities. Moreover, it ignores the internal source of many of the ruptures within Russian-Jewish society. One senses here the retrospective pull of Dubnov's ideology of Jewish autonomism and his tendency to cast the organic national community as the central force in Jewish history. For an insightful treatment of Dubnov's life and historical outlook, see Robert M. Seltzer, "Simon Dubnow: A Critical Biography of His Early Years," Ph.D. dissertation, Columbia University, 1970, esp. pp. 219–45.

108. RGIA, f. 1269, op. 1, d. 137, l. 135.

PART TWO

The Jews of St. Petersburg

His [Alexander II's] reign "carved a window on Russia for us Jews," through which the rays of citizenship and a freer life began to stream upon us like shafts of light. Jews moved forward by an entire century.

The Russian Jew, (MARCH 11, 1881)

As far as the Jews are concerned, it's apparent to everyone that their rights in choosing a place of residence have broadened immensely over the last twenty years. At least they have appeared in Russia in places where they weren't seen before.

DOSTOEVSKY, *Diary of a Writer* (1877)

Take a city like St. Petersburg, where a Jew is definitely not kosher.

SHOLEM ALEICHEM, *The Bloody Hoax* (1913)

We have lately had very bitter experiences in Russia. We are both too many and too few; too many in the southwestern provinces, in which the Jews are allowed to reside; and too few in all other provinces, where they are forbidden. If the Russian government, and the Russian people as well, realized that an equal distribution of the Jewish population would benefit the entire country, we might have been spared all our sufferings. Unfortunately, Russia cannot and will not realize this.

LEON PINSKER, *Autoemancipation!* (1882)

Jews in Moscow and Petersburg, and Jews over there, in that Russian Palestine of theirs, where they feel at home — those are two entirely different types.

IVAN AKSAKOV, *Rus´* (October 15, 1883)

Obviously the provinces are still the provinces — even if we're talking about Odessa.

ADOLF LANDAU, *letter of November 4, 1894*

Chapter 3

Language, Ethnicity, and Urban Space

The practice of selective integration gave rise to an unmistakable Jewish presence in late imperial Russian society. Beginning in the 1860s, tens of thousands of Jews settled legally in the Russian interior, learned Russian, and encountered specifically Russian forms of life. According to what must be regarded as very rough data compiled by the Ministry of Internal Affairs, in 1858 a total of 11,980 Jews resided in the provinces of European Russia outside the Pale, not including Siberia, Central Asia, the Caucasus, and the Baltic provinces. Most of these Jews were presumably soldiers. By 1880 the number had climbed to 59,779, and by 1897, the year of the first reasonably reliable empire-wide census, to 128,343. The census also recorded an additional 186,422 Jews living in Siberia, Central Asia, the Caucasus, and the Baltic provinces, though it is impossible to say how many of these left the Pale via selective integration and how many were descended from Jewish communities that had lived in these regions throughout the nineteenth century.[1] Whatever the circumstances of their residence, by the end of the century more than 300,000 Jews were living outside the Pale of Settlement.

The largest Jewish community outside the Pale formed in St. Petersburg, the political and cultural nerve center of the Empire, its most populous, modern, and industrialized city. For both Jews and Russians, Petersburg Jewry represented a kind of laboratory of selective integration, a case study on the front

---

1. RGIA, f. 821, op. 9, d. 122, ll. 7–116; *Evreiskaia entsiklopediia*, 11: 536–38. For a useful survey of Jewish communities outside the Pale, see Semyon Kreiz, "Toldot ha-yehudim be-eizorim she-mihuts le-tehum ha-moshav." M.A. thesis, University of Haifa, 1984.

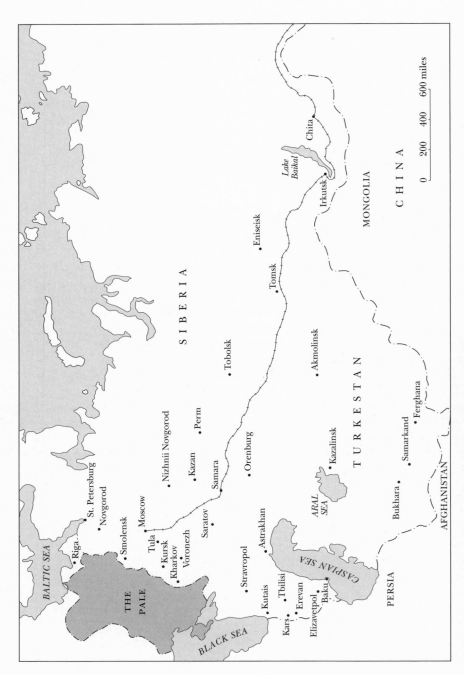

Map 2. Jewish communities outside the Pale of Settlement, 1897

line of the Russian–Jewish encounter.[2] For the tsarist autocracy, the experiment in Jewish integration that unfolded in the imperial capital served as a test of its ability to manage the "Jewish Question" in a highly visible arena—its own back yard. How successful would the policy of "merging" be, and what would success look like? Could Russia's estate system effectively absorb and assimilate Jews and, by analogy, other minorities as well? How would the carefully elaborated mechanisms of selective integration into Russia's social hierarchy function in a turbulent metropolis whose total population more than tripled, reaching some 2 million, during the half-century before the First World War? What influence would Petersburg Jewry exert on the masses of Jews in the Pale?

One of the distinguishing features of the "Jewish Question" in imperial Russia, as we have seen, was its strongly territorial dimension. Across the spectrum of contemporary viewpoints on what the Jews' place in the larger society ought to be, one finds a remarkable consensus that the entire question could ultimately be reduced to a single issue: whether or not to remove restrictions on Jewish residence. In the minds of proponents and opponents alike, dismantling the Pale of Settlement seemed synonymous with Jewish integration. This consensus was based to a large extent on the assumption that many Jews were eager, indeed desperate, to leave the territory to which they (and they alone) were confined by law. There is certainly no lack of evidence for this view: the constant campaign by Jewish spokesmen to abolish the Pale; the tsarist regime's oft-stated concern about a "flood" of Jews entering Russia proper; the periodic expulsion of "illegal" Jews from the interior; and above all, the mass emigration of some two million Jews from the

2. Aside from a handful of articles and chapters, there have been no scholarly studies of prerevolutionary Petersburg Jewry. Mikhail Beizer, *The Jews of St. Petersburg: Excursions through a Noble Past,* trans. Michael Sherbourne, ed. Martin Gilbert (Philadelphia, 1989), is a detailed guide to the city's Jewish historical sights, and is an expanded version of his *Evrei v Peterburge* (Jerusalem, 1989). Beizer's more recent monograph, *Evrei Leningrada, 1917–1939: Natsional'naia zhizn' i sovetizatsiia* (Jerusalem, 1999), offers a detailed study of Petersburg Jewry during and after the Russian Revolution. On the prerevolutionary period, see works by N. V. Iukhneva listed in the bibliography. See also Alexander Orbach, "The Russian-Jewish Leadership and the Pogroms of 1881–82: The Response from St. Petersburg," in *The Carl Beck Papers in Russian and East European Studies,* no. 308 (Pittsburgh, 1984); Stanislawski, *For Whom Do I Toil?* pp. 106–28; and Iu. P. Vartanov, "Nekotorye dannye o byte peterburgskikh evreev v 70-e gody na stranitsakh gazety 'ha-melits,'" in *Etnografiia Peterburga-Leningrada* (Leningrad, 1987), 1: 30–36. Shaul Ginzburg's *Amolike Peterburg* offers a series of portraits of important individuals. Most recently, see Yvonne Kleinmann, "Petersburger Juden im 19. Jahrhundert: Demographie und Religiosität," in Stefan Creuzberger et al., eds., *St. Petersburg–Leningrad–St. Petersburg: Eine Stadt im Spiegel der Zeit* (Stuttgart, 2000), and V. Iu. Gessen, *K istorii Sankt-Peterburgskoi evreiskoi religioznoi obshchiny: Ot pervykh evreev do XX veka* (St. Petersburg, 2000), which appeared too late to be used for my study.

Russian Empire during the late imperial period. All these circumstances have cemented the image of the Pale as a teeming, overpopulated "ghetto," a term used by contemporary writers and by more than a few historians.[3] The Pale itself, in other words, appeared to offer a self-evident explanation for why so many Jews should have felt the urge to leave it.

This urge requires closer examination. While the Pale confined its Jews to less than 5 percent of the territory of the Russian Empire, it nonetheless covered an area roughly the size of France—hardly the dimensions of a typical ghetto. The vast majority of those who lived in the territory of the Pale were non-Jews whose levels of out-migration were far lower than that of Jews. To be sure, Jews were concentrated in towns and cities, where they often constituted a sizable portion or even the majority of residents. But most Jews who migrated within or beyond the Pale moved to larger and even more densely populated cities. Thus overpopulation, however defined, cannot explain the dramatic emigration (in any direction) of Jews from the Pale beginning in the last third of the nineteenth century.

The far greater wave of pre-1914 Jewish emigration surged westward, of course, away from Russia entirely. Those who moved eastward into the Russian interior constituted, by comparison, mere ripples, while those who moved farther south, to Palestine, formed barely a trickle. A comparison is nonetheless instructive. As the economist Simon Kuznets demonstrated, skilled workers, mainly artisans, were markedly overrepresented among Jewish immigrants to the United States between 1899 and 1914, as compared to their proportion of the Jewish population of the Pale. Artisans were in fact the social group that, among all those permitted to settle in the Russian interior, were least likely to do so. Conversely, those most likely to take advantage of the privileges of selective integration, merchants and university graduates, were significantly underrepresented among immigrants to the United States.[4] In this sense, migration from the Pale can be divided into three vastly unequal currents: one, characterized by relatively high levels of wealth and/or education, to the Russian interior; another, driven by ideology or religious faith, to the land of Israel; and a third, poor, less educated, and far larger, to Europe or the New World. Each of these currents, like all migrations, was selective. Those who abandoned the tsarist empire, however, selected themselves, while those who moved to the empire's Russian interior were, at least in part, selected by the imperial state.

3. For examples of this usage see Iosif Lur´e, *Ukazanie o prave zhitel´stva dlia pereseli-aiushchikhsia vo vnutrenniia gubernii* (St. Petersburg, 1908), p. 1; a memorandum by the lawyer Menashe Morgulis in TsGIA-SPb, f. 422, op. 2, d. 1, l. 73; and the memoirs of Alexander Kerensky, *The Crucifixion of Liberty* (New York, 1934), p. 72.

4. Simon Kuznets, "Immigration of Russian Jews to the United States: Background and Structure," *Perspectives in American History* 9 (1975): 102–5.

A WINDOW ON RUSSIA

The granting of residential privileges to selected groups of Jews, as significant as it was, cannot by itself explain why considerable numbers of Jews chose to migrate to the Russian interior, far from the towns and villages of the Pale where their ancestors had lived for centuries. For many, the enormous commercial markets concentrated in Petersburg were the decisive attraction. This was true not only at the pinnacle of Jewish economic activity, among the Gintsburgs and others who were busy establishing banks and managing numerous financial interests, but at the humbler level of individual traders and skilled artisans. The enterprising watchmaker Chaim Aronson, for example, moved there in order to market his mechanical inventions to a wider public.[5] Others were drawn by Petersburg's dynamic urban life. The lawyer Genrikh Sliozberg, whose family had lived near Vilna, in his words, "since time immemorial," recalled his decision to take up university studies in Petersburg in the 1880s: "How attractive the capital seemed to me—the center of the country's intellectual life where, so I thought, one could meet writers, where life was in full swing, and enlightenment poured forth in broad streams, drawing all to culture and progress."[6] "From childhood on," reported the writer Vladimir Grossman, "the magnificent capital of the Russian Empire attracted us all like a magnet"; to the lawyer and writer Iosif Gessen, the capital was "charming—like an inaccessible woman."[7]

So alluring was the imperial capital that many Jews settled there who lacked the legal right to reside outside the Pale, and who therefore faced the constant threat of forcible expulsion by the city's police. A quasi-fictional example of such a person was Gershon ben Gershon, the protagonist of Gershon Lifshits's autobiographical novella *Confession of a Criminal* (1881), who in the course of his expulsion declares:

> What a pity to abandon Petersburg! A good job at the office, a circle of close friends, the Public Library right around the corner, every day a fresh newspaper, good theater, and in general, all the blessings of civilization. I am forced to leave and abandon all this—and the main question is: *Where to go?* To Moscow, Kiev, Orel, Kharkov? But the "Nota-Bene" in my passport [limiting residence to the Pale] rules out these cities. To Warsaw? But I am *Russian* and don't know Polish. . . . To "us"? To Vilna, Kovno, Grodno, Minsk, Berdichev?—Brrr!!

5. Chaim Aronson, *A Jewish Life under the Tsars: The Autobiography of Chaim Aronson, 1825–1888,* trans. Norman Marsden (Totowa, N.J., 1983), pp. 203–78. This work is to my knowledge the only published memoir by a Jewish artisan who lived in St. Petersburg.

6. Sliozberg, *Dela minuvshikh dnei,* 1: 111. Similar sentiments appear in Jacob Teitel, *Aus meiner Lebensarbeit: Errinerungen eines jüdischen Richters im alten Rußland* (Frankfurt a. M., 1929), p. 19; Ginzburg, *Amolike Peterburg,* p. 20; and Wengeroff, *Memoiren einer Grossmutter,* 2: 133.

7. Vladimir Grossman, *Amol un heynt* (Paris, 1955), p. 15; I. V. Gessen, *V dvukh vekakh: Zhiznennyi otchet* (Berlin, 1937), pp. 55–57.

Smelly streets, musty traditions—the whole place is caught in a quagmire. The dark, hungry Jewish masses wallow about, one tearing a piece of bread from the throat of another![8]

To be sure, the image of Petersburg as simultaneously magnetic and forbidding is ubiquitous in Russian literature of the nineteenth century, but among Jews these two poles carried rather different connotations. The city's magnetism was intensified by its capacity as a secular metropolis, a way of escaping from the Orthodox religious fetters and grinding poverty of life in the Pale. At the same time, the tenuous legal status of Jews there created a constant fear of expulsion and vulnerability to shifting political winds. "It was no Garden of Eden," recalled the Zionist writer Mordechai ben Hillel Ha-Kohen, who moved to Petersburg with his merchant father in 1877: "It was like being a hunted dog who trembles at the slightest noise. At the sight of a police officer or official you were overcome by panic and fear lest it occur to them to ask about your place of residence and to demand your identity card. We were especially fearful after every terrorist attack."[9]

For virtually all Jewish immigrants, Petersburg was the first "Russian" city they had ever experienced; for them, the northern capital served not as a "window on Europe" (the image immortalized in Pushkin's *Bronze Horseman*) but as a window on Russia itself. "For the first time," recalled the Yiddish writer Peretz Hirshbein of his initial glimpse of Petersburg, "I felt myself in a Russian atmosphere."[10] In the Pale, Jews lived for the most part among Ukrainians, Belorussians, Lithuanians, and Poles; in many small towns, moreover, Jews were the single largest group. Even in major cities within the Pale such as Kiev and Odessa, ethnic Russians accounted for just half the total population.[11] "In my native town I had hardly known any non-Jews," wrote Ha-Kohen of his childhood near Mogilev in the 1860s. "I had known some government officials, whose relations with Jews were those of the rulers to the ruled. In Petersburg our entire business was with pure Russians, and relations were natural and human."[12]

Native speakers of Russian constituted over 80 percent of Petersburg's population throughout the late imperial period.[13] To be sure, Russian literature

8. G. Lifshits, *Ispoved' prestupnika: Iumoristicheskii rasskaz iz zhizni peterburgskikh evreev* (St. Petersburg, 1881), p. 12 (emphasis in original). Lifshits was a staff writer for the Petersburg Jewish newspaper *Razsvet.*

9. Ha-Kohen, *Olami,* 1: 77, 106.

10. Peretz Hirshbein, *In gang fun lebn: Zikhroynes,* 2 vols. (New York, 1948), 1: 150.

11. Kappeler, *Rußland als Vielvölkerreich,* p. 327.

12. Ha-Kohen, *Olami,* 1: 81.

13. Most cities in the Great Russian provinces were ethnically even more homogeneously Russian than St. Petersburg. See N. V. Iukhneva, "Materialy k etnicheskomu raionirovaniiu gorodskogo naseleniia evropeiskoi Rossii (po dannym perepisi 1897 g.)," in I. I. Krupnik, ed.,

and Slavophile ideology had endowed the imperial capital with the aura of an alien city dominated by European influence.[14] But in Jewish memoirs one finds a rather different impression. Nevsky Prospect, easily the most cosmopolitan, European boulevard in the entire city, appeared to Pauline Wengeroff, the wife of a successful tax farmer, as the quintessential site for "Russian street life, in which all of Russian nature was reflected." The Bundist Vladimir Medem found Petersburg "an amazing city, deep and withdrawn, like the Russian soul."[15]

Among the various provinces of the Russian Empire, as the ethnographer Nataliia Iukhneva has shown, per capita levels of migration to Petersburg were inversely related to the distance of the point of origin from the capital. Immigration was also less pronounced from areas with significant non-Russian populations. In other words, the farther away or less ethnically Russian a given province, the less likely the inhabitants were to abandon their native surroundings for those of Petersburg.[16] Although there are no data on the geographical origins of Jewish immigrants to the capital, contemporaries were often struck by the wide range of cities and towns represented by Jews there.[17] And the mere fact that they came from the Pale—that is, from a relatively distant, non-Russian region of the empire—distinguished them from the vast majority of Petersburg's inhabitants.

Etnicheskie gruppy v gorodakh evropeiskoi chasti SSSR (formirovanie, rasselenie, dinamika kul'tury) (Moscow, 1987), pp. 112–26.

14. Demographically, foreigners—that is, citizens of foreign countries—were a marginal element; at their peak, around 1800, they constituted between 7 and 9 percent of the city's inhabitants. By 1850, foreigners in St. Petersburg were beginning to be outnumbered by non-Russian subjects of the empire such as Finns, Poles, and Baltic Germans, immigrants from territories conquered by the Romanovs over the previous 150 years. See Iukhneva, *Etnicheskii sostav*, pp. 20–23. For secondary literature on non-Russians in prerevolutionary St. Petersburg, see Klaus Zernack, "Im Sog der Ostseemetropole: St. Petersburg und seine Ausländer," *Jahrbücher für Geschichte Osteuropas* 35, no. 2 (1987): 232–40; Max Engman, "The Finns in St. Petersburg," in Engman, ed., *Ethnic Identity in Urban Europe* (New York, 1992), pp. 99–119; Ludwik Bazylow, *Polacy w Petersburgu* (Wroclaw, 1984); Anders Henriksson, "Nationalism, Assimilation, and Identity in Late Imperial Russia: The St. Petersburg Germans, 1906–1914," *Russian Review*, no. 52 (July 1993), pp. 341–53; and "Deutsche in St. Petersburg und Moskau," *Nordost-Archiv*, no. 1 (June 1994).

15. Wengeroff, *Memoiren einer Grossmutter*, 2: 169; Vladimir Medem, *The Life and Soul of a Legendary Jewish Socialist*, trans. Samuel Portnoy (New York, 1979), p. 452.

16. Iukhneva, *Etnicheskii sostav*, pp. 82–97. A similar point is made in James H. Bater, *St. Petersburg: Industrialization and Change* (London, 1976), pp. 146–47.

17. Ha-Kohen, *Olami*, 1: 77. Anecdotal evidence suggests that even after Jews arrived in St. Petersburg, regional affinities in the form of *landsmanshaftn* or *zemliachestva* continued to play an important part in their social and professional lives. See, e.g., Markus Kagan [Mordechai ben Hillel Ha-Kohen], "K istorii natsional'nogo samopoznaniia russko-evreiskogo obshchestva: Po lichnym vospominaniiam," *Perezhitoe* 3 (1911): 145; and L. O. Levanda, *Ispoved' del'tsa* (St. Petersburg, 1880), pp. 83–84.

The high percentage of ethnic Russians in Petersburg's population was due primarily to the large presence there of peasants, the most ethnically Russian estate within the city and the group about whose geographical origins we have the most detailed information.[18] With the abolition of serfdom in 1861, there began a large-scale and enduring flow of peasants from provinces in central Russia to the imperial capital. By the time of the 1869 census, in fact, peasants accounted for 31 percent of the population, the largest single estate in the city. By 1890 they made up over half the population and their absolute numbers and relative share continued to climb steadily thereafter.

In contrast to the large numbers of peasant immigrants to Petersburg, Jews were much more likely to have come from what official censuses described as towns or cities, as opposed to rural areas. By the time of the 1897 census, there was a far higher proportion of "urban dwellers" among the empire's Jews—49 percent—than in any other sizable ethnic group; Germans and Armenians followed at 23 percent, Poles at 18 percent, and Russians and Latvians at 16 percent.[19]

But since the 1897 census followed the longstanding official Russian practice of defining "urban" settings not by size of population or level of industry or trade but by administrative function, so-called cities or towns included settlements of as few as a thousand people. Thus many of the settings from which Jews emigrated were likely to have been little more than small towns, hardly comparable to the Russian capital. To the watchmaker Chaim Aronson, in the course of his journey in the 1860s from the Belorussian shtetl of Serednik to Petersburg, even Vilna—with a population one-tenth that of Petersburg—appeared as "a vast city."[20] The narrator of Lev Levanda's *Confession of a Wheeler-Dealer* (1880), arriving for the first time in Petersburg from his hometown of Bobruisk in Ukraine, was at a loss for words: "My head began to spin, I was dazzled by the huge, multistory buildings extending in long,

18. In 1869, 97 percent of Petersburg's peasants were native speakers of Russian; in 1897, 93 percent were. Among merchants, the equivalent figures were 78 and 80 percent, respectively. See Iukhneva, *Etnicheskii sostav*, p. 42.

19. "Sizable" here means over 200,000 total members of a given ethnic group. I have omitted two relatively urbanized ethnic groups from the non-European territories of the empire: Tadjiks (29 percent of whom were urban dwellers) and Sarts (21 percent). See Bauer et al., *Nationalitäten des Russischen Reiches*, 2: 69–74. Using the far more extensive available data regarding Jewish migration in the Austro-Hungarian Empire during roughly the same period and from a similar East European milieu, Marsha Rozenblit has calculated that the larger the town in which a Jew lived and the larger the Jewish community there, the more likely he or she was to move to Vienna. See Rozenblit, *The Jews of Vienna, 1867–1914: Assimilation and Identity* (Albany, 1983), p. 37.

20. The profound effect of exposure to urban settings is apparent in Aronson's subsequent comment that "when I returned from the big city of Vilna I realized how poorly we had lived—although before I had ever left my father's home I had always considered it a veritable paradise." See Aronson, *A Jewish Life under the Tsars*, pp. 69, 99.

even rows on both sides of the street, and by the noise and hubbub of the gaily colored crowd surging back and forth, in which I was unable to recognize even one familiar face. . . ."[21] And in the former cantonist Viktor Nikitin's short story "Seeker of Happiness" (1875), the protagonist arrives in Petersburg together with his fellow Jewish immigrants from a small town in the Pale, only to be nearly arrested for loitering in the street outside the train station as they nervously discuss where to spend their first night in the capital. "We looked around in wonder: where we came from, all sorts of private matters were discussed and decided in the middle of the street. . . . Here they won't let you stand for a minute."[22] The process of adjustment to Petersburg's distinctly metropolitan rhythms, therefore, was often scarcely less dramatic for newly arrived Jews than it was for their fellow immigrants from the villages of central Russia.[23]

THE CENSUS AS SOURCE: LANGUAGE, RELIGION, AND ETHNICITY

To reconstruct the evolving demographic profile of Petersburg Jewry during the second half of the nineteenth century, I have relied to a large extent on the five city censuses conducted roughly every ten years between 1869 and 1910 as well as the empire-wide census of 1897. To a lesser extent, I have employed police reports, annual statistical registers, and the vital records kept by the Jewish community. Like all historical sources, census and other demographic data must be treated with skepticism, perhaps with more than the usual dose, given their seductive veneer of precision and clarity. Accordingly, I have tried to recapture the specific conditions under which census data were gathered and interpreted in order not only to correct for possible quantitative flaws but to explore the qualitative interplay between contemporary debates about Jews and quasi-scientific attempts to depict their role within the larger society. Like the vocabulary of social identity explored in Chapter 2, statistical data need to be approached through the contemporary meanings attached to them. Like words, numbers have a history.

Until 1869, records concerning Petersburg Jewry were assembled by the police, who would periodically review registration documents for Jews residing in the capital. Apart from breaking down the Jewish population by gender or estate, police reports generally gave the total number of registered

---

21. Levanda, *Ispoved´ del´tsa*, p. 79.

22. Viktor Nikitin, "Iskatel´ schast´ia (iz rasskazov otverzhennogo)," *Evreiskaia Biblioteka*, 5 (1875): 89. Nikitin was a cantonist in Nicholas I's army, where he was baptized. He moved to Petersburg in the 1860s. See *Rossiiskaia evreiskaia entsiklopediia*, 4 vols. to date (Moscow, 1995–), 2: 330.

23. For an analysis of urban experience through peasant eyes, see Barbara Alpern Engel, "Russian Peasant Views of City Life," *Slavic Review* 52, no. 3 (Fall 1993): 446–59.

TABLE 1. Jewish and Total Population of St. Petersburg, 1826–1910, as Reported by Governor General, Police, and Census

	Jewish population			Total population, census
Year	Governor general	Police	Census	
1826		370		
1851		520		
1855	495			
1856	527			
1857	552			
1858	1,050			
1859	847			
1861	959			
1862	2,339			
1863	2,708			
1864	2,699	2,612		
1865	2,612			
1866	2,701			
1869[a]		2,179	6,624	667,207
1881[a]			16,826	861,303
1887		11,699		
1888		11,604		
1889		12,503		
1890[a]		11,627	15,331	954,400
1891		10,546		
1892		9,905		
1893		16,472		
1894		17,009		
1895		18,582		
1896		20,446		
1897[b]		26,962	16,944	1,264,920
1898		26,120		
1899		27,026		
1900[b]		28,268	20,385	1,439,521
1910[b]			34,995	1,905,589

NOTE: Missing years reflect the absence of population statistics for those years.

[a] Figures pertain to St. Petersburg's twelve urban boroughs (*chasti*) only.

[b] Figures pertain to both urban boroughs and suburbs (*uchastki*). Relatively few Jews lived in the suburbs.

SOURCES: *Governor general:* G. M. Deych, unpublished manuscript surveying population figures in *gubernskie otchety* of selected Great Russian provinces. *Police:* RGIA, f. 821, op. 8, d. 164, ll. 87–89, 118; *Evreiskaia entsiklopediia*, 13: 941. *Census: Sanktpeterburg po perepisi 10 dekabria 1869 goda* (St. Petersburg, 1872), no. 1, sec. 2, pp. 25, 38, 49, 59; *Sanktpeterburg po perepisi 15 dekabria 1881 goda* (St. Petersburg, 1883), vol. 1, pt. 1, pp. 242–43; *S.-Peterburg po perepisi 15 dekabria 1890 goda* (St. Petersburg, 1891), pt. 1, sec. 1, pp. 46–47; *Pervaia vseob-*

shchaia perepis´ naseleniia Rossiiskoi imperii, 1897 goda, 89 vols. (St. Petersburg, 1899–1905), vol. 37, pt. 2, p. 51; *S.-Peterburg po perepisi 15 dekabria 1900 goda* (St. Petersburg, 1903), pt. 2, sec. 1, pp. 152–59; *Petrograd po perepisi naseleniia 15 dekabria 1910 goda* (Petrograd, n.d.), pt. 1, sec. 1, p. 5.

Jews and nothing more. For police purposes, a Jew was anyone whose internal passport (obtained at one's point of origin) indicated "Jewish" in the line concerning religion; that is, police reports, in contrast to the census, involved no self-reporting. It is unclear whether the police counted all Jews or only heads of households. Jewish communal records, for their part, include vital statistics (births, deaths, marriages, divorces) but no data on Jewish population as a whole.[24]

The first more or less reliable measure of the city's population, including its Jews, came with the census of 1869, which, as Table 1 indicates, reported three times the number of Jews reported by the police for the same year. In the decades that followed, the gap between police and census data regarding Jewish population narrowed until the 1890s, when police estimates began significantly to exceed those of the census. The police may well have become more aggressive over time in their monitoring of the city's Jews—especially those residing there illegally, who presumably found it more difficult to decline a request for information from a police officer than from a census official.

Apart from attempting to establish the size of the city's population, the 1869 census also recorded its composition by gender, age group, estate, field of occupation, religious affiliation, native language, and other criteria. In fact, it inaugurated in the Russian Empire the practice of collecting data on a given population in the course of a single day. This method continued in subsequent Petersburg censuses.[25] The specific questions posed and categories employed changed significantly from one census to the next, and in ways that bear directly on our ability to discern the shifting roles of ethnicity and religious affiliation in the life of the city in general and for Jews in particular. Neither the five St. Petersburg censuses nor the empire-wide census of 1897 asked respondents directly to state their ethnicity. But contemporary commentary—including the prefaces of the censuses themselves—proceeded from the assumption that respondents' "ethnicity" (*narodnost´*) was synonymous with their "native language" (*rodnoi iazyk*), which respondents were asked to report.[26]

24. For Petersburg Jewry's communal records, see TsGIA-SPb, f. 422, op. 3, dd. 11–527.

25. Bater, *St. Petersburg,* pp. 184, 441.

26. The equation of ethnicity or nationality with native language was also common in European censuses of the time. See Bauer et al., *Nationalitäten des Russischen Reiches,* 1: 140.

This assumption, questionable to begin with, was particularly risky when it came to Jews, who might reasonably declare their native language to be Yiddish or Hebrew or—depending on education and background—Russian, Polish, or German. Whether any of these choices translated directly into a sense of ethnicity remained an open question. In the 1869 census, "native language," though not specifically defined, appears to have been understood (at least by the census's organizers) as the language of one's childhood.[27] In the 1890 census, by contrast, "native language" was explicitly described in the forms given to respondents as "that language in which you customarily express yourself within your family, at home"—meaning the language shared by parents and children at the time of the census.[28] The 1890 census also inaugurated the practice, followed in subsequent city censuses, of devoting an entire section to data exclusively concerning the city's Jews, without explaining why this was done. No other ethnic group, including Russians, was singled out for such close scrutiny.[29]

In the 1897 census, the significance of "native language" shifted yet again. Unable to agree on a compromise between "present family language" and "the language of one's childhood," census organizers instructed those gathering data in the field simply to record "that language which each [respondent] considers for himself to be native."[30] But the assumption that native language coincided with ethnicity remained unchanged, as the editors of the 1897 census volume on Petersburg explained:

> Native language does not signify conversational language; rather, it signifies belonging to a certain ethnicity [*narodnost'*]. For example, many people of Jewish background, while not practicing the Jewish faith, indicated the Jewish language [i.e., Yiddish], despite the fact that there is no such thing as the Jewish language; rather, there is a Jewish jargon, which educated Jews, in particular those who do not practice the Jewish faith, often do not even know. There-

27. In their preface to the published data, the editors drew readers' attention to "the remarkable situation of encountering Catholic and Protestant families where the parents indicated their native language as one or another non-Russian tongue, while giving the native language of their children as Russian": *Sanktpeterburg po perepisi 10 dekabria 1869 g.* (St. Petersburg, 1872), no. 1, p. xxv. This and other Petersburg censuses were published in bilingual Russian-French editions in which *evreiskii iazyk* ("the Jewish language," meaning Yiddish) was incorrectly rendered in French as *hébreu*.

28. Iukhneva, *Etnicheskii sostav*, p. 9.

29. For the 1890 census, see *S.-Peterburg po perepisi 15 dekabria 1890 goda* (St. Petersburg, 1891), pt. 1, sec. 2, pp. 56–75. As one Jewish commentator remarked, "We do not know what reasons led the compilers to construct this separate section, although it would be quite useful for correctly evaluating the statistics presented. But in any event we must thank them for this unintended kindness." See Mikhail Soloveichik, "Peterburgskie evrei po poslednei perepisi," *Voskhod* 5 (1892): 8.

30. Quoted in Bauer et al., *Nationalitäten des Russischen Reiches*, 1: 144. A proposal to ask respondents to indicate directly their *narodnost'* was rejected.

קול קורא ! לאחינו בני ישראל

מהרב הגאון ומהרב המאושר מטעם הממשלה ומהגבאים דבתי התפלות ·

עס איז ידוע , אז קורץ נאך נייא יאהר וועט זיין ביי אונז , אין רוסלאנד , אײן אַלגעמײנער
פּערעפּיס . דאַס הייסט מען וועט פּערשרייבּען אַללעמען , וואָס וואוינען אין רוסלאַנד : אַלט און יונג ,
זכרים און נקבות , פון יעדער אומה ולשון , מיט בּעצײכנונג , וויא יעדער הייסט , וויא אַלט ער איז , פון
וועלכע נאַציאָן און גלויבּען ער איז , אויף וועלכע שפּראַך ער רעט , וואָ ער וואוינט שטענדיג , צוא
איז ער אַ גרעמאַטענער , מיט וואָס ער בּעשעפטיגט זיך (מלאכה , מסחר , סלוזבּע) און דאָס גלייכען ;
אויך וועט וועם אַנגעצייכענט ווערען · וואָר עם איז רל בּלינד , טויבּ , שטום . נייסטיג קראַנק — דער נייער
פּערעפּיס האָם נים דיא בּעדייטונג פון דיא פריערדינע סקאַזקעס , און דאָס נים קיין שום כַּונה וועגען
געלד זאַכען אום צוא פערגרעסערען דיא אבּצאַלונגען , און נים וועגען נפשות , אום צוא נעמען מעהרער
מענטשען אין וואַיענע סלוזבּע ; דער צוועק איז מעהר נים-צו וויסען , וויפיל מענטשען עם געפינען זיך
אין לאַנד , אין יעדער גובערנע , יעדער אויעזד , שטאַט , דאָרף , און צוא האָבּען דיא איבּעריגע זאַכען
דערמאַנטע ידיעות , וואָ אָן דעם קען קין מלוכה נים אום קומען — אַזעלכע פערעפּיסען ווערען גענומען
אין אויסלאַנד זייער אפט , בּיי אונו איז דאָס דער ערשטער , און פון ציים צוא ציים וועלען אַזעלכע
פערעפּיסען גענומען ווערען · להבּא אויך ·

Figure 5. Excerpt from a public notice to Jews announcing the 1897 imperial census:

AN APPEAL TO OUR BROTHERS, SONS OF ISRAEL!
From the great learned rabbi and from the official government rabbi and from the heads of the houses of prayer: It is known that shortly after the new year a general census will be held here in Russia, that is, everyone who lives in Russia will be registered: old and young, male and female, from every nation and tongue, with a record of each person's name, his age, his nationality and faith, what language he speaks, his place of permanent residence, whether he is literate, his occupation (craft, trade, state service), and so forth. It will also be recorded who (heaven forbid) is blind, deaf, mute, or mentally ill. The new census does not have the same significance as surveys conducted in the past; its aim has nothing whatsoever to do with money and increasing revenues, nor with individual souls and raising the number of draftees for military service. The purpose is to know more about the number of people living in this country, in each province, district, town, and village, and to gather other information described above, without which no state can function. Such censuses are very often conducted abroad; here it will be for the first time. In the future such censuses will be conducted from time to time as well (Vilna, 1896).

fore, by indicating the Jewish language as their native tongue, they sought to articulate their tribal [*plemennoe*] background.[31]

Whatever the prejudices of this passage, Yiddish was indeed known by Jews as "jargon," and the question whether it should be regarded as a corrupt dialect of German or as an authentic, perhaps the authentic, Jewish language aroused strong feeling among Jewish intellectuals. On first meeting his cousins in Petersburg, for example, the future *Forverts* editor Abraham Cahan reported, "I envied them their inability to speak Yiddish."[32] There were in fact Jews in tsarist Russia who grew up without Yiddish—the lawyers Oskar Gruzenberg and Iosif Gessen, the poet Osip Mandel´shtam, the Bundist Vladimir Medem, and the Zionist Vladimir (Ze'ev) Jabotinsky admit as much in their memoirs. But such a condition appears to have been rare, even outside the Pale (leaving aside the non-Ashkenazic Jews of the Crimea, Caucasus, and Central Asia). More common among Petersburg Jews, perhaps, was the position taken by the fictional Yakov Vainshtein, an apprentice lawyer in Sholem Asch's novel *Petersburg*, set in the decade before the Russian Revolution. Asked to translate for a Yiddish-speaking client, Vainshtein "was offended that anyone could dare even to think that he understood 'jargon.'" In fact, he understands perfectly.[33] Clearly, in a setting of widespread multilingualism (by 1897, over 50 percent of Petersburg's self-declared native speakers of Yiddish were literate in Russian), the meaning of "native language" and its relation to ethnicity were in a state of considerable flux.[34]

In all the censuses considered here, Jews could leave two distinct kinds of traces: as native speakers of Yiddish and/or as adherents of the Jewish religion.[35] The degree of overlap between the two groups varied considerably over time. By the last quarter of the nineteenth century, for example, large

---

31. *Pervaia vseobshchaia perepis´ naseleniia Rossiiskoi imperii, 1897 g.*, 89 vols. (St. Petersburg, 1899–1905), vol. 37, pt. 2, p. xxii.

32. Abraham Cahan, *The Education of Abraham Cahan*, trans. Leon Stein, Abraham P. Conan, and Lynn Davison (Philadelphia, 1969), p. 161.

33. Sholem Asch, *Peterburg*, the first volume of the trilogy *Farn mabl* (Warsaw, 1929), p. 157 (the trilogy was published in English as *Three Cities* [New York, 1933]).

34. For a detailed discussion of the use of language as an indicator of nationality in Russian and European censuses across the nineteenth century, see Bauer et al., *Nationalitäten des Russischen Reiches*, 1: 137–58.

35. In accord with tsarist policy, census data registered Karaites separately from Jews (or "Talmudists," as the latter were occasionally called). The Karaites, a longstanding Jewish sect concentrated around the Black Sea and the Near East, recognized as sacred the Hebrew Bible but not the Talmud. In Petersburg, Karaites never numbered more than a few hundred, and I have excluded them entirely from my statistical analysis. On Karaites in the Russian Empire, see Phillip E. Miller, ed. and trans., *Karaite Separatism in Nineteenth-Century Russia: Joseph Solomon Lutski's "Epistle of Israel's Deliverance"* (Cincinatti, 1993), esp. pp. 1–49.

numbers of self-declared adherents of the Jewish religion in Petersburg described themselves as native speakers of Russian. Conversely, apostate Jews
often reported Yiddish as their native tongue, either because it literally was
or because they thereby sought to express the possibility of being a Christian of Jewish ethnicity.[36]

While each group—Jews as native speakers of Yiddish and Jews as adherents of Judaism—was subject to depletion via linguistic assimilation or
(more rarely) religious conversion, both were virtually free from statistical
infiltration by outsiders. That is, leaving aside apostates from Judaism, practically no non-Jews declared Yiddish their native tongue, while conversion
to Judaism was, until 1905, a punishable offense. The fact that these two Jewish markers—Yiddish and Judaism—were not shared by any other group represents a great advantage for the historian.[37] Other groups in the census can
be far more difficult or simply impossible to trace. Because the censuses did
not include explicitly national or ethnic categories, for example, Eastern Orthodox speakers of Russian who may have considered themselves ethnic
Ukrainians or Belorussians appeared in census data as Russians—as indeed
the tsarist government wished them to do. Similarly, it is impossible to determine the ethnic breakdown of the city's Catholics as among Poles, Germans, Ukrainians, and others.

The study of selective Jewish integration in the imperial capital nonetheless presents its own problems. For despite the silence of census takers on
the subject, it appears that the precarious status of Jews outside the Pale
led significant numbers of them to shun the official counts entirely. Accounts of Jews residing in Petersburg who did not belong to any of the "useful" categories, who lacked the necessary legal documents, who paid bribes
(known euphemistically among Jews as "tariffs") to the police, or who were
summarily expelled abound in contemporary sources.[38] In 1878 the city
governor Aleksandr E. Zurov went so far as to claim, in a report to the minister of internal affairs, that "the number of Jews living in the capital without

36. In the censuses of 1890 and 1897, for example, the breakdown of members of the Orthodox Church into ethnic groups (*narodnosti*) included the category of "Jewish"; the same breakdown was given among Catholics, Protestants, and other religious groups.

37. In the city censuses, most of the data concerning the breakdown of the Jewish population by gender, estate, occupation, literacy, etc. concerns those professing the Jewish faith.
The empire-wide census of 1897, by contrast, gives most such data only for speakers of Yiddish, thereby missing the roughly one-third of Petersburg's Jews who by then were declaring
themselves native speakers of Russian. In all statistical tables presented in this chapter I have
preserved this distinction: "Jew" indicates a religious category, while "Yiddish-speaker" signifies
declared native language.

38. See, e.g., Ginzburg, *Amolike Peterburg*, p. 22; L. Kliachko, "Za chertoiu: V Peterburge,"
Evreiskaia Letopis' 2 (1923): 114; A. E. Landau, "Pis'ma ob evreiakh: peterburgskie evrei," *Biblioteka dlia Chteniia* 187, no. 2 (1864): 1.

special permission and lacking this right under the law is considerably greater than the number living [there] on the basis of existing laws."[39] Ever since the Jews had become subjects of the tsar, in fact, state officials had complained that Jews throughout the empire underreported their own numbers in order to reduce the pressures of taxation and military conscription. For Jews whose legal right to live in St. Petersburg was subject to doubt, the additional threat of expulsion only increased the incentive to dodge the census.

The issue of illegal Jewish residence in St. Petersburg made its way into the popular press as well, where the specter was raised of an imperial capital flooded with Jewish immigrants from the Pale, uncounted and hence outside the control of the authorities. *Golos* (The Voice) warned its readers in 1874 that Petersburg Jews had suspiciously managed to misplace some of their own records of births and deaths.[40] While the 1881 municipal census data were still being sorted through, *Novoe Vremia* (New Times) and *Russkie Vedomosti* (Russian Gazette) rushed to assert that the census had found a "colossal number" of Jews, as many as 40,000 (which would have constituted just over 4 percent of the city's population), living in the imperial capital. One newspaper called for the city to be "cleansed" of such undesirable elements; another went so far as to claim that government officials were already considering the possibility of forcibly returning the city's Jews to the Pale.[41]

The Jewish press, which by the 1880s had shifted its center of gravity from Odessa to St. Petersburg, wasted little time in responding to such attacks. After publication of the 1881 census, *Russkii Evrei* (The Russian Jew) mocked the exaggerated fears of its journalistic opponents, emphasizing instead the minuscule number of Jews actually living in the capital, given in the census as just over 16,000. "Hasn't the distinguished correspondent [of *Russkie Vedomosti*]," asked another Petersburg Jewish newspaper, "been pouring on the salt a bit too heavily?"[42] But neither paper went so far as to suggest that even if there were 40,000 Jews in the Russian capital (as there soon would be), there would still be nothing to fear. *Russkii Evrei*'s praise for the census's accuracy and fairness, one suspects, had more to do with the newspaper's timid pleasure in the low reported Jewish head count than with any real certainty about the procedures employed. Signs had been posted at intersections throughout Petersburg, *Russkii Evrei* confidently noted, reassuring the pop-

---

39. RGIA, f. 821, op. 8, d. 24, l. 125. For similar impressions from Jewish sources, see Ginzburg, *Amolike Peterburg*, p. 22; A. E. Landau, "Pis´ma ob evreiakh: Peterburgskie evrei," *Biblioteka dlia chteniia* 187, no. 12 (1864): 2; Grossman, *Amol un heynt*, p. 15.

40. *Golos*, 1874, pp. 191, 203.

41. See the discussion and response to these articles in *Nedel´naia Khronika Voskhoda*, 1882, no. 7, p. 115, and *Russkii Evrei*, 1883, no. 46.

42. *Nedel´naia Khronika Voskhoda*, 1882, no. 7, p. 115.

ulation that "the census is not being used to further the goals of the police," that "those who are entered into the 'lists' will not be required to produce documents of any kind," and that "as a general matter the census does not threaten anyone in any way."[43] But given the ever-present threat of expulsion for Jews, one may doubt whether such assurances were convincing; and since in 1881 the majority of Petersburg Jews still could not read Russian, the signs are scarcely likely to have had the desired effect.

In light of the tenuous status of many Jews in the capital, it makes sense to take census data as representing only the "legal" population, meaning those officially qualified for residence outside the Pale. The interpretations I offer in this chapter therefore pertain to this population and may or may not apply to illegal Jewish residents. But the apparently expanding number of illegal Jewish residents in St. Petersburg, and presumably elsewhere outside the Pale, as suggested by police data and anecdotal evidence, is itself significant. It indicates not only the attraction of the empire's vast interior but the extent to which the policy of selective integration may have been losing its monopoly over how Jews got there.

Like many urban centers in late imperial Russia, St. Petersburg had the feel of what Daniel Brower has called a "migrant city" with a "fugitive population."[44] The peasant tradition of seasonal migration to urban jobs, combined with the capital's volatile economy, assured a high level of transience among the city's many recent arrivals. So pronounced was this pattern that by 1890 the proportion of native-born residents was actually higher among the city's Jews (42 percent) than among the population as a whole (32 percent).[45] But even among Jews, immigrants continued to form the majority, as wave after wave of new arrivals from the Pale continuously fortified traditional rhythms and habits of Jewish life within the capital's Jewish community. By 1878, the alarmed city governor Zurov was reporting that the increasing numbers of illegal Jewish immigrants "constitute a vagrant population that comes and goes . . . according to circumstances."[46]

Police vigilance with respect to Jews reached its apex under the harsh regime of Zurov's successor, Petr A. Gresser, who ruled Petersburg from 1882 until his death in 1892. This was the only decade between the 1860s and the Revolution of 1917 during which the city's Jewish population declined absolutely.[47]

---

43. *Russkii Evrei*, 1883, no. 46.

44. Daniel R. Brower, *The Russian City between Tradition and Modernity, 1850–1900* (Berkeley, 1990), pp. 7, 40.

45. *S.-Peterburg po perepisi 15 dekabria 1890 g.*, pt. 1, sec. 1, pp. 36–37, 52–53; sec. 2, p. 92.

46. RGIA, f. 821, op. 8, d. 24, l. 125.

47. The 1880s brought an economic depression that briefly retarded (without reversing) the growth of Petersburg's population as a whole. See Bater, *St. Petersburg*, p. 309. The depression may account for some of the absolute decline in Jewish population, but by no means all.

In fact, police data (see Table 1) show that the year immediately after Gresser's death witnessed a dramatic rise in the number of Jews. One contemporary newspaper, describing Gresser as "well known" for his zeal in limiting Jewish residence in the capital, reported that he had posted police at train stations to demand residence papers on the spot from all arriving Jews, rather than leaving it to the new arrivals to register with the authorities. Those lacking the necessary documentation were expelled at once.[48] Gresser insisted that in Jews' passports the section for "religion" be marked in red for easier inspection, and that Jewish shopkeepers display on their signs their first names as written in their passports—usually Yiddish forms such as Yankele and Yoshke—which readily identified the proprietors as Jews. For this and similar acts he was immortalized in a contemporary Yiddish pun: "Ver iz greser—a khazir oder a hunt?" (Which is bigger [Gresser]—a pig or a dog?).[49]

ESTATE, OCCUPATION, AND SOCIAL IDENTITY

In the Pale, Jews differed markedly from their neighbors in estate and occupational profile. The virtual absence of both a Jewish peasantry and a Jewish nobility left the vast majority of Jews engaged as petty traders, small shop- or tavernkeepers, artisans, moneylenders, or *luftmenshen* ("air people") who floated from one odd job to the next. Contemporary accounts of economic life in the Pale typically noted that "Jews constitute the entire middle class," that "commerce is entirely in the hands of the Jews," or some variation on this theme.[50] Such claims, while exaggerated, were far from pure fantasy. In Vilna province (including the city of Vilna) in 1861, for example, of the roughly 1300 merchants, three-fourths were Jews; in Odessa, Jews dominated the grain export business, the backbone of the local economy.[51]

Despite the expectation that those Jews allowed to reside in the Russian

---

48. *Novorossiiskii Telegraf*, Aug. 14, 1886. The article goes on to complain that Jewish would-be immigrants were circumventing Gresser's strategy by exiting their trains at stations outside the city and from there "triumphantly entering Petersburg in hired carts." It called for the re-institution of checkpoints on all roads leading into the city, "as in times past."

49. Ginzburg, *A molike Peterburg*, p. 22. For corroboration of Gresser's harsh regime, see S. M. Dubnov, *Kniga zhizni*, vol. 1 (Riga, 1934), p. 201, and Sliozberg, *Dela minuvhskikh dnei*, 1: 121–25. Sliozberg notes that a formal complaint by the Petersburg Jewish lawyer M. S. Varshavskii to the Senate (the highest court in tsarist Russia), protesting the "medieval" character of Gresser's policy of marking Jewish passports in red, was rejected after lengthy debate.

50. See, e.g., the annual reports submitted across the nineteenth century by the governors of the fifteen provinces that constituted the Pale, as quoted in G. M. Deych, comp., *Arkhivnye dokumenty po istorii evreev v Rossii v XIX—nachale XX vv.: Putevoditel'*, ed. Benjamin Nathans (Moscow, 1994), pp. 40–85.

51. Orshanskii, *Evrei v Rossii*, p. 24.

interior would "merge" with the surrounding population, census after census showed that Petersburg Jewry continued to differ markedly from the rest of the city's inhabitants in its distribution across the various estates. This was all but inevitable, given that half (in 1869) to two-thirds (in 1897) of the capital's Gentile residents were either peasants or members of the nobility. The policy of selective integration virtually guaranteed that a relatively narrow range of social groups would be represented among the city's Jewish population. In 1869, for example, nearly 90 percent of the city's Jews were classified as merchants (13 percent), soldiers (38 percent), or *meshchane,* a catchall category that included artisans, students, and employees of merchants (34 percent), while in Petersburg's population as a whole these categories together constituted just 40 percent.[52]

The unusual preponderance of active or retired soldiers among Petersburg Jews was a short-lived phenomenon. Once the military reform of 1874 replaced the draconian 25-year conscription policy instituted by Nicholas I with universal (and much briefer) service, Jewish veterans no longer gained the right to reside outside the Pale. Accordingly, the percentage of soldiers in Petersburg's Jewish community declined precipitously beginning in the 1880s.[53] At the same time, the proportion of meshchane ballooned rapidly. By the turn of the century, the estate composition of Petersburg Jewry looked remarkably similar to that of Jews in the Pale. In both cases, the overwhelming majority fell into the broad category of meshchane (87 percent in St. Petersburg, 94 percent in the Pale); the only other statistically significant group were merchants (5 percent in St. Petersburg, 1 percent in the Pale). Noblemen and honored citizens, almost unknown among Jews in the Pale, constituted 3 percent of the capital's Jewish population.[54]

---

52. *Sanktpeterburg po perepisi 10 dekabria 1869 g.,* no. 1, sec. 3, pp. 110–11, 124–27. In the 1869 census, "tsekhovye" (artisan guild members) were not included in the chart showing estate distribution among Jews. I am assuming that Jewish artisans are therefore included under "meshchane." Data on the clerical estate included only clergy of Christian denominations.

53. The 1869 census lists 2,513 Jewish soldiers (active and retired), including family members. By 1890 this number was 393. Judging by the number of births and deaths among the families of retired soldiers, as recorded in the vital records of the Petersburg Jewish community, the population of retired kantonisty began to decline in the 1880s and had all but disappeared by 1900. See the vital records for the years 1856 to 1917 in TsGIA-SPb f. 422, op. 3, dd. 11–527.

54. *Pervaia vseobshchaia perepis´ naseleniia Rossiiskoi imperii, 1897 goda,* vol. 37, pt. 2, pp. 232–47. Because data on estate membership in the 1897 census were broken down according to native language rather than religious confession (as in previous censuses), it is impossible to determine the estate membership in that year of the roughly one-third of Petersburg Jews who declared Russian rather than Yiddish to be their native language. The impression is thereby created, for example, that the number of Jewish merchants living in the capital declined between 1869 and 1897. By contrast, the vital records of the Jewish community (in

While the hierarchy of estates remained an important tool in the tsarist regime's administration of its various populations—not least in the case of selective Jewish integration—the Great Reforms weakened the lines of demarcation precisely in the middling, usually urban ranks, where the meshchane and the *raznochintsy* (literally, "people of various ranks") resided.[55] During the postreform period, census takers were increasingly aware that official estate categories often failed to capture actual social roles and identities. As early as 1866, the prominent statistician P. Semenov complained of the "uncertainty of our classification of estates. . . . In Russia, only the hereditary nobility, the clergy, and the rural estate [i.e., the peasantry] belong to sharply defined groups; among the remaining estates there are not sharp boundaries."[56] Thus census data on estate membership, while valuable as an index of how Jews were sifted into the official system of social classifications (and thereby in some cases became eligible for selective integration), tell us relatively little about actual occupations and socioeconomic roles.

Data on occupations, while varying widely in level of specificity from census to census, suggest that the majority of Petersburg Jews (at least those residing legally in the city) tended to cluster in a small number of professions and trades. In 1881 and thereafter, tailors and shoemakers—traditional occupations for Jews throughout Eastern Europe—accounted for between a fourth and a fifth of the city's working Jewish population. Those involved in commerce, whether as full-fledged merchants, brokers at the city's stock exchange, petty traders, or their employees, accounted for roughly another fifth.[57]

In a few cases, Jews formed a high proportion of the total number of those involved in a given occupation, far exceeding their share of the city's population as a whole (which fluctuated over the latter half of the century between 1 percent and 2 percent). This was particularly striking in the world of trade and finance. In 1881, 43 percent of all brokers (*komissionery po torgovle*), 41 percent of all pawnshop owners, and 12 percent of all employees of trading houses were Jews. Jews were similarly visible in the so-called free professions: they constituted 20 percent of all pharmacists, 11 percent of all

---

which religion, not native language, was the determining factor) suggest that the Jewish merchant population increased steadily throughout the late imperial period.

55. Hildermeier, *Bürgertum und Stadt*, pp. 309–10.

56. *Statisticheskii vremennik rossiiskoi imperii* (St. Petersburg, 1866), 1: xix, quoted in Iukhneva, *Etnicheskii sostav*, p. 35.

57. See S. O. Gruzenberg, "Evreiskoe naselenie Peterburga v sotsial'nom i sanitarnom otnoshenii: Statisticheskii ocherk," *Voskhod*, no. 1 (1891), pp. 15–23; Soloveichik, "Peterburgskie evrei po poslednei perepisi," pp. 11–16; and the unusually detailed *S.-Peterburg po perepisi 15 dekabria 1890 goda*, pt. 1, sec. 2, pp. 56–75. For an overview of typically Jewish artisan trades, see Ezra Mendelsohn, *Class Struggle in the Pale: The Formative Years of the Jewish Workers' Movement in Tsarist Russia* (Cambridge, 1970), p. 6 and sources cited there.

dentists, and 9 percent of all physicians. By the late 1880s, estimates of the proportion of Jews among the capital's lawyers ranged from 22 percent to 42 percent, while estimates for Jewish apprentice lawyers—the future generation of lawyers—were higher still, ranging from 43 percent to 55 percent. Among artisans, Jews accounted for 18 percent of all watchmakers and 14 percent of all furriers. Sixteen percent of all owners of brothels were Jews (as against 3 percent of all registered prostitutes).[58]

The prominence of Jews in certain occupations did not escape contemporary comment. With respect to the manufacturing sector as a whole, where Jews constituted under 3 percent of the workforce, the statistical bureau of the city administration (led by Iu. E. Ianson, the most prominent demographer of Petersburg) highlighted what it described as the Jews' tendency to shun subordinate positions as "workers" in favor of managerial or independent positions (see Table 2).

Despite the low percentage of Jews at every level, the statistical bureau commented that "relative to others, Jews are seizing privileged positions as managers, self-employed, and administrators."[59] These data and Ianson's accompanying commentary found a wide echo in public and official treatments of the "Jewish Question" in St. Petersburg. They were repeated verbatim, for example, in a report issued in 1888 by the High Commission for Review of Legislation Regarding Jews in the Empire, the Jewish Committee's nominal successor as coordinator of official policy toward the empire's Jews.[60] Concern about Jewish "overrepresentation" in privileged sectors of Russia's economy and society would soon shift to institutions of higher education and the professions, with results that called into question the entire logic of selective integration.

Though closer to lived experience than estate categories, census data on occupations had their own blind spots when it came to the Jews. Because the system of selective integration linked vital privileges to membership in cer-

---

58. *Obshchaia zapiska vysshei komissii dlia peresmotra deistvuiushchikh o evreiakh v imperii zakonov* (St. Petersburg, 1888), pp. 18–19. Upon learning that 11 of 52 pharmacies in Petersburg were owned by Jews, the Ministry of Internal Affairs decreed in 1880 that while Jews could work as pharmacists outside the Pale, they could not own pharmacies there. The decree was overturned by the Senate in 1882 after a successful appeal by several pharmacy owners. See *Nedel'naia Khronika Voskhoda,* Mar. 26, 1882, p. 315, and Dec.14, 1882, p. 1368. For data on Jewish lawyers, see *Vysochaishe uchrezhdennaia komissiia dlia peresmotra zakonopolozhenii po sudebnoi chasti: Ob"iasnitel'naia Zapiska k proektu novoi redaktsii uchrezhdeniia sudebnykh ustanovlenii,* vol. 3 (St. Petersburg, 1900), pp. 34–35; "Za mesiats (Iuridicheskaia khronika)," *Zhurnal grazhdanskogo i ugolovnogo prava,* no. 6 (June 1889), p. 146; and Vladimir Ptitsyn, *Russkaia advokatura i evrei* (St. Petersburg, 1905), app. 3.

59. *Statisticheskii ezhegodnik S.-Peterburga 1883 goda* (St. Petersburg, 1884), p. 34.

60. *Obshchaia zapiska vysshei komissii,* p. 18. See also Iu. E. Ianson, "Naselenie Peterburga po perepisi 1869 g.," *Vestnik Evropy,* no. 10 (1875), pp. 606–40, and no. 11 (1875), pp. 55–94.

TABLE 2. Jews and Non-Jews in St. Petersburg
Manufacturing Sector, 1881, by Position Held (%)

Position held	Jews	Non-Jews	Jews as % of total
Manager (*khoziaeva*)	29%	9%	5%
Administrator (*administratsiia*)	4	3	–
Worker (*rabochii*)	41	76	1
Self-employed (*odinochka*)	26	12	3
ALL POSITIONS	100%	100%	

SOURCE: *Statisticheskii ezhegodnik S.-Peterburga 1883 goda* (St. Petersburg, 1884), pp. 34ff.

tain groups such as artisans and the merchantry, it created enormous incentives for Jews to adopt fictitious professional identities. By far the most
attention-grabbing of such metamorphoses involved Jewish women who registered as prostitutes in order to gain the right to reside in Petersburg or
elsewhere outside the Pale. Having procured the prostitute's infamous "yellow ticket," Jewish women were in some cases discovered to have enrolled as
auditors in medical institutes or in the special "higher courses" for women,
or to be working a variety of odd jobs without ever making an appearance
in a brothel.[61]

While the "yellow ticket" story achieved the status of urban legend, a para-
ble of tsarist oppression as well as of the perils of assimilation, actual cases
appear to have been extremely rare.[62] Far more widespread was the strategy
practiced by Jewish intellectuals and what we would now call white-collar

61. The earliest mention I have found of such a case involved a Jewish stenographer who
registered in 1880 as a prostitute in order to be able to reside in Moscow. See "Sluchai
prozhivaniia chestnoi devushki-stenografistki po zheltomu biletu iz-za prava zhitel´stva v
Moskve," *S.-Peterburgskie Vedomosti*, 1881, p. 164, and additional commentary on the same case
in *Novoe Vremia*, 1881, p. 1932. In his novella *Ispoved´ prestupnika* (p. 21), G. Lifshits refers to a
similar case in Petersburg.

62. The 1897 empire-wide census recorded a total of seventeen Jewish prostitutes registered in Petersburg. An earlier census (1889) devoted exclusively to prostitutes recorded twelve.
On the latter, see Laurie Bernstein, *Sonia's Daughters: Prostitutes and Their Regulation in Imperial
Russia* (Berkeley, 1995), p. 211. Actual numbers were doubtless somewhat higher. In any event,
the sensational quality of the "yellow ticket" story, which managed to combine sex, nationality
(or what contemporary sources often referred to as "race"), life in the big city, and tsarist injustice, ensured that it achieved a notoriety far beyond the census data. In fact, it became something of a cottage industry for Jewish filmmakers in Eastern Europe, inspiring no fewer than
four films by the end of World War I, from the 1911 *Vu iz emes?* (Where Is Truth?) to the 1918
commercial hit *Der gelber shayn* (The Yellow Ticket), in addition to a Russian version, *Tragediia
evreiskoi kursistki* (The Tragedy of a Jewish Co-ed). See J. Hoberman, *Bridge of Light: Yiddish Film
between Two Worlds* (New York, 1991), pp. 23–45.

workers who lacked degrees from Russian institutions of higher education. As the journalist L. Kliachko recalled, "I knew many literary types . . . who were able to reside in Petersburg because they were fictitiously registered . . . as tailors, bookbinders, shoemakers, etc. I knew respected people, well known for their scholarly publications, who in order to be able to live in Petersburg had registered as domestic servants of their co-religionists."[63] One such person was the historian Simon Dubnov, who in his memoirs describes procuring a forged artisan certificate before embarking for Petersburg in 1880.[64] Another was Zalman Shazar (Rubashov), the future president of Israel; Shazar and his friends "were registered as painters, inkmakers, waiters, or doorkeepers in wealthy Jewish homes" while pursuing their own unofficial studies.[65] The poet Simon Frug was likewise registered as a domestic servant in the home of the Jewish banker A. M. Varshavskii.[66] A Russian newspaper, alarmed at the sudden prominence of Jews in the legal profession, claimed that Jewish lawyers in Petersburg were hiring as "servants" Jewish apprentice lawyers who would otherwise be barred from the capital. The apprentice lawyers would then quietly establish their own practices, and "thus, out of one Jewish lawyer . . . there emerge two."[67]

The absurdity involved in assuming fictitious identities was the source of bitter humor. Those who practiced the deception were often referred to as living *na dvorianskikh pravakh* (with a courtier's rights), where *dvorianskii* alluded both to aristocrats (*dvoriane*) and the apartment house courtyard superintendents (*dvorniki*) whom it was necessary to bribe in order to preserve the fiction.[68] Similarly, a Jew who bribed a doorman (*shveitsar*) to collaborate in the preservation of a fictitious identity (in case of a visit by the police) was known as a *shveitsarskii poddanyi*, a triple pun signifying "a subject of Switzerland," "a subject of the doorman," and—to a Yiddish ear—"a sweating subject."[69] Both expressions draw on the irony of upwardly mobile Jews who, in their desperation to live outside the Pale, had to adopt downwardly

---

63. Kliachko, "Za chertoiu," p. 119.

64. Dubnov, *Kniga zhizni,* 1: 106.

65. Zalman Shazar, *Morning Stars* (Philadelphia, 1967), pp. 173–74.

66. Sliozberg, *Dela minuvshikh dnei,* 1: 124. For further examples, see Ha-Kohen, *Olami,* 1: 102–3; Michael Ginsburg, "The Ginsburg Family: 1864–1947: A Memoir of Their Life and Times in Russia, Paris, and the U.S.," chap. 2, p. 5.

67. *Novorossiiskii Telegraf,* Aug. 14, 1886. The use of fictitious occupations to secure residence permits in areas off limits to Jews extended well beyond Petersburg. On such practices in Kiev, see Michael Hamm, *Kiev: A Portrait, 1800–1917* (Princeton, 1993), p. 127; on Samara, see Teitel, *Aus meiner Lebensarbeit,* p. 29. In 1912, several dozen young Jews were put on public trial in Moscow for residing there under false certification as dentists. See S. M. Brusilovskii, ed., *Za cherty osedlosti: Protsess dantistov v moskovskoi sudebnoi palate* (Moscow, 1913), pp. 1–22.

68. Beizer, *Evrei v Peterburge,* p. 137.

69. Kliachko, "Za chertoiu," p. 120.

mobile identities. "In order to be an accountant in Petersburg," exclaims Gershon Lifshits in his autobiographical novella, "I [had] to turn myself into a shoemaker! This is how I obtained the rights of citizenship."[70] Perhaps the most extreme example of fictitious identity could be found in a characteristic Jewish joke of the time, in which a certain Rosenberg, lacking the proper residence papers but determined to stay in Petersburg, is found crawling on all fours and barking up and down the capital's streets, in the hopes of being taken for a dog and thereby securing the right to residence.[71]

Conversely, Jews who came to Petersburg as genuinely certified artisans or merchants, or in other approved categories, often found themselves unable to make a living in their stated professions and therefore turned to different occupations, particularly petty trade. In so doing, however, they forfeited their legal right to live outside the Pale and thus became vulnerable to expulsion.[72] In one contemporary anecdote, two Jews, both coincidentally named Chaim Rabinovich, meet on a train after having just been expelled from Petersburg. In the course of their conversation it emerges that one of them is a dental assistant and has been expelled from the capital for engaging in commerce, while the other is an employee of a merchant and has been expelled for *not* engaging in commerce. Suggests one to the other: "You know what, let's trade places somehow. Does the government really care which Chaim Rabinovich buys and sells and which doesn't?"[73]

Just how widespread the practice of adopting fictitious professional identities was among Jews, and the seriousness with which it was viewed by city authorities, is suggested by the fact that in the 1880s the Petersburg police began a campaign of spot searches of Jewish artisan shops to verify that those registered as artisans were actually practicing their stated crafts at the declared locations. Official "Jewish" data sheets were printed specifically for inspectors handling such cases. In 1885, 252 fictitious Jewish artisans were caught in this manner and expelled to the Pale; in 1891, the number rose to 341.[74]

---

70. Lifshits, *Ispoved´ prestupnika*, pp. 53–57. Elsewhere in the same story, a proofreader passes himself off as a typesetter.

71. "Anekdoty o evreiskom bezpravii," *Evreiskaia Starina* 4 (1909): 269–70. A similar scene occurs in Lifshits, *Ispoved´ prestupnika*, p. 22.

72. The policy of selective integration required that those who qualified maintain their specific estate membership or face expulsion from the interior. Thus, a merchant who suffered a business failure and became unable to maintain his guild membership or an artisan who abandoned his official craft for another would automatically lose his residence rights. Similarly, if his grown children did not fit one or another of the categories for open residence established by the government, they would be required to return to the Pale. See Iosif Lur´e, *Ukazaniia o prave zhitel´stva dlia pereseliaiushchikhsia vo vnutrennie gubernii* (St. Petersburg, 1908), p. 9.

73. Kliachko, "Za chertoiu," p. 116.

74. TsGIA-SPb, f. 223, op. 1, dd. 5384, 5398, 5399, 5405–9, 5432, 5433; op. 3, d. 15, ll. 1–86.

When Jews reported their professions to census takers, did they indicate their official or actual occupations? A firm answer is impossible, but where the two did not match, one can only assume that the official occupation was reported, given the threat of possible expulsion. Census data regarding Jewish occupational patterns must therefore be treated with the same skepticism as data regarding estate membership.

It is true that during the late imperial period many non-Jewish inhabitants of large cities in the Russian Empire, particularly peasants and artisans, increasingly worked at jobs unrelated to their official estate status. But for Petersburg Jews engaged in such practices, the stakes were higher and the distance between official and actual occupations was greater. As the influential (and generally philosemitic) monthly journal *Vestnik Evropy* (Messenger of Europe) pointed out, "A pagan can live in the capital without being a merchant of the first guild, or his agent, or an artisan, but a Jew, outside these conditions, cannot."[75]

In examining the social fictions practiced by many Petersburg Jews, I seek not merely to cast a skeptical eye on official statistics. Rather, such fictions suggest that the officially sanctioned mechanisms of selective integration, as crafted by the Jewish Committee with input from self-appointed Jewish spokesmen, were failing to keep pace with the evolving roles played by Jews in Russia's urban economy and society. To be sure, throughout the late imperial period selective integration retained its important place within the formal legal structure that framed the Russian–Jewish encounter, and played a significant role as well in recasting social hierarchies within Jewish society. But in the wake of the Great Reforms, the everyday realities of that encounter took on a dynamic of their own. In a sense this was part of a larger phenomenon whereby the tsarist autocracy in the postreform era gradually lost its ability to steer the development of urban society, as Russia's cities were subjected to the increasingly autonomous forces of migration and industrialization. The official channels of selective Jewish integration into Russian society were designed to create incentives for Jews to engage in pursuits officially designated as "useful." By contrast, the experience of Petersburg Jewry, the largest Jewish community in Russia proper, suggests that considerable numbers of Jews were maneuvering around, rather than within, the framework of government policy.[76]

75. "Vnutrennee obozrenie," *Vestnik Evropy* 4, no. 5 (May 1869),: 389. The statement neglects to include graduates of Russian institutions of higher education and retired soldiers among the privileged Jewish groups.

76. This is one of the central themes of Lifshits's novella *Ispoved' prestupnika* (Confession of a Criminal), of Yakov Shteinberg's poem *Prestupniki* (The Criminals), and of other works of fiction in which the "crimes" committed by Petersburg Jews are all victimless, and originate in attempts to circumvent tsarist legislation on Jewish residence. See Chapter 4.

FAMILY AND GENDER

How did selective integration affect Jewish women and Jewish families? Most Jewish women who moved beyond the Pale did so in their capacity as wives or daughters of men who qualified as "useful." In the early decades of Jewish settlement in Petersburg this practice produced a significant gender imbalance. Among Jews living in the Pale there were approximately 104 females to every 100 males, a ratio that remained more or less constant across the second half of the nineteenth century and applied to urban and rural Jews alike. By contrast, the 1869 Petersburg census recorded 77 Jewish females for every 100 males; in 1897 the ratio was still 89:100.[77] In this respect the city's Jews differed little from their Gentile counterparts, among whom the gender imbalance was slightly greater. But the preponderance of Jewish males had its own specific causes, and was not simply an artifact of selective migration to a large city. The "useful" social categories whose reward was legal equality, after all, were typically occupied by men, the principal exceptions being midwives and, beginning in the 1880s, female students in institutions of higher education.[78] In large cities in the Pale and Poland where selective integration did not affect residency, Jewish women continued to outnumber their male counterparts slightly. The less balanced gender ratios in the Russian capital, moreover, were characteristic of most Jewish communities outside the Pale.[79]

Of course, male-female ratios alone tell us relatively little about the function of gender and family relations. More revealing, perhaps, are data on dependency, where the differences between Jews and non-Jews are striking. As Table 3 shows, Petersburg Jews displayed a far higher ratio of dependent family members to those "gainfully employed" (*samostoiatel'nye*) than did the population as a whole, even within the same profession.

As with data on Jewish occupational patterns, the issue of dependency served as ammunition for those ill disposed toward a Jewish presence in the Russian interior. In its commentary on the 1881 census, the St. Petersburg city council complained that the city's Jews, with their high proportion of dependents, were predominantly "consumers" (as opposed to producers), thereby perpetuating in the capital the allegedly parasitic role to which they had grown accustomed in the Pale.[80] The High Commission for Review of

---

77. *Sanktpeterburg po perepisi 10 dekabria 1869 goda*, no. 1, sec. 2, pp. 25, 38, 49, 59; *Pervaia vseobshchaia perepis' naseleniia Rossiiskoi imperii, 1897 goda*, vol. 37, pt. 2, p. 51.

78. It is worth noting that in 1846, the Jewish Committee had considered allowing only Jewish men of certain estates, without family members, to live and work outside the Pale. See Montefiore's account of his conversation with Kiselev in Montefiore and Montefiore, *Diaries*, 1: 336.

79. See data concerning gender ratios in Kishinev, Lodz, Odessa, Vilna, and Warsaw in Bauer et al., *Nationalitäten des Russischen Reiches*, 2: 399–402. For communities outside the Pale, see *Evreiskaia entsiklopediia*, 11: 536–37.

80. *Statisticheskii ezhegodnik S.-Peterburga 1883 goda* (St. Petersburg, 1884), p. 34.

TABLE 3. Number of Dependents per 100 Persons Gainfully Employed
in Jewish Families and in All Families, St. Petersburg, 1881 and 1897

	Year	Jewish families	All families
All occupations	1881	121	46
All occupations	1897	114	54
Tailor		128	52
Trader (torgovets)		160	76

SOURCES: S. O. Gruzenberg, "Evreiskoe naselenie Peterburga v sotsial´nom i sanitarnom otnoshenii: Statisticheskii ocherk," *Voskhod*, no. 1 (1891), pp. 8–9; *Pervaia vseobshchaia perepis´ naseleniia Rossiiskoi imperii, 1897 goda* (St. Petersburg, 1903), vol. 37, pt. 2, pp. 212–29.

Legislation Regarding Jews in the Empire repeated this judgment several
years later in its final report. In addition, the High Commission noted that
similarly large numbers of dependents could be found among Jews wherever they settled outside the Pale, despite the fact that the basic aim of selective integration had been to integrate only "useful" Jews into the surrounding society.[81]

Quite apart from the question of how to evaluate the role that "consumers"
played in Petersburg's economy, the reasons for the contrasting statistics on
dependency were rather more complex than official commentators implied.
First, a far lower proportion of Jewish women in the capital were gainfully
employed (in 1897, 24 percent) than was the case for non-Jewish women (46
percent)—or, for that matter, for Jewish women in the Pale. In his response
to official attacks on dependency among Petersburg Jews, the demographer
Mikhail Soloveichik argued that the practice of "'going off in search of a living' is practically unknown to the Jewish woman, and with few exceptions the
circle of her activities is limited to the family setting."[82] Those few exceptions
invariably involved Jewish women in search of higher education.

Not only were Jewish women less likely to go to Petersburg on their own in
search of work; Jews of both sexes were far more likely than non-Jews to im-
migrate to Petersburg in family units. In this respect they resembled Jewish
immigrants to other large cities, whether in the Pale or abroad or overseas,
who were far more likely than Gentile immigrants to move as families, thereby
expressing their intention to put down roots and stay.[83] Because of the higher
proportion of families, the Jewish population of Petersburg was significantly

81. *Obshchaia zapiska*, pp. 12–18.
82. Soloveichik, "Peterburgskie evrei," pp. 3–4.
83. S. M. Ginzburg, *Amolike Peterburg*, noted (p. 22) that even Jews who came to St. Petersburg illegally tended to bring their families with them. For other examples see Stephen D.
Corrsin, *Warsaw before the First World War: Poles and Jews in the Third City of the Russian Empire,*

younger than the non-Jewish, reflecting the larger numbers of children. In 1890, 25 percent of the city's Jews were under age ten, as compared to 15 percent of the population as a whole; in 1897, these figures were 20 and 14 percent, respectively.[84] Jews of both sexes were more likely to marry at a younger age.[85] The presence of spouses and families also helps account for the dramatically lower incidence of (reported) illegitimate births among Jews.[86]

Finally, because imperial Russian law automatically assigned all married women to the estate of their husbands (unless a woman inherited or was employed in an estate higher than that of her husband), Jewish women living outside the Pale were particularly vulnerable to expulsion in cases of divorce, which among Jews was not uncommon. In theory, even a divorced woman retained the estate status of her ex-husband (until she remarried), but in practice divorced Jewish women living outside the Pale often faced the prospect of lengthy court battles to avoid forcible return to the Pale.[87]

LANGUAGE AND ACCULTURATION

One of the more striking signs of acculturation among Petersburg Jews can be found in the arena of linguistic practices. Between 1869 and 1910, the declared native language of nearly half the city's Jews shifted from Yiddish to Russian, at nearly identical rates for men and women (see Table 4). Although it is impossible to reconstruct precise equivalent data for other ethnic groups (because of the absence of exclusive markers for both language and religion), it appears that no other group in Petersburg displayed anything close to this level of linguistic adaptation. N. V. Iukhneva's estimates of language use show that, on the contrary, groups such as Poles and Estonians actually grew *less* inclined to declare Russian their native language during the same period (see Table 5).

1880–1914 (Boulder, 1989), p. 25; Rozenblitt, *Jews of Vienna*, p. 18. On the high incidence of families among Jewish immigrants to the United States, see Kuznets, "Immigration of Russian Jews to the United States," p. 94.

84. *S.-Peterburg po perepisi 15 dekabria 1890 goda*, pt. 1, sec. 1, p. 11; sec. 2, p. 92; *Pervaia vseobshchaia perepis´ naseleniia Rossiiskoi imperii, 1897 goda*, vol. 37, pt. 2, pp. 248–61. In both years Jews are classified by religion, not language.

85. *Statisticheskii ezhegodnik S.-Peterburga 1881 goda* (St. Petersburg, 1882), p. 86.

86. Between 1881 and 1900, the incidence of illegitimate births among Petersburg Jews ranged between 3 and 12 per 1,000 reported births. For the city's population as a whole, the number ranged from 230 to 290 per 1,000. See *Statisticheskii ezhegodnik S.-Peterburga 1881 goda*, p. 95; *Statisticheskii ezhegodnik S.-Peterburga 1884 goda* (St. Petersburg, 1885), p. 62; *Statisticheskii ezhegodnik S.-Peterburga 1896–97 gg.* (St. Petersburg, 1899), p. 8; V. I. Binshtok and S. A. Novosel´skii, "Evrei v Leningrade [*sic*] 1900–1924 gg.," in Binshtok et al., eds., *Voprosy biologii i patologii evreev* (Leningrad, 1926), 1: 46.

87. See C. Freeze, "Making and Unmaking the Jewish Family," pp. 307–12.

TABLE 4. Native Language Reported by Jewish Men
and Women, St. Petersburg, 1869–1910 (percent)

Language	1869	1881	1890	1900	1910
Yiddish	97%	84%	67%	61%	54%
Men	n.a.	83	67	n.a.	54
Women	n.a.	86	68	n.a.	54
Russian	2	12	29	37	42
Men	n.a.	13	29	n.a.	42
Women	n.a.	11	28	n.a.	42

SOURCES: *Sanktpeterburg po perepisi 10 dekabria 1869 goda* (St. Petersburg, 1872), no. 1, sec. 2, p. 25; *S.-Peterburg po perepisi 15 dekabria 1890 goda* (St. Petersburg, 1891), pt. 1, sec. 2, p. 79; *Statisticheskii ezhegodnik S-Peterburga 1892 goda* (St. Petersburg, 1893), p. 67; *Petrograd po perepisi naseleniia 15 dekabria 1910 goda* (St. Petersburg, n.d.), pt. 1, sec. 1, p. 5; N. V. Iukhneva, *Etnicheskii sostav i etnosotsial'naia struktura naseleniia Peterburga, vtoraia polovina XIX–nachalo XX veka: Statisticheskii analiz* (Leningrad, 1984), p. 208.

The adoption by Jews of Russian as a native language, moreover, was consistently associated with a rise in literacy. To be sure, in census data the category of "literate" often indicated merely an affirmative answer to the question "Can you read?" and therefore cannot be taken as a completely reliable index of actual literacy skills, whether in reading or writing.[88] The meaning of literacy statistics with respect to Yiddish is perhaps even more ambiguous, since Jews and non-Jews alike were wont to question the status of Yiddish as a language, let alone a print language. Nonetheless, the basic pattern of a rise in literacy accompanying the acquisition of Russian is unmistakable: in 1890, literacy in Yiddish among its native speakers (of all ages) was reported as 52 percent, while among Jewish native speakers of Russian 78 percent were literate. In 1897, these figures were 67 percent and 83 percent, respectively.[89]

In one sense, of course, the declaration of Russian as one's native language

88. See the cautionary note in Bater, *St. Petersburg*, p. 441, and the detailed discussion of the category of literacy in Russian censuses in Bauer et al., *Nationalitäten des Russischen Reiches*, 1: 360–70.

89. *S.-Peterburg po perepisi 15 dekabria 1890 goda*, pt. 1, sec. 2, p. 80; *Pervaia vseobshchaia perepis' naseleniia Rossiiskoi imperii 1897 goda*, vol. 37, pt. 2, pp. 56–87. According to the 1897 census, among Jews of all ages throughout the empire, 38 percent were literate in some language. See Bauer et al., *Nationalitäten des Russischen Reiches*, 2: 94, and Shaul Stampfer, "Yedi'at kero ukhtov etsel yehude mizrah eropah ba-tekufah ha-hadashah," in Shmuel Elmog et al., eds., *Temurot ba-historiyah ha-yehudit ha-hadashah. Kovets ma'amarim: Shai li-Shmu'el Etinger* (Jerusalem, 1987), pp. 459–83. Outside of Petersburg and a handful of other major cities, the 1897 census did not distinguish literacy levels among Jews claiming different native languages.

TABLE 5. Members of Ethnic Groups Who Spoke Their
Own National Languages, St. Petersburg, 1869–1910 (percent)

Group	Language	1869	1881	1890	1900	1910
Jews	Yiddish	97%	84%	67%	61%	54%
Poles	Polish	78	82	81	90	94
Finns	Finnish	93	94	88	87	85
Estonians	Estonian	75	63	74	86	86

SOURCES: Adapted from N. V. Iukhneva, *Etnicheskii sostav i etnosotsial´naia struktura naseleniia Peterburga, vtoraia polovina XIX–nachalo XX veka: Statisticheskii analiz* (Leningrad, 1984), p. 24, and from *Statisticheskii ezhegodnik S-Peterburga 1892 goda* (St. Petersburg, 1893), p. 67.

was a powerful indicator of acculturation, a trait that would in all probability be passed on to one's children and that acted in highly significant ways in everyday life. Paradoxically, however, Jews who acquired Russian were in another sense becoming *less* like the surrounding population, insofar as their level of literacy, already higher to begin with, only moved further above that of the population as a whole. This divergence remains even when one excludes the considerable number of peasants residing in the imperial capital. Thus the simple equation of the acquisition of Russian with acculturation or assimilation—in the sense of becoming more like the surrounding population—is misleading.

The acquisition of Russian by Jews was associated with a second, related transformation that bears both on the Jewish world and on its relation to the surrounding society. As Table 4 suggests, Jewish men and women in Petersburg shifted from Yiddish to Russian at nearly the same pace throughout the late imperial period. The unusually detailed data on language in the 1897 census make it possible to trace the transformation in literacy for men and women that occurred with the acquisition of Russian (see Table 6). As Jewish men and women entered the Russian-speaking world, not only did their ability to manipulate the printed word grow; the gap between their respective levels of literacy shrank, thereby challenging the traditionally privileged position of men in the world of print culture. This transformation, moreover, again made the Jews *less* like the surrounding population of Petersburg, in which large discrepancies between male and female literacy (in 1897, 61 percent as against 41 percent; in 1910, 76 percent as against 57 percent) persisted down to the end of the tsarist regime.[90]

The relatively high level of Russian literacy among Jewish girls and women in Petersburg parallels their disproportionate presence in the city's primary

90. *Pervaia vseobshchaia perepis´ naseleniia Rossiiskoi imperii 1897 goda*, vol. 37, pt. 2, p. 91; *Petrograd po perepisi naseleniia 15 dekabria 1910 goda* (Petrograd, n.d.), pt. 1, sec. 2, p. 269.

TABLE 6. Literacy in Yiddish and Russian among Jewish Males
and Females, St. Petersburg, 1897, by Native Language (percent)

Native language	Language of literacy	Literacy		Gender gap
		Males	Females	
Yiddish	Yiddish	74%	59%	15%
Yiddish	Russian	59	48	11
Russian	Russian	86	80	6

SOURCE: *Pervaia vseobshchaia perepis' naseleniia Rossiiskoi imperii, 1897 goda* (St. Petersburg, 1903), vol. 37, pt. 2, pp. 99–119.

and secondary schools. By the 1880s, when Jews constituted 2 percent of the city's population, Jewish girls accounted for nearly 10 percent of all female students in city schools. They outnumbered Jewish boys in city schools 3 to 1, reflecting the abiding desire of many parents to educate their sons separately, in Jewish schools.[91]

ETHNICITY AND URBAN SPACE

At the beginning of this chapter I suggested that in the Russian Empire the "Jewish Question" had a strongly territorial component, insofar as it was seen as hinging largely on the question of the Jews' right to live and work beyond the Pale of Settlement. In a sense, the territorial dimension was reenacted daily on a smaller scale within urban settings across the Pale, for until the Reform era there was hardly a major city in the western and southwestern borderlands that did not contain certain streets or neighborhoods in which Jewish residence was either restricted or banned altogether. It is true that the Russian Empire, with the exception of the kingdom of Poland, had never known the Jewish ghetto in its classic European form of a contained space inhabited exclusively by Jews.[92] But in many cities of the Pale, legal restrictions on Jewish residence—often dating from the period of Polish rule— had created easily identifiable Jewish districts, a fact that took on great significance during pogroms. As late as 1860, cities such as Vilna, Kovno, and

91. S. O. Gruzenberg, "Evreiskoe naselenie Peterburga," p. 6. For information on Jewish primary education in Petersburg, see L. Berman, *S.-Peterburgskiia evreiskiia uchilishcha: Otchet za pervyia piatnadtsat' let ikh sushchestvovaniia 1865–1880, s prilozheniem (1880–1884)* (St. Petersburg, 1885); "Evreiskaia shkola v S.-Peterburge," *S.-Peterburgskie Vedomosti,* no. 193 (1867); V. A. Levin, "Ocherk istorii evreiskogo shkol'nogo obrazovaniia v dorevoliutsionnom Peterburge," in *Evreiskaia Shkola* (St. Petersburg, 1993), pp. 74–86.

92. See Iulii Gessen, "Geto v Rossii," in *Evreiskaia entsiklopediia,* 6: 449–57.

Zhitomir, where Jews made up half or nearly half the population, contained areas in which Jewish residences and businesses were officially prohibited.[93]

Before the partitions of Poland at the end of the eighteenth century, cities in Russia proper had had no need for such restrictions, as Jews were barred from residence altogether. But the principle of residential segregation according to nationality or religion was by no means unknown in the Russian interior. In earlier centuries many Russian cities, including Moscow and St. Petersburg, had relied on designated settlement areas, known as *slobody*, to house French, German, Tatar, and other groups. Certain occupational groups were residentially segregated as well.[94] Many cities in early modern Europe engaged in similar practices. Moscow's so-called German Suburb (*nemetskaia sloboda*), home to mercenaries and fortune seekers from across Europe, became famous for having given a teenaged Peter the Great his first glimpse of "Western" life. But by the middle of the nineteenth century settlements for foreigners in Petersburg had largely disappeared, their residents dispersed throughout the city, leaving only vestigial names such as the English Embankment, the Tatar Market, and German Street.[95]

During the first half of the nineteenth century, a trickle of Jewish merchants and traders—no more than a few hundred—began to appear in the Russian interior as temporary visitors on commercial or financial missions. In contrast to Moscow, where visiting Jews were required to stay at a designated inn (the Glebovskoe podvor´e, today the site of the hotel Rossiia) near the Kremlin, in Petersburg they were allowed to rent private rooms throughout the city. In 1838 this arrangement became the subject of a brief controversy involving the head of the infamous Third Section (the political police), Count A. K. Benckendorff. Ostensibly concerned about the lack of police control over visiting Jews, and citing the example of Moscow, Benckendorff argued that Jews in Petersburg should be restricted to a certain district within the city. The Council of Ministers, however, flatly rejected the idea, noting that a Jewish quarter in the imperial capital, where foreign embassies and foreign guests would surely notice it, would be "inappropriate" and an embarrassment for the government.[96] As the poet Yehudah

93. RGIA, f. 1269, op. 1, d. 136 ll. 59–62, 98–105, 254.

94. See John Armstrong, "Mobilized Diaspora in Tsarist Russia: The Case of the Baltic Germans," in Jeremy Azrael, ed., *Soviet Nationality Policies and Practices* (New York, 1978), p. 64. Armstrong cites a nineteenth-century historian, A. Bruckner, as comparing the *slobody* to the "Jewish Quarters" of cities in Western Europe. See also Iukhneva, *Etnicheskii sostav*, p. 107, and the maps of proposed settlement areas for *raznochintsy* within various cities in Wirtschafter, *Structures of Society*, pp. 113–17.

95. Iukhneva, *Etnicheskii sostav*, pp. 107ff.

96. RGIA, f. 1269, op. 1, d. 136, ll. 59–62, 98–105, 254. See also S. M. Ginzburg, "Idishe getos in amoligen rusland," in his *Historishe Verk*, 3: 343–47

Leib Gordon later put it in a different context, "through the window on Europe which we carved out [i.e., Petersburg], we are being watched by Europe as well."[97]

When the policy of selective integration made possible a more substantial Jewish presence in the Russian interior, the tsarist government, in the form of the Jewish Committee, reaffirmed the practice of open settlement within Petersburg by qualified Jews. Petersburg, moreover, was henceforth to serve as a standard for other cities across the empire. Condemning the "medieval" practice of enforced residential segregation, the Jewish Committee cast it as one of the chief obstacles to "merging" the Jews with the surrounding population:

> The privileges granted by Polish kings stem from the time when, because of intolerance toward them, Jews were kept apart from the general Christian population and their residence was restricted to a small number of cities and to certain neighborhoods or streets. Today, when our government has adopted precisely the opposite system—namely, merging the Jews with the native inhabitants and directing them to labor and useful commercial activity—retaining the ancient Polish privileges would be in utter contradiction to the government's intentions and the spirit of the times.[98]

The "spirit of the times," it should be noted, was primarily that of utility: again and again the committee reminded recalcitrant local officials that restrictions on Jewish residence lowered property values in the affected areas (by reducing demand) and in general stifled Jewish investment in local economies.

The striking contrast between the tsarist regime's zeal for dismantling spatial segregation in individual cities and its hesitance to do the equivalent on an imperial scale speaks to a profound divide in official thinking vis-à-vis urban and rural populations and their relations with Jews. On the whole, tsarist officials felt an obligation to protect the allegedly vulnerable and volatile Russian peasant masses from contact with Jews, if only to prevent outbreaks of popular violence.[99] Russia's urban population rarely inspired the same instinct. This remained the case even after it became clear that pogroms were an overwhelmingly urban, not rural, phenomenon. To be sure, the Municipal Reform of 1870 preserved existing proportional limits on the right

---

97. Gordon, "K istorii poseleniia evreev v Peterburge," *Voskhod* 1 (1881): 121.

98. RGIA, f. 1269, op. 1, d. 136, l. 54; d. 138, l. 63. In many cases (e.g., Vilna, Kiev, and Kamenets), restrictions on Jewish residence did go back to the medieval period, when much of the Pale had been under the control of the Polish-Lithuanian commonwealth. The Jewish Committee repeatedly noted that the "ancient privileges" (*de non tolerandis judaeis*) were of Polish, not Russian, origin.

99. Rogger, *Jewish Policies and Right-Wing Politics,* pp. 170–73.

of Jews to vote for and serve in city councils. As a rule, however, the autocracy vigorously combated local forms of urban segregation, not only in the empire's showcase capital but in cities such as Moscow, Kiev, Vilna, Kamenets-Podol´sk, Kovno, and Zhitomir, and after 1862 throughout Poland. Like the relatively weak urban social estates, cities themselves found it difficult to resist central authorities' determination to impose certain forms of Jewish integration at the local level.[100]

In the absence of both legal restrictions on residence and traditional Jewish neighborhoods, what form did Jewish settlement take in Petersburg? This question requires a brief review of the city's social geography. Despite the leading role Petersburg played in the industrialization of the empire, the geography of the city throughout the late imperial period remained a mixture of typically preindustrial and industrial formations. On the one hand, as James Bater has argued, census data suggest that Petersburg was residentially less segregated by class or social status than comparable European cities. Neighborhoods in the Russian capital tended to be socially and economically heterogeneous, and the limited socioeconomic segregation that did occur was more likely to be vertical—for example, a ground-floor apartment as opposed to a cellar or attic garret—rather than horizontal, by street or neighborhood.[101]

On the other hand, to a much greater extent than statistical evidence would suggest, different areas within the city had pronounced and enduring reputations based on class and estate.[102] As is often the case, the vernacular, everyday experience of the city in many respects did not correspond to the printed page of the census. The Admiralteiskaia borough, for example, running along the south bank of the Neva, which encompassed the Winter Palace and many government ministries, was regarded as an enclave for those of noble birth and great wealth. Here one could find the residences of the Gintsburg family and other Jewish notables. Beyond the Fontanka Canal, the boroughs at the city's periphery, as well as Vyborg to the north, had a pronounced working-class reputation.

Where did Jews who settled in the imperial capital fit into the city's social landscapes, statistical and imagined? "In Petersburg there is not and never was an official 'Jewish quarter,'" wrote Vsevolod Krestovskii in his quasi-ethnographic novel *Petersburg Slums*, "but ever since Jews were allowed to settle in the capitals, they have set up something similar on their own."[103] Other

---

100. RGIA f. 1269, op. 1, d. 136, ll. 98–105, 254; d. 137, ll. 1–7, 21–32, 154–58; d. 138, ll. 49–71, 253–56.

101. Bater, *St. Petersburg*, pp. 196–98. Bater further develops the notion of vertical segregation in "Between Old and New: St. Petersburg in the Late Imperial Era," in Michael Hamm, ed., *The City in Late Imperial Russia* (Bloomington, 1986), pp. 43–78.

102. Bater acknowledges this in "Between Old and New," p. 66.

103. Vsevolod V. Krestovskii, *Peterburgskie trushchoby* (Moscow, 1990), p. 520. Krestovskii's novel first appeared in serial form in the late 1860s.

contemporaries, too, referred to Petersburg's "Jewish quarter" or "Jewish ghetto."[104] The 1869 census shows that the roughly 7,000 Jews then present had in fact settled in all twelve of Petersburg's boroughs, but in highly uneven proportions. The majority of Jews (63 percent) resided in a cluster of six adjacent wards (*uchastki*) centered on the three parallel Pod˝iacheskaia streets, bounded by the Ekaterininskii Canal and Sadovaia Street, several blocks south of Nevsky Prospect, Petersburg's grand boulevard.[105] Several of the wards in this neighborhood featured the highest population densities and number of inhabitants per apartment in the entire city (and would continue to do so throughout the late imperial period), the highest concentration of prostitutes and brothels, and the highest mortality rates.[106] Equally important, however, it was an area known for its petty markets, small shops, and artisan workshops selling goods at retail, rather than by contract.[107] Pod˝iacheskii and its environs, in other words, were a poor man's Nevsky Prospect.

Thus, in the absence of any legal restrictions on residence within the city, Petersburg Jews—the majority of whom were artisans and petty traders—settled largely in an area where their trades were already well established. When the watchmaker Chaim Aronson came to the Russian capital with his family in 1868, he rented rooms near the corner of Sadovaia and Voznesenskaia streets, in the heart of Pod˝iacheskii.[108] According to a number of accounts, there were entire apartment buildings in the area known to be inhabited, legally or illegally, by Jews. Here one could easily find kosher food and informal houses of prayer.[109] In the 1880s, the historian Simon Dubnov and his brother would often meet for lunch at the corner of Sadovaia and Voznesenskaia, in one of the area's Jewish cafeterias, as did the protagonist of Levanda's *Confession of a Wheeler-Dealer*, who frequented a cafeteria full of Jewish salesmen talking "with the usual gesticulations" about "gesheft."[110] One contemporary journalist reported that cabbies would approach newly arriving Jews (often distinguishable by their attire) at train stations and, without prompting, begin barking out names of guesthouses in Pod˝iacheskii. Another writer portrayed Jewish immigrants being duped by eager landlords

104. Lifshits, *Ispoved´ prestupnika*, p. 15. In his autobiography, Osip Mandel´shtam described his neighborhood in fin-de-siècle Petersburg as the "Jewish quarter." See Osip E. Mandel´shtam, "Shum vremeni," in his *Sobranie sochineniia*, 3 vols. (Moscow, 1991), 2: 65.

105. *Sanktpeterburg po perepisi 10 dekabria 1869 goda*, no. 1, sec. 2, p. 25. The six wards were Spasskaia 3 and 4, Kolomenskaia 1, Narvskaia 1 and 2, and Moskovskaia 4.

106. Bater, *St. Petersburg*, pp. 167, 204, 319, 345–50.

107. Iukhneva, *Peterburg i guberniia*, pp. 108–9.

108. Aronson, *A Jewish Life under the Tsars*, pp. 206–19.

109. Ginzburg, *Amolike Peterburg*, p. 22; Kliachko, "Za chertoiu," p. 120; A. E. Landau, "Pis´ma ob evreiakh: peterburgskie evrei," *Biblioteka dlia Chteniia* 187, no. 2 (1864): 4.

110. Beizer, *Evrei v Peterburge*, p. 307; Levanda, *Ispoved´ del´tsa*, p. 93.

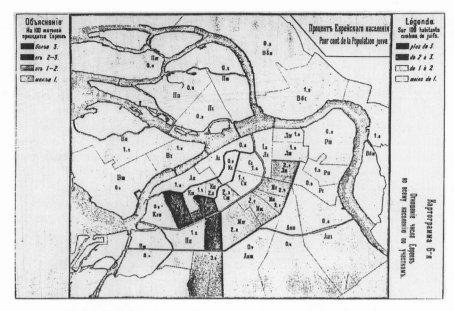

Figure 6. Map showing Jews as a percentage of the total population of St. Petersburg, by ward (drawn by the St. Petersburg police ca. 1890).

into believing that they were forbidden to live elsewhere in the city.[111] Indeed, this area was so identifiably Jewish that a retired cantonist contrasted the Petersburg he had seen under Nicholas I to that of the 1870s with the memorable remark, "What was Petersburg then—a desert! But now—it's like Berdichev!"[112] By the 1880s, in fact, the Pod″iacheskii neighborhood had been jokingly nicknamed Peterburgskii Berdichev.[113]

The humor in these expressions derived precisely from the juxtaposition of two starkly contrasting images, the crowded, unwashed provincial shtetl in the midst of the resplendent imperial metropolis. Both images, however, were highly selective refractions of reality. Late nineteenth-century Petersburg was

111. Landau, "Pis′ma ob evreiakh: Peterburgskie evrei," pp. 3–4; V. Nikitin, "Iskatel′ schast′ia," p. 90.

112. Quoted in N. N., "Iz vpechatlenii minuvshago veka: Vospominaniia srednogo cheloveka,"*Evreiskaia Starina* 6, no. 3 (1914): 430. In Jewish folklore, Berdichev often figured as an archetypal Jewish town. According to the 1897 census, among towns with more than 15,000 inhabitants, Berchidev featured a higher proportion of Jews (42,000 out of a total population of 53,000, or just under four-fifths) than any other town or city in the Pale. See Evreiskoe Statisticheskoe Obshchestvo, *Evreiskoe naselenie Rossii po dannym perepisi 1897 g. i po noveishim istochnikam* (Petrograd, 1917), p. 29.

113. S. O. Gruzenberg, "Evreiskoe naselenie Peterburga," p. 6.

an astonishingly diseased city, demographically dominated by impoverished peasant-workers, and Pod˝iacheskii, for its part, bore little resemblance to a shtetl or a ghetto, where Jews were often in the majority.[114] According to census data, even in the area of highest identifiable Jewish concentration within Pod˝iacheskii—the fourth ward of the Spasskaia borough—Jews never constituted more than 8 percent of the population. The decline of Yiddish as a declared native language proceeded almost as rapidly in Pod˝iacheskii as among Jews in the city as a whole.[115]

Although the portion of the city's Jews who lived in Pod˝iacheskii declined steadily during the late imperial period, the neighborhood's reputation as a Jewish enclave persisted.[116] In fact, compared to most other ethnic groups in Petersburg, Jews continued to live in a relatively segregated fashion.[117] The index of residential segregation, which designates the percentage of a given group that would have to relocate in order to be dispersed throughout the city to the same degree as a control group (in this case, those of the Russian Orthodox faith), has been calculated for the years 1869 and 1910 as shown in Table 7.

Leaving aside the Muslim and Gregorian groups, who in 1910 each numbered fewer than 3,500, as against roughly 35,000 Jews, the latter were not only, as James Bater puts it, "the only sizable minority concentrated to any considerable degree," but the only sizable minority whose degree of segregation increased over the course of four decades.[118] In 1910, Jews in Pe-

---

114. On health and sanitation in St. Petersburg, see Bater, *St. Petersburg*, pp. 188–90.

115. By 1910, 64 percent of Jews residing in Pod˝iacheskii listed Yiddish as their native language, as opposed to 51 percent across the entire city.

116. If we define Pod˝iacheskii as comprising the six wards described in n. 105, the neighborhood's share of the city's Jewish inhabitants declined as follows: 1869, 63 percent; 1881, 52 percent; 1890, 43 percent; 1910, 30 percent. See *Sanktpeterburg po perepisi 10 dekabria 1869 goda*, no. 1, sec. 2, p. 25; Gruzenberg, "Evreiskoe naselenie," p. 7; *S.-Peterburg po perepisi 15 dekabria 1890 goda*, pt. 1, sec. 1, pp. 46–47; *Petrograd po perepisi naseleniia 15 dekabria 1910 goda*, pt. 1, sec. 1, p. 5.

117. A similar trend seems to have occurred in Moscow, where Jews remained concentrated in the Zaradie neighborhood even after formal residential restrictions were abolished. See Landau, "Pis´ma ob evreiakh: peterburgskie evrei," *Biblioteka dlia Chteniia* 187, no. 2 (1864): 298ff.

118. Commenting on the anomaly of Jewish residential patterns, Bater suggests that "in view of the pogroms occurring in the Pale it is not at all surprising that some measure of residential segregation occurred" (*St. Petersburg*, pp. 377–78). But it was precisely their highly visible segregation within the towns and cities of the Pale that made Jews *more* vulnerable to pogroms. This point was understood by Petersburg Jews, as evidenced in a letter written by Yehudah Leib Gordon during the wave of pogroms that swept the Pale in 1881: "There is truly no reason to fear such outbreaks in [Petersburg], where the Jews live dispersed throughout the city and not concentrated in any one area, as in the provincial towns. . . ." (quoted in Stanislawski, *For Whom Do I Toil?*, p. 160). A similar point is made in S. Grinberg, *Jewish Life in St. Petersburg: A Paper Read before the Cambridge Branch of the Anglo-Jewish Association on Friday, February 13, 1914* (Cambridge, 1914), p. 3.

TABLE 7. Percentage of St. Petersburg's Non–Russian
Orthodox Population That Would Have to Relocate
to Achieve Residential Distribution Equal to That of the
Russian Orthodox Population, 1869 and 1910, by Religious Group

Religious group	1869	1910
Catholics (Uniates)	20.6%	13.5%
Protestants	20.8	20.0
Schismatics	38.1	29.6
Armenians (Gregorians)	41.7	37.6
Jews	40.7	52.0
Muslims	39.9	56.1

SOURCE: James H. Bater, *St. Petersburg: Industrialization and Change* (London, 1976), pp. 200, 377.

tersburg were considerably more segregated spatially than their counterparts in Vienna, despite the legacy of its ghetto.[119]

The available data for Petersburg do not allow one to reconstruct the spatial segregation within Jewish society according to occupation or social class. But the highly detailed census of 1897 reveals that, just as among the city's population as a whole, Jewish literacy (in any language) varied little from one borough to the next. What did vary considerably, however, was declared native language. In this respect the linguistic map of Jewish Petersburg closely followed the social reputations of the city's neighborhoods: from the elite Admiralteiskaia borough, where the language spoken in Jewish homes was more likely to be Russian (49 percent) than Yiddish (43 percent), to the mixed but largely working-class outlying areas of Aleksandro-Nevskaia, Rozhdestvenskaia, and Vyborg, where Yiddish was spoken in roughly 85 percent of Jewish homes.[120]

It is a measure of the complexity of the process of acculturation—or "merging," to use the contemporary term—that Petersburg Jews exhibited both

119. Rozenblit, *Jews of Vienna*, p. 225n26, gives the index of residential segregation for Viennese Jews in 1910 as 44.2.

120. The census of 1897 included particularly detailed data on literacy and language use in each of St. Petersburg's boroughs. Jewish literacy rates ranged from a low of 63 percent (in the outlying Rozhdestvenskaia borough) to a high of 78 percent (in the central Admiralteiskaia borough). Among the population as a whole, literacy ranged from 46 percent (Vyborg and Aleksandro-Nevskaia) to 54 percent (Admiralteiskaia). *Pervaia vseobshchaia perepis´ naseleniia Rossiiskoi imperii, 1897 goda*, vol. 37, pt. 2, pp. 56–87.

remarkable adaptation to their new surroundings and abiding separateness. The most striking example of this contrast is to be found in the simultaneous movement toward unparalleled linguistic assimilation, on the one hand, and continued, even intensified, residential segregation, on the other. Neither of these phenomena was the direct result of regulation by the tsarist state, notwithstanding the latter's penchant for social control. Rather, they reflected the largely unregulated encounter of Jews with the dynamic, turbulent world of the imperial capital.

That world, whatever its reputation among Russian intellectuals, was for its Jewish inhabitants the paramount symbol of Russia itself, the imperial "center," and thus of escape from the peripheral confines of the Pale. But the sense of having "arrived" is nonetheless conspicuously absent from the lives of Petersburg Jews. The reason is not simply continued vulnerability to the threat of expulsion by a venal police force. Relatively few people, whether Jewish or not, ever really "arrived" once and for all in St. Petersburg: throughout the late imperial period, out-migration from the city, seasonal or permanent, was extraordinarily common. And although Jews were, ironically, becoming natives of Petersburg at a higher rate than Russians, what distinguished their migratory patterns most was their pronounced tendency to move as families, a practice that helped to reinforce inherited social behaviors and attitudes.

Despite the official policy of seeking to "merge" the Jews with the surrounding population, Petersburg Jews continued to work largely in a few well-defined sectors of the economy, as they did in the Pale.[121] If anything, as *Vestnik Evropy* (Messenger of Europe) pointed out, selective integration ensured that outside the Pale the professional concentration of Jews would intensify.[122]

The fact that the "Jewish Question" in the Russian Empire was talked about and managed largely as an issue of spatial containment corresponds to the persistence of extraeconomic forms of coercion and agrarian-territorial modes of thought in both the tsarist regime and Russian society. But as the experiment with selective integration in Petersburg shows, the lifting of territorial and other restrictions for an elite minority of Jews did not in itself resolve the "Jewish Question" within the limited framework of the Russian capital any more than did legal emancipation in Western Europe. As we have seen, in their collective profile as well as in contemporary commentary, Petersburg Jews continued to diverge markedly from the surrounding population in ways that built upon those seen in the Pale. Even the characteristics that distinguished Jews in the Russian capital from their counterparts in the Pale—greater concentrations of wealth, literacy (especially among women),

---

121. The same was true, one might note, of East European Jewish immigrants to Vienna, except that the particular sectors differed somewhat in each case, reflecting the different economies of the two cities. See Rozenblit, *Jews of Vienna*, p. 49.

122. "Vnutrennee obozrenie," *Vestnik Evropy* 4, no. 5 (May 1869): 390.

secular education, and employment in free or independent professions—also distinguished them from the city's non-Jewish inhabitants. Moving beyond the Pale—whether to Petersburg or elsewhere in Russia—was associated with a level of urbanization far higher than that among Jews in the Pale as well as among Russians.[123]

Well before establishing themselves in Petersburg, newly emerging Jewish elites, with the Gintsburg family at their pinnacle, had gained prominence as self-appointed intercessors on behalf of Russian Jewry. In addition to this function vis-à-vis the state, the new elites sought to dominate Jewish communal institutions in the capital and from there to assert their authority across the Pale. In the two chapters that follow, I turn to the history of Petersburg Jews as a community, from the intramural struggles that attended the formation of communal institutions, to the community's relations with city and imperial authorities, and finally, to relations between Petersburg as the would-be center of Russian Jewry and the provincial communities of the Pale.

123. According to data compiled by the Ministry of Internal Affairs in 1880, 84 percent of Jews residing outside the Pale in European Russia lived in places defined as urban. See RGIA, f. 821, op. 9, d. 122, ll. 7–116. The 1897 census shows a similar proportion, as compared to Jews in the Pale, of whom roughly half lived in urban areas, and to the population of the entire empire, of whom some 13 percent lived in urban areas. See Bauer et al., *Nationalitäten des Russischen Reiches*, 2: 212–30.

Chapter 4

Conflict and Community

The Jews who settled by the thousands in the Russian imperial capital beginning in the 1860s found a city with no collective Jewish past and virtually no Jewish presence. The legacy of Jews in Petersburg during the century and a half after its founding in 1703 offered only a haze of anecdotes and legends concerning sojourns by individual Jews or crypto-Jews, rumored influence in high places, and unceremonious expulsions. In 1714 Peter the Great brought back with him from Amsterdam a new court jester, Jan d'Acosta—said to be a descendant of Portuguese Marranos. Another alleged Marrano, Anton Manuilovich de Vier (also from Holland), became Petersburg's first chief of police.[1] Tsar Alexander I's reforming minister, Mikhail Speranskii, was once rebuked for secretly meeting in the capital with the wealthy tax farmer Avram Perets, while the founder of the Hasidic Habad movement, Rabbi Shneur Zalman ben Baruch, was reportedly held prisoner in Petersburg's notorious Peter and Paul fortress.[2] The young German rabbi Max Lilienthal, on a visit to the Russian capital in 1841, was informed by a Jewish convert there that, upon ascending to the Russian throne, Nicholas I had presented the city's temporary Jewish residents the choice of conversion or expulsion.[3]

Out of these and similar stories there formed among Petersburg Jews in the postreform period a certain mythology of the capital's allure and the

---

1. *Evreiskaia entsiklopediia*, 1: 652–53, 7: 164; Ginzburg, *Amolike Peterburg*, pp. 13–14.

2. Y. L. Gordon, "K istorii poseleniia evreev v Peterburge," *Voskhod*, no. 2 (February 1881), p. 29; *Evreiskaia entsiklopediia*, 16: 55–60.

3. Philipson, *Max Lilienthal*, p. 176. For an account of an expulsion of Jews from Petersburg under Nicholas I, see S. Beilin, "Posledstviia poseshcheniia stolitsy dlia dvukh evreev," *Evreiskaia Starina* 3, no. 3 (1911): 418–19.

difficulty of Jewish existence there. In the Pale of Settlement, Jewish folklore had long since assigned distinct personalities and reputations to various towns and regions. Vilna was "Yerushalayem de Litva" (the Jerusalem of Lithuania), famous as a center of rabbinic learning and Hebrew publishing. Odessa, that southern bastion of hedonism and assimilation, was said to be encircled by seven miles of hellfire ("zibn mayl arum Ades brent der gihenum"). Chelm was mocked in countless Jewish folktales for its residents' pseudo wisdom. And the Jewish name for Poland—Polin—was creatively read to mean "here abide" (*po lin*), suggesting a divine sanction for Jewish settlement there.[4]

In Petersburg, by contrast, neither the pious nor the assimilated were imagined to have felt fully at home. To be sure, Russians had their own tropes for the artificial quality of existence in the northern capital, centering on the city's unnatural origins and inhospitable climate.[5] To Jews, the city seemed unnatural in a different way: according to the mid-eighteenth-century rabbi Arieh Leib Epstein, Providence itself had ordained that Jews should not live in the imperial capital, since during the white nights in June the sun never sets, making it impossible to determine the correct time for morning and evening prayers.[6] Insofar as this remark came at a time when Jews were still banned from Petersburg, one might well interpret Epstein's words as seeking to make a virtue of necessity.

Even a century later, after the ban had been partially lifted, the sense of being out of place persisted, if in a more secular vein. The theme of the Jewish presence in the capital as itself a potential crime, quite apart from actual behavior, appeared in an array of fictional works, beginning with Gershon Lifshits's *Confession of a Criminal.*[7] A particularly memorable version of the Petersburg Jew as involuntary outlaw appeared in Yakov Shteinberg's poem "Prestupniki" (The Criminals), published in 1881. Borrowing at times word for word from Pushkin's celebrated *Bronze Horseman,* Shteinberg substitutes for Pushkin's poor clerk Evgenii a young Jew who has come to the imperial capital "thirsting for knowledge," only to find himself hunted like an animal because he lacks the proper residence papers. Following in Evgenii's footsteps, the anonymous Jew turns in desperation to the statue of Peter the Great, the city's founder and preeminent symbol of state-sponsored modernization:

4. The popular epithets described here are to be found in many sources. For specific examples, see Israel Cohen, *Vilna* (Philadelphia, 1943), p. 105; Zipperstein, *Jews of Odessa,* p. 1; Aronson, *A Jewish Life under the Tsars,* p. 18.

5. Well-known examples can be found in Pushkin, *The Bronze Horseman;* Gogol, *The Overcoat;* and esp. Dostoevsky's *White Nights, Notes from Underground,* and *Crime and Punishment.*

6. Iu. Gessen, "Sankt-Peterburg," in *Evreiskaia entsiklopediia,* 13: 939; Ginzburg, *Amolike Peterburg,* p. 16.

7. Lifshits, *Ispoved´ prestupnika.*

Centuries of slavery have crumbled,
Your people [i.e., the serfs] have been liberated
And recognize their calling
As citizens of the world.
But there is here one unhappy tribe,
A stepson of Russia,
And from it alone has the yoke not been lifted,
Only to it has freedom not been granted!
Great Peter, I stand before you,
I am not a criminal, I am a Jew,
Yet I am hunted down;
I cannot live among my fellow human beings!
Why should sons of Russia
Be denied a fatherland and freedom![8]

Despite the poem's Pushkinian references, Shteinberg's Peter diverges tellingly from Pushkin's: he is a sympathetic listener, "as if touched by [the Jew's] tears," and the poem ends with the statue representing not persecution of the individual by an autocratic state but implicit endorsement of Jewish equality by an enlightened monarch.

If, however, one judges by sheer frequency of telling and retelling, then the defining story of the Jewish predicament in Petersburg comes in a letter written by Catherine the Great in 1773. Responding to an inquiry from her admirer Denis Diderot about whether there were any Jews in Russia, Catherine wrote that the newly conquered Polish territories were "swarming with Jews." In addition, she noted, "There are three or four [Jews] in Petersburg. For eight or nine years I have had a confessor with whom they have been lodging; they are tolerated in spite of the law. One pretends not to notice that they are here."[9] A century later, this episode became an obligatory reference for virtually every Russian-Jewish writer who touched upon the life of Jews in the imperial capital.[10] Its allegorical resonance, at least among educated Jews, provides an important clue about Russian-Jewish self-

---

8. Shteinberg, "Prestupniki," *Voskhod,* no. 4 (1881), p. 161. A later example of the Petersburg Jew as outlaw can be found in the poem by David Shimonovich (Shimoni), "Sfinksy" (The Sphinxes), written in Hebrew in 1910 and published in Russian translation in V. F. Khodasevich and L. B. Iaffe, eds., *Evreiskaia antologiia: Sbornik molodoi evreiskoi poezii* (Moscow, n.d.), pp. 145–48.

9. Diderot's and Catherine's letters, in French with Russian translation, were reproduced in *Russkii Arkhiv,* no. 3 (1880), pp. 2–3.

10. See, e.g., Orshanskii, *Evrei v Rossii,* p. 234; Gordon, "K istorii poseleniia evreev," p. 122; Gessen, "Sankt-Peterburg," in *Evreiskaia entsiklopediia,* 13: 939; M. B. Epshtein, "K istorii evreiskoi kolonii v Peterburge," *Evreiskaia Letopis´* 2 (1923): 104; and Ginzburg, *Amolike Peterburg,* p. 16. Some of these authors may have borrowed from others, but this does not weaken my argument that the incident resonated widely.

understanding and the ambiguities of the Jews' relation to Petersburg's imperial authorities. In Catherine's letter, the Jewish guests, despite their illegal presence in the capital, appear to have gained a remarkable if precarious proximity to the autocracy's inner sanctum: they are, after all, lodged
with a court priest. Equally significant, however, is the fact that what Catherine chose to ignore was not that the visitors were Jews but that they existed
at all ("on fait semblant d'ignorer qu'ils y sont"). To overlook their Jewishness was inconceivable.

THE NEW JEWS

In 1858, *Sankt-Peterburgskie Vedomosti* (St. Petersburg News) could still report
a sighting of Jews in the imperial capital as a special event, given that "we in
St. Petersburg are unfamiliar [with] those with Jewish features."[11] The history of a permanent and visible Jewish presence in the imperial capital was
to begin soon thereafter, when the policy of selective integration made it possible for certain categories of Jews to reside beyond the Pale. In a remarkably short period of time, Petersburg Jewry gave rise in Russia to a new image of the Jew as modern, cosmopolitan, and strikingly successful in urban
professions (such as law, banking, and journalism) that were emerging in
the wake of the Great Reforms. This new profile did not supplant but instead coexisted uneasily with the enduring figure of the Russian Jew as backward, fanatically separatist, and frequently impoverished. In this respect the
effects of selective Jewish integration in Russia were remarkably similar to
those of full-scale emancipation in Europe: in the one as in the other, observers identified the Jews as harbingers of a protean modernity (especially
its more menacing aspects) even as they clung to Christian conceptions of
Jews as stubborn relics of an obsolete past.

The impression made by Petersburg's "new Jews" did not register with their
enemies alone. When the British-Jewish philanthropist Sir Moses Montefiore
visited Petersburg in 1872, he marveled at the contrast between the Jews there
and those he had met in the Pale during his previous visit to Russia in 1846.
In the imperial capital, he wrote in his diary,

> I had the happiness of seeing a considerable number of our co-religionists dis-
> tinguished by decorations of different grades from the Emperor. The Jews now
> dress like ordinary gentlemen in England, France or Germany. Their schools
> are well attended, and they are foremost in every honorable enterprise des-
> tined to promote the prosperity of their community and the country at
> large. . . . Looking back to what the condition of our co-religionists in Russia
> was twenty-six years ago, and having regard to their present position, they have

---

11. *Sankt-Peterburgskie Vedomosti,* July 20, 1858, quoted in Christian, *'Living Water,'* p. 168.

Figure 7. Yarmulke and bow tie: The new Jew.
(*Pluvium*, 1906.)

> "I am the one whom no one likes
> Whom every living thing curses . . .
> I am the one who destroys Holy Russia
> And sucks the blood of the people!"

now indeed abundant reason to cherish grateful feelings towards the Emperor,
to whom their prosperity is in so great a measure to be attributed.[12]

To take the relatively small and privileged community of Jews in Petersburg
as representative of Russian Jewry as a whole was of course misleading. But
Montefiore was neither alone nor mistaken in imagining the future of Russia's Jews through the experience of those in the imperial capital.

Despite the numerical predominance of artisans and petty traders among

12. Montefiore and Montefiore, *Diaries*, 2: 251–52.

the city's Jewish population, it was, not surprisingly, the merchants, bankers, and financiers who usually caught the public eye. In no other Jewish community in Russia was there such extraordinary and visible affluence. Petersburg quickly became the address of choice for the Russian-Jewish plutocracy, many of whom played a major role in the burgeoning fields of private banking, stock market speculation, and railroads. A Jewish resident of the capital was perhaps only slightly exaggerating when she wrote of the 1860s and 1870s that "never before or since did the Jews in Petersburg live so richly, for the institutions of finance lay to a large extent in their hands."[13]

During the heyday of private banking in Russia, roughly from the 1860s to the reestablishment of the state credit system in the 1880s, Russian-Jewish bankers played a role in imperial finances comparable to that of Gerson Bleichröder in Germany and the Rothschilds in France.[14] The 1860s witnessed what one Jewish newspaper in Petersburg called "a feverish decade of enterprise-building."[15] In the words of a former employee of the Gintsburg bank,

> A complete metamorphosis could be observed in those who left the Pale of Settlement. The tax farmer was transformed into a banker, the contractor into a high-flying entrepreneur, and their employees into Petersburg dandies. A lot of crows got dressed up in peacock feathers. Bigshots from Balta and Konotop quickly came to consider themselves "aristocrats" and would laugh at the "provincials."[16]

Beneath its mocking tone, this passage encapsulates the evolving role of the Jewish financial elite as Russia moved from a rural serf economy toward the early stages of commercial capitalism. Whether as "feudal" tax farmers or as "capitalist" investment bankers, Jewish financiers (at least those in Petersburg) continued to make their fortunes largely in state-sponsored undertakings and to cultivate close ties to government officials.

The House of Gintsburg was the most prominent example. Building on their role as liquor tax farmers and suppliers of goods and clothing to the Russian army during the Crimean War, Evzel Gintsburg and his son Horace established their bank in Petersburg in 1859, and subsequently floated enor-

---

13. Pauline Wengeroff goes on to report that "Jewish banking houses were founded, as were joint-stock companies led by Jews. The stock exchange and banking took on unexpected dimensions. At the stock exchange the Jew felt in his element; there people often became rich overnight, but others were toppled just as quickly. This sort of occupation was something new in Russia. But it was taken up in a positively brilliant manner by the Jews, even by those whose only training had been in Talmud": *Memoiren einer Grossmutter,* 2: 135.

14. Anan'ich, *Bankirskie doma,* p. 4.

15. *Razsvet,* (June 12, 1880, p. 921.

16. [N. N.], "Iz vpechatlenii minuvshago veka: Vospominaniia srednogo cheloveka," *Evreiskaia Starina* 6, no. 3 (1914): 431.

mous loans for many government projects, including the war against the Ottoman Empire in 1877–78.[17] The Poliakov brothers (Samuel, Yakov, and Lazar) were instrumental in financing the construction of railroads, and as a result were elevated by Alexander II to the Russian hereditary nobility, an extremely rare achievement for Jews. In 1871, Avram I. Zak, a former employee of the Gintsburgs, became director of the Petersburg Discount Lending Bank, one of the largest banks in the empire, whose owner was the Polish-Jewish magnate Leopold Kronenberg. Many more names and enterprises could be added to this list.[18] Indeed, the Jewish railroad contractor loomed large enough in the Jewish popular imagination to become known in Yiddish as a *shemindefernik* (chemin-de-fer-nik).[19]

The meteoric rise of such Jews inspired predictable outbursts against upstart philistines. In one of his deservedly lesser-known works, the populist poet Nikolai A. Nekrasov, then eking out a living in Petersburg, intoned in the poem "Ballet" (1866):

> One has only to glance at the box seats,
> Where the bankers' wives are seated,
> Hundreds of thousands of rubles on their bosom. . . .
> Valor, youth, and strength captured
> A woman's heart in days gone by.
> Our girls are more practical, cleverer;
> Their ideal is the golden calf,
> Embodied in the gray-haired Jew,
> Whose filthy hand causes these bosoms
> To quiver with gold.[20]

A German resident, for whom the city's poorer Jews were similarly invisible, reported in 1881 that the only Jews to be found in Petersburg were

17. Anan'ich, *Bankirskie doma*, p. 43. In 1878 the Gintsburg bank provided the government with a loan of 10 million rubles, more than any private bank had hitherto lent the tsarist regime. The Russian-Jewish banker Ippolit Vavel'berg lent an additional 2 million in the same year.

18. Other prominent Jewish financiers in Petersburg included Leon Rosenthal, Lev Fridland, and Avram Varshavskii. See ibid.; Alfred Rieber, "The Formation of 'La Grande Societé des Chemins de Fer Russes,'" *Jahrbücher für Geschichte Osteuropas* 21 (1973): 375–91; [N. N.], "Iz vpechatlenii minuvshago veka," pp. 434–6; and individual entries on these figures in *Evreiskaia entsiklopediia*.

19. See Wengeroff, *Memoiren einer Grossmutter*, 2: 137, and Gershon Badenes, "Zapiski otshchepentsa," *Voskhod*, no. 3 (1884), pp. 23–25 (the latter cited in Slutsky, *Ha-itonut ha-yehudit-rusit*, p. 20).

20. Quoted in Beizer, *Evrei v Peterburge*, p. 69 (translation mine). For the original text in full see N. A. Nekrasov, *Polnoe sobranie sochinenii i pisem*, 15 vols. (Leningrad, 1981), 2: 235–36. In the poem Nekrasov wavers between, on the one hand, lashing out at commercially adept minorities in the Russian capital (not only Jews but Greeks and Germans), and on the other, bitterly (and inaccurately) noting that "there is no Russian merchantry (has the bitter cold frightened them away, perhaps?)."

"a few hundred 'protected' families. . . . The proletariat of government bureaucrats, owing to their miserable salaries, are forced to cultivate relations with financiers of Mosaic origin . . . , speculators in construction and railroads."[21]

Petersburg's Jewish intellectuals, too, were often critical of the newly emerged plutocracy, though less out of fear of their influence than from anger at their apparent self-distancing from less prosperous Jews. The intellectuals' ire was only intensified by the fact that many of them (or the newspapers and journals that employed them) were at various times financially dependent on the wealthy elite.[22] Uri Kovner, a struggling journalist who proudly carried the epithet of "the Jewish Pisarev," published his short story "Around the Golden Calf" as an indictment of the banker A. I. Zak, his former employer.[23] Zak's personal secretary, Grigorii I. Bogrov, left to become co-editor of the Petersburg Jewish weekly *Razsvet* (1879–83), where he joined forces with Mark S. Varshavskii, nephew of the railroad magnate A. M. Varshavskii, in crafting editorials condemning the communal role of the rich.[24] Later generations of writers, including those with few direct links to the Russian capital, expanded these criticisms to the point of vilification, as in Sholem Asch's historical novel *Petersburg* (1929), which depicts the prerevolutionary Jewish plutocracy as wallowing in decadence, gluttony, and, in one case, near incest.

LEVANDA'S *CONFESSION*

By far the most highly developed portrait of the Petersburg Jewish financial elite appeared in Lev Levanda's novel *Confession of a Wheeler-Dealer,* a rags-to-riches-to-rags story that received wide attention in the contemporary press.[25] The novel was part of a small but growing body of fiction dealing with the

21. Julius Eckardt [presumed author], *Aus der Petersburger Gesellschaft* (Leipzig, 1881), p. 44. The municipal census of the same year counted over 16,000 Jews in the city.

22. On Horace Gintsburg's financial support of Jewish writers, see Ginzburg, *Historishe verk,* 2: 141.

23. See I. S. Tsinberg, "Arkadii (Abram-Uri) Kovner: Pisarevshchina v evreiskoi literature," *Perezhitoe* 2 (1910): 130ff. Dmitrii Ivanovich Pisarev was a nihilist literary critic who came to prominence in the 1860s. Kovner later achieved brief fame through his correspondence from a Siberian prison with Dostoevsky. See L. P. Grossman, *Ispoved´ odnogo evreia* (Moscow, 1924), and Max Weinreich, *Fun bayde zaytn ployt: dos shturemdike lebn fun Uri Kovner, dem nihilist* (Buenos Aires, 1955).

24. Sliozberg, *Dela minuvshikh dnei,* 1: 122.

25. Lev Levanda, *Ispoved´ del´tsa* (St. Petersburg, 1880). See contemporary reviews cited in *Sistematicheskii ukazatel´ literatury o evreiakh na russkom iazyke s vremeni vvedeniia grazhdanskogo shrifta (1708 g.) po dekabr´ 1889 g.* (St. Petersburg, 1892), p. 369, no. 6522.

lives of Jews who lived among Russians.[26] As the leading Jewish writer in Russian of his time, Levanda (1835–88) published fiction and nonfiction in nearly every contemporary Russian-Jewish periodical, as well as in Russian newspapers such as *Sankt-Peterburgskie Vedomosti* and *Novoe Vremia*. Employed since 1860 as an "expert Jew" in the offices of the governor general of Vilna province, Levanda was an ardent integrationist and Russophile until the wave of pogroms in 1881–82 induced a crisis of confidence and a late flirtation with the idea of emigration to Palestine.[27]

The narrator of *Confession* is one Mordechai Shmalts, who during the era of Great Reforms leaves his native shtetl in the Pale determined to become a millionaire in Petersburg—in his words, "the bubbling center of the broadest and most diverse empire in the world." He is part of a stream of young, ambitious Jewish immigrants (women as well as men) leading his hometown rabbi to exclaim, "Everyone is running off to Petersburg these days, whether on business or not! As if manna from heaven fell on everyone there!"[28] Once in Petersburg (without the necessary permit), Shmalts finds himself caught up in ruthless competition with other seekers of a fast ruble, including the Russified Polish aristocrat Bliznevich, the Baltic German Baron von Werner, and a host of Jewish would-be millionaires. Shmalts is instantly successful at the stock exchange and in various commercial deals of questionable legality; he buys a palace in a fashionable Petersburg neighborhood and adopts all the trappings of aristocratic life. But his wealth, like that of so many char-

26. In addition to Levanda's novel, there are a number of rich and suggestive fictional representations of Jewish life in Petersburg (some of the following works have been previously cited): V. N. Nikitin, "Vek prozhit'—ne pole pereiti (iz razskazov otstavnogo soldata)," *Evreiskaia Biblioteka* 4 (1874): 300–358; idem, "Iskatel' schast´ia," *Evreiskaia Biblioteka* 5 (1875): 74–110; G. G. Lifshits, *Ispoved´ prestupnika. Iumoristicheskii razskaz iz zhizni peterburgskikh evreev* (St. Petersburg, 1880); Y. L. Gordon, "Rahamei-'em," reprinted in *Kitve Yehudah Leib Gordon: Prozah* (Tel Aviv, 1960), pp. 99–104; Ia. Shteinberg, "Prestupniki," *Voskhod*, no. 4 (1881), pp. 159–62; M—khin, "Ne ko dvoru," *Voskhod*, nos. 8–12 (1886); S. Iaroshevskii, "Potselui," *Voskhod*, nos. 7–10 (1888); N. Pruzhanskii, "Katorzhnik," *Voskhod*, no. 7 (1903), pp. 69–81; P. Smolenskin, *Gemul Yesharim* (Warsaw, 1905); D. Shimonovich, "Sfinsky" (1910), in V. F. Khodasevich and L. B. Iaffe, eds., *Evreiskaia Antologiia: Sbornik molodoi evreiskoi poezii* (Moscow, n.d.), pp. 145–48; Asch, *Peterburg*. See also "Anekdoty o evreiskom bezpravii," *Evreiskaia Starina* 1, no. 4 (1909): 269–81, a collection of bittersweet jokes set largely in Petersburg. On selected literary representations of Jewish assimilation in late imperial Russia, see Gabriella Safran, *Rewriting the Jew: Assimilation Narratives in the Russian Empire* (Stanford, 2000).

27. On Levanda see N. A. Bukhbinder, *Literaturnye etiudy (russko-evreiskie pisateli)* (Leningrad, 1927); B. A. Gol´dberg, *L. O. Levanda kak publitsist: Po sluchaiu 40-letnego iubeleia vozniknoveniia russko-evreiskoi pechati* (Vilna, 1900); Shimon Markish, "Stoit li perechityvat´ L´va Levandu," *Vestnik evreiskogo universiteta v Moskve*, no. 3 (10) (1995): 89–140 and no. 2 (12) (1996): 168–93. See also Dubnov's description of his encounter with a broken Levanda one year before the latter's death, in Dubnov, *Kniga zhizni*, 1: 203–5.

28. Levanda, *Ispoved´ del´tsa*, pp. 56–58.

Figure 8. Lev Levanda (1835–1888).

acters in the novel, slips away as easily as it arrived, and at the conclusion of
the story he is a broken man, his wife in a state of nervous collapse, and his
children utterly estranged (in one case to the point of apostasy).

Levanda himself had spent relatively little time in the Russian capital.
Nonetheless, the Petersburg newspaper *Russkii Evrei* (The Russian Jew) singled out his *Confession* for its "highly realistic" portrayal of Jewish life there.[29]
While the portions of Levanda's narrative that concern traditional shtetl life
derive largely from the well-worn repertoire of Haskalah satire, the story as
a whole is notably free of typical maskilic heroes, whether enlightened Jews
or benevolent Gentiles. On the contrary, it is Shmalts's father, a quintessential
shtetl Jew, who is made to prophecy his worldly son's downfall:

> "I know, my son, that you are rich, very rich . . . , but—you won't get angry?—
> I have little faith in your wealth."

29. L. Kantor, "Chem my sdelalis′ v poslednie dvatsat′ piat′ let?" *Russkii Evrei*, no. 13 (1879),
pp. 485–88.

"Why?"

"Because it was acquired in a strange way, and that which has not been acquired through labor is not secure. A divine curse lies on it."

"Father, I do not understand what you are saying."

"This is what I want to say: in my time people also got rich—from what? From trade, commerce. A person would trade in, say, grain, or timber, or manufactured goods . . . , would travel around to fairs, work hard, and God would bless his labor and he would become a wealthy merchant . . . From what have you gotten rich, my son? I have asked everywhere, and no one can explain to me clearly what you trade in. They spoke about some sort of 'shares,' 'companies,' 'stock exchange,' and I wrote down all these mysterious words and again asked: What is that—timber? No, they say. Grain? No. Hemp? No again. So what is it? What is there to get rich from?"[30]

If the sudden rise of the Petersburg Jewish elite was a mystery to Jews in the Pale, it often appeared both mysterious and menacing to non-Jews. Much of Levanda's *Confession* is in fact designed to combat the popular impression of Jewish clannishness by illustrating again and again how Jews compete as mercilessly with one another as with everyone else. "They tried to ruin me," Shmalts laments of his fellow Jewish financiers, "and I them, at every convenient opportunity and with particular pleasure. There's our vaunted solidarity for you." Where non-Jews were prepared to see the kahal at work in every Jewish success, Shmalts insists that Jewish commercial ascendancy resulted from "our temperament, our asceticism, our intensive and inexhaustible activity. While wheeler-dealers of other nationalities are more often than not people with human passions and desires, epicureans easily distracted from business by music, or painting, or women, or horses, dogs, hunting, sports, card games—we Jewish wheeler-dealers are neither fascinated nor distracted by anything not directly related to business."[31]

The contrast of restless Jewish ascetic to Gentile (usually Russian) epicurean functioned as a remarkably consistent boundary marker for acculturated Jews. For them, older, starker forms of everyday differentiation (language, dress, dietary rules) no longer applied, and new ones were emerging. At the conclusion of Levanda's earlier novel, *Goriachee vremia* (Hot Times, 1875), the protagonist, Sarin, had confronted the limits of Jewish assimilation by observing that "we will be Russians, but for us Russian idleness, Rus-

---

30. Levanda, *Ispoved´ del´tsa*, p. 294.

31. Ibid., pp. 232–34. The novel abounds in examples of ruthless competition among Jews; see pp. 104, 152, 179–80, 195, 300. The reality of such competition, in Petersburg as in the Pale, is confirmed in many contemporary sources, including the memoirs of Chaim Aronson, *A Jewish Life under the Tsars*, p. 278.

sian lightheartedness, dissolution, impassivity, and what is called the broad Russian nature will forever remain foreign."[32] Traces of this contrast are found far beyond the works of Levanda. It is practically a cliché in contemporary Jewish sources that Jews tended to gesticulate and appear anxious more than Russians. One memoirist notes that after his family moved from a peasant village to a largely Jewish town, "I became more and more of a Jew. . . . I gestured more, and I was livelier."[33] In Jewish sources there is a strikingly consistent tendency to highlight the unusual "energy" of individual Jews, in implicit contrast to the aura of Oblomovian languor surrounding their Russian counterparts. (Oblomov was a lethargic character who snored his way to fame in a popular novel by Ivan Goncharov.)[34] The cultivation of sensual pleasures (especially regarding nature and food) is a staple of Russianness in contemporary Jewish fiction.

From the standpoint of Petersburg Jews on the front line of acculturation, the ascetic/epicurean contrast elaborated a self-understanding of the Jews as a spiritual people, distinguished from the worldly physicality of non-Jews.[35] The pioneering ethnographer, writer, and Petersburg resident Solomon Rapoport (1863–1920; better known by his pseudonym, Ansky), creator and exemplar of an emerging secular Jewish identity in an East European setting, went so far as to argue that "in works of Jewish folk art we find nearly all the basic elements of the folklore of other peoples. But [these works] have all been transformed from a material to a spiritual level, imbued with the biblical-Talmudic spirit, and colored by a powerful religious temperament."[36] The historian Simon Dubnov, officially registered as an artisan in the imperial capital, developed a grand theory of "spiritual nationalism" as the guid-

---

32. The orginial reads: "My budem russkimi, no dlia nas ved´ vsegda ostanutsia chuzhdymi russkaia len´, russkaia bezzabotnost´, zabubennost´, bezstrastie i to, chto nazyvaetsia russkoiu shirokoiu naturoiu." See Levanda, *Goriachee vremia* (St. Petersburg, 1875), p. 327.

33. Carole Malkin, ed., *The Journeys of David Toback* (New York, 1981), p. 13. Further examples of the Jewish propensity to gesticulate are to be found in Gessen, *V dvukh vekakh*, p. 12; Sliozberg, *Dela minuvshikh dnei*, 1: 30; Lifshits, *Ispoved´ prestupnika*, p. 14.

34. Il´ia Orshanskii, for example, contrasted the "persistence" and "energy" of the Jews to the Russians' "age-old Oblomovism," which he described as "somewhere between easygoingness [*blagodushie*] and indifference [*ravnodushie*]." See Orshanskii, *Evrei v Rossii*, pp. 180, 194, 233. For similar characterizations see Ginzburg, *Amolike Peterburg*, p. 47; Wengeroff, *Memoiren einer Grossmutter*, 2: 133, 174; Tsitron, *Shtadlonim*, p. 343.

35. Elements of this contrast appear in Yiddish folk sayings as well, e.g., "Az der yid iz hungerig—zingt er; der poyer—shlogt dos vayb" (When the Jew is hungry, he sings; the peasant beats his wife) (quoted in S. Vaisenberg, "Evrei v russkikh poslovitsakh," *Evreiskaia Biblioteka* 7, no. 2 [1915]: 230; despite its title, this article contains Yiddish folk sayings as well). Also "The Jew eats in order to live; with the Christian it's the other way around: he lives in order to eat," quoted in Eliakum Tsunzer, *Tsunzers biografiye, geshribn fun im aleyn* (New York, 1905). *Apikoyres* (epicurean) was a standard Yiddish epithet for an irreligious person.

36. S. A. Ansky [Solomon Rapoport], "Evreiskoe narodnoe tvorchestvo," *Perezhitoe* 1 (1909): 278.

ing force of Jewish history, in contrast to conventional European nationalisms grounded in physical territory and state power.[37]

Remarkably, the basic elements of contrast between restless ascetic and broad-natured epicurean inform the depiction of Jews in many Russian sources as well, albeit with a wide range of moral undertones. At the outset of selective integration, the liberal newspaper *Russkii Invalid* declared that "we will use [the Jews'] energy, resourcefulness and cleverness as a new means of satisfying the needs of society," while several decades later the populist revolutionary Aleksandr Mikhailov praised his comrade Aaron Zundelevich as "incredibly energetic and lively—in short . . . truly astonishing."[38] More often, however, the stereotypically energetic, gesticulating Jew was seen as irritating or worse—a symbol of Jewish rootlessness, preference for talk over physical labor, and exploitation of the ostensibly generous and tolerant Russian peasantry. "Chase the Jew out the door and he'll return through the window," warned a popular folk saying.[39] Whether in openly anti-Semitic diatribes such as Dostoevsky's *Diary of a Writer* and *Novoe Vremia*'s influential 1880 article "Zhid idet!" ("The Kike Is Coming!") or, more subtly, in the widespread belief among ruling elites that gullible Russian peasants required protection from the Jews' overdeveloped entrepreneurial spirit, the culturally coded contrast between indefatigable Jew and easygoing Russian defined contemporary attitudes toward ethnic difference.[40]

A Russian version of the ascetic/epicurean opposition was unexpectedly thrust upon Levanda in the form of a critical response to his *Confession*. The author of this critique was none other than Levanda's literary patron, Mikhail Fedorovich De-Pulé (1822–85), the editor of *Vilenskii Vestnik* (Vilna Herald), an official government newspaper to which Levanda was a frequent contributor. De-Pulé had high hopes for Jews such as Levanda. When official Russification in the western provinces began, he noted, "We had no more appreciative arena for our activities, no more ardent accomplices, than educated Jews."[41] In a letter of 1879 dripping with condescension, De-Pulé con-

---

37. The concept of Jewish spiritual nationalism, adapted by Dubnov from the French historian of religion Ernst Renan, first appeared in Dubnov's *Ob izuchenii istorii russkikh evreev i ob uchrezhdenii russko-evreiskogo istoricheskogo obshchestva* (St. Petersburg, 1891), esp. pp. 5–8, and was later elaborated in his *Pis'ma o starom i novom evreistve* (St. Petersburg, 1907).

38. Quoted respectively in John Klier, *Imperial Russia's Jewish Question*, p. 39, and Erich Haberer, *Jews and Revolution in Nineteenth-Century Russia* (Cambridge, 1995), p. 144.

39. *Evreiskii vopros v kartinkakh* (Kiev, 1885), p. 2.

40. "Zhid idet!" *Novoe Vremia*, Mar. 23, 1880. On Dostoevsky, see David Goldstein, *Dostoevsky and the Jews* (New York, 1981); and more generally, Felix Dreizin, *The Russian Soul and the Jew: Essays in Ethno-Literary Criticism* (Philadelphia, 1990). For attitudes among political elites, see Rogger, *Jewish Policies and Right-Wing Politics*, pp. 110, 170–73.

41. *Sankt-Peterburgskie Vedomosti*, no. 331 (1868), quoted in Grigorii Vol'tke, "Russkie liudi po voprosu ob obrazovanii evreev," *Sbornik v pol'zu evreiskikh shkol* (St. Petersburg, 1896), p. 510.

gratulated Levanda for finally writing a novel in a setting outside the Pale. "It is time," De-Pulé announced, "to emerge from the Jewish sphere and to take part in the broader horizons of a *Russian* writer." *Confession of a Wheeler-Dealer* represented an important step in this direction, but fell short in its treatment of Russian life:

> Be bold! Be bold! The Russian loves to swear, and loves when others swear at him. Instead of Jews, Poles, Armenians, Germans, you should have taken up all sorts of Russians—swindlers, thieves, rogues, nihilists, socialists, etc. The plot unfolds in Petersburg—but there is not a single Russian woman, Russian bureaucrat, bribe-taker, stockbroker. . . . The novel smells of Petersburg, but the life is Jewish: Jews, Jews, and more Jews. This will not entirely please the Russian reader.[42]

Whatever the prejudices of De-Pulé's letter, the virtual absence of Russian characters—epicurean or otherwise—in a novel set in Petersburg and written by one of the period's most ardent Jewish integrationists is indeed striking. It suggests a counterpart in the realm of literary imagination and, I would argue, of lived experience as well, to the Jews' abiding physical segregation in the Russian capital. Apart from the pursuit of their livelihood, many Jews who lived in Petersburg appear to have had little social contact with the city's predominantly Russian population. If they were prone to regard Petersburg as a "window on Russia," they remained largely spectators at that window.

THE STRUGGLE FOR COMMUNAL LEADERSHIP (I)

Despite Levanda's attempt to dispel popular notions of Jewish solidarity, non-Jews were wont to take such intramural cohesion for granted, and more often than not to regard it as a serious problem. Government officials such as P. A. Gresser, Petersburg's city governor, and Minister of the Interior I. N. Durnovo were convinced that Horace Gintsburg and other wealthy Jewish financiers held sway over Jewish students, who were suspected of organizing nihilist disorders at St. Petersburg University and elsewhere. More than once Gintsburg was threatened with expulsion from the city if the disorders did not stop.[43] Yehudah Leib Gordon, well acquainted with the internal workings of Petersburg Jewry from both personal experience and service as sec-

42. "Iz perepiski L. O. Levandy," *Evreiskaia Starina* 5, no. 2 (1913): 280–81.

43. See the account of a conversation with Gresser in W. T. Stead, *The Truth about Russia* (London, 1888), p. 247; Durnovo's position is recounted in *Dnevnik gosudarstvennogo sekretaria A. A. Polovtsova* (Moscow, 1966), 2: 433. As the moving force behind the Society for the Spread of Enlightenment among Russian Jews, Gintsburg did help supervise the distribution of stipends to Jewish students at Russian universities, including that of St. Petersburg. But he and the society were loyal to the tsarist regime and had no sympathy whatever for radicals.

retary of the communal governing board, lamented that the Russian government was "haunted by the specter of the kahal."[44] Nowhere was the inaccuracy of the government's view more evident than in the communal history of Petersburg Jews, in which one finds in heightened form many of the intramural tensions that were to be found within Russian Jewry as a whole.

Like the "port Jews" of Odessa and other frontier communities, Jewish immigrants to Petersburg were confronted with the challenge, and opportunity, of building communal institutions virtually from scratch, far removed from the centuries of tradition that lay behind age-old Jewish centers such as Vilna, Lublin, and Berdichev.[45] In Petersburg, moreover, the filling in of this tabula rasa (as one Jewish newspaper called it)[46] began in the 1860s, several decades later than in Odessa, and therefore at a more advanced stage in the internal differentiation of Russian Jewry. Like everything else in the capital, Jewish communal institutions there came under intense official scrutiny, not only by local administrators but by the highest organs of the tsarist government. Thus on top of the heightened self-consciousness that came from the deliberate designing of communal life, Petersburg Jews were acutely aware of their representative function vis-à-vis the larger world. Jews and non-Jews alike regarded the capital's Jewish community as both a yardstick by which the policy of selective integration would be measured and—if successful—a potential model for Russian Jewry as a whole.

The Jewish elites who began to gather in Petersburg in the 1860s were determined to fashion institutions of Jewish life equal to those of their counterparts in Berlin and Paris.[47] To this end, a group of some one hundred prominent Jewish residents of the capital met in July 1863 to elect delegates to a governing board charged with organizing communal affairs. Of the fifteen delegates selected, two-thirds were merchants (with Evzel and Horace Gintsburg heading the list), the rest physicians, dentists, or graduates of Russian institutions of higher education.[48] The board's first act was to hire Dr. Avram Neiman (1809–75), a German-born follower of Reform Judaism,

44. Yehudah Leib Gordon, "K istorii poseleniia evreev v Peterburge," *Voskhod*, no. 2 (1881), p. 45. The charge of Jewish solidarity must have struck Gordon as particularly ironic in the wake of what he believed was a Hasidic conspiracy against him. See Stanislawski, *For Whom Do I Toil?* p. 136 and the sources cited there.

45. On Odessa see Zipperstein, *Jews of Odessa*, esp. pp. 9–40.

46. *Razsvet*, May 29, 1880, p. 843.

47. Comparisons with Jewish communities in West European capitals were common and explicit; see, e.g., remarks by Yehudah Leib Gordon in the records of the Petersburg synagogue board, TsGIA-SPb, f. 422, op. 1, d. 157, l. 84 (I am indebted to V. A. Levin for bringing Gordon's remarks to my attention), and "Zadachi peterburgskikh evreev," *Razsvet*, May 29 and June 26, 1880.

48. RGIA, f. 821, op. 8, d. 24, ll. 7–9.

to become the first—and because of official restrictions, the sole—rabbi of the Petersburg community. Neiman had spent the previous twenty years in Riga, where he had succeeded the German maskil Max Lilienthal as rabbi of the city's Reform congregation.[49] Barely able to speak Russian or Yiddish, Neiman conducted services in German and Hebrew for a congregation of merchant notables in a temporary prayer house in the heart of Pod˜iacheskii, the area of densest Jewish population. With his characteristically German-Jewish combination of yeshiva and university training, Neiman presided over what one observer termed the city's first "orderly congregation, at least in the intellectual sense."[50]

For the more traditionally religious among Petersburg Jewry, Neiman's arrival and his status as the sole officially sanctioned rabbi were hardly welcome. But even among those sympathetic to religious reform, there was considerable dissatisfaction. Six years after Neiman's appointment, the journalist (and future publishing giant) A. E. Landau publicly criticized Neiman's lack of initiative; apart from lending a certain "enlightened" decorum to Jewish ritual, Neiman had accomplished remarkably little in the way of building communal institutions in the capital.[51] For the younger generation of educated Jews, eager to be regarded as citizens of the newly reformed Russia, Neiman's inability to speak the language of state was an uncomfortable reminder of the Haskalah's lingering cultural ties to Germany. Equally disturbing, Neiman had been chosen by a self-selected governing board rather than by representatives of the community as a whole, in contrast to traditional Jewish practice in the Pale.[52]

It was this latter issue that became the subject of a protracted series of skirmishes among various Jewish factions in the capital. In a report of 1867

---

49. Adolf Ehrlich, *Entwickelungsgeschichte der israelitischen Gemeindeschule zu Riga* (St. Petersburg, 1894).

50. *Razsvet,* May 15, 1880, p. 763.

51. Landau ["Gamabbit"], "Peterburgskie pis´ma," *Den´,* no. 43 (1870), p. 765; for similar views of Neiman's lack of initiative, see *Razsvet,* May 29, 1880, pp. 843–45. Landau quoted an unidentified fellow Jew as asking, "For whom is the rabbi necessary: for the Jews or for the Christians?" In one sense Neiman was indeed a rabbi for the Christians. His appointment had been carefully supervised by state authorities, and by 1864 he was being referred to in official government correspondence as "functionary [*chinovnik*] for special assignments in Jewish affairs" in the office of the governor general of St. Petersburg province. In this capacity, and not unlike the "expert Jews" employed by numerous government offices, Neiman occasionally submitted reports to state officials on developments within Petersburg Jewry, together with suggestions for reform. This practice was in accord with the official policy of seeking to use the clergy—of whatever religion—as sources of information about various segments of the population. See RGIA, f. 821, op. 8, d. 16, ll. 1–10; d. 24, ll. 33–35; dd. 400, 417, 427.

52. The tsarist government itself took seriously the right of Jewish communities in the Pale to elect their own rabbis, and frequently blocked plans by maskilim to restrict or do away with such elections. See RGIA, f. 1269, op. 1, d. 138, ll. 125–28, 167–68, and d. 139, ll. 141–55.

Figure 9. Frontispiece of David Maggid's *Chronicle of the Congregation of the Merchant (mitnagdic) Bet Midrash in Petrograd* (1917). (By permission of Sankt-Peterburgskii filial Instituta vostokovedeniia Rossiiskoi Akademii Nauk).

to the governor of St. Petersburg province, Neiman candidly discussed the problem. Characterizing the city's rapidly expanding Jewish community as plagued by "disorders and stagnation," he noted that members of the governing board were frequently away from Petersburg for business purposes and hence unable to attend to communal affairs. In an effort to add greater legitimacy to the governing board—and, by extension, to his own position—Neiman urged that new elections be held in which "all estates within the Jewish community" (artisans, soldiers, merchants, and intellectuals) would separately elect representatives. The governor turned for advice to Horace Gintsburg, whom he characterized as "a person familiar with the communal affairs of the Jews, but neutral, standing to the side of petty local squabbles." Gintsburg, similarly interested in putting an end to intramural conflicts, endorsed Neiman's proposal.[53]

Had it become formalized, the division of Petersburg Jews into voting blocs according to estate would have introduced an entirely new and decidedly Russian hierarchy into the structure of the Jewish community. But imperial authorities were wary of anything resembling autonomous, quasi-representative institutions.[54] In any event, the first communal elections by estate, held in 1868, were also the last, owing to widespread charges of corruption and string-pulling. As Horace Gintsburg (then in Paris) learned in a letter from his secretary, Emanuel Levin, a minority of "progressives" had scored "a complete victory over the conservatives," but only through a series of intrigues.[55] Though sympathetic to the "progressives," Levin was forced to concede that

> the mass of Jews here is disturbed by the results of the election, and one can't help but admit that Neiman and his party committed a blunder by exclusively promoting the opposition. This has aroused great anger against them. I have kept my distance from all the various intrigues and parties and sincerely wish only one thing: that there be no mutual slander and complaints to officials, which could greatly damage us in the opinion of the supreme authorities.[56]

Levin's fears were only too well grounded. Complaints by Jews against their communal authorities began to flood the desks of various government officials. Many petitioners confirmed Neiman's observation that members of the governing board spent long periods of time abroad and were usually

53. RGIA, f. 821, op. 8, d. 24, ll. 33–35, 53–58.

54. Ibid., ll. 35, 48.

55. RNB, f. 183, op. 1014, d. 1746, ll. 3–4. The intrigues included announcing the time and place of the balloting for artisans only in the Russian newspaper *Golos*, which few Jewish artisans were likely to read. See also RGIA, f. 821, op. 8, d. 24, l. 37, and *Razsvet,* May 29, 1880, p. 844.

56. RNB, f. 183, op. 1014, d. 1746, ll. 4–5.

Figure 10. Baron Goratsii (Horace) Gintsburg
(1833–1909), a.k.a. "Papasha." (Courtesy of
V. E. Kel´ner.)

too busy with commercial affairs to devote significant energy to the needs of
the community.[57] In 1868, Shaul Katsenelenbogen, a "certified translator,"
requested in a petition to the Ministry of Internal Affairs that the results of
the recent election be nullified. Jewish artisans and retired soldiers, he argued, had been wholly excluded from the decision-making process, despite

57. See, e.g., RGIA, f. 821, op. 8, d. 24, ll. 33, 45, 120. This charge was reiterated by Landau in *Den´*, no. 22 (1869), p. 347, and by the editors of *Razsvet*, June 12, 1880, who noted that
members of the governing board frequently missed meetings, with the result that the board
first met weekly, then monthly, then only irregularly. One petition (in 1873) complained that
of eleven current board members, six (listed by name, including Horace Gintsburg) spent
significant parts of the year abroad, and three others were completely absorbed with business
affairs. See RGIA, f. 821, op. 8, d. 24, l. 120.

the fact that they constituted the overwhelming majority of the capital's "native Jewish population."[58]

At this point, the issue of representation was joined by the equally potent matter of communal taxation on kosher meat. In Jewish communities across the Pale, the ritual slaughterer (*shohet*) frequently served as a lightning rod for religious and social controversies. As Katsenelenbogen and others emphasized, it was precisely the lower ranks of Jews who, as consumers, paid the lion's share of the tax on the slaughter and sale of kosher meat (the *korobka*) and thereby financed the community's budget:

> Communal revenues come primarily from artisans . . . , who observe the rituals of their faith. With very few exceptions, the merchants and the educated—bowing to the progress of the times—reject such rituals, and differ from Christians neither in their diet nor in any other way. The artisan estate is hard-pressed and driven nearly to starvation by the merciless price of [kosher] meat—up to 40 kopeks per pound![59]

In effect, the wealthy, self-elected members of the board were using communal funds from the pockets of the poor in an attempt to finance "reformed" Jewish institutions alien to the religious practices of their brethren. The resulting tensions at times led to violence, as when a group of artisans, furious at the high price of kosher meat, scuffled with the elite congregants at Neiman's prayer house over what one Jewish journalist called the "exploitation of the poor folk by Jewish kulak-butchers."[60]

58. RGIA, f. 821, op. 8, d. 24, ll. 37–38.

59. Ibid., l. 37. Pinkhus Khaimovich Rozenberg, variously described as a tailor and a merchant of the first guild (he may well have been both), submitted a similar petition in 1869; see ibid., ll. 45–46, and RNB, f. 183, op. 1014, d. 1746, ll. 3–4. A. E. Landau echoed Katsenelenbogen a year later in *Den'*, no. 12 (1870), p. 201: "In Petersburg—entre nous, dear reader—one rarely finds a kosher kitchen in the home of the wealthy. Their Jewish patriotism notwithstanding, the wealthy quietly eat *tref* like the 'simple goys' and thus the entire weight of the kosher meat tax falls exclusively on the poor."

60. Gershon-ben-Gershon [Gershon Lifshits], "Kartinki iz zhizni peterburgskikh evreev," *Razsvet*, no. 3 (1879), pp. 85–87. Looking back on communal life in the 1860s, *Razsvet* noted that "whoever so desired could name himself and be a representative; whoever so desired could have access to communal funds" (May 29, 1880, p. 843).

An official at the Ministry of Internal Affairs charged in 1877 that "the poor majority [of Petersburg Jews] are deprived of active participation [in communal affairs] and are subject to exploitation by the wealthy minority. This is a phenomenon generally noticed in the areas of permanent Jewish settlement": RGIA, f. 821, op. 8, d. 24, l. 78. Empire-wide commissions in 1844, 1858, 1881, and 1888 made similar charges, citing in particular misuse by elites of revenues from the kosher meat tax. See Iu. Gessen, "Korobochnyi sbor," *Evreiskaia entsiklopediia*, 9: 759–67. Maskilic writers were known to scathingly satirize the workings of the korobka, as in the play *Di takse* (The Tax), published in 1869 by S. Y. Abramovich ("Mendele Mokher Sforim").

SOCIAL AND RELIGIOUS FAULT LINES

By the mid–nineteenth century, Russian Jews had already acquired a reputation among government officials as being, among other things, a litigious people.[61] Internecine conflicts (chiefly, but not exclusively, between Hasidim and their opponents), the elaborate maze and arbitrary application of discriminatory legislation, combined with relatively high rates of literacy and a culture imbued with legal norms, led to extraordinary numbers of formal appeals by various Jewish groups and individuals for state intervention on their behalf.[62] One well-placed observer describes a campaign among Orthodox Jews that culminated in "thousands of petitions, each with hundreds of signatures, pouring down on the Ministry of Public Enlightenment."[63] Even against this background, Jews in the capital stood out. Scarcely a decade after the policy of selective integration made it possible for Jews to settle in Petersburg, the minister of internal affairs complained of "the constant disagreements among the Jews here, mutual incriminations, and petitions to city authorities."[64] *Razsvet* similarly bemoaned the "endless intrigues" among the capital's Jews.[65]

This was a far cry, one might note, from the specter of Jewish solidarity. Landau, in his usual partisan way, was one of many who commented on the extraordinary contrasts among the capital's Jews:

> The diversity of the Jewish population of Petersburg is truly remarkable. Among the Jews here you will find . . . people from all classes of society, in terms of both material status and moral development, from extreme conservatives to ardent reformers, from unregenerate fanatics and sanctimonious hypocrites to those who are genuinely religious but at the same time enlightened and tolerant.[66]

Until late in the nineteenth century, when significant numbers of Russian-Jewish intellectuals began to cultivate a specifically Jewish form of populism

---

61. Early examples of this reputation are to be found in the annual *vsepoddanneishie otchety* of the provincial governors of Podolia (1832) and Mogilev (1843); see Deych, *Arkhivnye dokumenty po istorii evreev v Rossii*, pp. 68, 72. For similar attitudes expressed by the Jewish Committee in 1863 and Minister of Internal Affairs Ignat´ev in 1882, see RGIA, f. 1269, op. 1, d. 139, l. 175, and GARF, f. 730, op. 1, d. 1623, l. 1. For a later period, see I. V. Gessen and V. Fridshtein, eds., *Sbornik zakonov o evreiakh s ras˝iasneniiami po opredeleniiam Pravitel´stvuiushchago Senata i tsirkuliaram Ministerstv* (St. Petersburg, 1904), p. vii.

62. On the government's role in Hasidic controversies, see Deych, *Tsarskoe pravitel´stvo i khasidskoe dvizhenie.*

63. Sliozberg, *Dela minuvshikh dnei,* 1: 293.

64. Letter of Dec. 12, 1869, to the governor of St. Petersburg province, RGIA, f. 821, op. 8, d. 24, ll. 49–50. If anything, the volume of complaints only increased as the capital's Jewish population grew, especially after the government sought to shut down many of the prayer houses that had sprung up throughout the city. See d. 164, l. 117.

65. *Razsvet,* May 29, 1880, p. 843.

66. Landau, "Peterburgskie pis´ma," *Den´,* June 30, 1869, p. 72.

(many of them having already passed through its Russian counterpart), openly critical remarks about popular Jewish practices were a staple of mask-ilic commentary. Reporting in 1864, for example, on a wedding he had witnessed involving two Jewish soldiers' families in Petersburg, Landau ridiculed the "yelling, noise, bustle, and disorder," the "wild" mixture of languages, the faulty reading of the prayer book. He was particularly incensed that the bride was forbidden to eat the entire day and had to have her hair plucked out by the guests, her head smeared with sugar and honey (for good luck) and covered with a heavy wig. Normally, Landau assured his readers, one would find such "ignorance and religious superstition only in the most remote, backward Lithuanian shtetls." Neiman's excessively long sermon at the wedding, in German no less, only added to the incongruity of such an event in the Russian capital.[67]

Similarly, the editors of *Razsvet*, reviewing a visit to Petersburg by Adolphe Crémieux, the head of the Paris-based Alliance Israélite Universelle, worried aloud: "Imagine if Monsieur Crémieux . . . had taken it into his head to ask our notables to show him their house of worship, and instead of magnificent Parisian-style synagogues, with their well-ordered, harmonious services, they had had to show him our dark, dirty, stinking kennels, ruled by noise and uproar and other similar attributes of our quasi-Orthodox prayer houses."[68] Nor were foreign Jewish dignitaries the only potentially important audience for Petersburg's Jews.[69] According to a memorandum circulated among the communal governing board, the Russian political elites who were concentrated in the imperial capital would also draw certain conclusions from what they witnessed of Jewish life there:

> One must not forget that the life of Petersburg Jews unfolds before the eyes of those on whom depends the fate of all Jews in Russia, the granting to the Jews of the right to life [*sic*], labor, and education. If Petersburg Jews, even in their lower ranks, will demonstrate by their example a capacity for productive labor, good manners, and good morals—all this will produce the appropriate impression and will serve to uproot the reigning prejudices among influential circles of Russian society in the capital.[70]

67. Landau, "Pis´ma ob evreiakh: Peterburgskie evrei," *Biblioteka dlia Chteniia* 187, no. 12 (1864): 8.

68. *Razsvet*, June 5, 1880, p. 884.

69. When the time came to attend Sabbath worship during his first visit to Petersburg in 1846, Sir Moses Montefiore had had to settle for a visit to the Jewish soldiers' barracks; there was not a single prayer house, let alone synagogue, in the entire city. In the absence of a rabbi, a soldier was assigned the task of leading the service, and with characteristic restraint, Sir Moses observed that the congregants "appeared very devout, and joined loudly in the prayers": Montefiore and Montefiore, *Diaries*, 1: 335. Educated Russian Jews were apt to be more blunt.

70. TsGIA-SPb, f. 422, op. 1, d. 64, ll. 76–77; quoted in V. A. Levin, "Ocherk istorii evreiskogo shkol´nogo obrazovaniia v dorevoliutsionnom Peterburge," in *Evreiskaia Shkola* (St. Petersburg, 1993), p. 74.

Figure 11. Adolf Landau (1842–1902).

At first glance, religious tensions among Petersburg Jews appeared to match lines of social division, separating traditionally observant soldiers and artisans from "progressive" (or indifferent) merchants and intellectuals. One should not, however, be misled by Neiman's proposal to hold separate elections according to social estate, or by petitions in the name of "artisans" or "soldiers" or "merchants," into seeing the fault lines as simply following the categories of estate. To begin with, as Chapter 3 suggested, such categories, while crucial for a Jew's legal status, were in practice often fictitious. Moreover, according to an 1878 report by the city governor, in at least three of Petersburg's eight prayer houses, one could find Jews of different estates worshiping side by side.[71]

71. RGIA, f. 821, op. 8, d. 24, ll. 127–28. The number of legal prayer houses in Petersburg varied considerably over time. The census of 1869 reported ten (see *Sanktpeterburg po perepisi*

The limited available evidence concerning religious practices among Petersburg Jews suggests that dissatisfaction with Orthodoxy occurred in varying degrees at all social levels of the city's Jewish population. But whereas among the well-to-do and educated such disaffection often led to a search for a reformed Judaism, among poor and/or uneducated Jews it seems to have translated into a departure from organized religion altogether.[72] Religious conflicts within Petersburg Jewry were less a matter of competing theologies than of everyday practices and forms of community: the orderliness and severity of the synagogue service, decorum, dress, the use of choral singing and of non-Jewish languages, and the turn to new and large-scale forms of philanthropy as a defining communal activity. Petersburg Jewish elites rapidly adopted modes of fund-raising from the surrounding society, including charity balls, ladies' committees, bazaars, and limited-edition publications. The range of beneficiaries of all this activity expanded, too, reflecting a new set of social concerns: funds were earmarked for vocational and agricultural training, inexpensive housing, and aid to poor women, students, and artists, among others. Philanthropies in the capital were more likely to target Jews in the Pale than those living in Petersburg itself.

The confusion of contemporary terms for the opposing camps suggests that by the second half of the nineteenth century, religious categories were becoming less rather than more sharply definable, certainly less than our received notions of Hasidism, Mitnagdism, Orthodoxy, Musar, and others would

---

10 dekabria 1869 goda, no. 2, pp. 128ff); *Razsvet,* June 5, 1880, reported twenty. Of the eight listed in the 1878 city governor's report, three were described as having congregants of various estates; one was singled out for its "predominantly educated" congregation and "more proper external appearance, choral singing, and less severe ritual practices"; another was referred to as the "merchant prayer house," and yet another as the "artisan prayer house."

72. I have found only a handful of descriptions by poor Jews of religious disaffection. In the portion of his memoirs dealing with his life in Petersburg in the 1870s and 1880s, the artisan Chaim Aronson, appalled at the superstition of traditional Jews, makes no mention whatsoever of Jewish religious life in the capital; the same holds for V. N. Nikitin's autobiographical vignettes. By contrast, acculturated Jewish intellectuals in Petersburg such as Dubnov, Sliozberg, Gordon, and Landau exhibited considerable interest in the synthesis of Judaism and modernity. Of course, significant numbers of Russian-Jewish intellectuals remained aloof from all forms of organized religion.

There is as yet no major study of Reform Judaism's impact on Russian Jewry. Michael A. Meyer's essay "The German Model of Religious Reform and Russian Jewry," in I. Twersky, ed., *Danzig, between East and West: Aspects of Modern Jewish History,* Harvard Judaic Texts and Studies IV (Cambridge, Mass., 1985), pp. 67–86, focuses on synagogue services in "German"-style congregations in Warsaw, Riga, Odessa, and Vilna. Meyer makes the important point that, in contrast to Germany, where Reform Judaism was developed to a considerable extent by rabbis, in Russia the movement for religious reform was almost exclusively in the hands of laymen. Michael Stanislawski's biography of Yehuda Leib Gordon analyzes one layman's attempt to fashion an "enlightened" Judaism for Russian Jewry, but as Stanislawski repeatedly notes, Gordon's views were highly idiosyncratic for his time. See Stanislawski, *For Whom Do I Toil?* pp. 73, 90, 131, 153, 170.

suggest.[73] Landau, noting that in Petersburg within the same Jewish family one could often find those who prayed thrice daily and thrice yearly, vaguely pitted "reformers" and "the enlightened" against "conservatives" and "fanatics." Gintsburg's secretary, Emanuel Levin, preferred "progressives" and "conservatives," while *Razsvet* referred to "reform" and "orthodox." Decades later, the historian Shaul Ginzburg (who came to Petersburg in 1886 as a student) cast the struggle as between the governing board and the *frum* (pious) camp, which, according to him, brought together mitnagdim and their erstwhile Hasidic enemies. Gordon, tracing much the same religious landscape, depicted a governing board guided by "rational, modern principles" and its opponents as "inspired by the familiar charms and routines [of] Shklov and Berdichev."[74]

As one of the few surviving accounts of Petersburg Jewry that makes no secret of its preference for the "charms of Berdichev," the memoirs of Pauline Wengeroff offer a useful contrast to the views of Landau, Levin, Gordon, and other would-be reformers. Upon arriving in Petersburg in the 1870s with her merchant husband, Wengeroff was shocked to find that among the wealthy elite, certain families had restricted their observance to three days each year: Passover, Yom Kippur, and Christmas (the last ostensibly for the benefit of the servants). Some would travel to the prayer house on the Sabbath by carriage rather than by foot, and would eat during intermissions of the Yom Kippur service. The Passover seder was drastically abridged, and as often as not was celebrated in remembrance of the exodus not from Egypt but from the Pale; conversation during dinner would move quickly to the latest headlines and trends in the stock market.[75] But Wengeroff was care-

---

73. In Germany, by contrast, the terms "Reform" and "Orthodox" had crystallized in Jewish discourse as early as the 1840s.

74. Landau, "Pis´ma o evreiakh. Peterburgskie evrei," *Biblioteka dlia Chteniia*, 187, no. 12 (1864): 4; idem, "Peterburgskie pis´ma," *Den´*, no. 5 (1869), pp. 72–73; E. B. Levin to Horace Gintsburg, Mar. 21, 1868, in RNB, f. 183, op. 1014, d. 1746, ll. 3–4; *Razsvet*, May 29, 1880, p. 845; Ginzburg, *Historishe verk*, 1: 128 (Ginzburg appears, moreover, to use the terms "Orthodox" and "Hasidic" interchangably); Gordon, "K istorii poseleniia evreev," pt. 2, p. 47.

75. Wengeroff, *Memoiren einer Grossmutter*, 2: 172–73. The trope of Petersburg as the Promised Land and the Pale as Egypt also appears in Orshanskii, *Russkoe zakonodatel´stvo o evreiakh*, p. 10, as well as in a humorous Passover scene in Levanda's *Ispoved´del´tsa*, pp. 120–21. A glimpse into the atmosphere of the Passover Seder among Petersburg's Russian-Jewish intelligentsia can be found in the following tongue-in-cheek invitation (from the period between 1906 and 1914) from Roza Vinaver, wife of the prominent Jewish lawyer Maksim Vinaver, to the literary critic and editor of *Russkoe Bogatstvo*, A. G. Gornfel´d (RNB, f. 211, op. 1, d. 410, l. 11):

Most esteemed Arkadii Georgievich,
    I hasten to remind you that, as a loyal and pious Jew, you are called upon to fulfill your duty, which we will try to make as pleasant as possible. It's all happening on the 21st of March at 9 p.m., and incidentally I suggest that on that day you eat only lightly (I'm sure that this "lightly" will have to be examined under a microscope).
                                                                    Your devoted Roza Vinaver

Figure 12. Pauline (Pessele) Wengeroff,
née Epstein (1833–1916). (Courtesy of
Electra Yourke.)

ful to note that among the Jewish financial elite were also families who followed traditional forms of observance.

The high degree of diversity within Petersburg Jewry was often blamed for its relative lack of internal cohesion.[76] "We have communal representatives, a communal rabbi, and . . . some ten prayer houses," Landau lamented in 1869, "but you will search in vain for a Jewish community [*evreiskoe obshchestvo*] here."[77] Aside from a single orphanage for the children of Jewish

76. Landau, "Peterburgskie pis´ma," *Den´*, June 30, 1869, p. 72; *Razsvet,* June 26, 1880, p. 1003.

77. Landau, "Peterburgskie pis´ma," *Den´*, no. 22 (1869), p. 346. Similar remarks may be found in *Razsvet,* June 12, 1880, p. 924.

soldiers and a single elementary school for some seventy-five children of the poor, there were as yet few of the traditional institutions that made Judaism in Eastern Europe a social order as well as a religion: burial and mutual aid societies, subsidized kosher cafeterias, hospitals, interest-free lending agencies, a *talmud-torah,* or, for that matter, a proper synagogue.[78] "Impoverished in body and spirit" was Ha-Kohen's lapidary verdict on Petersburg Jewry.[79] In 1869, the lone Jewish orphanage found itself threatened by a rival orphanage, sponsored by the Imperial Society of Lovers of Humankind, expressly for "Jewish children baptized or entering baptism into the Russian Orthodox faith."[80]

The self-styled reformers who complained of communal discord nonetheless insisted that, because of its representative function, Petersburg Jewry could not afford to split formally into separate denominational camps, as Jews had done in Vilna, Odessa, and other cities in the Pale. Particularly in centralized countries such as Russia and France, argued the editors of *Razsvet,* the capital was the natural center of cultural and political activity, no less for Jews than for other groups. Not only among Jews in the Pale but in Russian society and the government "it is desired and expected that we serve as models for our provincial brothers. . . . And let us admit that we are not averse to regarding ourselves as the leaders and architects of the fate of Russian Jewry." But *Razsvet* was forced to concede that the exemplary Jews in West European capitals were themselves already divided into separate Reform and Orthodox communities. Insisting rather obscurely that such an arrangement would be "premature" in Petersburg, *Razsvet* could only note that "our Jewish orthodoxy does not at all correspond to the meaning of the term in Western Europe."[81]

THE STRUGGLE FOR COMMUNAL LEADERSHIP (II)

Petersburg Jewry brought to full boil the intramural tensions simmering throughout the Pale. Because of Petersburg's special political and cultural role, and because of the absence of a Jewish past there, Jewish institutions in the capital were fashioned within the context of a particularly fierce struggle for exclusive communal authority and exclusive recognition from the tsarist government.

---

78. *Otchet pravleniia S.-Peterburgskoi evreiskoi obshchiny za vremia s 10 aprelia 1870 goda po 1 ianvaria 1873 goda* (St. Petersburg, 1873), p. 10.

79. Ha-Kohen, *Olami,* 1: 78.

80. TsGIA-SPb, f. 542, op. 1, d. 1. In 1886 the orphanage was renamed Mariinsko-Sergievskii priiut dlia kreshchaemykh i kreshchenykh v pravoslavnuiu veru evreiskikh detei.

81. *Razsvet,* May 15, 1880, pp. 761–63; June 26, 1880, pp. 1004–5.

One year after the failed 1868 elections to the governing board, new elections were held in which, by private agreement between Horace Gintsburg and city authorities, only registered merchants and graduates of institutions of higher education took part. Composed entirely of merchants and financiers, and with Gintsburg again at its head, the newly elected board quickly took a number of decisive steps. First, with official approval, it limited the right to vote in future elections to those—of whatever estate—who contributed at least 25 rubles to the communal treasury, a sum beyond the reach of most Petersburg Jews.[82] Despite frequent protests in subsequent years against the voting fee, these guidelines remained unchanged until the Revolution of 1917, thereby assuring at least the formal ascendancy of the "reformers."[83] Second, the board put its own financial dealings in greater order, and in 1873 began publishing annual (or nearly annual) reports on its budget and activities. No other Jewish community in the Russian Empire made itself available for public scrutiny in this way.

Finally, in response to the many charges of fiscal abuse and again with official approval, the board eliminated the kosher meat tax as a source of communal revenue.[84] This measure put the Petersburg community on a dramatically different fiscal footing than that of Jewish communities in the Pale. As a community-wide, more or less mandatory consumption tax specifically linked to religious practice, the tax on kosher meat was the last significant vestige of the Jews' right to govern themselves as a corporate entity. The abandonment of internal taxation significantly weakened communal authorities' control over the community of practicing Jews and transformed the latter into a strictly voluntary collectivity. As it turned out, the number of Petersburg Jews who were willing and able to pay the 25 ruble voting fee never ex-

82. Gessen (*Evreiskaia entsiklopediia*, 13: 939) asserts that the 25 ruble fee was imposed on the governing board by city authorities. Other sources, however, suggest that Horace Gintsburg first proposed the idea in a petition of 1869. See RGIA, f. 821, op. 8, d. 24, l. 53. Mordechai ben Hillel Ha-Kohen (Markus Kagan) traces the idea to Yehuda Leib Gordon, who was then secretary of the St. Petersburg Jewish Community. See Kagan, "K istorii natsional'nogo samosoznaniia russko-evreiskogo obshchestva: Po lichnym vospominaniiam," *Perezhitoe* 3 (1911): 141. Kagan's broadside against Gordon first appeard in *Ha-Tsefirah*.

83. For a summary of debates regarding the voting fee, see the minutes of the governing board for 1911 in TsGIA-SPb, f. 422, op. 1, d. 266, ll. 1–3; see also *Nedel'naia Khronika Voskhoda*, Sept. 2, 1895, p. 987, and Kagan, "K istorii natsional'nogo samopoznaniia," *Perezhitoe* 3 (1911): 141.

84. The board's stated reasons for the abolition of the korobka were that other religious groups did not levy such internal taxes, and that the burden of the tax fell disproportionately on the poor. See *Otchet pravleniia S.-Peterburgskoi evreiskoi obshchiny za vremia s 10 aprelia 1870 goda po 1 ianvaria 1873 goda* (St. Petersburg, 1873), p. 3. But in petitions to various branches of the government, Gintsburg and other notables had indicated as early as 1863 that the korobka was "unreliable" as a source of revenue. See RGIA, f. 1269, op. 1, d. 139, l. 212, and f. 821, op. 8, d. 24, l. 53.

ceeded 500.[85] Revenue from the fee (even when combined with the lesser dues paid by the far larger number of nonvoting members) consistently proved too meager to finance the board's projects and, as before, the communal budget depended heavily on individual donations.[86] The board's annual reports invariably included a jeremiad against the paucity of donors and the resulting budgetary constraints.

After the reorganization of the governing board in 1869, virtually all aspects of Jewish communal life in the capital (leaving aside the now largely separate and rarely visible activities of the more traditional groups) were dependent on the voluntary contributions of a handful of extraordinarily wealthy families. At the head of the community, the barons Gintsburg—first Evzel, then his son Horace, followed by Horace's son David—formed a quasi-dynastic leadership with access to high tsarist officials and considerable fame throughout the Pale as philanthropists and intercessors. Something of the family's standing can be gleaned from the fact that in private, Petersburg Jews referred to Horace Gintsburg simply as "papasha" (papa). He was a man of aristocratic bearing and, like many Russian aristocrats, felt more at home in French than in Russian. Among the guests at the fashionable Gintsburg mansion on the English Embankment could be found prominent Russian writers, artists, generals, jurists, and government officials.[87] On their peri-

85. A list of voting members of the Petersburg community in 1876 gives 185 names; see RGIA, f. 821, op. 8, d. 24, ll. 70–72. The published annual report of the governing board for 1881 gives the number of voters as 304; see *Otchet pravleniia S.-Peterburgskoi evreiskoi obshchiny za 1881 god* (St. Petersburg, 1882), p. 6. Gessen reports the number in 1911 as approximately 300, at a time when the city's official Jewish population was roughly 35,000. See *Evreiskaia entsiklopediia*, 13: 948. On the eve of tsarism's collapse, in 1916, there were 500 voting members; see Beizer, *Evrei Leningrada*, p. 173.

86. Before it was abolished, the korobka had generated approximately 13,000 rubles annually, at a time when annual communal expenses averaged around 30,000 rubles. See *Otchet pravleniia S.-Peterburgskoi evreiskoi obshchiny za vremia s 10 aprelia 1870 goda po 1 ianvaria 1873 goda*, pp. 3–4. In 1876, seven years after the abolition of the korobka, the 185 voting members of the community generated only 4,625 rubles in dues. But an additional 14,489 rubles appeared in the form of donations, of which over two-thirds came from just six individuals, with Horace Gintsburg topping the list at 4,740 rubles. See RGIA, f. 821, op. 8, d. 24, ll. 70–72. To appreciate the abiding importance of the korobka for Jewish communities in the Pale, one has only to take the example of Odessa, where at the beginning of the twentieth century the tax produced annual revenues of well over 300,000 rubles, which were used to finance communal institutions as well as to pay mandatory fees to the city administration. See *Evreiskaia entsiklopediia*, 12: 63.

87. The term appears in several private letters from the turn of the century. The author of one such letter that had been intercepted by the Petersburg police, when asked to explain who "papasha" was, responded that "'papasha' is how Jews refer to Goratsii Osipovich Gintsburg." See GARF, f. 102, deloproizvodstvo 3, 1891, op. 89, d. 445, l. 86. For another example of the term, see RNB, f. 183, op. 1014, d. 1160, l. 15. On Gintsburg's acquaintances, see Sliozberg, *Baron G. O. Gintsburg*, pp. 52–53, 60–66; "Mémoire du baron Alexandre de Gunzburg," pp. 33–37.

odic visits to their sprawling estate in Podolia (a province in the Pale), the Gintsburgs were often besieged by crowds of poor Jews begging for assistance or intercession of various kinds.[88] In the popular Jewish imagination, hungry for all-powerful protectors, various prominent Petersburg Jews who happened to bear the name Ginsberg, Ginsburg, Ginzburg, or Günzburg were merged into a single "Baron Gintsburg," to whom all good deeds were attributed.[89]

Despite the appearance of orderliness that the new arrangement gave to the capital's Jews, intramural conflict did not disappear entirely. Though financially separate from the elites, the city's Orthodox and Hasidic Jews often depended on the governing board to procure residence permits for their clandestine rabbis, who in many cases were formally registered as "assistants" to Neiman and his successor as "official" rabbi, Avram Drabkin.[90] Nor did the new order please the small but vocal minority of Jewish intellectuals with populist leanings. For them it was as if the nouveaux riches depicted in Levanda's *Confession* had come to life and taken control of Russian Jewry's flagship community. In a direct challenge to the Gintsburgs and the Jewish plutocracy, the editors of *Razsvet* wrote in 1880:

> We Jews are still unable to shake off that sad, centuries-old legacy, thrust upon us from without by our . . . historical past, we are still utterly unable to liberate ourselves from that regrettable conviction, unfortunately based on sad experience, that everything can be achieved only through money. Money, and money alone, saved us from expulsion, from bonfires; money secured us, and in some states even today secures us, respect and a privileged position. Why then, it is asked, shouldn't our communal affairs be resolved as needed by money, and money alone? This, however, turns out to be impossible. *Within* Jewry, different levers, different moving forces are required as well. . . . We are not, incidentally, opposed to the involvement of our well-known financiers in communal affairs. . . . We are merely against their exclusive participation at the expense of everyone else. Only those communal undertakings which are the business not of isolated individuals but of the people as a whole can be truly successful.[91]

88. See the account by David Gintsburg's daughter Sophie Gintsburg, "David avi," *He-ʿavar,* no. 6 (1958), p. 159.

89. Beizer, *Evrei v Peterburge,* p. 131. Additional testimony concerning the near-mythic status of the Gintsburg family in popular Jewish lore can be found in Tsitron, *Shtadlonim,* pp. 334–76, esp. 335, and Shaul Ginzburg (no relation), "Di familiye Baron Gintsburg: drey doros shtadlonos, tsedokeh un haskoleh," in his *Historishe verk,* 2: 117–59.

90. Ginzburg, *Historishe verk,* 1: 125–29. In contrast to Neiman, Drabkin was a native of the Russian Empire (Mogilev), although his training included a period of study with the German-Jewish scholars Heinrich Graetz and Zacharias Frankel at the Breslau rabbinical seminary. See *Evreiskaia entsiklopediia,* 7: 316.

91. *Razsvet,* June 12, 1880, p. 923 (emphasis in original).

RELATIONS WITH CITY AND STATE AUTHORITIES

The struggle among different groups within the Jewish population proved to be only part of the story of how communal institutions were formed. For no sooner had the "reformers" won the upper hand (in the wake of the 1869 elections) than they found themselves confronted with unexpected interventions by the state, which had its own visions of Petersburg Jewry as a tabula rasa. Official policy, in fact, played nearly as great a role in the shaping of communal institutions in the capital as did the struggles between various Jewish factions.

A bewildering array of tsarist bureaucratic offices had a hand in regulating the communal affairs of Petersburg Jewry.[92] Over time, and depending on the personalities involved, the constraints and pressures applied to Jewish communal life varied, but as with official Jewish policy as a whole, certain broad contours are discernible. In essence, these amounted to an attempt to strip Jewish life in the capital of all elements not directly related to religious ritual.

In 1870, the newly reconstituted governing board submitted a charter to the Ministry of Internal Affairs, detailing the proposed legal rights and responsibilities of the city's Jewish community.[93] The charter reiterated the board's desire to construct a grand synagogue in the imperial capital, as well as an array of related charitable and religious institutions. All the proposed institutions were typical components of Jewish communal life in the Pale. In its response to the charter, however, the ministry announced that Jewish communal life in Petersburg was to be organized differently. A burial society, for example, could not be financed or controlled by the governing board, for that "would resemble the structure of the kahal," which had been formally banned by Russian law in 1844. Similarly, philanthropic institutions would have to be wholly independent of the board, lest they promote an "artificial centralization" of authority within the community. With the exception of the planned synagogue, the ministry declared, the board lacked the right even to own property in its own name. At the very least, each communal organization would have to apply separately for permission to carry out its activities.[94]

The governing board, already beleaguered by its opponents within the Jewish community, was stunned by the drastic limitations imposed on its au-

---

92. The municipal police, the city governor, the governor of St. Petersburg province, and, within the Ministry of Internal Affairs, the Administrative Department and the Department of Spiritual Affairs of Foreign Faiths were all regularly involved in overseeing the affairs of the city's Jews. Individual episodes produced sporadic involvement by the Senate and the secret police as well.

93. A copy of the charter is in RGIA, f. 821, op. 8, d. 24, ll. 63–69.

94. Ibid., ll. 78–83, and d. 164, l. 193.

thority by the government. At a time when the board was struggling to shed its reputation among the city's (and the empire's) Jews as an instrument of the wealthy elite, the government's policy required that all communal capital, buildings (other than the planned synagogue), and land be registered as the property of individuals rather than of the community as a whole. Such an arrangement could only strengthen the appearance, if not the reality, of corruption.[95] Moreover, official resistance to Jewish communal organizations in Petersburg only increased with time, even as the size of the Jewish population and its needs grew. By the late 1870s, the Ministry of Internal Affairs was questioning whether specifically Jewish philanthropic and educational institutions were necessary in Petersburg at all, since they strengthened the Jews' status as "a distinct corporation."[96] In its published annual report for 1882, the board explained its relatively meager accomplishments by noting tersely that it had "not exceeded the program drawn up for it by the government."[97]

The policy of curtailing the activities of Jewish communal institutions was certainly not unique to Petersburg. In addition to abolishing the kahal throughout the Pale, since the 1860s the tsarist government had sought to eliminate Jewish burial societies, though without much success.[98] What distinguished the case of Jews in Petersburg was the vigor with which the government pursued its aim there.

The government's highly restrictive approach to all Jewish institutions not immediately connected to religious ritual (narrowly understood), first applied in Petersburg, became the explicit model for official policy in respect to Jewish communities everywhere outside the Pale.[99] In this sense, the attempt to reduce Jewish communal life in the Russian interior to purely religious and strictly voluntary functions can be seen as extending the logic of selective integration, according to which residence outside the Pale was con-

95. *Evreiskaia entsiklopediia,* 13: 949.

96. RGIA, f. 821, op. 8, d. 24, l. 82. Similarly, in 1884 Lazar and Anna Berman, a husband and wife in Petersburg who ran a pair of private Jewish schools (one for boys, another for girls), requested that, as in the Pale, their schools receive a portion of the revenues generated by the candle tax. The superindendent of the Petersburg school district responded that since Russian schools were open to Jews and in fact allowed them to have separate lessons in religion, "there can no longer be a compelling need for a separate Jewish school." See RGIA, f. 733, op. 189, d. 170, l. 103.

97. *Otchet pravleniia S.-Peterburgskoi evreiskoi obshchiny za 1882 god* (St. Petersburg, 1884), p. 5.

98. John Klier, "Russkaia voina protiv 'Ḥevra kadisha,'" in D. A. El´iashevich, *Istoriia evreev v Rossii: Problemy istochnikovedeniia i istoriografii* (St. Petersburg, 1993), pp. 109–14.

99. The distinction between communities within and those outside the Pale and Petersburg's role as a model for the latter are mentioned explicitly in official documents; see, e.g., RGIA, f. 821, op. 8, d. 24, l. 35, and d. 164, l. 193.

ditional upon integration into certain social estates. Having left the Pale, Jews in theory were no longer supposed to require the array of services provided by specifically Jewish organizations, from health care to interest-free loans. As an official report by the Ministry of Internal Affairs on the Jews of Petersburg asserted in 1877, "the concept of a distinct 'Jewish community' [*osoboe 'evreiskoe obshchestvo*'], apart from membership by Jews in the existing estates—merchants, meshchane, artisans—has lost its meaning."[100]

THE SYNAGOGUE CONTROVERSY

Perhaps in no other area were relations between the communal governing board and the tsarist government so tangled—and so fraught with symbolism—as in the construction of Petersburg's first synagogue.[101] For the "reformers," this project took precedence over all others: a synagogue in the political and cultural center of the empire would serve as a glorious statement, impressing the Jews' worthiness upon Russian society, the government, and the Jews themselves. Jewish newspapers, in Petersburg as well as other cities, kept their readers regularly informed of developments in the synagogue's planning and construction. As Landau put it,

> A Jewish temple in Petersburg—this is a matter of utmost importance. Everyone understands and agrees with this. And every Jew, no matter where he lives, whether in Petersburg or in Odessa, in the foothills of the Caucasus or the cold snows of Siberia—each will make his full contribution to this great cause . . . , this temple, in which Russian society will become acquainted with the most profound side of Jewish existence: with the Jewish religion![102]

Perhaps unintentionally, Landau's imagery suggests the extent to which the Petersburg Jewish elite, taking a cue from its Russian counterpart, had begun to view the world through an imperial lens, with itself at the center, surrounded by far-flung and diverse peripheries. This vision is particularly striking given that all but a sliver of the empire's expansive territory—including Siberia and the Caucasus—was in fact off limits to the majority of the Jewish population. But the perceived audience for a national synagogue extended even beyond the far reaches of the empire. "The future synagogue in Petersburg," argued Gordon, "must not be inferior in any way to the syn-

100. Ibid., op. 8, d. 24, l. 82.
101. In the following discussion of the synagogue controversy, apart from my own research, I have benefited from previous treatments of certain aspects of this issue by Michael Stanislawski (*For Whom Do I Toil?* p. 131) and V. A. Levin ("Peterburgskaia khoral´naia sinagoga," an unpublished paper kindly provided to me by the author).
102. Landau, "Peterburgskie pis´ma," *Den´*, Dec. 20, 1869, pp. 10–11.

agogues of other countries and capitals."[103] After all, the Russian Empire had by far the world's largest Jewish population, more than all the rest of Europe combined. The frequency with which Petersburg Jews (again like their Russian neighbors) compared themselves and their planned synagogue with their counterparts in West European capitals lends credence to the claim that it was in part concern over Western Jewish opinion, and in particular Adolphe Crémieux's visit to Russia in 1869, that sparked plans for the synagogue's construction.[104]

In a rather different way, comparisons with the West also inspired one of the preeminent Russian art historians and liberal critics of the day, V. V. Stasov (a non-Jew), to launch a public discussion of the future synagogue. Writing in the Petersburg "thick journal" *Evreiskaia Biblioteka* (Jewish Library) in 1872, Stasov noted that "it is somehow embarrassing" that Jews in Petersburg, "right next door to Europe," should not have their own synagogue in which to worship freely and openly. A grand synagogue in the capital would add to Russia's "honor and glory, because it would once again prove that we are increasingly putting an end to our former shameful prejudices [and that] we do not want to lag behind the rest of Europe in the brightness and breadth of [our] attitudes."[105] With its kaleidoscopic range of ethnic and religious groups, the Russian Empire had the potential to far outstrip European countries as a showcase of tolerance, human diversity, and universalist aspirations. For Stasov, a synagogue in Petersburg—alongside the already existing Russian Orthodox, Catholic, Lutheran, Protestant, Armenian, and other churches, as well as a mosque—would reinforce the image of a broad and generous Russian national character.

As one might expect from an art historian, Stasov also had ideas about the proposed synagogue's appearance. To highlight the empire's diversity, it would necessarily have to look distinctively and recognizably Jewish. Much

---

103. TsGIA-SPb, f. 422, op. 1, d. 157, l. 84, quoted in Levin, "Peterburgskaia khoral´naia sinagoga" (see n. 101). For similar views, see Landau, "Peterburgskie pis´ma," *Den´*, no. 24 (1869), p. 379.

104. This argument first appeared in *Razsvet,* June 5, 1880, pp. 882–84. Crémieux, as head of the Alliance Israélite Universelle, had visited Russia in 1869 in part because of reports of widespread famine in the western provinces, where the Jewish population was at its densest. This alone, according to *Razsvet,* was a source of embarrassment to Russian-Jewish notables, who were concerned lest they be seen as incapable of tending to their own flock. But Crémieux went further: after a particularly unceremonious expulsion (during his visit) of a group of Petersburg Jews lacking the proper residence permits, he submitted a formal letter of protest to the Russian government. Several Russian newspapers reacted with indignant cries against foreign interference in domestic affairs, and a leading Jewish newspaper of the time, *Den´*, concurred (May 16, 1869).

105. Stasov, "Po povodu postroiki sinagogi v S.-Peterburge," *Evreiskaia Biblioteka* 2 (1872): 435–36.

of Stasov's argument, in fact, took the form of a polemic against Richard Wagner's recently published anti-Semitic diatribe, *Das Judentum in der Musik,* and defended the idea that the Jews had their own aesthetic styles to draw upon and were not mere parasites of other traditions. For Stasov, an authentically Jewish synagogue would look "Oriental" and "Eastern," built in the Arabic-Moorish style of synagogues in medieval Spain and, more recently, Germany.[106]

However welcome Stasov's sentiments may have been to many of the capital's Jews—and in the context of Russian public discourse in the 1870s his remarks were unusually sympathetic—they nevertheless provoked strong opposition from several prominent Jewish voices. In a private letter to Stasov, the well-known sculptor of Jewish origin Mark Antokol´skii endorsed the call for an authentically Jewish design for the Petersburg synagogue, but questioned whether a Moorish style would meet this goal. "I am concerned," he wrote, "that it not be an imitation of the Berlin synagogue, which was designed in imitation of a Protestant church, which in turn is an imitation of a Catholic church." To follow such a pattern would be "to imitate precisely what we should least of all be imitating."[107]

Yehudah Leib Gordon took nearly the opposite view. In his published response to Stasov, Gordon denied that the Jews had their own distinct architectural style, arguing instead that throughout their history, "the Jews borrowed the style of the dominant nation at any given time and place."[108] Consistent with his well-known slogan—"Be a man in the streets and a Jew at home"—Gordon argued that only the internal aspect of Jewish ritual had ever mattered to the Jews, who were "completely indifferent to the external appearance of their houses of worship . . . as long as it did not contain anything shocking, tendentious, or anti-Jewish."[109] If Jews had once built synagogues in an Arabic style, they did so only because they had lived among

---

106. On the use of Moorish styles in synagogues in Germany, see Harold Hammer-Schenk, *Synagogen in Deutschland: Geschichte einer Baugattung im 19. und 20. Jahrhundert* (Hamburg, 1981), vol. 1.

107. V. V. Stasov, ed., *M. M. Antokol´skii: Ego zhizn´, tvoreniia, pis´ma, i stat´i* (St. Petersburg, 1905), pp. 386–87. I am grateful to Musya Glants for bringing Antokol´skii's letter to my attention.

108. Gordon, "V kakom stile dolzhna byt´ postroena sinagoga v Peterburge?" *Razsvet,* Oct. 11, 1879, p. 190. In his rejoinder to Gordon (the last public episode in this debate), Stasov condemned this notion as "a bizarre slander on the Jewish people." See Stasov, "Otvet g. L. Gordonu," *Razsvet,* Nov. 15, 1879, p. 384.

109. Gordon, "V kakom stile," p. 190. The slogan "Be a man in the streets and a Jew at home" appeared in Gordon's well-known poem "Hakitsah ʿami!" (Awake, My People!), literally as "Be a man in your going out and a Jew in your tents," itself a variation on Deuteronomy 33:18. For a detailed discussion of the meanings of this slogan, see Stanislawski, *For Whom Do I Toil?* pp. 50–52.

Arabs. To reproduce such a style in Petersburg made no more sense than for the Jews to speak Arabic there, rather than Russian. Instead, a synagogue in the Russian capital ought to follow the style of Russian Orthodox churches, exclusive of all explicitly Christian symbols.[110] Nor should a star of David be placed on the synagogue's cupola, since, according to Gordon, Jewish teaching rejects visual representation altogether, and in any case the star of David was a product of "popular superstition" inspired by the Kabalah. In essence, Gordon's response sought to remove all appearances of "Oriental" qualities in Jewish religious practice. Except for the fact that they pray toward the east (in the direction of Jerusalem), Gordon maintained, Jews were not intrinsically an Eastern people.

By implication, then, the Petersburg synagogue was supposed to demonstrate that Judaism was fully compatible with Western norms and traditions. Of course, Gordon's position took for granted that copying the architecture of a Russian Orthodox church would advance this goal, and thus avoided the complex problem of Russia's own shifting identity between East and West. But more important for our purposes, beneath the surface of a scholarly debate about architectural history, Stasov and Gordon had staked out unexpectedly opposed positions on the Jews' proper role in the Russian Empire. Gordon's insistence on complete external assimilation directly undermined Stasov's hope that Russia's glory would reside in its diversity, while Stasov's call for the Jews to emphasize their distinctiveness could only work against Gordon's dream of Jewish integration and acceptance.[111]

While the debate over architectural style was being carried out, another was being waged over the synagogue's location. Where could one find a suitable setting for a synagogue with representational ambitions within Petersburg's already symbol-laden urban landscape, with its grand imperial facades, foreign luxury stores, grimy factories, and crowded tenements? And, one should add, its churches: prerevolutionary Petersburg was a city filled with imposing churches, a fact that considerably complicated the placement of a synagogue. An imperial *ukaz* dating from the reign of Nicholas I instructed that no synagogue in the empire could be built closer to a Russian Orthodox church than 100 *sazhen* (just over 200 yards) if on the same street, or

110. It is worth noting that a decade after Gordon's article appeared, the Moscow Jewish community was ordered by city authorities to replace the immense cupola of its synagogue, apparently in order to reduce its resemblence to a Russian Orthodox church, which, it was feared, might confuse Christian passers-by. See A. Katsnel´son, "Iz martirologa Moskovskoi obshchiny (Moskovskaia sinagoga v 1891–1906 gg.)," *Evreiskaia Starina* 1, no. 2 (1909): 175.

111. On the debate over a Jewish national style in art and architecture, see Mirjam Rainer, "The Awakening of Jewish National Art in Russia," *Jewish Art*, no. 16–17 (1990–91), pp. 98–121. I am grateful to Richard Cohen for bringing this article to my attention. On parallel developments in Russian-Jewish music, see Albert Weisser, *The Modern Renaissance of Jewish Music: Events and Figures, Eastern Europe and America* (New York, 1953).

50 sazhen if on a different street.[112] Stasov was sufficiently concerned about this restriction to recommend to city authorities that it be dropped as archaic. It was not.[113]

The search for a site began in 1869 and lasted over a decade. The seemingly endless delays only fueled accusations within the Jewish community of absenteeism and lethargy on the part of the governing board.[114] In reality, the board's many proposals were invariably taken up and chewed on at length by various departments of the city and imperial administrations, only to be rejected. The first proposal targeted a fashionable site at the intersection of the Fontanka Canal and Gorokhovaia Street, one of the three radial boulevards (including Nevsky Prospect) that gave the downtown area its distinctive layout. The neighborhood with the greatest Jewish settlement, Pod˜iacheskii, as well as a temporary "merchant prayer house," were nearby. But General F. F. Trepov, the Petersburg police commandant (1866–73) and city governor (1873–78), vetoed the plan, citing the fact that important government officials often traveled along Gorokhovaia on their way to the Tsarsko-Selskoe train station, and "it would not be good if masses of Jews were to gather there on Saturdays and Jewish holidays."[115] Trepov proposed instead a site on the outskirts of the city, in the northeastern corner of the Vyborg district, in an area where very few Jews, or anyone else for that matter, lived. The board in turn rejected this idea since it was several miles from Pod˜iacheskii, thus making it impossible for congregants to walk to synagogue on the Sabbath and other holy days.[116]

The board rebounded with a new proposal for another spot near Pod˜iacheskii, on Bol´shaia Masterskaia street (currently Lermontovskii Prospekt). This time Trepov's objections were more explicit: "A Jewish synagogue should not be permitted to be built in a populated part of the city, in order to avoid the gathering there of a mob and the associated filth."[117] This

---

112. *Ukaz ego imperatorskogo Velichestva kasatel´no togo, v kakom razstoianii ot pravoslavnykh tserkvei dolzhny byt´ ustraivaemy evreiskie sinagogi i molitvennyia shkoly* (St. Petersburg, 1844). The decree pertains only to Russian Orthodox churches, and does not mention churches of other denominations. No reasons for the restrictions are given.

113. Stasov, "Po povodu postroiki sinagogi," pp. 436–37.

114. See, e.g., charges against the board leveled in *Razsvet,* June 12, 1880, p. 925, and Landau's fear that continued delays would cause "our provincial brothers to laugh at us and completely lose faith," in *Den´,* Dec. 20, 1870, p. 705.

115. The quotation is Landau's rendering of Trepov's position, in *Den´,* Aug. 1, 1870, p. 527.

116. TsGIA-SPb, f. 422, op. 1, d. 250, l. 1. Although contemporary sources make no such suggestion, it is possible that Trepov was proceding from a bizarre sense of history—or worse. The site he proposed was on Shafirovskii Prospekt (currently Bestuzhevskii Prospekt), named for Pavel Shafirov, a converted Jew who served as a diplomat and was ennobled by Peter the Great. See *Evreiskaia entsiklopediia,* 15: 920.

117. As quoted in the minutes of the communal governing board, TsGIA-SPb, f. 422, op. 1, d. 157, l. 83.

position appeared to place the issue of walking distance in jeopardy; appeals by the board to higher authorities, including Tsar Alexander II, were of no avail.

Trepov's resignation in the wake of his near assassination by the populist Vera Zasulich in 1878 inspired a new round of proposals. Gordon, for one, again addressed himself in public to the issue of the synagogue:

> The masses of the Russian people are like a good-natured, trusting child, who listens to what his elders say. Their "way of thinking" depends on the direction given them from above. Place a Jewish synagogue on Nevsky Prospect and the common Russian, passing by, will take off his hat and cross himself: "Must be, well, holy, if they put it here." But hide it beyond the Narvsky Gates [at the southwestern edge of the city], and he not only will regard the banished synagogue as something foul, but will infer that it is pleasing to God and the authorities to throw out all the yids.[118]

This passage is remarkable in several respects. It graphically illustrates the enduring maskilic habit of looking to the state as both potential ally of the Jews and all-powerful shaper of popular Russian attitudes and behavior. In Gordon's view, moreover, the state's power of persuasion expresses itself not just in the form of Petersburg, the imposing metropolis created by Peter the Great, but of Nevsky Prospect in particular. Granted, by anyone's definition Nevsky was charged with symbolic significance, but in Gordon's telling (mis)reading, it is supposed to be perceived by Russians as a sacred space, in contrast to its more typical reputation as an arena of Western commercial influence, of mixing among disparate social groups, and increasingly of political demonstrations—in a word, of an uncertain modernity.[119]

In any event, as a site for the synagogue Nevsky never came under serious consideration. Trepov's resignation did ease matters, however, and in 1880 the lot on Bol´shaia Masterskaia was approved by all the necessary city and imperial authorities. In the meantime, a pledge campaign among the Jewish financial elite had already secured more than 125,000 rubles in fund-

118. Gordon, "K istorii poseleniia evreev," p. 118. In the same essay (p. 119), Gordon lamented that if only Peter the Great had included tolerance of Jews among the values he imported from the West, "there would not now be a 'Jewish Question'" in Russia.

119. Nevsky's importance in Gordon's mental map of Petersburg emerged again in a letter to Sholem Aleichem, in which Gordon argued that to raise one's children in Yiddish (instead of Russian) "would be like forcing them to promenade down Nevsky Prospect in tattered rags and worn-out shoes" (paraphrased in Stanislawski, *For Whom Do I Toil?* p. 226). For similar Jewish perceptions of Petersburg and Nevsky, see the section "A Window on Russia" in Chapter 3. For an imaginative look at the representation of Nevsky Prospect in Russian literature, see Marshal Berman, *All That Is Solid Melts into Air: The Experience of Modernity* (New York, 1988), pp. 173–286.

ing (as against a projected cost of some 800,000 rubles), with Horace Gintsburg topping the list at 70,000.[120] The governing board convened a jury to review submissions for the synagogue's design, and in the spirit of integration included a non-Jew, none other than V. V. Stasov. Stasov's wide reputation gave him far greater authority than his three fellow jurors, and thus the chance to carry out the ideas he had promoted in his exchanges with Gordon and Antokol'skii. One submission, for example, Stasov rejected out of hand precisely because of its resemblance to a church. More important, he singled out the winning entry, by Leon I. Bakhman (the first Jew to graduate from the Academy of Arts in Petersburg) and I. I. Shaposhnikov (a Russian professor at the academy), "not only for its Arabic style, but in general for its Eastern character. . . . In its cumulative effect the building resembles neither a church . . . nor a mosque."[121]

This was not the end of the matter, however. When the governing board submitted Bakhman and Shaposhnikov's design to the tsar for final approval, Alexander II—in what may have been his last pronouncement vis-à-vis Russian Jewry before his assassination in March 1881—returned it with the terse comment: "Redo the project in more modest dimensions."[122] Even Gordon, who opposed the winning design, was dumbstruck by what he understood this remark to mean: "Jews ought not to assume that they are already full-fledged residents, rather than mere guests." Struggling to maintain his optimism, he could only shake his head at such "inexplicable mistrust."[123]

The synagogue opened its doors in 1893 with a ceremonial dedication, including a customary prayer for the royal family. The cantor recited the "El male rahamim" ("God full of compassion," a prayer for the departed) on behalf of Alexander II, presumably in his capacity as "tsar liberator" rather than as critic of the original plans for the synagogue's construction.[124] Horace Gintsburg, loyal as ever, even commissioned a statue of Alexander II by the sculptor Antokol'skii for the synagogue, but religious principle prevented it from being placed there, and instead it went to the Academy of Fine Arts.[125]

It is difficult to know how much smaller the synagogue was than originally

120. *Otchet pravleniia S.-Peterburgskoi evreiskoi obshchiny za vremia s 10 aprelia 1870 goda po 1 ianvaria 1873 goda*, p. 17. As several commentators noted, the Orthodox and Hasidic camps showed no interest in a grand synagogue, especially one designed to conform to "reformed" ritual practices. See Landau, *Den'*, June 30, 1869, p. 73.

121. TsGIA-SPb, f. 422, op. 1, d. 7, ll. 1–4; *Evreiskaia entsiklopediia*, 13: 946.

122. TsGIA-SPb, f. 422, op. 1, d. 7, l. 43.

123. Gordon, "K istorii poseleniia evreev," p. 46.

124. *Seder ha-ʿavodah le-hanukat bet ʾadonai le-ʿadat yisrael be-kiryat melekh rav sʾt peterburg* (St. Petersburg, 1893), pp. 10, 14.

125. Sliozberg, *Baron G. O. Gintsburg*, p. 59.

Figure 13. St. Petersburg Choral Synagogue.

מורה

Figure 14. Dedication ceremony at the St. Petersburg Choral
Synagogue, 1893. (Courtesy of V. A. Levin.) "All of a sudden
two gentlemen in top hats, splendidly dressed and exuding
wealth, with the refined movements of wordly people, touch
the heavy book, step out of the circle and on behalf of everyone, with the authorization and commission of everyone, perform some kind of honor, the principal thing in the ceremony.
Who is that? Baron Gintsburg. And that? Varshavskii" (Osip
Mandel´shtam, "Shum Vremeni," in his *Sobranie sochinenii v
chetyrekh tomakh* [Moscow, 1991], 2: 66).

planned; the cost of construction was just over half the original estimate.[126]
With a reduced seating capacity of 1,200, it was still large by contemporary
standards, but smaller than the two grand synagogues of Odessa (the Brody
and the Bet Knesset Hagadol), as well as the imposing Oranienburg syna-

126. *Evreiskaia entsiklopediia*, 13: 946.

gogue in Berlin. A dozen pseudo minarets and various ornamental details gave the building the desired Eastern flavor—"an exotic fig tree," in the words of the poet Osip Mandel´shtam, who ventured inside only under duress.[127] Services, however, carried a distinctly Western flavor, with named seats for wealthy donors and choral singing. Known officially as the Choral Synagogue (as it is today), for a time the building also bore the more informal name of Baron Gintsburg Synagogue.[128]

127. Mandel´shtam, "Shum vremeni," in his *Sobranie sochineniia,* 2: 66.
128. Beizer, *Jews of St. Petersburg,* p. 106.

Chapter 5

The Geography of Jewish Politics

At the outset of the era of selective integration, Odessa could justly lay claim to being the center of an emerging Russian-Jewish culture, indeed of a self-consciously innovative Jewish modernity in Eastern Europe. During the middle of the nineteenth century, immigrants from elsewhere in the Pale had begun streaming into this frontier city on the Black Sea, creating the fastest-growing Jewish community in the Russian Empire, soon second in size only to that of Warsaw.[1] Ukraine's reputation as the "breadbasket of Europe" depended in no small measure on Odessa's thriving port, where a substantial portion of the grain export business was in the hands of the city's Jewish merchants. Like their counterparts in Petersburg, Odessa's Jews built their communal institutions more or less from scratch, and like the imperial capital, Odessa became a closely watched staging ground for maskilic efforts to reform synagogue practices and communal life in general.[2] In the 1860s, the first Russian-language Jewish newspapers as well as new periodicals in Hebrew and Yiddish were founded there, transforming the city into a center of debate about the future of the Jews in a reformed Russia.

By the 1870s, however, St. Petersburg had displaced Odessa as the headquarters of the struggle for Jewish integration and of an emerging Russian-Jewish culture. Petersburg maintained this role, moreover, until the tsarist state collapsed and the Bolsheviks transferred the capital back to Moscow. St. Petersburg's Jewish community held the lead against considerable odds, including its small size, the internal fault lines that plagued its communal organizations, various state-imposed restrictions on its public activity, and

1. Bauer et al., *Nationalitäten des Russischen Reiches*, 2: 395–409.
2. Zipperstein, *Jews of Odessa*.

eventually the emergence of Jewish movements opposed to gradualism and in some cases to integration itself.

How did a relatively small and isolated community come to assume such a role? To begin with, selective integration produced an extraordinary concentration of wealth and (secular) learning among Petersburg's Jews. The fact that the imperial capital was the nerve center of Russia's political, cultural, and economic life, moreover, fostered analogous ambitions among Jews there, who came to regard themselves as the natural leaders of Russian Jewry as a whole. And while the pogrom that erupted in Odessa in 1871 (and another a decade later) erased a good deal of that city's cosmopolitan luster, in Petersburg collective violence against Jews was unknown. In the imperial capital, Jewish public organizations and periodicals blossomed, their life span measured in years or decades rather than in months, as had often been the case in Odessa. Their members and subscribers, while concentrated in the capital, could also be found throughout the Pale, and unlike the handful of Jewish newspapers published in Odessa, those in Petersburg, as one resident put it, transcended mere *provintsialishkeyt* by concentrating on events and issues relevant to Russian Jewry as a whole.[3]

Geographically, of course, Petersburg seemed an even less likely candidate than Odessa for such a role. Whereas Odessa was located at the extreme southern periphery of the Pale, at a considerable distance from the areas of densest and longest-standing Jewish settlement in the former Polish and Lithuanian territories, Petersburg was entirely outside the Pale, separated by hundreds of miles and by walls of restrictive legislation barring the vast majority of Jews from the Russian interior. In this sense the geography of Jewish life in late imperial Russia differed from that in many other European countries, where over the course of the nineteenth century capital cities became the home not just of Jewish elites but of a substantial portion of the Jewish population. In the eastern half of Europe, however, as the ethnographer Nataliia Iukhneva has noted, ethnic elites commonly developed outside their traditional ethnolinguistic territories, particularly in the great multinational empires.[4] Whether it was Slovenes in Vienna, Serbs in Budapest, or Latvians in Petersburg, the intelligentsias of stateless minorities frequently launched national movements—and in some cases national print languages—from imperial centers far removed from the target population. As one observer reported in the 1880s, "One can say without exaggeration that . . . every national and religious group whose interests are separate from

3. Ginzburg, *Amolike Peterburg*, p. 24. On the flowering of Jewish periodicals in Petersburg in the 1880s, see Slutsky, *Ha-itonut ha-yehudit-rusit ba-mea ha-tsha-esre*, pp. 102–20.

4. Iukhneva, "Peterburg kak tsentr natsional´no-kul´turnykh dvizhenii narodov Rossii," *Etnografiia Peterburga-Leningrada*, no. 1 (1987), pp. 4–12.

those of the state and the ruling church has in Petersburg its secret representatives, its agents, spies, and advocates."[5]

On at least one point, the Petersburg Jewish elite differed from those of other minorities (and from its eventual Zionist and Bundist rivals): it sought to promote not Jewish national distinctiveness, which it regarded as already sufficiently developed, but integration into Russian society. As we have seen, the policy of selective integration was designed with active participation by Jewish elites, who were eager to create tangible incentives for Jews to emerge from their traditional isolation and enter "useful" occupations. Even as they gravitated to the imperial capital, however, the Gintsburgs and other advocates of Jewish integration sought to position themselves as spokesmen for those they had left behind, that is, the Jews of the Pale. The tension involved in this literal and figurative distancing from their putative constituents never disappeared. As one might expect, it found expression in contemporary discourse: while Petersburg Jews often referred imperiously to the Pale as "the provinces," they just as frequently described themselves as a "colony" and the Pale, or individual towns therein, as "home."[6] The language of empire was seemingly inescapable, but for the empire's Jews it was not always clear where to assign center and periphery. For all the talk of the Pale as a new Egypt, from which the chosen might flee in order to resettle in the empire's grand metropolis, those who did so often found themselves in a kind of second diaspora, forever animated by the sense of attachment—desired or not—to the dense web of Jewish life in the Pale.

In the annals of Russian-Jewish history, the complexity and the significance of the relationship between Petersburg and the Pale has often been lost in retrospective shadows cast by the radical Jewish political movements that emerged in the final decades of the nineteenth century. In their search for the sources of modern, autonomous Jewish politics, historians have tended to reduce the Petersburg elites to a passing phenomenon, the last ineffective gasp of the medieval tradition of *shtadlanut* (personal intercession by notables), destined to be swept away by the stronger currents of Jewish nationalism and socialism.[7] In this narrative, the pogroms that erupted across much of the Pale in the early 1880s exposed with maximum clarity the crisis confronting Russian Jewry and the bankruptcy—if not utter irrelevance— of the Petersburg notables' struggle for Jewish integration. This view is by no means an ex post facto invention of historians: it draws directly upon contemporary criticism of Petersburg's Jewish elite as obsolete and self-serving, cut off from the realities of Jewish life in the Pale and from the emerging

---

5. Eckardt, *Aus der Petersburger Gesellschaft*, p. 45.
6. See, e.g., Sliozberg, *Dela minuvshikh dnei*, 3: 136; Ginzburg, *Amolike Peterburg*, p. 111.
7. See, e.g., Vital, *Origins of Zionism*, p. 76; Frankel, *Prophecy and Politics*, pp. 57–64, 74–81.

spirit of populist, not to say democratic, politics. Indeed, attempts to dismiss the notables as a historic anachronism began to surface as early as the 1860s and continued more or less without interruption across the late imperial period, extending through the revolutions of 1905 and 1917 and into the early years of Bolshevik rule.

And therein lies the problem: the Petersburg Jewish notables were constantly being consigned by their critics to the dustbin of history but steadfastly refused to go there. The sheer longevity of opposition toward them suggests, at the very least, that they were of far more than passing importance. What can it mean when, half a century after public criticism of Evzel Gintsburg first surfaced, opponents such as the Zionist Mikhail Aleinikov were still railing in 1918 against "Petersburg Jewish activists" as the "unnatural offspring of discrimination and self-appointment," declaring that henceforth they would "no longer rule over Jewry"? "The role and significance, authority and influence of Jewish Petersburg," Aleinikov intoned, echoing two generations of critics, "has been lost forever."[8]

The antipathies voiced by Aleinikov and his predecessors are undeniably significant for the history of Russian Jewry and the Russian–Jewish encounter. Embedded as they are in contemporary polemics, however, they cannot serve as a reliable description either of the character of the Petersburg elite or of its relation to the Jewish masses of the Pale, whose loyalty the notables' opponents hoped to secure. The goal of the present chapter, therefore, is to take a fresh look at the geography of Jewish politics in the late imperial period. I want to suggest that while the integrationist agenda was put on the defensive in the wake of the pogroms of 1881–82, it was by no means defeated. Across the late imperial period, in fact, Jews from the Pale continued to look to Petersburg notables for leadership and assistance in all arenas of life, large and small. "Whenever there was misfortune, whenever there was a harsh edict, a fire in a Jewish town, or any kind of disaster," recalled one contemporary, "people would turn to Horace Gintsburg. They knew that there, in Petersburg, was the Jewish Baron."[9] The Petersburg elites not only survived the crisis of the pogroms but reinvented themselves in a thoroughly modern idiom.

"BROTHERS IN THE PALACE"

Ever since the Jews had become subjects of the Russian Empire at the end of the eighteenth century, official and unofficial deputies representing in-

---

8. *Rassvet*, no. 9 (March 1918), p. 8, quoted in Mikhael Beizer, *Evrei Leningrada, 1917–1939: Natsional'naia zhizn' i sovetizatsiia* (Jerusalem, 1999), p. 54.

9. Ginzburg, *Historishe verk*, 2: 144.

dividual Jewish communities or religious factions had journeyed to the capital to defend their interests against excessive intrusion by the state or by local rivals.[10] By the mid–nineteenth century, when Evzel Gintsburg and his fellow merchants were already regular visitors to the imperial capital, more than one provincial governor complained that Jews in the Pale were learning of new laws well in advance of their publication, and in some cases before the governors themselves were informed.[11]

In the wake of selective integration, locally chosen deputies from the Pale were largely eclipsed by self-appointed representatives on permanent location in the capital, who claimed to speak for the empire's entire Jewish population. As one newspaper put it in 1880:

> We Petersburg Jews embody . . . so to speak the *fine fleur* of Russian Jewry. Here are concentrated more or less all of our best intellectual forces, people who occupy by no means the last place in the fields of law, medicine, and scholarship in general, people active in the press. Here there are material resources as well. Here, finally, under the mutual influence of common interests, the line that everywhere separates Jewish from non-Jewish society is not so sharp. . . . To whom, one asks, should be put the demand for a rapid and expedient reorganization of Russian Jewry, if not to us? Who, if not we, ought to realize these demands with the necessary effort and the required energy?[12]

Even their critics grudgingly acknowledged that the Petersburg elites had become the focus of enormous hopes among broad segments of the Jewish population in the Pale. As the partisan of orthodox rabbinical authority Ya'akov Halevi Lifshitz lamented, "In the most recent period, ever since there arose among our people the great ones and the enlightened ones, the people began to say: 'Now we have brothers in the palace'. . . , so that only they were deemed fit for public activity, and it was to them that the people looked for salvation."[13] At the pinnacle of this elite, of course, stood the Gintsburg dynasty. If not literally "in the palace," the Gintsburgs enjoyed unparalleled access to the upper echelons of the tsarist bureaucracy. Having successfully established themselves and their banking house in the Russian capital, they in no way retreated from their assumed role as spokesmen for what Horace Gintsburg had taken to calling "my Jews."[14] On the contrary, during the 1860s and 1870s they continued to press the tsarist government to expand the range of social groups subject to selective integration. An 1862 petition from

10. Iulii Gessen, "'Deputaty evreiskogo naroda' pri Aleksandre I: Po arkhivnym istochnikam," *Evreiskaia Starina* 1, no. 3 (1909): 17–29, and no. 4 (1909): 196–206.

11. RGIA, f. 1269, op. 1, d. 40, ll. 1–3, 10; d. 136, ll. 105–7, 190–94.

12. *Razsvet*, May 15, 1880, p. 764.

13. Lifshitz, *Zikhron Ya'akov*, 2: 188, quoted in Lederhendler, *Road to Modern Jewish Politics*, p. 79.

14. G. B. Sliozberg, "Baron G. O. Gintsburg," p. 111.

Evzel Gintsburg, for example, bluntly criticized the "excessively slow pace" of reform, noting that only "a very small number" of Jews had as yet reaped tangible benefits from the new turn in official policy.[15] In 1866, Gintsburg together with nine other merchants and honored citizens petitioned to extend selective integration to the rapidly growing number of Jewish graduates of Russian gymnasia, and urged that merchants of the lower guilds and additional categories of artisans be included as well.[16] Other petitioners requested rights for additional groups within the Jewish population.[17]

Whether because of a pragmatic belief that Russia's rulers were not yet prepared to grant civil rights to all Jews or because they themselves continued to favor the differential granting of rights as an instrument of internal Jewish reform, Jewish elites in Petersburg worked strictly within the paradigm of selective integration, urging only that its scope be widened.[18] Even those bold enough to use the term "emancipation"—as did the Gintsburgs—continued to assert that rights should be granted only to "useful citizens."[19] In fact, this approach at first worked reasonably well. Evzel Gintsburg's 1862 petition, for example, was forwarded by the Jewish Committee with a request for comments to over two dozen senior officials, including several ministers, the head of the Holy Synod, and numerous provincial governors and governors general.[20] The positive evaluation it received from the majority of respondents soon led to a modest broadening of selective integration, to include certain categories of artisans, veterans of Nicholas I's army, and a wide array of students in Russia's institutions of higher education.

---

15. RGIA, f. 821, op. 9, d. 77, ll. 8, 13. This copy of the petition is undated, but another copy preserved from Gintsburg's personal papers is dated July 6, 1862. See YIVO, RG 89, folder 756, doc. 27. According to Sliozberg (*Dela minuvshikh dnei,* 1: 301), Emanuel Levin was the actual author of the petition.

16. RGIA, f. 821, op. 9, d. 77, ll. 227–32. This petition begins with the highly atypical proposition that henceforth the principle of gradualism should apply to the rights granted (Jews as a group should gradually receive more and more rights) rather than dividing the Jewish population into those with equal rights and those without. It quickly retreats, however, to the standard approach based on different rights for different, if broader, categories within the Jewish population.

17. See, e.g., RGIA, f. 821, op. 9, d. 77, ll. 251–64, and d. 78, ll. 1–33.

18. Apologists for the Gintsburgs tended to stress their pragmatism as the motive for their requesting less than full emancipation; see, e.g., Ginzburg, *Historishe verk,* 2: 126.

19. E. Gintsburg, "Zapiska, predstavlennaia pochetnym grazhdaninom Ginzburgom [*sic*], po voprosu o postepennoi emansipatsii russkogo Evreiskogo naseleniia," in *Materialy Komissii po ustroistvu byta evreev* (St. Petersburg, 1879), pt. 1, item 15. For use of the term "useful citizens," see YIVO, RG 89, folder 756, doc. 59, p. 3.

20. For the responses of various officials, see RGIA, f. 821, op. 9, d. 77, ll. 51–265. According to Genrikh Sliozberg, the 1862 Gintsburg petition was originally composed by Emanuel Levin and was forwarded to all governors general of the Pale. Judging by what was preserved in the archives, however, not all governors general responded. See Sliozberg, *Dela minuvshikh dnei,* 1: 301.

A number of tsarist officials along with a significant portion of the Reform-era Russian press proposed reforms more far-reaching than those put forth by Jewish notables. In 1863, for example, the ministers of enlightenment and finance endorsed the call for all Jewish merchants and all graduates of secondary schools to be granted rights equal to those of their Russian counterparts. At least one provincial governor privately urged that rights be granted to Jews "not only to the extent requested by Gintsburg but to the extent already in effect for subjects of all other confessions," a move that would have abolished the Pale.[21] Over the course of the 1860s, newspapers ranging from the provincial *Kievlianin* (Kievan) and *Vilenskii Vestnik* (Vilna Herald) to the *Sankt-Peterburgskie Vedomosti* similarly called for an end to the Pale.[22] The arguments put forth were not always philo-Semitic; they ranged from the need to emulate European states whose emancipated Jewish citizens had contributed to economic growth to the desire to lower the concentration of Jews, with all their allegedly negative influences, within the territory of the Pale.[23]

This was not the first time individual tsarist officials went further than Jewish notables in their advocacy of increased rights for Jews.[24] What was new, however, was the fact that in the comparatively open atmosphere of the 1860s, the unexpected constellation of views became public knowledge via the press. Writing in the Odessa Jewish weekly *Den´*, for example, Adolf Landau castigated the notables for their timidity:

> Even Russian public opinion, insofar as it is expressed in the periodical press, requests far more for the Jews than the Jews themselves request. This is a remarkable fact, which demonstrates the destructive effect of enduring discrimination upon the character of its victims. They become intimidated creatures who dare not even wish for themselves what others request on their behalf.[25]

To be sure, those journalists and tsarist officials who called for the abolition of the Pale had no more success in shaping official policy than did the notables. As Landau was soon forced to concede, it was unclear whether bolder demands from Jewish notables would have secured more rights, or none at all.[26] Nevertheless, the public nature of Landau's criticism and the fact that he

21. RGIA, f. 821, op. 9, d. 77, ll. 51–52, 137. The quotation comes from the response to Gintsburg's 1862 petition by Count Sivers, governor general of Kharkov province, located just outside the Pale.

22. Klier, *Imperial Russia's Jewish Question*, pp. 66, 198, 373–75.

23. See, e.g., RGIA, f. 821, op. 9, d. 77, ll. 88–143; d. 78, ll. 67–68.

24. See Chapter 2, n. 45.

25. Landau, "Peterburgskie pis´ma," *Den´*, no. 10 (1869), p. 157.

26. Landau, "Peterburgskie pis´ma," *Den´*, no. 19 (1869), p. 297.

had obtained copies of supposedly confidential memoranda and petitions signaled the emergence of a new factor in the relationship between Petersburg and the Pale: the contest for public opinion.[27]

As they freely admitted, the Petersburg notables preferred to manage Jewish affairs discreetly, away from what Emanuel Levin called the "passions of the parties."[28] Before the Reform era, Evzel Gintsburg was rarely mentioned in print, and then usually under a pseudonym. In Abraham Mapu's roman à clef 'Ayit tsavu'a (Painted Bird), for example, he makes a cameo appearance as "Emanuel the Great," a heroic intercessor on behalf of the Jews, while in the Petersburg weekly Illiustriatsiia he appeared in a less flattering light as the affluent "Mr. N."[29] Once installed in the capital in the 1860s, however, the Gintsburgs became increasingly public figures, subject for the first time to criticism from some of their supposed constituents. At a time when Jewish emancipation appeared a natural corollary of the emancipation of the serfs, virtually every meeting between government officials and Jewish notables inspired extravagant hopes among the Jewish population. With hindsight, moreover, it seems clear that the fantasy of having "brothers in the palace" was by no means limited to the Jewish masses. Indeed, it may have been strongest among those intellectuals who initially looked to the notables as a vehicle for fundamental reform of Jewish mores and legal status—and whose disappointment at the comparatively modest results of the notables' efforts transformed them into their most vocal critics.

Unrealized hopes shadowed the relationship between Petersburg and the Pale almost from the moment the notables established themselves in the imperial capital. In some cases, expectations were simply unrealistic. In others, a genuine divergence of viewpoint developed between the notables and the masses whose interests they claimed to represent.

The Rabbinical Commission that convened in Petersburg in 1861–62, for example, initially inspired visions among reformers of a kind of supreme court of the Haskalah, empowered both to impose sweeping reforms on Jewish communities across the Pale and to articulate the case for Jewish rights before the tsarist regime. The presence of Evzel Gintsburg on the commis-

---

27. For a pioneering investigation of the role of public opinion, real or imagined, in Russian-Jewish society during the second half of the nineteenth century, see Lederhendler's *Road to Modern Jewish Politics.*

28. Levin, "Zapiska," p. 302.

29. On Mapu's novel, see Lederhendler, *Road to Modern Jewish Politics,* p. 82. The figurative meaning of the novel's title is "hypocrite," a term that applies to the protagonist rather than to the character of Emanuel. Mapu's brother Metatyahu was a member of Evzel Gintsburg's staff; see "Mémoire du baron Alexandre de Gunzburg," p. 19. On the coded reference to Gintsburg in *Illiustriatsiia,* see Klier, *Imperial Russia's Jewish Question,* p. 51. Additional references to Gintsburg in the contemporary Jewish press are noted in Lederhendler, *Road to Modern Jewish Politics,* p. 207n116.

sion only heightened expectations of a breakthrough. Tsarist authorities saw things differently, however, and restricted the commission's work to strictly religious (as opposed to civic or political) matters, an area where the majority of members, including Gintsburg, proved reluctant to dictate change from above. After examining a total of ten cases, the commission disbanded without noticeable effect. When it reconvened seventeen years later, with Horace Gintsburg taking the place of his recently deceased father, expectations swelled again, only to be frustrated once more by the commission's narrow purview.[30]

Similarly grand hopes for both internal Jewish reform and legal equality attended the founding of the Society for the Spread of Enlightenment among the Jews of Russia (commonly known by its Russian acronym, OPE).[31] Inaugurated in Petersburg in 1863 by a coalition of wealthy merchants, including Evzel Gintsburg, the sugar magnate A. M. Brodskii, and the financier L. M. Rosenthal, the society was the first and longest-lasting public Jewish organization in Russia. Its members included not just plutocrats but prominent intellectuals, as well as several high-level tsarist officials. From the very beginning, as John Klier has shown, each of the OPE's constituencies had its own distinct agenda. Old-style maskilim longed for patronage for scholarly and literary works in Hebrew, while a younger generation of Jewish reformers imagined the society as a central command post in the *Kulturkampf* against the religious obscurantism of the Jewish masses.[32] Across the Pale, the Jewish masses demonstrated their own hopes for the society by flooding it with personal requests for aid in all matters large and small, from tuition assistance to helping secure residence rights for individuals or groups. Many such requests went far beyond the scope of activity permitted by the society's charter. Actual membership levels, in the meantime, remained low even among the OPE's supporters, partly because of the substantial dues required. During the 1860s and 1870s there were never more than 500 members at any given time, roughly half of whom lived in Petersburg—a condition that only reinforced the society's image as distant and elitist.[33] Before the turn of the century, the society's only real success in putting down institutional roots in "the provinces" occurred in Odessa, where an affiliate opened in 1867. Other attempts at grass-roots growth were blocked by local or imperial authorities.[34]

30. ChaeRan Freeze, "Making and Unmaking the Jewish Family," pp. 143–44, 426–31; Lederhendler, *Road to Modern Jewish Politics,* pp. 73, 150. Freeze argues that the 1879 Rabbinical Commission did have a significant impact on Jewish divorce law, at least in theory.

31. Tcherikover, *Istoriia Obshchestva dlia rasprostraneniia prosveshcheniia,* p. 29.

32. Klier, *Imperial Russia's Jewish Question,* pp. 245–62.

33. See, e.g., *Otchet Obshchestva rasprostraneniia prosveshcheniia mezhdy evreiami v Rossii za 1875 god* (St. Petersburg, 1876), pp. 26–31.

34. Klier, *Imperial Russia's Jewish Question,* p. 264.

Lack of consensus about the OPE's mission—what "enlightenment" consisted of, to whom it should be addressed, and in what language—produced widespread impatience among Jews eager for reform. Contemporary criticism of the society's alleged political timidity has tainted its image ever since, leaving the impression of an ineffective, cravenly assimilationist organization.[35] It is worth noting, however, that from the beginning, the society's wealthy founders had in mind a program more philanthropic than political. Critics tended to focus far more on what members had failed to say or do than on their actual accomplishments, and in particular on how they were spending their money. For the OPE became in essence an organization devoted to financial aid for Jewish students, and as Chapter 6 will demonstrate, in this—in contrast to its other ventures—it proved enormously successful.

While reform-minded critics contended that the society was doing too little, others, inspired by darker visions, insisted that it was doing too much. Iakov Brafman, an apostate Jew and ardent opponent of all forms of Jewish communal authority, was the first to attack the society as a covert substitute for the banned kahal, a would-be governing institution for Russian Jewry as a whole. When Brafman's accusations found a receptive audience in the conservative Russian press, their intensity only increased. By the mid-1870s, the OPE was being demonized in the pages of *Golos* as the Russian arm of the Paris-based Alliance Israélite Universelle, part of an alleged international Jewish plot to undermine Christian civilization.[36] Judeophobic newspapers began to pounce on any form of Pale-wide coordination as an act of conspiracy, forcing the society to adopt an increasingly defensive posture, even as it faced charges of inactivity from Jewish reformers.[37]

THE VILNA COMMISSION

Brafman also helped trigger an episode that elicited the first open dissent by Jews in the Pale concerning the policy of integration, and that therefore

---

35. In 1870, Adolf Landau, frustrated by the OPE's failure to become a forum for public debate, urged that it disband; twenty years later, Simon Dubnov described the society as "barely alive." See Landau, "Peterburgskie pis´ma," *Den´*, no. 8 (1870), p. 126; Dubnov, "Literaturnaia letopis´: Itogi obshchestva prosveshcheniia evreev," *Voskhod*, no. 10 (1891), p. 41. In his memoirs, Dubnov maintained his negative assessment of the society's "merely philanthropic" mission: see Dubnov, *Kniga Zhizni*, 1: 119. For additional expressions of disappointment, see Klier, *Imperial Russia's Jewish Question*, pp. 258–59.

36. Klier, *Imperial Russia's Jewish Question*, p. 261.

37. In 1872 OPE member Avram Neiman petitioned the Ministry of Internal Affairs to bar *Golos* from publishing articles that "openly strive to incite popular passions against the Jews," and raised the possibility of a lawsuit. YIVO, RG 89, folder 757, doc. 85, p. 1. In 1873 Emanuel Levin noted in a memorandum to Horace Gintsburg that enemies of the Jews were winning the battle for public opinion in Russia. See ibid., doc. 92, pp. 1–3.

tested the commitment to that policy on the part of the Petersburg elite. In 1866, Brafman's accusation that the kahal survived as a secret brotherhood mired in religious fanaticism and fiscal abuse led Rabbi Ya'akov Barit of Vilna to request an official investigation in order to repudiate the charge. Thus was born the so-called Vilna Commission.[38] The governor general of Vilna, Count E. T. Baranov, was already convinced of the truth of Brafman's charges, and wanted not just an inquiry but an opportunity to dismantle Jewish communal separatism once and for all. The "Baranov Circular," published in 1867—well before the commission had completed its work—called for the complete merging of Jewish communal institutions into those of the surrounding population, in both urban and rural areas. The Jews' "privileged position," argued Baranov, whereby they remained a distinct entity in matters pertaining to taxation (including internal taxes) and military service, had to end.[39] So did the long-standing fiction that allowed rural Jews to be counted as members of urban communities; henceforth they were to be merged into the peasant estate, where they would be subject to corporate institutions (*volosti*) established for peasants by the 1861 emancipation decree.

When Baranov was unexpectedly replaced in 1868, local Jewish leaders in Vilna persuaded the new governor general, A. L. Potapov, to convene a delegation of Jews to respond to the Brafman-Baranov proposals. Delegates were to be selected by Jewish communities in Vilna and the surrounding provincial capitals. As in the case of the Rabbinical Commission, the prospect of a quasi-representative body deliberating on issues central to Jewish life stimulated enormous interest—as well as jockeying for influence—among Jews of all stripes.[40] A dozen delegates gathered in Vilna in October 1869, hailing from Grodno, Kovno, Minsk, Vilna, and Vitebsk. They were accompanied by an unknown number of self-appointed "observers" intent on monitoring the delegation's activities, including Rabbi Israel Salanter, leader of the orthodox *musar* movement, and Alexander Tsederbaum, the editor of the weekly *Ha-Melits*, which did much to stir up public interest in the commission's proceedings.[41]

One of the two delegates "representing" Vilna was in fact Emanuel Levin,

38. The story of the Vilna Commission has been told a number of times, most recently and comprehensively by Eli Lederhendler (*Road to Modern Jewish Politics*, pp. 142–45) and John Klier (*Imperial Russia's Jewish Question*, pp. 173–81). My account incorporates previously untapped archival material from YIVO and uses the commission to shed light on the relationship between Jewish elites in Petersburg and their putative constituents in the Pale.

39. "Tsirkuliar b[yvshego] glavnogo Nachal'nika Severo-zapadnogo kraia, grafa E. T. Baranova," reprinted in Iakov Brafman, *Kniga Kagala* (Vilna, 1869), pp. 156–58. The circular was originally published in *Vilenskie Gubernskie Vedomosti*, no. 92 (1867).

40. YIVO, RG 89, folder 756, doc. 68, p. 3.

41. For a complete list of participants, official as well as unofficial, see ibid., pp. 3–22.

Figure 15. Delegates to the Vilna Commission of 1869. At the closing
ceremony, Governor General A. L. Potapov presented each delegate with
a copy of this photograph. As unofficial head of the delegation, Emanuel
Levin presented Potapov with a finely bound copy of his translation into
Russian of *Pirkei 'Avot*, the mishnaic ethical treatise. Seated from left to
right are M. Solomonov (representing the Jewish community of Minsk),
S. Bul´kovshtein (Grodno), Rabbi Ya'akov Barit (Vilna), L. Sel´tser
(Vitebsk), and S. Fogel´son (Vitebsk); standing from left to right are
Rabbi Zalkind Minor (Minsk), I. Levi (Kovno), G. Shapir, M. Knorozovskii
(Grodno), and Emanuel Levin (Vilna).

who had no particular connection to the city, having grown up in Minsk and
lived in Petersburg since 1859 as secretary to the Gintsburgs and (as of 1863)
to the Society for the Spread of Enlightenment. It was probably Evzel Gintsburg who arranged for Levin not only to participate but to serve as de facto
head of the Jewish delegation. Levin alone enjoyed privileged access to the
commission's chairman, P. N. Spasskii, who informed him that Governor
General Potapov would be eavesdropping on the proceedings from a con-
cealed adjacent room. It was Levin who addressed the crowds of Vilna Jews
anxious to learn of the commission's work, and Levin who, by his own account,
was constantly trailed by Tsederbaum, ever eager for breaking news. Levin
also became the focus of envy on the part of the Gentile population of Vilna:

They expressed this openly, saying that if it had been an issue concerning them, all the policies would have been worked out behind closed doors, without asking anyone, while the Jews were honored with an invitation to send delegates. This envy came to the fore whenever I arrived [for a meeting] or was walking down the street. People would point at me, saying, "Look, there's the president of the Jewish delegation!"[42]

As John Klier has pointed out, the fact that elected Jewish delegates were invited to respond to the Vilna Commission's findings was indeed extraordinary.[43] The opinions of individual Jews had certainly counted in previous government committees. Indeed, in the case of Kiselev's Jewish Committee, I have suggested, they played a decisive role. With the exception of the rabbinical commissions, however, those opinions had never been actively solicited, and certainly not in such a nominally democratic fashion. Equally unprecedented was the fact that the deliberations of the Vilna Commission were open to public scrutiny via the press. Both factors—the calling forth of Jewish opinion and its widespread publicity—were to have important reverberations for the relationship between Petersburg's Jewish notables and the masses of the Pale.

Jewish reactions to Levin, whom everyone regarded as the plenipotentiary of the Petersburg notables, were decidedly mixed. On the one hand, his success in neutralizing Brafman's attacks on Jewish religious practices gained him considerable popularity. A celebratory crowd formed outside Levin's quarters after the commission, at its third meeting with the Jewish delegation, declared religious issues outside its purview.[44] For the hopeful, events in Vilna suggested a new possibility for consensus among traditionalist and maskilic leaders when vital Jewish interests were threatened.[45] Levin's response to Baranov's proposed merging of Jewish and Gentile communal institutions, on the other hand, proved far more contentious. For Levin and the Petersburg notables, this was an extraordinarily delicate issue, since in principle Baranov's proposals were entirely consistent with the policy of selective integration. Indeed, Levin regarded them as "an essential step toward emancipation."[46] In certain key respects, however—as Levin and many others recognized—they involved a form of integration and equality that was clearly disadvantageous for Jews. Complete integration into the corporative institutions of the surrounding Gentile population, for example, could easily increase the Jews' vulnerability when it came time for

42. Ibid., p. 15.
43. Klier, *Imperial Russia's Jewish Question*, p. 174.
44. YIVO, RG 89, folder 756, doc. 68, p. 14.
45. Lederhendler, *Road to Modern Jewish Politics*, pp. 142–45.
46. YIVO, RG 89, folder 756, doc. 68, p. 16.

local communities to apportion taxes or select draftees for the army. In addition, Jews were hardly likely to gain from the merging of charitable organizations, since, as Levin noted, most Jewish communities already sponsored (and funded) a far more elaborate network of such organizations than did their Gentile counterparts.[47] Jewish law, moreover, prohibited Jews from accepting certain forms of assistance from non-Jews.[48] The disadvantages of integration were especially apparent in rural communities, where relatively small numbers of Jews faced an ocean of impoverished peasants, only recently liberated from centuries of near slavery and still subject to customary peasant law.

The majority of Jewish delegates assembled in Vilna vehemently opposed Baranov's proposed merger in both urban and rural settings, preferring a state of affairs that one could roughly characterize as separate but equal. From Levin's perspective, this was a result of intense pressure from "backward Orthodox" elements and "individuals who profited from their control over communal affairs, [who] were not at all eager to abandon Jewish communal autonomy." Opponents delivered rousing sermons in synagogues and prayer houses, and at one point an apparently well-rehearsed crowd appeared at Levin's door to announce, "We have come to request of Mr. Levin that we be permitted to remain Jews."[49] Levin, for his part, was eager to demonstrate to the government that Jews could be constructive partners in the process of integration. To be sure, he rejected outright those aspects of Baranov's circular that violated the principle of equality, such as the stipulation that Christians were to retain the majority of seats in institutions of local government, and the ban on Jewish ownership of rural land.[50] He also expressed misgivings regarding the abolition of Jewish charitable organizations and of the Jews' right to administer the military draft among themselves. For Levin, however, and for the Petersburg notables whose views he represented, the basic idea behind the Baranov proposal was not only sound but essential to the progress of Jewish integration. "First, out of principle, and second, out of a desire not to compromise the delegation in the eyes of the administration," Levin concluded that delegates ought to endorse the proposal to merge urban Jewish and Gentile communities, on the condition that Jewish reli-

47. Recent scholarship has confirmed the extraordinarily high proportion of charitable organizations among Jews as compared to other ethnic and religious groups in late nineteenth-century Russia. See Adele Lindenmeyr, *Poverty Is Not a Vice: Charity, Society, and the State in Imperial Russia* (Princeton, 1996), pp. 203–4.

48. YIVO, RG 89, folder 756, doc. 68, p. 17.

49. Ibid., p. 28.

50. "Tsirkuliar b[yvshego] glavnogo Nachal'nika Severo-zapadnogo kraia, grafa E. T. Baranova," in Brafman, *Kniga Kagala*, p. 157. For Levin's position, see YIVO, RG 89, folder 756, doc. 68, p. 16–18.

gious institutions—including charitable groups—be left undisturbed, and that local political representation be established without regard to religion.[51]

Another principle, of course, namely that of majority rule among the Jewish delegates who had gathered in Vilna, threatened to torpedo Levin's plan. "I admit," he later recalled, "that this was the most difficult part of my assignment. What would the commission have done, what would the governor general have thought of us [i.e., the Jewish delegates], if we had departed without having reached a consensus?" Surviving accounts of how Levin resolved this conundrum vary widely. Levin himself maintained, improbably, that he secured the delegation's unanimous consent to his proposal, a feat he described as nearly miraculous, given the "well-known" fact that "as soon as three Jews get together, there can be no agreement."[52]

Other accounts suggest a more ambiguous outcome. M. L. Knorozovskii, one of the Jewish delegates from Grodno, publicly criticized Levin's "self-appointed" position and tactical maneuvering.[53] In a closing statement to Governor General Potapov, a group of delegates sharply distanced themselves from the aims and methods of the Petersburg Jewish elite. Responding both to a recent petition by Evzel Gintsburg requesting equal rights for Jews with higher education and to Levin's intervention in Vilna, the group declared,

> Several of our co-religionists in the capital have petitioned for a small number of educated Jews to be permitted to settle in Russia. We do not share this view. We consider the broadening of the rights of the *few* incommensurate with the suffering of the *masses*. We also declare ourselves not in solidarity with certain other individuals who, from afar, and without consulting us, are trying to use inappropriate means to help us.[54]

While hardly a full-fledged revolt, the delegates' resentment and impatience vis-à-vis the notables were a portent of things to come.[55] It is worth noting,

51. YIVO, RG 89, folder 756, doc. 68, p. 28.
52. Ibid., pp. 29, 30.
53. Ex-deputat, "O deiatel´nosti byvshei vilenskoi delegatsii," *Den´*, Jan. 10, 1870, quoted in Klier, *Imperial Russia's Jewish Question*, p. 472n38.
54. YIVO, RG 89, folder 756, doc. 73, p. 2 (emphasis in original). The Tcherikover Collection inventory attributes this document, I believe mistakenly, to Emanuel Levin. Its wording is nearly identical to what the historian Iulii Gessen described as a letter to Governor General Potapov from a group of Jewish delegates at Vilna. See Gessen, "Iz letopisi minuvshogo: Vilenskaia komissiia po ustroistvu byta evreev, 1866–1869 gg.," *Perezhitoe* 2 (1910): 306.
55. The inability and/or failure of the Petersburg Jewish elite to respond effectively to the famine that struck large numbers of Jewish communities in Lithuania in 1869 provoked similar expressions of frustration at roughly the same time. See Eli Lederhendler, "Modernity without Emancipation or Assimilation? The Case of Russian Jewry," in Frankel and Zipperstein, *Assimilation and Community*, p. 334.

however, that as early as 1862, Evzel Gintsburg had privately expressed a similar impatience with the slow progress of selective integration, and had repeated that sentiment in numerous petitions to the tsarist regime during subsequent years. In addition, by focusing on the unequal distribution of residential rights among Jews, the delegates in Vilna glossed over their main source of contention with Levin, namely, the extent to which integration should apply not only to individuals but to communal institutions. Evzel Gintsburg, for his part, continued to lobby for further integration, at least in urban settings. In an 1873 memorandum, for example, he proposed that the tsarist state cease to treat Jewish communities as separate legal entities. Records of birth, death, marriage, and divorce, he argued, should be kept not by rabbis but by town councils; the tax on kosher meat should be abolished (the governing board of the Petersburg Jewish community, it will be recalled, had just renounced the tax on kosher meat as a source of revenue) in favor of a poll tax; and individual Jews should enjoy all the rights of the urban social estates to which they belonged.[56]

In the end, neither Baranov's circular nor the Vilna Commission, nor for that matter Gintsburg's petitions, had any discernible impact on the relationship between Jewish communal institutions and those belonging to other entities, whether estates, towns, or *volosti*. For all its professed opposition to Jewish separatism, the tsarist regime proved profoundly reluctant to increase the Jewish presence among peasants. Even the Jewish agricultural colonies established at various times across the nineteenth century, whose aim was to transform Jews into peasants, were kept rigidly separate from peasant institutions.[57] If anything, the abolition of serfdom, which exposed tens of millions of peasants to the perils and opportunities of an emerging market economy, heightened rather than reduced official anxiety about the presence of Jews in the Russian heartland.

With regard to communal integration in urban settings, the empire-wide municipal reform of 1870—preparation for which had begun before the Vilna Commission was convened—followed a similarly conservative line. Although henceforth Jews would no longer constitute a separate voting bloc in municipal elections, they would continue to be limited to a maximum of one-third of the seats in local governing institutions, regardless of their proportion of the local population, and were barred from holding the office of mayor (*gorodskoi golova*). The municipal reform also left fully intact the separate legal and fiscal status of individual Jewish communities.[58]

56. RGIA, f.821, op. 9, d. 100, ll. 432–35.
57. Sliozberg, *Dela minuvshikh dnei*, 1: 295.
58. *Evreiskaia entsiklopediia*, 6: 713–16.

MILITARY SERVICE

In a similar fashion, the controversies regarding military service that swirled around the Vilna Commission were eclipsed by the Military Reform of 1874, and in a way that again cast the diverging viewpoints of the Petersburg notables and the Jewish masses of the Pale into sharp relief. Since 1827, when mandatory military service was first imposed on the empire's Jews, no arena of integration had produced greater Jewish resistance. Although the practice of seizing minors had ceased in 1856, the traumatic memory of the cantonist experience—along with the continued drafting of non-minors for service in the imperial army—remained a notable source of anxiety in Russian-Jewish life for generations thereafter.[59] Under Alexander II and his reform-minded minister of war, Dmitrii Miliutin, Russia's army was struggling to transform itself into a *vsesoslovnaia* (all-estate) organization, based on universal male service and promotion according to merit rather than birth. For the Petersburg Jewish notables, as indeed for anyone who believed that Jews should earn emancipation by demonstrating their utility to the state, Jewish military service appeared to offer the strongest argument for expanded rights. With this quid pro quo in mind, Horace Gintsburg lobbied strenuously against government officials who sought to exclude Jews from the draft, urging instead that Russia's reformed army treat Jews no differently than other subjects.[60]

Gintsburg also lobbied Russian Jews themselves to accept military service as a prerequisite of equality. In a highly unusual gesture, he published an open letter in 1874 on the front page of the Hebrew weekly *Ha-Magid* praising the recent military reform and condemning Jews who sought by fraudulent means to escape service in the army. Henceforth, he announced, all Jewish veterans "will be full citizens, partaking of all the rights of the state, like all soldiers who have served." In Gintsburg's view, the 1867 decree granting rights to Jewish veterans of Nicholas I's army equal to those of Gentile veterans, including the right to reside throughout the empire, was now to apply to all Jewish veterans under the new system of universal male conscription:

> Your eyes have seen that the new law regarding military service . . . does not distinguish between Israel and the nations. Our merciful ruler did not withhold his righteousness and truth from us, he has faith in us and has rewarded us in advance of the deed. . . . The government will find a way to detect the

59. Litvak, "Literary Response to Conscription."
60. RGIA, f. 821, op. 9, d. 103, ll. 216–17; for further evidence of the importance Gintsburg attached to Jewish military service, see Sliozberg, *Baron G. O. Gintsburg*, pp. 31–32, and Ginzburg, *Historishe verk*, 2: 134.

tricks of the crooked ones, and if they continue on this path, doctoring the official record books and changing their ages despite the truth, the government will likewise change the law concerning us. [In that case] the law will not distinguish between the righteous and the wicked, it will apply not to the individual but to the community as a whole, and the righteous shall suffer with the wicked.[61]

For Gintsburg, the specter of collective Jewish punishment stood in stark contrast to the far more preferable principle of selective integration, whereby rights and privileges were intentionally granted not to the community as a whole but rather to deserving individuals, and thus created an incentive for self-reform. And it must be said that Gintsburg strove to carry out the obligation of military service in his own family: he insisted that his sons and at least one grandson enlist in the army, where three Gintsburgs attained the rank of officer.[62]

For the vast majority of Jews, however, the full-scale overhaul of the army in 1874 failed to live up to the promise of Gintsburg's open letter. To be sure, the reform legislation was relatively free of discrimination against Jews, thanks in part to Gintsburg's behind-the-scenes efforts. Jews were to be drafted at the same age, according to the same criteria, and in the same proportion as Gentiles. Once in the army, moreover, Jewish soldiers were to serve on an equal footing, including, for volunteers, the possibility of promotion to the rank of officer. But the 1874 reform failed to extend to Jewish veterans the rights granted in 1867 to the cantonists who had served under Nicholas I, and it therefore failed to uphold the larger quid pro quo envisioned by Gintsburg and others. While active military service, now reduced from twenty-five years to six, continued to exercise an enormous social influence on Jewish soldiers, in legal terms the reformed army was eliminated as an instrument of selective integration. Within a decade of the 1874 military reform, moreover, the possibility of Jews rising to the rank of officer was effectively eliminated; between 1874 and 1917 only nine Jews were promoted to the rank of officer.[63]

Had the 1874 military reform included the granting of equal rights in exchange for service, tens of thousands of Jewish veterans would in all likelihood have become the single largest constituency for selective integration. Moreover, their right to settle and work outside the Pale, like that of Jewish graduates of institutions of higher education, would have been unconditional, based on prior service rather than on continued adherence to a particular occupation or estate, as was the case for Jewish artisans and mer-

61. *Ha-Magid,* Nov. 11, 1874, p. 387.
62. "Mémoire du baron Alexandre de Gunzburg," pp. 6–7.
63. *Evreiskaia entsiklopediia,* 3:164; Petrovsky-Shtern, "Jews in the Russian Army," pp. 119–27.

Figure 16. Jewish soldiers celebrating Passover, ca. 1905. (By permission of
YIVO Institute for Jewish Research.)

chants.[64] These considerations may in fact have contributed to the decision
not to link military service with civil rights.[65] Whatever the motives, the absence of such provisions represented a stunning defeat for Horace Gintsburg.
Even his most ardent supporters admitted that Gintsburg's position on military service had put him at odds with the vast majority of Russian Jews, in
whose minds the army still conjured up the nightmare of kidnapped children and forced conversion.[66] In the wake of the 1874 reform, Gintsburg
was left with the knowledge of having helped ensure that Russia's Jews would
bear their full share of the burden of military service without the expected
reward of equal rights.

STALEMATE

The 1870s marked a period of inertia in official Jewish policy as a whole,
during which the range of social groups subject to selective integration remained nearly frozen. While the successor to the Jewish Committee, the so-

---

64. Although there was some ambiguity in the laws governing residence by Jewish merchants
and artisans outside the Pale, in practice, changing one's occupation brought with it the risk
of forcible return to the Pale. See, e.g., the discussion in G. Samoilovich, *O pravakh remeslennikov-evreev* (St. Petersburg, 1894), pp. 31–39.

65. Gessen, *Istoria evreiskogo naroda v Rossii*, 2: 206n.

66. "Mémoire du baron Alexandre de Gunzburg," p. 6; Sliozberg, *Baron G. O. Gintsburg*, p.
31; Ginzburg, *Historishe verk*, 2: 134.

called Commission for Restructuring Jewish Life (1872–81), was highly receptive to the integrationist agenda, its influence within the tsarist government was negligible. In contrast to its predecessor, the commission met only sporadically; its members stood far lower in the tsarist bureaucracy and as a consequence their generally liberal recommendations could be safely ignored.[67] Various Jewish groups, building on the experience of Vilna in 1869, requested that delegates from individual communities across the Pale be sent to Petersburg to take part in the commission's deliberations, which, as one particularly hopeful petition put it, "promise to lay the groundwork for the complete elimination [of the] Jewish question."[68] Such requests, however, were flatly denied, with the explanation that, in the wake of the municipal reform of 1870, Jewish interests would henceforth be represented by nonethnically specific urban institutions. Horace Gintsburg was the sole Jewish contributor of any consequence to the commission's deliberations, and even in this role subsequently found himself subject to attack by the young historian Simon Dubnov, who dismissed Gintsburg's activism as little more than "filling the archives of various government commissions."[69]

The loss of momentum in the autocracy's pursuit of selective integration during the 1870s cannot be explained solely within the domain of Jewish policies. The perceived results of the still quite limited experiment in Jewish integration, in fact, seem to have had little impact—favorable or unfavorable—on official thinking. None of the legislated paths out of the Pale, including the 1865 decree on artisans, had produced the much-feared "flood" of Jews into the Russian interior. To be sure, the 1870s witnessed a noticeable rise of anti-Jewish opinion across much of the Russian press, leading several newspapers to abandon their previous support for abolition of the Pale. But there is little evidence that public opinion shaped official policy in any significant way before the 1880s.[70] Rather, it was the unsettling changes unleashed by the Great Reforms that tipped the balance toward greater conservatism in virtually all arenas of official policy, including the "Jewish Question." In the wake of the emancipation of the serfs, paternalist concern for the vulnerable muzhik (poor peasant), combined with the

---

67. For a detailed account of the commission's deliberations, see Vitalii Nakhmanovich, *Evreiskaia politika tsarskogo pravitel'stva v 1870-kh gg.: Deiatel'nost' Komissii po ustroistvu byta evreev* (Moscow, 1998). This unpaginated article was published as a preprint by the Jewish Heritage Society of Moscow. The Commission's proceedings have been preserved in RGIA, f. 821, op. 9, dd. 77–129.

68. RGIA, f. 821, op. 9, d. 91. ll. 1–4 (quotation on l. 3).

69. Quoted in Seltzer, "Simon Dubnow," p. 208.

70. The definitive study of the shift in tone in the Russian press is John Klier, *Imperial Russia's Jewish Question,* esp. chap. 16. Klier nonetheless concludes (p. 455) that until 1881, "official policy did not yet follow the lead of public opinion."

more pragmatic fear of peasant unrest, acted as an increasingly effective counterweight to arguments for broader Jewish integration. Furthermore, the Polish uprising of 1863 focused official attention on the unwelcome ambitions of non-Russian minorities in the western borderlands, where the overwhelming majority of Jews lived. Finally, various attempts by radical conspirators (none, for the time being, Jews) to assassinate Alexander II did much to dampen the will to reform that had previously animated the tsar-liberator and his enlightened bureaucrats.

In other words, just as selective integration rose on the larger political tide of the Reform era, it was left more or less stranded as that tide began to recede across the 1870s. Stranded, but not drowned: apart from the failure to extend to Jewish veterans of the reformed army the residential and other rights bestowed on their predecessors from the era of Nicholas I, the existing mechanisms of selective integration remained intact during the latter half of Alexander II's reign—and indeed until the collapse of the tsarist regime. Much the same could be said of Horace Gintsburg, who found himself increasingly isolated in official circles but by no means without influence. In 1879 he succeeded in persuading the government to extend the benefits of selective integration to Jewish graduates of all institutions of higher education (not just universities). The following year, again after Gintsburg's intervention, Minister of Internal Affairs L. S. Makov granted a virtual amnesty to all Jews who had settled illegally outside the Pale before 1880.[71] One estimate put the number of such Jews at 70,000.[72]

That selective integration, after a promising beginning, had entered a period of inertia was nonetheless clear, both to the Jewish notables in Petersburg and to the growing number of reform-minded Jews in the Pale. Surveying the meager results of a decade and a half of lobbying, a group of Jewish merchants, honored citizens (including Horace Gintsburg), and holders of advanced degrees protested to the minister of internal affairs:

> [Our] petitions have been repeated almost annually, but without success. Jews assumed that the system of gradualness . . . had completed its mission and would at last be put aside. They have been patiently waiting, over the course of many beneficent [general] reforms, for their turn finally to be released from the yoke of restrictive laws. To our great sorrow, this hope, too, has proved il-

71. For a discussion of the "Makov Circular," see ibid., p. 299. On Gintsburg's involvement, see Ginzburg, *Historishe verk*, 2: 135, and Sliozberg, "Baron G. O. Gintsburg i pravovoe polozhenie russkikh evreev," *Perezhitoe* 2 (1910): 102, 110.

72. Sliozberg, "Baron G. O. Gintsburg," p. 110. Sliozberg claims that the Makov Circular, which did not have the status of law, was rescinded in 1892, and tens of thousands of Jews were suddenly placed in legal jeopardy. Another source, however, asserts that it remained in effect until 1904. See Grigorii Rubinshtein, *Vospominaniia starogo advokata* (Riga, 1940), p. 26.

lusory. Not only has the final granting of civil rights to Jews not followed, but even the former system of gradualism has, apparently, been abandoned.[73]

POGROMS AND JEWISH POLITICS

The greatest test of the Jewish notables' claim to leadership came in the wake of Alexander II's assassination in Petersburg on March 1, 1881, by members of the terrorist group The People's Will. As fear of popular unrest spread, Jews across the Pale looked to local authorities for protection. In the middle of April, still mourning his father, Tsar Alexander III canceled the popular festivities that normally occurred during the Orthodox Church's week-long celebration of Easter. This ruling was apparently misconstrued in certain areas as a purely local decision, made by venal police who had allegedly been bribed by Jews to limit Christian festivities so as to prevent public disorder. To complicate matters, the Jewish Passover (the original occasion for the Last Supper of Jesus and his disciples) began that year on April 14, precisely during the now substantially truncated Easter holiday. Still in shock at the murder of their tsar, Christians commemorated the Crucifixion even as Jews celebrated their liberation from slavery in Egypt. In the city of Elizavetgrad, the confluence of these holy days, historically linked and fraught with theological tension, sparked an explosion of violence that cut a destructive path through Jewish communities across the southern provinces of the Pale for over two years.[74] A confidential government report later described the scene in Elizavetgrad on April 15:

> The city presented an extraordinary sight: streets covered with feathers and obstructed with broken furniture which had been thrown out of the residences; houses with broken doors and windows; a raging mob, running about yelling and whistling in all directions and continuing its work of destruction without let or hindrance, and as a finishing touch to this picture, complete indifference displayed by the local non-Jewish inhabitants to the havoc wrought before their eyes.[75]

From Elizavetgrad, violence quickly spread to nearby cities, including Kiev and Odessa, and soon engulfed hundreds of communities. These were by no means the first pogroms against Jews in the Russian Empire, but 1881 inaugurated a new pattern of anti-Jewish violence in which national political events acted as decisive catalysts, and rioting occurred not just in isolated settings but across large regions, for months or years on end. The abolition

---

73. RGIA f. 821, op. 9, d. 87, l. 4.

74. Aronson, *Troubled Waters*, p. 47; Stanislawski, *For Whom Do I Toil?* p. 158; on the timing of Passover, see Sliozberg, *Dela minuvshikh dnei*, 1: 100.

75. Quoted in Dubnov, *History of the Jews in Russia and Poland*, 2: 250.

of serfdom and the spread of railroads had drastically increased geographic mobility in the European parts of the empire, leading to substantial population growth in towns and cities, where virtually all the pogroms occurred. By the time the violence triggered by Alexander II's assassination began to subside in 1883, thousands of Jewish homes and businesses had been devastated by roaming mobs, several dozen Jews murdered, and unknown numbers assaulted and raped.[76]

In recent decades, a growing body of historical research has carefully reexamined the origins of the 1881 pogroms, one of the severest episodes of ethnic violence in the Russian Empire during the nineteenth century. The result has been a vigorous challenge to the received notion that the tsarist regime or other organizations, eager to deflect popular discontent from the government, conspired to organize attacks against Jews.[77] Instead, the pogroms now appear to have drawn on what contemporaries referred to as "spontaneous"—that is to say, deeply embedded—rather than consciously manipulated antipathies in certain sectors of the population. The pogroms' *effects*, however, have largely escaped such critical reexamination. A virtually unchallenged consensus holds that 1881 dealt a fatal blow to the regime of the notables in all its manifestations: the faith in integration into surrounding societies as the sole path to modernity for the Jews, the method of petitioning and personal intercession, the Haskalah. The pogrom crisis thus occupies a pivotal place in the historiography of Russian Jewry, and indeed of modern world Jewry, as a decisive step in the genesis of autonomous political solutions to the Jewish predicament in the Diaspora.[78]

While there is little doubt that the pogroms helped transform the landscape of Jewish politics in Russia, the notion that they permanently crippled the Petersburg Jewish elite and the broader hopes for integration and emancipation cannot withstand scrutiny. Let us begin by recalling the precise nature of the crisis *within* the Jewish fold; that is, not the outbreak of violence itself but the debate over how to respond to it. Criticism of the notables focused less on their failure to persuade their supposedly high-level contacts in the tsarist government to stop the attacks against Jews than on their specific refusal to support Jewish emigration from Russia as a response to anti-Jewish violence. The spontaneous and disorganized bursts of emigration that did occur in 1881 and 1882 were inspired largely by false rumors of material

76. See John Klier and Shlomo Lambroza, eds. *Pogroms: Anti-Jewish Violence in Modern Russian History* (Cambridge, 1992).

77. Hans Rogger inaugurated the revisionist approach in his *Jewish Policies and Right-Wing Politics;* the most comprehensive analysis of the causes of the pogroms of 1881–82 can be found in Aronson, *Troubled Waters.*

78. The strongest case for the centrality of the 1881–82 crisis in the development of modern Jewish ideologies and movements is made by Frankel, *Prophecy and Politics,* pp. 49–132. See also Lederhendler, *Road to Modern Jewish Politics,* pp. 154–57.

assistance from Jewish organizations in the West, as well as by careless statements (subsequently retracted as contrary to Russian law) by the minister of internal affairs, Nikolai Pavlovich Ignat´ev, to the effect that "the Western border is open to the Jews."[79]

Because the pogroms of 1881 were the first to encompass an entire region rather than just an individual city, they posed an unprecedented challenge to the Petersburg elite to produce a coordinated "national" response. In this context, the opposition of Petersburg notables to mass Jewish emigration rested on several considerations. To begin with, it was illegal. It would mark a cowardly retreat from two decades of struggle for Jewish equality in the Russian Empire; it would play into the hands of anti-Semites by confirming charges of Jewish rootlessness and thereby encouraging further anti-Jewish violence; and finally, even under the most favorable conditions for emigration, the vast majority of the empire's roughly 4 million Jews would inevitably remain where they were (and where their ancestors had lived for centuries), with the same needs and concerns as before the pogroms.[80] As a matter of principle, moreover, the elites were reluctant to take their cues from below. At a conference of notables organized and convened in Petersburg in April 1882, G. I. Ernburg from Kharkov declared to his fellow delegates that "to sponsor emigration would be sinful, no matter how strong the urge [to emigrate] might be. There are occasions when a human being wants to die, but to help him carry out this wish is clearly a crime."[81] In response to suggestions that failure to support emigration would foment hostility among the Jewish masses toward the Petersburg leadership, the Petersburg writer G. M. Rabinovich asserted:

> Gentlemen, fortunately we do not have a *narod* [folk, people] in its fashionable meaning, in the sense of an antipode and rival of the intelligentsia, although, unfortunately and to our shame, among us are beginning to appear *narodniki* [populists] who would very much like to arouse in the people a distrust toward the intelligentsia. However, we can be sure that these gentlemen

79. Frankel, *Prophecy and Politics*, pp. 58–64. Rogger, *Jewish Policies and Right-Wing Politics*, pp. 176–87, documents the tsarist government's consistent opposition to Jewish emigration. Ignat´ev, a notorious anti-Semite, explained his initial endorsement of Jewish emigration in an interview several years later as a "misunderstanding." When Jewish representatives had complained to him in autumn 1881 that Russian Jewry was suffering under a yoke of bondage like that in ancient Egypt, Ignat´ev reported that he replied, "Why do you not make an Exodus? Where is your Moses? I shall only be too glad to give him full powers to take all your people off to the land of Canaan. Pharoah would not let you go; I, on the contrary, will be delighted to give you every facility for your departure": quoted in Stead, *Truth about Russia*, pp. 305–6. See also Ben-Tsiyon Dinur, "Tokhniyotav shel Ignatev le-fitron 'she'elat ha-yehudim' u-veidat net-sige ha-kehilot be-peterburg bi-shnot 1881–82," *He-'Avar* 10 (1963): 5–82.

80. Orbach, "Russian-Jewish Leadership," pp. 3, 29.

81. *Nedel'naia Khronika Voskhoda*, Aug. 21, 1882, p. 929.

will have very little success with our masses, for they [the Jewish masses] lack the two main factors that make chaotic mass unrest possible: they are perpetually sober and literate almost without exception. Therefore they are entirely unsuitable material for various disturbances and disorders.[82]

The final word in this discussion belonged to Horace Gintsburg. "The notion that we ought to adjust our decisions to the wishes of the masses, come what may," he told the delegates, "is false. We ought to do only what our conscience dictates to us. Only then will we have fulfilled our duty in the highest manner."[83]

Whereas nearly all elements of Russian society and government viewed the pogroms as a popular protest against Jewish economic exploitation, a majority of delegates to the Petersburg conference traced the violence to the absence of legal equality for Russia's Jews. As the delegates' final report asserted:

The whole problem lies in the restrictive legislation against Jews. The mob instinctively understands that the Jews are singled out in the law and that those who attack them will not be punished according to the normal pattern. . . . If the current restrictive legislation against Jews were to fall on another class of the population—the merchantry, the nobility, etc.—it would elicit the same horrifying pogroms against that class.[84]

The state rabbi Zalkind Minor offered a similar analysis, emphasizing that the emancipation of the serfs in 1861 had left the Jews as the only group with restricted rights, and that therefore the masses "had every reason to suppose that there was no need to stand on ceremony with the Jews."[85]

A small but vocal cohort of Jewish writers, students, and intellectuals vehemently rejected both the juridical explanation of the pogroms and the refusal to support would-be Jewish emigrants. Horrified at the lack of visible response to month after month of public violence against Jews, and to the pitiful condition of thousands of refugees desperately attempting to flee, crit-

---

82. Ibid, Sept. 4, 1882, p. 977.
83. Ibid., p. 975.
84. TsGIA-SPb, f. 422, op. 2, d. 1, ll. 18–24. It is important to note that despite their fierce disagreement on the proper response to the pogroms—chiefly, whether to promote Jewish emigration—delegates to the conference were nearly unanimous in the view that discriminatory legislation was the root cause of the violence. Other, secondary factors mentioned were the deliberate incitement of anti-Semitism by certain Russian newspapers and the government's failure to censor such incitement, thereby giving the appearance of official approval. See ibid., l. 24, and the protocols of the conference debates in *Nedel'naia Khronika Voskhoda*, nos. 30, 33, 34, and 36 (1882), esp. no. 34, pp. 926–27. For Russian attitudes, see John Klier, "The Russian Press and the Anti-Jewish Pogroms of 1881," *Canadian-American Slavic Studies* 17, no. 1 (1983): 199–221.
85. Zalkind Minor, *Posle pogromov, ili tri glavy o evreiskom voprose* (Moscow, 1882), p. 4.

ics launched an unprecedented series of printed attacks against the Petersburg elite. Some of these charges were clearly wide of the mark, such as the
suggestion that the Petersburg notables opposed emigration by the poor because they did not want to be stuck with paying for it, or even that they had
provoked the pogroms in the first place. "One thing that our men of wealth
should not forget," warned a writer for the Warsaw Jewish newspaper *Izraelita*,
"is that everywhere and at all times the main ground for persecution of the
Jews has been given by them, with their *gesheft*, their greed, their swagger-
ing, and . . . their ostentatious lifestyle."[86] The writer Grigorii Bogrov, echoing earlier criticisms of the way Petersburg Jewry handled its own communal affairs in the imperial capital, reported that "because of the intrigues and
lack of consensus on the part of Petersburg Jews, provincial Jews are forced
to remain chained to places where their enemies' fists continue to pound
them."[87] And a student in Kiev charged that "Gintsburg would like the mass
of Jews to emigrate but he would like it done his way, secretly, so that he could
declare his loyal feelings and attachment to Russia and so gain equal
rights."[88]

The most powerful criticisms, however, struck not only at the particular
policies of the notables but at their very status as self-appointed leaders of
Russian Jewry. Addressing the notables directly in the name of "the people,"
the newspaper *Ha-Melits* proclaimed:

> Who has the right to speak for the people? Only those who live the life of the
> people, who feel the pain and the sorrow of Jewish life directly—not those who
> enjoy the benefits of life. . . . Such "spokesmen" are inauthentic by virtue of
> their experience. . . . We, the masses of the people, have looked on this land
> as our homeland, we have loved it more than you. Day in and day out we strove
> to draw near to the native population, but look, they are attacking us with crow-
> bars. . . . We are leaving because we are forced to. . . . Get you away from the
> people! Let our brothers in distress see that they have no one to rely on but
> themselves.[89]

Similar emotions were evident in M. G. Orshanskii's survey in 1883 of the results of nearly two years of sustained anti-Jewish violence. Casting Petersburg—
where no pogroms had occurred—as hopelessly cut off from life in the Pale,
or what he called "Jewish Russia" ("for Russia, besides its division into Asi-
atic and European territories, can be divided into Jewish and non-Jewish"),
Orshanskii intoned:

86. Quoted in *Nedel'naia Khronika Voskhoda*, July 10, 1882, p. 761.
87. Ibid., Feb. 26, 1882, p. 209.
88. Quoted in Frankel, *Prophecy and Politics*, p. 76. For further examples of unsubstantiated
charges, see M. O. [Mikhail Grigorievich Orshanskii], "Za proshlyi god," *Voskhod*, no. 3 (1883),
p. 40, and Stanislawski, *For Whom Do I Toil?* p. 165.
89. *Ha-Melits*, Mar. 9, 1882, pp. 171–73.

During this period Petersburg stood at the head of the Jewish communities, as a kind of capital of Russian Jewry. Whether this was justified is open to question. . . . If the capital is to decide questions of national significance, and if it is to understand them—then the location of the Jewish capital can hardly be in Petersburg, but must by necessity be somewhere in the Pale of Settlement, with all its charming characteristics. Those who decide the fate of their people should be acquainted with the countless and varied legal restrictions and the so-called disorders not from newspaper articles and memoranda prepared by obedient secretaries, not so to say "vom Hören-sagen," but from life itself, from bitter experience and from direct observation.[90]

With its thinly veiled jibe at Emanuel Levin, personal secretary to Evzel and Horace Gintsburg and author of dozens of petitions and memoranda on their behalf, Orshanskii tapped a rich vein of resentment. Again and again, letters to the editors of Jewish newspapers complained of the "indifference" and "egotism" of Petersburg Jews, accusing them of allowing their own internal rivalries to interfere with decisive action to assist the cause of mass emigration.[91]

In assessing the extraordinarily bitter accusations against the Petersburg notables by the proponents of emigration, it is important first of all to distinguish fact from fancy. Charges of miserliness toward pogrom victims on the part of Horace Gintsburg and others, for example, are not supported by the evidence.[92] Nor is it the case, despite much of the rhetoric of the time, that the opponents and advocates of organized emigration were neatly divided between Petersburg and the Pale. The two leading forums for attacks against the notables, *Razsvet* and *Ha-Melits,* were both based in Petersburg. In fact, their very proximity to the Jewish plutocracy may well have added fire to their criticism. This was almost certainly the case with the editor of *Ha-Melits,* Alexander Tsederbaum. Although he fancied himself a man of influence, Tsederbaum was forever being kept at arm's length by Horace

90. Orshanskii, "Za proshlyi god," *Voskhod,* no. 3 (1883), p. 41, and no. 4 (1883), p. 28.

91. See the summary of letters in *Nedel´naia Khronika Voskhoda,* Feb. 26, 1882, pp. 201–6. In one case, the editors noted, they "received from different cities the exact same statements, copied word for word, letter for letter. Clearly, they were not composed according to any inner conviction, but by rote [*tak sebe*], and signed as if by a herd, according to purely superficial conviction." One might well conclude that, on the contrary, this practice suggests a remarkable degree of coordination on the part of the pro-emigrationists.

92. In his memoirs, Mordechai ben Hillel Ha-Kohen claims that by the end of April 1881 (i.e., less than two weeks after the first pogrom, in Elizavetgrad) relief funds collected by wealthy Jews in Petersburg amounted to only a few thousand rubles. In fact, Horace Gintsburg had already given 5,000 rubles to Jewish victims in Elizavetgrad, and within a year over 60,000 rubles had been collected, including 25,000 from Gintsburg and 15,000 from Samuel Poliakov. At the same time, the Petersburg leadership sought (without success) to persuade the tsarist regime to force local communities to compensate Jewish victims for property damages. See Ha-Kohen, *Olami,* 1: 159–60; TsGIA-SPb, f. 422, op. 2, d. 1, l. 29; *Vseobshchaia Gazeta,* no. 17 (1881).

Figure 17. Alexander Tsederbaum (1816–1893).

Gintsburg and others. Incensed at not being invited to the April 1882 conference of Jewish notables, Tsederbaum attempted to force his way into the opening session at Gintsburg's mansion on the English Embankment, declaring that "I have come here as a deputy in the name of seventy thousand Russian Jews!" When one delegate dryly asked who these 70,000 Jews might be, Tsederbaum replied that they were *Ha-Melits*'s readers (as opposed to actual subscribers, who numbered fewer than 1,000). His protests notwithstanding, Tsederbaum—grandfather of the future Menshevik leader Iulii Martov—continued to be kept at bay, a circumstance that may well have encouraged him to open the pages of *Ha-Melits* to some of the most strident attacks on those who had refused to recognize him.[93]

93. A. E. Kaufman, "Za mnogo let: otryvki vospominanii starogo zhurnalista," *Evreiskaia Starina* 5, no. 2 (1913): 217.

Conversely, opponents of emigration could be found across the Pale, especially (but not only) in the northern provinces that had largely escaped violence. At the April 1882 conference in Petersburg, delegates from the provinces of Grodno, Vilna, Vitebsk, Kharkov, and Chernigov opposed active support for emigration.[94] While it is true that delegates had been invited by the Petersburg notables, in at least one known case (Chernigov) a local committee of Jews had already formed and selected its representatives (who opposed mass emigration) several months before the announced conference in the imperial capital.[95] In fact, the range of opinion at the conference was as wide as in the public debates in the press. Thus there is little reason to assume that the delegates were any less representative of their communities than those writers at *Razsvet* and *Ha-Melits* who criticized the Petersburg leadership and who were similarly unelected.

Who were the critics of the Petersburg notables during the pogrom crisis? In contrast to earlier tensions between Petersburg and the Pale in connection with the Society for the Spread of Enlightenment, the Vilna Commission, and the various rabbinical commissions, those who condemned Gintsburg and others in 1881 and 1882 were almost exclusively intellectuals. Conspicuously absent from their ranks were rabbis, who in general opposed emigration, especially to the New World, out of fear that it would weaken communal authority and religious observance among the uprooted, and who in any case regarded Gentile oppression as an inevitable burden of exile.[96] Many if not most pro-emigration intellectuals were in fact former partisans of integration. Indeed, the trajectory of men such as Moshe Leib Lilienblum, Leon Pinsker, and Lev Levanda, all of whom sharply repudiated their former integrationist views during 1881–82 in favor of national, autonomous solutions to Jewish dilemmas, has become something of a paradigm for the transformation wrought by the pogrom crisis.

Even among intellectuals, however, the pogroms produced effects far more diverse than is implied by the paradigm of a repentant "return" to the Jewish people. For some integrationists, such as the historian Simon Dubnov and the poet Yehudah Leib Gordon, the pogroms produced no fundamental realignment, at least in the short term.[97] The writer Ansky (Shlomo

---

94. *Nedel'naia Khronika Voskhoda*, nos. 31–36 (1882), pp. 904, 927, 930, 977. Kharkov province was adjacent to the Pale; its sizable Jewish population was not the target of pogroms. Chernigov province was the site of several pogroms during 1881.

95. RGIA, f. 821, op. 9, d. 155, ll. 1–3.

96. Vital, *Origins of Zionism*, pp. 72–73.

97. Dubnov, *Kniga zhizni*, 1: 83–86. In his 1883 review of Pinsker's nationalist manifesto, *Autoemancipation!* Dubnov rejected mass emigration as a solution to Russian Jewry's woes, focusing instead on the need for legal emancipation as in Western Europe and on internal

Rapoport) proceeded to devote himself to the plight of the Russian peasantry, becoming an important figure in the Populist movement; only much later, at the turn of the century, did he reinvent himself yet again, this time as a Jewish populist. Josef Rabinovich, born into a Hasidic family in Bessarabia and a recent convert to the Haskalah, emerged from the trauma of the pogroms to found the New Israelites, a small sect of Jews who accepted Jesus as Messiah.[98] When one considers Russian Jewry as a whole, the pogroms appear to have produced not a paradigm or a moment of truth but profound disorientation, a recasting of aspirations and identities in multiple directions.

A PARTING OF WAYS

Jewish notables in Petersburg were part of this larger process of transvaluation. The eruption of violence forced them, too, to confront old assumptions and methods, and to search for new ones. Nowhere is this reorientation more clearly visible than in the case of Emanuel Levin, a man who had been at the epicenter of Petersburg Jewry's campaign for Jewish integration into Russian society. Near the end of 1882, even before the dust had settled in Balta, Ivanovka, Konotop, and countless other towns and cities across the Pale, Levin was working furiously on what became the first sustained analysis of the causes of the pogroms. The result was a 250-page indictment titled *The Jewish Question and the Anti-Jewish Movement in Russia in 1881 and 1882*, which charged the tsarist government with conspiring to instigate mass violence against Jews and then deliberately withholding police protection from them. The accusations were sufficiently sensational to prevent the publication of Levin's work until 1909 (and then only in fragments); in the immediate aftermath of the pogroms only a handful of hectographed copies were produced. "Representatives of the regime in the provinces," Levin charged, "even high-ranking ones, must have been personally involved in the anti-Jewish movement. With few exceptions, complete freedom to beat the Jews, to injure and mutilate them, to violate their wives and daughters, and to steal their property was granted [by the authorities]."[99] On top of all this, Levin noted,

---

Jewish reform. See Dubnov, "Kakaia samoemansipatsiia nuzhna evreiam?" *Voskhod*, nos. 5–8 (1883). On Gordon's response to the pogroms, see Stanislawski, *For Whom Do I Toil?* pp. 168–70.

98. David Roskies, "S. Ansky and the Paradigm of Return," in Jack Wertheimer, ed., *The Uses of Tradition: Jewish Continuity in the Modern Era* (New York, 1992), pp. 243–60; Steven Zipperstein, "Heresy, Apostasy, and the Transformation of Joseph Rabinovich," in Endelman, *Jewish Apostasy in the Modern World*, pp. 206–31.

99. [E. B. Levin], *Evreiskii vopros i anti-evreiskoe dvizhenie v Rossii v 1881 i 1882 g.*, quoted in Aronson, *Troubled Waters*, p. 12. Aronson, who is interested in Levin as the progenitor of the conspiracy theory that Aronson convincingly refutes, provides a detailed discussion of the history of Levin's text in *Troubled Waters*, pp. 239–40. In addition to the copy housed in the

the government publicly blamed the Jews themselves for the pogroms, citing their alleged exploitation of poor peasants recently freed from the bonds of serfdom. In May 1882, before the pogrom wave had fully subsided, Alexander III promulgated a law forbidding new Jewish settlement in rural areas within the Pale, thereby reversing the trend toward greater residential freedom. The assumed alliance between reform-minded Jewish elites and the tsarist regime, a cornerstone of the maskilic worldview since the 1820s, was shattered; gone too was Levin's former confidence in the superiority of autocratic over democratic politics and any of the other alleged advantages of Russia's archaic social order.

Levin's conspiracy theory regarding the pogroms' origins, which has now been largely refuted by historians, nonetheless marked the beginning of a decisive shift in the way Jewish notables understood their position vis-à-vis the imperial state. Convinced that tsarist officials had helped instigate violence against Jews, and further shocked by the government's subsequent decision to punish the victims with new discriminatory legislation, Petersburg's Jewish elites gradually ceased to regard the autocracy as an engine of reform. Instead, they came to see it as the source of the Jews' deepest trouble—their legal inequality, and therefore their vulnerability to arbitrary treatment and violence. In 1883 Levin accelerated this process by publishing the first guide to tsarist legislation concerning the Jews. Two years later, a revised and hugely expanded version of this work appeared, nearly 700 pages in length, fully documenting the maze of discrimination constructed by the regime over the course of the preceding eight decades.[100] A reviewer for the liberal *Vestnik Evropy* lamented that Russian laws regarding Jews "exceed in volume the Code Napoleon, which constitutes the complete legal code of an entire country."[101] For Levin, whose formative intellectual milieu had been the Russian Haskalah, the state continued to occupy center stage. Only now, in the wake of the pogroms, its role there was starkly inverted: no longer an ally of progress among Jews but an opponent; no longer a bulwark against mob violence but rather its instigator. Assessing the role of urban mobs in the recent pogroms, Levin insisted that "the people were deceived, confused, led into error, by inspirers and leaders who have not been exposed."[102]

Jewish National Library at the Hebrew University in Jerusalem (cited by Aronson), copies can also be found in the Russian National Library and Widener Library at Harvard University.

100. *Obzor nyne deistvuiushchikh iskliuchitel´nykh zakonov o evreiakh, sostoiashchikh v poddanstve Rossii* (St. Petersburg, 1883); *Svod uzakonenii o evreiakh: S izmeneniiami, posledovavshimi po 15 oktiabria 1884 goda* (St. Petersburg, 1885).

101. *Vestnik Evropy*, January 1885, p. 461.

102. Quoted in Aronson, *Troubled Waters*, p. 13.

At the same time that the Jewish elite in Petersburg were distancing themselves from the tsarist regime, the regime, in particular Minister of Internal
Affairs Ignat´ev, was doing much the same in return. To be sure, the government had never formally recognized the Gintsburgs or other notables as
representatives of Russian Jewry, since doing so would have violated the autocratic principle as well as the long-standing preference for administering
the empire's population according to region or estate rather than by nationality or religion.[103] But before 1881 the tsarist regime had certainly
looked to Petersburg Jewry as a model for Jews in the Pale, and had dealt
with the Gintsburgs and other notables as informal Jewish spokesmen on a
wide range of issues.

Alarmed at the widespread breakdown of public order evident in the
pogroms, Ignat´ev and other leaders (including the new tsar, Alexander III)
did not hesitate to blame the Jews themselves, whose exploitation of the peasants, they claimed, was now reaping its bitter fruit. Petitions from Petersburg
notables urging that various towns and cities be required to compensate Jewish victims and that more Jews be allowed to move into the Russian interior,
away from the regions where pogroms had occurred, met with terse rejec-
tions from tsarist officials.[104] As with the criticisms hurled by the pro-emi-
grationist camp of Jewish intellectuals, here too the Petersburg elites found
not just their specific proposals but their position as spokesmen for Russian
Jewry called into question. At a meeting early in 1882 with Horace Gintsburg, Samuel Poliakov, and other notables, Ignat´ev began by announcing
to the assembled group that "I did not want to receive you together, since I
obviously cannot recognize a solidarity of interests among Russian subjects
of the Mosaic law who live in different cities."[105] In a note to Alexander III
describing the meeting, Ignat´ev warned that the Jews were in fact danger-
ously well organized: Gintsburg, he wrote, was the secret Petersburg representative of the Alliance Israélite Universelle, the "universal kahal," and "in
this capacity [he] has not only taken to considering himself the representative of the Jews, but has even addressed himself in their name to Your

103. Aside from Congress Poland, the duchy of Finland, and the "protectorates" of Bukhara
and Khiva, the tsarist regime recognized only nonethnic administrative units.

104. Ignat´ev did, however, briefly propose allowing Jews to settle in Central Asia, much as
Catherine the Great had done with regard to the provinces of New Russia at the end of the
eighteenth century. In both cases, the motives were purely instrumental, based on the state's
interest in colonizing and developing newly conquered territories. See *Nedel´naia Khronika
Voskhoda*, Aug. 14, 1882, p. 901.

105. GARF, f. 730, op. 1, d. 1627, l. 1. A similar pattern had already been established at
the local level, as when the governor general of Chernigov province refused to receive a delegation of Jews in September 1881, arguing that "Jews do not have the right to send deputies,
since by law they constitute neither a distinct *soslovie* within the state nor a distinct society":
RGIA, f. 821, op. 9, d. 155, l. 1.

Figure 18.   Count Nikolai Pavlovich Ignat´ev (1832–1908).

Majesty."[106] Alluding to the extraordinary recriminations against them from various Jewish quarters, delegates at the Petersburg conference of April 1882 noted by contrast that the popular image of a secret Jewish brotherhood, directed by all-powerful figures in the imperial capital, "strikes us, especially in the present time, as a cruel irony."[107]

Along with populist assaults in the Jewish press and Ignat´ev's denial of Gintsburg's status as Jewish spokesman (which took place in private), Jewish notables found virtually all of their proposals for responding to the pogroms dismissed by the regime. Just as the government had severely circumscribed their role within the Petersburg Jewish community, so it undermined the no-

106. GARF, f. 730, op. 1, d. 1623, ll. 1–8.
107. TsGIA-SPb, f. 422, op. 2, d. 1, l. 20.

tables' claims to leadership in the Pale, and this during the most extreme episode of violence to visit the Jews since the Haidamak massacres of 1768. Such a policy was especially damaging for an elite whose qualifications to lead had rested in good measure on its putative influence in high government circles. After 1882, what was true for Russian society held for the Jews as well: the government refused to make allies of, or even to prop up, those Jewish elites who had been most favorably disposed toward it, and thereby gave unintended nourishment to new ideas and new movements offering far more radical solutions to the Jewish predicament.

In the aftermath of the pogroms, the tsarist regime in effect withdrew whatever legitimacy it had lent to the would-be national Jewish leadership centered in Petersburg, just as it had done with local Jewish communal leadership in the Pale a half century earlier. To be sure, the formal abolition of the kahal in Congress Poland in 1822 and in the Pale in 1844 struck at an institution of internal authority far more deeply rooted in Jewish society and tradition than the Petersburg elite, who by comparison were relative newcomers in Jewish politics. Yet like the kahal, the notables retained a good deal of their importance in Jewish life and in Russian-Jewish relations even after their effective derecognition by the tsarist state. Horace Gintsburg and his son (and designated successor) David continued to receive thousands of pleas every year for legal and financial help from Jews across the Pale, eloquent testimony to their enduring status in a country where the personal petition remained the most common form for expressing grievances.[108] By the 1890s, moreover, the Gintsburgs no longer understood themselves as traditional *shtadlonim,* intercessors who would plead the cause of their coreligionists before the tsar. Instead, they increasingly turned their efforts to Russia's reformed legal system, and eventually to its first parliament, in an attempt to force the regime at least to live up to its own laws. Part IV of this book explores these developments in detail, including the remarkable work of a generation of Jewish lawyers who collectively recast the modus operandi of the Petersburg elite and its relation to the tsarist regime as well as to the Jewish masses of the Pale. Before that story can be told, however, we need to understand how Jews became lawyers—and doctors and journalists and engineers—in the empire of the tsars.

---

108. See Sliozberg, *Dela minuvshikh dnei,* 2: 93. Some 1,500 letters and telegrams requesting help from the Gintsburgs have been preserved among the papers of David Gintsburg. See RNB, f. 183, op. 1014, dd. 143–1583.

PART THREE

Jews, Russians, and the Imperial University

And why shouldn't a Jew look upon education with a career in mind? Do you think his father has an estate, a title, an official rank and protection, so that he can afford to look upon education as an adornment?

GERSHON LIFSHITS, *Confession of a Criminal* (1881)

For [Jews], sooner or later, it had to become clear that education puts one in a privileged position. For them, education and education alone is the path of salvation, leading them out of that dead end into which they have been placed by the restrictive laws and prohibitions. Education returns to them their civil rights.

The Russian Jew, OCTOBER 15, 1880

Kulonu khakhomim, kulonu nevoynim, as it says in the Haggadah — nowadays everyone wants to be a student. Where? How? Why, a cow can sooner jump over a roof than a Jew get into a Russian university!

SHOLEM ALEICHEM, *Tevye the Dairyman* (1911)

We have rebelled against the worship of diplomas among our intelligentsia.

BERL KATZENELSON, *Revolution and Tradition* (1934)

Abraham-Leib could see no advantage these days for a Jew to be educated. It was all the same, gymnasium or no gymnasium. On the contrary, a Jew with a gymnasium education was a thousand times more unkosher than a Jew without a gymnasium education. And let us suppose he has completed gymnasium — then what? And between us, let us suppose he has even completed university too. So? What next? Peh — nothing would come of it. He would be the same Hershke, but a thousand times worse, because Hershke without a diploma was to them still Hershke, but once he earned a diploma he would no longer wish to be called Hershke, but Grisha or Grigorii, and when a Hershke acts like a Grisha or a Grigorii, that they won't tolerate.

SHOLEM ALEICHEM, *The Bloody Hoax* (1913)

The universities have been to this nation, as the wooden horse was to the Trojans.

THOMAS HOBBES, *Leviathan* (1651)

Chapter 6

The University as Melting Pot?

In his first novel set outside the shtetl—the archetypal locus for Yiddish fiction—Sholem Aleichem chose the bustling city of Kiev, where he himself had lived for many years, as the scene for an inspired tragicomedy. While *Der blutiger shpas* (*The Bloody Hoax,* 1913) bears many of the hallmarks of his earlier work, from the comic send-ups of social "types" to the ever-present concern with assimilation and authenticity, it nonetheless marks an important thematic departure.[1] The story unfolds not merely beyond the shtetl, in an environment where Jews are decidedly in the minority, but in a city that, although geographically within the Pale of Settlement, was legally off limits to the majority of Jews. In Kiev, as in cities in the Russian interior, the right of residence was extended only to Jews in those privileged categories enumerated in the policy of selective integration. But the story's novelty goes beyond its setting: rather than simply presenting the Gentile world through the eyes of Jewish characters, *The Bloody Hoax* offers a dual odyssey of "passing," in which Hershel Rabinovich and Grigorii Ivanovich Popov secretly decide to exchange identities so that each can learn how the other really lives. To make this rather farfetched "trading places" scenario plausible, Sholem Aleichem made a telling choice: he cast Hershke and Grisha, the Jew and the Russian, as students.

As with most stories of exchanged identities, this one winds its way inexorably toward the moment of unmasking. And it is again telling that when that moment occurs—when Hershke and Grisha are forced to return to their former selves—it is the result of forces entirely outside the student milieu. The university was, indeed, the setting in which selective Jewish integration

---

1. Sholom [*sic*] Aleichem, *The Bloody Hoax,* trans. Aliza Shevrin (Bloomington, 1991).

achieved its most dramatic success. In its effort to draw the Jews out of their separate existence and to "merge" them into the Russian social hierarchy, the tsarist autocracy experimented with a remarkable range of institutions, including the army, agricultural settlements, schools, and selected social estates. Army and school were of course the classic arenas in which nineteenth-century European states (and twentieth-century America) pursued social integration across lines of estate, class, ethnicity, and race. While many of the tsarist government's efforts at Jewish integration achieved no more than modest results, in the educational arena, the policy of "merging" not only succeeded but did so far beyond the regime's own expectations. Its success, in fact, was to prove its undoing.

As sites of integration, gymnasia and universities are noteworthy for the relative youth of their populations. The 1897 census revealed that 48 percent of the population of the Russian Empire was under the age of twenty; among Jews the figure was 52 percent.[2] Much of the dynamism of the various political and intellectual movements that flourished in the late nineteenth century may in fact have stemmed from a broader youth culture, in which the relatively small number of students in institutions of higher education played a disproportionate part.

Because they have played a highly visible role in modern revolutions of both the right and the left, students have tended to attract historians' keenest attention when they revolt. As Konrad Jarausch notes in his study of students in imperial Germany, "The methodological approaches linking them with society and polity tend to center around sociological, psychological, or historical explanations of dissent."[3] At the same time, the distinctive subculture and "hidden curriculum" that took shape in late imperial Russia's institutions of higher education functioned as a profound source of continuity in the face of students' inescapable transience, socializing generations of newcomers, including, by the final third of the nineteenth century, thousands of Jews.

I am interested primarily in higher education not as an incubator of revolution but as a setting for interethnic contact at the production site of future social elites. Before the 1860s, the vast majority of Jews shunned secular education, viewing it as little more than an instrument of forced assimilation by the tsarist regime. Between 1861 and 1887, however, young Jews flooded into Russia's gymnasia and universities, forming for the first time the seed bed of a Russian-Jewish intelligentsia. How can we explain the sudden influx of Jews into Russia's institutions of higher education? Why did

---

2. Bauer et al., *Nationalitäten des Russischen Reiches*, 2: 84–85.
3. Konrad Jarausch, *Students, Society, and Politics in Imperial Germany: The Rise of Academic Illiberalism* (Princeton, 1982), p. 15.

the tsarist state first promote this trend, only to inhibit it later by imposing quotas? What did Jews absorb from Russia's egalitarian student milieu, and what kind of collective presence did they establish in a subculture whose central mythology was the transcendence of social difference? Why did the imperial university, which of all the arenas of Russia's highly segmented society was the one where Jewish integration achieved its most striking success, nonetheless become the site of a new, secular Jewish particularism, and this at the high point of the student movement?

RUSSIAN AND JEWISH VIEWS OF SECULAR EDUCATION

Nowhere did the influence of the Enlightenment express itself so clearly in the lives of both Russians and Jews as in the realm of education. On the Russian side, the Russian Orthodox Church had remained well into the eighteenth century the single most important sponsor of educational institutions, including a network of parish schools, seminaries, and theological academies. Although Peter the Great and his successors inaugurated a number of secular institutions of learning, including Russia's first university (in Moscow) in 1755, not until the beginning of the nineteenth century did higher education come into its own. In 1802 Alexander I created the Ministry of Public Enlightenment to oversee a new, empire-wide system of schooling; its very name speaks to the cultural climate of the time.[4] Among elites in Russia no less than in Europe, the Enlightenment inspired an expansive confidence in the power of education to mold human character and behavior. By 1825 universities had appeared in St. Petersburg, Kazan, Kharkov, and Vilna, along with a growing network of secondary schools.[5] Also under Alexander I, universities in Dorpat and Helsinki were annexed and revived as part of Russia's westerly expansion.

The fact that higher education in Russia was born under the sign of the Enlightenment and as a result of state initiative had important consequences for the role it played in the Russian–Jewish encounter. First, unlike their older European counterparts, whose origins lie in the medieval period, universi-

---

4. The translation of the Russian term *Ministerstvo narodnogo prosveshcheniia* has a curious history. Most English-language works render it as "Ministry of Education," despite the fact that the final word is plainly "enlightenment," not "education," which would correspond to the Russian *obrazovanie*. When dealing with the Soviet period, by contrast—and perhaps for the purpose of contrast—scholars have tended to write of the "People's Commissariat of Enlightenment." I prefer the literal "Ministry of Public Enlightenment" for the tsarist institution, precisely because it faithfully reflects the central role of the Enlightenment project in Russia's state-driven educational system before 1917. If anything, it is translating the term *narodnyi* that is most difficult, since it partakes of both "popular" and "national," but in both cases only in a limited sense. "Public" is an admittedly imperfect compromise.

5. Patrick L. Alston, *Education and the State in Tsarist Russia* (Stanford, 1969), pp. 20–30.

ties in Russia lacked theological faculties and in general allowed students—including Jews—to take the oath required for enrollment and graduation in a form appropriate to the student's religion.[6] By contrast, mandatory Christian oaths had long served as the formal barrier to Jewish enrollment at many European universities, in some cases well into the nineteenth century.[7]

Second, the state's eagerness to achieve rapid international acclaim in scholarship and research led it to build its educational system from the top down. As has often been noted, Russia's Academy of Sciences came into being (in 1725) before a single university existed. Until near the end of the tsarist period the state consistently favored higher education over primary schooling in its allotment of resources. No other major nineteenth-century European country produced such high ratios of secondary and postsecondary enrollments to primary enrollments—or such low levels of popular literacy.[8] In this respect, the Jewish educational system offered a stark contrast to Russia's: elementary education (in the *heder*) was widespread among males, and literacy levels were significantly higher among Jews than among the Russian Orthodox as well as among Catholics.[9]

Third, insofar as Russian universities were created almost entirely from state initiative, they remained highly dependent on the state and its policies. Being a student placed one (temporarily) in a distinct legal category, and a university degree automatically served as an entrance ticket into the Table of Ranks, the basic hierarchy of Russian officialdom and an important index of social status.[10] While elsewhere in Europe the requirement of taking a Christian oath had often complicated the admission of and/or the granting of degrees to Jews, in pre-Reform Russia it was the eligibility for state service conferred by graduation that would repeatedly cause the government to waver in its treatment of Jewish students.

6. The single exception was the Lutheran theological faculty at the University of Dorpat (Tartu), a holdover from the university's medieval German origins. See Bauer et al., *Nationalitäten des Russischen Reiches*, 1: 327. On student oaths, see Iulii Gessen, "Pervyi evrei-iurist v Rossii—Simon Levin Vul´f," *Perezhitoe* 2 (1910): 315.

7. On Oxford and Cambridge, see Cecil Roth, "The Jews in the English Universities," *Jewish Historical Society of England: Miscellanies* 4 (1942): 108. See also *Encyclopedia Judaica*, 15: 1677–78.

8. James C. McClelland, *Autocrats and Academics: Education, Culture, and Society in Tsarist Russia* (Chicago, 1979), pp. 49–50.

9. Protestants in the Russian Empire displayed the highest literacy levels of all. The contrast between Jewish, Russian Orthodox, and Catholic literacy levels virtually disappears when one confines the analysis to urban populations. See Shaul Stampfer, "Yedi'at kero ukhtov etsel yehude mizrah eropah ba-tekufah ha-hadashah," in Shmuel Elmog et al., eds., *Temurot ba-historiyah ha-yehudit ha-hadashah. Kovets ma'amarim: Shai li-Shmu'el Etinger* (Jerusalem, 1987), esp. p. 466.

10. Alston, *Education and the State*, p. 52.

Finally, because the establishment of universities in Russia was part of the state's effort to reduce its dependence for service on the hereditary nobility, higher education was relatively open, at least in theory, to members of the lower estates.[11] Moscow University was the brainchild of Mikhail Lomonosov, a son of peasants who became eighteenth-century Russia's greatest scholar, and who insisted that even serfs be eligible for admission.[12] While many European universities, especially those with medieval origins, jealously guarded their guildlike autonomy and the privilege of restricting admission by various social and religious criteria, their younger counterparts in Russia were designed to serve one of the central aims of the enlightened absolutist state: to foster an obedient, meritocratic service class. As one study of Russian higher education puts it, "The Russian state offered more concrete educational opportunity to the propertyless and the obscure at the university preparatory level and beyond than did any other major European power."[13]

These characteristic traits of Russian higher education emerged early in the nineteenth century, at roughly the same time that the tsarist state was formulating its first attempts at Jewish reform. It is hardly surprising, then, that education played a central role in the thinking of tsarist bureaucrats concerned with drawing Jews out of their traditional isolation and transforming them into useful subjects. The opening paragraph of the 1804 Statute on the Jews, the government's first attempt to articulate an official Jewish policy, announced that Jews were eligible to enroll in "all primary schools, gymnasia, and universities," and to receive degrees in "medicine, surgery, physics, mathematics, and other branches of knowledge" on an equal basis with the empire's other subjects.[14] The leading liberal journal of the time, *Vestnik Evropy*, noted approvingly that "Alexander has ordered the opening of the doors of the universities and the gymnasia to young Jews. . . . It is necessary for the state to create useful citizens, and moral upbringing is the only way."[15] On paper, at least, few European states could match such a policy. Supremely confidant in the power of education to transform human character, the committee responsible for drafting the 1804 statute set as its goal the "perfection" of the Jews, thereby aligning itself with the rhetoric of "civic

---

11. I draw here on Marc Raeff's interpretation of tsar Peter III's "Charter to the Nobility" (1762): "Far from marking the nobility's 'victory' over the state, as frequently stated, the decree of 1762 marked rather the state's declaration of 'independence' from the service of the nobility." See Raeff, *Origins of the Russian Intelligentsia: The Eighteenth-Century Nobility* (New York, 1966), p. 109.

12. Alston, *Education and the State*, p. 9.

13. Ibid., p. 244.

14. Georgievskii, *Doklad*, p. 1.

15. *Vestnik Evropy*, no. 10 (May 1805), p. 139, quoted in Klier, *Russia Gathers Her Jews*, p. 130.

improvement" and "regeneration" that characterized contemporary debates about Jews in Germany and France.[16]

For much of the first half of the nineteenth century, however, such language—and the liberal admissions policy itself—had almost no practical effect on Russian Jewry's outlook or behavior. In many cases, theory failed to translate into practice, as local administrators arbitrarily blocked the admission of lone Jewish applicants to Russian gymnasia. Much of the resistance, however, came from Jews themselves. In traditional Jewish society, secular knowledge was formally countenanced strictly as a tool for greater understanding of Torah, or for the more complete fulfillment of divine commandments. The notion that non-Jewish learning was worthy of study carried with it the unsettling implication that not all truth was contained within the Torah. Compared to other Jewish communities, those of Eastern Europe were among the least interested in non-Jewish learning, and resistance only deepened with the spread of Hasidism in the late eighteenth century.[17] During the preceding centuries, only a handful of Polish Jews are known to have found their way to universities, nearly all in Italy and Germany, where they tended to study medicine. Indeed, traffic was far heavier in the other direction, as pious Jews from as far west as France sent their sons to East European yeshivas, renowned for their exclusively Jewish form of higher learning.[18]

With most of Russia's Jews suspicious of Gentile learning and the specter of apostasy lurking behind it, few parents chose to send their sons to anything but a heder and, for the gifted, a yeshiva. The fact that educational reform was central to the Haskalah thus helps account for the tremendous resistance the movement encountered among East European Jews. Although recent research has shown that small outposts of the Haskalah, including calls for greater openness to European ideas, emerged in the Russian Empire as early as the 1770s, none produced a large or lasting legacy before the middle of the nineteenth century.[19] "Among [all other peoples]," complained the maskil M. A. Ginzburg in 1834, "men of knowledge [i.e., arts

16. The expression "perfect the Jews" (*vesti evreev k sovershenstvu*), which occurs in the committee's proceedings in 1802, is quoted in S. V. Pozner, *Evrei v obshchei shkole: K istorii zakonodatel'stva i pravitel'stvennoi politiki v oblasti evreiskogo voprosa* (St. Petersburg, 1914), p. 3. For the idea of "civic improvement" in West European settings, see Katz, "The Term 'Jewish Emancipation'," pp. 33–41.

17. For an overview of recent scholarship on early modern Jewish attitudes toward secular, particularly scientific, knowledge, see David Ruderman, *Jewish Thought and Scientific Discovery in Early Modern Europe* (New Haven, 1995), pp. 1–11; on Eastern Europe see ibid., p. 91, and Stanislawski, *Tsar Nicholas I*, pp. 49–51.

18. Monika Richarz, *Der Eintritt der Juden in die Akademischen Berufe: Jüdische Studenten und Akademiker in Deutschland, 1678–1848* (Tübingen, 1974), pp. 24–30.

19. David Fishman, *Russia's First Modern Jews: The Jews of Shklov* (New York, 1995).

and science] are the pride of their people; among us they must conceal themselves like criminals."[20]

The memoirs of maskilim from the pre-Reform period frequently recount episodes in which young protagonists are caught reading forbidden literature—whether a Hebrew newspaper or a novel by Schiller—and the social ostracism that inevitably resulted even from such informal contact with non-Jewish learning. For those few who took the more extreme step of enrolling in a gymnasium or university, the turn to formal secular education often involved a near total rupture from community and/or family. One gymnasium student in the 1840s, fearing reprisals, would wait until safely inside the school building to trade his Jewish garb for the official school uniform, tuck his *peyes* behind his ears, and "become a different person."[21] Another, after attempting to enroll in a gymnasium in 1840, was offered up by the local kahal leadership as a recruit for the army.[22] "Dear brothers and fellow human beings!" pleaded the university graduate Arnold Dumashevskii in a Russian newspaper in 1858, "If only you knew how many hurdles stand before the Jew who . . . strives toward a [Russian] educational institution!"[23]

Although comprehensive data on enrollment are lacking, official sources indicate that in 1833, among the 2,105 gymnasium students within the territory of the Pale, only twelve (just over 0.5 percent) were Jews. In 1840, among the approximately 2,594 students at Russian universities across the empire, 15 were Jews (also just over 0.5 percent), including several who converted to Christianity before graduating.[24] Even at the University of Vilna, in a city with a substantial Jewish population as well as a strong maskilic presence, fewer than 0.5 percent of students were Jews.[25] An official history of Kiev University noted that the few Jewish students there before the 1860s

---

20. Quoted in Lederhendler, *Road to Modern Jewish Politics*, p. 87.

21. Quoted in Pavel Marek, *Ocherki po istorii prosveshcheniia evreev v Rossii: Dva vospitaniia* (Moscow, 1909), p. 167.

22. A. Beletskii, *Vopros ob obrazovanii russkikh evreev v tsarstvovanii Imperatora Nikolaia I* (St. Petersburg, 1894), p. 10.

23. Arnold Borisovich Dumashevskii, "Razmyshleniia po povodu podniatogo v nashei zhurnalistike voprosa o evreiakh," *Odesskii Vestnik*, Dec. 30, 1858, p. 763. Formally, at least, Jews attending Russian schools were required to produce documents showing that their Jewish communities had discharged them from all collectively borne fiscal obligations.

24. Pozner, *Evrei v obshchei shkole*, p. 8; M. Kosven, "K voprosu o vysshem obrazovanii russkikh evreev," *Evreiskaia Zhizn'*, no. 7 (July 1904), pp. 164–66.

25. For data pertaining to 1822–23, see Daniel Beauvois, *Lumières et société en Europe de l'Est: L'Université de Vilna et les écoles polonaises de l'Empire russe, 1803–1832* (Paris, 1977), 1: 322. For similar impressions, see Marek, *Ocherki po istorii prosveshcheniia evreev v Rossii*, p. 21.

"felt themselves in an alien environment" and therefore tended to drop out or convert.[26]

Those few Jews who somehow found their way to a university education soon discovered the practical limitations of the statute of 1804. We have, it is true, no evidence during the first half of the nineteenth century of Jews' being denied admission to a Russian university because of their religion. Within a European context, this is undeniably significant. *After* graduation, however, problems arose concerning the legal and professional privileges normally associated with a university degree, about which the statute of 1804 had maintained an ambiguous silence. In 1811, for example, as part of its strategy of attracting individuals from nonnoble estates to institutions of higher education, the government ruled that henceforth all university graduates would be exempt from the poll tax, the basic dividing line between the privileged and the unprivileged in Russian society. But in response to an inquiry from officials at the University of Vilna, the Ministry of Enlightenment ruled that the decree did not apply to Jewish graduates.[27]

With time, more such qualifications chipped away at the Enlightenment rhetoric of the 1804 statute. Of particular interest is the case of Simon Wolf (Vul´f), who enrolled at the University of Dorpat in 1810 and petitioned to be examined for a doctorate in jurisprudence in 1816. The law faculty refused to administer the exam, citing two concerns. First, the recipient of a doctorate automatically entered the Table of Ranks at a level that was, in the faculty's view, inconsistent with the ban on Jews' holding public office and various other functions associated with the administration of the law. Second, unlike medicine or philosophy, which were grounded in natural law, jurisprudence rested on "positive law," including "teachings incompatible with the religion of the Jew," who was therefore unable to teach or apply the law without violating his faith. These teachings included the various legal ordinances regarding oaths, blasphemy, sacrilege, desecration of holy objects, curses, heresy, and other phenomena in which Jews did not share Christian beliefs.[28]

Wolf's efforts to reverse the faculty's decision, including petitions to Tsar Alexander I and Minister of Enlightenment A. K. Razumovskii, were without success. On the contrary, in the wake of Wolf's case, Jews were formally barred from taking doctoral exams in jurisprudence at all universities. The reign of Nicholas I (1825–55) witnessed further rulings limiting the ability

26. M. F. Vladimirskii-Budanov, *Istoriia imperatorskogo universiteta Sv. Vladimira* (Kiev, 1884), 1: 145.

27. Pozner, *Evrei v obshchei shkole,* p. 4. On the exception for converts to Christianity, see James Flynn, *The University Reform of Alexander I, 1802–1835* (Washington, D.C., 1988), pp. 79–80.

28. Gessen, "Pervyi evrei-iurist v Rossii," pp. 311–15.

of Jewish university graduates to enter state service or otherwise to reap the practical benefits of their degrees.[29].

Jewish protests against such measures invariably reinforced the widespread notion that Jews looked upon education—as upon everything else—primarily with material benefits in mind. Maskilic reformers themselves often made such claims regarding the Jewish masses. Emanuel Levin, for example, asserted that Russian Jews "cannot understand and appreciate education without a visible, practical goal."[30] "Our people," wrote a group of Jewish medical students to the government in response to an 1845 decree barring Jewish physicians from state employment, "judges enlightenment according to its practical advantages."[31] Similarly, in a letter to Count Uvarov, the visiting German rabbi Max Lilienthal asserted that "Without a tangible, material benefit before his eyes, the Jew would rather not send his children to school at all. He cannot grasp the idea of study for the sake of education."[32] As regards Jewish learning, of course, this claim was untenable. From heder to yeshiva, the Jewish curriculum kept a safe distance from any sort of vocational training, except for those few who intended to become rabbis. And the rabbis themselves had long ago enshrined the principle of *Torah lishmah*—the study of sacred texts as a good in itself. To the extent that Jews were concerned with the tangible benefits of a diploma or university degree, moreover, they were hardly alone. The practical utility of knowledge played a central role in the Russian state's creation of institutions of higher education in the first place, as it would—with different political purposes—in the life of the Russian intelligentsia.

Whatever the limitations on their employment after graduation, Jews continued to be eligible to matriculate at nearly all educational institutions throughout the pre-Reform period. This peculiar state of suspended mobility led Simon Wolf, in his petition to the minister of enlightenment, to express what would become a leitmotif for the small number of Jewish students in Russian institutions of higher education before the 1860s. "If a Jew," Wolf asked, "having acquired knowledge, finds the path to prosperity and usefulness blocked, then his superlative education will have accomplished nothing more than to cause him to feel all the more acutely the disgrace that oppresses his nation. . . . What could lead Jews to send their children to Russian schools?"[33]

29. RGIA, f. 1269, op. 1, d. 19, ll. 40–41 and d. 136, l. 53; Georgievskii, *Doklad*, pp. 181–84.

30. E. B. Levin, "Zapiska ob emansipatsii evreev v Rossii (1859)," *Evreiskaia Starina* 8, no. 3 (1915): 306.

31. YIVO, RG 89, folder 755, doc. 6, p. 2.

32. Quoted in Georgievskii, *Doklad*, p. 21. This view was fully shared by the Jewish Committee: see RGIA, f. 1269, op. 1, d. 137, l. 180.

33. Quoted in Gessen, "Pervyi evrei-iurist," p. 315.

Precisely this dilemma can be found in the experiences of Leon Mandelshtam. In September 1840, poised to enroll as the first Jew at Moscow University, Mandelshtam was asked by a fellow Jew, a cantor in Minsk, to explain his purpose. The idea of studying at a university had come to Mandelshtam from conversations with Russian army officers who frequented his father's tavern near Vilna. Impressed with young Leon's skill at chess, they enthralled him with their accounts of educated Russian society, of "the new, the free, the sublime," as he later recalled. Copies of the German-Jewish journal *Ha-Me'asef* brought back by his father from business trips to Berlin introduced him to Haskalah views on education, which he consumed "like the biblical Adam, tasting the juice of the heavenly fruit—Enlightenment." After enduring an arranged marriage to a bride he had never met (and whom he promptly divorced), Mandelshtam adopted a critical maskilic stance toward "corrupted" Jewish mores. The curriculum of the heder and yeshiva, he argued, isolated Jews from educated society and condemned them to perpetual scorn.[34] Thus when asked by the cantor in Minsk why he should want to study in Moscow when he could be a leader among the Jews, Mandelshtam responded with a Mishnaic aphorism: "Better to be last among the lions than first among the hares."[35]

It is instructive to contrast this supremely condescending reply with that offered by Mandelshtam to his new peers at Moscow University, who were similarly perplexed by the sight of a Jew attending a Russian institution of higher education. To Mandelshtam, the motives for university study were self-evident: he sought enlightenment, knowledge, and self-perfection. He wanted only "to listen humbly and obediently, like a child, to the conversations and stories about science and poetry":

> But here they didn't understand me, they could not see the purely childlike feelings in me. . . . "A Jew"—therefore I could not simply have a desire to become educated, a pure desire, without any self-interested motives. And so, everyone asks me to what end I am studying. At first I didn't understand this question and would look foolishly at the questioners' eyes. I wanted to answer that I wished to become a poet, but that would have been even more foolish. In the midst of my confusion I would often hear a further question, that perhaps I wanted to be a teacher—and I let it serve as an answer to the first question.

34. S. M. Ginzburg, "Iz zapisok pervogo evreia-studenta v Rossii (Lev Iosifovich Mandel'shtam, 1819–1889)," *Perezhitoe* 1 (1909): 13–25. See also idem, *Amolike Peterburg*, pp. 74–86.

35. The original, in *Pirke 'Avot* 4:20, reads literally "Be a tail to lions rather than a head to foxes."

Figure 19. Leon Mandelshtam (1819–1889).

Flustered and misunderstood, Mandelshtam searched for sympathetic friends among the students. His thick accent, he wrote in a private letter, seemed only to double the prejudice against him, "as a yid and as an ignoramus."

> So, was I treated poorly? No, on the contrary, very charitably. But this charity, for which I was supposed to beg, like alms, gnaws at my heart and devours my sensitive pride. I am not a beggar! I do not take alms! I, who hoped to be one of the representatives of our people, even if that people has no present— it is still a people with the greatest antiquity in the world. . . . No, this I cannot endure![36]

36. Ginzburg, "Iz zapisok pervogo evreia-studenta," pp. 47–48.

By the following year, his second, Mandelshtam had succeeded in publishing a collection of poems on biblical motifs and thereby winning at least a few acquaintances. But evidently his discontent lingered, for he then transferred to the law faculty of St. Petersburg University, where in 1844 he became the university's first Jewish graduate.[37] Upon receiving his degree, Mandelshtam secured one of the few forms of state employment open to Jews, replacing the disillusioned Max Lilienthal in 1845 as "expert Jew" in the Ministry of Enlightenment.

Given the fragmentary evidence from Mandelshtam's student years, a certain caution is in order when one reconstructs the effect of those years on his outlook. At a minimum, his university experience seems to have tempered his impulse to issue sweeping indictments of Jewish practices, as well as to express self-abnegation in the presence of Christians. In a series of articles published in the Russian press in the 1850s, Mandelshtam vigorously refuted charges of backwardness and fanaticism leveled against Russian Jewry and the Talmud.[38] Lavishly praising the Jews as the most literate people in Europe, creators of the model for the great codes of Western law (Roman and Justinian), and discoverers of scientific laws well before Europeans, Mandelshtam now asked why it was that in Russia "educated Jews are not given those civil rights that the very lowest sort of other people possess."[39]

Reuven Kulisher, born in 1828 in the Ukrainian province of Volhynia, followed a trajectory similar to Mandelshtam's. After a maskilic upbringing, he enrolled in a gymnasium in Zhitomir and from there followed Mandelshtam at St. Petersburg University (1848–52).[40] In his second year as a university student, Kulisher composed a lengthy sentimental poem titled "A Reply to the Slav," which, after failing to pass the censor, was distributed in manuscript to a small circle of acquaintances. While it is not clear what induced him to write such a work, the title and the content suggest an affront, possibly by a fellow student, to Kulisher's newly sensitized Jewish pride.[41] Like

---

37. The poems were apparently composed in Hebrew and published in Russian translation as *Stikhotvoreniia* (Moscow, 1840). See *Evreiskaia entsiklopediia*, 10: 591. See also Ginzburg, *Amolike Peterburg*, p. 81, and Georgievskii, *Doklad*, p. 44.

38. L. I. Mandel'shtam, *V zashchitu evreev: Stat'i* (St. Petersburg, 1859). This pamphlet appeared originally in *Sankt-Peterburskie Vedomosti*, no. 101 (1858).

39. The quotation is from Mandel'shtam's article in *Russkii Invalid*, no. 58 (1859), as cited in Klier, *Imperial Russia's Jewish Question*, p. 49.

40. *Evreiskaia entsiklopediia*, 9: 904–5.

41. The poem was first published in its entirety in *Perezhitoe* 3 (1911): 365–77. There the editors suggest that Kulisher was responding to anti-Semitic articles in the Russian press. The poem itself, however, contains no direct evidence of such motives. Similarly, there is nothing in the poem to directly substantiate Michael Stanislawski's claim that the text "was couched in the 'Aesopian' language of the Russian intelligentsia and hence addressed the 'Slavs' rather than the government" (*Tsar Nicholas I*, p. 122). Like most maskilic writers of the time, Kulisher

Mandelshtam, Kulisher found it necessary, having entered the student world, to strike a new balance between criticizing the Jews' backwardness and defending them against the "slander of their enemies." "Be assured," he replies to the anonymous Slav,

> I am able to appreciate
> A reproach that is useful to me;
> I do not spare my prejudices
> And I am ready to improve myself.
> But I recognize a hostile voice
> Even if it rings sweetly.

While conceding that traditional Jewish education tended to "wear down the spirit" and "constrict the passions," Kulisher countered:

> What use are feelings to the Jew,
> And for what the flight of passion?
> Perhaps so that he might sooner understand
> How he is despised by all? . . .
> What for others are the blessings of enlightenment
> For me are only a cause of torment:
> I merely see more clearly
> How unlucky is my star.
> An exile from society, without rights,
> I remain just what I was before,
> But my sleeping spirit has been awakened
> By the agitation of wayward thoughts.[42]

Expressed here in heightened form, the theme of secular education's equivocal effect on Jews—which one Jewish university graduate likened to the playwright A. S. Griboedov's *Gore ot uma* (Grief Due to Understanding)—weaves its way through the handful of known accounts of Jewish students at Russian universities in the pre-Reform period.[43] Even those who experienced the "whirl of student exaltation," as Arnold Dumashevskii called it, soon found themselves transformed into Jewish versions of the "superfluous men" who populate Russian fiction of the mid–nineteenth century: highly educated yet

---

was inclined to regard the Russian state as an ally in the struggle for enlightenment and reform. I have therefore taken Kulisher's references to "Slavs" and "opponents" as reflecting conflicts that arose in his immediate surroundings—that is, in the student milieu—though I cannot link them to particular individuals or incidents.

42. Kulisher, "Otvet Slavianinu," *Perezhitoe* 3 (1911): 369–70.

43. For the Griboedov analogy, see Shaul Ginzburg's preface to E. Tcherikover, *Istoriia Obshchestva dlia rasprostraneniia prosveshcheniia*, p. vi. For similar sentiments, see Tarnopol, *Opyt sovremennoi i osmotritel'noi reformy*, pp. 262–63; M. G. Morgulis, *Voprosy evreiskoi zhizni: Sobranie statei* (St. Petersburg, 1903), p. 23; and the petitions from Jewish medical students cited in Chapter 2, notes 49 and 52.

unable to secure a place in Russian society, forced to return to the Pale only to be branded on the Jewish street as a *trayfnik* (a violator of the laws of kashrut).[44]

THE MAKING OF THE RUSSIAN-JEWISH INTELLIGENTSIA

By the 1850s the government's Jewish Committee was well aware that merely throwing open the doors of Russian schools had failed to attract a significant number of Jewish students. The special elementary schools created by the state for Jewish children, as a kind of halfway house on the road to full integration into the general educational system, had so far produced disappointing results, prompting the minister of enlightenment to suggest in 1859 that they be shut down.[45] Even a highly unusual decree *requiring* Jewish merchants and honorary citizens to send their sons to Russian schools—at a time when mandatory elementary education was virtually unknown in Russia—produced few results, and was acknowledged by the Jewish Committee as unenforceable.[46] To be sure, a number of incentives were offered to Jewish graduates of institutions of higher learning, such as a reduction in military service from twenty-five to ten years and the right to apply for employment in the civil service (with little hope of acceptance, especially for positions outside the Pale). But these were little more than token adjustments in the dense network of official discrimination and had no discernible effect.[47] As a dozen Jewish merchants informed the minister of enlightenment: "If even such Jews . . . are destined to remain deprived of basic human rights, then the condition of their brothers who continue to live in ignorance is far more enviable. They, at least, do not feel such deprivations; they are consoled by the

44. Dumashevskii, "Razmyshleniia po povodu podniatogo v nashei zhurnalistike voprosa o evreiakh," *Odesskii Vestnik*, Dec. 30, 1858. Dumashevskii took a degree in law at St. Petersburg University in the 1850s. See also the petition from Jewish students at the Military-Medical Academy, RGIA, f. 1269, op. 1, d. 19, ll. 40–41. On Jews with medical degrees as violators of ritual law, see Garkavi [Harkavi], *Otryvki vospominaniia*, p. 6. For *trayfnik* see *Nedel'naia Khronika Voskhoda*, Apr. 3, 1883, p. 320.

45. RGIA, f. 1269, op. 1, d. 137, l. 171.

46. The idea of mandatory secular education for sons of Jewish merchants was raised in 1858 in a coordinated series of petitions from merchants across the Pale to the Jewish Committee. See ibid., d. 3b, ll. 151–56, and Pozner, *Evrei v obshchei shkole*, p. 26. Primary education was already mandatory (for Gentiles) in some areas of the Baltics, but only in 1908 did the autocracy decide to require primary schooling for children throughout the empire, a goal meant to be achieved by 1922.

47. A petition from Jewish merchants to the Ministry of Enlightenment noted that Jews "are prepared to make every sacrifice to have their children completely exempted from the draft, but are not very concerned about extensions or reductions of its duration": RGIA, f. 1269, op. 1, d. 3b, l. 134.

thought that they are suffering for their faith, while the educated Jew lacks even that comfort." If Jews truly required "a practical goal and sufficient incentive" in order to be drawn into Russia's educational system, as the government's Jewish Committee concluded in 1859, then the current approach stood little chance of success.[48] In fact, it could even backfire: one anonymous Jewish writer claimed in 1860 that the sorry state of Jewish university graduates had only strengthened the hand of retrograde forces in Jewish society. "Pointing their fingers at the educated," he asserted, "the obscurantists say, 'Look at them, how are they better than we? They get expelled from the same places we do, they get the same [lack of] respect we do. Why should we become enlightened?'"[49]

Against this background, the government's decision in November 1861 to grant Jewish university graduates the rights and privileges of their Gentile counterparts—including unrestricted residence and choice of occupation—stands out as a sharp departure. Jewish merchants of the first guild had been accorded an analogous status two years earlier. Now the government was targeting those whose distinction lay not in commerce and wealth but in learning, the cornerstone of the Haskalah strategy for transforming the Jews into a modern European people. Whereas the estate-based privileges granted to Jewish merchants were designed to foster and reward utility, the November 1861 decree sought that and more: to alter, by means of education, the Jews' character and outlook.

The decree made an enormous impression on Jewish partisans of reform. The fact that it appeared in the same year as the epochal proclamation liberating tens of millions of Russian serfs from near slavery caused several commentators, Jewish as well as Russian, to highlight what appeared to be a historical connection between the two.[50] A letter to the editor in *Ha-Melits* from a Jewish student asserted that the new statute was equivalent to the emancipation of Russian Jewry.[51] Lev Levanda, then a recent graduate of the state-sponsored rabbinical seminary in Vilna, wrote excitedly to a friend, "How do you feel after the publication of the Imperial decree granting rights to the Jews? What are you going to do—give private lessons or become a student? Wait around for civil rights or possess them?"[52] The hero of Levanda's first novel, *Goriachee vremia* (Hot Times), exclaims, "Having re-

48. Ibid., l. 136; d. 137, l. 180.

49. Ibid., d. 108, l. 7. This passage was part of an article intended for publication in the fledgling Odessa Jewish weekly *Razsvet,* and was excised by censors.

50. See, e.g., *Nashe Vremia,* no. 45 (Mar. 4, 1862), cited by Klier, *Imperial Russia's Jewish Question,* p. 130.

51. *Ha-Melits* 2, no. 19 (1861): 301.

52. Quoted in Tcherikover, *Istoriia Obshchestva dlia rasprostraneniia prosveshcheniia,* p. 129.

ceived from Russia the key to education, we will acquire for ourselves, God willing, Russian nationality [*narodnost´*], Russian citizenship, and a Russian fatherland."[53]

When news of the decree reached Minsk, Rabbi Zalkind Minor stunned worshipers at the central prayer house there by reading aloud the full text of the new statute and then proceeding to an impassioned sermon—in Russian— celebrating the virtues of general education. "O my brothers," he implored, "have you grasped the full import of this decree for the fate of our people? Do not say that the granting of these rights concerns only a small portion of our people, no!" On the contrary, Minor insisted, an offer of full equality was being made to any Jew willing to pursue an advanced secular education: "O brothers! Let the American Jews take pride in their Franklin and Washington, the English Jews in [Queen] Victoria and their John Russells, let the French and Dutch Jews take pride in the Revolution, the German Jews in Napoleon I, and finally the Italian Jews in Victor Emanuel—we Russian Jews will be proud of our Emperor Alexander II!" With this inventory of leaders who had ostensibly ushered in Jewish emancipation in their respective countries over the course of the preceding century, Minor pressed his claim that the November 1861 decree shared the same lofty intent—if only Russia's Jews would open themselves to secular learning. To the parents in the prayer house he pleaded,

> Behind us is a dark and difficult past full of bitter memories, which has caused us to become slaves to fanaticism and superstition, and has subjected us to unimaginable poverty. Before us lies a bright, joyful future. Behind you— ignorance and death; before you—education and life. Choose! . . . If you prevent your sons from obtaining equal rights through study at gymnasia and universities, you will destroy the future of your own children. Become enlightened, and enlighten others! In the enlightenment of the nations, and your own, is your only salvation.[54]

Enthusiastic reports about the benefits of secular education dominated the budding Jewish press throughout the 1860s.[55] Though lower in pitch, the reaction to the 1861 decree in the Russian press was also overwhelmingly positive. When a lone critic, the Slavophile Ivan Aksakov, complained that

53. L. O. Levanda, *Goriachee vremia* (St. Petersburg, 1875).

54. Zalkind Minor, *Glas radosti. Rech´ po sluchaiu Vysoch. darovannykh, v 27 den´ noiabria 1861 goda, preimushchestv evreiam, poluchivshim obrazovanie i sluzhashchim pri evreiskikh uchebnykh zavedeniiakh. Proiznesena 21-go ianvaria 1862 g. v Minskom bol´shom Molitvennom Dome* (Minsk, 1862), pp. 7, 17, 19, 25. For a critical review of Minor's career, see Azriel Shochat, "Hashkafotav ha-asimilatoriyot shel Zalkind Minor, ha-rav mi-ta'am shel kehillat moskvah," *Tsiyon* 44 (1979): 303–20.

55. Orbach, *New Voices of Russian Jewry,* pp. 72, 90, 159–62; Tcherikover, *Istoriia Obshchestva dlia rasprostraneniia prosveshcheniia,* p. 19; Greenberg, *Jews in Russia,* 1: 81.

Russian liberals were showering the new law with "loud and luxurious phrases" simply to reinforce their misguided self-image as "modern" and "tolerant," he was roundly attacked in half a dozen newspapers.[56]

By opening the gate to social and geographic mobility, the 1861 decree attached a concrete, immediately tangible benefit to higher education. True, entrance into the civil service, eagerly sought by university-educated Jews before 1861, remained elusive because of abiding informal discrimination against Jews in the tsarist bureaucracy. But even as the dismantling of the serf economy dealt a serious blow to Jewish petty trade, the Great Reforms—the higher tide on which selective integration was borne—were creating new arenas of white-collar employment outside the Table of Ranks. Jewish graduates of institutions of higher education were well positioned to take up jobs as lawyers in the new judicial system, as engineers in the expanding network of railroads, as well as in journalism, publishing, finance, and a host of other burgeoning fields. In a series of articles in 1869 under the headline "What Does Education Provide the Russian Jew for his Practical Life?" the Odessa Jewish newspaper *Den´* encouraged Jewish students to move beyond their traditional concentration in medicine into other professions. The paper noted with particular pleasure a recent case in which a Jewish graduate, denied employment in the Corps of Communications Engineers because of his failure to produce a baptism certificate, successfully appealed to the State Senate and was promptly hired.[57]

The prospect of gainful employment after graduation and the freedom to settle where one pleased, including St. Petersburg, proved a powerful draw for young Jews. To be sure, the student population as a whole expanded significantly during the Reform era, which witnessed the founding of Novorossiiskii University in Odessa (1865), the reopening of Warsaw University (1869), and substantial growth in enrollment at most other universities. But the results in the Jewish case were even more dramatic, as Table 8 indicates. Whereas the gymnasium population as a whole increased nearly sixfold between 1853 and 1886, the Jewish portion of that population expanded by a factor of nearly 50, with the most rapid growth for both groups occurring in the decade between 1865 and 1875. The timing of this surge casts doubt on the argument—widely credited in the Russian press, and subsequently by a number of historians—that the military reform of 1874, which reduced the duration of army service for graduates of secondary schools, was the main factor in attracting large numbers of Jews to

---

56. I. Aksakov, "Sleduet li dat´evreiam v Rossii zakonodatel´nye i administrativnye prava?" *Den´*, Feb. 16, 1862. For contemporary reactions, see Klier, *Imperial Russia's Jewish Question*, pp. 129–32.

57. S. Rozenberg, "Chto nakhodit russkii evrei v obrazovanii dlia svoei prakticheskoi zhizni?" *Den´*, nos. 8–9 (1869).

TABLE 8. Number of All Students
and of Jewish Students in Gymnasia and Progymnasia
and in Universities, Russian Empire, 1840–1886

	Gymnasia and progymnasia			Universities[a]		
		Jewish students			Jewish students	
Year	All students	#	%	All students	#	%
1840	n.a.	n.a.	n.a.	2,594	15	0.6
1853	12,007	159	1.3	n.a.	n.a.	n.a.
1865	26,789	990	3.7	4,084	129	3.2
1876	47,639	4,674	9.8	4,959	247	5.0
1886	69,564	7,562	10.9	12,793	1,856	14.5

[a] Exclusive of technical institutes and other institutions of higher education.

SOURCES: M. Kosven, "K voprosu o vysshem obrazovanii russkikh evreev," *Evreiskaia Zhizn'*, no. 7 (July 1904), pp. 167–73; S. V. Pozner, *Evrei v obshchei shkole: K istorii zakonodatel'stva i pravitel'stvennoi politiki v oblasti evreiskogo voprosa* (St. Petersburg, 1914), app. 2, p. 55; app. 4, p. 61.

gymnasia.[58] By the late 1870s, Jews constituted over 10 percent of gymnasium and progymnasium students across the empire. Within the Pale they accounted for 19 percent, and in the Odessa educational district for over a third.[59]

At the university level, a fivefold increase in the total student population between 1840 and 1886 was proportionately more than matched by growth in the number of Jewish students, which ballooned by a factor of more than 100. Predictably, the period of most rapid growth at the university level came roughly a decade after that in the gymnasium, between 1875 and 1885. By 1886, one in seven university students in the Russian Empire was Jewish, and at universities such as Kharkov and Odessa, that figure was closer to one in four or even one in three.[60]

No matter how one arranged the data—and by the 1870s both Russian and Jewish periodicals were beginning to take careful note of the ethnic and religious composition of the imperial student body—the trend was unmistakable. Jews were flocking to educational institutions more enthusiastically than any other group. In 1876, for example, for every 1,000 secondary-

58. In moderated form this argument was taken up by the historian Yehuda Slutsky, who argued that the 1874 military reform had a "revolutionary" impact on Jewish educational patterns. See Slutsky, *Ha-itonut ha-yehudit-rusit*, p. 25. The military reform of 1874 also cannot account for the significant rise in the number of Jewish women in institutions of higher education.

59. Pozner, *Evrei v obshchei shkole*, app. 4, pp. 58–61.

60. Ibid., app. 2 and 4, pp. 54–59.

Figure 20. A law degree conferred by Novorossiiskii University, Odessa, on Solomon Mandel´kern, "of the Jewish faith," confirming his right to enter the Table of Ranks of the Russian civil service at the tenth rank, and to forgo military service. (Courtesy of the Center for Judaic Studies Library, University of Pennsylvania.)

school-age Jewish children, 28 were enrolled in state-run schools. The corresponding figure for Lutherans was 26, for Catholics 20, and for Russian Orthodox 8.[61] Within the hierarchy of secondary schools, in which graduates of gymnasia, with their elite classical curriculum, were far more likely to gain admission to a university than were those of the more vocationally oriented *realschule,* Jews were more highly represented in gymnasia. And among gymnasium graduates, Jews were more likely than non-Jews to continue on to postsecondary study.[62]

Another indication of the significance of the November 1861 decree is the stream of petitions it inspired from Jewish graduates of technical institutes and state-run rabbinical seminaries, requesting that they too be granted the privileges enjoyed by their Jewish counterparts who had passed through Russian universities. In 1862, a seminary graduate expressed the hope that "our blessed government, . . . having granted unlimited rights to certain of

61. A. Kaufman, "Uchatsia li evrei?" *Razsvet,* Feb. 14, 1880, pp. 269–71. These data presumably do not include private and parochial schools.

62. Pozner, *Evrei v obshchei shkole,* app. 4 and 5, pp. 61–65; Georgievskii, *Doklad,* p. 196.

our colleagues who completed university studies, will not fail to give its attention to the small brotherhood of rabbis."[63] Beginning in 1867, a series of petitions from Jewish dentists, pharmacists, and veterinarians requested permission to settle and work outside the Pale, arguing that advanced technical training qualified Jews for legal equality as much as did a university education. Still other petitions, including one co-signed by Evzel Gintsburg, pointed out the "strange anomaly" whereby certain Jewish artisans enjoyed broader legal rights than did Jewish holders of advanced technical degrees.[64] As Chapter 2 demonstrated, these petitions were remarkably successful. Proceeding in its usual cautious manner, the tsarist government extended the privileges outlined in the decree of November 1861 to non-university-trained Jewish physicians and medics in 1865; to graduates of the St. Petersburg Technological Institute in 1872; and finally, in 1879, to Jewish graduates of virtually all institutions of higher education, including dentists, pharmacists, veterinarians, physicians' assistants (*fel'dshery*) and midwives.[65] The extension of the 1861 decree to Jewish graduates of institutions of higher education other than universities appears to have produced a noticeable jump in Jewish enrollment at institutions such as the Agricultural and Forestry Institute of New Alexandria (near Moscow), and the Military-Medical Academy of St. Petersburg.[66]

As before, considerations of utility combined with the goal of social integration to shape official policy. One tsarist official involved in broadening the 1861 decree cited "the pressing demand for educated technicians in our manufacturing industry," while another noted that "there are shortages everywhere" of physicians' assistants and midwives.[67] That *both* utility and "merging" were regarded as necessary criteria for the extension of rights can be seen in the decision to deny rights to certain categories of students. The November 1861 decree was not extended to graduates of the official rabbini-

63. Quoted in I. Sosis, "Obshchestvennye nastroeniia 'epokhi velikikh reform,'" *Evreiskaia Starina* 4, nos. 3–4 (1914): 353. For similar petitions, see RGIA, f. 1269, op. 1, d. 137, ll. 213–16.

64. RGIA, f. 821, op. 9, d. 78, ll. 1–33; d. 103, l. 407; d. 87, l. 2.

65. M. Krol', "K voprosu o pravakh i preimushchestvakh evreev, poluchivshikh vysshee obrazovanie," *Voskhod*, no. 10 (1900), pp. 66ff. These "extensions" of the 1861 decree did, however, place certain restrictions on the rights of the relevant categories of Jews.

66. M. Kosven, "K voprosu o vysshem obrazovanii russkikh evreev," *Evreiskaia Zhizn'*, no. 12 (December 1904), p. 155, and *Evreiskaia entsiklopediia*, 1: 601. Most higher technical institutes lack data on Jewish enrollment before the 1880s, so it is difficult to measure the impact of the granting of residence rights to Jewish graduates. In the case of the Institute of Communications Engineering in St. Petersburg, Jews already accounted for over 9 percent of the student body in 1878, at a time when they were still legally required to return to the Pale after graduating.

67. RGIA, f. 821, op. 9, d. 78, l. 47; d. 103, l. 410.

cal seminaries, whose education, while desirable from the state's point of view, did not bring them into contact with non-Jews. Nor was the November 1861 decree applied to Jewish "externs" who had passed equivalency examinations for advanced technical degrees. "Completion of an entire course of study in a [Russian] educational institution," noted one government committee in 1877, "involving constant interaction with Russian youth, doubtless exercises an enormous moral influence. It pulls Jews out of that narrow and harmful milieu in which they wither away and are intellectually and morally corrupted. The same cannot be said of those who prepare at home for an [equivalency] exam."[68]

However strong the enticement of legal privileges conferred by a diploma after 1861, it is doubtful whether Jews would have flocked to Russian institutions of higher education without a shift in attitudes toward secular learning and the non-Jewish world itself. The process by which the traditional Jewish reverence for textual study could be extended—or transferred—to nontraditional domains is perhaps the most elusive of all the forces that propelled Jews into Russia's universities. "We were absolutely convinced," wrote Mikhail Krol´, a student at St. Petersburg University in the 1880s, "that a university education would necessarily raise a person to a higher moral level. This was a consequence of the Jewish conception of scholarship as enlightening and transformative."[69] In Jewish memoirs, first encounters with secular learning are often presented—in hindsight, of course—as part of an inevitable coming of age, bound up with the end of childhood in a culture in which there was no adolescence as such. The metaphors used, whether of "awakening" from sleep or "reaching for the light" or escaping from the "stifling ghetto" into the "fresh air" of secular knowledge, reveal frustratingly little about the actual process of change.[70] "None of us, including myself," recalled Vladimir Harkavi, "knew what a university was, and what a university education consisted of. For me it was a lamp, a symbol of freedom toward which I strove from the ghetto, not only geographically but also intellectually. Russia, unknown to us . . . , appeared radiant, made up primarily of people imbued with the ideas of Belinskii, of *Notes of the Fatherland, The Contemporary,* Turgenev, Nekrasov, etc."[71] Simon Dubnov, the great historian

---

68. Ibid,, d. 103, l. 409.

69. M. A. Krol´, "Vospominaniia o L. Ia. Shternberge," *Katorga i Ssylka* 27/28 (1929): 221.

70. Metaphors of awakening and illumination can be found in many East European Jewish memoirs and fictional accounts; for paradigmatic examples, see Y. L. Gordon's "Hakitsah 'ami!" in his *Kitvei Yehudah Leib Gordon: Shirah* (Tel Aviv, 1956), pp. 17–18; and Shlomo Rapaport [Ansky], *Zikhroynes* (Warsaw, 1925), 1: 5–6.

71. Garkavi [Harkavi], *Otryvki vospominaniia,* p. 9. In similarly laconic fashion, Mark Vishniak reports that at age sixteen he abruptly ceased observing Jewish religious law after reading Dostoevsky's *Brothers Karamazov:* "I became cognizant of my lack of faith." Mark Veniaminovich Vishniak, *Dan´ proshlumu* (New York, 1954), p. 25.

who had tried but failed to qualify for admission to a Russian university in 1881, was moved to ask, "What drove . . . the young fledglings from many Jewish nests and drew them to the big university cities?" His answer, a collage of material and intellectual motives, faithfully captures the inchoate ambitions of his generation:

> They were spontaneously attracted by new currents carried in the air, the consciousness that it was impossible to live in the old way, . . . to remain in the old swamp, to get married, have children, to sit in the store calling to customers, making deals, hunting for profit or just a plain piece of bread—in sum, to remain on the lower rungs of the social ladder at a time when a new culture was on the rise.[72]

Just how powerfully the new ideas and the prospect of a new way of living attracted young Jews to Russian universities is highlighted by an important subgroup of Jewish students to whom the November 1861 decree applied only in limited fashion, but who nonetheless established a noticeable presence in Russian higher education. The ascent of Jewish women up the Russian educational ladder was in many respects even more dramatic than that of their male counterparts.[73] Virtually excluded from the heder and served by only a handful of the government primary schools for Jews, the vast majority of Jewish girls across the nineteenth century received no formal education of any kind. Nonetheless, literacy among Jewish women was relatively widespread, and those few Jewish girls who were formally educated were far more likely than Jewish boys to attend Russian primary schools.[74]

Postsecondary education for Jewish women, as for all women in Russia, was extremely rare until the 1870s, when the first "women's higher courses" appeared. As with the opening of universities to Jews at the beginning of the century, here too Russia unexpectedly anticipated many of its European neighbors. Beginning in Moscow in 1872 and spreading over the following decade to Petersburg, Kiev, and Kazan, Russian postsecondary educational institutions graduated several thousand women at a time when only a small number of European universities (primarily in Switzerland) admitted women, many of whom in fact came from Russia. By 1882, more than two hundred

72. Dubnov, *Kniga zhizni*, 1: 74–75. On Dubnov's failed attempt to pass the equivalency exams for a gymnasium diploma, see ibid., pp. 83–84.

73. Enrollment in women's courses gave Jewish women temporary right of residence outside the Pale during the period of study. Only in 1911 was this right made permanent, as it had been for Jewish men since 1861. See Ruth Dudgeon, "The Forgotten Minority: Women Students in Imperial Russia, 1872–1917," *Russian History/Histoire Russe*, no. 9 (1982), p. 18.

74. Shaul Stampfer, "Gender Differentiation and Education of the Jewish Woman in Nineteenth-Century Eastern Europe," *Polin* 7 (1992): 63–87; Sliozberg, *Dela minuvshikh dnei*, 1: 110.

female physicians had been trained in Russia—more than in any other European state.[75]

Jewish women were quick to put these opportunities to use. Their motives appear to have been similar to those of other students, as in the case of Eva Broido, who recalled her ambitions as a teenager in the Lithuanian town of Dvinsk in the 1880s:

> A preoccupation with the ideas of freedom, discontent with the stagnant provincial life, a vague desire for an ideal country peopled with perfect men and women, a passion for knowledge which would show the way to a better and more glorious future—yes, such moods and ideas were almost general [sic] among us. Young men and women alike strove to enter universities or technical schools, there to learn the "truth about life." This thirst for knowledge and learning, for self-improvement and a free unfolding of one's personality, however vague and aimless, was so typical of all of us, that the then current ludicrous term "a young girl with strivings" described the condition most aptly.[76]

Expressions of idealism notwithstanding, Jewish women were often suspected of multiple forms of social climbing—as Jews and as women. "We often heard," wrote a Russian female student, "that in poor Jewish families, the gymnasium diploma served as a kind of dowry. . . . It was astounding with what tenacity the tavernkeeper or small shopkeeper would obtain a place in the gymnasium for his daughter."[77] Nor were Jewish males immune to such sentiments, as the St. Petersburg University student L. D. Liakhovetskii demonstrated in a letter to the leading Jewish weekly in September 1882. With an approving note by the editors, Liakhovetskii charged that most Jewish *kursistki* (as students in the "higher courses" were known) were simply out to "catch a good husband"—perhaps even a Gentile. For the following two months a stormy debate over this claim raged on the newspaper's pages. One respondent expressed his doubts that Jewish kursistki were driven by matrimonial interests, since one was hardly likely to find a good husband among students. Another expressed her view that Jewish women often pur-

---

75. Before the founding of the higher courses, women had briefly (from 1859 to 1861) been allowed to audit lectures at certain universities. However, women were not permitted to take the state examinations, since a passing grade would have qualified them for the Table of Ranks. See Christine Johanson, *Women's Struggle for Higher Education in Russia, 1855–1900* (Montreal, 1987), pp. 5, 19, 23; and Susan Morrissey, *Heralds of Revolution: Russian Students and the Mythologies of Radicalism* (New York, 1998), p. 13.

76. Eva Broido, *Memoirs of a Revolutionary*, trans. and ed. Vera Broido (London, 1967), p. 9.

77. "Eine versunkene Welt: Erinnerungen aus dem alten Russland," unpublished memoirs of Natalie Oettli-Kirpichnikova, a native of Odessa; quoted in Daniela Neumann, *Studentinnen aus dem Russischen Reich in der Schweiz (1867–1914)* (Zurich, 1987), pp. 80–81. I am grateful to Samuel Kassow for bringing Neumann's work to my attention.

Figure 21. Students in a dining hall at the Bestuzhev Higher Courses for Women, 1900.

sued higher education "partly in order to escape from the profitable fiancés thrust upon them by their parents, which happens quite frequently precisely in Jewish families."[78]

Whatever their motives, real or imagined, Jewish women entered the "higher courses" at a remarkable pace. In 1868 Varvara A. Kashevarova, an orphan of Jewish descent, became the first woman to receive a medical degree in Russia.[79] By the 1880s, Jewish women accounted for 16 percent of the students enrolled at the Kiev Higher Courses and the Liubianskie Courses in Moscow, 17 percent at the elite Bestuzhevskie Courses in Petersburg (to which Horace Gintsburg was a major donor), and 34 percent at the Women's Medical Courses, also in Petersburg. Within the total population of female students, Jewish women constituted the single largest non–Russian Orthodox element, outnumbering Catholics, Lutherans, and

78. Liakhovetskii's letter appeared in *Nedel'naia Khronika Voskhoda*, Sept. 25, 1882, p. 1071. For responses, see issues of Oct. 16, 1882, p. 1127; Oct. 23, 1882, p. 1153; Oct. 30, 1882, p. 1186 (where the response quoted above appears); and Nov. 16, 1882, pp. 1264–72. Liakhovetskii also published a short story that takes a critical stance toward a romance between a Jewish *kursistka* and a Russian university student: see L. L. Liakhovetskii, *Mechta i deistvitel'nost': Razskaz iz zhizni evreiskoi molodezhi* (St. Petersburg, 1884).

79. Jeanette Tuve, *The First Russian Women Physicians* (Newtonville, Mass., 1984), pp. 46–50.

Muslims combined.[80] Though smaller in absolute numbers, they were as much or more of a presence among the much-discussed kursistki as their Jewish male counterparts were within the university and technical school population.[81]

THE ECONOMICS OF HIGHER EDUCATION FOR JEWS

Thus far we have addressed the "why" of the Jewish presence in Russian institutions of higher education. But the "how" is also of interest, especially since it reveals the continuing influence of the Jewish notables who helped broker the policy of selective integration in the first place. In addition to petitions to government officials, that influence now took the form of a large-scale, privately endowed system of financial aid for Jewish students. Granted, it is impossible to isolate the specific impact of financial aid on the rise in the number of Jewish students, since we have almost no reliable data concerning their financial need prior to 1910.[82] Nonetheless, the story of how the Jewish presence in higher education was subsidized is of considerable significance.

For centuries, yeshivas in Eastern Europe had enjoyed a wide range of private financial assistance, whether from local individuals who provided "eating days" (*esn teg*) for students or from distant communities responding to appeals by traveling fund-raisers. This elaborate system of aid allowed large numbers of Jews to fulfill the commandment to support study of the Law.[83] By contrast, most Jews in nineteenth-century Russia, as a contemporary

---

80. These data are drawn from various years between 1872 and 1885, with chronological gaps that reflect incomplete records concerning religious affiliation. See Johanson, *Women's Struggle*, pp. 45, 69, 82; Ruth Dudgeon, "Forgotten Minority," p. 16; G. M. Gertsenshtein, "Evreiki-studentki," *Razsvet*, no. 37 (1880), p. 1466; Ekaterina Nekrasova, "Zhenskie vrachebnye kursy v Peterburge: Iz vospominanii i perepiski pervykh studentok," *Vestnik Evropy* 17, no. 6 (1882): 817.

81. See, e.g., Nekrasova, "Zhenskie vrachebnye kursy," p. 817. Once women began to be admitted to institutions of higher education in Germany at the beginning of the twentieth century, Jewish women similarly made up a larger proportion among female students there than did Jewish men among male students. See Marion Kaplan, *The Making of the Jewish Middle Class: Women, Family, and Identity in Imperial Germany* (New York, 1991), p. 138.

82. The single source of information on the financial standing of Jewish students before 1910 that I have been able to find is M. Kosven, "K voprosu o vysshem obrazovanii russkikh evreev," *Evreiskaia Zhizn'*, no. 10 (October 1904), p. 151, where the author notes that of 260 Jewish students at Kiev University between 1860 and 1880 for whom records exist, 44 (17 percent) were expelled for inability to pay tuition. Roughly the same proportion of non-Jewish students were expelled during the same period for the same reason.

83. For a description of the financing of the reknowned Volozhin yeshiva, see Shaul Stampfer, *Ha-yeshivah ha-lita'it be-hithavutah* (Jerusalem, 1995), pp. 39–43.

noted, "did not include students [at non-Jewish schools] in their under-standing of the concept of 'the needy.'"[84]

Even before the decree of November 1861 granted Jewish university grad-uates legal parity with their Gentile counterparts, a handful of wealthy mer-chants led by the ever-present Evzel Gintsburg began to adapt the traditional Jewish system of charity to strikingly new purposes. In 1857 Gintsburg es-tablished a 5,000-ruble fund, the interest on which would help defray ex-penses for Jews at institutions of higher education in Petersburg. In the fol-lowing year a group of 33 merchants in Kiev led by the sugar magnate A. M. Brodskii created a similar fund of 7,500 rubles to support Jews at Kiev Uni-versity. To underscore his "sincere rapprochement with his fellow Russian citizens," Brodskii endowed an additional scholarship for needy Christian students. Like-minded efforts followed at the universities of Kharkov and Moscow.[85]

Efforts to persuade the tsarist government to supplement these privately endowed scholarships with funds drawn from Jewish tax revenues were only modestly successful. At the Technological Institute in Petersburg, five state-funded stipends were earmarked in 1859 specifically for Jewish students.[86] At the same time the Ministry of Public Enlightenment, having solicited the opinions of superintendents of educational districts across the Pale, began to divert 10 percent—roughly 24,000 rubles—of the annual budget of state-sponsored Jewish schools to stipends for Jewish students attending Russian primary and secondary schools. The diversion of these funds reflected the fact that the state's ultimate aim was and always had been to mainstream Jew-ish students, and thereby to render separate Jewish schools superfluous. An additional motive was the desire, as the government's Jewish Committee put it, "to free these young Jews, at least during their studies, from dependence on their communities and relatives, who for the most part are fanatics."[87]

The annual 24,000-ruble subsidy, however, was strictly for Jewish students at the primary and secondary levels, and thus the burden of supporting those whose sights were set on a university education remained with private indi-viduals. They received much encouragement from Dr. Nikolai Pirogov, a pi-

84. Sliozberg, *Dela minuvshikh dnei*, 1: 89.

85. On Gintsburg, see RGIA, f. 1269, op. 1, d. 136, ll. 261–62; d. 139, l. 116. Gintsburg's scholarship was limited by imperial order to students at Petersburg's Medical-Surgical Acad-emy. On the Kiev group, see RGIA, f. 733, op. 149, d. 39, ll. 1–2, and *Razsvet*, Feb. 24, 1861. On Kharkov and Moscow, see Tcherikover, *Istoriia Obshchestva dlia rasprostraneniia prosveshcheniia*, pp. 134–35.

86. Tcherikover, *Istoriia Obshchestva dlia rasprostraneniia prosveshcheniia*, p. 139.

87. RGIA, f. 1269, op. 1, d. 139, ll. 104–15. For similar views, see *Materialy, otnosiashchiesia k obrazovaniiu evreev v Rossii* (St. Petersburg, 1865) p. 37. The latter document is a detailed re-port on the state schools for Jews prepared for the Ministry of Public Enlightenment by its in-spector, F. Postel's.

oneering Russian advocate of progressive educational reform, including access to higher education for women, who wrote in the pages of the Odessa Jewish weekly *Razsvet* in 1861, "I am convinced that nowhere does philanthropy yield such outstanding results as in the matter of university education for young people."[88] Another Odessa Jewish weekly, *Sion*, spoke for many when it asserted that "educated Jews will play an especially vital role in the fate of their people: they must improve its moral life, raise it in the eyes of the dominant population, and in this way bring us closer to our cherished goal."[89]

The decree of November 1861 galvanized such opinions and led directly to the formation of a new kind of organization, unprecedented in Russian-Jewish history, whose primary contribution would be to transform the economics of higher education for Jews. With the founding in 1863 of the Society for the Spread of Enlightenment among Jews in Russia, nongovernmental subsidization of Jewish students took on an entirely new dimension. While the society's founders failed to satisfy the hope that they would establish a headquarters for the Haskalah and a quasi-representative organ for Russian Jewry vis-à-vis the autocracy, they did make it possible for thousands of young Jews to take advantage of selective integration by means of a university or equivalent degree. The society typically devoted between two-thirds and three-fourths of its annual budget to financial aid for Jews in Russian institutions of higher education, beginning in 1863 with some 3,000 rubles (half of which came from Evzel Gintsburg) and cresting in 1893 at over 35,000 rubles. During the first quarter-century of its existence, a total of 268,000 rubles was distributed to Jewish students. Data on recipients suggest that in certain years roughly half of all Jewish students in the Russian Empire were beneficiaries of the society's largess.[90] This remarkable fact is underscored by the constant stream of petitions for support that made their way to the society's headquarters in St. Petersburg from Jewish students across the empire.[91] In an 1889 article on the growing exclusion of Jews from pri-

---

88. *Razsvet*, no. 42 (1861), p. 669. On Pirogov's role in the movement for women's higher education, see Richard Stites, *The Women's Liberation Movement in Russia: Feminism, Nihilism, and Bolshevism, 1860–1930* (Princeton, 1978), p. 30.

89. *Sion*, 1861, p. 205.

90. These data are drawn from the society's annual reports between 1864 and 1894. Most reports do not include the budget and activities of the society's Odessa branch. See also Zvi Halevy, *Jewish University Students and Professionals in Tsarist and Soviet Russia* (Tel Aviv, 1976), p. 18.

91. See, e.g., *Otchet Obshchestva dlia rasprostraneniia prosveshcheniia mezhdu evreiami v Rossii za 1870 god* (St. Petersburg, 1871), p. 11; *Otchet Obshchestva dlia rasprostraneniia prosveshcheniia mezhdu evreiami v Rossii za 1875 god* (St. Petersburg, 1876), p. 14; Tcherikover, *Istoriia Obshchestva dlia rasprostraneniia prosveshcheniia*, pp. 137, 146–47. Selected petitions are reproduced in Y. L. Rosenthal, *Toldot hevrat marbe haskalah*, vol. 2.

vate and state scholarship competitions, a journalist concluded that "their only source of support, which at least saves Jewish students from expulsion for failure to pay tuition, is the assistance provided by the Society for the Spread of Enlightenment."[92] No wonder, then, that the hostile but perceptive director of the Vilna District of Education, I. Kornilov, once accused the society of trying to act like "a Jewish Ministry of Enlightenment."[93]

In terms of strategy, the society did resemble the Ministry of Enlightenment in certain respects. Its priorities were decisively at the higher, more prestigious end of the educational spectrum, to the detriment of secondary and especially elementary schooling. The society even urged the Ministry of Enlightenment to shift the state's financial aid for Jewish students in Russian primary and secondary schools (the roughly 24,000-ruble annual fund) to the university level.[94] The only elementary-level education to receive funding from the society before the 1890s was that for Jewish girls, in large measure because girls were virtually excluded from both the heder and the government's Jewish schools. As for the heder itself—where the vast majority of Jewish boys continued to receive their primary and in most cases only formal education—the society's members were reluctant to press for reform lest they offend traditional sensibilities. They were similarly loath to subsidize state-run Jewish schools—including the rabbinical seminaries—for fear that the government might respond by shifting its resources elsewhere. Even after the tsarist Ministry of Enlightenment drastically reduced its support for the network of state-sponsored Jewish schools in 1873 and canceled its annual 24,000-ruble scholarship fund in 1875—having correctly concluded that Jewish students no longer needed to be coaxed into Russian schools— the society continued its top-heavy pattern of financial aid.[95]

By the mid-1880s, as Table 9 demonstrates, the Jewish presence in Russian educational institutions reproduced the top-heavy structure of the Rus-

92. *Nedel'naia Khronika Voskhoda*, Feb. 17, 1889, p. 171. *Russkii Evrei*, Mar. 19, 1880, p. 454, noted that of the 93 privately endowed scholarships at Kharkov University, Jews were eligible for only 3; the rest were limited to adherents of the Russian Orthodox faith.

93. Klier, *Imperial Russia's Jewish Question*, p. 165, citing I. Kornilov, *Russkoe delo v severno-zapadnom krae* (St. Petersburg, 1908).

94. *Otchet Obshchestva dlia rasprostraneniia prosveshcheniia mezhdu evreiami v Rossii za 1865 god* (St. Petersburg, 1866), p. 35.

95. In the 1880s a handful of members called for a fundamental shift in the society's priorities, toward elementary education, especially in rural Jewish communities, where schools of any kind were scarce. But only at the end of the century did this idea begin to become a reality, driven in large measure by the 1887 quotas on Jews in higher education and gymnasia, which effectively limited the pool of upper-level financial aid recipients. See *Otchet Obshchestva dlia rasprostraneniia prosveshcheniia mezhdu evreiami v Rossii za 1883 god* (St. Petersburg, 1884), pp. 81–82; *Otchet Obshchestva dlia rasprostraneniia prosveshcheniia mezhdu evreiami v Rossii za 1889 god* (St. Petersburg, 1890), p. 4; see also RGIA, f. 1532, op. 1, d. 353a, l. 7, and YIVO, RG 89, folder 757, doc. 106.

TABLE 9. Number and Percent of Jewish Students in Non-Jewish
Educational System, Russian Empire, 1886, by Type of Institution

Type of institution	#	%
Elementary school		
Parish and rural	15,619	1
District	938	5
Urban	1,604	4
Real'nye (secondary) school	1,579	8
Gymnasium and progymnasium		
Boys'	7,640	11
Girls'	5,213	8
Women's Higher Courses	236	16
Veterinary institute	101	14
Technological institute	271	17
University	1,856	15

SOURCE: A. Georgievskii, *Doklad po voprosu o merakh otnositel'no obrazovaniia evreev* (St. Petersburg, 1886), p. 200.

sian educational system itself: it was proportionally weakest at the elementary level and increased steadily as one moved up the educational ladder.

Table 9 requires careful interpretation. The low absolute and relative numbers of Jews in Russian primary schools reflect the fact that most Jewish males, whatever their ultimate educational path, began their studies in a heder or, less often, in a state-sponsored Jewish school, rather than in a Russian school. At the end of the century, the Jewish Colonization Association estimated that there were 370,000 students in heders and 60,000 Jews in Russian or state-sponsored Jewish schools.[96] Furthermore, had the data in Table 9 been restricted to the territory of the Pale of Settlement, where roughly 95 percent of the Jewish population lived, instead of encompassing the empire as a whole, the proportion of Jews in Russian primary and secondary schools would have appeared somewhat higher. Nonetheless, the data's empire-wide scope is appropriate insofar as enrollment not only in universities but in gymnasia was drawing more and more Jews out of the Pale. In 1870, roughly 10 percent of all Jewish gymnasium and progymnasium students in the Russian Empire lived outside the Pale. By 1900, this figure had grown to an astounding 38 percent.[97]

96. Slutsky, *Ha-itonut ha-yehudit-rusit*, p. 13.

97. Among Jewish students at *real'nye uchilishche*, the figure was even more striking: in 1900, 47 percent lived outside the Pale. Pozner, *Evrei v obshchei shkole*, app. 4 and 5. On the legal status of Jewish gymnasium students outside the Pale and the government's concern, see *Nedel'naia Khronika Voskhoda*, Aug. 5, 1884, p. 877.

Like the tsarist government, the Society for the Spread of Enlightenment allocated its resources in a way that reinforced the privileged status of educational institutions in Russia proper, especially in the two capitals, at the expense of those located in or near the Pale. Over the course of the society's first two decades (1863–83), approximately 80 percent of its financial aid went to students enrolled at institutions in St. Petersburg, and much of the remainder went to those in Moscow, utterly eclipsing the funds provided to their peers in Odessa, Dorpat, Riga, Kiev, Kharkov, and Kazan. Jewish students at Warsaw University, which reopened in 1869, were considered part of the Polish sphere and received no funding from the society.[98] In part, this pattern reflected the geographical concentration of the society's members, of whom the single largest contingent, ranging over time from 25 to 50 percent, lived in the imperial capital—more than in any other city. Nearly all the major donors, beginning with the Gintsburg family and Leon Rosenthal, lived there. More broadly, the society's distribution of funds reflected its members' sense of ethnic hierarchy, their belief that the acquisition of *Russian* learning and culture was the key to progress for the empire's Jews.

THE QUESTION OF RUSSIFICATION

Did the tsarist government share this belief? The question whether and in what manner the tsarist state pursued a policy of Russification of its ethnic minorities (and for that matter, of those considered ethnic Russians) has become a source of considerable controversy among historians.[99] By and large, the debate as it concerns the Jews has focused on policy pronouncements by high officials, and has paid surprisingly little attention to actual practices on the ground.[100] Beyond the acquisition of the Russian language, what

98. Halevy, *Jewish University Students*, p. 18. Data on geographical distribution apply to approximately half of the funds given away by the society; there are no such data for the rest. It is also worth noting that most of the early petitions to establish local branches of the society came from university towns such as Odessa, Kiev, Moscow, and Kazan, where members specifically sought the right to steer a portion of their dues to scholarships for local Jewish students. See *Otchet Obshchestva dlia rasprostraneniia prosveshcheniia mezhdu evreiami v Rossii za 1865 god* (Petersburg, 1866), p. 33, and *Otchet Obshchestva dlia rasprostraneniia prosveshcheniia mezhdu evreiami v Rossii za 1880 god* (St. Petersburg, 1881), p. 11. On the denial of funding to Jewish students at the University of Warsaw, see Tcherikover, *Obshchestva dlia rasprostraneniia prosveshcheniia mezhdu evreiami v Rossii*, p. 150.

99. For recent, wide-ranging discussions, see Kappeler, *Rußland als Vielvölkerriech*, pp. 224–29, and Goeffrey Hosking, *Russia: People and Empire* (Cambridge, Mass., 1997), pp. 367–97. On the western borderlands, see Theodore Weeks, *Nation and State in Late Imperial Russia: Nationalism and Russification on the Western Frontier, 1863–1914* (De Kalb, Ill. 1996).

100. Rogger, *Jewish Policies and Right-Wing Politics*, pp. 26–27; Klier, *Imperial Russia's Jewish Question*, pp. 152–58, examines contemporary debate in the Russian press.

specific values and cultural norms did the government want Jewish students to absorb?

An ideal site in which to search for answers to this question is the series of government-sponsored textbooks prepared specifically for Jews at the secondary level (universities enjoyed a certain autonomy in matters of curriculum, and in any event did not offer courses or readings specifically aimed at Jews). Under titles such as *Useful Readings for State Jewish Schools, Russian Readings for Jewish Youth,* and *Russian Readings for Jewish Children,* these books were produced in mass quantities, in several cases going through multiple editions of well over 10,000 copies from the 1860s to the 1880s.[101] They consist of roughly four kinds of material: fables and homilies, short sketches of Russian geography and historical figures, brief adaptations (in Russian) of Jewish texts, and descriptions of scientific and natural phenomena. The largest category, that of fables and homilies, strove above all (and, it must be said, with a minimum of subtlety) to instill a work ethic and upright behavior. Apart from the fact that they were conveyed in Russian, however, the folktales and stories transmitted no overtly Russian content: typically, their main characters were animals (e.g., "The Bee and the Sheep"), and some were translated into Russian from other languages.

The texts concerning Russian history and geography—on average no more than a tenth of the total content—concentrated on individual tsars and territories, with an eye toward cultivating loyalty to the monarchy and the Russian lands. They lend weight to the argument that the tsarist government was more comfortable expressing itself in an ethnically neutral, dynastic idiom than in the rhetoric of nationhood. In the various readers, moreover, Russian history was more than offset quantitatively by ancient Jewish history and texts concerning leaders such as Abraham, Moses, and King Solomon. If anything, the spirit of the readers was remarkably cosmopolitan. One finds there not just the fabulist I. A. Krylov but E. T. A. Hoffmann and the brothers Grimm; not just the historical popularizer Vladimir Novakovskii but Thomas Jefferson and the Talmud. When it examined *Russian Readings for Jewish Youth* for publication in 1865, the Ministry of Enlighten-

---

101. *Poleznoe chtenie dlia upotrebleniia v kazennykh evreiskikh uchilishchakh* (Vilna, 1873) came out in an initial run of 3,100 copies; *Russkoe chtenie dlia evreiskogo iunoshestva* (Vilna, 1865–88) went through at least eight editions and 14,000 copies, and its commercial success inspired a companion volume, *Kratkii slovar´ ili ob˝iasnenie slov vstrechaiushchikhsia v knige "Russkoe chtenie dlia evreiskogo iunoshestva"* (Vilna, 1873); *Pervye uroki russkoi gramoty: Bukvar i pervonachal´noe chtenie prednaznachennye dlia evreiskogo iunoshestva* (Vilna, 1866–75) went through at least five editions and 17,000 copies; *Russkoe chtenie dlia evreiskikh detei* (Kiev/Zhitomir, 1885–88) went through at least three editions and 5,800 copies. The title pages of most of the readers indicate that they received official approval from the Ministry of Enlightenment, and of course all had to pass the censor. The remarks that follow, summarizing the readers' contents, draw on all the works named in this note.

ment questioned the inclusion of excerpts from the Talmud, but in the end gave the book its full endorsement.[102]

Jewish students who enrolled in Russian gymnasia encountered a similarly cosmopolitan curriculum.[103] Thanks largely to the influence of the long-serving D. A. Tolstoi (minister of enlightenment, 1866–80; minister of internal affairs, 1882–89), the Russian gymnasium—the main conduit to higher education—required its students to immerse themselves in the languages and literatures of ancient Greece and Rome. The choice of a classical curriculum owed less perhaps to the perceived affinity between Russia and the civilizations of antiquity than to the urge to emulate Russia's European neighbors, whose gymnasia in the nineteenth century tended to be thoroughly classical. But in European societies, a veritable cult of classical antiquity often served as (among other things) a vehicle for national self-exaltation.[104] While students in Russia frequently derided the official curriculum as tedious, reactionary, and far removed from present-day needs (in stark contrast to the unofficial curriculum of radical Russian writers and critics), it was not—nor could it have been—accused of fomenting Russian nationalism. "One has only to examine the textbooks . . . recommended by the authorities," recalled one former Jewish student, "to be convinced that young people had nowhere from which to draw the juices of national identity."[105] Thus to the extent that anything resembling *cultural* (as opposed to strictly linguistic) Russification occurred among Jewish students, it was only indirectly the product of official policy, and owed far more to the unofficial curriculum of the student subculture, about which more below.

But official policy did foster, unwittingly, another dimension of Russification. For insofar as Russia's educational system, with its pronounced preference for higher learning, helped create the characteristically Russian chasm between a small, Europeanized intelligentsia and an enormous mass of unschooled peasants with their own distinctive norms and practices, it increasingly exerted a roughly analogous pressure on Russia's Jews. Russian institutions of higher education were the primary incubators not just of Jewish intellectuals but of a Jewish intelligentsia, a new social formation that did not exist before the 1860s and had no direct counterpart in any other Jew-

---

102. RGIA, f. 733, op. 189, d. 116, l. 2.

103. An official survey conducted in 1864 also confirms the absence of any overt Russification in the state-sponsored rabbinical seminaries. See *Materialy, otnosiashchiesia k obrazovaniiu evreev v Rossii*, pp. 11–19.

104. Frank Turner, *The Greek Heritage in Victorian Britain* (New Haven, 1981); Suzanne Marchand, *Down from Olympus: Archeology and Philhellenism in Germany, 1750–1970* (Princeton, 1996).

105. G. B. Sliozberg, "Dorevoliutsionnoe russkoe studenchestvo," in P. A. Bobrinskoi et al., eds., *Pamiati russkogo studenchestva: sbornik vospominanii* (Paris, 1934), p. 87. In this connection I take issue with Patrick Alston's characterization of Tolstoi's pedagogic policies as "bureaucratic nationalism." See Alston, *Education and the State*, chap. 3.

ish community.[106] The forces that shaped the Jewish encounter with Russia's institutions of higher education virtually guaranteed such an outcome; it was, quite simply, overdetermined. These factors included the government's decision in 1861 to set the highest educational threshold for selective integration (a postsecondary degree); the fact that the first concrete benefit of such integration was the freedom to remove oneself from the Pale; the decision by the Society for the Spread of Enlightenment to support Jewish students almost exclusively at the postsecondary level; the society's marked preference for students at institutions outside the Pale; and the generally fragmented state of Jewish society in nineteenth-century Russia.

For a considerable number of Jewish students, higher education involved a physical departure from the centers of Jewish life in the Pale. For nearly all, as we have seen, it fostered a psychological self-distancing as well. By the 1860s, contemporaries began to speak of a Jewish "intelligentsia" and imported the Russian word into Hebrew and Yiddish, which like most languages had lacked a singular noun to designate a collective entity of intellectuals. The fact that there was never such a collective singular noun for maskilim (in contrast to *rabanut,* or rabbinate) further highlights the significance of the Russian context for the emergence of the Jewish intelligentsia as a social entity. By the 1870s, in fact, a pair of spin-off terms—*diplomirovannaia intelligentsiia* (diploma intelligentsia) and *polu-intelligent* (half/pseudointellectual)—had acquired specific inflections in the Jewish context, signifying the distinction between Jewish graduates of Russian institutions of higher education and those whose formal training had taken place exclusively in the heder, talmud torah, and/or yeshiva.[107]

In the minds of the new Russian-Jewish intelligentsia, there emerged the parallel, populist-tinged idea of a Jewish *narod,* or folk. To be sure, the term *narod,* with its highly charged overtones of ignorance, suffering, and au-

106. The entrance of Jews into the German educational system produced—as one would expect, given the structure of German society in the nineteenth century—a Jewish *Bildungs-bürgertum* rather than an intelligentsia per se. While both the *Bildungsbürgertum* and the intelligentsia purported to transcend inherited divisions of estate and religion, the former was nonetheless solidly bourgeois in orientation and far less dependent for self-definition on projects for radical reform. See Norbert Kampe, "Jews and Antisemites at Universities in Imperial Germany (I). Jewish Students: Social History and Social Conflict," in *Leo Baeck Institute Year Book,* vol. 30 (1985), p. 357; George Mosse, "Jewish Emancipation between *Bildung* and Respectability," in Jehuda Reinharz and Walter Schatzberg, eds., *The Jewish Response to German Culture from the Enlightenment to the Second World War* (Hanover, 1985), pp. 1–16; Keith Pickus, *Constructing Modern Identities: Jewish University Students in Germany, 1815–1914* (Detroit, 1999), pp. 134–39.

107. For examples of this terminology, see "Zadachi peterburgskikh evreev," *Razsvet,* June 26, 1880, p. 1004; I. Sosis, "Period 'obruseniia': Natsional'nyi vopros v literature kontsa 60-kh i nachala 70-kh godov," *Evreiskaia Starina* 7, no. 2 (1915): 129; Sliozberg, *Dela minuvshikh dnei,* 1: 41; Marek, *Ocherki po istorii prosveshcheniia evreev,* p. iii.

thenticity, did not enter Hebrew or even Yiddish (an exceptionally absorbent language), as did "intelligentsia." But for those who passed through the gates of Russia's gymnasia and universities, the traditional division of the Jewish world into *proste un sheyne yidn* (roughly, "common and refined Jews") was giving way to that of "the people" and "the intelligentsia." The Jewish social landscape, in other words, was being reimagined in distinctively Russian categories.

UNIVERSITY *vs.* YESHIVA

The postreform encounter with Russian higher education produced a fundamental realignment for Jewish intellectuals, bringing them for the first time within the orbit of their Russian counterparts and dramatically reconfiguring their relationship with Jewish society.[108] Russian institutions of higher education decisively shifted the balance of forces in the Kulturkampf inaugurated by the Haskalah. "The former stable stratification along religious lines," wrote I. V. Gessen, who graduated from St. Petersburg University in the 1880s, "[in which] the descendants of rabbinical families were considered aristocrats, yielded to that of educational qualifications."[109] Pauline Wengeroff, whose son and two daughters pursued advanced degrees in Russia and abroad, observed— with regret—that "the doctor, the lawyer, etc. were taking the place of the traditional aristocracy."[110] In truth, the "diploma intelligentsia" challenged, rather than displaced, that portion of the traditional elite whose status was grounded in Jewish learning.[111] During the second half of the nineteenth century, after all, the traditional elite were busy reinvigorating their own institutions of higher education, the yeshivas.[112] Nonetheless, though we lack aggregate data on yeshiva enrollments, it is likely that by the end of the century the number of Jews studying in Russian universities and technical institutes surpassed that of their counterparts in the yeshivas. And if one includes the thousands of Russian Jews who after the 1890s enrolled at European institutions of higher education, then the trend becomes unmistakable: while the heder was for the time being holding its own against the state-sponsored primary school, the yeshiva found itself increasingly eclipsed by the university.[113]

---

108. Sosis, "Obshchestvennye nastroeniia 'epokhi velikikh reform,'" *Evreiskaia Starina* 6, nos. 3–4 (1914): 360; Ginzburg, *Amolike Peterburg*, p. 29; Dubnov, *Kniga zhizni*, 1: 103.

109. Gessen, *V dvukh vekakh*, p. 20.

110. Wengeroff, *Memoiren einer Grossmutter*, 1: 140.

111. On the social hierarchy sustained in part by learning in East European Jewish society, see Shaul Stampfer, "Heder Study, Knowledge of Torah, and the Maintenance of Social Stratification in Traditional East European Jewish Society," *Studies in Jewish Education* 3 (1988): 271–89.

112. Stampfer, *Ha-yeshivah ha-lita'it be-hithavutah*.

113. On Russian Jews enrolled in European universities, see *Novyi Voskhod*, no. 11 (1914), p. 4, and my discussion in Chapter 7.

The contest among Jewish youth between university and yeshiva was about far more than numbers. Just as university life threatened to pull Jewish students away from collective Jewish concerns, so most yeshivas in late nineteenth-century Russia vigorously defended their curriculum against any and all secular incursions—including the study of non-Jewish languages. While yeshivas successfully consolidated their monopoly on the training and certification of rabbis (a monopoly they had lacked during the first half of the century), most did so at the expense of engagement with the Haskalah, let alone with more recent currents within Russian-Jewish society.[114] The emergence of a Jewish "diploma intelligentsia" and, in part as a reaction against it, the sharp turn inward of the yeshivas thus marked a fateful parting of ways within Jewish society.

Originally, as we have seen, the tsarist government had hoped to fashion not a Jewish intelligentsia but a modernized rabbinate, along the lines charted by various European states. In nineteenth-century Germany, a combination of state policy and internal Jewish reform had made a university education practically a necessity for ambitious rabbis, whether Reform or Orthodox.[115] The failure of the Russian-Jewish version of this "middle way," combining secular and religious learning, cast into sharp relief the internal and external pressures acting on Russian-Jewish society. Graduates of the state-sponsored rabbinical seminaries in Vilna and Zhitomir found it extraordinarily difficult to find employment, since Jewish communities elected their own rabbis and rarely considered the seminary graduates qualified.[116] Attempts by Horace Gintsburg and the Society for the Spread of Enlightenment to establish an independent and more prestigious Jewish theological institute, combining religious and secular study at the advanced level (and modeled on the renowned Breslau seminary in Germany, founded in 1854), were repeatedly thwarted by the Orthodox.[117]

The result was the so-called dual rabbinate—one group ("official rabbis") trained and recognized by the government, literate in the language

114. Stampfer, *Ha-yeshivah ha-lita'it be-hithavutah*, pp. 314–15. There were a few exceptions to this pattern, such as the Odessa yeshiva where, beginning in 1905, the Hebrew poet Chaim Nachman Bialik and the literary critic Yosef Klausner taught. See *Evreiskaia entsiklopediia*, 8: 739–40.

115. Ismar Schorsch, "Emancipation and the Crisis of Religious Authority: The Emergence of the Modern Rabbinate," in Werner Mosse, Arnold Paucker, Reinhard Rürup, eds., *Revolution and Evolution: 1848 in German-Jewish History*, (Tübingen, 1981), pp. 205–244.

116. Shochat, *Mosad "ha-rabanut mi-ta'am,"* pp. 104–8.

117. The earliest mention of such a project apparently came in 1868 in a proposal to the OPE by the Odessa physician and future Zionist Leon Pinsker. See *Otchet Obshchestva dlia rasprostraneniia prosveshcheniia mezhdu evreiami v Rossii za 1868 god* (St. Petersburg, 1869), pp. 22–23. The idea was shelved in the 1890s, in response to a massive letter-writing campaign by Orthodox rabbis. See Shochat, *Mosad "ha-rabanut mi-ta'am,"* pp. 93–98.

of state but unable to navigate the "sea" of the Talmud; the other ("spiritual rabbis") shaped by rigorous textual study in the yeshiva but removed from European thought and lacking official sanction. A phenomenon peculiar to Russia, the dual rabbinate may represent a short-lived projection onto Jewish society of deep Russian binary patterns of "dual belief" and "dual power."[118] But we should not be fooled into thinking that the fundamental battle was between two kinds of rabbis, or that conservative Jewish resistance alone undermined the creation of a modernized rabbinate. For the lure of the university and the rights it conferred played an equally important if not greater role. At the Vilna rabbinical seminary, for example, during the decade from 1862 to 1872 (that is, in the aftermath of the 1861 decree on the rights of Jewish graduates of Russian institutions of higher education), only fifty-three students graduated with rabbinical certification. By contrast, ninety-two students left the seminary to attend a Russian university or technical institute (and many more left but failed to gain admission elsewhere).[119] According to a contemporary account, the rabbinical seminaries had lost their original function of training an "enlightened clergy" and were now full of students seeking "a general Russian education" as a springboard to a university degree.[120] Students at the rabbinical seminaries repeatedly petitioned to have Greek and Latin included in their curriculum, the better to prepare themselves for university entrance examinations.[121] M. P. Shafir, an 1866 graduate of the Zhitomir seminary who went on to study law at St. Petersburg University, offered the following account:

> Despite the fact that this was a Jewish seminary and was supposed to train rabbis and teachers for Jewish schools, we spent more time on general subjects, and above all on Russian literature. We read with utmost enthusiasm the Russian classics, as well as Belinskii, Dobroliubov, and others. On the sly we read Herzen's *The Bell*, which made its way into Russia then, and whoever did not

---

118. Iurii Lotman and Boris Uspensky, "The Role of Dual Models in the Dynamics of Russian Culture," in idem, *The Semiotics of Russian Culture* (Ann Arbor, 1984), pp. 3–35.

119. *Ukaz ministru narodnogo prosveshcheniia*, p. 51. Several of the fifty-three students certified as rabbis also went on to Russian institutions of higher education and were never employed as rabbis. The majority of students at both the Vilna and Zhitomir seminaries did not graduate.

120. S. Rozenberg, "Chto nakhodit russkii evrei v obrazovanii dlia svoei prakticheskoi zhizni," *Den´*, no. 8 (1869), p. 121. This view was confirmed by F. Postel´s in *Materialy, otnosiashchiesia k obrazovaniiu Evreev v Rossii*, p. 21, and *Ukaz ministru prosveshcheniia*, p. 52, as well as in the memoirs of M. G. Morgulis, who relates his decision to enroll in the Zhitomir seminary to the enthusiasm he felt among seminary students for the world of Pushkin and Zhukovskii. See Morgulis, "Iz moikh vospominanii," *Voskhod* 15, no. 4 (April 1895): 30.

121. *Ukaz ministru narodnogo prosveshcheniia*, p. 52.

have the opportunity to become acquainted with this illegal journal was initiated into its secrets by those who did. I remember how we used to quote and sing the ditties from *The Bell:* "God of potholes, there he is / God of frosts, there he is—the Russian god!"[122]

Born in controversy, the rabbinical seminaries were constantly dogged by rumors of their immanent demise. From the government's point of view, of course, they were far from total failures: at a minimum, they successfully channeled many of their students into Russian educational institutions, and those who remained and were certified as "official rabbis" often served the regime as "expert Jews" or as keepers of vital records (in Russian) in various Jewish communities. But there was no denying that the project of fashioning an "enlightened clergy" among the Jews, and using it as an instrument of official policy, had reached a dead end. As a group of some twenty influential Jewish merchants asserted in 1870 in a petition to the Ministry of Enlightenment, the entire project was doomed from the start:

> In the Jewish religion there are no sacraments upon whose fulfillment the salvation of the soul depends. There are not even dogmas in the Christian sense of that word. Given this essential character of Judaism . . . there is no clergy, or perhaps one should say there are no laymen, as Holy Scripture says: "And you shall be unto Me a kingdom of priests." Among a people who do not recognize any mediation between themselves and God, a clerical hierarchy is unthinkable.[123]

This was by no means the first time that reservations had been expressed about Count Uvarov's 1840 plan to recast (and co-opt) the rabbinate as a Russian-style clerical estate.[124] It was precisely such criticism, moreover—rather than the opposition of the traditional rabbinate—that ultimately persuaded the Ministry of Enlightenment to put an end to the training of "official rabbis" and limit the function of the rabbinical seminaries to training teachers for state-sponsored Jewish schools.[125] In 1873, in its explanation for its closing of the seminaries, the Ministry reproduced much of the argument offered by the merchants' petition:

> [Official policy] has proceeded from the assumption that rabbis have the same significance among Jews that priests have among the Russian Orthodox. In fact,

---

122. M. P. Shafir, "Moi vospominaniia," *Evreiskaia Letopis´* 4 (1926), p. 106.

123. RGIA, f.733, op. 189, d. 387, l. 3. The biblical passage is from Exod. 19:6.

124. See, e.g., the discussion by the Jewish Committee in 1860, in RGIA, f. 1269, d. 139, ll. 209–10.

125. The seminaries had always had two tracks, one for those who wished to become state rabbis and one for those who wished to become teachers in the government schools for Jews; after 1873 only the second remained.

the Jews have no clergy. [Such an estate] was possible only when the Temple in Jerusalem existed. The fulfillment of religious commandments is in no way a privilege of the rabbis. Circumcisions, weddings, etc. can be performed by any Jew. For this reason, petitions have frequently appeared from among educated Jews regarding the pointlessness of the rabbinical seminaries and the necessity of closing them.[126]

The closing of the rabbinical seminaries marked the end of any kind of institutional basis for a "middle way" between university-educated and yeshiva-trained elites. Reactions to the ever-widening chasm between the Jewish intelligentsia and the rabbinate varied widely. At one extreme, individual rabbis urged the tsarist regime to curtail admission of Jews to gymnasia and universities, while at the other, newspapers such as the Petersburg *Razsvet* celebrated the triumphant march of enlightenment among Jewish youth, and at least one anonymous petitioner encouraged the government to shut down the yeshivas.[127] Between these two poles was the widespread concern with what Steven Zipperstein has aptly dubbed the "Jewish brain drain."[128] The Odessa Jewish weekly *Den'*, for example, warned that the education of Jewish youth was splitting Russian Jewry into two mutually exclusive camps, one conservative and backward, the other lacking knowledge of and sympathy for Jewish tradition.[129]

A parting of the ways was already evident when Genrikh Sliozberg decided in 1875 to attend a gymnasium in Poltava. His father, a heder teacher, quickly found himself unemployed, since "one could not imagine combining the title 'father of a gymnasium student' with that of 'melamed.'" Relatives rebuked his parents for "spoiling a Jewish soul," while Sliozberg realized upon entering the gymnasium that he had "de facto dismissed and excluded myself from [Jewish] society, even in a spiritual sense."[130] B. Krugliak, in his ac-

126. *Ukaz ministru narodnogo prosveshcheniia*, p. 49.

127. On the rabbis, see *Nedel'naia Khronika Vokhoda*, Mar. 12, 1882, p. 269. A Jewish petition recommending that Jews be steered away from secular educational institutions can be found in RGIA, f. 821, op. 150, d. 395, ll. 1–10. For examples celebrating the influx of Jews into Russian gymnasia and universities, see G. Gertsenshtein, "Universitetskie studenty-evrei: Statisticheskaia zametka," *Razsvet*, Aug. 31, 1880; A. Kaufman, "Uchatsia li evrei?" *Razsvet*, Feb. 14, 1880; G. M. Gertsenshtein, "Evreiki-studentki," *Razsvet*, July 3, 1880. The petition to close the yeshivas is in RGIA, f. 1269, op. 1, d. 136, ll. 212–40.

128. Steven Zipperstein, *Elusive Prophet: Ahad Ha'am and the Origins of Zionism* (Berkeley, 1993), p. 107.

129. E. Trubich, "Odnostoronnee vospitanie evreiskogo iunoshestva," *Den'*, no. 11 (1869), p. 172. For similar concerns, see Tsunzer, *Tsunzers biografiya;* the letter from a certain Orenshtein to Deputy Minister of Enlightenment A. I. Georgievskii in RGIA, f. 846, op. 1, d. 131, ll. 3–8; and the views expressed by B. I. Gorovits (Horowitz), the Jewish delegate to the Ekaterinoslav Provincial Commission of 1881, in S. A. Panchulidzev, *Spravka k dokladu po evreiskomu voprosu*, vol. 8 (St. Petersburg, 1908), p. 24.

130. Sliozberg, *Dela minuvshikh dnei*, 1: 64–65, 91.

count of preparing to take an admission examination in Odessa, remembered imagining the magnificent reception he would receive after graduating from a university:

> You start to dream about how pleasant it will be when you appear in the provinces as a student, in your peaked cap with the blue band around it. Won't that be great! With reverence and envy the provincials will say: "Ah, the former *melamed*—what a fellow, he's preparing for his doctorate!" And your wife and parents, even though they're Orthodox, will stop looking askance at you, and instead will feel nothing but pride.[131]

He was soon disabused: his family reacted in horror at the sight of the "dandy" shorn of beard and *peyes*. Similarly, M. B. Slutskii, recalling his departure from pious family members in Kishinev to attend Kharkov University (in the company of two Christian fellow students), likened the experience to the tearful farewells organized for Jews departing for the New World—presumably never to be seen again.[132]

THE STUDENT SUBCULTURE

As if in compensation for such ruptures, Jewish students in the postreform era found themselves swept into a student milieu in which a powerful collective ethos was taking shape. The 1860s witnessed the first stirrings of a youth movement that would gain force during the late imperial period, reaching its peak in the form of student demonstrations that rocked cities across Russia between 1899 and the Revolution of 1905. The student ethos was grounded in the pursuit of "consciousness," understood as a unified, usually radical, worldview from which flowed both ethical imperatives and a new collective identity.[133] It thrived in the small, elite, face-to-face communities of Russia's institutions of higher education.

Students' self-perception in the late imperial period owed much to the Russian intelligentsia's master narrative of its own development. According to that extraordinarily influential narrative, universities were the first institution in Russia where oppressive social distinctions had begun to dissolve in a shared ethos of idealism and public responsibility. In no other arena of

---

131. B. Krugliak, "Vospominaniia o zhizni eksternov v Odesse (1896 g.)," *Evreiskaia Starina* 9 (1916): 282.

132. M. B. Slutskii, *Moi vospominaniia iz detstva, iunosti i poluvekovoi vrachebnoi i obshchestvennoi deiatel'nosti* (Kishinev, 1927), pt. 1, p. 22.

133. Among many works on students in late imperial Russia, I have found most helpful the following: Alain Besançon, *Éducation et société en Russie dans le second tiers du XIXe siècle* (Paris, 1974); Daniel R. Brower, *Training the Nihilists: Education and Radicalism in Tsarist Russia* (Ithaca, 1975); Samuel Kassow, *Students, Professors, and the State in Tsarist Russia* (Berkeley, 1989); and Morrissey, *Heralds of Revolution.*

Russian society—save perhaps Russian literature—were the hopes of transcending inherited social divisions so powerfully invested; the university appeared, in the historian Martin Malia's words, as "one of the few islands of democracy in the most unequal society of Europe."[134] Looking back on his experience at Moscow University in the 1830s, Alexander Herzen, one of the architects of the student mythology, proclaimed:

> The youthful strength of Russia streamed to it from all sides, from all strata, as into a common reservoir; in its halls they were purified of the prejudices they had picked up at the domestic hearth, reached a common level, became like brothers. . . . Young men of all sorts and conditions coming from above and from below, from the south and from the north, were quickly fused into a compact mass of comradeship. Social distinctions had not among us the offensive influence that we find in English schools and barracks, let alone in English universities.[135]

Herzen's friend and classmate Nikolai Ogarev similarly observed that "university youth . . . serves as a unifying bridge for the estates," while the St. Petersburg University professor Dmitrii Kavelin likened student life, with its solidarity and egalitarian ethic, to that of the celebrated peasant commune.[136] Indeed, like the peasantry and other social groups, students in the late imperial period came to be described, and to conceive of themselves, as a kind of estate. Despite their temporary and nonhereditary status, they constituted a self-perpetuating subculture known as the *studenchestvo*. In the words of one student newspaper, "The studenchestvo is a separate corner of Russian life. [It] is not a random, mechanically assembled mass of separate individuals. No, it is like a miniature people, its firm sense of solidarity coming from the basic aspects of its collective existence."[137]

Even Herzen, however, did not fail to recall the existence of certain "external" distinctions—which he insisted "did not go very deep"—among his fellow students of the prereform period. "The majority of the medical students," he noted, "consisted of seminarians and Germans. The Germans kept a little apart and were deeply imbued with the Western bourgeois spirit. The

---

134. Martin Malia, *Alexander Herzen and the Birth of Russian Socialism* (New York, 1971), p. 61.

135. Aleksandr Gertsen [Herzen], *Byloe i dumy* (Moscow, 1982), 1: 109–10. My translation is an amended version of that by Constance Garnett, published as *My Past and Thoughts: The Memoirs of Alexander Herzen* (New York, 1968), pp. 95–96.

136. Ogarev quoted in Rafail Vydrin, *Osnovnye momenty studencheskogo dvizheniia v Rossii* (Moscow, 1908), p. 18; on Kavelin, see Brower, *Training the Nihilists*, p. 124.

137. *Studencheskii Mir*, no. 1 (1910), quoted in Kassow, *Students, Professors, and the State*, pp. 49–50. Even harsh critics of student life conceded that students had created a distinctive and enduring culture of their own. See, e.g., the controversial essay by A. S. Izgoev, "Ob intelligentnoi molodezhi," in *Vekhi: Sbornik statei o russkoi intelligentsii* (Moscow, 1909).

entire education of the seminarians, all their luckless ideas, were utterly different from ours; we spoke different languages."[138] Other accounts confirm the impression that not only graduates of theological seminaries and ethnic Germans but Polish students as well often formed distinct minorities within the imperial student body.[139] Both phenomena—the celebration of the student body as an egalitarian collective and the quiet persistence of fault lines based on religion and ethnicity—are important in establishing the context for the Jewish encounter with institutions of higher learning.

In the 1860s the mythology of students as a supra-estate entity took on added force. It now appeared that the enrollment of ever larger numbers of plebeian "sons" (the fabled *raznochintsy*, or members of various social estates between the peasantry and the nobility) was helping to pull the aristocratic generation of "fathers" (such as Herzen and Ogarev, both from gentry families) down from the clouds of idealism, thereby making the studenchestvo and the intelligentsia as a whole more realist, more radical, and more socially inclusive. At last the university appeared poised to live up to its name (and Herzen's vision): a universe in microcosm. Historians have, to be sure, substantially qualified this claim by exposing its ideological rather than sociological roots.[140] They have done so first by demonstrating that institutions of higher education continued until the end of the nineteenth century to be dominated by students from gentry and other socially elite families, and second, by deflating the notion of any direct or necessary correlation between social origin and ideological orientation. Nonetheless, the mythology of the raznochintsy must be reckoned with as a force in itself, and not only among the intelligentsia: the tsarist regime's repeated attempts to reduce radicalism in the universities by constricting the number of poor or nonnoble students shows that it too accepted the idea of a nexus between class (or estate) and worldview.

The mythology of the studenchestvo's transcendence of social diversity— of the university as melting pot—was critical for the Jewish encounter with higher education in Russia. For much of the second half of the nineteenth century, students' obsession with the problem of difference based on estate and class effectively eclipsed all other forms of difference, including those grounded in ethnicity or religion. Particularly among left-leaning students, attention to ethnic and religious distinctions was regarded not merely as irrelevant but as evidence of reactionary impulses. As a result, a largely benign

138. Gertsen, *Byloe i dumy,* 1:82.

139. See the sources cited in Brower, *Training the Nihilists,* p. 115; Kassow, *Students, Professors, and the State,* pp. 53, 77, 112; and Iu. Badrakh, ed., *Pol'skie professora i studenty v universitetakh Rossii, XIX–nachalo XX v.* (Warsaw, 1995).

140. See esp. Besançon, *Éducation et société en Russie,* pp. 82–83. For a useful summary of the debate see Wirtschafter, *Structures of Society,* pp. 3–17.

but unstable silence enveloped the entire issue, a condition that has made the job of investigating interethnic relations in the universities especially complex.[141] Any historical approach to the Russian university as an imperial institution, whose student body reflected a good deal of the staggering diversity of the empire, must acknowledge the enormous influence of the mythology of supra-estate student solidarity as embodied in the story of the raznochintsy. For many members of the intelligentsia, that mythology exerted a far greater unifying force than did the ethnically neutral dynastic idiom favored by the tsarist regime. Indeed, Jews typically understood their own dramatic entrance into institutions of higher education—and more broadly into Russian society—as having been made possible by the social pluralism that arose with the alleged displacement of aristocratic "fathers" by plebeian "sons."[142]

During the Reform era, a distinct code of behavior and sense of mutual obligation developed among the growing number of students who participated in discussion circles, informal assemblies, and collective organizations. Initially, grievances centered on student life, in particular the right to form mutual aid societies and the struggle to prevent the government from raising tuition and thereby blocking access to higher education by the poor. Though far from revolutionary, such goals nonetheless placed students at the front line of public self-assertion vis-à-vis the autocracy.[143] By the second half of the nineteenth century the university had displaced the salon as the key institutional locus of Russia's intellectual life. With the student subculture rather than the official curriculum in mind, the aging Herzen declared in 1861 that "the idea of Russian citizenship has been bred in the universities."[144]

Just such a sentiment struck Vladimir Harkavi as he made his way from Vilna to Moscow University in the summer of 1864. Sitting face to face with a Polish student in a train compartment—the nineteenth century's favorite site for encounters across lines of ethnicity and class—Harkavi "tasted the feeling of equality for the first time: it was not a *zhid* and a *pan* who were traveling, but two students. . . . We conducted our conversation in Russian."[145] If Russian was the imperial lingua franca uniting the various nationalities, then the Russian university would serve as the setting in which the newfound equality found its fullest expression. After passing the entrance examinations, Harkavi and another Jewish student from Vilna were exultant:

---

141. A recent analysis of imperial Russian student life notes that "the issue of ethnicity proved a tantalizing but elusive topic": Morrissey, *Heralds of Revolution,* p. 10.

142. See, e.g., Israel Tsinberg's entry on "assimilation" in *Evreiskaia entsiklopediia,* 3: 334.

143. Kassow, *Students, Professors, and the State,* p. 52.

144. Quoted in Alston, *Education and the State,* p. 49.

145. Garkavi, *Otryvki vospominaniia,* p. 10.

Figure 22. Vladimir Harkavi (1846/47–1911) as a student in the 1860s.

When we emerged from the old university building we crossed to the opposite sidewalk, respectfully took off our hats, bowed to the temple that had given us sanctuary, and kissed each other. With pride we walked home, and we were ready to exclaim to every passer-by, "Do you know what, we are students!" It was as if the feeling of alienation from the Christians around us collapsed all at once. We felt that we had been inducted into a new community [*korporat-siia*], in which there were neither Jews nor Hellenes.[146]

Once dressed in the official student uniform, young Jews often found that observers were indeed unable to distinguish them from their Gentile peers,

146. Ibid., p. 14. That Harkavi would borrow the language of the New Testament (Gal. 3:28: "There is neither Greek nor Jew, there is neither bond nor free, there is neither male

in effect transforming Jewish students from a visible to an invisible minor-ity.[147] And while traditional anti-Jewish stereotypes were by no means absent, they rarely found fertile ground in institutions of higher education. Vladimir Medem, the future Bund leader, went so far as to claim that "in the Kiev stu-dent environment, differences between Christian and Jew were nonexistent." Recounting a rare anti-Semitic slur by a student in one of the auditoriums of the university, Medem described the uproar that swiftly ensued:

> An anti-Semitic catcall in a student environment! This was something unheard of in those halcyon days! The student conscience found it intolerable. The cul-prit was seized, placed in the defendant's dock [of the student court] and tried. The trial ran for two days. On the first day it involved a closed meeting of the particular class in which the incident had occurred. The following day a mass meeting of the whole university was convened. There were angry speeches. The young anti-Semite received his due.[148]

To be sure, social differences between Christians and Jews remained: Medem himself records the existence of a Jewish student kitchen at Kiev University (where kosher food was probably served), and anti-Jewish sentiment seems to have briefly erupted among medical students at Kharkov University in 1885.[149] But a wide selection of memoirs leaves one with the impression of student life as relatively free of anti-Jewish incidents. Looking back after half a century, Grigorii Rubinshtein recalled his four years in the 1880s at the Demidov School of Jurisprudence in Iaroslavl as "the happiest time of my life."[150] Even Jews generally critical of Russian student life noted the absence of ethnic exclu-sivity.[151] More common was the "utter ignorance of Judaism and Jewish life" encountered by a pseudonymous memoirist in the 1860s at the Petrovskaia Academy of Agriculture and Forestry near Moscow. There, in a student body composed of Russians, Armenians, Poles, Germans, and Jews, one found "no

nor female, for ye are all one in Christ Jesus") to express a new, transcendent identity speaks both to the power of the studenchestvo mythology and to Harkavi's high degree of accultura-tion. See Lucy Dawidowicz, ed., *The Golden Tradition: Jewish Life and Thought in Eastern Europe* (New York, 1967), p. 89n.

147. Landau, "Pis'ma ob evreiakh. Peterburgskie evrei," *Biblioteka dlia chteniia* 187, no. 12 (1864): 11; I. Brutskus, "Ha-studentim ha-yehudim ba-universitah ha-moskva'it," *He-ʿAvar*, no. 18 (1971), pp. 63–65. As a student at Kharkov University in the 1870s, the populist Osip V. Aptekman had doubts about whether he, as a Jew, could effectively participate in the "going to the people" movement, which involved propaganda work directly with peasants. His Russian fellow students reassured him that he was "not typically Jewish in appearance and speech," and therefore could "pass for a Russian": quoted in Haberer, *Jews and Revolution*, p. 101.

148. Medem, *Life and Soul of a Legendary Jewish Socialist*, p. 108. The incident occurred in the 1890s.

149. Ibid., p. 130; on the Kharkov incident, see *Nedel'naia Khronika Voskhoda*, Oct. 6, 1885.

150. Rubinshtein, *Vospominaniia starogo advokata*, p. v.

151. See, e.g. Sliozberg, "Dorevoliutsionnoe russkoe studenchestvo," p. 94.

Figure 23. Vladimir Medem (1879–1923) as a student in the 1890s.

strict grouping by nationality, and the Jews tended to mix with the Russians." Living in a group house composed of Russian and Jewish students who addressed one another with the informal *ty*, this writer recalled that in the course of a discussion with his housemates concerning religion, he chanced to refer to the Jewish injunction "You shall love your neighbor as yourself." "'Excuse me,' interrupted a Russian housemate, 'that's not in the Old Testament. Jesus Christ said that. I should know—I attended a seminary.'"[152]

If anything, Jewish students were more likely to note incidents of prejudice involving professors. The mathematician N. I. Bugaev (father of the Sym-

152. The phrase appears in Lev. 19:18. It reappears in the New Testament in Matthew, Romans, and Galatians. The source of this vignette is N. N., "Iz vpechatlenii minuvshago veka: Vospominaniia srednogo cheloveka," *Evreiskaia Starina* 6, no. 3 (1914): 436–37.

bolist writer Andrei Bely) informed Julius Brutskus, a student at Moscow University in the 1880s, that he considered Jews enemies of the human race.[153] The renowned chemist and Russian nationalist D. I. Mendeleev, a professor at St. Petersburg University, was well known for sharing his anti-Semitic views during lectures. Such attitudes, however, generally did not find favor among students, and could even strengthen student solidarity in opposition to authority figures perceived to be bigoted. When a colleague of Mendeleev's began a lecture on socialism by announcing that its founders were all Jews, "who know only how to destroy," his listeners, among whom were a number of budding Marxists, were unimpressed. "Well," shrugged one, "what about the Jew David Ricardo?"[154] Although there were certainly professors who expressed sympathy for the cause of Jewish emancipation, such as the renowned historian Vasilii Kliuchevskii and the liberal jurist Boris Chicherin, to many students the majority seemed to be on the other side.[155]

During the 1860s and 1870s, even as they were achieving a critical mass at institutions of higher education, Jewish students typically avoided identifying themselves with Jewish issues, instead immersing themselves in the world of the Russian studenchestvo. A considerable number went so far as to formally request permission to use Russian first names in place of the diminutive Yiddish forms that typically appeared on official documents, including class rosters and diplomas.[156] A student registered as Itsko (Hebrew: Yitshak) might wish to formally change his name to Isaak, rare but not wholly unfamiliar among Russians. A name such as Haim, lacking a phonetic equivalent in Russian, might be changed to the semantically linked Vitalii (both names drawing on respective roots meaning "life"). "Jews with a certain level of education," wrote the dean of the Medical-Surgical Academy to the minister of enlightenment in 1871 on behalf of dozens of Jewish students at

153. Brutskus, "Ha-studentim ha-yehudim ba-universitah ha-moskva'it," p. 64.

154. A. E. Kaufman, "Za mnogo let: otryvki vospominanii starogo zhurnalista," *Evreiskaia Starina* 5, no. 2 (1913): 213. For further examples of professorial prejudice, see M. Rozengardt, "Nechto o evreiakh, nakhodiashchikhsia v 'bolee blagopriiatnom polozhenii,'" *Russkii Evrei*, no. 12 (1880), and L. Liakhovetskii, "Nashi professora-iudofoby," *Nedel'naia Khronika Voskhoda*, Jan. 9, 1883.

155. On Kliuchevskii, see Brutskus, "Ha-studentim ha-yehudim ba-universitah ha-moskva'it," p. 64, and Robert Byrnes, *V. O. Kliuchevskii, Historian of Russia* (Bloomington, 1995), p. 147; on Chicherin, see Boris Chicherin, *Pol'skii i evreiskii voprosy* (Berlin, 1901), and Gary Hamburg, *Boris Chicherin and Early Russian Liberalism, 1828–1866* (Stanford, 1992), p. 135.

156. Jewish names were registered at birth by local rabbis, who were legally responsible for maintaining the metrical books of their communities and who typically insisted on Yiddishized forms of Hebrew names. The names recorded in these books then became the basis for all subsequent official documents. Russian law forbade the changing of surnames except by permission of the tsar himself, and until the end of the nineteenth century such cases were extremely rare. On changing surnames see Andrew M. Verner, "What's in a Name? Of Dog-killers, Jews and Rasputin," *Slavic Review* 53, no. 4 (Winter 1994): 1046–47.

THE UNIVERSITY AS MELTING POT?

the Academy, "feel severely burdened by their diminutive first names, which sharply distinguish them."[157] An unpublished government report from the 1870s noted that the majority of requests by Jews for name changes came from students and merchants.[158] To be sure, the significance of those requests and the effect produced by Russifying one's name can be inferred only indirectly. It may well be that Jewish students, precisely because of their relatively high degree of integration, registered more acutely than other Jews the psychological or other penalties associated with a publicly marked Jewish identity, even in the comparatively tolerant student milieu. Those who sought permission to use a Russian name also presumably regarded a mere change of name as promising significant dividends, perhaps even the ability to pass as a non-Jew.[159] Nearly a century earlier Jews had petitioned the Russian government to use the proper descriptive term for "Jew" in official documents (*evrei* rather than *zhid*). Now, as selective integration opened up new social arenas to a small but significant minority of Jews, it was a ques-

157. RGIA, f. 733, op. 189, d. 431, l. 1. For further examples of requests by Jewish students for name changes, see RGIA, f. 821, op. 9, d. 92, ll. 3–108. On the perception by certain acculturated Jews that Yiddishized names bore a social stigma, see Klier, *Imperial Russia's Jewish Question,* chap. 1, and Verner, "What's in a Name?" pp. 1058–61.

158. RGIA, f. 821, op. 9, d. 92, l. 104. Jewish merchants, or those in Petersburg at any rate, also showed a striking tendency to register their children under Russian first names in official documents. See Igor´ B. Kotler, "Spravochnaia kniga o litsakh Sankt-Peterburgskogo kupechestva kak istochnik po etnicheskoi antroponimike Peterburga," in I. I. Krupnik, ed., *Etnicheskie gruppy v gorodakh evropeiskoi chasti SSSR (formirovanie, rasselenie, dinamika kul´tury)* (Moscow, 1987), p. 133.

The problem of Jews seeking to change their first names was sufficiently widespread—and sufficiently relevant to issues of taxation, military service, and social control—for the tsarist government to attempt on several occasions to create a standardized system of correspondence among Yiddish (diminutive), Hebrew (biblical), and Russian names, and to tightly regulate changes from one to another. See, e.g., K. S. Zhurakovskii and S. M. Rabinovich, eds., *Polnoe sobranie evreiskikh imen s napisaniem ikh na russkom i evreiskom iazykakh* (St. Petersburg, 1874), which was originally prepared for the Ministry of Internal Affairs, and N. N. Glubokovskii, *Po voprosu o "prave" evreev imenovat´sia khristianskimi imenami: Traktat i istoricheskaia spravka* (St. Petersburg, 1911). Other such works, including one by Iakov Brafman, were commissioned by the government but apparently never published. See RGIA, f. 821, op. 9, d. 92, ll. 3–53, and *Evreiskaia entsiklopediia,* 8: 149–53.

159. A member of the Committee for the Transformation of Jewish Life reported in the 1870s that "even though a Russian would have no doubts as to whether the merchant Yokhel Girshovich, having been renamed Mikhail Grigorevich, is Russian by nationality, nonetheless he might suppose that such an individual is a foreigner, rather than a Jew": RGIA, f. 821, op. 9, d. 92, l. 105. Anti-Semitic writers were reluctant to state directly that a change of name might actually make it possible for a Jew to be mistaken for a Christian, since that would imply that the differences between the two were disturbingly subtle. But their strenuous concern about Jews' "hiding their Jewishness" suggests the possibility of precisely such a scenario. See Glubokovskii, *Po voprosu o "prave" evreev imenovat´sia khristianskimi imenami,* p. 9.

tion of the desired form of individual names rather than that of the group.[160]

Jewish students by and large appear to have kept their distance from Jewish communities in university towns, rarely setting foot inside a synagogue.[161] One searches in vain for self-organized Jewish student groups until the end of the nineteenth century, long after Polish and Ukrainian students had formed underground societies at several universities.[162] Describing his first student rally in Kiev, Vladimir Medem records that "the speakers included representatives of various nationalities, Russians, Georgians, Armenians. A number of Jews also spoke, but not as representatives of the Jews."[163] Within the student body as a whole, the dominant form of associational life was the *zemliachestvo*, in which social intercourse and mutual assistance were based on shared geographic rather than ethnic origins. Although the evidence is anecdotal—the tenuous legal status of the *zemliachestva* left little room for any other kind—it appears that Jewish students commonly participated as equals in the system of local affiliations.[164]

Most of the first post-1861 generation of Jewish students, in other words, were hardly inclined to distinguish themselves publicly from their non-Jewish peers. This impression is confirmed, if tendentiously, by critics such as Aron Liberman, who in the mid-1870s issued a stinging attack on "the youth at the institutions of higher learning who have left the Jewish environment."[165] A graduate of the Vilna rabbinical seminary who briefly audited courses at the Technological Institute in Petersburg, Liberman issued a manifesto, "To the Educated Jewish Youth," in which he excoriated Jewish students—"You 'enlightened' slaves of gold and power!"—for "having put on the mask of European civilization."[166] In a similar vein, the Bundist Avrom Lesin condemned "the national betrayal by the *intelligenty* who . . . sought individual

160. On the controversies regarding *evrei* and *zhid*, see John Klier, "*Zhid:* The Biography of a Russian Pejorative," *Slavic and East European Review* 60, no. 1 (1982): 1–15, and Fishman, *Russia's First Modern Jews*, p. 81.

161. On Jewish students in Moscow, see *Den'*, Aug. 1, 1870, p. 525. On Petersburg, see Sliozberg, *Dela minuvshikh dnei*, 1: 144, and Ha-Kohen, *Olami*, 1: 77.

162. Sliozberg, *Dela minuvshikh dnei*, 1: 119. On Polish students at Russian universities, see Badrakh, *Pol'skie professora i studenty*. On Ukrainian and Polish student groups at Kiev University in the 1860s, see V. M. Iuzefovich, "Tridtsat' let tomu nazad: Ocherk iz studencheskoi zhizni," *Russkaia Starina* 84, nos. 10 (1895): 167–99 and 11 (1895): 95–130.

163. Medem, *Life and Soul of a Legendary Jewish Socialist*, pp. 108–9.

164. Ibid., pp. 107–8, 130; Sliozberg, *Dela minuvshikh dnei*, 1: 119; Iakov Teitel, *Iz moei zhizni* (Paris, 1925), p. 18.

165. Quoted in Frankel, *Prophecy and Politics*, p. 37.

166. Aron Liberman, "K evreiskoi intelligentnoi molodezhi," *Vpered* (London), no. 38 (Aug. 1, 1876), p. 474.

salvation by escape from the Jewish masses into higher education . . . , casting off the ghetto and the legal restrictions."[167]

Perhaps the most dramatic evidence of integration across ethnic and religious lines was the prominence achieved by a number of Jews in underground student revolutionary groups. Samuel Kliachko and Mikhail Grinshtein at Moscow University, Solomon Chudnovskii at Odessa University, Pavel Akselrod at Kiev University, Roza Frank at the Bestuzhev Higher Courses in Petersburg, and Mark Natanson and Osip Aptekman at the Military-Medical Academy in Petersburg all established themselves as leaders of radical student groups during the 1860s and 1870s. Before the 1880s, in fact, it would have been difficult to find a Jewish revolutionary outside the student milieu. In this respect, the comparatively tolerant attitude toward Jews among radical students prefigured and contributed to that within the revolutionary movement as a whole, where individuals of Jewish background gained extraordinary access.

One should bear in mind, however, that while Jewish students played a significant role in Russia's small but growing revolutionary movement—even in its pre-Marxist, populist phase, as Erich Haberer has shown—they represented only a small fraction of the total Jewish student population.[168] And as self-described cosmopolitans whose political commitments often led them to abandon university studies as an unjustifiable privilege (or distraction), revolutionary Jews had a limited impact on the lives of most Jewish students. If we want to understand fully the dynamics of the Russian–Jewish encounter within the student milieu, and if we want to avoid the pitfall of paying attention to students only when they revolt, then we shall have to free ourselves from an exclusive focus on revolutionary activities.

It is telling that the first specifically Jewish organizations to appear in Russian institutions of higher education were established not by Jewish students themselves but by the Society for the Spread of Enlightenment. By 1875 the society had helped create Jewish *kassy* (mutual aid funds) at a half-dozen institutions of higher education to facilitate the distribution of its financial aid.[169] Whereas typically such organizations were generated from below by students seeking to protect their collective welfare as well as their interests, the Jewish kassy, founded and funded from without, lacked any sort of remotely political agenda. In keeping with the goal of rationalizing Jewish char-

---

167. Quoted in Frankel, *Prophecy and Politics,* p. 195.
168. Haberer, *Jews and Revolution,* pp. 94–115.
169. These institutions included the universities of St. Petersburg and Dorpat, the Medical-Surgical Academy, the Riga Polytechnic Institute, the St. Petersburg Technological Institute, and the St. Petersburg Mining Institute. See *Otchet Obshchestva dlia rasprostraneniia prosveshcheniia mezhdu evreiami v Rossii za 1875 god* (St. Petersburg, 1876), p. 13.

ity, moreover, the society sought to distribute its financial aid on the basis of merit more than of need, again in contrast to the usual practice.[170] The meritorious, according to the society, were those who demonstrated not only high academic ability but the willingness to "defend their nation, rather than irresponsibly reprove it—such as we unfortunately often encounter among students."[171] For many Jewish students, these distinctive features of the Jewish kassy were a source of acute discomfort. Like their egalitarian Russian counterparts, they insisted that financial aid be distributed solely on the basis of need. In a November 1879 letter intercepted by the secret police, Elena Kaplanskaia, a medical student in Petersburg, wrote to a fellow student in Moscow,

> I was at a meeting with Dr. Harkavi, the local representative of the Society for the Spread of Enlightenment, and I vigorously opposed the formation of a special Jewish mutual-aid fund, since it would lead not to improved material circumstances for female Jewish students but only to their union. Having formed a private mutual-aid fund, we would have to remove ourselves from the general one.[172]

The substantial amounts of money given to Jewish kassy made government officials uneasy as well, such as the director of the Kiev educational district who complained that such funds had no official sanction and were therefore subject to abuse, and who worried that student participation in the distribution of funds would necessarily involve illegal gatherings.[173]

It is also telling that when *self*-organized Jewish student associations first appeared, in 1881, they did so exclusively in the Baltic provinces, at Dorpat University and the Riga Polytechnic Institute, both of which were outposts of German academic culture. At Dorpat (where the university was reopened under Russian rule in 1802) and Riga (where the Polytechnic Institute was founded in 1862), the predominantly Baltic-German student body enjoyed an officially tolerated tradition of living in fraternities (*Burschenschaften*), each with its own name, house, uniform, customs, forms of entertainment, and songs.[174] In fact, the student bodies at the two institutions were divided be-

170. *Otchet Obshchestva dlia rasprostraneniia prosveshcheniia mezhdu evreiami v Rossii za 1865 god* (St. Petersburg, 1866), p. 32.

171. Quoted in Tcherikover, *Istoriia Obshchestva dlia rasprostraneniia prosveshcheniia*, p. 141.

172. GARF, f. 109-SA, op. 3, d. 2330, l. 1. The following day, Kaplanskaia herself was criticized by several Jewish classmates for her extreme "antinational" position. The Dr. Harkavi referred to here is Avraham Harkavi, a prominent Semitic philologist employed by the Imperial Public Library in St. Petersburg, not to be confused with the Vladimir Harkavi quoted earlier.

173. RGIA, f. 733, op. 149, d. 39, ll. 1–2.

174. Rafael Abramovich, *In tsvey revolutsiyes: Di geshikhte fun a dor* (New York, 1944), p. 36; Ministerstvo narodnogo prosveshcheniia, *Trudy vysochaishe uchrezhdennoi komissii po preobrazovanniiu vysshykh uchebnykh zavedenii* (St. Petersburg, 1903), 2: 218–27.

tween mostly German fraternity members, on the one hand, and those unaffiliated students whom the fraternity brothers disdainfully dubbed "the sav-
ages" (*die Wilde*), on the other.[175] An enduring rivalry arose between the two
groups, the fraternities contemptuous of the lack of organization among the
unaffiliated and the unaffiliated disgusted by the "medieval separatism" and
"childish" drinking and dueling that characterized the fraternities.[176] Jewish students were largely among the unaffiliated, and frequently were spokesmen for the ideals of the Russian *studenchestvo*, for example as co-founders
of inexpensive student cafeterias and Russian-language reading rooms.[177]

By the 1870s, many of the unaffiliated students in Dorpat and Riga had
organized themselves by nationality, establishing fraternities such as Polo-
nia, Estonia, Livonia, Fraternitas Rigensis, and Ruthenia (the last for Russian students).[178] Jewish students found themselves isolated from their formerly unaffiliated comrades, and were shocked when many of the new
organizations refused to admit Jews, even those who had identified with the
Polish or Russian cause. The rejection by Russian students in particular, as
an alumnus of the Riga Polytechnic Institute later put it,

> made a spectacular impression on the Jews. Jewish students suddenly came to
> see their friends as they really are. They saw how sincere their liberal talk re-
> ally was—about free, brotherly relations among all students, in contrast to the
> closed corporate spirit, about the harm of national prejudices, etc. Only now
> did they understand that their Russian comrades had merely tolerated them

175. By the turn of the century, use of the term "savage" (*dikii*) had spread to students at
universities in Russia proper. Tellingly, however, it referred to those who were not members of
political parties (a synonym of *bezpartiinye*) rather than of fraternities. See Vladimir M. Purishkevich, *Materialy po voprosu o razlozhenii sovremennogo russkogo universiteta* (St. Petersburg, 1914),
p. 180. This meaning also exists in German, but only secondarily.

176. See the reminiscences by the former Riga Polytechnic students Ch. Galmudi, "Evreiskoe
studenchestvo rizhskogo politekhnikuma," *Nedel'naia Khronika Voskhoda*, Dec. 30, 1884, pp.
1505–9, and M. Kovarskii, "Byvshii kruzhkovets," ibid., Mar. 17, 1885, pp. 305–8.

177. Galmudi, "Evreiskoe studenchestvo rizhskogo politekhnikuma," p. 1506; "Evrei-studenty
rizhskogo politekhnikuma," *Nedel'naia Khronika Voskhoda*, Apr. 26, 1887, p. 457.

178. Ministerstvo narodnogo prosveshcheniia, *Trudy vysochaishe uchrezhdennoi komissii*, 2:
218–23. See also Heinz von zur Mühlen, "Deutsch-Baltische Korporationen und die Studen-
tenschaft der Universität Dorpat (1802–1939)"; Erik Amburger, "Die Bedeutung der Universität Dorpat für Osteuropa, untersucht an der Zusammensetzung des Lehrkörpers und der Stu-
dentenschaft in den Jahren 1802–1889"; and Clara Redlich, "Das Rigaer Polytechnikum
1862–1918," all in Gert von Pistohlkors, Toivo Raun, and Paul Kaegbein, eds., *Die Universitäten
Dorpat/Tartu, Riga und Wilna/Vilnius, 1579–1979: Beiträge zu ihrer Geschichte und ihrer Wirkung
im Grenzbereich zwischen West und Ost* (Cologne and Vienna, 1987), pp. 152–53, 173, and 247–48.
In the case of Dorpat, several non-German fraternities were actually founded earlier, as far
back as the 1820s, but did not achieve substantial membership until the 1860s and 1870s. The
ethnic fragmentation of student life at Dorpat persisted through the post-1905 period; see
V. V. Sviatlovskii, "Studencheskiia perepisi v Rossii," in M. Benasik, comp., *Studenchestvo v tsifrakh
po dannym perepisi 1907 goda v Iur'eve* (St. Petersburg, 1909), pp. 55–56.

for the time being, [only now] did they comprehend what an abyss remained between them, and how fruitless had been all their efforts toward genuine integration, which earlier seemed so imminent.[179]

In both Dorpat and Riga, attempts to form a full-fledged Jewish fraternity (Judonia) came to naught. In January 1881, however, a Jewish Circle (Evreiskii Kruzhok), also known as the Jewish History and Literature Club (Verein für jüdische Geschichte und Literatur) was established in Riga. It was the first and possibly the longest-lasting self-organized Jewish student association in the Russian Empire. Within a few years, some 20 percent of the Polytechnic Institute's Jewish students had joined.[180]

To the extent that events in Dorpat and Riga belong to a larger framework, it is to be found not in Petersburg or Odessa or Kharkov but in Berlin and Heidelberg and Vienna. In German and Austrian universities, the first Jewish student organizations were organized during the same period as those in the Baltics, in the early 1880s, and were likewise a direct response to anti-Semitism among fellow students, but of a far more virulent kind. Institutions of higher education in Central Europe, in fact, were traditionally among the most potent arenas of anti-Jewish agitation, a trend that dated back at least to the early modern period and continued well into the twentieth century.[181] By the 1880s the University of Vienna had emerged as a crucible of anti-Semitic, Pan-German agitation, and in the following decade a convention of fraternities from across Austria-Hungary declared Jews ineligible to take part in the defining fraternity ritual, the duel.[182] In Germany, students played a key role in promoting a popular referendum to exclude Jews from certain professions.[183] As more and more self-described "Aryan" student groups barred Jews from their ranks in the 1880s, the first Jewish student associations appeared, followed by Jewish fraternities and eventually a national umbrella organization for Jewish fraternity students.[184] Similarly, in Vienna the

179. M. Kovarskii, "Byvshii kruzhkovets," *Nedel'naia Khronika Voskhoda,* Mar. 17, 1885, p. 306.

180. Ibid.; "Evrei-studenty Rizhskogo politekhnikuma," *Nedel'naia Khronika Voskhoda,* Apr. 26, 1887, p. 458.

181. On early modern Poland, see Bernard Weinryb, *The Jews of Poland: A Social and Economic History of the Jewish Community in Poland from 1100 to 1800* (Philadelphia, 1973), p. 153; and Janusz Tazbir, "Images of the Jew in the Polish Commonwealth," *Polin* 4 (1989): 26, both of whom note the frequent involvement of Polish students (including Jesuit seminarians) in physical attacks on Jews during the sixteenth and seventeenth centuries. On modern Germany, see Norbert Kampe, *Studenten und "Judenfrage" im deutschen Kaiserreich: Die Entstehung einer akademischen Tragerschicht des Antisemitismus* (Göttingen, 1988).

182. Robert Wistrich, *The Jews of Vienna in the Age of Franz Joseph* (Oxford, 1989), pp. 59, 217.

183. Kampe, *Studenten und "Judenfrage,"* pp. 23–25.

184. The founding in 1880 of the explictly anti-Semitic Association of German Students, for example, prompted the establishment of the Free Academic Union, a de facto Jewish organization, as well as the Academic Association for Jewish History and Literature. See Pickus,

Zionist student group Kadimah (Forward/Eastward) came into being in 1883 in large part as a response to the exclusion of Jews from Pan-German student associations. Although its founders were East European Jews, by the late 1880s it was dominated by students born in Vienna, who transformed it from an "academic society" into a fraternity—the mirror image, in fact, of the Burschenschaft.[185]

The point of this brief excursion to the Baltics and Central Europe is to highlight, by way of contrast, the remarkable inclusiveness of the late imperial Russian university—at least as far as Jewish students were concerned—and as a corollary, the striking absence of Jewish student groups in the Russian Empire (except for the Baltics) before the 1890s. At first glance one might reasonably have expected the reverse. By the 1870s, after all, German and Austrian Jews had achieved full legal emancipation, were more acculturated, and constituted a smaller proportion of both the total population and the university population than did their counterparts in the Russian Empire. Jewish students in Central Europe would seem to have been far better positioned to merge with their Gentile peers. In this case, however, the decisive factor was not the character of the Jewish populations from which they came but rather the student subcultures into which they sought entrance. Russian students not only lacked the medieval guildlike traditions of the Central European fraternities but by the 1860s had forged a powerful collective spirit grounded in opposition to the tsarist regime and much of what it stood for—including its legally inscribed discrimination against Jews. German and Austrian students had once (before and during the revolutions of 1848) played a similar oppositional role, but even then, especially in Germany, that role included considerable opposition to state-sponsored Jewish emancipation.[186] In the latter half of the century, Central European students either abandoned political activism or moved to a right-wing and virulently anti-Semitic agenda, inspired in part by the notion that Jewish students were somehow responsible for the saturation of the academic labor market (the so-called *Überfüllungskrise*).[187] In Russia, by contrast, the massive entrance of Jews into higher education coincided with the zenith of left-wing student activism and ethnic tolerance between the 1860s and the Revolution of 1905.

Constructing Modern Identities, pp. 81–110. Among the founders of the first Jewish student associations in Germany were Russian Jews studying abroad.

185. Wistrich, *Jews of Vienna*, pp. 246–47, 363–69.

186. See Richarz, *Eintritt der Juden in die akademischen Berufe*, p. 85, where the author notes that universities became the prime institutional locus of the post-1815 antiemancipation campaign.

187. Charles McClelland, *State, Society, and University in Germany, 1700–1914* (Cambridge, 1980), p. 234. Robert Wistrich gives a similar explanation for Austrian student anti-Semitism; see his *Jews of Vienna*, p. 64.

This comparison further illuminates the first and only significant episode of collective self-assertion by Jewish students in Russia (apart from the Baltics) before the 1890s, the burst of activity to promote mass emigration in response to the pogroms of 1881–82. In an extraordinary outpouring, a considerable number of Jewish students at universities in Petersburg, Moscow, Odessa, Kharkov, and Kiev reacted to the violence against Jews by participating in communal fasts and penitential prayers (*selihot*) at local synagogues, where most had never set foot before. They were joined by other acculturated Jews such as lawyers, doctors, and merchants, many of whom likewise rarely appeared in a house of worship or otherwise publicly identified with Jewish causes.[188] A smaller number of students, not content with the traditional response to catastrophe—the selihot, after all, cast Jewish suffering as a consequence of Jewish sins—set out to establish utopian colonies in Palestine or America, the ultimate goal being nothing less than a mass exodus of Jews from Russia. In his renowned autobiographical work *Derekh Teshuvah* (The Way of Repentance), Moshe Leib Lilienblum recounted the traumatic effect of the pogrom that swept through Odessa in May 1881:

> The pogroms taught me their lesson, and I was in despair about our future. My studies seemed a sin against my unfortunate people. . . . Our people were fleeing the sword, misfortune all around, the present bitter, the future fearful— and I was thinking of entering the university! For years I had striven toward this. But now I am convinced that our misfortune is not the lack of general education but that we are aliens. We will still remain aliens when we are as stuffed with education as a pomegranate is with seeds. I terminated my studies.[189]

Between spring 1881 and summer 1882, the groups Ahavat Tsiyon (Love of Zion) in Petersburg, Am Olam (Eternal People) in Odessa and Kiev, and BILU (a Hebrew acronym for "House of Jacob come, let us go" [Isa. 2:5]) in Kharkov and elsewhere all attempted a kind of Jewish "going to the people," loosely modeled on the famous 1873–74 pilgrimage of Russian student Populists to the villages, in both cases with the hope of rousing the suffering masses to action.[190]

Though of enormous symbolic significance for the subsequent history of Zionism, the burst of activism unleashed by the pogroms was in fact short-lived and had remarkably little impact on Jewish student life, for several reasons. First, in contrast to the pivotal role of anti-Semitic fraternities in Central European and Baltic universities, the stimulus for Russian-Jewish student

188. For an eyewitness account of these events in Petersburg, see Ha-Kohen, *Olami*, 1: 192–93; more generally, Frankel, *Prophecy and Politics*, pp. 54–96.

189. Moshe Leib Lilienblum, *Ketavim otobiografiyim*, ed. Shlomo Breiman (Jerusalem, 1970), 2: 199.

190. See Jonathan Frankel's superb reconstruction of these events in *Prophecy and Politics*, pp. 49–51, 90–97.

activism in 1881–82—and in virtually every case thereafter, as Chapter 7 demonstrates—came entirely from outside the academy. It is true that for some Jewish students the shock of the pogroms was compounded by the apparent indifference, and in some cases approval, expressed by their fellow students as well as the Russian intelligentsia at large.[191] But Russian students were not among the actual perpetrators of violence, nor were Jewish students singled out as targets. Second, just as the pogroms had no direct link to student issues, neither did any of the Jewish groups that emerged, however briefly, in their wake. With the exception of the BILU, in fact, students were a minority in most of the various pro-emigration groups.[192] Finally, like their Jewish counterparts in the Russian revolutionary movement, the number of Jewish students who actively participated in the emigration drive was relatively small: a total of fifty-three BILU members, mostly students, left for Palestine, some of whom subsequently returned to Russia. In the meantime, the tapering off of the pogroms caused the movement to evaporate by 1883, barely a year after its founding. Leadership of Am Olam and Ahavat Tsiyon rapidly passed out of student hands and into the small circles of proto-Zionists scattered across the Pale. Just as the Russian populists had effectively reduced their influence in institutions of higher education by insisting that students abandon their studies in order to "go to the people," so the ranks of Jewish student activists in 1881–82 were rapidly depleted by the perceived

191. The positive response to the pogroms of 1881–82 on the part of certain members of the People's Will and other Russian revolutionary groups has frequently been cited as an important stimulus of national sentiment among otherwise left-leaning Russian-Jewish intellectuals. Certain contemporary accounts and subsequent memoirs lend some credence to this view. See, e.g., L. L. Liakhovetskii's novella on student life, *Mechta i deistvitel'nost': Razskaz iz zhizni evreiskoi molodezhi* (St. Petersburg, 1884), pp. 59–60, and Pavel Akselrod's reminiscences, "Pogromen un di revolutsionere bavegung mit 43 yor tsurik," *Di tsukunft*, no. 29 (1924), pp. 553–55. Historians, too, have largely subscribed to this version of events; e.g., Vital, *Origins of Zionism*, pp. 56–57, and Frankel, *Prophecy and Politics*, pp. 98–102. Lucy Dawidowicz further argued that the favorable interpretation of the pogroms by the People's Will—as the first stage of the longed-for revolution—is part of a long history of "the trauma of betrayal by the Left," which again and again has brought radical Jews back to the Jewish fold (Dawidowicz, *What Is the Use of Jewish History?* [New York, 1992], p. 230). More recently, however, Erich Haberer has offered a substantially different view. First, he has shown that the reaction to the pogroms of 1881–82 among Russian socialists and populists (including the People's Will) was anything but unified; only a small minority expressed outright endorsement. Second, rather than simply unmasking Russian radicals' deeply ingrained revolutionary anti-Semitism, the pogrom crisis marked a turning point for the left itself: after 1884, argues Haberer, "it was no longer in good taste to greet popular anti-semitic outbursts as manifestations of the 'people's' revolutionary temperament." This observation was certainly born out during subsequent waves of pogroms in 1903–6 and 1919–21. Finally, Haberer shows that whatever trauma may have been felt by Jewish radicals, Jews continued to flock to Russian radical parties after 1882, including the People's Will. See Haberer, *Jews and Revolution*, pp. 206–29.

192. Frankel, *Prophecy and Politics*, pp. 55–56, 90.

need to act, and to act immediately, on the imperative of emigration. As the BILU proclaimed in 1882, "We have to show that we do not believe in the possibility of a bearable existence in Russia."[193]

Enrollment figures suggest that the vast majority of Jewish students thought otherwise, and in any event they did not draw the same lessons from the pogroms as Lilienblum. During the five years after the outbreak of pogroms (1881–86), Jews continued to outpace all other groups in their enthusiasm for higher education, more than doubling their numbers (from 783 to 1,856) and substantially increasing their proportional presence (from 9 to 15%) in Russia's eight universities.[194] If we can learn anything from the rhetoric employed by student supporters of emigration, who cast themselves as repentant members of a privileged intelligentsia determined to lead the Jewish masses to salvation, it is the extent to which they too had absorbed the norms of the studenchestvo.

While plans for a mass Jewish exodus to the ancient homeland rapidly faded from view, the national impulses unleashed by the pogrom crisis among a small number of Jewish students were far from dead. As the next chapter shows, they later resurfaced in altered form, giving rise for the first time to Jewish student organizations across Russia. But before Jewish students organized, they first had to become targets of discrimination, as the "Jewish Question" insinuated its way into the academy.

193. Quoted ibid., p. 97.

194. Pozner, *Evrei v obshchei shkole,* app. 2, p. 55. These data do not include technical institutes and other nonuniversity institutions of higher education.

Chapter 7

A Silent Pogrom

Until the 1860s, the idea of using secular education to assimilate Russia's Jews met with little opposition from non-Jews. At worst, critics claimed that it might require generations to work.[1] More typical was the confidence expressed by Nikolai Pirogov, the noted physician and head of the Kiev educational district: "Enlightenment has such an ability to amalgamate, to humanize [*ochelovechivat´*], that Jews, Slavs, and every other one-sided nationality yield to it."[2] Indeed, as we have seen, many young Jews fully embraced a student identity that seemed to dissolve the barriers separating them from their Russian peers. As early as the mid-1860s, however, certain conservative Russian observers began to express alarm at what they saw as the persistence of "Jewish" characteristics in the growing number of university-educated Jews. A Vilna newspaper warned in 1866, for example, that educated Jews were on a mission to infiltrate and de-Christianize Russian society.[3] The influential *Moskovskie Vedomosti* (Moscow News) told its readers that without curbs on Jewish admissions, Russia's universities and then its civil service would soon be dominated by Jews.[4] In 1876, the apostate Iakov Brafman painted a still more sinister picture in the Petersburg newspaper *Golos* (The Voice):

---

1. See, e.g., E. Karnovich, "Ob obrazovanii evreev v Rossii," *Russkii Pedagogicheskii Vestnik,* no. 5 (St. Petersburg, 1857), p. 39; Mikhailo Serebriakov in *Vitebskie gubernskie vedomosti* 14–15, no. 4 (Apr. 11, 1859), cited by Klier, *Imperial Russia's Jewish Question,* pp. 67–68.

2. *Razsvet,* Nov. 14, 1860, p. 792. For further examples of positive statements by prominant Russians regarding the impact of secular education on Jews, see Grigorii Vol´tke, "Russkie liudi po voprosu ob obrazovanii evreev," in *Sbornik v pol´zu evreiskikh shkol* (St. Petersburg, 1896), pp. 493–513.

3. *Vilenskii Vestnik,* June 3, 1866, quoted in Klier, *Imperial Russia's Jewish Question,* p. 260.

4. Quoted in *Den´,* June 27, 1869.

The difference between Jews trained in the Talmud and Jews receiving a general education lies only in the following: those trained in the Talmud wait for the restoration of the Judaic kingdom to occur suddenly, unexpectedly, without the participation of the Jews, by some miracle; educated Jews preach that the restoration of the Judaic kingdom will occur naturally, and that the Jews ought to prepare for it through education, which will give their nation good generals, engineers, lawyers, and people required for the restoration and survival of the state.[5]

A year later, in his serialized *Diary of a Writer,* Fedor Dostoevsky took up the theme of secularly educated Jews, "whose numbers have now suddenly multiplied in our midst," and issued his well-known dictum that "a Jew without God is somehow unthinkable. I do not even believe in educated Jewish atheists; they are all of one essence, and God only knows what the world has to expect from educated Jews!" Quite apart from its theological agenda, Dostoevsky's pronouncement placed him in the camp of those conservative writers whose anxiety over the erosion of traditional identities in postreform Russia led them alternately to condemn and deny the transforming impact of modern education. Educated Jews, Dostoevsky argued, eerily echoing the sentiments of Simon Wolf and other prereform Jewish university students, lost none of their Jewishness, and only grew more sensitive to criticism by Christians: "It is difficult to find anything more irritable and overly scrupulous than an educated Jew and more ready than he to take offense—as a Jew."[6]

The bombshell in this escalating campaign came in 1880 with the publication of an anonymous letter to the editor of *Novoe Vremia,* Russia's leading daily, under the headline "The Kike Is Coming!" (*Zhid idet!*). Contemporary readers no doubt caught the allusion to the recently coined phrase "the commoner has arrived" (*raznochinets prishel*), by which the populist N. K. Mikhailovskii had celebrated the ascent of nonnoble elements into Russia's universities and intelligentsia.[7] As a sequel, however, "The Kike Is Coming!" was anything but celebratory. Rather, it warned that the composition of Russia's intellectual elite was on the verge of a second major shift, this time across lines not of rank or estate but of nationality. "Who in Russia," the letter asked, "has made most active use of our finest educational resources, which raise people, if not yet to the highest, then at least to the in-

---

5. *Golos,* Apr. 28, 1876, quoted in Klier, *Imperial Russia's Jewish Question,* p. 261.

6. F. M. Dostoevskii, *Dnevnik pisatelia,* in his *Polnoe sobranie sochinenii v tridtsati tomakh* (Leningrad, 1983), 25: 75–82.

7. Mikhailovskii first used the slogan *raznochinets prishel* in *Otechestvennye Zapiski* (March 1874), and concluded that "this event . . . is of epoch-making importance:" quoted in Christopher Becker, "*Raznochintsy:* The Development of the Word and of the Concept," *American Slavic and East European Review* 18 (1959), p. 71.

termediate rungs of the social ladder? Least of all, we Russians, and most of all, the Jews." Using statistics on educational patterns among various ethnic/religious groups (which had been published only four weeks earlier, with evident satisfaction, in the Jewish newspaper *Razsvet*),[8] the anonymous author of "The Kike Is Coming!" demonstrated that Jews had achieved a presence in educational institutions that was far above their proportion within the population as a whole: "In another decade or so, we will see that in certain areas of Russia, Jews will dominate not only the practical [i.e., financial and commercial] professions, but also the so-called liberal professions; that is, they will hold in their hands both the material and the intellectual power. This of course cannot be allowed. We must fight against this phenomenon." To make matters worse, Jewish upward mobility was being subsidized by tax revenues extracted from the Russian muzhik. "Every Ioshka and Hershka who passes through a gymnasium," it was argued, "prevents a poor Russian from doing the same, and acquires the means to oppress many such poor Russians while advancing himself and his kin."[9]

"The Kike Is Coming!" may well have been the most influential Judeophobic statement produced in Russia between Brafman's *Book of the Kahal* (1869) and the infamous *Protocols of the Elders of Zion* (1905). Whereas the *Book of the Kahal* drew readers' attention to the dark machinations of an internal Jewish institution, "The Kike Is Coming!" crystallized concerns about the Jewish presence in *Russian* institutions, and in particular those whose mission was to train the future intellectual elite. It unleashed a stream of like-minded articles and letters in the Russian press, especially in the southwest territories, and its arresting headline became a common slogan of the reactionary right.[10]

Arguments against the influx of Jews into Russia's institutions of higher education boiled down to four claims: that the flood of Jews was depriving non-Jews of educational opportunities; that Jewish students were exercising a negative moral influence on their Christian counterparts; that Jewish students were supporting the revolutionary movement; and that the disproportionate Jewish presence in higher education threatened to shift the bal-

8. A. Kaufman, "Uchatsia li evrei," *Razsvet*, Feb. 14 and 21, 1880. On the use of his article by the author of "The Kike Is Coming!" see Kaufman, "Za mnogo let: Otryvki vospominanii starogo zhurnalista," *Evreiskaia Starina* 5, no. 2 (1913): 215.

9. "Zhid idet! Pis´mo v redaktsiiu," *Novoe Vremia*, Mar. 23, 1880.

10. Reactions in the press to "The Kike Is Coming!" are summarized in Klier, *Imperial Russia's Jewish Question*, pp. 404–7. Years after its initial appearance, the slogan continued to be used; see the examples cited in *Nedel'naia Khronika Voskhoda*, July 6, 1886, p. 737. It also provided the title for a novel by V. V. Krestovskii, *Zhid idet!* (St. Petersburg, 1899). Given its wide public resonance, the original "Kike Is Coming!" was almost certainly read by tsarist officials; at the very least, a copy made its way into the files of the Ministry of Internal Affairs: see RGIA, f. 821, op. 9, d. 8, ll. 68–69.

ance of power among technical and professional elites into the hands of a non-Russian, non-Christian minority whose loyalty to the tsarist state appeared at best doubtful. Initially, the campaign against Jewish students placed its conservative spokesmen at odds with official policy, which remained confident in the power of education to transform Jews into loyal and useful subjects. When Minister of Enlightenment D. A. Tolstoi addressed a Jewish audience in Odessa in 1875, he commended his listeners for their pursuit of secular education and expressed his "sincere hope that the surge of Jews into educational institutions" would "become even stronger."[11] During a visit to the city of Kherson he proclaimed:

> Our government makes no distinctions in its schools, neither by religious faith nor by estate. . . . There exists a single distinction among students—that of merit. You of course have read and heard about the criticisms of me . . . alleging that I instituted the classical curriculum only in order to block access to our gymnasia and universities for all except the aristocrats. This is true. Our gymnasia should produce aristocrats, but what sort? Aristocrats of the mind [audience: "bravo, bravo!"], aristocrats of knowledge ["bravo, bravo!"], aristocrats of labor. God grant that we might have more such aristocrats.[12]

Both speeches were published in the official journal of the Ministry of Enlightenment. Nor did the government share critics' growing concern that instead of assimilating, Jewish students would "de-Christianize" their peers. As we have seen, when government officials decided in 1877 not to extend the privileges of university graduates to Jewish "externs," they specifically cited the absence of the beneficial "moral influence" of interaction with Russian students.[13] Above all, the government's decision in 1879 to extend residence and employment privileges to Jewish graduates of nearly all institutions of higher education, rather than just to those of universities, highlights the contrast between continuing official support for selective integration through education and an emerging backlash among conservative commentators.

A key turning point in this burgeoning public debate came with the pogroms of 1881. Jewish students were not especially singled out for attack, nor did non-Jewish students participate in any noteworthy way in the violence.[14] But insofar as the pogroms were widely interpreted by the Russian

11. *Zhurnal Ministerstva narodnogo prosveshcheniia*, November 1875, p. 63.

12. Ibid., December 1875, pp. 131–32.

13. RGIA, f. 821, op. 9, d. 103, l. 409.

14. It should be noted, however, that the social identity of the pogrom perpetrators was subject to many wild rumors and cannot be determined with confidence; see Aronson, *Troubled Waters*, pp. 101–7. Also, some right-wing newspapers attempted to incite pogroms specifically against Jewish students, arguing that they had "taken over our three southern universities": *Novorossiiskii Telegraf*, Mar. 19, 1881, p. 2.

state and society as a protest against Jewish exploitation, the official response was to search for means to reduce all manifestations of Jewish power over non-Jews. Remarkably, the autocracy's first gesture, in the autumn of 1881, was to convene provincial commissions across the Pale of Settlement to solicit local opinion concerning possible responses to the pogroms. Though the commissions were hardly lacking an agenda—their official mandate was to propose ways to restrain the Jews' harmful activities—they nonetheless produced a series of vigorous and revealing debates, the first approximate sampling, in fact, of educated public opinion on Russian-Jewish relations.[15]

Commission members consisted of local state and zemstvo officials together with a variety of notables, including, in most cases, one or two Jews, usually prominent local merchants. In thirteen of the seventeen commissions, participants debated the possibility of establishing quotas on admission of Jews to schools and universities—a sign that by 1881 the idea was already widely current. In several commissions, a minority of members voted to exclude Jews entirely from Russian schools. The arguments in favor of quotas were much the same as those that had begun to appear a decade earlier in the press. Because of the flood of Jews into Russian gymnasia, claimed the Kherson commission in its final report, "The children of poor noblemen, bureaucrats, and landowners lack the means to compete."[16] In a personal testimony, a student at Kharkov University related:

> In the first class of those gymnasia where there are already significant numbers of Jews, the Russian boy, having come from a Christian family, learns from his [Jewish] peers that Christ was a faker and a magician. Gradually such ridicule and contempt . . . have their effect. By the fourth or fifth class the boy is already a bad Christian. There begins the battle of opinions so characteristic of young minds, and by the upper levels both sides have entirely rejected their religions. In the upper levels begins the mockery of everything Russian, everything patriotic, as being slavish and illiberal, to which is contrasted the Jews' cosmopolitanism. I experienced this myself and I confess that only my patriotic feelings preserved my religious faith. This was the atmosphere in which Zheliabov and Trigoni [prominent Russian left-wing terrorists] came of age, both of whom had been students in jewified [*evreizirovannye*] gymnasia.[17]

---

15. I. Michael Aronson, "Russian Commissions on the Jewish Question in the 1880s," *East European Quarterly* 14, no. 1 (1980): 59–74. As Aronson points out, the commissions were designed in part to gather useful information and in part to convince local populations that the government was actively trying to remove the root causes of anti-Jewish violence, which continued even as the commissions met.

16. Extensive selections from the commissions' deliberations are reproduced in S. A. Panchulidzev, *Spravka k dokladu po evreiskomu voprosu*, 12 vols. (St. Petersburg, 1909–12); the passage here is from vol. 8 (*Prosveshchenie*), p. 36.

17. Ibid., pp. 1–2 (Kharkov commission).

One of the two Jewish members of the Kharkov commission came out forcefully against such views, noting that a significant proportion of "wayward
youth" came from Russian Orthodox seminaries, where one could hardly
blame Jewish influence. B. I. Gorvits of the Ekaterinoslav commission went
even further, offering the opinion (widely held by traditional Jews) that "Jews
are being corrupted by Christians. Until Jews began attending Russian
schools there was no sedition among them."[18]

Concern about the impact of Jewish students extended well beyond their
years of study. In the Ekaterinoslav commission, the landowner Miklashevskii
proclaimed that "in our time every government in the civilized world is necessarily dependent on its national intelligentsia; government personnel itself is drawn from this very intelligentsia. What will happen if the Jewish intelligentsia pushes aside the Russian intelligentsia?"[19]

Others, however—and not only the Jewish members of the various commissions—opposed the zero-sum mentality as regards educational opportunity. A zemstvo official from Kherson argued that Russians should expand
their educational system rather than seek to exclude minorities from it. Noting that even poor Jewish parents considered it their moral duty to have their
children taught to read, he added, "It would be extremely useful for us to
adopt this praiseworthy example from the Jews." Another commission member, responding to a proposal to limit the number of Jewish students in the
medical faculty at Kharkov University, declared that such a step could be
taken only "if it were to be proved that Russian physicians know their trade
better than Jews."[20]

In the end, eight commissions voted in favor of some form of *numerus
clausus* (closed number) on admission of Jews to gymnasia, five voted against,
and four took no position. Of those in favor, nearly all supported the notion
that Jewish students ought to constitute a proportion of the total student body
no higher than the proportion of Jews in the population at large. For proponents there was an irresistible logic to such a formula: it simply did not
make sense for Russia's educational institutions to bestow their benefits on
Jews in greater proportion than on the rest of the population. The application of the formula, however, varied considerably according to how one
defined "the rest of the population." If it were taken as that of the empire as
a whole, then the numerus clausus would be set at 5 percent or less; if it were
that of the Pale, 10 percent; if it were that of individual educational districts,

18. Ibid., pp. 9 (Kharkov) and 24 (Ekaterinoslav). For other instances of the view that Christian students were corrupting Jews rather than vice versa, see RGIA, f. 846, op. 1, d. 131, ll.
3–8; *Nedel'naia Khronika Voskhoda,* Mar. 12, 1882; Tsunzer, *Tsunzers biografiya;* Levanda, *Ispoved
del'tsa,* p. 125.

19. Panchulidzev, *Spravka k dokladu po evreiskomu voprosu,* 8: 23.

20. Ibid., pp. 38 (Kherson commission), 7 (Kharkov commission).

as high as 30 percent. And since Jews were multiplying at a higher rate than most other ethnic groups in the empire, all these estimates would, in theory, be subject to change over time.

Such variations notwithstanding, the fact remained that nearly half the provincial commissions convened in 1881 sought to limit the use of educational institutions as channels of Jewish integration. In subsequent years, moreover, government officials often chose to count only the thirteen commissions that had expressed an opinion, in order to argue that a decisive majority (eight) had supported the introduction of anti-Jewish quotas.[21] It would be a mistake, of course, to portray tsarist policy makers in the 1880s as beholden to public opinion in any meaningful way. But it is difficult to escape the conclusion that the pogroms of 1881–82, and more significantly the perception of the pogroms as an attack against selective Jewish integration, added enormous weight to the arguments presented in "The Kike Is Coming!" and similar pronouncements.

The actual establishment of the numerus clausus on admission of Jews began not as a single, coordinated plan but in piecemeal fashion, beginning with individual higher technical institutes under the control of branches of the government other than the Ministry of Enlightenment. In 1882 the War Ministry inaugurated a 5 percent quota on Jewish admissions at the Military-Medical Academy in St. Petersburg, where Jewish students had first petitioned for equal rights in the 1850s. The following year the Ministry of State Domains adopted an identical quota at its Mining and Forestry Institutes.[22] By 1886 quotas were in place at the St. Petersburg Institute of Communications Engineering, the Kharkov Technological Institute, and the Dorpat Veterinary Institute, while the Kharkov Veterinary Institute banned admission of Jews altogether.[23]

The majority of Russia's institutions of higher education, however—including all its universities—were controlled by the Ministry of Enlightenment. Under the direction of Count I. D. Delianov (1882–98), the ministry still reflected, if increasingly dimly, the Enlightenment notion of education as the great assimilator, and in fact Delianov put up considerable resistance to the establishment and implementation of anti-Jewish quotas.[24] The piecemeal introduction of quotas at educational institutions controlled by other

21. For examples, see RGIA, f. 821 op. 8, d. 246, l. 126; op. 9, d. 188, ll. 284–90, and d. 215, ll. 245–47.

22. TsGIA-SPb, f. 184, op. 8, d. 10, ll. 1–4.

23. RGIA, f. 733, op. 190, d. 58, ll. 3–5; Georgievskii, *Doklad,* pp. 233–36. Several other institutes administered by the Ministry of State Domains were spared quotas only because Jewish enrollment was already less than 6 percent of the total.

24. Guido Hausmann, "Der Numerus clausus für jüdische Studenten im Zarenreich," *Jahrbücher für Geschichte Osteuropas* 41 (1993): 520.

ministries, however, inevitably increased the number of Jewish applicants at those administered by the Ministry of Enlightenment.[25] As early as 1884, for example, the superintendent of the Kiev educational district, with the support of the Academic Council of Kiev University, wrote to Delianov requesting the imposition of a 10 percent quota on admission of Jewish medical students. The letter specifically mentioned the pressures created by the recent quota on admission of Jews to the Military-Medical Academy in St. Petersburg. A similar initiative appeared at Kharkov University the following year, with support from at least some non-Jewish medical students.[26] Apart from the Kharkov case, however, none of the pressure to institute quotas appears to have come from students themselves.

It was the renewed student unrest of the 1880s that transformed the numerus clausus from an ad hoc response by individual ministries into a broad government policy. In 1882, student demonstrations spilled over into the streets of St. Petersburg and Kazan, and police and government officials claimed to have observed Jewish students playing a prominent role.[27] Even D. A. Tolstoi, in his new capacity as minister of internal affairs, began to lose faith in strictly meritocratic admissions. In a series of memoranda to Alexander III, Tolstoi began on a positive note: "Eighty years of effort on the part of the government to draw Jews into general educational institutions have been crowned with complete success. The Jews have come to recognize the value of general education for their children, and undoubtedly will continue to strive for it, especially in light of the substantial reductions in military service that it provides."[28] But Tolstoi now saw disturbing aspects to this trend as well. There had been an "extraordinary growth," he reported to the tsar, in the proportion of Jewish students among those under investigation for revolutionary activity in the southern provinces of the empire. Of 182 individuals indicted in 1886 for sedition, for example, 87 were Jews, and of these, 62—including 10 women—were students. "In the recent past," Tolstoi added, "those of Jewish origin have assumed the leadership of the revolutionary movement" in Russia as well as among exiles abroad. Tolstoi's initial suggestion, approved by the tsar, was to sentence convicted Jewish revolutionaries to ten years' administrative exile in Siberia, rather than the usual five. By 1888 Tolstoi was a firm supporter of admission quotas in institutions of higher education as well.[29]

25. This effect did not escape the attention of the government; see RGIA, f. 821, op. 9, d. 215, l. 257.

26. Ibid., d. 188, ll. 4–5. On Kharkov, see *Nedel'naia Khronika Voskhoda*, Oct. 6, 1885.

27. TsGIA-SPb, f. 139, op. 1, d.7253, ll. 1–2. For police surveillance of Lev Kogan-Bernshtein, a prominent student revolutionary at St. Petersburg University, see GARF, f. 102, deloproizvodstvo 7 (1886), d. 103, ch. 1, ll. 1–2.

28. RGIA, f. 821, op. 8, d. 246, l. 123.

29. GARF f.102, deloproizvodstvo 7 (1886), d. 103, ch. 1, ll. 1–2; RGIA, f. 821, op. 8, d. 246, l. 126.

Other officials, well aware of the extensive financial support provided to Jewish students by the Society for the Spread of Enlightenment, were convinced that it was in Baron Horace Gintsburg's power to curb unrest in the universities. A highly placed observer recorded Tolstoi's successor as minister of internal affairs, I. N. Durnovo, as claiming that "every time disorders have broken out in [St. Petersburg] University, Gintsburg has been threatened with expulsion [from the capital], and the disorders ceased immediately." Similarly, the St. Petersburg city governor, P. A. Gresser, assured a British visitor that "the Nihilist disorders in the university were all the work of the Jewish students." After threatening the leaders of the capital's Jewish community with mass expulsion if they failed to use their influence with the students, Gresser boasted, "from that day there has not even been an audible whisper in the university against the authorities."[30]

By far the most thorough official analysis of the "Jewish Question" in higher education came from A. I. Georgievskii, the second highest ranking official in the Ministry of Enlightenment. Georgievskii submitted his conclusions in 1886 to the High Commission for Review of Legislation Pertaining to the Jews of Russia (1883–88), of which he was a member and which was charged with devising a comprehensive Jewish policy in the wake of the pogroms. Having published a series of articles in the 1860s portraying Jewish emancipation in Europe in highly favorable terms, Georgievskii was as close to a Judeophile as one could find in the tsarist bureaucracy.[31] To his mind, student disorders were the direct result of the social democratization of the universities that had begun in the 1860s, and had little to do with the influx of non-Russians per se. A numerus clausus for Jews, wrote Georgievskii, would be "arbitrary, inappropriate, and unjust," threatening the government's highly successful policy of integration and pushing even more young Jews into the arms of hostile elements. But if Georgievskii rejected specifically Jewish quotas on moral as well as political grounds, he did not hesitate to endorse the goal of reducing the number of lower-class Jewish students as part of a general program to reassert the elite social composition of higher education. In fact, his proposed alternative to quotas—barring admission of Jews whose fathers were not merchants of the first or second guild, honored

---

30. On Durnovo, see *Dnevnik gosudarstvennogo sekretaria A. A. Polovtsova*, 2: 433; on Gresser, see Stead, *Truth about Russia*, p. 247; both cited by Rogger, *Jewish Policies and Right-Wing Politics*, p. 75. Needless to say, Gresser's claim, as reported by Stead, did not stand the test of time. A different source reports an instance in which Horace Gintsburg tipped off Jewish students at St. Petersburg University who faced arrest in the event of their participation in a planned demonstration. See M. P. Shafir, "Moi vospominaniia," *Evreiskaia Letopis´* 4 (1926): 110.

31. See the analysis of Georgievskii's views on Jews and Judaism in Klier, *Imperial Russia's Jewish Question*, pp. 91–93. Klier (p. 467n19) observes that Georgievskii's unusually Judeophilic views led to (false) rumors that he was of Jewish origin.

citizens, or civil servants—adhered to the tradition of selective integration, whose logic consisted of strategically differentiating between social classes within the Jewish population.[32]

Neither Tolstoi's plan for tougher sentencing of Jewish revolutionaries nor Durnovo's and Gresser's fantasy of inducing Horace Gintsburg to quell student unrest nor Georgievskii's plan for class-based exclusions (the latter endorsed by a majority of the fifteen-member High Commission) was able to satisfy a regime that felt itself increasingly under siege by radical students. Indeed, the High Commission's two most powerful members—Prince N. N. Golitsyn and the chairman, Minister of Justice K. I. Pahlen—appended a dissenting memorandum to Georgievskii's report, calling for the "complete segregation" of Jewish and Christian students at the secondary level, to be achieved by the creation of a separate network of gymnasia for Jews, financed by Jewish taxes. While expressing confidence that the classical curriculum could "conquer the Talmud," Golitsyn and Pahlen nonetheless took a dark view of the encounter between Jews and higher education:

> In spite of their European education and milder external form, [Jewish students] nonetheless remain Jews with the same qualities that Christian society has found particularly harmful (and these qualities sometimes become even stronger). . . . Social intercourse by Jews with their Christian fellows, which is enormously harmful to the latter, does not substantially advance the goal of transforming the Jew for the better. . . . In an exclusively Jewish milieu, surrounded by the *demokratizm* of the Jewish community (which recognizes an aristocracy only in the form of its advanced interpreters of Talmudic learning), Jewish children will not be so harmful to one another.[33]

Like the vast majority of proposals submitted by the High Commission, this one was dismissed by the Council of Ministers.[34] Instead, the council voted in July 1887 to establish the numerus clausus for admission of Jewish males to all institutions of higher as well as secondary education run by the Ministry of Enlightenment. At the time, Jewish female students were not re-

---

32. Georgievskii, *Doklad,* pp. 227–29, 265. Georgievskii also proposed prohibiting Jewish students from giving private lessons, thereby depriving the poorer among them of their chief source of income, and recommended that Jewish applicants to institutions of higher education be separately evaluated for their "moral qualities" and knowledge of Russian.

33. K. I. Palen and N. N. Golitsyn, *Osoboe mnenie po dokladu A. I. Georgievskogo* (St. Petersburg, 1887) (copy located in RGIA, f. 821, op. 150, d. 381, ll. 31–33).

34. Despite its impressive name, and in contrast to the Jewish Committee (1840–63), most of whose members were heads of ministries, the High Commission for Review of Legislation Pertaining to the Jews of Russia was composed largely of second-tier bureaucrats. The sole exceptions were Pahlen and Golitsyn.

garded as warranting such drastic action—though that would begin to change in the 1890s.[35] Quotas were set at 10 percent for institutions within the Pale (corresponding roughly to the Jewish proportion of the total population of the Pale), 5 percent outside the Pale (corresponding roughly to the Jewish proportion of the total population of the empire), and 3 percent in Moscow and St. Petersburg (where the most prestigious and arguably most "Russian" universities were located, along with the most rebellious students). With an eye toward minimizing potential student protests, quotas took the form of a "temporary" administrative decree, rather than formal legislation.[36]

Jews were not the first targets of quotas on admission to institutions of higher education in late imperial Russia. At various times the autocracy had attempted to manipulate the composition of the student body according to ethnicity and religion (quotas against Polish Catholics), estate (quotas or outright bans on admission of graduates of religious seminaries), wealth (by raising tuition expressly to exclude the poor), and, of course, gender.[37] In many cases, suspicion of disproportional participation in revolutionary movements was the prime motive, as with the 10 percent quota instituted against Polish students in 1864 in response to the Polish uprising of the previous year. This was also the case with the infamous "Cook's Circular" of 1887, which limited the admission to gymnasia of children of "coachmen, menials, cooks, washerwomen, small shopkeepers, and the like."[38]

Ethnically based quotas such as those targeting Jews and Poles were distinctive insofar as they stemmed not only from concerns over revolutionary activity but from fears that non-Russians would soon dominate the professions and other public arenas. Thus, for example, as an internal government memorandum justifying the 1883 quota at the St. Petersburg Mining Institute asserted:

> Individuals of Polish and Jewish descent, having a particular capacity for mathematics, are more successful than others on the entrance exams, and therefore

---

35. In 1892 Jewish quotas were instituted at the Bestuzhevskie Higher Courses for Women and at midwifery institutes associated with medical schools at the universities of Warsaw, Dorpat, and Kazan, and in 1897 at the St. Petersburg Women's Medical Institute. See *Evreiskaia entsiklopediia*, 13: 53.

36. Pozner, *Evrei v obshchei shkole*, p. 85.

37. On the origins of anti-Polish quotas, see TsGIA-SPb, f. 14, op. 1, d. 7303, ll. 1–2; RGIA, f. 821, op. 9, d. 188, l. 224; and Franciszek Nowinski, *Polacy na uniwersytecie petersburgskim w latach 1832–1884* (Wroclaw, 1986), pp. 192–93. I am grateful to Theodore Weeks for bringing this work to my attention and for translating the relevant passages. For seminarians, see Gregory Freeze, *The Parish Clergy in Nineteenth-Century Russia: Crisis, Reform, Counter-Reform* (Princeton, 1983), p. 405. Admission restrictions based on estate and class are discussed in Alston, *Education and the State*, pp. 32–33, 128–39; on women, see Dudgeon, "Forgotten Minority," and Johanson, *Women's Struggle for Higher Education.*

38. The circular is quoted in Alston, *Education and the State*, p. 129.

are enrolling in very considerable numbers. . . . Every year the percentage of non-Russians among mining engineers increases, and one can already roughly calculate the time, according to the theory of probability, when a large portion of the management positions in factories and mines will pass into the hands of individuals of Polish and Jewish origin. This situation poses an even greater political danger to the extent that masses of Russian workers in factories, mines, and gold fields are entrusted to the authority of our mining engineers, including factories responsible for supplying the Russian army and navy.[39]

As Chapter 9 will show, the entrance of Jews into the professions and other positions of public authority was to have important repercussions for the development of civil society in fin-de-siècle Russia.

THE IMPACT OF QUOTAS

The quota on admission of Jews to Russian educational institutions marked the tsarist state's most significant retreat from the policy of selective integration during the entire late imperial period.[40] It is not merely that the quota was discriminatory; that much could be said of the policy of selective integration itself, which treated different groups within the Jewish population differently and preserved the inferior legal status of the majority of Jews. Rather, what was significant about the quota was that it perversely constricted the Jews' ability to carry out the quid pro quo implicit in official policy since the 1840s: that those who demonstrated their utility—as defined by the state—would be rewarded with legal rights. What the Pale was for Jewish geographical mobility the numerus clausus threatened to be for Jewish social mobility. For the Russian-Jewish intelligentsia and for an ever-expanding portion of the Jewish population as a whole, secular education had become virtually synonymous with progress, and to be denied its benefits was tantamount to being shut out from modernity itself.

The notion of restricting rather than fostering access to education was so unthinkable to Jewish elites that their initial reaction to the idea was sheer disbelief.[41] *Razsvet* mocked "The Kike Is Coming!" with the headline "Confusion Is Coming!," reminding its readers that "if Jews were to enroll in lower proportions than Russians, *Novoe Vremia* would be screaming that Jews are

39. GARF, f. 102, deloproizvodstvo 3, op. 79 (1883), d. 583, l. 1.

40. A letter to the editor of the leading Jewish weekly at the time proclaimed the quotas "an extraordinarily heavy blow—more serious in terms of their consequences, perhaps, than all the other restrictive measures introduced recently." See "K voprosu o normirovke uchashhikhsia v universitetakh evreev: Pis'mo Dr. S. Gruzenberga," *Nedel'naia Khronika Voskhoda*, Aug. 2, 1887, p. 779; for a similar assessment with greater hindsight, see Sliozberg, *Dela minuvshikh dnei*, 1: 258.

41. John Klier makes this point in *Imperial Russia's Jewish Question*, p. 405–6.

alien to contemporary civilization and prefer blind ignorance."[42] Soon thereafter, *Razsvet* began publishing installments of a satirical novel under the title "The Kike Is Coming!," a send-up of the perceived hysteria of the original letter to the editor.[43] For their part, the editors of *Russkii Evrei*, playing on the theme of the Jew as congenital lawbreaker, wrote, "Yes, we confess. We confess completely. The facts show that we are guilty of a criminal propensity toward education."[44]

For Jews who aspired literally or figuratively to move beyond the Pale, the quotas were to have a more sustained impact than any of the government's other anti-Jewish measures during the late imperial period. In contrast to the spontaneous outbursts of pogrom violence, in which the role of the tsarist state and the identity of the perpetrators were a source of ongoing controversy among contemporaries, the quotas of 1887 were openly premeditated, debated first in the press and then by local authorities before being approved at the highest levels of the autocracy. Though billed as "temporary," they would remain in place for thirty years, until the collapse of the Romanov dynasty in February 1917. In the bitter words of Chaim Weizmann, an early victim of the quotas as a gymnasium student in Pinsk (and later the first president of Israel), "Nothing in tsarist Russia was as enduring as 'Temporary Legislation.'"[45] The future Zionist leader Shmarya Levin went so far as to compare the "tortures" of his cohort of Jewish students—"they had been made thirsty for knowledge, and the means of slaking their thirst was withheld from them"—with those of Jewish cantonists under Nicholas I.[46] In the memoirs of the founding generation of the Bund, too, the quotas loom much larger than the pogroms as a source of animus against the Russian state.[47]

The quotas had their greatest impact at the gymnasium level, where after 1887 the number of Jewish students rapidly shrank both absolutely and in relation to the student body as a whole (see Table 10). Enrollment data, of course, indicate only the number of students who successfully navigated the quotas, and do not reflect the proportion of those who sought but were denied admission. The critical factor was not simply how many "Jewish slots" were available at any given school but the ratio of Jewish applicants (whose quantity is unknown) to available Jewish slots; that is, demand to supply. In one case—that of Vilna, the most densely Jewish educational district—the

42. "Sumbur idet! Popovodu stat'i: Zhid idet!" *Razsvet*, Mar. 27, 1880.

43. "Zhid idet!" *Razsvet*, nos. 14–16, 22–24, 26–27, 31–33, 44–48 (1881).

44. *Russkii Evrei*, Oct.15, 1880, p. 1643.

45. Chaim Weizmann, *Trial and Error: The Autobiography of Chaim Weizmann* (New York, 1949), p. 17.

46. Shmarya Levin, *Youth in Revolt*, trans. Maurice Samuel (New York, 1930), p. 150.

47. Henry Tobias, *The Jewish Bund in Russia from Its Origins to 1905* (Stanford, 1972), pp. 11–12.

TABLE 10. Jewish and Non-Jewish Students in Gymnasia
and Progymnasia Within and Outside the Pale, 1886 and 1896

| | Within the Pale | | | Outside the Pale | | |
| | | Jewish | | | Jewish | |
Year	Non-Jewish	#	%	Non-Jewish	#	%
1886[a]	25,142	5,547	18	36,860	2,015	5
1896[b]	24,555	2,945	11	41,334	1,686	4
Net change	-2%	-47%		+12%	-16%	

[a] On eve of implementation of quotas.
[b] Year by which all students admitted before quotas had passed through the maximum eight years of secondary schooling.

SOURCE: S. V. Pozner, *Evrei v obshchei shkole: K istorii zakonodatel'stva i pravitel'stvennoi politiki v oblasti evreiskogo voprosa* (St. Petersburg, 1914), app. 4.

Society for the Spread of Enlightenment was able to demonstrate a dramatic decline in the proportion of Jewish applicants admitted, from 58 percent in 1888 to 16 percent in 1900, even as the student body as a whole expanded.[48]

The quotas' quantitative effect at the university level was considerably more ambiguous.[49] In 1886, Jews accounted for 15 percent of all students at Russia's eight universities. Over the course of the following decade, their proportion declined to 12 percent, thereby reversing the steady rise that had begun in the 1860s but by no means erasing the Jewish presence in higher education.[50] Among the universities, moreover, there was tremendous variation, as Table 11 indicates. The most prestigious universities, those in Moscow and St. Petersburg, initially registered a sharp drop in the number of Jewish students, even as overall enrollment increased. But in the early decades of the twentieth century, and in fact down to the collapse of the Old Regime, only the University of Kazan achieved the proportions for Jewish enrollment set by the 1887 decree. In several others the percentage of Jews actually went up. Similarly varied results obtained at the higher technical institutes.[51]

48. RGIA, f. 1532, op. 1, d. 353-a, l. 14. These figures reflect applications and admissions at both gymnasia and *realuchilishche*. I have been unable to locate data on the ratio of applications to admissions among Gentiles.

49. This point is raised in Halevy, *Jewish University Students*, p. 44.

50. Pozner, *Evrei v obshchei shkole*, app. 2.

51. By the end of the nineteenth century, the following institutions for technical training had ceased to admit Jews altogether: the Institute of Communications Engineering and the Military-Medical Academy, both in St. Petersburg; the Electrotechnical Institute, the School of

TABLE 11. Non-Jewish and Jewish Students
in Universities, Russian Empire, 1886 and 1896, by University

| University | 1886 | | | 1896 | | |
| | Non-Jewish | Jewish | | Non-Jewish | Jewish | |
		#	%		#	%
St. Petersburg[a]	2,012	268	12	3,211	109	3
Moscow[a]	2,683	298	10	4,053	153	4
Kharkov[b]	1,047	414	28	1,061	391	27
Dorpat[b]	1,349	235	15	698	179	20
Kazan[b]	907	60	6	728	95	12
Warsaw[c]	947	172	15	811	193	19
Kiev[c]	1,588	237	13	2,041	604	23
Odessa[c]	404	172	30	465	145	24

[a] 3% quota beginning July 1887.
[b] 5% quota beginning July 1887.
[c] 10% quota beginning July 1887.

SOURCE: S. V. Pozner, *Evrei v obshchei shkole: K istorii zakonodatel'stva i pravitel'stvennoi politiki v oblasti evreiskogo voprosa* (St. Petersburg, 1914), app. 2.

These discrepancies appear not to have been due to active resistance on the part of individual universities, whose autonomy (including control over admissions) had been severely curtailed by the government's University Statute of 1884. Nor were they the result of opposition in Russian society at large. While the overt social discrimination of the "Cook's Circular," as one historian has put it, "aroused public resentment against the regime of Alexander III as no other act of his reign," the anti-Jewish quotas elicited at best silence, and in many cases approval, in the Russian press.[52] Rather, the irregular enforcement of the quotas at the postsecondary level appears to have been the work of the Ministry of Enlightenment itself, particularly under the administration of I. D. Delianov. Under Delianov, who reluctantly oversaw the application of the 1887 decree until his death in 1898, the op-

Engineering, and the Agricultural Institute, all in Moscow. See RGIA, f.1532, op. 1, d. 353-a, l. 21. By contrast, in 1896 Jews still constituted 20 percent of the student body at the Riga Polytechnic Institute and 11 percent at the Kharkov Technological Institute, both outside the Pale. See Pozner, *Evrei v obshchei shkole*, app. 3.

52. Alston, *Education and the State*, p. 129. The "Cook's Circular" may well have inspired Lenin's oft-quoted remark that under socialism, a cook would be able to run the government. On the reaction of the Russian press to anti-Jewish quotas, see "Otgoloski pechati," *Nedel'naia Khronika Voskhoda*, Aug. 2, 1887, p. 782.

portunities for bypassing the quota system were stunning.[53] Jewish applicants who had passed the university entrance examination but had failed to secure a slot in the "Jewish quota" (*evreiskii komplekt*) could petition to be admitted "above the norm," and as early as 1888 many hundreds did so. Isaak Lipkovich, for example, an 1887 graduate of the Minsk classical gymnasium who was initially rejected by Kiev University, gained admission above the norm after sending an impassioned plea to Delianov: "Bitterly lamenting my fate, I nonetheless supposed that the seeds of goodness and truth planted in me by the gymnasium would help me find at least some modest station in life. But, having sorted through all spheres of activity, I had to conclude that the gymnasium did not prepare me for them. And in the meantime my impulse toward higher education has not diminished."[54] In certain instances, the number of Jewish applicants admitted above the norm actually exceeded the number admitted under the quota system. In 1887 the Demidov School of Jurisprudence in Iaroslavl filled its 5 percent Jewish quota with six applicants and admitted somewhere between thirty-five and sixty additional Jews above the norm.[55] At a ceremony for new students that fall, the school director's proclamation that for him "there are neither Jews nor Hellenes" elicited enthusiastic applause from the audience.[56] In 1897, eleven Jews were admitted under the quota to Odessa University, while an additional seventy-one gained entrance after petitioning Delianov.[57]

These and other similar instances were enough to raise the hopes of Jewish students everywhere that they could escape what one Jewish newspaper called the "silent, invisible pogrom" in higher education.[58] "Who among the Jews does not hope," wrote Genrikh Sliozberg, "that for him an exception will be made in the general anti-Semitic atmosphere?"[59] The quotas added yet another category to the staggering array of issues about which Jews regularly wrote petitions, whether directly to state offices or via notables such as the Gintsburgs.[60] By the turn of the century, the Ministry of Enlighten-

53. *Materialy po voprosu o prieme evreev v sredniia i vysshiia uchebnyia zavedniia* (St. Petersburg, 1908), pp. 63–64. Dubnov, *History of the Jews in Russia and Poland*, 2: 351, describes Delianov as "good-natured . . . despite his reactionary proclivities."

54. RGIA, f. 733, op. 150, d. 382, ll. 14–15. Lipkovich's petition was one of 147 submitted by Jewish applicants who had been denied admission to Kiev University in 1888.

55. GARF, f. 102, deloproizvodstvo 3, op. 83 (1887), d. 507, ll. 1–8.

56. Rubinshtein, *Vospominaniia starogo advokata*, p. v.

57. RGIA, f. 733, op. 150, d. 571, l. 11; Pozner, *Evrei v obshchei shkole*, p. 89.

58. *Nedel'naia Khronika Voskhoda*, July 31, 1882, p. 835.

59. Sliozberg, *Dela minuvshikh dnei*, 1: 159.

60. Among the roughly 1,500 personal letters sent to David Gintsburg (son of Horace and grandson of Evzel) and preserved in his archive, a substantial number are from students seeking assistance in gaining admission to a gymnasium or institution of higher education. See RNB, f. 183, op. 1014, dd. 143–1583.

ment faced an annual flood of petitions from thousands of Jewish graduates of Russian secondary schools, desperate to be admitted to a university or technical institute above the norm. Preserved in the archives literally by the thousands, such petitions offer remarkable testimony to the mass hunger for higher education among Russian Jews.[61] Many petitioners came to the imperial capital in person, in what one contemporary described as a "mass pilgrimage" to the ministry's doors.[62] Indeed, having witnessed "the rather considerable number of Jews who every year, from August to December, come to Petersburg . . . to petition," Delianov urged local school officials in 1893 to forestall such trips, reminding them that Jews were barred from the capital unless already enrolled in an institution of higher education there.[63] "A new category has been created among Jews," observed the Jewish activist Solomon V. Pozner, referring to the young gymnasium graduates desperately seeking to bypass the quota.[64] The new social type of the Jew seeking admission above the norm was familiar enough to find its way into contemporary works of fiction, Russian as well as Yiddish.[65]

Although we generally think of quotas as operating covertly, behind the curtains of the admission process, in imperial Russia they were applied with surprising openness. Indeed, despite their extralegislative status, their existence was common knowledge. "I don't have to go into detail," the wry narrator of one of Sholem Aleichem's novels laments to the reader, "to explain what I mean by the quotas."[66] It was not uncommon, on the eve of each new semester, for a university or technical institute to compile a ranked list of Jews who had passed the admission exam, and to publicly post the list while those on it awaited the opening of Jewish slots according to the volume of non-Jewish enrollment. A January 1904 telegram to the Minister of Enlightenment from an anxious Wolf Herzfeld (Vul´f Gertsfel´d) conveys the mechanics of such a system:

AUGUST 1903 REJECTED FROM IUR´EV [Dorpat] UNIVERSITY. NOW AT BE- GINNING OF [spring semester] 1904 — 30 CHRISTIANS ACCEPTED. WAS CON-

61. For a sampling of petitions from Jewish students preserved in the archive of the Ministry of Enlightenment, see RGIA, f. 733, op. 151, dd. 67–68, 164–66, 236–37, 347–50, 478–80, and op. 152, dd. 28–34. For students seeking to study in St. Petersburg in particular, see inter alia TsGIA-SPb, f. 139, op. 1, d. 7447.

62. Pozner, *Evrei v obshchei shkole,* p. 88. For a personal account of one such visit—which ended in expulsion from St. Petersburg—see L. Aizenberg, "Vidy pravitel´stva v evreiskom voprose: Pleve i evreiki-bestuzhevski," *Evreiskaia Letopis´* 2 (1923): 73–74.

63. Pozner, *Evrei v obshchei shkole,* app. 1, doc. 7.

64. Ibid., p. 88.

65. See, e.g., Boris Gegidze, *V universitete: Nabroski studencheskoi zhizni,* 6th ed. (St. Petersburg, n.d.), pp. 30–34. Jewish student petitioners also appear in Sholem Aleichem's novel *Der blutiger shpas.*

66. Sholom [*sic*] Aleichem, *In the Storm,* trans. Aliza Shevrin (1907; New York, 1984), p. 22.

SIDERED NUMBER ONE JEWISH CANDIDATE WAS SURE OF ENROLLMENT BUT ANOTHER ADMITTED INSTEAD. ACCORDING TO QUOTA FOR EVERY 30 CHRISTIANS MORE THAN ONE JEW TO BE ADMITTED. HUMBLY REQUEST YOUR EXCELLENCY TO ADMIT ME BASED ON EXTRA 10 CHRISTIANS [i.e., under a 5 percent quota, thirty Christian enrollments correspond to one and a half Jewish slots, which Herzfeld asks be rounded up to two]. NATIVE OF RIGA STUDIED FOR 8 YEARS IN RIGA ALEKSANDROVSKAIA GYMNASIUM WITH GOOD DIPLOMA. PARENTS SACRIFICING EVERYTHING TO MAKE CHILDREN HONEST USEFUL CITIZENS AS OLDEST SON DREAMED OF BEING ANCHOR FOR THEM IN OLD AGE EAGERLY AWAIT YOUR GENEROUS DECISION.[67]

The Ministry of Enlightenment rejected Herzfeld's plea until April, by which time a full complement of forty Christians had enrolled, the number necessary for the creation of a second Jewish slot.[68]

Quotas introduced a broad array of new attitudes and strategies into the Jewish pursuit of higher education, not only for those seeking admission but for those actually admitted. To begin with, after 1887, admission to a secondary school—and somewhat less frequently to a university or technical institute—joined the list of items for which Jews routinely offered bribes. In cities like Mogilev, where Jews constituted over half the population but were limited (as everywhere in the Pale) to 10 percent of the seats in local secondary schools, a common response was to present the appropriate official with what one former student called the "Magna Carta of the Jewish people"—cash.[69] "What his shield is to the soldier in battle," mused Mary Antin, "that was the ruble to the Jew."[70] In some instances, Jewish slots were reportedly sold to the highest bidder.[71] The proportion of Jews in any given institution, as well as that in the local population, became crucial factors in the decision about where to apply. Ambitious parents—now, more often than not, ardent proponents rather than foes of secular education—increasingly took the step of sending their sons to secondary schools outside the Pale, where by and large the Jewish presence was sparse, and the chances for admission therefore greater, despite the more restrictive quota.[72] By the year 1900, more than a third of Jewish gymnasium students in the Russian Em-

---

67. RGIA, f.733, op. 152, d. 27, l. 62.

68. Ibid., ll. 70–81.

69. The quotation comes from the account in B. Ia. Koprzhiva-Lur´e, *Istoriia odnoi zhizni* (Paris, 1987), p. 33. For similar impressions, see Levin, *Youth in Revolt,* p. 149, and Grinberg, *Jewish Life in St. Petersburg,* p. 7.

70. Antin, *Promised Land,* p. 23.

71. Pozner, *Evrei v obshchei shkole,* p. 186.

72. For a historical example, see Koprzhiva-Lur´e, *Istoriia odnoi zhizni,* pp. 33–35; for a fictional one, see Sholem Aleichem, *Bloody Hoax,* p. 225.

pire attended schools outside the Pale (where roughly 6 percent of the total Jewish population lived).[73]

Popular advice books such as *What Kind of Education Jews Need and Where
to Get It: Sensible Advice for Jewish Parents* (Odessa, 1900) and the *Handbook for
Questions of Education for Jews* (St. Petersburg, 1901) offered tips to anxious
parents, steering them away from the gymnasium, with its classical, univer-
sity-preparatory curriculum, since so few Jews could hope to gain admission
to a university. Instead, the guidebooks counseled, parents should send their
children to the growing number of private commercial and technical high
schools, where quotas were far more relaxed or did not apply at all and the
curriculum was more vocationally oriented.[74] Another widespread Jewish strategy was "external" study and auditing, in the hope that one would eventually
be able to take and pass examinations for a higher degree.[75] In a survey of
Jewish students at Kiev University in 1910, 38 percent reported having received their gymnasium diplomas as externs.[76]

In his short story "Gymnasium" (1902), Sholem Aleichem—who had
himself attended a gymnasium in the prequota era—deftly captures the predicament faced by the fictional Katz family in the wake of the numerus
clausus. Determined to secure an elite education for their young Moshke,
the parents are informed by school officials that even with straight 5s (the
highest possible score) on the entrance exams, Moshke is by no means assured admission to the local gymnasium. The eighty-three Christians in the
incoming class allow for only eight Jewish slots (i.e., 10 percent). A clumsily
offered bribe is graciously accepted but fails to produce the desired result
because of a bureaucratic mixup. The despairing parents then set out in
search of a school with more favorable odds. "Wherever there was a town,
wherever there was a gymnasium," relates the father, "there we were. There

73. Data adapted from Pozner, *Evrei v obshchei shkole,* app. 4. The high proportion of Jewish gymnasium students outside the Pale is doubtless due in part to the fact that Jewish families who lived outside the Pale, by virtue of belonging to privileged social categories, were more
likely to send their children to gymnasia. Among Jewish students at the more vocational *realuchilishche,* the data are even more striking: in 1900, 47 percent lived outside the Pale. See
ibid., app. 5. On the legal status of Jewish gymnasium students outside the Pale and the government's concern, see *Nedel'naia Khronika Voskhoda,* Aug. 5, 1884, p. 877.

74. Romish, *Kakoe obrazovanie nuzhno evreiam i gde poluchit' ego? Blagorazumnyi sovet roditeliam
evreiam* (Odessa, 1900), pp. 9, 34–35; *Spravochnaia kniga po voprosam obrazovaniia evreev: Posobie
dlia uchitelei i uchitel'nits evreiskikh shkol i deiatelei po narodnomu obrazovaniiu* (St. Petersburg, 1901),
Introduction. Other Jewish manuals similarly favored practical or vocational education; see,
e.g., the introduction to the conference proceedings *Trudy s"ezdov po evreiskomu professional'nomu
obrazovaniiu* (St. Petersburg, 1911), vol. 1.

75. Sliozberg, *Dela minuvshikh dnei,* 3: 290; B. Krugliak, "Vospominaniia o zhizni eksternov
v Odesse (1896 g.), *Evreiskaia Starina* 9 (1916): 276–99.

76. Pozner, *Evrei v obshchei shkole,* p. 160.

Figure 24. "An auditor at the Imperial University
in the uniform prescribed by the Ministry [of Public
Enlightenment]." (*Pluvium*, 1906.) In fact, unlike
regular students, auditors did not wear special
uniforms. With its stereotypical Jew in traditional
garb, this caricature blends hostility and anxiety
regarding the growing ranks of Jewish auditors.

we presented ourselves. There we took the exam. There we passed the exam.
As a matter of fact, there we passed the exam with flying colors. And there
we were denied admission. Why? All because of the quotas!" As if heeding
the advice books, the Katzes set aside their dream of eventual university study
and settle for a commercial high school. Their problems, however, are far
from over, as the father explains:

> And the Almighty had compassion, and sent me a gymnasium in Poland, a "com-
> mercial" one, where they took in one Jew to every Christian (no comparison
> intended)—that is, where the quota was 50 percent. There was just one little
> catch: the Jew had to bring his own Christian with him, and only if he passed—
> that is, the Christian—and you were ready to treat him to tuition did you stand

a fighting chance. In other words, instead of one millstone around my neck, there were two. Do you follow me? As if it weren't enough to knock my brains out for my own boy, now I had someone else's to worry about, because if Esau doesn't pass, Jacob can pack his bags too. But what I went through before I got that Christian, a shoemaker's son named Kholiava, is not to be described. Wouldn't you know it, he went and flunked! And in religion [*zakon bozhii*], of all subjects! My own son had to take him in hand and coach him for the makeup. Now here's a tough question: how does my son know anything about Christianity? No need to ask. For what does he have a head on his shoulders?[77]

A further bribe is required, this time to persuade the shoemaker to enroll his son in a school with so many Jews. In the end, the vain pursuit of secular education literally and symbolically tears apart the Jewish family: the mother leaves the father to be with her son at the distant commercial high school, causing the family business to collapse, while Moshke proceeds to drop out of school to become a revolutionary. In his later novel *The Bloody Hoax,* Sholem Aleichem takes the theme of secular education's corrosive power even further: a would-be university student converts to Christianity in order to gain admission for himself (now as a Christian) *and* tip the scales so that an additional Jewish slot opens up for his unconverted friend.[78] Real-life incidents of Jewish students' converting for the sake of admission were frequent enough to provoke bitter debates in the Jewish press.[79]

Along with his warning about the perils of enlightenment and assimilation— characteristically submerged beneath a humorous surface—Sholem Aleichem conveys an important psychological dimension of the Jewish experience of quotas. It is certainly true that long before 1887, indeed well before the nineteenth century, a sense of collective intellectual superiority was embedded in the worldview of most Jews.[80] Among secularly educated Jews, however, the encounter with European civilization had begun to effect a kind of Copernican shift, decentering the formerly privileged status of Jewish knowledge, and with it the belief in Jewish intellectual preeminence. It is thus worth noting that along with the humiliations they brought, the anti-Jewish quotas in Russia also had the unintended effect of reinvigorating the image of the "smart Jew." Jews, it seemed, displayed such mental prowess that others, even the "dominant nationality," felt the need to block their advance.

77. Sholem Aleichem, "Gimnaziye," in *Ale verk fun Sholem Aleichem* (New York, 1944), 7: 188–89. The above translation draws on that by Hillel Halkin in Sholem Aleichem, *Tevye the Dairyman and the Railroad Stories* (New York, 1987), p. 226.

78. Sholem Aleichem, *Bloody Hoax,* p. 25.

79. On the problem of apostasy for the sake of gaining admission, see A. Press, "Ch´ia vina?" *Novyi Voskhod,* no. 37 (1912), p. 12.

80. Raphael Patai, *The Jewish Mind* (Detroit, 1977), pp. 324–27. On late nineteenth-century and more recent versions of this view, see Sander Gilman, *Smart Jews: The Construction of the Image of Jewish Superior Intelligence* (Lincoln, Neb., 1996).

Nowhere was this sentiment more powerfully expressed than in the image of Jewish parents recruiting, subsidizing, and coaching a Christian pupil simply in order to be able to enroll their own child in a Russian school. Although it is virtually impossible to find specific evidence that such a practice actually occurred (in contrast to apostasy for the sake of admission, which certainly did occur), its existence was almost universally credited by contemporary Russian Jews. A wide range of figures, from the historian Simon Dubnov to the Duma member Eliezer Nisselovich, insisted that Jewish sponsorship of Christian students for the purpose of manipulating admission quotas was "not an anecdote, but a fact."[81]

While the quotas were intended to restrict the Jewish presence in educational institutions, and while on a quantitative level they partly achieved their goal, qualitatively they had quite the opposite effect. Those Jews who gained admission to institutions of higher education were now seen—and saw themselves—as having demonstrated a level of talent and drive beyond that required of Gentiles. Numerous memoirs register the conviction that after 1887, only a gold or silver medal (indicating first or second ranking in one's class) would secure a Jewish gymnasium student admission to a university.[82] "I have a son who is a gymnasium student," exclaims a woman in *The Bloody Hoax,* "and I've been badgering him for almost three years, every morning and every night, 'A medal, a medal, a medal!' . . . A Jew without a medal is like a . . . is like a . . . "[83] Dr. Vladimir M. Bekhterev, one of Russia's preeminent psychiatrists, wrote of having encountered various emotional disorders in young Jewish patients who had become obsessed with winning a gold medal.[84]

In reality, of course, the majority of Jewish university students had not won medals. But the quotas created enormous pressure for early academic distinction, and the result of such pressure, predictably, was to intensify Jewish academic competitiveness as well as the perception of Jewish intellectual prowess. In seeking to explain why his social circle at a Minsk gymnasium in the 1890s, despite its cosmopolitan worldview, was composed exclusively of Jews, Vladimir Medem un-self-consciously remarked, "It developed quite au-

81. The quotation is from Pozner, *Evrei v obshchei shkole,* p. 121. See Dubnow, *History of the Jews,* 3: 30. In one of his speeches to the Third Duma, Nisselovich remarked that Jewish parents were known to subsidize Russian students in order to create additional slots for Jews: *Razsvet,* May 3, 1909, p. 26, cited in Christoph Gassenschmidt, *Jewish Liberal Politics in Tsarist Russia, 1900–1914* (New York, 1995), p. 198n. Another account appears in the memoir by A. N. Trainin, "Ia zhil za chertoi," *Sovietskoe Studenchestvo,* no. 8 (1937), p. 42.

82. Koprzhiva-Lur´e, *Istoriia odnoi zhizni,* pp. 35–36; Sofiia Dubnova-Erlikh, *Khleb i matsa* (St. Petersburg, 1996), p. 64; Vishniak, *Dan´ proshlomu,* p. 47; Trainin, "Ia zhil za chertoi," p. 43.

83. Sholem Aleichem, *Bloody Hoax,* p. 14.

84. V. Bekhterev, "Iz mraka k svetu," in L. Andreev, M. Gor´kii, and F. Sologub, eds., *Shchit: Literaturnyi sbornik,* 3d ed. (Moscow, 1916), pp. 37–39.

tomatically: of the thirty-odd pupils in my class, the seven or eight Jews were the more intelligent."[85] On the Russian side, in a report to the Ministry of Enlightenment in 1896, the superintendent of schools for the Vilna educational district noted that the "very high scores" required of Jewish students meant that those accepted were "superbly prepared, with comparatively outstanding abilities."[86] It is of course difficult, if not impossible, to arrive at reliable generalizations regarding the academic performance of students from different ethnic and religious groups in late imperial Russia. But there can be little doubt that the quotas intensified both the Jewish drive to excel and the assumption of Jewish intellectual talent. Indirect evidence for such an impression can be found in the fact that those Jews who failed to gain admission to institutions of higher education after 1887 invariably blamed the quotas for their fate. Inadequate academic performance virtually disappeared as an explanation of failure.[87]

For those unable or unwilling to endure the humiliation of quotas, petitions, bribes, external study, or conversion, there was a final option: study abroad. Before 1887, the number of Russian Jews enrolled at institutions of higher education across Central and Western Europe in any given year could be measured in the hundreds. Many of them were Jewish women responding to the general dearth of opportunities for higher learning for women in Russia, especially in the field of medicine.[88] Others, such as Aaron Zundelevich and Pavel Akselrod in the 1870s, studied abroad in order to avoid arrest for prior political activities in Russia.[89] With the introduction of quotas, however, this latter sequence was typically reversed: the thousands of

---

85. Medem, *Life and Soul of a Legendary Jewish Socialist*, p. 89. For similar impressions, see Dubnova-Erlikh, *Khleb i matsa*, p. 64, and Weizmann, *Trial and Error*, p. 21.

86. Quoted in Pozner, *Evrei v obshchei shkole*, p. 145. Pozner quotes a similar statement from the Kiev district superintendent in 1898.

87. Vishniak, *Dan´ proshlomu*, p. 18.

88. Available data on Russian-Jewish students in institutions of higher education in Europe are fragmentary; for an overview, see Arthur Ruppin, "Russische Studierende an westeuropäischen Universitäten," *Zeitschrift für Demographie und Statistik der Juden* 1, no. 11 (1905): 9–11. In 1888 a total of 57 Russian-Jewish students were enrolled at German universities (data on enrollments at other institutions of higher education in Germany are unavailable). Thereafter the number rose dramatically, and by 1912 over 850 Russian Jews were enrolled at German universities and another 1,650 at higher technical institutes (*Hochschulen*). See Jack Wertheimer, "The Ausländerfrage at Institutions of Higher Learning—A Controversy Over Russian-Jewish Students in Imperial Germany," *Leo Baeck Institute Year Book* 27 (1982): 187–215. On Russian-Jewish women studying abroad, see Neumann, *Studentinnen aus dem Russischen Reich*, who notes (p. 51) that between 1880 and 1914 the percentage of Jews among the "Russian" female students in Switzerland ranged from 60 to 80 percent, depending on the university.

89. To this list could be added the revolutionary activists Grigorii Gurevich, Leizer Tsukerman, Vladimir Iokhelson, Iosel Efron, Khasia Shur, Avgustina and Nadezhda Kaminer, Nakhman and Leizer Levental, and Shimon Lur´e. See Haberer, *Jews and Revolution*, p. 124, and Halevy, *Jewish University Students*, p. 45.

young Russian Jews who after 1887 flocked to institutions of higher learning in Germany, Switzerland, Austria-Hungary, and France rarely did so because of prior political activism, but once abroad, they displayed a high degree of politicization.[90] In his 1886 report to the High Commission for Review
of Legislation Pertaining to the Jews, in which he criticized plans for anti-
Jewish quotas, A. I. Georgievskii had warned, "Given the Jews' well-developed
inclination toward education, Jewish youth, unable to find a place in Russian educational institutions, will migrate by the masses to foreign schools.
When they finish such schools, they will return to Russia more dangerous
than Jews who have studied in Russian educational institutions."[91]

This passage was to prove remarkably prescient. It is not simply that
"masses" of young Russian Jews opted to study abroad. By the beginning of
the twentieth century, we come face to face with an extraordinary fact: more
Russian Jews were studying in institutions of higher education in Europe (between seven and eight thousand) than in the Russian Empire itself (approximately five and a half thousand).[92] The first Russian-Jewish student periodical, *Evreiskii Student* (The Jewish Student), appeared not in Odessa or
Kiev or Petersburg but in Berlin, and its inaugural issue (Feb. 1, 1913) alerted
readers to the fact that the majority of Russian-Jewish students were now outside the Russian Empire.[93] Among non-Jewish students from the Russian Empire, by contrast, less than 5 percent were studying abroad. After a century
of attempting to mold Jewish minds by drawing young Jews into Russian educational institutions, and after in many respects succeeding beyond its own
expectations, the tsarist regime had created a new set of circumstances in
which European institutions exerted the dominant influence on Russian-
Jewish students. Within Russian-Jewish society, students were now the major
conduit to Western ideas and practices.

The impact of study abroad on Russian-Jewish students was complex and
varied, and lies beyond the scope of this book. In European institutions of
higher education, especially those in Germany, where approximately half
of Russian-Jewish students abroad were enrolled, students were typically ex-

90. Neumann, *Studentinnen aus dem Russischen Reich,* p. 92; Jack Wertheimer, "Between Tsar
and Kaiser: The Radicalization of Russian-Jewish University Students in Germany," *Leo Baeck Institute Year Book* 28 (1983): 329.

91. Georgievskii, *Doklad,* p. 221.

92. For contemporary estimates, see A. Press, "O prosvetitel'nom fonde," *Novyi Voskhod,* no.
11 (1914), p. 4, and idem., "Bor'ba za vysshee obrazovanie evreev pri Nikolae II," *Evreiskaia
Letopis'* 3 (1924): 137. Press notes that in 1913 Jews accounted for roughly 60 percent of all
Russian subjects studying abroad.

93. In the same year, a group calling itself the Union of Eastern Jewish Student Associations in Western Europe (Farband fun mizrekh yidishe studenten-faraynen in mayrev eyrope)
published two issues of the short-lived newspaper *Di yidishe studentenshaft.* See Wertheimer, "Between Tsar and Kaiser," p. 345.

posed not only to world-class scholarship and teaching but to virulent anti-Semitism. By the turn of the century, German students were publicly demonstrating for restrictions on foreign Jews in their ranks, while at the University of Vienna nationalist students were known to barge into lecture halls shouting "Juden hinaus!" (Jews out!).[94] Such episodes, inconceivable in Russian universities, may account in part for the far greater intensity of Jewish nationalism among Russian-Jewish students abroad, who in fact became the single most important recruiting ground of future Zionist leaders, "the cradle of the modern Zionist movement," as Chaim Weizmann put it.[95] Similarly, among student members of the Bund, which oscillated between internationalist and nationalist agendas, national sentiment was far stronger abroad than in Russia.[96] One could certainly draw analogies to the heightened national consciousness produced by European study in non-Western intellectuals generally, from Mohandas Ghandi in England to Zhou Enlai in France, but it would be difficult to find a group of expatriate students among whom this effect occurred on as great a scale as among Russian Jews.

If the hallmark of the Jewish encounter with higher education between 1861 and 1887 was rapid, unprecedented integration into one of the elite institutions of imperial Russian society, the period thereafter left a far more ambiguous legacy. To be sure, the Jewish demand for secular education continued unabated and even intensified—not least because all the incentives created by the law of 1861, including freedom of residence, continued to apply to those who successfully navigated the quotas. But for Jews the quotas dealt a significant blow to the ideal of the Russian university as melting pot. They did so in two ways. First, by creating a separate and more arduous admissions process for Jews, the quotas fostered a sense of distinctiveness among Jewish students that persisted even after admission. Trends outside the academy in the 1880s and 1890s, such as the heightened attention to the "Jewish Question" in official policy and the press, as well as the emergence of Jewish political movements, only strengthened Jewish student particularism. Second, the quotas thrust the "Jewish Question" for the first time directly into the academy, into the studenchestvo itself, and kept it there per-

94. Wertheimer, "Ausländerfrage," p. 199; Wistrich, *Jews of Vienna*, p. 60.
95. Weizmann, *Trial and Error*, p. 36. Evidence of anti-Jewish sentiment among students in Russian institutions of higher education in the 1890s does surface here and there, but one must look hard to find it. See, e.g., T. Shatilova, "Epizody iz zhizni evreev-studentov (1886–1910)," *Evreiskaia Letopis'* 2 (1923): 147–48, who acknowledges that non-Jewish students often defended their Jewish peers from attacks by anti-Semites.
96. Tobias, *Jewish Bund in Russia*, p. 137.

manently. Without expanding the scope of its grievances beyond the purely academic, the student movement was now forced to confront state-sponsored anti-Jewish discrimination in its own midst.

THE GROWTH OF JEWISH STUDENT ORGANIZATIONS

The change in climate among Jewish students was palpable: by the end of the century there began to emerge, for the first time, a broad network of Jewish student organizations across European Russia. As we saw in Chapter 6, Russian-Jewish students had previously organized themselves only in the Baltic territories (Dorpat and Riga), where the Germanic fraternity tradition prevailed, or in the extraordinary circumstances of the pogroms of 1881–82, and then only briefly. The decisive turning point in their associational life came after the "silent pogrom" unleashed by the quotas: in the late 1880s, underground Jewish student societies not only sprang up at many institutions of higher education but in several cases coordinated their activities throughout the empire, with links to Russian-Jewish students abroad.

The activities of Jewish student organizations in imperial Russia have yet to be reconstructed by historians—a surprising fact given the amount of attention scholars have devoted to student life generally and to Jewish students in their later incarnation as members of various Jewish parties. The little that we know of such organizations comes largely from private letters preserved by participants or intercepted by the tsarist police, and for the time being these yield a fragmented picture, further blurred by the frequent use of pseudonyms, aesopian language, invisible ink, and other necessary rituals of the underground.[97] In 1889, for example, police uncovered correspondence indicating the formation of a society of Jewish students (including the future historian Shaul Ginzburg) at the universities of St. Petersburg and Dorpat. The following year, students in Moscow and Kharkov formed a circle devoted to studying and improving the conditions of Russian-Jewish life.[98] By the turn of the century, a clandestine Union of Jewish Students (initially named the Center for Jewish Student Circles) had been established at St. Petersburg University as a kind of clearinghouse for Jewish student organizations throughout Russia, one of whose goals was "to come to the aid of Russian Jews studying abroad and suffering from a level of need unknown to their

97. The most important and almost entirely untapped source of such letters is the enormous archive of the tsarist police housed in GARF, f. 102. A selection of private letters pertaining to Zionist student circles is included in Alter Druyanov and Shulamit Laskov, eds., *Ketavim le-toldot hibat-tsiyon ve-yishuv Erets-Yisrael,* 7 vols. (Tel Aviv, 1982).

98. GARF f. 102, deloproizvodstvo 3, op. 87 (1889), d. 460, ll. 1–4, 32; op. 88 (1890), d. 153, ll. 1–3; op. 90 (1892), d. 446, ll. 1–4.

more fortunate comrades in Russian educational institutions."[99] Its principal representative at Warsaw University was Heinrich (Wolf Hersh) Erlich, the future Bund leader. A Russian-Jewish student congress was planned (originally to convene in Berlin, then in Vilna or Minsk) but may never have been held.[100]

A second society to emerge from post-1887 Jewish student activity was the Jewish Comradely Union (Evreiskii tovarishcheskii soiuz), which brought together gymnasium and university students. A mutual-aid society as well as a forum for discussion and debate, the union was notable for the breadth of its commitments. It held benefit concerts and lectures to raise money for its members' tuition and living expenses in Russia and abroad, established clandestine libraries, sponsored study groups on the national question and on Jewish history, and donated a portion of collected money to a fund for the establishment of a Jewish university in Palestine.[101] Many of the union's members were recruited from—and continued to be active in—radical Russian student groups.

This last point is worth emphasizing: none of the various Jewish student groups appears to have been organized in response to hostility or exclusion on the part of other students. In at least several cases, non-Jews were welcomed as members, and despite widespread concern with ideological correctness and *partiinost'* (loyalty to a particular party), overlapping membership seems to have been common. Indeed, the Jewish Comradely Union called on its members to participate simultaneously in the general struggle of Russian students and in specifically Jewish causes. One member, who like many had come of age reading Dobroliubov and Darwin, described the typical path trod by self-proclaimed Jewish "cosmopolitans" toward a specifically Jewish activism:

> After all, for such youths the Russian agrarian question was far more important than distant and abstract national questions. Nonetheless, all the young Jews I knew from the general student revolutionary organizations joined the Jewish Comradely Union . . . . They explained this step in terms of practical considerations: as long as the quotas existed, it was essential to organize mu-

---

99. Ibid., osobyi otdel, op. 226 (1898), d. 3, ch. 189, l. 1; ch. 245, l. 55. In Russian, Soiuz evreiskoi uchashcheisia molodezhi, previously Tsentr kruzhkov evreiskogo iunoshestva. The union was acutely aware that Russian-Jewish students abroad were ineligible for financial assistance from the Society for the Spread of Enlightenment. Funds collected by the union were to be distributed via Jewish students at the University of Berne (Switzerland).

100. Ibid., ch. 245, l. 48; deloproizvodstvo 3, op. 91 (1893), d. 644, ll. 1–4; osobyi otdel, op. 226 (1898), d. 3, ch. 189, l. 6.

101. Ibid., osobyi otdel, op. 226 (1898), d. 3, ch. 235, ll. 7–34, 40–52, 75–87, 99–106, 185–89, 204–8. See also Agasfer (pseud.), "Evreiskii Tovarishcheskii Soiuz: Nastroeniia uchashcheisia molodezhi v pervye gody XX v.," *Evreiskaia Starina* 10 (1918): 177.

tual aid for Jewish students. They were above all attracted by the idea of an illegal [Jewish] organization whose goal was oppositional. In joining the union,
the cosmopolitans cherished the dream of putting it to use for "higher" political goals.[102]

The prior (and continuing) experience of the members of Jewish student
groups in parallel Russian organizations expressed itself at every level: in their
organizational strategies, in their rhetoric, in their relationship with the Jewish population at large. "What is to be done—as Jews?" was the leading topic
of many a discussion. Devotion to the ideal of action above all else was accompanied by endless debate over principles, often preventing much action
from being taken. Jewish community leaders representing the status quo were
dubbed "fathers," as distinct from more radical "sons," who perceived their
distance from and yet were strongly attracted to "living Jewry," its needs and
wants.[103]

Jewish students struggled to justify their emerging particularism, returning again and again to the question (as one group formulated it): "Do Jews
have the right to stand apart in some way in the fight against the common
enemy, and to issue their own Jewish demands?"[104] Part of the difficulty of
justifying the existence of separate Jewish student groups lay in the fact that
Russian students themselves, or at least the more vocal among them, repeatedly expressed their own opposition to anti-Jewish quotas at educational
institutions. Even during the relative lull in activism in the 1890s, students
at Moscow University used the occasion of Nicholas II's accession to the
throne in 1894 to petition for (among other things) the removal of national,
religious, and gender criteria in the admission process. The third All-Russian
Student Congress in 1897 adopted a similar platform and specifically condemned discrimination against Jewish applicants.[105] When the student movement exploded back into public view in February 1899 with a series of mass
demonstrations (which continued periodically up through the Revolution
of 1905), calls for the abolition of quotas were frequently high on the list of
demands.[106]

At the same time, as the gates separating the university from the street
flew open, the student movement found itself increasingly swept up by the

102. Agasfer, "Evreiskii Tovarishcheskii Soiuz," p. 185.

103. Ibid., pp. 186–90.

104. This was the subject of a heated debate among students, as recounted ibid., p. 188.

105. Vydrin, *Osnovnye momenty studencheskogo dvizheniia*, p. 38; Shatilova, "Epizody iz zhizni
evreev-studentov," p. 150. More generally: Soiuz Studentov S.-Peterburgskogo Universiteta i Akademicheskii Soiuz Slushatel´nits S.-Peterburgskikh Vysshikh Zhenskikh Kursov, *Universitet i politika* (St. Petersburg, 1906), p. 84.

106. See, e.g., the case at Kiev University in 1901, as recounted in *Krasnyi Arkhiv*, 1938,
p. 266.

larger tide of revolutionary upheaval. With the spread of unrest among peasants and workers, students began to face pressure from the left to rise above "narrow" academic agendas—including admission policies—in favor of "universal" social transformation. It was a dynamic not unlike that faced previously by Jewish students themselves. But Russian students were subject to a second kind of pressure as well, from the right, which created an additional incentive to distance themselves from the particular grievances of their Jewish peers. By the turn of the century, the passage of significant numbers of Jews through Russia's institutions of higher education had given rise to the negative conflation of "intellectuals" and "Jews" in the minds of many non-Jews, especially those with conservative or reactionary inclinations. "Jewishness" was becoming a highly elastic label, not infrequently applied to individuals with no Jewish ancestry or beliefs (a practice not unknown in Russia and Eastern Europe today). Echoing this effect, the writer Iosif Bickerman, a graduate of Odessa University, wrote in 1911 that "the Russian intellectual is in fact a 'zhid': like the Jew, he is an alien in his own land."[107] The fear of being branded as Jews, or as lackeys of Jews, proved a potent factor among Russian students as they entered the revolutionary fray.

THE SMUGGLERS

The confluence of these two forms of extra-academic pressure and their impact on the Russian–Jewish encounter within the arena of higher education can best be glimpsed through the prism of a memorable episode in the student movement. In the fall of 1900, the publisher A. S. Suvorin, whose *Novoe Vremia* was then Russia's most widely read daily newspaper ("The Kike Is Coming!" had appeared in its pages in 1880), decided to bring an obscure drama called *Kontrabandisty* (The Smugglers) to the renowned Malyi Theater in St. Petersburg, which he owned.[108] The play had already been performed in smaller venues in the imperial capital under the title *Syny Izrailia* (Sons of Israel) with little public resonance.[109] Its plot featured a crude assemblage of stereotypes of Jewish depravity: the curtain rises to reveal Moshe Gol´den-veizer, a wealthy merchant, and his hangers-on planning a smuggling operation as they mark the Sabbath in a Jewish tavern. The local rabbi announces

107. I. M. Bickerman, *Cherta evreiskoi osedlosti* (St. Petersburg, 1911), p. 136.

108. On *Novoe Vremia* see Louise McReynolds, *The News under Russia's Old Regime: The Development of a Mass-Circulation Press* (Princeton, 1991), p. 74 and app. A, table 6.

109. *Zhizn'*, no. 1 (April 1902), p. 241; Hoover Archive, Boris Nikolaevskii Collection, box 215, folder 1, "Zametki o volneniiakh sredi studentov po povodu postanovki p'esy 'Kontrabandisty' v noiabre 1900 g. v SPb.," in the manuscript "Dnevnik studenta-tekhnologa N.," pt. 2, p. 8. *Sons of Israel*, however, had met with protests at previous performances in Odessa. See *Novosti i Birzhevaia Gazeta*, Nov. 19, 1900, p. 19.

that since smuggling does not involve work, it is permitted on the Sabbath. When a customs official stumbles on their illegal activity, the Jews murder him, again with the blessing of the rabbi, who declares that the commandment "Thou shalt not kill" is valid only among Jews. Eventually one of the smugglers discovers that Gol´denveizer's daughter Sarah has fallen in love with a Russian soldier; to prevent her from converting to Christianity and eloping to Petersburg—and with the predictable blessing by the rabbi—the father kills his daughter. Here the play ends.[110]

The real drama, however, was just beginning. News of the play's impending performance began to spread as students were returning from their summer vacations to Petersburg's many institutions of higher learning. There was already a certain seasonal pattern to student unrest, as those returning in the fall searched for ways to rekindle the previous year's unresolved struggles. Thus when one of Novoe Vremia's local rivals, the liberal Severnyi Kur´er (Northern Courier), condemned Suvorin's plan to air the "vile contents" of The Smugglers, a group of students at St. Petersburg University seized the opportunity to renew the struggle against the forces of oppression. Several weeks in advance of the November 23 premier at the Malyi, copies of the play were distributed in the student cafeteria, and organizers purchased large blocks of tickets—as well as whistles and other noisemaking devices—in order to disrupt the opening performance.[111]

Police spies in the university dutifully notified their superiors of the impending demonstration, and theatergoers on the evening of November 23 found the Malyi Theater surrounded by uniformed officers and large crowds of students, male and female. As it became clear that the majority of ticket holders were students, the police began refusing admission to anyone in a student uniform. Those who protested such treatment were promptly arrested.[112] But plenty of students and their sympathizers were able to enter the theater, and as soon as the curtain went up, a prearranged cacophony of yelling, stomping, rattling, and whistling erupted from the audience, completely drowning out the play. Refusing to capitulate, the actors went on with their roles, using exaggerated gestures to convey as much of the plot as possible. Infuriated by this resistance, the audience continued its noisemaking, now supplemented

---

110. Apparently several variants of the play were performed. I have summarized a published version: V. Krylov and S. Litvin, Syny Izrailia: Drama v 4-kh deistviiakh i 5-i kartinakh (St. Petersburg, 1899).

111. GARF, f. 102, osobyi otdel, op. 226 (1898), d. 3, ch. 1, l. 19; Elena Semenova Kots [Katz], "Kontrabandisty (Vospominaniia)," Byloe: Zhurnal, posviashchennyi istorii osvoboditel´nogo dvizheniia 3, no. 37 (1926): 47.

112. See the eyewitness account by Vladimir Levitskii, Za chertvert´ veka (Moscow, 1926), p. 141–42. Levitskii, like his brother Iulii Martov (the Menshevik leader), was the grandson of Alexander Tsederbaum.

by a variety of projectiles, including potatoes, cucumbers, rotten apples, binoculars, gloves, and boots (one newspaper assured its readers that boots were thrown exclusively by Jews).[113] The actors did their best to return the projectiles to their source, and soon abandoned what remained of the plot in favor of gesticulations meant to suggest that members of the audience were imbeciles. At this point, the director of the theater appeared on stage, appealing for calm, only to be shouted down with cries of "Curtain!"; "Suvorin is a scoundrel!"; and "Enough!" Soon thereafter, the curtain came down.

Taking advantage of the relative quiet that ensued, the theater director telephoned the city governor for advice, and was told that the play must continue. When the curtain went back up, the confrontation between audience and actors began to repeat itself, only this time for less than a minute: police now stormed the theater, beating and dragging out anyone who looked like a student. Mounted Cossacks with whips—for students, an icon of the regime's violation of their personal dignity—dispersed the crowds outside. In all, some seventy individuals (nearly all students) were arrested for disturbing the peace.[114] It was, in fact, the worst riot in the history of Russian theater.[115] The trial was set for mid-December.

Protesters were jubilant: they had scored a direct hit against a flagrantly anti-Semitic play. The brutal intervention of Cossacks, moreover, conveniently linked this event to the already legendary demonstrations of February 1899, while the looming trial of those arrested promised to provide an additional public forum for the students' case.[116] Yet the meaning and consequences of the events of November 23 and their impact on relations between Russian and Jewish students were to prove far more complex than students anticipated. Public opinion outside the academy, in particular the press, was to play a decisive role. The next morning the fiasco at the Malyi Theater was front-page news in virtually all of the capital's newspapers. *Novoe Vremia* denounced the disturbance as the work "primarily of Jews and natives of the happy East";[117] *Peterburgskii Listok* (The Petersburg Page), under the head-

113. For the remark on Jews and boots, see *Peterburgskii Listok,* Nov. 24, 1900.

114. "Pis´mo iz Peterburga," *Nakanune: Sotsial´no-Revoliutsionnoe Obozrenie* (London), no. 24 (December 1900), pp. 1–2; *Novosti i Birzhevaia Gazeta,* Nov. 24, 1900, pp. 13–14; Kots, "Kontrabandisty," p. 46; GARF, f. 102, osobyi otdel, op. 226 (1898), d. 3, ch. 1, ll. 59–60.

115. Catherine A. Schuler, *Women in Russian Theatre: The Actress in the Silver Age* (London, 1996), p. 142. Schuler describes the role played in the *Smugglers* episode by the actress Lidia Iavorskaia, who refused to join the production and with her husband established the newspaper *Severnyi Kur´er* as a rival to Suvorin's *Novoe Vremia.* My thanks to Richard Stites for bringing Schuler's book to my attention.

116. On the perceived link between the protests of Nov. 23, 1900 and Feb. 9, 1899, see G. Engel´ and V. Gorokhov, *Iz istorii studencheskogo dvizheniia, 1899–1906* (St. Petersburg, n.d.), p. 18.

117. *Novoe Vremia,* Nov. 24, 1900.

line "Yesterday's Gevalt in the Malyi Theater," condemned the "outrageous scandal organized by the Jews."

> In the parterre, in the box seats, in the galleries, everywhere there were typical Jewish faces; in the corridors of the theater, in the vestibule, on the adjacent streets the sons and daughters of Israel roamed, like conspirators, waiting for something, hoping for something. . . . They transformed the stage into a bazaar, where they threw whatever came to hand. The actors fell victim to the kahal. In order to put an end to the power of these Jewish scandalmongers, who do not wish to have negative Judaic characteristics displayed on stage . . . , *The Smugglers* should be performed several more times. Otherwise, instead of "Sons of Israel" there will be "Triumphant Israel."[118]

In contrast to these and other newspapers whose attacks on the demonstration relied on branding the perpetrators as Jews, those who supported the protest avoided all mention not only of Jews but of anti-Semitism as the original motivating issue: "This was a broad demonstration against an assault upon the sanctity of the stage, whose mission is to teach, to foster the feeling of goodness in people"; "It is impossible to offend the moral feeling of the public with impunity."[119]

A large number of students—900, by one account—gathered at the university on the afternoon of the 24th to discuss the previous evening's events. According to a police informer, "students read and discussed excerpts from the newspapers. . . . All were upset by the article in *Peterburgskii Listok;* the question arose as to how to prove that Jews had not participated in the disturbance." A solution was quickly settled upon: all those who had taken part in the demonstration at the theater would put their names (first, last, and patronymic, so as to maximize ethnic identification) and religion on a list to be circulated at the university, the Military-Medical Academy, the Forestry Institute, the Technological Institute, and the Higher Courses for Women. The list would then be sent to the *Severnyi Kur´er* for publication—an act of considerable daring, given the impending trial of those arrested at the scene of the demonstration.[120] In the meantime, a majority of students demanded that the rector of the university file a formal complaint against

118. *Petersburgskii Listok,* Nov. 24, 1900.

119. *Novosti i Birzhevaia Gazeta,* Nov. 24, 1900; *Severnyi Kur´er,* Nov. 24, 1900. For similar reactions see *Peterburgskaia Gazeta,* Nov. 24, 1900, and *Rossiia,* Nov. 24, 1900.

120. GARF, f. 102, osobyi otdel, op. 226 (1898), d. 3, ch. 1, l. 16. This police report was filed the following day, Nov. 25. The fate of the list of participants in the disturbance is unknown, but it is unlikely that it was published, since on Nov. 25 government censors banned further mention of the incident pending the trial of those arrested (the ban lasted until January 1901), and *Severnyi Kur´er* was in the meantime shut down. See *Nakanune: Sotsial´no-Revoliutsionnoe Obozrenie* (London), no. 26/27 (February/March 1901), and *Osvobozhdenie* (Stuttgart), no. 1 (1903).

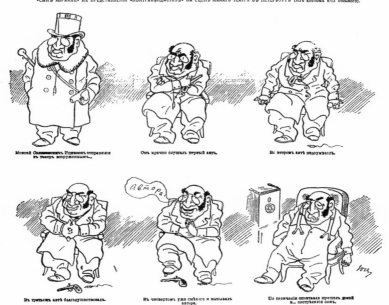

Figure 25. A judeophobic fantasy in Russia's most widely read daily newspaper, *Novoe Vremia*, Nov. 25, 1900: "A 'son of Israel' at the performance of *The Smugglers* at the Malyi Theater in Petersburg." Left to right, from top: "1. Moisei Solomonovich Itsikson made his way, armed, to the theater. 2. He gloomily watched the first act. 3. In the second act he became perplexed. 4. The third act put him in a better mood. 5. The fourth had him laughing and calling out 'Author!' 6. At the conclusion of the show he went home and . . . shot himself."

the brutality of the police, and that Suvorin be expelled from the Union of Writers.[121]

At a second gathering on the following day (again according to a police spy), Boris Raikov, a participant in the original protest and now one of the leaders of the follow-up meetings, read aloud additional press reports concerning the events of November 23. A majority of students condemned the "cavalier" behavior of the police and the violation of their personal freedom

121. Hoover Archive, Boris Nikolaevskii Collection, box 215, folder 1, "Zametki o vol-neniiakh sredi studentov po povodu postanovki p´esy 'Kontrabandisty' v noiabre 1900 g. v SPb.," in the manuscript "Dnevnik studenta-tekhnologa N.," pt. 2, p. 8.

and dignity. Again and again Raikov emphasized the broader significance of the clash:

> The events of November 23 are analogous to what happened on February 8, 1899. Then as now we see the insult to the person as human being and citizen. Then as now the rights of the individual were trampled. We have to confront this not as a special [*chastnoe*] case but as a societal [*obshchestvennoe*] one. It's irrelevant whether or not this matter concerns Jews or those of another nationality—the issue is not nationality but the person as human being. . . . I am not going to take up the question as to whether I like Jews or not; that's a different matter.[122]

In a sign of growing differentiation within the student movement, a minority argued that disrupting the performance of *The Smugglers* amounted to censorship, and that in any case the police had little choice but to remove those who were violating norms of public behavior. As a counterweight to the list of names gathered at the previous meeting, several hundred so-called Academists vowed to draft a letter apologizing for the "Scythian" behavior of their peers and expressing their sympathy to Suvorin.[123] By now the Jewish dimension of the incident had virtually disappeared from student debates, yielding the floor to issues of police misconduct, university autonomy, inspectors, and spies.[124]

Or so it seemed to the students. *Novoe Vremia* presented a very different picture. In its November 25 coverage of the previous day's student gathering, the newspaper informed its readers that "this was a meeting of Jews. Among those who held forth, almost all were Jews. The person who chaired the meeting was also a typical Jew [who] refused to allow Russians to speak, extending this right exclusively to Jews and to those Russians whom the former succeeded in seducing." When a Russian student called out that Suvorin's only crime had been to stage a play that the "Chosen People" disliked, without asking their permission, he was allegedly shouted down. *Novoe Vremia* concluded:

---

122. GARF, f. 102, osobyi otdel, op. 226 (1898), d. 3, ch. 1, ll. 19–22.

123. Ibid., ll. 19, 40; *Nakanune: Sotsial'no-Revoliutsionnoe Obozrenie* (London), no. 25 (January 1901), p. 3.

124. See, e.g., the report concerning the next student gathering, on Nov. 26, in GARF. f. 102, osobyi otdel, op. 226 (1898), d. 3, ch. 1, ll. 24–31. A lone exception to the decreasing visibility of the Jewish dimension occurred on Nov. 25 in the Bestuzhevskie Higher Courses for Women. A certain Professor Shliapkin, who decided to take a detour in one of his lectures in order to discuss the incident at the Malyi Theater, offhandedly used the term *zhid*. At his next lecture 150 students walked out of the hall in protest, leaving only a handful behind. See Hoover Archive, Boris Nikolaevskii Collection, box 215, folder 1, "Zametki o volneniiakh sredi studentov po povodu postanovki p'esy 'Kontrabandisty' v noiabre 1900 g. v SPb.," in the manuscript "Dnevnik studenta-tekhnologa N.," pt. 2, p. 9.

Mr. Suvorin has the right to stage whatever plays he chooses, and does not have to ask the Jews whether they approve. We Russians do not assault actors and directors when they perform Gogol's *Inspector-General*. It is a fact that 90 percent of the audience on November 23 were Jews, [together with] a herd of young noisemakers driven on by the Jews to defend the inviolability of Jewish kulaks and scoundrels.[125]

Two days later, on November 27, an estimated 2,000 students from over half a dozen of the capital's institutions of higher education gathered in the university courtyard to continue their protest against the police and against Suvorin, in his capacity as owner of both the Malyi Theater and *Novoe Vremia*. The chair of previous meetings, a Georgian student named Mikhail Tageev, requested that a new chair be selected, since he had "heard allusions made regarding his alleged Semitic face and origins" (having been mislabeled by *Novoe Vremia*). Boris Raikov, an ethnic Russian, took his place, and students elected a committee to draft a letter to the Union of Writers demanding Suvorin's expulsion. "We categorically assert," the letter read, "that the overwhelming majority of representatives of student youth who took part in the protest were not Jews. *Novoe Vremia*'s assertion that the protest was organized by the 'Jewish kahal' is false."[126] In December the revolutionary émigré newspaper *Nakanune* (On the Eve), published in London, went even further, informing its readers that "well in advance [of the original Nov. 23 protest] it was decided that only Christians should take part, because otherwise the demonstration would lose all significance."[127]

We will never know precisely what proportion of the demonstrators were Jews. The only available data concern the roughly seventy individuals arrested on November 23, of whom just under a third were listed as Jews (consisting of equal numbers of men and women).[128] Beyond the numbers, however, the nature of the controversy after the aborted performance of *The Smugglers* suggests that most observers found it nearly impossible to distinguish Russian and Jewish students. And more important, the question of the identity of the protesters overshadowed all other issues, initially in the minds of conservative critics of the protest and then—the agenda having been set— among students as well, who felt a need to refute the portrayal of the entire student movement as being "in the hands of 'oppressed nationalities.'"[129]

125. *Novoe Vremia*, Nov. 25, 1900; for the remark about "chosen people," see GARF, f. 102, osobyi otdel, op. 226 (1898), d. 3, ch. 1, ll. 37–38.

126. GARF, f. 102, osobyi otdel, op. 226 (1898), d. 3, ch. 1, ll. 39–42.

127. *Nakanune: Sotsial'no-Revoliutsionnoe Obozrenie* (London), no. 24 (December 1900), p. 1.

128. Estimates of the number arrested ranged from 60 to 73. See GARF, f. 102, osobyi otdel, op. 226 (1898), d. 3, ch. 1, ll. 59–60, 92–94; Kots, "Kontrabandisty," p. 47.

129. Engel' and Gorokhov, *Iz istorii studencheskogo dvizheniia*, p. 12. The ethnic identity of other "participants" became the subject of controversy as well. One of the authors of *Kontra-*

This pattern repeated itself as *The Smugglers* toured from city to city, frequently encountering protests by mixed crowds of students and others, Jews and Gentiles, who were then invariably described in the right-wing press—and in internal police correspondence—as Jews.[130] Looking back in 1908, a high-ranking police official, determined to see a Jewish conspiracy as the driving force behind Russia's recent revolutionary upheaval, reported to Prime Minister Stolypin that "the beginning of the Russian Revolution must be reckoned not January 9, 1905 ["Bloody Sunday," the massacre of peacefully marching workers in front of the Winter Palace], as the revolutionary parties are accustomed to doing, but November 23, 1900."[131]

JEWS, STUDENTS, AND POGROMS

Seen through the prism of Russian-Jewish relations within the academy, the *Smugglers* episode appears as a way station along the path of differentiation that began in 1887 with the imposition of quotas and culminated in 1905 with the revolutionary puncturing of the ideal of the university as melting pot. Having sparked a new and much broader wave of unrest at the turn of the century, the student movement unexpectedly found its own corporative solidarity sundered by the larger logic of class identity and universal social transformation. To be sure, academic concerns never entirely disappeared from the student agenda, and the majority of students before and after 1905 continued to support what they called the "open door" policy, in opposition to all forms of discrimination in admission to institutions of higher education. But academic grievances were increasingly taking a back seat to

---

bandisty, S. K. Litvin, was an apostate from Judaism whose original name was Efron; the leading actor in Suvorin's troupe, Iakov Tinskii (original surname: Shif), who played the merchant Gol´denveizer, was also Jewish by origin.

130. For a partial list of cities where protests occurred, see Dubnov, *History of the Jews,* 3: 38. For examples of descriptions by the police of protesters as Jews, see GARF, f. 102, otdelenie 2, op. 58 (1901), d. 19, ll. 2, 7. Other anti-Semitic plays met with student protests as well, such as the 1903 Warsaw production of *The Golden Calf.* See Shatilova, "Epizody iz zhizni evreev-studentov," p. 149.

131. "S.-Peterburgskoe okhrannoe otdelenie v 1895–1901 gg. 'Trud' chinovnika Otdeleniia P. Statkovskii," *Byloe: Zhurnal, posviashchennyi istorii osvoboditel´nogo dvizheniia,* no. 16 (1921), p.

132. The protests against *Kontrabandisty* produced quite a different effect in Jacob Raisin, an immigrant from the Russian Empire to the United States, who in 1913 published one of the first histories of Russian Jewry in English. Raisin concludes his *Haskalah Movement in Russia* (Philadelphia, 1913) with the hopeful assertion that "the attitude lately manifested both in St. Petersburg and the provinces against the *Kontrabandisti* [*sic*] will become more and more general. Then the heroic effort and the unexampled progress of the Russian Jews will be more fully appreciated, and a patriotic nation will gratefully acknowledge its indebtedness to that smallest but most energetic and self-sacrificing portion of its heterogeneous population, the Jews" (p. 303).

grander efforts on behalf of the empire's peasant and worker masses and to calls for dismantling the tsarist autocracy itself. As the *Smugglers* episode illustrated, students engaged in revolutionary struggle were reluctant to identify themselves publicly with extra-academic Jewish concerns, or for that matter with Jews—and this at a time when more and more of their Jewish peers, having created their own circles and underground organizations, were increasingly inclined to seek a hearing for the grievances of Russian Jewry as a whole.

Nowhere was this contrast sharper than in student reactions to anti-Jewish violence. As we have seen, the first, small spurt of Jewish student activism was directly tied to the outbreak of pogroms in 1881. The resurgence of pogrom violence in the spring of 1903 in Kishinev, where Jewish fatalities now numbered not in the dozens but in the hundreds, again met with silence on the part of the student movement, which was more comfortable opposing the anti-Semitism of Nicholas II or Suvorin than that of urban crowds. In a sign of how much had changed in the student milieu during the previous two decades, however, Jewish student groups now voiced their outrage over this silence directly to their Gentile peers at student meetings.[132]

The most savage pogroms of the first revolutionary period occurred in the pivotal year of 1905 and reached their greatest intensity in the aftermath of the manifesto issued by Nicholas II on October 17, in which the tsar acceded to liberal demands for a duma (parliament) and fundamental civil rights. The timing of the violence left no doubt that Jews were now firmly linked, at least in the minds of the perpetrators of pogroms, with the revolutionary cause. Other social groups typically associated with opposition to the autocracy were also subject to violent attacks by the same mobs, none more so than students, who by virtue of their distinctive uniforms were easily identifiable. In Odessa, Kiev, Kharkov, Kazan, and elsewhere, students and Jews alike (though not in anything approaching equal numbers) were subject to random attacks on the streets, and cries of "Beat the yids!" were easily transposed to "Beat the students!"[133]

Although one might expect that shared victimization would foster a certain solidarity, and although there is evidence of some coordination by Jewish and student self-defense groups in Odessa,[134] the net effect of the counter-revolutionary pogroms, as well as the perceived failure of the revo-

---

132. See D. [A. Diakonov], *1905 i 1906 god v Peterburgskom Universitete* (St. Petersburg, 1907), p. 25.

133. Rallying cries quoted in Charters Wynn, *Workers, Strikes, and Pogroms: The Donbass-Dnepr Bend in Late Imperial Russia, 1870–1905* (Princeton, 1992), p. 218. For Odessa, see Robert Weinberg, *The Revolution of 1905 in Odessa: Blood on the Steps* (Bloomington, 1993), pp. 164–72; and more generally Kassow, *Students, Professors, and the State*, p. 271.

134. Weinberg, *Revolution of 1905 in Odessa*, pp. 171–72.

lution itself, was to magnify the distance between Russian and Jewish students. On more than one occasion in 1905 and 1906, bitter arguments broke out at student meetings over the question whether and how to address the specifically Jewish component of antirevolutionary violence. At a gathering on September 15, 1905, for example, during a discussion of the open-door admissions policy (for Jews, women, seminary graduates, and others), a group of Jewish students insisted on a separate and far broader resolution concerning Jews:

> Ever since the 1880s, we have lived under the weight of unbearable conditions. We, the Jewish masses, have already recognized the necessity of the sacred battle against slavery. . . . For the future good of Russia all Jews have come forth as fighters, just like the Russians. Jews are dying not only for their own freedom but for Russia's! Therefore—we are equals. Our demand—not request—to you, Russians, is that you recognize our rights. . . . Students have shamefully besmirched themselves: when the bloody Kishinev pogrom occurred, they went ahead and took their exams! Such was their "passionate" defense of our human rights! We turn now to all student citizens and demand full equality of rights with them. [We demand] complete freedom for Jews to enroll at the university! We demand it in return for the victims of the Russian revolution![135]

With its "we" ambiguously signifying now Jewish students, now the "Jewish masses," this speech embodied the merging of academic and extra-academic grievances in the revolutionary era. While the general student response at the meeting was described by one observer as "entirely sympathetic," the majority voted against a separate resolution condemning the pogroms and Jewish quotas. As one respondent put it, "The Jews, who have been deprived of their rights, obviously can count on our defense. But we must not isolate this question, since our general tactics for the entire country include national self-determination for the ethnic groups. . . . One must not for the sake of logic transform a particular incident into a general one."[136]

In protest against the majority's opinion, Jewish students left the meeting. Three days later they held their own gathering (also in the university), at which some 200 Jewish students and nearly 2,000 Jewish residents of Petersburg were present.[137] Returning to a general student meeting the next day (September 19), Jewish students again failed to persuade their peers to adopt a separate resolution addressing Jewish concerns. Insisting that "the national question has been clarified once and for all," the majority stuck to

---

135. Quoted in D., *1905 i 1906 god*, p. 25. On a similar incident at a student meeting at the St. Petersburg Technological Institute, see TsGIA-SPb, f. 14, op. 3, d. 16323, ll. 49–52.

136. Quoted in D., *1905 i 1906 god*, p. 26.

137. TsGIA-SPb, f. 14, op. 3, d. 16323, ll. 39–40. Summaries of the speeches given at this meeting were not included in the relevant police report.

their original endorsement of the open-door admissions policy.[138] Right-wing critics, however, would persist in characterizing student protests as a thinly disguised "uprising of yids" (*zhidovskii bunt*).[139]

Such was the pattern at student rallies across 1905 and 1906. If anything, the heightened militancy of the revolutionary student left in reaction to the regime's renewed self-assertion after 1905 only further eclipsed Jewish students' demands. "The liberal compromisers are busy with protests," proclaimed a Bolshevik student in September 1906. "But the revolutionary army, understanding the situation, does not protest against capital punishment or pogroms. There's no need. Those who are capable of fighting need not protest!" Another student, downplaying the specific grievances of Jewish, Polish, and Latvian students, reminded his colleagues that "our task is to build a social-democratic state within the [existing] state. And we are its avant-garde. . . . Look at how the [ethnic] cadres of the proletariat are uniting— the studenchestvo still has its role to play in the revolution!"[140]

Despite their reluctance to engage extra-academic Jewish issues, Russian students nonetheless made good on their commitment to nondiscriminatory admissions. Taking advantage of the ever greater autonomy granted by the regime, university after university (and technical institutes as well) acted on student demands to unilaterally abandon Jewish quotas. In 1905 the All-Russian Academic Union, a new umbrella group representing professors and scholars from institutions of higher education and the Academy of Sciences, officially endorsed the open-door policy.[141] Indeed, even a majority of the Council of Ministers, facing a fait accompli, voted in January 1906 to recommend to Nicholas II that Jewish quotas be abolished. The tsar, however, ignored the advice. Nicholas also rejected a petition from the reactionary Union of Russian People requesting that henceforth only "Russians by faith and origin" be admitted to certain institutions of higher education, and that Jews be barred altogether from the two capitals.[142]

With institutions of higher education virtually dictating their own admission policies, Jewish enrollment during the revolutionary years skyrocketed. The results (reproduced in Table 12) provide a glimpse of what quota-free admissions might have looked like in the Russian Empire as it entered the twentieth century.

138. D., *1905 i 1906 god*, p. 29.
139. Purishkevich, *Materialy po voprosu o razlozhenii sovremennogo russkogo universiteta*, p. 41.
140. D., *1905 i 1906 god*, pp. 75, 97.
141. GARF, f. 518, op. 1, d. 29, l. 27.
142. A. E. Ivanov, *Studenchestvo Rossii kontsa XIX–nachalo XX veka: Sotsial´no-istoricheskaia sud´ba* (Moscow, 1999), p. 221; RGIA, f. 1284, op. 224, d. 131, ll. 1–5.

TABLE 12. Jews in Incoming Classes
in Universities, Russian Empire, 1905 and 1906,
by University and Quota (percent)

University	1905	1906
3% quota		
St. Petersburg	13%	18%
Moscow	7	10
5% quota		
Kharkov	23	12
Dorpat	12	9
Kazan	4	5
Tomsk	10	10
10% quota		
Warsaw	46	n.a.
Kiev	23	20
Odessa	33	34

SOURCE: Ministerstvo narodnogo prosveshcheniia, *Materialy po voprosu o prieme evreev v sredniia i vysshiia uchebnyia zavedeniia* (St. Petersburg, 1908), p. 69.

While the non-Jewish university population grew by some 50 percent between 1903 and 1907, the number of Jewish students tripled. Their greatest absolute and proportional rise occurred in the universities of St. Petersburg and Moscow, where the quotas had been most severe.[143] The gains would no doubt have been even greater if quotas at gymnasia had not continued to be enforced during the revolutionary period. Moreover, among the thousands of auditors admitted to universities during the revolution (most of them women, who had not been allowed to audit university courses since 1861), approximately one-third were Jewish.[144]

This dramatic growth was short-lived. By the summer of 1907 the tsarist regime had reasserted its power over an exhausted and divided opposition, and wasted no time in resuming its efforts to reinstate the quotas. To regain control over admissions policies, the numerus clausus was transformed from a "temporary" administrative measure into formal law. Henceforth it was to be applied not only to incoming classes but to each institution's student body as a whole—a maneuver designed to reverse as rapidly as possible what a government memorandum called the "flood of Jews into the uni-

143. Pozner, *Evrei v obshchei shkole,* app. 2.

144. *Materialy po voprosu o prieme evreev,* p. 70. Among those who responded to a survey of female auditors at Dorpat University in 1907, nearly half were Jewish. See Benasik, *Studenchestvo v tsifrakh,* p. 120.

Figure 26. Students and auditors in a dining hall at the Imperial University of St. Petersburg, 1910.

versities," if necessary by suspending their admission or by expelling current students. The latter tactic resulted in the resignation, out of protest, of nearly half the faculty of the Kiev Polytechnical Institute.[145] Taking up yet again the paternalist mantle of protecting the weak against an alleged Jewish conspiracy, the Ministry of Enlightenment insisted that during the revolution "the universities had proved powerless" against the onslaught of Jewish students.[146]

In the increasingly desperate climate of late tsarism, state officials were determined to go beyond merely reinstating the quotas. Their efforts began with the rescinding of residence rights for Jewish graduates of the growing number of private and public (as opposed to state) institutions of higher education, most of which had far less restrictive quotas (or none at all) and were therefore a haven for Jews. By the turn of the century, such schools—sponsored by local societies, individuals, city councils, and rural councils (zemstvos)—were training tens of thousands of students in business, den-

145. Stephen P. Timoshenko, *As I Remember: The Autobiography of Stephen P. Timoshenko*, trans. Robert Addis (Princeton, 1968), p. 116.

146. *Materialy po voprosu o prieme evreev v sredniia i vysshiia uchebnyia zavedeniia*, p. 69.

tistry, midwifery, and other vocations.[147] Attempts to intervene in the admission policies of private institutions began before the Revolution of 1905, when then minister of internal affairs Viacheslav Plehve sought to force the withdrawal of Jews enrolled in Petersburg's prestigious Bestuzhev Higher Courses for Women by stripping the school of its legal status as an institution of higher education (it was this status that gave the school's Jewish students the right to live in the capital). A court case brought by a Bestuzhev student, Dvora Rafailovich, eventually blocked Plehve's plan.[148] After the failed revolution, tsarist officials again targeted private educational institutions, threatening to withdraw their accreditation and the legal rights conferred on their graduates (Gentile as well as Jewish), unless they adopted the numerus clausus. School directors and occasionally the Ministry of Finance (when so-called commercial schools were at issue) invariably opposed such encroachments by the state.[149] A pair of examples will stand for many.

At the turn of the century, a group of merchants from Vilna petitioned to establish a school of commerce, offering to use their own funds for any costs not covered by tuition revenue. Negotiations with the government became snarled over the issue of anti-Jewish quotas—four-fifths of Vilna's merchants were Jews, as presumably were most of the petitioners—but by 1901 a compromise was reached, and the Pushkin Commercial School opened its doors that year with Jewish enrollment formally limited to 40 percent. In 1909 Minister of Enlightenment A. N. Shvarts demanded that the quota be lowered to 15 percent (at the time, Jews actually constituted 60 percent of the school's student body). The merchant sponsors refused, noting that nearly all the private funds poured into the school had come from Jews, and that the proposed quota would leave Christian slots unfilled and thereby threaten the school's solvency. In 1912 the Ministry of Finance stepped in (there being no clear jurisdiction in matters pertaining to private educational institutions) to offer a compromise: rather than immediately adopting the 15 percent quota, the school could gradually lower the proportion of Jews admitted, by 1 percent annually, so that the reduction would be spread out over twenty-five years, ending in 1937. The merchants rejected the offer, and after failing to win their case in court, they abandoned the school to an uncertain fate.[150]

Shvarts's successor as minister of enlightenment, L. A. Kasso, imposed a 5 percent quota on Kiev's two commercial schools, where nearly 2,000 Jews—

147. McClelland, *Autocrats and Academics,* p. 34; Pozner, *Evrei v obshchei shkole,* pp. 119–21.

148. See the account by Rafailovich's lawyer in the case: L. Aizenberg, "Vidy pravitel´stva v evreiskom voprose," pp. 73–86.

149. See, e.g., the cases cited in RGIA, f. 1284, op. 224, d. 133, ll. 31, 44–45, 51–52, and TsGIA-SPb, f. 113, op. 1, d. 108, ll. 94–98.

150. Materials pertaining to this case were gathered by Paul Miliukov, the historian and Kadet leader. See GARF, f. 579, op. 1, d. 1962, ll. 5–13.

Figure 27. A Jewish student at a commercial high school. (By permission of YIVO Institute for Jewish Research.)

among them the young Isaac Babel and Solomon Mikhoels—constituted 60 percent of the combined student body. Now it was the Kiev branch of the Council of Representatives of Trade and Industry, a private business group, that rose to defend the schools and their Jewish students. The council reminded the government that the schools had been established with private funds, with "broad participation" by Jewish donors, in line with the regime's goal of promoting business education according to the European model. In fact, Jewish donors had contributed over four-fifths of the 280,000-ruble start-up funds for Kiev's two commercial schools.[151] The council also reminded the government of the logic behind the 1887 quotas: Jews should

151. Pozner, *Evrei v obshchei shkole*, p. 157.

not benefit from state-financed educational institutions to an extent greater than their proportion of the total population. Since the commercial schools depended not on state funding but rather on the tuition paid equally by the students and on private subsidies, that logic did not apply. In the end, however, the council was forced to settle for a quota of 10 percent, matching that at the local university.[152]

Similar battles were waged against a wide range of private institutions in which there were substantial contingents (in some cases, majorities) of Jewish students, including the Bekhterev Psycho-Neurological Institute in Petersburg, the renowned conservatories and provincial music schools run by the Russian Musical Society, and dentistry schools in cities across European Russia.[153] In this manner, the numerus clausus set off multiple skirmishes over accreditation of entire institutions and their graduates, and more profoundly, over the boundary between state and private authority.

To reduce the number of Jewish students further, the tsarist regime employed other techniques as well. In 1911 it extended quotas to Jewish externs—those seeking an equivalency degree by studying on their own and then taking state exams—despite the fact that there was no necessary limit on the number of external students a given institution could accept, and therefore no zero-sum scenario between Jews and Gentiles. "This is a new assault on our culture," wrote Simon Dubnov, "or more precisely, on our culturedness [*kul'turnost'*]."[154] Even the conservative Third Duma demanded an explanation.[155] In secret negotiations with Germany, moreover, the Russian government pressed first for heightened surveillance of the thousands of Russian subjects studying in German institutions of higher education (of whom the vast majority were Jews) and then for outright quotas against them—in effect endorsing the demands of German students. Bavaria obliged in 1909, followed by Prussia in 1912.[156] Finally, in a desperate attempt to assemble not just a quantitatively but a qualitatively diminished Jewish student body, the Ministry of Enlightenment ruled in 1913 that henceforth applicants for the Jewish slots in Russian universities would be admitted not according to their academic performance, letters of recommendation, and other usual

152. Materials on this case were collected by the lawyer Mikhail Sheftel'. See TsGIA-SPb, f. 2049, op. 1, d. 82, ll. 1–6.

153. *Materialy po voprosu o prieme evreev v sredniia i vysshiia uchebnyia zavedeniia*, pp. 16–22; Sliozberg, *Dela minuvshikh dnei*, 3: 291–92; GARF, f. 579, op. 1, d. 2057, ll. 1–2.

154. *Evreiskii Mir*, Mar. 25, 1911.

155. Pozner, *Evrei v obshchei shkole*, p. 115.

156. Wertheimer, "Ausländerfrage," pp. 199–202. German quotas targeted foreign students, with exceptions for those from Western Europe and the United States. The University of Zurich adopted similar quotas in 1913, although no one has produced evidence that the Russian government was involved in this decision. See A. Press, "Bor'ba za vysshee obrazovanie evreev pri Nikolae II," *Evreiskaia Letopis'* 3 (1924): 137.

criteria but by lottery. The turn to an essentially random system of selection among Jewish applicants to institutions of higher learning represented a moral and intellectual "dead end," as one contemporary put it, a virtual abandonment by the tsarist regime of the logic of utility to the state that had inspired the policy of selective integration.[157]

A SELF-PORTRAIT

What were the results of the experiment with selective integration in Russia's institutions of higher learning? What had become of the imperial university as melting pot in the wake of the quotas? Significantly, it was at its moment of greatest disillusionment and disarray, after the failed Revolution of 1905, that the studenchestvo produced the richest and most nuanced portrait of itself, in an outpouring of books, journals, and statistical surveys based on questionnaires distributed to many thousands of students. With the mythology of revolutionary heroism rapidly receding, students now turned a collective eye inward to confront the full force of their own diversity: of class and estate, of the material conditions of daily life, of political orientation, of sexual behavior—and all the complex correlations among them, real or imagined. "Differentiation" became the anxious watchword of the post-1905 era.[158]

The small number of student surveys conducted before 1905 showed little or no interest in the ethnic and religious composition of the student body, preferring to relate the broad spectrum of student behaviors and beliefs to differences in class and social origin.[159] The resulting near-invisibility of Jewish students led them to produce their own journals and statistical surveys.[160] To be sure, when it came to subjects such as motives for study, favorite authors, and living conditions, the profile of Jewish students was virtually indistinguishable from that of the student population as a whole (questions regarding sexual behavior, it should be noted, were conspicuously absent from Jewish surveys). In fact, internal "differentiation" was as much a leit-

---

157. Pozner, *Evrei v obshchei shkole*, p. 100.

158. See the excellent treatment of this theme in Morrissey, *Heralds of Revolution*, esp. pp. 146–49.

159. Ibid.

160. D. I. Sheinis, *Evreiskoe studenchestvo v tsifrakh (po dannym perepisi 1909 g. v Kievskom universitete i politekhnicheskom institute)* (Kiev, 1911); *K kharakteristike evreiskogo studenchestva (po dannym ankety sredi evreiskogo studenchestva g. Kieva v noiabre 1910 g.)* (Kiev, 1913); *Odesskoe studenchestvo: Itogi ankety sredi evreiskikh studentov, proizvedenoi v 1911–1912 gg.* (Odessa, 1913); D. I. Sheinis, *Evreiskoe studenchestvo v Moskve po dannym ankety 1913 g.* (Moscow, 1914). Taken together, these surveys incorporated responses from over 2,000 Jewish students at a dozen institutions of higher education in Moscow, Kiev, and Odessa between 1909 and 1913. The 1909 Kiev survey specifically invokes (p. ii) the absence of data on issues pertaining to nationality in the general student surveys.

motif among Jewish students as among students generally, leading some (Jewish) respondents to question the need for separate surveys.[161] In a provocative article titled "We and the Russian Studenchestvo," the Bundist Sarah Brenner concluded that the concept of an ethnically defined "us and them" was simply a fiction—though a widespread one.[162]

The sources and nature of differentiation, however, varied substantially among Russian and Jewish students. While significant numbers of both groups were moving away from left-wing causes, Jewish students were more likely to retreat from politics altogether, while their Russian counterparts fanned out across the entire political spectrum. The interrevolutionary period witnessed the founding of several nationalist groups, such as the Union of Russian Students, which combined the rituals of German fraternities with the conservative Russian platform of "orthodoxy, autocracy, and nationality."[163] A survey conducted at the St. Petersburg Technological Institute in 1909, noting that "in recent times we have observed open manifestations of anti-Semitism in the student milieu," solicited students' opinion regarding Jewish legal equality. Over a third of the respondents declared themselves opposed (25 percent), indifferent (8 percent), or uncertain (4 percent)—results that would have been shocking a decade earlier.[164] A survey at the Riga Polytechnicum in 1910 produced roughly similar figures.[165] And while some left-wing students continued to protest against the numerus clausus as well as against extra-academic manifestations of anti-Semitism such as the 1913 trial of Mendel Beilis on charges of ritual murder, there were far fewer than had participated in the 1900 demonstrations against the performance of *The Smugglers.*[166]

The Beilis trial, as the Jewish student journal *Nash put´* (Our Path) noted with shame, produced no distinct, organized response on the part of Jewish students either.[167] Whether Jews participated in general student protests is unknown. What seems clear, however, is that Jewish students were increasingly divided or uncertain regarding fundamental issues. In survey after survey, roughly half of all Jewish students responded affirmatively to the question "Do you sympathize with the preservation and development of the Jewish nation?" while most of the rest declared themselves either "indifferent"

---

161. Sheinis, *Evreiskoe studenchestvo v Moskve,* p. iv.

162. Sarra Brenner, "My i russkoe studenchestvo," *Nash Put´: Sbornik, posviashchennyi interesam evreiskogo studenchestva* (Petrograd, 1916), pp. 31–33.

163. Morrissey, *Heralds of Revolution,* p. 144.

164. *K kharakteristike sovremennogo studenchestva (po dannym perepisi 1909–10 g. v SPb-skom Tekhnologicheskom Institute)* (St. Petersburg, 1910), pp. 23–24.

165. "Studencheskaia anketa," *Evreiskii Mir,* no. 12 (1911), pp. 16–18.

166. TsGIA-SPb, f. 14, op. 25, d. 48, ll. 28–38.

167. *Nash put´,* p. 4.

(roughly a fourth) or in favor of "assimilation" (roughly a fifth).[168] Half did not endorse the goals of any political party; of those who did, a slim majority favored All-Russian parties (in particular the Social Democrats) over Jewish (usually the Bund, but also various Zionist parties). Actual membership in parties was extremely rare. "I used to be a Bundist," declared one student; "now I don't consider myself one, because I have grown tired."[169] Many students found it difficult to characterize their worldview, political or otherwise, as the following sample of responses to a 1909 questionnaire indicates:

I haven't yet worked out a worldview. It's not so easy.

My shortcoming, which I think is characteristic of today's youth, is a great lack of principle.

Unfortunately, I am unable to establish a worldview. I love life and have faith in it. I agree with Alesha Karamazov that "one has to love life before logic, and only then can one understand its meaning."

I keep my distance from all orthodox worldviews.

At the moment, historical materialism. Last year—Tolstoyan idealism.[170]

Behind the confusions and divisions of worldview—according to contemporary thinking—lay those of experience. Whereas Russian student surveys tended to look exclusively to social origin as the "objective" reality underlying "subjective" worldviews, Jewish surveys revealed that the majority of respondents came from families representing a comparatively narrow slice of society, concentrated in commerce and white-collar professions. The Jewish search for "objective" sources of heterogeneity led instead to factors such as language (Yiddish, Hebrew, and Russian—what one survey called "the tragic Jewish multilingualism"), primary education (heder vs. state school), and geographic origin (within the Pale vs. outside it).[171] Here, too, stark contrasts among students emerged. Between a fifth and a third of Jewish students reported no knowledge of Yiddish, the native language of 95 percent of Russia's Jews. Younger students, moreover, were far less likely to know Yiddish than their older peers. A third of all male students and two-thirds of all female students reported no knowledge of Hebrew, with ignorance again higher among the young.[172] Less than half of male students had attended a heder, and virtually no female students. Those who grew up outside the Pale—among Jewish students in Moscow, one in three; among those in Kiev, one in eight—were far less likely to know Jewish languages. One of the few

168. Sheinis, *Evreiskoe studenchestvo v tsifrakh*, p. 37; idem, *Evreiskoe studenchestvo v Moskve*, p. 42; *K kharakteristike evreiskogo studenchestva*, p. 48.

169. Sheinis, *Evreiskoe studenchestvo v tsifrakh*, pp. 44–46.

170. Sheinis, *Evreiskoe studenchestvo v Moskve*, p. 54.

171. Ibid., p. 35. The quotation is from *K kharakteristike evreiskogo studenchestva*, p. 44.

172. *K kharakteristike evreiskogo studenchestva*, pp. 32–34.

characteristics common to nearly all Jewish students (ninety to ninety-five percent) was their lack of religious belief and observance.[173]

"If, in the future," warned *Nash put'*, "the distinction between the intelligentsia and the masses will consist not only of the degree of culturedness (*kul'turnost'*) but of the culture (*kul'tura*) itself, if we admit that a member of the intelligentsia is in need not only of different words but of a different language [i.e., Yiddish], then we are faced with an unbridgeable gap between the popular masses and those elements who are positioned to serve them."[174] In one sense, of course, this was true, and represented an advanced symptom of the parting of ways within Jewish society that resulted from the combination of selective integration, Russia's topheavy educational system, and the sustained encounter with the world of the Russian studenchestvo. But the urge to reverse that trend by returning to the Jewish masses and their language owed much to the encounter with Russian students as well. "In the sixties," wrote Arnold Margolin, a graduate of Kiev University, "it was customary to speak in Yiddish about the necessity of assimilating and studying the Russian language." Half a century later, he reported, "one could . . . hear Jews advocating in Russian the necessity of national rejuvenation and study of the Jewish language. . . . In the sixties, Jewry, of its own accord, began to drink the brew of assimilation, but it could only do it by the spoonful. Later, when new watchwords had been sounded and Jewry, in a paroxysm of exaltation and pride, resolved to tread the path of national rejuvenation, it began to absorb the same brew by the bucketful, without even noticing it."[175] As long as the Russian university remained a kind of self-contained arena, Jewish integration proceeded there at a breathtaking pace. Only when that autonomy broke down—first with the imposition of quotas by the tsarist state, then as a result of the absorption of the student movement by a broader social revolution— did integration stall and a significant portion of Jewish students set out in search of a distinct group identity. Even then, they took with them much of the worldview—mythological and otherwise—of the Russian studenchestvo.

Given the centrality of education to the way both government officials and Jewish reformers imagined Jews becoming integrated in Russian society, the

---

173. On self-reported religious belief (or absence thereof), see Benasik, *Studenchestvo v tsifrakh*, p. 116–17, who shows that Jews were the least likely of all confessional groups among the students of Dorpat University to profess adherence to a religion or belief in a personal God. It should be noted, however, that Benasik's data are sufficiently sloppy to cast doubt on the finer points of his conclusions.

174. *Nash put'*, p. 10. The editors of the 1916 volume noted that they would have preferred to publish the journal in Yiddish but were prevented from doing so, presumably by wartime censorship.

175. Arnold D. Margolin, *The Jews of Eastern Europe* (New York, 1926), p. 45.

establishment of quotas represents the most serious assault on the policy of selective integration during the entire late imperial period. To be sure, both before and after 1887, the tsarist government enacted various laws that intensified rather than lessened the burden of anti-Jewish discrimination. But such laws left the various paths toward selective integration open and intact. That is, they did not formally alter the system of incentives for Jews to disperse themselves into selected arenas of what was formally still a corporative society. By contrast, quotas on admission to educational institutions reduced Jewish access to those very incentives, and as an internal government report acknowledged in 1908, "they have done much to arouse hostile feelings toward the government on the part of Jews in general and Jewish youth in particular."[176] The numerus clausus narrowed what was supposed to be the royal road to progress and modernity. Deliberately constricted in Russia, that road increasingly led abroad, with the result that by any measure—numerical, organizational, ideological—the center of gravity of Russian-Jewish student life moved to universities and other institutions of higher education in Central and Western Europe.

The numerus clausus also added urgency and legitimacy to the call for the establishment of a separate university exclusively for Jews. The idea had been raised as early as 1884 (i.e., before the introduction of quotas) by the Lovers of Zion, who dreamed of founding a Jewish university in Palestine, and was officially endorsed at the first Zionist congress in Basel in 1897. In the wake of the drastic tightening of quotas after the Revolution of 1905, even non-Zionist Jews began to think in terms of a separate Jewish institution of higher learning, but in Russia rather than Palestine. In 1911 a group of university-educated Jews led by the engineer Aleksei Press and the lawyer Yakov Gal´pern, alarmed at the sudden rise in the number of conversions by young Jews seeking admission to institutions of higher education, petitioned the tsarist government for permission to establish a technological institute specifically for Jews. It was a gesture that would have been inconceivable—to Jews, Russians, and the tsarist government alike—just a quarter century before. Under the transformed circumstances of the First World War, when the demand for technical know-how rose sharply, the autocracy gave its consent, by which time the favored site—Vilna, now under German occupation—had to be abandoned for another, Ekaterinoslav. When the privately funded Jewish Polytechnicum held its opening ceremony on January 21, 1917, it marked the birth of the world's first Jewish institution devoted to higher secular education—and a stunning departure from the ideal of the melting pot.[177]

176. *Materialy po voprosu o prieme evreev*, p. 68.

177. My brief account is based on the following articles in the journal *Novyi Voskhod:* "Ch´ia vina?" no. 37 (1912); "Universitet ili politekhnikum," nos. 14–15 (1913); "Uchrezhdenie Po-

In order to place in perspective the complex forms of privilege and exclusion, of acculturation and particularism, that characterized the Jewish encounter with higher education in late imperial Russia, it may be helpful to compare them briefly with those of another group whose encounter with higher education proceeded nearly simultaneously, namely, women.[178] Because Russia's estate-based social order could accommodate neither women's suffrage nor European-style emancipation of Jews as citizens, education, with its own transformative potential, took center stage in the struggles of both groups for civic and social equality.[179] In both cases, observers commonly assumed that only material motives lay behind the pursuit of higher education, whether residential privileges and escape from military service for Jews or better matrimonial prospects for women. Furthermore, in both cases access to institutions of higher education raised the controversial question of admission to the Table of Ranks, and therefore to state employment—a privilege hitherto automatically conferred upon Christian male graduates. Finally, both Jewish and women students were required to confront the argument that their "particular" concerns were secondary to, and would ultimately be fully resolved by, an all-embracing revolutionary upheaval.

But it is the contrasts between the two encounters that are most illuminating. While the tsarist regime initially attempted to assimilate Jews by drawing them into state-run educational institutions, it showed little interest in transforming women, and after a brief, reluctant experiment with female auditors at universities between 1859 and 1861, it again barred them from the halls of higher learning. Only the resulting enrollment of Russian women abroad and the specter of their radicalization induced Alexander II to permit the creation of a kind of domestic safety valve, and then strictly in the form of separate "higher courses" for women.[180] The higher courses, moreover, were the result of private, not state, initiative, and their graduates received only certificates of completion, which conferred neither a place in the Table of Ranks nor the privilege of entering state service.

By contrast, it was the dramatic *success* of Jewish integration in the acad-

litekhnikuma," no. 16–17 (1913); "Strakh pered neudachei," no. 26 (1913); "Osnovnaia zadacha vysshei shkoly," no. 45 (1913); "O prosvetitel´nom fonde," no. 11 (1914). See also Press, "Bor´ba za vysshie obrazovanie," pp. 138–140. Sliozberg, *Dela minuvshikh dnei*, 3: 301, gives slightly different dates. Scarcely a month after the Jewish Polytechnicum's founding, the February Revolution put an end to the autocracy. Students and faculty continued their work until the school was absorbed into the Soviet Commissariat of Enlightenment.

178. A systematic comparison with the experiences of Polish and other non-Russian students would also be useful, but apart from the sparse material presented in this chapter I have been unable to locate the necessary sources.

179. See Stites, *Women's Liberation Movement*, pp. 30, 75–87; Johanson, *Women's Struggle for Higher Education.*

180. Johanson, *Women's Struggle for Higher Education*, p. 58.

emy that led the autocracy to limit the number of Jewish students, and only then—as a direct result of the quotas—did significant numbers of Jewish students migrate to institutions of higher education in Europe. After the Revolution of 1905, the divergence of the two trajectories was unmistakable. For women, it was a decade of unprecedented educational growth: more than twenty new women's institutions of higher education opened in a dozen cities from Warsaw to Tomsk. In 1911 the Ministry of Enlightenment recognized the curriculum of the "higher courses" as equivalent to that of the universities. Women thereby became eligible to take university examinations and, if successful, to enjoy the rights they conferred (except for entrance into the Table of Ranks). Even as Jewish enrollment was frozen or in some cases cut back, the number of women students skyrocketed, from 5,500 in 1905 to 44,000 in 1915.[181]

While the tsarist autocracy severely curtailed Jewish access to higher education, it did not close the door entirely. In the academic year immediately preceding the outbreak of World War I, some 4,440 Jews were still enrolled at Russian universities and technical institutes (just under 8 percent of the total male student population), while the number and proportion of Jewish students at the lower end of the state educational system were growing.[182] Furthermore, during the entire thirty-year history of the numerus clausus, the state proved extraordinarily reluctant to tamper with the privileges granted to those Jews who did manage to obtain a postsecondary degree. By the beginning of the twentieth century, such Jews numbered in the tens of thousands. In Part IV we turn our attention to one of the largest groups among them, professionals in Russia's newly established, European-style legal system.

181. McClelland, *Autocrats and Academics,* pp. 34–39; Johanson, *Women's Struggle for Higher Education,* pp. 100–101; Dudgeon, "Forgotten Minority," p. 9.

182. Georgievskii, *Doklad,* p. 200; Z. M., "Evreiskaia uchashchaiasia molodezh´ v tsyfrakh," *Vestnik Obshchestva prosveshcheniia evreev,* no. 11 (1912), pp. 122–27; Ivanov, *Studenchestvo Rossii,* p. 197.

PART FOUR

In the Court of Gentiles

"Since when have the yids started worrying about Russia's interests?"

"Since they stopped being yids," *answered Sarin, "and started thinking of themselves as Russian citizens."*

"Citizens?" sputtered the official. "Citoyens? In Russia there are no citizens, citoyens, there are subjects, understand? Ugh, what have they dreamed up—citizens! What is this, a republic?"

LEV LEVANDA, *Hot Times* (1875)

David Shapiro was utterly convinced that today's world was not the same as it once was; once a Jew had no recourse, but today there were laws and courts, justice, a Duma, and newspapers.

SHOLEM ALEICHEM, *The Bloody Hoax* (1913)

Chapter 8

The Judicial Reform and Jewish Citizenship

Within the Jewish "diploma intelligentsia" of the late imperial period, lawyers occupied a special place. They were founders of many of the leading public Jewish organizations and the most visible activists on behalf of Jewish causes. By the turn of the century, several of them had become well-known names on the Jewish street. Lawyers played a central role in transforming the goals and strategies of the Petersburg Jewish elite, moving the struggle for emancipation to Russia's reformed courts of law as well as to the court of public opinion. More than in any other profession, moreover, Jews achieved quantitative and qualitative prominence in the Russian bar, arguably the most important institutional component of Russia's embryonic civil society. Numerous memoirs by Russian-Jewish lawyers testify to their sense of calling in both Russian and Jewish society, and illuminate the manner by which they became mediators between the two.

The Judicial Reform of 1864, which fashioned a modern judiciary and introduced the preconditions for the rule of law in Russia, "fundamentally altered the political face of the tsarist empire."[1] Although other components of the Great Reforms—the emancipation of the serfs in 1861, the military reform of 1874—had a greater and more immediate impact on relations between Jews and Russians, the judicial reform stands out because of the extent to which it broke with the tradition of official discrimination against Jews. In the entire text of the 1864 legislation, in all the regulations governing the creation of independent courts open to the public, a professional class of lawyers, prosecutors, and judges, and a modern jury system, the word "Jew"

---

1. Jörg Baberowski, *Autokratie und Justiz: Zum Verhältnis von Rechtsstaatlichkeit und Rückständigkeit im ausgehenden Zarenreich, 1864–1914* (Frankfurt a. M., 1996), p. 11.

appeared only once.[2] The judicial reform thus held out the promise that, despite the myriad Jewish disabilities inscribed in Russian law, the application of that law, the legal process itself, would henceforth be impartial and open to scrutiny.

Until 1864, the judiciary had been a mere appendage of the executive — that is, of the autocracy—and courtrooms were at the mercy of political expediency, corruption, and caprice. Lawyers as such did not exist; in fact, under Nicholas I the imported word for "lawyer" (*advokat*) was banned from the press.[3] An individual appearing in court was accompanied ("represented" would overstate the case), if at all, by a *striapchii,* an occupation more akin to notary than attorney. Consistent with the segmentation of prereform society, juries, when used, were composed according to the social estate of the contending parties. Since Jews belonged de facto to two estates— one ethnic/religious, the other social/occupational—they also participated in two separate legal systems. Within Jewish society, rabbinical courts (*batai-din,* sing. *bet-din*) meted out justice based on Jewish law in a tradition dating back to antiquity. The typical bet-din involved no lawyers or other intermediaries acting on behalf of plaintiffs or defendants. Judges, however, would occasionally solicit the opinions of "experts in the law" (*morei hora´a*).[4] As members of various urban estates, Jews had been declared eligible in 1783 to participate in municipal courts, despite the protest of individual Jewish communities that wished to retain the bet-din's monopoly on dispensing justice to Jews. At the same time, the tsarist government repeatedly sought (and largely failed) to restrict the jurisdiction of the rabbinical courts to purely religious matters, in order to leave secular affairs in the hands of the municipal courts. Such a distinction was largely foreign to traditional Jewish practice, in which the domain of "religious" law (halakhah) extended to nearly all aspects of civil life, and the principle of *dina demalkhuta dina* ("the law of the kingdom is law [for the Jews]") had always been applied selectively.[5]

To the extent that they did participate in the prereform Russian legal system (at a minimum, in cases involving both Christians and Jews), Jews and their elected representatives were eligible to sue and to take oaths in municipal courts. They were also permitted to serve on juries, but only in civil trials involving Jews and in criminal cases not involving the Christian faith

---

2. The single instance of the word "Jew" in the text of the 1864 reform occurs in a passage forbidding the use of Jews as witnesses in cases involving Jewish apostates. See L. B. [L. M. Bramson], "Sudebnaia reforma i evrei," *Voskhod,* nos. 11–12 (1889), p. 7.

3. Richard Wortman, *The Development of a Russian Legal Consciousness* (Chicago, 1976), p. 12.

4. Isaac Levitats, *The Jewish Community in Russia, 1844–1917* (Jerusalem, 1981), pp. 140–43.

5. See "Bet-din," *Evreiskaia entsiklopediia,* 4: 410–13; Klier, *Russia Gathers Her Jews,* pp. 142–46; Lederhendler, *Road to Modern Jewish Politics,* pp. 16–17.

or church matters. Furthermore, Jews could neither serve as jury foremen nor constitute more than a third of the members of a given jury, regardless of their proportion in the local population (which in towns of the Pale was often much more than a third).[6]

In prereform Russia, however, juries mattered little, since the real verdicts were commonly dictated from the chancelleries, and often with little regard to the evidence or the law. It is therefore of considerable significance that when the 1864 reform shifted genuine decision-making power to juries and justices of the peace, none of the previous restrictions—in fact, no restrictions at all—were placed on Jews. As plaintiffs and defendants, too, Jews were to participate as equals. These circumstances stand out in even greater relief when one considers that under the judicial reform, the peasantry—roughly 80 percent of the population—continued to be subject, at the local level, to a separate body of customary law in traditional *volost'* (peasant district) courts.

Ideally, an assessment of the impact of judicial reform on the Russian–Jewish encounter would begin by exploring the extent to which Jewish litigants brought their grievances to reformed state courts rather than to rabbinical courts. Unfortunately, such an assessment is difficult to make, if only because official efforts to restrict the jurisdiction of rabbinical courts resulted in much clandestine Jewish activity, whose scope we may never know. Contemporary accounts suggest, however, that the popularity of the reformed courts was growing among Jews, especially in cases involving commercial or family law. The Jewish lawyer Il'ia G. Orshanskii, for example, noted in the 1870s the "powerful decline throughout southern Russia of the judicial activities of the rabbis since the introduction of the new courts, [which are] literally overflowing with cases brought by Jews, owing to their commercial activities, which generate a considerable quantity of disputes and lawsuits."[7] The state-sponsored *Vilenskii Vestnik* reported in 1872 with evident enthusiasm (and probably some exaggeration) that, "having learned about the straightforward and uncomplicated mechanisms of the new courts, their accessibility to all in matters of every kind, beginning with the most trivial, Jews have eagerly turned to the new institutions, abandoning their bet-din almost

---

6. "Prisiaga evreev po russkomu zakonodatel'stvu," *Evreiskaia entsiklopediia*, 12: 933–37; G. Litovskii [Iakov Markovich Gal'pern], "Uchastie russkikh evreev v otpravlenii pravosudiia: Po arkhivnym materialam," *Perezhitoe* 3 (1911): 158. Gal'pern was the highest-ranking unconverted Jew in the Ministry of Justice.

7. Orshanskii, *Evrei v Rossii*, pp. 381–82. It is worth noting that Orshanskii made these remarks in an article whose general aim was to defend the rabbinical courts against the charges levied against them in Iakov Brafman's *Kniga kagala*, and to explain their historical longevity before various European states had introduced fair and open courts. For similar contemporary assessments of the decline of rabbinical courts in Russia after the judicial reform, see L. B., "Sudebnaia reforma i evrei," p. 9, and Gal'pern, "Uchastie russkikh evreev," p. 162.

completely." It went on to cite instances of Jews in Vilna turning to the new courts even in cases involving customary issues such as marital law and the right of *aliya* (being called up to read from the Torah in synagogue services).[8] Indeed, cases of Jewish women turning to reformed state courts in matters of divorce have now been substantially documented.[9]

In addition to having free access to the new courts and serving as equals on juries, Jews became eligible for the entire range of new positions connected with the administration of justice: lawyers, state prosecutors, investigators, justices of the peace, and judges. Russia's judiciary was therefore at the time more open than those of the Austrian Empire (where Jews were first admitted to the bar in 1867) and Great Britain (where they were first admitted in 1883).[10] Looking back on the judicial reform on its twenty-fifth anniversary in 1889, the lawyer Leontii Bramson remarked that "in no other reform did the principle of the equality of all citizens before the law and the rejection of all exclusions find such full, deep, and consistent expression."[11] At the time of Bramson's remarks, Jews constituted some 14 percent of the empire's certified lawyers (249 out of a total of 1,771) and 43 percent of all apprentice lawyers (456 out of a total of 1,069)—the primary pool from which future members of the bar would be drawn, and thus an unmistakable sign that their presence in the profession was rapidly rising. Indeed, during the preceding five years, 22 percent of those admitted to the bar and an astounding 89 percent of those who became apprentice lawyers were Jews.[12] Only slightly less dramatic was the Jewish presence among so-called private attorneys, practitioners lacking formal legal training but certified and regulated by the state beginning in 1874. Fragmentary available data suggest that in the empire's nine western provinces (all of them within the Pale), Jews constituted between a quarter and half of all private attorneys.[13] With employment in academia and the civil service all but closed to them, Jewish

8. "Ob otnoshenii vilenskikh evreev k sudu," *Vilenskii Vestnik*, no. 241 (1872).

9. ChaeRan Freeze, "The Litigious Gerusha: Jewish Women and Divorce in Imperial Russia," *Nationalities Papers* 25, no. 1 (1997): 91–92.

10. With the exception of France, where Jews were first admitted to the bar in 1791, most European countries did not open the practice of law to Jews until the mid–nineteenth century. See "Lawyers," *Encyclopedia Judaica*, 10:1490–98.

11. L. B., "Sudebnaia reforma i evrei," p. 1.

12. *Vysochaishe uchrezhdennaia komissiia dlia peresmotra zakonopolozhenii po sudebnoi chasti: Ob˝iasnitel'naia zapiska k proektu novoi redaktsii uchrezhdeniia sudebnykh ustanovlenii*, vol. 3 (St. Petersburg, 1900), pp. 34–35.

13. William Pomeranz, "Justice from Underground: The History of the Underground *Advokatura*," *Russian Review* 52 (July 1993): 329n. I am using "lawyer" or "attorney" throughout for *prisiazhnyi poverennyi* and "apprentice lawyer/attorney" for *pomoshchnik prisiazhnogo poverennogo*. A five-year apprenticeship (usually after graduation from a law faculty) was required before one could apply for admission to the bar, although a significant minority of applicants

graduates of law faculties were far more likely than their non-Jewish counterparts to join the bar and take up private practice, thereby further expanding their presence in the legal profession.

The Russian legal profession's aspirations for the rule of law (*zakonnost'*)
and corporate independence, enshrined in the judicial reform and sustained in the decades thereafter by university law departments and the bar
(though only sporadically by the government itself), helped recast the worldview of its Jewish members, and through them the outlook of a significant
portion of the Russian-Jewish intelligentsia. Three areas in particular were
reshaped by the introduction of juridical categories and norms: the attempt
to create a usable narrative of the Russian-Jewish past, the struggle for emancipation, and the search for self-definition as Jews in a reformed multinational state. While recognizing that these three enterprises—historiography,
political struggle, and self-definition—were often inseparable, I shall consider the relevance of legal categories to each in turn.

LAW, HISTORIOGRAPHY, AND THE JEWS

Although Jews had resided in Eastern Europe since at least the eleventh century, and by the seventeenth century their numbers were greater there than
in all the rest of the European continent, historical research largely passed
over them until the appearance of the Haskalah. Among literate Jews in the
Russian Empire, historical self-knowledge in the modern, critical sense took
root in the mid-nineteenth century and blossomed with the emergence of
the Jewish intelligentsia during the Reform era. Before that time, and as had
been the case among Jews throughout medieval Europe, historical memory
was grounded in cycles of liturgy and ritual in which an ancient, sacred history was continually projected into the present.[14]

Beginning in the Reform era, the historiography of Jews in the Russian
Empire took as its central concern the Jews' legal standing, which is to say,
the development of official policy and legislation regarding the Jewish pop-

---

to the bar came directly from government service. Unless otherwise indicated, statistics presented here on lawyers exclude both private attorneys (*chastnye poverennye*) and the underground
bar (*podpol'naia advokatura*), in which Jews played a significant role as well, although reliable
data are lacking. See Baberowski, *Autokratie und Justiz*, pp. 500–510, and Joan Neuberger, " 'Shysters' or Public Servants? Uncertified Lawyers and Legal Aid for the Poor in Late Imperial Russia," *Russian History/Histoire Russe* 23, nos. 1–4 (1996): 301–4.

14. See the influential works by Yosef Hayim Yerushalmi, *Zakhor: Jewish History and Jewish
Memory* (New York, 1989), and Shmuel Feiner, *Haskalah ve-historiyah: toldoteha shel hakarat-'avar
yehudit modernit* (Jerusalem, 1995), esp. pp. 210–373.

ulation.[15] There was more than a sufficient number of reasons for this focus. First, emancipation, the guiding issue in the pan-European relationship between Jews and the societies in whose midst they lived, was understood across the nineteenth century largely in terms of legal rights and restrictions. For Russia's Jews, of course, legally prescribed disabilities were an inescapable fact of everyday existence, lending a special urgency to the analysis of their origins and history. The living counter-example of legal equality for Jews elsewhere in Europe exercised a powerful teleological pull on conceptions of Jewish history in the continent's eastern half, just as the European example guided the imagination of much of the Russian intelligentsia. In addition, Russian historiography during the Reform era was dominated by the "State School," which emphasized the role of law and the state in Russia's development; the source materials most frequently employed by historians were still the voluminous published and relatively organized imperial law codes.

Perhaps most significant, the majority of prerevolutionary Russian-Jewish historians were in fact lawyers by training, occupation, and outlook.[16] Not a single Russian-Jewish historian was educated in a historical-philological faculty or held an academic position, though several (including Il'ia Orshanskii, and Genrikh Sliozberg) were offered such positions at the price of conversion, only to refuse.[17] The first semi-organized forum for the study of Russian-Jewish history began as a weekly professional colloquium led by Alexander Passover for apprentice lawyers in Petersburg and eventually became the Jewish Historical-Ethnographic Society (under the aegis of the Society for the Spread of Enlightenment among the Jews of Russia).[18] The extra-academic position of Russian-Jewish historians only intensified their social and political engagement.

Taken together, all these factors ensured that contemporary legal issues constantly shadowed and illuminated representations of the Jewish past in

15. For an analysis of major trends in Russian-Jewish historiography from 1860 to 1930, see Benjamin Nathans, "On Russian-Jewish Historiography," in Thomas Sanders, ed., *Historiography of Imperial Russia: The Profession and Writing of History in a Multinational State* (Armonk, N.Y., 1999), pp. 397–432.

16. For two important exceptions to the model of the historian-lawyer, Simon Dubnov and Iulii Gessen, and their significant departures from the juridical approach to Russian-Jewish history, see ibid., pp. 410–13. See also Viktor Kel'ner, "'Ia smotriu na Vas kak na svoego uchitelia . . .' (Pis'ma Iu. I. Gessena k S. M. Dubnovu)," *Vestnik evreiskogo universiteta v Moskve* 4, no. 22 (2000): 291–310.

17. On Orshanskii, see Yitshak Maor, "Eliyahu Orshanski u-mekomo be-historiografiyah shel yehudei rusiyah," *He-ʿAvar* 20 (1973): 56–59; on Sliozberg, see his *Dela minuvshikh dnei*, 1: 152–59. See also Nathans, "On Russian-Jewish Historiography," pp. 417–19.

18. Maksim Vinaver, "Kak my zanimalis' istoriei," pp. 41–53, and idem, *Nedavnee (vospominaniia i kharakteristiki)* (Paris, 1926), pp. 112–15.

Russia. Many works on the Russian-Jewish past produced in the late imperial period were in fact hardly histories as we understand the term today, but analyses of legislative acts culled from successive volumes of the law codes. Their stated purpose was to give practical guidance to Jews as well as tsarist bureaucrats attempting to navigate their way through the enormous maze of legislation and court rulings concerning Jews and Jewish issues.[19] Beyond this immediate goal, however, Russian-Jewish lawyers in effect used legal history to make the case for emancipation before the court of public opinion. Despite their often modest self-descriptions as "handbook," "collection," or "index," the best of these works offered an impressive depth of historical interpretation. Instead of tracing the development of official Jewish policy across successive reigns, the manuals were organized by topic (residence law, property law, commercial law, etc.), within which the analysis moved chronologically. If measured in terms of sheer number and variety, the manuals appear to have reached nearly as many readers as more conventional histories of Russian Jewry.[20]

The first attempt at a narrative legal history of Russian Jewry came from the pen of Il'ia Orshanskii (1846–1875). Denied a lectureship in civil law at Odessa's Novorossiiskii University because of his refusal to convert, Orshanskii entered private practice in Odessa while pouring his frustrated ambition into a broad range of publications as well as communal activism. Speaking for himself and other engagé Jewish lawyer-historians, Orshanskii alerted his readers in typically incisive fashion that "the ideal toward which we strive consists precisely of expelling the Jews once and for all from the legal codes."[21] For decades his essays on Jewish topics, which first appeared in the press and were then collected in two volumes published in the 1870s, were unsurpassed among scholarly treatments of the "Jewish Question" in the Russian Empire.[22] As Michael Stanislawski has suggested, it was Orshanskii who established the

19. More than twenty such manuals were published between 1860 and 1917, and several went through multiple editions. The most comprehensive—in part because they were published toward the end of the imperial period—are I. V. Gessen and V. Fridshtein, eds., *Sbornik zakonov o evreiakh s ras˝iasneniiami po opredeleniiam Pravitel´stvuiushchago Senata i tsirkuliaram Ministerstv* (St. Petersburg, 1904); Ia. I. Gimpel´son, comp., *Zakony o evreiakh: Sistematicheskii obzor deistvuiushchikh zakonopolozhenii o evreiakh,* ed. L. M. Bramson, 2 vols. (St. Petersburg, 1914–15); and M. I. Mysh, comp., *Rukovodstvo k russkim zakonam o evreiakh,* 3d ed. (St. Petersburg, 1904).

20. One of the best-selling manuals was N. D. Gradovskii's *Torgovye i drugie prava evreev v Rossii v istoricheskom khode zakonodatel´nykh mer* (St. Petersburg, 1885), which went through twelve editions.

21. Orshanskii, *Russkoe zakonodatel´stvo o evreiakh,* p. 336.

22. I. G. Orshanskii, *Evrei v Rossii: Ocherki ekonomicheskogo i obshchestvennogo byta russkikh evreev* (St. Petersburg, 1877), and idem, *Russkoe zakonodatel´stvo o evreiakh: Ocherki i issledovaniia* (St. Petersburg, 1877). Orshanskii's writings on general Russian civil law also achieved widespread recognition.

enduring pattern of treating anti-Jewish legislation as an anomaly within the larger framework of Russian law.[23] A talented polemicist with an affinity for abstraction, Orshanskii argued:

> Our legislation regards the Jews from precisely the opposite perspective as it does all other classes of the population. With respect to the latter, the law operates on the entirely correct principle that everything not prohibited by law is permitted. . . . Thus nowhere in the law will you encounter a ruling that a Greek, a Tartar, or a Mordvinian has the right to practice all branches of commerce, to acquire property . . . , to educate his children in public schools, etc. All this is assumed as a matter of course, as a result of the general human and civil rights of every Russian subject. But with regard to Jews the law takes as its point of departure the idea that they, as Jews, do not have any [a priori] rights in Russia and therefore that everything not explicitly permitted them by law is forbidden.

Orshanskii could point to numerous examples of Russian laws declaring that "Jews are permitted to engage in agricultural labor," "Jews may oversee all kinds of factories in the areas where they are allowed to reside," and "Jewish children enjoy unrestricted access to public schools." Moreover, Jewish citizens of other countries visiting or residing in Russia had never shared the legal status of other foreigners, but rather were subject to many of the restrictions imposed on Russian Jews.[24]

While Orshanskii's analysis of the jurisprudential logic at work in the examples he cited was compelling, it ignored numerous counter-examples of anti-Jewish discrimination based on a different logic. Just as often, in fact, tsarist law would outline the privileges and obligations of a given estate or social group, only to introduce the qualifier *krome evreev* (except Jews). To take a single but prominent example, the landmark decree of February 19, 1861, ending the institution of serfdom, stated that owners of landed estates might henceforth lease their lands to members of all estates, "except Jews." The popular Jewish imagination, resigned to the seeming inevitability with which this phrase surfaced at the end of every ostensibly promising decree, knowingly dubbed it *di klausele* (the little clause).[25]

More significant, Orshanskii's assertion that the non-Jewish population was protected by "the general human and civil rights of every Russian subject" assumed an imagined standard, a uniformity in the legal status of the rest of the empire's population, that had more to do with Western legal theory than with the actual legal hierarchy of the Russian soslovie system. His position parallels the legal fiction adopted by Kiselev and the Jewish Committee in

23. Stanislawski, *Tsar Nicholas I*, pp. 5–8.
24. Orshanskii, *Russkoe zakonodatel'stvo o evreiakh*, pp. 3–6.
25. Maor, *She'elat ha-yehudim*, p. 85.

1856, that "existing regulations on the Jews" should be brought into agreement with "the general laws for other subjects of the empire." And like Kiselev, Orshanskii appeared at times to recognize the fictitious nature of this uniformity:

> The Jews are not the only class of people for whom there exist exclusions from and limitations on general laws. . . . Our legislation allows for an enormous and varied mass of exceptions from general laws for different territories and classes of the population. It is well known that in no other European legislation is the principle of uniformity and equality so weakly applied as in that of Russia. . . . The fundamental abnormality [of the Jews' legal status] lies in the character and quality of [their particular] limitations.[26]

In Russia, in other words, anomalies were not anomalous. In order to assess properly the degree of distinctiveness in the Jews' legal status, one would have had to compare their position systematically with that of other groups. Except for occasional allusions to the Russian Orthodox sect of Old Believers and to groups who shared the Jews' classification as "aliens" (*inorodtsy*), however, such a comparative approach was absent from Russian-Jewish historiography. This is hardly surprising, given that Russia's Jews themselves had barely begun to receive scholarly attention, and in any event the implicit comparative framework was much more likely to be the experience of Jews in Central and Western Europe.

Orshanskii's work thus displays an underlying tension between, on the one hand, presenting the Jews' legal standing as utterly unique, and on the other, viewing the Jews within an imperial Russian context in which legally inscribed inequalities were the norm. This tension, moreover, insinuated itself in various guises into the work of nearly every prerevolutionary Russian-Jewish historian, and as we shall observe, into other areas of Jewish activity as well. In the works of Orshanskii's successors such as Menashe G. Morgulis (1837–1912), Pesakh S. Marek (1862–1920), Genrikh B. Sliozberg (1863–1937), Shaul M. Ginzburg (1866–1940), Leontii M. Bramson (1869–1941), Solomon V. Pozner (1876–1946), and Grigorii Ia. Krasnyi-Admoni (1881–1970)—all lay historians trained in the law—one finds a similar pattern of official legislation regarding Jews analyzed as an arena unto itself, governed by an autonomous ebb and flow of official anti-Semitism, and yet, on a different level of the narrative, utterly in sync with the general rhythms of reform and reaction.[27] In his study of Jews and tsarist educational policy, for

---

26. Orshanskii, *Russkoe zakonodatel´stvo o evreiakh*, p. 3.

27. Examples of this dissonance can be found in treatments by these and other first-generation Russian-Jewish historians of the extension of military conscription to the Jews (in the context of Nicholas I's general militarization of Russian society), the policy of selective Jewish integration (and its place within the Great Reforms), as well as the establishment of quotas for

example, Pozner presented the Jews' legal status both as distinctive and as a finely calibrated "barometer" of changes in the larger political climate: "General political shifts here [in Russia] have always affected Jews earlier than anyone else."[28] Quite apart from its explanatory value, this point of view may well derive from two contrasting needs on the part of Russian-Jewish historians: to preserve a sense of distinctiveness in the Jewish experience of discrimination and at the same time to see the Jews as bound up and participating in the fortunes of Russian society as a whole.

THE PROFESSIONALIZATION OF *SHTADLANUT*

By the end of the nineteenth century, the dilemma of whether to view legal discrimination against the Jews as an independent problem requiring an independent solution or rather as part and parcel of the broader structures of inequality in Russian society had moved from the pages of history books into the arena of Jewish political activism. It was destined to become, in fact, one of the most profound and profoundly divisive issues in Russian-Jewish life. Jewish socialists, in particular, were bitterly divided over whether to subsume specifically Jewish grievances within those of the revolutionary movement as a whole. Liberal Jewish delegates to the first two dumas would similarly struggle with the question whether to form a distinct Jewish party or faction. But the legacy of Orshanskii and his successors began to make itself felt well before the era of mass movements and parliamentary campaigns, in a way that gradually transformed the strategy and politics of the Petersburg Jewish elite.

The earliest sign of the potential influence of lawyers in Jewish society, and in the Russian–Jewish encounter, appeared in the aftermath of the Odessa pogrom of May 1871. This was the first incident of popular anti-Jewish violence after the emancipation of the serfs and the reform of Russia's judicial system, as well as the first to elicit public comment from the fledgling Russian-Jewish intelligentsia.[29] As an eyewitness to the pogrom—his law

---

Jewish students in the late 1880s (within the general reintroduction of estate-based university admissions).

28. Pozner, *Evrei v obshchei shkole*, p. xii. Casting their position as a kind of political barometer, it should be noted, was by no means unique to Russian Jews. The hero of a novel by the German-Jewish writer Berthold Auerbach remarks that "the position of the Jews has always been the barometer of humanity": cited in Salo W. Baron, "The Impact of the Revolution of 1848 on Jewish Emancipation," in Abraham Duker, ed., *Emancipation and Counter-Emancipation* (New York, 1974), p. 147.

29. Pogroms occurred in Odessa in 1821, 1849, 1859, 1871, 1881, and 1905. For an insightful discussion of continuities in the unfolding and subsequent explanation of these and other pogroms, see John Klier, "The Pogrom Paradigm in Russian History," in Klier and Lambroza, *Pogroms*, pp. 13–34. On the 1871 pogrom in particular, see Zipperstein, *Jews of Odessa*, pp. 114–28.

office was located at the corner of Rishelevskaia and Evreiskaia streets, near the center of rioting—Orshanskii offered an interpretation of the event that was to dominate future Jewish understanding of the underlying causes of anti-Jewish violence, at least until the far more devastating pogrom in Kishinev in 1903. In stark contrast to the traditional Jewish tendency to view mass violence as an instrument of divine punishment for Jewish sins, Orshanskii's analysis of the events of May 1871 focused on juridical factors, and in particular on how the position of the tsarist state vis-à-vis the Jews, as expressed in its laws, conditioned popular attitudes. The fundamental cause of the violence, he argued, was the Jews' inferior legal status, and the gap between it and their relative economic strength. Because they were known to lack legal rights, the Jews appeared as a group that could be attacked with impunity. "Until such time as the divergence between the Jews' actual and juridical position in Russia is permanently removed by eliminating all existing limitations on their rights," Orshanskii wrote shortly after the violence subsided, "hostility toward Jews will not only not decrease, but in all likelihood will grow."[30]

Orshanskii did more than subject the so-called Jewish Question to an influential if questionable juridical analysis.[31] He was also the first to respond to collective violence against Jews by attempting to mobilize Russia's new judicial system. Immediately after the Odessa pogrom, Orshanskii, together with fellow Odessa lawyers Menashe Morgulis, Alexander Passover, and Mikhail Kulisher, conducted a systematic survey of the violence, neighborhood by neighborhood, identifying victims, perpetrators, and eyewitnesses, and prepared a report sharply criticizing the feeble response by city authorities. They then took the unprecedented step of turning to the recently

30. Orshanskii, *Evrei v Rossii*, p. 164. The article in which this passage appeared was originally written for the Odessa Jewish newspaper *Den'* in 1871, but was cut by the censor. See John Klier, "The Jewish *Den'* and the Literary Mice, 1869–1871," *Russian History* 10, no. 1 (1983): 31–49.

31. The subsequent history of popular violence against fully emancipated Jews in the twentieth century—beginning in 1919 with the massive pogroms in the territories of the former Pale of Settlement—casts significant doubt on Orshanskii's analysis. Nor must one appeal solely to a future that Orshanskii obviously could not have predicted. As Hans Rogger has noted, older examples such as the anti-Jewish riots of 1819 in the German principalities (associated with the Hep-Hep movement) raise similar doubts about the relation between legal rights and vulnerability to violence. See Rogger, "Conclusion and Overview," in Klier and Lambroza, *Pogroms*, pp. 318–19. Rogger concludes (p. 325) that "the way Europe's governments dealt with their Jewish subjects—that is, their legal status—[cannot] be considered decisive in determining whether they were set upon by groups of their neighbors over a larger or smaller territory for various periods of time. Pogroms or riots were experienced by Jews who were emancipated and by those who were not, by rich and poor, under monarchical and republican regimes of the most diverse political coloration, in cities as well as in country districts, in times of peace, war, and revolution." Nonetheless, the notion that the Jews' inferior legal status was the root cause of violence against them retained considerable currency in Russia.

reformed courts, where trials were open and uncensored testimony could be printed in the newspapers, in order to seek official compensation for damages inflicted on the city's Jewish population.[32] In classic nineteenth-century liberal fashion, and taking the judicial reform at its word, Orshanskii and his colleagues sought to harness the power of the Russian state not so much to manipulate the internal affairs of Jewish communities as to reform and regulate relations between Jews and Russians, whether as groups or individuals. The tsarist regime, however, saw matters differently: caught off guard by the sudden outbreak of public violence, it insisted on trying accused perpetrators in closed-door military courts, where public order rather than the Jews was understood to be the primary victim. Evidence gathered by Orshanskii and others went unheeded and was barred from publication.[33]

At roughly the same time, the juridical approach to advancing Jewish interests began to influence the modus operandi of the Petersburg Jewish elite. By the 1870s, Orshanskii's ideas were making their way into the petitions of Horace Gintsburg and other Petersburg notables.[34] An 1871 petition to the minister of internal affairs from a group headed by Gintsburg, for example, complained that "while according to the general spirit of justice everything not forbidden by law is permitted, when it comes to the Jews, unfortunately, the interpretation is just the opposite: everything not permitted them by law is considered, for them, forbidden."[35] When Jewish merchants were told by bureaucrats in Kiev province in 1879 that they could not purchase land in the area because there was no law explicitly allowing Jews to do so, or when officials in the military town of Nikolaev attempted to bar Jewish settlement, citing the absence of a decree specifically permitting Jews to reside in Nikolaev, Gintsburg questioned why the government should "find it necessary to enact laws that read, 'Jews may freely . . . ,' 'All Jews are permitted to . . . ,' etc."[36] Commenting in 1882 on an attempt to bar certified Jewish druggists from owning pharmacies outside the Pale, a leading Jewish newspaper asked whether Jews were excluded from the principle that "everything that is not directly forbidden by law is permitted."[37]

---

32. The official police report on the three days of rioting, during which hundreds of shops and homes were vandalized and looted, set the total damages at 10 million rubles. See Klier, "Pogrom Paradigm in Russian History," p. 24.

33. For accounts of the lawyers' efforts, see M. G. Morgulis, "Bezporiadki 1871 goda v Odesse (po dokumentam i lichnym vospominaniiam)," in *Teoreticheskie i prakticheskie voprosy evreiskoi zhizni: Prilozhenie k zhurnalu "Evreiskii Mir"* (St. Petersburg, 1911), pp. 42–44, and *Evreiskaia Nedelia,* Apr. 29, 1910, pp. 8–14.

34. Sliozberg, *Baron G. O. Gintsburg,* p. 50.

35. RGIA, f. 821, op. 9, d. 87, l. 2. Further examples of Orshanskii's ideas in petitions from Petersburg Jews can be found ibid., l. 56, and d. 100, l. 435.

36. Ibid., op. 9, d. 87, ll. 55–67.

37. *Nedel'naia Khronika Voskhoda,* Mar. 19, 1882, p. 281.

Orshanskii's juridical approach also helped shape the response by Petersburg Jewish elites to the pogroms that erupted across southern Russia in 1881 and that, as Chapter 5 suggested, severely tested the relationship between those elites and the Jewish masses of the Pale. While the government and much of Russian society viewed the pogroms as a protest by former serfs now exposed to Jewish economic exploitation, Gintsburg and others adopted Orshanskii's view that official discrimination against Jews was the root cause of popular violence against them. Once again Jewish advocates trained in the law, this time led by Orshanskii's colleague Menashe Morgulis, attempted to take local communities to court to sue for damages, and once again the tsarist regime blocked attempts to use the legal system to extract compensation from perpetrators, apart from the return of stolen goods.[38]

As the historian I. Michael Aronson has pointed out, whatever the government's intentions regarding the victims and perpetrators of pogroms, the tsarist legal system was simply ill equipped to render justice in cases involving thousands of arrests for a wide range of acts committed under highly chaotic conditions. Local officials were as likely to resort to extrajudicial punishments, such as on-the-spot flogging or the billeting of troops in communities suspected of criminal behavior, as to formal trials. Charges brought against accused *pogromshchiki* were limited to those of disorderly conduct in public places and simple theft, both of which carried relatively light sentences. In Odessa in 1882, moreover, the charge of disorderly conduct was brought against some 150 Jews who had dared to defend themselves and their property against violent crowds. Only occasionally were individual rioters tried for the more serious charge of damage to movable and immovable property, and only in 1891 did the government issue a law specifically dealing with attacks by one social group against another.[39]

For Jews and non-Jews, however, the response of the legal system to anti-Jewish violence was utterly eclipsed by the larger verdict rendered by the Russian state in the years after 1882. Even before the wave of pogroms had subsided, the tsarist regime moved to enact legislation restricting Jewish residence in rural areas *within* the Pale (the so-called May Laws of 1882), thereby in effect endorsing the charge that Jewish exploitation of the peasantry was

---

38. TsGIA-SPb, f. 422, op. 2, d. 1, ll. 16–17; Aronson, *Troubled Waters*, pp. 154–55.

39. Aronson, *Troubled Waters*, pp. 145–60. In his unsuccessful attempts in 1882 to persuade the tsarist government to require local communities to compensate Jews for damages they had suffered, Morgulis had to appeal to the example of a German law that held local communities responsible for damages caused by mob violence. See TsGIA-SPb, f. 422, op. 2, d. 1, ll. 16–17. Although Morgulis did not mention it, the principle of local responsibility for damages suffered by Jews was in fact applied in Bavaria after the Hep-Hep riots of 1819. See Rogger, "Conclusion and Overview," in Klier and Lambroza, *Pogroms*, p. 319.

the root cause of the violence. The promulgation of additional restrictions on Jewish activity over the course of the 1880s only further called into question the efficacy of the juridical approach.

Despite its evident lack of success, the turn by Orshanskii and his followers to Russia's reformed judiciary represents an important chapter in the development of new strategies by Russian-Jewish elites. These strategies and the Jewish lawyers who adopted them were in many ways analogous to their counterparts in post-emancipation Europe, such as one finds in the Alliance Israélite Universelle in Paris (founded in 1860), the Österreich-Israelitische Union in Vienna (1886), and the Central-Verein deutscher Staatsbürger jüdischen Glaubens in Berlin,(1893). To be sure, Russian-Jewish elites retained some of the political naiveté of the Haskalah, as demonstrated by their reliance on petitions from individuals and their faith in the power and reasonableness of the tsarist state, or at least its judicial system. But the juridical approach broke decisively with the Haskalah myth of an implicit alliance between the Russian state and reform-minded Jews, and this in two respects: first, by attributing the problem—discrimination against Jews—to the state itself (or its laws) rather than to Jewish practices, and second, by appealing to state authority not to force internal reforms in Jewish life but to regulate relations between Jews and non-Jews.

It is crucial to appreciate that while the pogroms of 1881–82 and the government's decision to punish the Jews in response were an important catalyst of Jewish political movements devoted to revolution and/or emigration, they hardly put an end to the Petersburg elites and their integrationist politics. On the contrary, the declining efficacy of their lobbying and petitioning during the 1870s and, most dramatically, during the pogrom crisis led the Petersburg notables to invent new methods to fight old battles. When Alexander III in effect withdrew the informal status his father had bestowed on the Gintsburgs as representatives of Russian Jewry before the tsar, Horace Gintsburg turned to Jewish lawyers and the reformed Russian judiciary as the cornerstone of a new strategy of using state institutions to challenge the state itself.

The influence of the juridical approach on the strategies of the Petersburg Jewish elite took a decisive turn in 1893, when Emanuel Levin retired at age seventy-three from his post as secretary to the Gintsburgs, after nearly four decades of service during which he had drafted countless petitions and memoranda. As Chapter 5 demonstrated, the pogroms of 1881–82 had drawn Levin's attention late in his career to the maze of discriminatory legislation directed against the Jews, inspiring him to publish some of the first popular guides to the relevant Russian laws. As a member of the generation of maskilim that preceded the rise of the "diploma intelligentsia," however, Levin remained an autodidact, with little practical experience in the Rus-

Figure 28. Genrikh Sliozberg (1863–1937): "a good Jew and a good Russian citizen." (Courtesy of V. E. Kel'ner.)

sian legal system.[40] The same could not be said of his successor as the Gintsburgs' right-hand man, Genrikh Borisovich Sliozberg, a young lawyer who had recently graduated with the gold medal in law from St. Petersburg University.[41] One could hardly wish for a better symbol of the transformation of *shtadlanut* (personal intercession by notables) in late imperial Russia: the maskil replaced by the lawyer.

40. S. Gol'dshtein, "Emmanuil Borisovich Levin (1820–1913): Po avtobiograficheskim zametkam," *Evreiskaia Starina* 8, no. 3 (1915): 253; *Evreiskaia entsiklopediia*, 10: 114. Aronson, *Troubled Waters* p. 74, incorrectly identifies Levin as a lawyer.

41. Sliozberg, *Dela minuvshikh dnei*, 1: 156, 301.

Driven by his profession's ideal of replacing autocratic arbitrariness (*proizvol*) with the rule of law (*zakonnost´*), Sliozberg shifted the emphasis of Gintsburg's efforts from personally petitioning high-placed officials (although this certainly continued) to systematically defending Jewish rights in the reformed courts, and at the highest levels. By the late 1880s, when the momentum behind the policy of selective integration had stalled, Sliozberg recalled,

> I became convinced that the time had come for a determined struggle to re-tain those few rights that had been granted the Jews. Arbitrariness threatened to destroy the very possibility of existence for the Jewish masses, if those rights were not defended point for point by means of the legal resources that were still at our disposal. It was necessary to begin to apply purely juridical meth-ods, to show a little imagination in arguing for the appropriate interpretation of laws that were at times unclear [and] frequently contradictory.[42]

Two factors, according to Sliozberg, caused the government of Alexander III to pursue anti-Jewish policies in a particularly arbitrary way and often out-side the normal channels (e.g., by administrative decree rather than by pub-lic legislation). These were the government's inability to formulate a new overall direction for Jewish policy even as its confidence in selective inte-gration receded, and the increasing attention paid by Jewish financial cir-cles in Europe and America to the plight of Russian Jewry. "The lack of clar-ity in laws about Jews," Sliozberg noted, "and the impossibility of determining the exact range of persons and subjects covered by every restrictive law . . . created ample room for interpretations that introduced new restrictions."[43] Toward this end, the government came to rely particularly on the State Sen-ate, the highest court in the land, to deliver the desired interpretations of the law.

Sliozberg became an eyewitness to this process.[44] Shortly after graduat-ing from St. Petersburg University in 1886, he was unofficially hired as an assistant by the legal counsel to the Ministry of Internal Affairs, Ia. A. Pliushchevskii-Pliushchik, whose busy social life in the imperial capital led him to depend on hired hands to do much of his office work for him. This position in turn brought Sliozberg into nearly constant contact with the Sen-ate over the course of some fifteen years. Through contacts, he gained ac-cess to hundreds of appeals annually brought by Jews, in advance of their consideration by the Senate. In many cases he would arrange, with Horace Gintsburg's financial support, to serve as attorney for the plaintiffs.[45]

---

42. Ibid, p. 302.

43. Ibid, vol. 2, p. 7.

44. For another lawyer's account of how Jewish issues played themselves out in the State Senate, see L. Aizenberg, "Vidy pravitel´stva v evreiskom voprose," pp. 80–84.

45. Sliozberg, *Dela minuvshikh dnei*, 1: 216–18, 2: 7–15. According to another source, "ap-peals concerning 'Jewish' issues constituted a very considerable percentage of the total num-

Sliozberg himself also helped initiate countless suits against local officials whose actions went beyond the letter even of openly discriminatory laws, in the hopes that they would reach "the highest courts in the capital," where they stood a better chance of favorable resolution.[46] By the turn of the century, his reputation had spread throughout the Pale.[47] As one colleague put it, "Sliozberg's continuous client over the course of many years was the Jewish people."[48]

One example from the many appeals handled by Sliozberg will give a sense of the stakes involved. A tailor named Kagan, having resided legally in a suburb of Petersburg for some fifteen years, was without warning issued a summons by the police expelling him from his residence and ordering him to return to the Pale within thirty days—a not uncommon fate for the tens of thousands of Jewish artisans (not to mention fictitious Jewish artisans) who had put to use the residence privileges granted by the law of 1865. Kagan's right to reside outside the Pale depended on the approval of the executive board of the tailors' guild of his native town, and this, it had been discovered, he lacked. But as Sliozberg pointed out to the Senate during the case's hearing, in Kagan's hometown there was no tailors' guild, so Kagan had obtained permission instead from the local bureau of artisans (*remeslennoe upravlenie*). Persuaded that this step satisfied the intent of the 1865 law, and in light of the fact that Kagan had been lawfully practicing his stated craft, the Senate annulled the expulsion order. In a legal system that relied heavily on precedent, Sliozberg noted, "defending the interests of a [single] plaintiff in the Senate served as a defense of the Jewish population in general."[49]

But frequently such appeals did not turn out so well. As Sliozberg himself conceded, there was a "sisyphian" quality to his strategy of working within the legal system to combat discrimination: he took on the majority of cases "in full awareness of the hopelessness of achieving a favorable outcome, of convincing those who would not or could not be convinced as a result of pressure from above."[50] Dubnov, a largely unsympathetic observer of the Petersburg elites, noted a certain frustration among "the Baron's young guard"

---

ber of cases in the First Department [of the Senate]": Gessen and Fridshtein, *Sbornik zakonov o evreiakh*, p. vii.

46. Sliozberg, *Baron G. O. Gintsburg*, p. 49.

47. Ginzburg, *Amolike Peterburg*, pp. 88–100. In his preface to Sliozberg's memoirs, Jabotinsky goes so far as to claim that Sliozberg's fame among the Jewish masses outshone that of his patron, Horace Gintsburg. This seems an exaggeration. See Sliozberg, *Dela minuvshikh dnei*, 1: x.

48. M. L. Gol´dshtein, *Advokatskie portrety* (Paris, 1932), p. 27.

49. Sliozberg, *Dela minuvshikh dnei*, 1: 303, 2: 15 (quotation).

50. Ibid, 1: 145, 2: 223.

of Jewish lawyers.[51] The general tide of reaction under the last two tsars meant that, for Sliozberg, success usually consisted merely of preserving, rather than expanding, the limited scope of selective integration. The arcane legal language of Senate rulings and the absence of positive, progressive results ensured that the content of Sliozberg's work remained largely opaque to the Jewish masses. Like a character in one of Sholem Aleichem's novels, he risked being dismissed as "a specialist in the law and commentary on residence permits."[52] Indeed, Sliozberg's memoirs seek again and again to defend (retrospectively) the juridical approach to Jewish interests against charges of political timidity and excessive focus on the individual victim rather than on Russian Jewry as a whole. Among most Jews, he lamented, "there was no legal consciousness, only a feeling of injustice. . . . Nothing that occurred outside the walls of the ghetto concerned them; they were not familiar with the available means, within the general structure of political life, for struggle against repression."[53]

Public and often sensational trials of Jews accused of ritual murder likewise produced mixed results for the juridical approach to Jewish rights. The first such trial under the reformed legal system was held in 1879, in the Kutais district of the eastern Caucasus, in connection with a young Christian girl found dead under mysterious circumstances.[54] Although the paucity of evidence prevented local prosecutors from formally linking the alleged murder to ritual purposes, nonetheless, by repeatedly noting that the body had been found "on the eve of the Jewish Passover," the charge was implicitly registered. Pioneering a new approach that sought to exploit the openness of Russia's reformed courts in order to expose the blood libel to the critical light of public opinion, the defense attorneys, L. A. Kupernik and P. A. Aleksandrov (the latter an ethnic Russian), set out to refute the charge not only of murder but of ritual intent.[55] Successful in the first respect, they

---

51. Dubnov, *Kniga zhizni*, 1: 236. Dubnov, it should be noted, failed to register the change in strategy of the Petersburg Jewish elites after Gintsburg's hiring of Sliozberg and other lawyers, whose work he belittled as mere "filling of archives of various ministries." Of Horace Gintsburg at the turn of the century, Dubnov remarked, "A petitioner, having secured favors, is unsuitable for the role of fighter for justice" (ibid., p. 236).

52. Sholem Aleichem, *Bloody Hoax*, p. 34.

53. Sliozberg, *Dela minuvshikh dnei*, 1: 9–11.

54. The charge of ritual murder involved the notion that Jews required the blood of Christian children for rituals (ostensibly the making of matzoh) associated with the Passover holiday, which not coincidentally is celebrated close to the time of Easter, the commemoration of Jesus' crucifixion. Before the Kutais affair, trials involving the blood libel had been held in Russia in 1799, 1805, 1811, 1816, 1827, and 1852. In all but the last case, the Jewish defendants had been acquitted. See Iulii Gessen, "Obvinenie evreev v prestupleniakh s ritual'noi tsel'iu," *Evreiskaia entsiklopediia*, 11: 869–71.

55. "Kutaiskoe delo," *Evreiskaia entsiklopediia*, 9: 939–40.

failed to persuade the jury, even after a subsequent appeal, to disavow the blood libel. Similar results—acquittal of the Jewish defendant by a jury that nonetheless declined to take a position on the question of ritual murder—obtained in nearly every subsequent trial involving the blood libel in pre-revolutionary Russia. In the infamous 1913 trial of Mendel Beilis in Kiev, jurors acquitted the defendant but found that a ritual murder had in fact been committed.

Though they lie beyond the scope of my investigation, the court trials after the wave of pogroms in Kishinev, Gomel, Odessa, Bialystok, and dozens of other cities between 1903 and 1906 fall into much the same pattern. A team of lawyers led by Sliozberg, Oskar Gruzenberg, and Vinaver set out not only to continue Orshanskii's strategy of suing local communities for damages but to publicly accuse tsarist officials of deliberately fomenting anti-Jewish violence.[56] At the turn of the century, Sliozberg and other Jewish lawyers teamed together to create what they called the Defense Bureau, an organization based in Petersburg that offered free legal services to victims of anti-Jewish discrimination throughout the empire. In the wake of the new wave of pogrom violence, the Defense Bureau not only participated in numerous trials against alleged instigators but enlisted prominent members of the Russian intelligentsia (including Lev Tolstoy, Maxim Gorky, Vladimir Korolenko, and Vladimir Solov'ev) as well as Jewish groups abroad in a campaign to condemn the Russian government.[57]

While the trials and related publicity campaigns did much to expose the horrible violence inflicted on Jews (including over a thousand killings) and made household names of lawyers such as Gruzenberg, Sliozberg, and Vinaver, not a single government official was made to stand trial, and among those convicted of crimes were not only pogromshchiki but dozens of members of Jewish self-defense units. Indeed, the Jewish lawyer Arnold Gillerson found himself subject to prosecution. Incensed that the defendants put on trial for the 1906 pogrom in Bialystok did not include local officials who in his view had instigated the violence, Gillerson addressed the court in Bialystok with a fiery speech denying the charge that the pogrom had erupted spontaneously from conflicts between Christian and Jewish workers. "Such discord cannot exist," he declared, "because the slogan of Christian and Jewish workers is the same: 'Working men of all countries, unite!'—and not 'devour each other,' which is the slogan of the bourgeoisie and the bureaucracy." For this pronouncement Gillerson was tried and convicted of violating the 1891 law against inciting one social group against another—a law originally

---

56. On the trials held after the pogrom in Kishinev, see Edward Judge, *Easter in Kishinev: Anatomy of a Pogrom* (New York, 1992), chap. 6, esp. pp. 109–19.

57. On the Defense Bureau, see Gassenschmidt, *Jewish Liberal Politics*, pp. 8–10; on foreign reactions to the pogroms, see Judge, *Easter in Kishinev*, pp. 84–91.

Figure 29. Mendel Beilis (center) and the prominent Christian and Jewish attorneys who successfully defended him at his 1913 trial for the alleged ritual murder of a Christian child. They include Oskar Gruzenberg (upper left) and the Constitutional Democratic party leader Vasilii Alekseevich Maklakov (upper middle, with incorrect middle initial). (By permission of YIVO Institute for Jewish Research.)

Figure 30. "Commemorating the Beilis trial. Beilis innocent, but the Jews guilty as usual." With a pair of gallows in the background, Tsar Nicholas II (center) addresses the fleeing Mendel Beilis: "Go, Mendel, you're free! Enjoy yourself with your American friends, but in return for your liberation I will get even with your Russian brothers who remain." The elderly man, identified as "the Jewish people," sits handcuffed to a ball and chain labeled "blood libel." (By permission of YIVO Institute for Jewish Research.)

promulgated in response to anti-Jewish violence—and sentenced to a year in prison.[58]

Seen against the full spectrum of Jewish political strategies in fin-de-siècle Russia—intercession by wealthy notables, lobbying and petitions by sub-groups within the Jewish population, a labor movement, and various political parties—the juridical approach pioneered by Orshanskii, Sliozberg, and other Jewish lawyers reveals both innovative and conservative elements. It abandoned the assumption that Jews needed to earn legal rights by demonstrating utility to the state or upright moral character, or by any other ostensible form of "merging" or assimilation. It refused to accept any necessary link between the Jews' status in the surrounding society and internal reform of Jewish society. Even the assumption of a confluence of interests

58. Gillerson's conviction elicited strong but unsuccessful protests from the bar. See *Prot-sess A. I. Gillersona* (St. Petersburg, 1910), esp. pp. 24–25. Gillerson's relationship with the legal profession was stormy: he had once been expelled from the Moscow bar for his vehement protest against the decision to restrict the number of Jewish apprentice lawyers. See Sliozberg, *Dela minuvshikh dnei*, 3: 216.

between Jewish reformers and the tsarist autocracy was jettisoned. If anything, the state was now seen as the source and guardian of the legislation that lay at the heart of Jewish inequality. Like their non-Jewish colleagues in the legal profession, Jewish lawyers understood their calling as that of promoting the rule of law in order to check the autocracy's abuse of power.

At the same time, despite their recognition of the autocracy's restrictive role in Jewish life, Jewish lawyers clung to a thoroughly state-centered strategy for reform, at least until 1907, when Russia's experiment with parliamentary government was sharply curtailed.[59] By employing the legal system to address unlawful discrimination against Jews, they were in effect attempting to use state institutions to combat the state itself. Given the bureaucracy's procedural labyrinths and often profoundly conservative bent, such a strategy inevitably involved considerable compromise. The absence of dramatic successes in Sliozberg's work was noted even by staunch allies like Oskar Gruzenberg:

> Only those who themselves have trod the tortuous path of the *everyday* struggle for justice and for the interests of individual *people,* who have fought on their behalf in courts, in ministries, against the mighty of this world—only they know the price of giving out one's heart in small pieces. [Sliozberg] understood perfectly well that "history" remembers the names only of those who fight on behalf of the distant, not the nearby. And nonetheless the pain and suffering of *isolated individuals* compelled him to decline the entrance ticket to history.[60]

Pronounced at Sliozberg's funeral in Paris in 1937, this eulogy reflected more than just retrospective bitterness at the fact that the Bolshevik Revolution derailed the integrationists' hopes for a European-style civic emancipation in Russia. It offered a response to countless charges of elitism, anachronism, and naiveté leveled at Sliozberg and other partisans of integration, and marked a self-distancing from what appeared to be the adventurist politics of Jewish socialists and Zionists, with their far-off utopias of a workers' paradise or a return en masse to Zion.

It is therefore all the more surprising to discover a rather different assessment of Sliozberg's career by none other than the militant Zionist—and

---

59. After Stolypin's June 1907 coup d'état, Jewish lawyers turned their energies to grassroots reform within Jewish communities, above all in the areas of education and economic reform. They joined forces with and revitalized the Society for Artisan Labor (better known under its Russian acronym, ORT) and the Society for the Spread of Enlightenment among the Jews. As Christoph Gassenschmidt has shown, this was in no way a retreat to a "premodern" politics. See his *Jewish Liberal Politics,* pp. 72–135, and Benjamin Nathans, "The Other Modern Jewish Politics: Integration and Modernity in Fin-de-Siècle Russia," in Zvi Gitelman, ed., *A Century of Modern Jewish Politics* (forthcoming).

60. O. O. Gruzenberg, *Ocherki i rechi* (New York, 1944), p. 159; emphasis in original.

lawyer—Vladimir Jabotinsky.[61] Describing a typically chilly encounter at a Jewish political gathering around 1905, Jabotinsky quotes Sliozberg as saying to him,

> "I envy you—for you the Jewish Question is a dream about the future. But for me a clause in this or that statute concerning the liquor trade is also a big part of the Jewish Question." Sliozberg probably had no idea that that night, after the meeting, we, his opponents, the young people of our camp, had a long conversation among ourselves about this statement. Prosaic, as if issued from a chancellery, and pronounced without passion, it struck us like a thunderbolt. It reminded us of the terrible tragedy of everyday existence, of the fact that in three lines of an official text there was sometimes contained a nearly fatal verdict for hundreds of thousands of people. It reminded us of the enormous idealistic value of realism.[62]

Despite the emergence in fin-de-siècle Russia of Jewish political movements that prided themselves on issuing demands rather than requests, the business of responding to injustice in the daily encounters between Jews and the surrounding society was concentrated to a remarkable extent in the hands of people like Sliozberg. A Jew struggling to maintain residence rights in Kiev or Moscow, seeking to get a son or daughter into an institution of higher education "above the norm," or looking for restitution after an anti-Semitic attack—in short, those with individual here-and-now problems involving non-Jewish society—were unlikely to turn to the Bund or the various Zionist parties for assistance. These groups were fighting for fundamental collective change in an undetermined future.

"The Jewish people, like other peoples," wrote the lawyer M. L. Gol´dshtein, "in addition to their vital problems, have thousands of small needs, concerns, and fears, they have so to say not only their great festivals but also their weekdays. With other peoples these concerns are handled by thousands of bureaucrats, hundreds of chancelleries, departments, and bureaus. With the Jewish people in Russia this entire titanic job . . . was performed by one person—Sliozberg."[63] Despite its exaggerated focus on Sliozberg, this statement fairly captures the day-to-day import of the work performed by Jewish lawyers connected to the Petersburg Jewish elites. However modest the results of the juridical approach, whether in response to crises like pogroms and blood libels or on the more quotidian level of residence permits and

---

61. Jabotinsky studied law in Europe but eventually received a law degree as an extern at the Demidov School of Jurisprudence in Iaroslavl. See Iakov I. Aizenshtat, "Ze'ev Zhabotinskii—iurist," in Mikhail Parkhomovskii, ed., *Evrei v kul´ture russkogo zarubezh´ia: Sbornik statei, publikatsii, memuarov i esse 1919–1939* (Jerusalem, 1992), 1: 420.

62. See Jabotinsky's preface to Sliozberg, *Dela minuvshikh dnei*, 1: x.

63. Gol´dshtein, *Advokatskie portrety*, p. 29.

court appeals, we should not be blind to the profound transformation that occurred in the modus operandi of Russian-Jewish elites under the influence of lawyers like Sliozberg, Gruzenberg, and Vinaver. Their failures were in the end a result of the chasm between the ideals of the judicial reform of 1864 and the reality of the tsarist state, a chasm that would eventually emerge within the legal profession, at great cost to Jewish lawyers themselves.

IDENTITY AND LEGAL CONSCIOUSNESS

"We considered ourselves *Russian Jews* (*russkie evrei*)," Sliozberg wrote in his memoirs, giving deliberate emphasis to a term that neither he nor other Jewish integrationists could take for granted in late imperial Russia.[64] Such emphasis conveys, subtly but unmistakably, the sense that the combination of "Russian" and "Jew" was as much an aspiration as a self-description. Despite its current broad usage in English—a reflection perhaps of the tendency to subsume everything in the Russian Empire (and later the Soviet Union) under the general rubric of "Russian"—the term "Russian Jew" made its first tentative appearance only in the Reform era, that is, three-quarters of a century after the Jews' incorporation into the empire.[65] Even then its use was essentially programmatic, meant to extend the imagined confluence of interest between reform-minded Jews and the tsarist autocracy to include some form of Russian identity, despite the fact that the majority of "Russian" Jews continued to live among non-Russians. That Sliozberg, following the typical usage of the late imperial period, prefaced the Jewish noun with the adjective "Russian" (*russkii*, a term associated with ethnic Russianness) rather than "imperial Russian" (*rossiiskii*, a term associated with the tsarist state and its empire) reflects the relative weakness of supranational identity in the Russian Empire. The term "Russian Jew" also marks a departure from the contemporary practice of describing compound identities through a string of nouns (e.g., "Jew-merchant" [*evrei-kupets*] or "a merchant from the Jews" [*kupets iz evreev*]), instead clearly subordinating one aspect of identity in the form of an adjective.

Sliozberg's self-characterization therefore needs to be read as a kind of credo. To articulate one's identity as a "Russian Jew," as an integrationist, meant not only swimming against a tide of official and social anti-Semitism

---

64. Sliozberg, *Dela minuvshikh dnei,* 2: 301 (emphasis in original).

65. As I note in my introduction, the earliest usage of the term "Russian Jew" I have been able to find occurred in a petition from Evzel Gintsburg and other Jewish merchants to the Jewish Committee in 1856 (RGIA, f. 1269, op. 1, d. 61, l. 4). Several Jewish newspapers of the 1860s and 1870s (e.g., *Razsvet, Sion,* and *Den´,* all published in Odessa) described themselves in their mastheads as "the organ of Russian Jews."

but bearing the additional weight of the Zionist polemic against the "spiritual slavery" of assimilation. For Jewish intellectuals in Russia across the political spectrum, the extreme assimilation of self-styled "Poles of the Mosaic faith" played a crucial role in shaping—often by contrast—ideas about national identity.[66] This, at any rate, was the basis for the Zionists' invidi-
~~s characterization of Sliozberg and other opponents as "Russians of the
~~ faith," a formula they never applied to themselves. The term "Rus-
~~" thus performed the function of distinguishing its bearers from
~~ssively assimilated Polish-Jewish elite, not simply in terms of alle-
~~ one polity or another but in the nature of that allegiance. As
~~argued,

> ⌐here ⌐as a huge divide between Poles of the Mosaic faith and non-Zionist Russian Jews, conditioned not only by the attitudes of the Jews themselves but by the general conditions of Russian and Polish life. We, [even as] non-Zionists, recognized the Jewish nationality. . . . In the life of the all-Russian [*rossiiskoe*] state we, Jews by nationality, were not an alien element, since in Russia there resided many nationalities, united in Russian statehood.[67]

Expanding the comparison, Maksim Vinaver wrote in a similar vein:

> In France, in England, even in Germany . . . the Jews have been transformed into "citizens of the Mosaic faith," and the course of their history has almost completely fused with that of their fellow citizens. Things are different for Jews in the East. There the multitudinous Jewish masses are united not only by bonds of religion but by those of culture, history, and, in part, language.[68]

By girding the Jewish noun with a Russian adjective, the term "Russian Jew" sought to articulate a layered identity in which an inner, national core was suspended in and shielded by an outer framework defined by the state.

To cast the relationship between the Jew and his Russianness in semantic terms alone was clearly not enough; here too Jewish lawyers invoked juridical categories. Refusing to accept demands for exclusive allegiance, Sliozberg wrote:

> To be a good Jew does not prevent one from being a good Russian citizen, and vice versa, to be a proper Russian citizen does not at all interfere with one's remaining a good Jew, believing in Jewish national culture, being devoted to one's people and serving them according to one's strength. Acquisition of Russian culture . . . is entirely consistent with faithfulness to Jewish national culture.[69]

66. Jonathan Frankel makes a similar point with regard to Russian-Jewish socialists and their Polish-Jewish counterparts in the 1890s; see *Prophecy and Politics,* p. 198.

67. Sliozberg, *Dela minuvshikh dnei,* 2: 301–2.

68. Vinaver, *Nedavnee,* p. 257.

69. Sliozberg, *Dela minuvshikh dnei,* 1: 4.

Figure 31. Maksim Vinaver (1862–1926). (By
permission of YIVO Institute for Jewish Research.)

The asymmetries in the preceding passage were carefully chosen. Not only
is "Jew" paired with "Russian citizen," but Jewish culture is specifically described as national, while Russian culture acts as the medium for a civic, legal relationship with a multinational society and the imperial state.[70] Since
the dominant values of educated Russian society, according to Sliozberg, were
imported from Europe, and since the "Russian national idea" was almost exclusively the creation of the state in opposition to the multinational charac-

70. Sliozberg employed these categories more than once in his memoirs (see ibid., pp.
91–92, 2: 301) and asserted elsewhere that Horace Gintsburg "considered himself a Russian
citizen in the best sense of that word" (*Baron G. O. Gintsburg*, p. 58).

ter of the country, what passed for "Russian" culture was in fact more pan-European than national. Even assimilated Jews, Sliozberg insisted, "became 'Russians,' at best, only in the official [*gosudarstvennyi*] sense, not in the national sense."[71] The lawyer and historian Solomon Pozner expressed similar views, urging that "Jews should take part in the civic life" of Russia "while guarding their national-cultural independence."[72] Vinaver, too, was wont to distinguish between two types of nations: those grounded in law and the state (Russia) and those formed by culture and history (the Jews).[73] He in turn was eulogized by the lawyer Moisei Gol´dshtein as "the greatest Russian Jew and a great Russian citizen."[74]

In the call to be "a good Jew and a good Russian citizen" one hears a clear if perhaps unintended echo of Yehudah Leib Gordon's earlier Haskalah maxim, "Be a man in the streets and a Jew at home." But it is important to appreciate the distance separating the two declarations as well. To begin with, where Gordon appealed to the ideal of a universal anational "man," for Sliozberg and his peers this entity has descended somewhat from the stratosphere and taken the more limited form of a transnational "Russian citizen." Furthermore, Gordon's division of identity into public and private components—his virtual domestication of its Jewish aspect ("be a Jew at home")—finds no parallel in Sliozberg and other integrationists, who insisted in word and deed on a public, national Jewishness. If anything, Sliozberg's vision of the "Russian Jew" draws on the Enlightenment categories of "man" and "citizen," adapting them to the specific national and imperial dimensions of tsarist Russia.

The aspiration of acculturated Jews to a compound identity that somehow transcended conventional ethnic and national divisions was of course hardly unique to Russia. Modern European history is replete with poignant and unsettling examples of Jews adopting, or being assigned, cosmopolitan identities even as ethnic and national fault lines hardened. In the last decades of Habsburg rule, acculturated Jews appeared to some as the only Austrians in Austria.[75] A Zionist leader once asserted, in a conversation with Tomáš Masaryk, president of the then newly independent Czechoslovakia, that "among you there are either Czechs or Slovaks; only we, the Jews, are Czechoslovaks."[76] In her analysis of modern anti-Semitism, Hannah Arendt

---

71. Sliozberg, *Dela minuvshikh dnei*, 1: 91–92.

72. Pozner, "Bor´ba za ravnopravie," in Vinaver, *Maksim Moiseevich Vinaver i russkaia obshchestvennost´ nachala XX veka: Sbornik statei* (Paris, 1937), p. 168.

73. Ibid., p. 167.

74. M. L. Gol´dshtein, *Rechi i stat´i* (Paris, 1929), p. 49.

75. See the sources cited in Rozenblit, *Jews of Vienna*, p. 170n.

76. Quoted in Eli Barnavi, *A Historical Atlas of the Jewish People* (New York, 1992), p. viii.

concluded that Jewish elites in Germany and France prized the "grandeur of their consistently European existence."[77] These and similar claims of trans-national identity offer a useful mirror in which to view the condition of ac-culturated Jews in late imperial Russia, who similarly cultivated a sense of civic identity that transcended conventional boundaries. But in contrast to "Aus-trian," "Czechoslovakian," "European," and other historically significant compound identities, *rossiiskii*—the qualities associated with the Romanovs' dynastic empire—provided little emotional resonance for acculturated Jews. No one would have described the Jews of the Russian Empire, or even their secular elites, as embodying the equivalent of an Austrian identity. As if in compensation, however, Sliozberg and other acculturated Jews in the tsarist empire came to regard Russian culture and Russia itself as a transnational phenomenon, a potentially fertile site for a juridically, as opposed to ethni-cally, defined citizenship and therefore a bulwark against assimilation.[78]

Although with hindsight it appears utopian, the vision of a pluralist Rus-sian Empire should be distinguished from the earlier Haskalah utopia that Jacob Katz aptly characterized as the "neutral society."[79] Russia's kalaido-scopic ethnic and religious diversity, together with the density of Jewish set-tlement, allowed Sliozberg and others to seek to secure at one and the same time a neutral society (Russian and therefore transnational) and a nonneutral community (Jewish and national). In fact, there is much in the distinction between a Jewish national identity and a Russian civic identity that fits the typology developed by the nineteenth-century German sociologist Ferdinand Tönnies, in which a distinction is drawn between community (Gemeinschaft) and society (Gesellschaft).[80] Unlike Tönnies, however, Jewish integrationists in late imperial Russia conceived of community as coexisting within, rather than being engulfed by, society—the Jewish noun wrapped in the Russian adjective, as it were.[81]

77. Hannah Arendt, *The Origins of Totalitarianism* (Cleveland, 1969), p. 23; see also p. 58 on the expectation that educated, emancipated Jews would become "exceptional specimens of humanity."

78. The distinction between civic and ethnic bases of citizenship came to define an im-portant school of thought on modern nationalism, beginning with Hans Kohn, *The Idea of Na-tionalism: A Study in Its Origins and Background* (New York, 1944), and more recently with Rogers Brubaker, *Citizenship and Nationhood in France and Germany* (Cambridge, Mass., 1992), and Liah Greenfeld, *Nationalism: Five Roads to Modernity* (Cambridge, Mass., 1993).

79. Jacob Katz, *Out of the Ghetto: The Social Background of Jewish Emancipation, 1770–1870* (New York, 1978), pp. 42–56.

80. Ferdinand Tönnies, *Community and Society*, trans. and ed. Charles P. Loomis (New York, 1963).

81. It is worth recalling that the attempt to legally secure both individual civil and political rights and collective cultural rights of stateless ethnic groups did not gain significant momen-tum until the Paris Peace Conference in 1919. In the decade before the First World War, the

The concept of a juridically, as opposed to ethnically, defined citizenship lay at the heart of the remarkable intersection of legal consciousness and national identity among Jewish lawyers and their fellow integrationists. By making possible the articulation of a civic identity, the legal profession's ideal of the rule of law and the contractual nature of public relationships exercised a profound influence on the integrationists' sense of their place as Jews in Russian society.

---

idea of Jewish minority rights in the Russian Empire—educational, linguistic, and communal—had achieved a profound legitimacy across virtually the entire Jewish political spectrum, but largely on the level of party slogan rather than precise legal formulation. In the interwar period, formal treaties guaranteeing minority rights were signed by the League of Nations and most of the newly created states of Central and Eastern Europe, though not by the Soviet Union, where the Bolsheviks pursued a radically different approach to nationalities policy. See Oscar Janowsky, *The Jews and Minority Rights (1898–1919)* (New York, 1933).

Chapter 9

Ethnicity and Civil Society

The Russian Legal Profession

Long after the liquidation of the tsarist judiciary by the Council of People's Commissars in November 1917, former Russian lawyers, now refugees in Berlin, Paris, or New York, would gather annually on November 20 to commemorate the day in 1864 when their profession, and with it a modern legal system, were born in the Russian Empire.[1] In the face of the Bolsheviks' contemptuous attitude toward the idea of the rule of law—an attitude with deep roots in the prerevolutionary intelligentsia—exiled lawyers continued to celebrate the values of judicial independence and professionalism inspired by the 1864 reform and to mourn the loss in Russia of their collective calling. In a speech to a gathering of the Association of Former Russian Lawyers in Paris in 1929, M. L. Gol´dshtein, an eminent trial lawyer who had defended everyone from pogrom victims to members of the Duma, declared, "We have organized ourselves in the sense of having a fund not only of mutual material assistance but of mutual moral assistance. The past of the Russian legal profession has left priceless values, and in the dark days that we are now experiencing, we can draw on these for spiritual comfort and support."[2] Iakov L´vovich Teitel, a former justice of the peace in Saratov, looked back on the prerevolutionary judiciary as "an oasis in the midst of a desert," while the former Kiev attorney Samuel L. Kucherov, recalling the satisfaction of defending individuals against the tyranny of the tsarist regime, wrote that "the

---

1. Samuel L. Kucherov, *Courts, Lawyers, and Trials under the Last Three Tsars* (New York, 1953), p. 313. The reformed judiciary was inaugurated Nov. 20, 1864. The bar was established slightly later, in 1866, but the former date came to stand for the judicial reform as a whole.

2. Gol´dshtein, *Rechi i stat´i*, p. 12. On Gol´dshtein's legal career, see Stanislav Kel´ner, "Soiuz dlia dostizheniia polnopraviia evreiskogo naroda v Rossii i ego lidery," *Iz glubiny vremen* 7 (1996): 6.

individual person is the greatest value society possesses. . . . To be his knight and defender is the noblest function a man can fulfill."[3]

The tradition of lawyers celebrating the judicial reform's anniversary had begun well before the collapse of tsarism, at a time when the reform was still very much alive, if increasingly under assault. Speaking to the St. Petersburg Juridical Society on November 20, 1897, Maksim Vinaver reflected on the origins of the legal profession in absolutist France and the distinguished legacy upheld by his audience: "Lawyers are not simply master artisans. They are the sacred servants of an order. Conscious of the sacredness of their mission, they rally together in a union, but this union stands out from the ranks of others even by its name: it is neither a guild nor a corporation—that would be too base—but rather it is called an estate [*soslovie*], an 'order,' with the same right as the knighthood that bore this name." Oskar Gruzenberg, the renowned trial attorney who defended Mendel Beilis, among others, echoed this sentiment two decades later at the fiftieth anniversary celebration of the St. Petersburg bar (1866–1916), declaring, "My speech concerns that great, invincible entity, that gathering force which created and creates our history—no, not our history, our life: my speech concerns the estate. Outside the estate a lawyer does not and cannot exist. . . . What pride, what joy, that the Russian bar, having just begun to live, has from the very first day taken its place alongside the oldest European estates."[4]

That these and other Jewish jurists were among the most ardent champions of their profession should perhaps come as no surprise. For secularly educated Jews, the bar appeared to hold the hope of social advancement and integration, of freedom from the constraints of discrimination, such as were unmatched in any other arena of Russian society. Within the horizon of their own experience, in fact, Jewish lawyers in Russia appear to have come closest to their oft-invoked sense of ethnically neutral citizenship in the context of their profession itself, the fraternity of attorneys established in the wake of the judicial reform. For Vinaver, the Russian legal profession represented a kind of civil society in miniature, a voluntary, transparent association open to talent:

> Is [the legal profession] a hereditary caste, a medieval guild, a closed circle of a limited number of immortals? It is none of these. It does not bind anyone for life, like a caste, nor does it encompass one's entire existence, like the medieval guild. It is accessible to anyone who can satisfy criteria that are set in advance. It is a free union of individuals, unlimited in number, who are

3. Jakov Teitel, *Aus meiner Lebensarbeit*, p. 46; Kucherov, *Courts, Lawyers, and Trials*, p. 311.
4. M. M. Vinaver, *Ocherki ob advokature* (St. Petersburg, 1902), p. 3; O. O. Gruzenberg, *O petrogradskoi advokatskoi gromade* (Petrograd, 1916), pp. 3, 13. Throughout this chapter I have translated *advokatura* as either "the legal profession" or "the bar" in order to avoid constant use of a foreign word.

united by a common goal . . . and who have placed themselves under public scrutiny.[5]

Gruzenberg found within the bar "a beneficial atmosphere of scrutiny and criticism . . . that shaped the lawyer's moral outlook, drew him out of narrow-mindedness, and provided him with a public bearing."[6] To be sure, Jewish lawyers were not the only ones to extol the legal profession's independence and openness within the absolutist system. The Polish-born lawyer Vladimir Danilovich Spasovich (Spasowicz), the widely acknowledged doyen of the profession and the chairman of the governing council of the Petersburg bar, celebrated the profession as the "*magnum asylum* for all races and nationalities" in a climate of rising chauvinism.[7] But as their testimonies suggest, Jewish lawyers were especially fervent—and prominent—in their tributes to the profession as a lone citadel of equality and independence. The eminent lawyer Alexander Passover, denied an academic career because of his refusal to adopt Christianity, was fond of telling his protégés, "Instead of converting to Russian Orthodoxy, I converted to the legal profession."[8]

THE RISE OF JEWS IN THE LEGAL PROFESSION

For Jewish graduates of law faculties, the impossibility of an academic career and the near impossibility of government service left the bar as virtually the sole arena in which to apply the knowledge gained in university studies.[9] For this reason, the proportion of Jews in the legal profession grew quickly, a fact that, like the presence of Jews in institutions of higher education, quickly caught the attention of contemporary observers, including the press. In 1876, scarcely a decade after the judicial reform, *Odesskii Vestnik* charged that "in the new system of open courts . . . Jews have greedily thrust themselves into the legal profession, and by this means they cleverly transfer their clients'

---

5. Vinaver, *Ocherki ob advokature,* p. 36.

6. Gruzenberg, *O petrogradskoi advokatskoi gromade,* pp. 4, 7.

7. V. D. Spasovich, *Zastol'nyia rechi V. D. Spasovicha v sobraniiakh sosloviia prisiazhnykh poverennykh okruga S.-Peterburgskoi sudebnoi palaty (1873–1901)* (Leipzig, 1903), p. 51. Spasovich had joined the bar after leaving his position as lecturer at St. Petersburg University in the wake of the government's crackdown on student unrest there in the early 1860s.

8. Quoted in Vinaver, *Nedavnee,* p. 95. Throughout his long career, Passover remained bitter over having been denied an academic career. See L. Aizenberg, "Vidy pravitel'stva v evreiskom voprose," *Evreiskaia Letopis'* 2 (1923): 80.

9. G. Litovskii, "Uchastie russkikh evreev v otpravlenii pravosudiia: Po arkhivnym materialam," *Perezhitoe* 3 (1911): 163–64. Litovskii (pseudonym of Yakov Markovich Gal'pern) describes a brief post-1864 "honeymoon" during which several dozen Jews were hired by the Ministry of Justice as state prosecutors and justices of the peace; by the mid-1870s, the tsarist bureaucracy virtually ceased to hire Jews and withheld promotions from many of those already employed.

money into their own pockets." One Jewish lawyer in Odessa, the newspaper maintained, "having only just acquired Russian literacy," was allegedly making a scandalous annual income of over 1,000 rubles. "Fleecing the ignorant common folk at every turn," *Odesskii Vestnik* continued, "the Jew sells his conscience even in the sanctuary of the court."[10] The commission established to investigate the pogroms of 1881 in Chernigov province stated in its final report that the legal profession there "has been attracting thoroughly unsavory social groups, among whom Jewish lawyers occupy a noticeable position," and complained of several instances in which Jews had "fleeced their simple-minded clients."[11] The tsarist government was also quick to develop doubts about the role of Jews in the reformed judiciary, though its concerns were initially limited to restricting Jewish influence in the new jury system. A decree of 1877, for example, forbade non-Christians to serve as foremen of juries in the nine western provinces (the areas of greatest Jewish settlement in the Pale), and in 1884 the government required that the proportion of Jews on any given jury not exceed their proportion of the population of the local district (*uezd*).[12]

As the proportion of Jews in the legal profession continued to climb, the nature of public and official concern shifted. By 1885, Jews accounted for 13 percent (201 out of a total of 1,549) of all lawyers and 19 percent (135 out of 710) of all apprentice lawyers.[13] These figures applied to the empire as a whole; in some areas they were considerably higher. By 1886, for example, Jews accounted for 26 percent of all lawyers in the Warsaw circuit, 30 percent in the Odessa circuit, and 49 percent in the city of Odessa.[14] By 1888, in the Petersburg bar—the most prestigious and influential branch of all—Jews (not counting converts) constituted 21 percent of all lawyers and 30 percent of all apprentice lawyers.[15] Moreover, Jews were present in the

10. "Evreiskaia advokatura v uezdnykh mirovykh uchrezhdeniiakh," *Odesskii Vestnik*, May 18, 1876.

11. *Trudy Chernigovskoi komissii po evreiskomu voprosu* (Chernigov, 1881), pp. 78–79. For similar impressions of Jews as private and underground attorneys, see Neuberger, "'Shysters' or Public Servants?" p. 304.

12. In addition, in 1879 non-Christians were barred altogether from juries in cases involving crimes against the Christian faith or church rules. See L. B. [L. M. Bramson], "Sudebnaia reforma i evrei," *Voskhod*, nos. 11–12 (1889), pp. 7–8; and Pravitel'stvuiushchii Senat, *Sobranie uzakonenii i rasporiazhenii pravitel'stva*, no. 74 (St. Petersburg, 1884), art. 547.

13. *Vysochaishe uchrezhdennaia komissiia dlia peresmotra zakonopolozhenii po sudebnoi chasti*, 3: 34–35.

14. "Evrei—prisiazhnye poverennye," *Novorossiiskii Telegraf*, Aug. 27, 1886.

15. Z, "Za mesiats (Iuridicheskaia khronika)," *Zhurnal grazhdanskogo i ugolovnogo prava*, no. 6 (June 1889), p. 146. I have found no data on the number of apostates from Judaism in the legal profession. Persons who warned of Jewish dominance, however, commonly asserted that because of the considerable number of converts, data on religious affiliation failed to convey the full extent of Jewish control.

highest ranks of the profession: in 1880 Passover was elected to the governing council of the Petersburg bar, and by the mid-1880s half of the dozen senior lawyers chosen to lead seminars for apprentice lawyers were Jews.[16]

The growing prominence of Jews in the profession met with increasingly aggressive attacks in anti-Semitic newspapers such as *Novoe Vremia* and *Novorossiiskii Telegraf,* which argued that Jewish lawyers were forming a "kahal" within the bar in an attempt to take over the profession:

> An entire horde of jurists of the Mosaic law are swarming into the legal profession, since other paths are blocked. It is not difficult to see where this will lead: if Jewry's flood is not restrained in a timely manner, then in a very short time the bar will be entirely filled with Jews and this profession will take its place alongside that of usury and other such national Jewish "institutions." . . . Christians will then have to flee from the estate.[17]

Lawyers, so the argument went, had already squandered their initially positive reputation by taking sides in cases simply according to who offered the highest fees, and this practice had developed precisely "since the time when Jews achieved a dominant position in the soslovie."[18]

The initial enthusiasm for lawyers, at least in some quarters of the intelligentsia, derived primarily from their outspoken courtroom defense of arrested revolutionaries in the 1870s.[19] Perhaps the most celebrated political trial of the late imperial period pitted the tsarist autocracy against the populist Vera Zasulich, who in 1878 had shot and wounded the military governor of St. Petersburg after he flogged a political prisoner. At her trial, Zasulich's lawyers created a sensation, amplified by extensive press coverage, when they persuaded a jury to acquit her. For the government, of course, this display of political independence on the part of defense attorneys was an unexpected and highly undesirable effect of the judicial reform. In the wake of Zasulich's acquittal, the Ministry of Justice decided that future po-

---

16. On Passover, see Spasovich, *Zastol'nye rechi,* p. 25; on the seminars, see *Vestnik Evropy,* no. 5 (1888), p. 421.

17. "Kagal v molodoi advokature," *Novorossiiskii Telegraf,* Feb. 22, 1885. Despite the insinuation that Jewish lawyers might be following their own "Mosaic law," this point was not explicitly developed.

18. "Ogranichenie chisla evreev v prisiazhnoi advokature," *Novorossiiskii Telegraf,* June 17, 1886. Another issue of the same newspaper (Aug. 23, 1887) claimed that "it is hardly necessary to hold forth on the influence of the Jewish element on our still young but already powerfully corrupted legal profession. Everyone is fully aware that it is precisely the Jews who cultivate the type of lawyer whom society treats with deserved disdain, the wheeler-dealer type, for whom there is no such thing as black and white, but only sky-high fees for which he is ready to crucify truth and conscience and anything else several times a day."

19. On the role of the bar in political trials in the 1870s, see Kucherov, *Courts, Lawyers, and Trials,* pp. 212–25.

litical trials would be held behind closed doors. But this was not enough. By the mid-1880s, the government was determined to chip away at the autonomy of the profession itself by regulating the admission process.

Jewish lawyers, one should note, did not play a significant part in any of the celebrated political trials of the 1870s and 1880s. Nor should the bright halo surrounding those lawyers who became famous for defending opponents of the autocracy obscure the fact that in Russia, as elsewhere, lawyers were subject to broad criticism for greed and lack of scruples. On the left, the satirist Mikhail Saltykov-Shchedrin attacked lawyers for being interested "not in the question as to whether a crime was really perpetrated but in the question as to whether there are some excuses for it in the law and as to how the evidence presented can be refuted."[20] On the right, Dostoevsky charged that in many cases, a lawyer "deliberately defends, and tries to acquit, a guilty person. . . . A lawyer is actually never able to act according to his conscience. He is a man doomed to dishonesty. . . . Finally—and this is the most important and serious matter—this sad situation has actually been somehow legalized by someone and something, so that it is not considered as being in any sense a deviation but, on the contrary, as a most normal state of affairs."[21] Many equally prominent names could be added to the list of Russian critics of lawyers and the law, from the Slavophiles through Herzen, Tolstoy, and Lenin.[22]

Ever since the jurist B. A. Kistiakovskii concluded in the aftermath of the 1905 revolution that "the Russian intelligentsia's legal consciousness is at an extremely low level of development," it has been widely accepted that the formal demands of legal procedure did not find especially hospitable soil in Russia.[23] Among conservatives and radicals alike, personal and moral rather than legal categories tended to dominate debates about social and political justice. Even before Kistiakovskii, Vinaver had observed in 1902 that "juridical thought is still foreign to our society. In opposition to the chain of juridical reasoning with its particular ways of guaranteeing the fullest and most expedient realization of justice, society insists on its confused, unexamined *feeling* for justice . . .—a feeling that may serve as a point of departure, but not at all as the final factor in the juridical process."[24] It was precisely this atti-

---

20. Quoted ibid., p. 172.

21. Dostoevsky, *Diary of a Writer*, quoted in Kucherov, *Courts, Lawyers, and Trials*, pp. 171–172.

22. For a survey of critical Russian attitudes toward law and legal culture (and to a lesser extent lawyers), see Andrzej Walicki, *Legal Philosophies of Russian Liberalism* (Oxford, 1987), pp. 9–104.

23. B. A. Kistiakovskii, "V zashchitu prava: Intelligentsiia i pravosoznanie," in *Vekhi: Sbornik statei o russkoi intelligentsii,* 2d ed. (1909; rpt. St. Petersburg, 1990), p. 126.

24. Vinaver, *Ocherki ob advokature,* p. 10; emphasis in original. Sliozberg, as we have seen, criticized the Jewish masses for a similar lack of legal consciousness.

tude that inspired in much of educated Russian society, as one study puts it, "a distaste for members of the judicial profession as officials cold and un-Russian in their rational adherence to legal science."[25]

In the Ministry of Justice, where the bar was viewed with suspicion for its unprecedented professional and increasingly political independence, proposals to scale back the judicial reform of 1864 had been circulating since the mid-1870s.[26] Not only were political trials moved behind closed doors; the government also became interested in the bar's internal activities, particularly the supervision—or lack thereof—of apprentice lawyers and the standards used for admission to full membership. The latter decision, based on professional and ethical criteria, was in the hands of elected bar councils (where such existed). In essence, the government was caught between, on the one hand, its desire to stem the rapid and unregulated growth of the legal profession and, on the other, its reluctance to grant the bar the necessary authority, in the form of a professional monopoly, to accomplish this task.

Many senior lawyers shared the view that the apprenticeships lacked rigor and were a poor training ground for future lawyers. At the same time, jealous of their unusual degree of corporate autonomy, they were loath to see control over admission to the bar transferred from the profession to the state. As the sine qua non of professional independence, the factor that literally determined who and what the legal profession would be, the issue of control over admission was to prove the "main theater of war" in the ongoing struggle between the Ministry of Justice and representatives of the bar.[27]

THE GENESIS OF ETHNIC RESTRICTIONS

The debate over admission to the bar was complex and often arcane; in theory, it concerned matters that had nothing to do with Jews or the "Jewish Question." And yet, in a remarkable chain of events, Jews and control over admission became inextricably and fatefully bound up with each other.

No sooner had the Ministry of Justice announced the formation in 1885 of a commission under the chairmanship of G. A. Evreinov to overhaul the

25. Wortman, *Development of a Russian Legal Consciousness*, p. 288. Non-Russians were in fact a significant presence in the legal profession. Spasovich, a Pole, was a lightening rod for xenophobic criticism of the bar. See Walicki, *Legal Philosophies*, pp. 76–77.

26. In the following summary of debates about post-1864 reform of the legal profession, I draw upon William Pomeranz, "The Emergence and Development of the Russian *Advokatura*: 1864–1905," Ph.D. dissertation, University of London, 1990, esp. pp. 169–223. I gratefully acknowledge the author's permission to cite this work.

27. I. V. Gessen, *Istoriia russkoi advokatury*, vol. 1: *Advokatura, obshchestvo i gosudarstvo, 1864–1914* (Moscow, 1914), p. 286.

rules by which the legal profession governed itself than voices began to be heard calling for restrictions on admission of Jews to the bar.[28] *Novorossiiskii Telegraf* led the way, approvingly reporting rumors in 1886 and again in 1887 that the commission was planning to impose a quota on Jews in the profession, and providing statistical data on the percentages of Jews in various judicial circuits. The rumors had caused "a sensation among lawyers."[29]

But the press was not alone. For the first time, voices from within the legal profession openly supported restrictions on Jewish colleagues, less for their supposedly underhanded dealings with gullible clients than allegedly to protect the profession from encroachments by the state.[30] In 1886 *Sudebnaia Gazeta* (Court Gazette) printed a letter to the editor from a lawyer complaining that Jewish lawyers were ruining the reputation of their Christian colleagues and of the courts as well. This "parasitic element," the letter concluded, "must be eliminated . . . in order to maintain the high place given to the courts by the judicial reforms of Emperor Alexander II."[31] Two years later a committee of apprentice lawyers in Moscow, responding to the influx of Jews into its ranks, urged its senior colleagues in the bar to impose a quota.[32] An alarmed law student responded in a letter to *Odesskii Listok* (Odessa Page) that a university education ought to be assurance enough that Jewish lawyers shared the convictions and morals of their Russian colleagues. Although no action had yet been taken in Moscow, the student wrote, "we must nevertheless register the fact that the question was raised. And it was raised not in government circles, where this or that regulation is promulgated for political reasons of state, but by the corporation of lawyers, educated people who only recently left the university family."[33]

Evreinov's unexpected promotion to a ministerial position brought his commission's work to an abrupt end before it could produce a final report. But the diverse political and professional agendas for reform of the bar's admission procedures had already begun to converge. The decisive push came

28. On the Evreinov Commission, see ibid., p. 335.

29. "Ogranichenie chisla evreev v prisiazhnoi advokature," *Novorossiiskii Telegraf,* June 17, 1886, and "Uchastie evreev v prisiazhnoi advokature po novoi reforme," ibid., Aug. 23, 1887. Similar rumors for the period 1886–88 surfaced in *Russkaia Mysl′*, no. 3 (1888), p. 197.

30. In an article published in the early 1870s Orshanskii referred to complaints among Moscow lawyers of excessive numbers of Jews in their ranks, but other than this passing reference I have found no evidence of discussion of restrictions against Jews by members of the legal profession before the late 1880s. The article is reprinted in Orshanskii, *Russkoe zakonodatel′stvo o evreiakh,* pp. 233–34.

31. *Sudebnaia Gazeta,* no. 23 (1886), pp. 10–11.

32. Between 1885 and 1887, the percentage of Jews among apprentice lawyers in Moscow had risen from 3 to 17 percent. See Gessen, *Istoriia russkoi advokatury,* 1: 280.

33. Student-Iurist, "Pis′mo v redaktsiiu," *Odesskii Listok,* no. 27 (1888).

TABLE 13. Lawyers and Apprentice Lawyers
in St. Petersburg Judicial Circuit, 1888, by Religious Affiliation

Religion	Lawyers		Apprentices	
	#	%	#	%
Russian Orthodox	160	54	109	41
Jewish	62	21	104	39
Roman Catholic	38	13	34	13
Lutheran	36	12	17	7
All religions	296	100%	264	100%

SOURCE: *Zhurnal grazhdanskogo i ugolovnogo prava*, no. 6 (1889), p. 146.

in 1889, when for the first time the Petersburg bar included in its published annual report a section on the religious affiliations of its members and apprentice members (see Table 13).

Within weeks of the data's publication, Alexander Passover, the most prominent Jewish member of the profession, resigned in protest from the St. Petersburg Governing Council.[34] At two stormy meetings of the General Assembly of the Petersburg bar on April 16 and 30, 1889, some members demanded "radical measures" to curtail the admission of Jews, while others argued that information on religious affiliation should never have been published in the first place. In a speech to the assembly responding to the latter charge, V. D. Spasovich, who as chairman of the council had been responsible for the decision to publish the data, defended the move as a necessary step to induce the bar to take the Jewish issue into its own hands and thereby avoid state intervention and the loss of professional autonomy that would go with it.[35] If present trends continued, he noted, within a few years Jews would comprise over half the capital's apprentice lawyers, and not long thereafter, of the profession itself. Responding to the position taken by the liberal journal *Russkaia Mysl'* that of all the various estates the Bar had the greatest obligation to follow "strict logic and principled rigor," Spasovich argued, "Simple logic may say, 'what concern is it of yours if one particular group grows in relation to another?' I cannot follow such logic. We

34. Ginzburg, *Amolike Peterburg*, p. 109.

35. Spasovich, *Zastol'nyia rechi*, p. 51 (speech of Apr. 30, 1889); *Zhurnal grazhdanskogo i ugolovnogo prava* no. 6 (June 1889), p. 145. There is scattered contemporary testimony that other regional branches of the bar—e.g., in Kharkov—had informally taken it upon themselves to limit or obstruct Jewish enrollment before 1889. See, e.g., *Evreiskaia entsiklopediia*, 1: 470; L. B., "Sudebnaia reforma i evrei," p. 8; and *Zhurnal grazhdanskogo i ugolovnogo prava*, no. 3 (1890), p. 146.

Figure 32. Vladimir Danilovich Spasovich (Spasowicz) (1829–1906).

are dealing with a colossal problem, one which cannot be solved according to the rules of cliché liberalism."[36]

The full import of these words can be measured only when one bears in mind that Spasovich himself was a self-described liberal, a leading representative of the reform-minded intelligentsia who only a few years before had closed a speech to the Petersburg bar with a ringing toast "to those people who stand firmly for progress, for liberalism!"[37] He was also a frequent guest at Horace Gintsburg's table.[38] Because of his prominence in the legal

36. *Russkaia Mysl'*, no. 3 (1888), p. 197; Spasovich, *Zastol'nyia rechi*, p. 53 (speech of Apr. 30, 1889).

37. Spasovich, *Zastol'nyia rechi*, p. 29 (speech of May 5, 1881).

38. Ginzburg, *Historishe verk*, 2: 141.

world—Spasovich liked to remind his listeners that he had helped draft the judicial reform—and because he resists easy categorization, his defense of the publication of data on religious affiliation deserves special attention.

While according to Spasovich the presence of individual non-Russians, whether Jews, Poles, or Germans, posed no particular threat to the legal profession,

> if, as a consequence of the artificial influx of an alien ethnic group, the composition [of the profession] changes fundamentally . . . , if it is in danger of changing from Russian to Jewish, then I am obliged to see to it that this sort of change does not occur. I must do so not from my own personal point of view, but from a more elevated, public one. I would justify this resistance to the sudden influx of Jews in terms of the Jews' own interests. This was a good corporation, this was the *magnum asylum* for you too. If you quickly overflow it, the state may not tolerate this and may abolish . . . the council. For this very reason no councils were established in Odessa. Und das Kind wird mit dem Bade ausgeschüttet [and the baby gets thrown out with the bath]. . . . We may lose our elected justices of the peace, perhaps all justices of the peace, perhaps juries as well. Our corporation's councils are for the time being its only stronghold. . . . Perhaps these too will be abolished. For now we have to be acrobats, to maintain our balance on the wire, to be opportunists not for the sake of growing but in order simply to preserve our current station and somehow prevent the diminution of what we inherited from our predecessors.[39]

Spasovich was under no illusions about the virtual impossibility of employment in the academy and the state bureaucracy for Jewish lawyers and their resulting overrepresentation in the legal profession. But given the recent reactionary turn of official policy, he argued, there was little hope that these circumstances would change. Again addressing the Jews in his audience directly, he urged,

> Do what we Poles do. . . . We direct our young generation not to law departments but to secondary and vocational schools, where they can build careers without leaving their home territory. You don't have a home territory, you are a race; try to ensure that your generation prepares itself for useful careers in those arenas to which no state law can deny you access. How is one to reduce the flood of the law school proletariat into the ranks of apprentice lawyers? By having the government set a percentage? I am against this method. Should the

39. Spasovich, *Zastol'nyia rechi*, pp. 51–54 (speech of Apr. 30, 1889). One is reminded in this context of the assertion by the eminent liberal German historian Friedrich Meinecke, in the midst of a critical discussion of anti-Semitism in imperial Germany, that "the Jews, who are inclined to make careless use of a temporarily favorable political climate, had occasionally given cause for offense since their full emancipation. They contributed greatly to that gradual devaluing and discrediting of liberal thought which began at the close of the nineteenth century": *Die deutsche Katastrophe* (Wiesbaden, 1965 [1946]), p. 29.

council set it? The council is your executive and judicial power—and nothing more. Only the General Assembly of Lawyers, not the council, can set general norms. If it does not take this matter into its own hands, then . . . the Damoclean sword of government-enforced quotas on admission will fall upon us. This is a mind-numbing, difficult question. . . . Let us resolve this threatening issue peacefully and without offense to anyone![40]

For Spasovich, then, the future autonomy of the profession required the bar, by its own internal democratic means, to remove the temptation for the state to take unilateral action regarding the flood of aspiring lawyers, of whom an alarming percentage were Jews. It bears repeating, however, that in principle the issue of admission and the presence of Jews in the profession were entirely distinct. By conflating them, Spasovich aimed at what appeared to be a strategic compromise: to preserve part of the legacy of 1864, professional autonomy, at the expense of another, an admissions policy based strictly on individual training and merit.

Spasovich had numerous and diverse links to Jewish colleagues. His relationship with Passover was known to be testy.[41] At the 1880 banquet marking Passover's election to the Petersburg council—a move that had met with considerable resistance, including calls to strip the bar of its corporative privileges[42]—Spasovich congratulated the profession for demonstrating its "cosmopolitanism." He also noted that Russia faced a more difficult task in dealing with the Jews than it had with the Poles, since the Jews, left to their own devices, would exploit the peasants and monopolize trade. His endorsement of equal Jewish rights, moreover, could not have entirely pleased Passover and other Jews present: "The same holds in relations among ethnic groups as in the lives of individuals. You find someone distasteful—don't live together, don't interact, don't become relatives, but you have no right to refuse admission to that person wherever people are admitted according to their merits."[43] And yet throughout his career Spasovich was more actively sympathetic to the Jewish plight than the vast majority of his professional colleagues, or for that matter than the Russian intelligentsia as a whole.[44] In 1882 he publicly condemned the pogroms that had begun the previous year and criticized the Russian intelligentsia for their silence on the subject. Later he successfully defended before the State Senate the right of Jewish phar-

40. Spasovich, *Zastol'nyia rechi*, pp. 54–55.

41. Vinaver, for whom both men were mentors, testifies (*Nedavnee*, p. 85) that "there was a kind of elemental antagonism" between the two.

42. Gessen, *Istoriia russkoi advokatury*, 1: 279.

43. Spasovich, *Zastol'nyia rechi*, p. 26 (speech of Apr. 27, 1880).

44. On the liberal Russian intelligentsia and their attitudes toward Jews and the "Jewish Question," see Maor, *She'elat ha-yehudim*, pp. 1–97, and Klier, *Imperial Russia's Jewish Question*, pp. 370–83.

macists to own drugstores in Petersburg, and in 1900, toward the end of his life, he took a leading role in the defense of David Blondes against charges of ritual murder in Vilna.[45] Even a close observer of the debates on Jews in the bar such as Sliozberg, while inclined to blame Spasovich for succumbing to a government strategy of pitting national minorities against each other (in this case, Poles against Jews), insisted that his motives were not anti-Semitic.[46] Vinaver, who along with several other Jews served as an apprentice lawyer under Spasovich's patronage, dedicated his first book to him; Gruzenberg praised him as "the great unsurpassed teacher" of the profession.[47]

If Spasovich's justification for discriminating against Jews in the bar was the seemingly higher goal of preserving professional independence from the state, the same cannot be said for many of his colleagues. In a June 1889 report on trends in the legal profession, the journal of the prestigious St. Petersburg Juridical Society fairly begged the government to institute a quota on admission of Jews to the bar. Here, in contrast to Spasovich, the emphasis was on the alleged internal threat posed by Jewish lawyers to the profession. If one took into account the presence of converted Jews, the journal argued, then the Petersburg bar was already half Jewish. "This state of affairs," it continued, "is of course abnormal if only because in the capital of the Russian tsardom there ought not to be a legal profession composed of foreigners, or more precisely, of 'those professing a different faith,' since Jews do not have a fatherland." But more important, because of the Jews' "well-known solidarity among themselves," it was becoming "physically impossible for a Russian lawyer to compete with them."

> Here, as everywhere, free competition between Jews and Christians is dangerous and even simply impossible, and this impossibility is grounded in racial characteristics with which one cannot avoid reckoning. A person is not to blame for having been born with blond hair nor is he to blame if, for historical reasons, he has a certain character, certain inclinations and abilities. Historical factors have fostered in the Jewish people a resourcefulness that stops at nothing, such a love for grubbing and such an awareness of commonalities of interest that one cannot place in servitude to Jews those people in whom other historical factors have not fostered those qualities. The task of government is to come to the aid of such people, to prevent the exploitation of one by the

---

45. Spasovich, *Zastol'nyia rechi*, p. 31 (speech of May 2, 1882); *Nedel'naia Khronika Voskhoda*, Apr. 15, 1882, p. 419, and Dec. 14, 1882, p. 1368; *Evreiskaia entsiklopediia*, 4: 663.

46. Sliozberg, *Dela minuvshikh dnei*, 1: 208–10.

47. Vinaver, *Ocherki ob advokature*, after title page; Gruzenberg, *O petrogradskoi advokatskoi gromade*, p. 7. In their respective memoirs, Vinaver and Gruzenberg praise Spasovich as the pillar of the legal profession and strangely overlook his involvement in the issue of anti-Jewish quotas. In fact, Vinaver specifically portrays Spasovich as a steadfast opponent of any and all ethnic restrictions in the bar, despite irrefutable evidence to the contrary. See Vinaver, *Nedavnee*, pp. 1–49, esp. 44, and the conclusion of this chapter.

other. . . . The government has not only the right but the duty to limit Jewish exploitation.[48]

The Darwinian, or perhaps one should say Lamarckian, pessimism inherent in this discussion (and similar voices could be found in other forums) is all the more striking given the elite status and education of the Russian lawyers it sought to defend. In fact, the journal of the St. Petersburg juridical society extended this reasoning to other elite segments of Russian civil society: "One or the other—either we recognize that Jews in Russia ought to have the same rights as Russians, in which case there would be no need to limit their admission to educational institutions, or, recognizing the danger of their predominance, we also limit their numbers in all professions that require a special higher education."[49]

The word "competition" comes up frequently in attacks on Jewish lawyers from within the profession. It is therefore tempting to suggest that ethnic and religious rivalries within the professions in Russia were driven primarily by competition for employment and status. But as critics of quotas pointed out again and again, the facts indicated otherwise. In contrast to the competition for the limited number of slots for university students, there was no upper limit ("zero sum") on membership in the bar. Indeed, the evidence points to a severe shortage of lawyers in the Russian Empire: in 1889, the year Spasovich released data on religious affiliation, there were fewer than 3,000 lawyers in a country of over 100 million people, or one lawyer for every 35,000 people.[50] And unlike many previous arguments for limiting the Jewish presence in the legal profession, the June 1889 report of the St. Petersburg Juridical Society rejected the idea that Jews were inordinately responsible for the bar's low moral reputation. Among their colleagues in the capital, it noted, Jewish lawyers were known for being "far more attentive to the interests of their clients than non-Jews."[51] Thus we should understand "competition" not simply in terms of supply and demand but of perceived ethnic and cultural dominance.

Spasovich's urging notwithstanding, divisions of opinion within the General Assembly of Lawyers in Petersburg prevented an internal resolution of the now burning issue of Jewish quotas. An appeal by Spasovich in October 1889 to the minister of justice, N. A. Manasein, to help reduce the flow of

48. *Zhurnal grazhdanskogo i ugolovnogo prava,* no. 6 (1889), pp. 147–49.

49. Ibid., p. 154.

50. In 1889 there were 1,772 lawyers and 1,069 apprentice lawyers in the Russian Empire. This calculation does not take into account "private attorneys" (*chastnye poverennye*) and "scriveners" (*striapchie*), whose numbers are uncertain. See M. N. Gernet, ed., *Istoriia russkoi advokatury,* vol. 2: *Soslovnaia organizatsiia advokatury, 1864–1914* (Moscow, 1916), pp. 3–4.

51. *Zhurnal grazhdanskogo i ugolovnogo prava,* no. 6 (1889), p. 148.

TABLE 14. Jewish Lawyers and Apprentice Lawyers
in Selected Judicial Circuits, Russian Empire, 1890 and 1895

	1890			1895		
		Jews			Jews	
Circuit	Total	#	%	Total	#	%
St. Petersburg						
Lawyers	303	68	22	419	57	14
Apprentices	270	115	43	262	99	38
Warsaw						
Lawyers	400	80	20	495	75	15
Apprentices	156	79	51	207	91	44
Odessa						
Lawyers	141	43	30	179	30	17
Apprentices	190	130	68	155	81	52
Moscow						
Lawyers	346	16	5	375	15	4
Apprentices	n.a.	n.a.	n.a.	n.a.	n.a.	n.a.
Kharkov						
Lawyers	167	9	5	174	7	4
Apprentices	n.a.	n.a.	n.a.	n.a.	n.a.	n.a.
Saratov						
Lawyers	61	1	2	87	0	0
Apprentices	n.a.	n.a.	n.a.	n.a.	n.a.	n.a.
Kazan						
Lawyers	61	4	7	72	3	4
Apprentices	n.a.	n.a.	n.a.	n.a.	n.a.	n.a.

SOURCE: *Vysochaishe uchrezdennaia komissiia dlia peresmotra zakonopolozhenii po sudebnoi chasti: Ob"iasnitel'naia zapiska k proektu novoi redaktsii uchrezhdeniia sudebnykh ustanovlenii* (St. Petersburg, 1900), 3: 34–36.

Jews into the bar by lifting the ministry's unofficial internal ban on hiring Jews fell on deaf ears.[52] Manasein instead obtained Tsar Alexander III's approval in November for a temporary administrative decree that required every admission of a non-Christian to the bar to receive the personal approval of the minister of justice. No explicit explanation for this restriction was offered, but the fact that it was presented as an amendment to the section of the judicial reform dealing with the ethical requirements for admission to the bar amounted to an official endorsement of the view that the morals of Jewish lawyers were less than satisfactory.

52. Sliozberg, *Dela minuvshikh dnei*, 1: 210.

For Spasovich, the November 1889 decree represented a resounding defeat. By granting personal discretionary powers to the minister of justice, it increased state control over admission to the bar far more than quotas would have done, thereby setting a dangerous precedent. And like many "temporary" administrative measures in late imperial Russia, the November 1889 decree remained in force, apart from a brief lapse during the upheavals of 1904–7, until the February 1917 Revolution. Its effect on the relative and absolute presence of Jews in the bar was felt within several years (see Table 14).

Between 1889 and 1896, not a single Jewish candidate for admission to the bar was approved by the minister of justice, and between 1896 and 1904 only 15 Jewish candidates were so approved.[53] Vinaver, Sliozberg, Gruzenberg and other Jews were forced to remain apprentice lawyers for a decade and a half or more instead of the normal five years, even as their publications and trial performances achieved national prominence. Jokes began to circulate among Jewish lawyers about tombstones reading "Here lies an apprentice lawyer."[54]

Within the legal profession, those who had pushed for quotas quickly moved to broaden the effects of the November 1889 decree. In the following year one Moscow lawyer demanded that the official registry of bar members list Jews by their Yiddish names rather than the Russian versions.[55] The Odessa bar summarily expelled thirty-two Jewish apprentice lawyers from its ranks.[56] In 1890 the Moscow bar council voted to stop accepting Jews as apprentice lawyers, while the Petersburg council voted to require that Jewish apprentice lawyers be given a maximum of three years (rather than the usual five) to gain admission to the bar, after which they would be expelled from the profession. Both these votes were overturned in 1895 upon appeal to the Senate (where the November 1889 decree was held to apply only to applicants for membership at the bar, not for apprenticeships), but at least in Moscow no Jews were accepted as apprentice lawyers during the intervening five years.[57]

PROFESSION, CIVIL SOCIETY, AND EMPIRE

The restriction on the admission of non-Christians to the bar introduced in November 1889 did little to address the various diagnoses of the profession's

---

53. Pomeranz, "Emergence and Development of the Russian *Advokatura*," pp. 79–80.
54. Vinaver, *Nedavnee*, p. 260.
55. Gessen, *Istoriia russkoi advokatury*, 1: 281.
56. *Russkaia Mysl'*, no. 4 (1890), p. 212.
57. S. L. Kucherov, "Evrei v russkoi advokature," in *Kniga o russkom evreistve*, vol. 1 (New York, 1960), p. 407, and idem, *Courts, Lawyers, and Trials*, p. 275. In addition, as part of its efforts to curtail the power of the zemstva, the government ruled in 1890 that Jewish private attorneys could not appear in the new district appeals courts (*uezdnye s"ezdy*) except by personal permission of the minister of justice. See *Evreiskaia entsiklopediia*, 1: 471.

wider malaise, whether those offered by the government or by members of the bar itself. The first thing that strikes one in the aftermath of 1889 is the extent to which public debates about ethnicity and the legal profession not only did not subside but intensified. Moreover, precisely because the 1889 decree was fashioned outside the normal legislative channels, groups of jurists continued to search, officially and unofficially, for a more durable set of regulations regarding not only the status of Jewish lawyers but the bar's entire system of apprenticeships and its right to self-government. Although none of the recommendations arrived at by these groups was ever implemented, they nonetheless offer a valuable glimpse into the spectrum of contemporary legal opinion.

After the abortive Evreinov Commission of 1885, the next comprehensive attempt to revise the judicial statutes of 1864 occurred under the aegis of Minister of Justice Nikolai Valerianovich Murav´ev (1894–1905), a man whom Alexander Passover once described as a "sophist, who takes the law into consideration only insofar as it corresponds to his personal advantage."[58] The Murav´ev Commission counted among its twenty-four members leading jurists such as Spasovich and Anatolii Fedorovich Koni, the St. Petersburg University law professor N. S. Tagantsev, and Murav´ev's eventual successor, I. G. Shcheglovitov.[59] The overwhelming majority of members agreed that the large number of Jews in the bar had a "damaging influence" on the profession, and that quotas on admission of Jews were a necessary response. Although Koni and two other members argued against quotas, only one— V. O. Liustikh (a non-Jew), the head of the Petersburg bar—refused to endorse the majority's recommendations.[60]

In justifying the imposition of quotas, the Murav´ev Commission pointed to the allegedly low moral standards of Jewish lawyers as well as the extent of their influence in the legal profession. Among the factors governing human behavior, it noted, the most important was conscience, which found its most consistent expression in religion. The commission was therefore particularly concerned to uphold what it saw as Christian morality in the burgeoning public arena, where new and unfamiliar forces were emerging:

---

58. The Murav´ev Commission produced the *Vysochaishe uchrezhdennaia komissiia dlia peresmotra zakonopolozhenii po sudebnoi chasti*. A similar (at least in terms of Jewish issues) but shorter report was published under the preceding minister of justice, M. V. Krasovskii: *Vysochaishe uchrezhdennaia pri Ministerstve iustitsii komissiia* (St. Petersburg, 1897). For Passover's characterization of Murav´ev, see Aizenberg, "Vidy pravitel´stva v evreiskom voprose," *Evreiskaia Letopis´* 2 (1923): 77.

59. For some reason Spasovich's name is not given in the official list of Murav´ev Commission members, but his name, pronouncements, and votes appear in the commission's protocols.

60. *Vysochaishe uchrezhdennaia komissiia dlia peresmotra zakonopolozhenii po sudebnoi chasti*, 3: 31–42.

One cannot ignore the danger for state and society that can result from the subordination of an entire institution to points of view alien to Christian morality. This danger, so easy to confront in government institutions by simply barring the admission of non-Christians above a certain quantity . . . , presents a particularly serious problem for those public institutions that are accessible to all persons who can satisfy certain legally established requirements. To such institutions unquestionably belongs the legal estate, for which the danger of being flooded with morally unreliable individuals is compounded by the practice of estate self-government. Any group of individuals, having achieved numerical predominance, acquires thereby a dominant position in the estate.[61]

As several critics subsequently noted, the commission's final report, while amply documenting the proportion of Jews in the legal profession, contained no evidence whatsoever concerning the ethical behavior of Jewish and non-Jewish lawyers. Over a decade later, an ad hoc committee of attorneys used Murav´ev's own data on disciplinary actions against lawyers to show that there was no correlation between the frequency of such actions and the proportion of Jews in any given judicial circuit.[62]

But the commission went further, giving voice to the same pessimism heard in earlier rounds of debate:

Given the Jewish tribe's characteristic unity and capacity for cohesive, coordinated, and determined action—as opposed to the lack of organization and happy-go-lucky attitude toward one's interests that make up the usual qualities of the Russian character—there is no doubt that, even without achieving numerical predominance, the Jewish portion of the legal estate might be able to secure power over estate governance and subordinate the remaining lawyers to its moral viewpoint.[63]

As this passage suggests, commission members were not content to keep Jews a minority in the legal profession. A fearful arithmetic yielded far more restrictive recommendations. Since regional general assemblies of the bar re-

---

61. Ibid., pp. 33–34. Here as elsewhere in the contemporary discussion of quotas the terms "non-Christian" and "Jewish" were used more or less interchangeably to refer to the objects of restrictive policies. As the Murav´ev Commission noted (ibid., p. 40), in 1896 there were a total of four Muslim lawyers in the Russian Empire. Other religions were not represented in the profession.

62. *Materialy k sozyvu Vserossiiskogo Advokatskogo S˝ezda: Protokoly soveshchanii predstavitelei sovetov prisiazhnykh poverennykh v Petrograde i Moskve* (Moscow, 1916), p. 114. In fact, this report showed that in Saratov, where in 1895 there was not a single Jewish lawyer, the frequency of disciplinary action against lawyers was higher than in Odessa and Warsaw, where in the same year Jews constituted 17 and 15 percent of the lawyers, respectively.

63. *Vysochaishe uchrezhdennaia komissiia dlia peresmotra zakonopolozhenii po sudebnoi chasti,* 3: 36.

quired a minimum of one-third attendance for binding votes, one-sixth (17 percent) of the total membership could in theory form a majority; and since a small number of Christian lawyers typically voted "on the side of the Jews," who in turn were assumed always to vote as a block, the commission determined that Jews should be allowed to constitute no more than 10 percent of the lawyers in any circuit. Suggestions by Spasovich and Koni that the quota be set at 15 or 20 percent were rejected as leaving the Jews too wide a margin of influence. In addition, commission members—including Spasovich and Koni—voted to forbid the election of a Jewish lawyer to the post of chairman or vice chairman of any regional bar council, finding that "it would be impossible for such individuals to serve as representatives of the entire estate of lawyers."[64]

Among the twenty-four members of the Murav´ev Commission, only one (Liustikh) rejected any form of religious or ethnic discrimination whatsoever. The fact that all other members, including highly respected representatives of the bar such as Spasovich and Koni, had endorsed the use of quotas provided ready ammunition for subsequent commentators who favored limitations on the admission of Jews. But Liustikh was not without public allies elsewhere in the profession. The Jewish lawyer Alexander S. Gol´denveizer blasted the commission for recommending quotas even after it had acknowledged the lack of alternatives outside the bar for Jewish graduates of law faculties. "And this," he proclaimed, "is being proposed by the ministry that bears the name 'Justice'?" Ridiculing the crude application of national stereotypes within an educated estate such as the bar, Gol´denveizer insisted that if Jewish lawyers in fact abused their clients, the latter were free to turn to Russian lawyers without any necessary interference by the state. The real issue, he argued, was not Jewish quotas but the meaning of education: "The question here is about the significance of intellectual enlightenment and the rights associated with it. This question has been put point-blank with respect to Jewish graduates of institutions of higher learning, but if it is decided against the Jews, it will represent a grave verdict on the results of education in general."[65] Similarly, a committee of Petersburg lawyers responding to the Murav´ev report drew attention to its "insulting" portrayal of Christian lawyers as "some kind of inert, meek gathering, estranged from the interests of the estate and from any initiative whatsoever." Rejecting all restrictions

---

64. Ibid., pp. 39–42. A decade earlier, *Vestnik Evropy*, no. 5 (1888), p. 424, had argued that a ban on the election of Jews to bar councils would be acceptable "if this should turn out to be the only means of putting an end to the suspicions and criticisms that have undermined the authority of the corporation." Such a restriction, the journal wrote, would be infinitely less burdensome to Jews than a quota on admission.

65. Alexander Gol´denveizer, "Po povodu zakonoproekta ob advokature," *Severnyi Vestnik*, no. 12 (1897), p. 50.

based on religion or ethnicity, the committee insisted that "a self-governing and independent estate can, on its own, protect itself from undesirable elements, [if it is] guided by recognition of duty and the feeling of honor rather than by the external measures" proposed by the commission. Referring to the proposed ban on electing Jews to the posts of chairman and vice chairman of regional bar councils, the committee concluded, "To suggest that people who have received higher education and long years of practical training, and who now occupy prominent social positions, are not capable of selecting their own representatives with sufficient care . . . is hardly justified."[66]

But alongside the dissenting voices one could find others willing to endorse the Murav´ev Commission's findings, or even to push for harsher restrictions. Two commission members urged that the Jewish quota be set at 5 percent for regional bars outside the Pale. In a separate appendix to the Murav´ev report, the lawyer Fedor Nikiforovich Plevako, a future Duma representative, argued that the quota should apply to people of "non-Christian origin" rather than simply to "non-Christians," so as to include Jewish converts to Christianity. In the name of an integral Russian-Christian nationalism, Plevako carried the commission's stated position on legal culture and national identity to its logical extreme:

> Law, like religion, can be the subject of knowledge. But can someone who knows our dogma in great detail, and yet remains outside it for want of acknowledging its truth, can such a person be a teacher of faith . . . ? No, he cannot, for he *knows* but does not *believe*. The same holds for the law. It is not enough to know it, one must live it, embody it in oneself by means of ideas transmitted through native speech, native customs, native conditions. . . . Herein lies the justification for the government's concern to restrict the admission of non-Christians to the corporation (and not only that of lawyers).[67]

For Sliozberg, Vinaver, and other Jewish lawyers, of course, such a conception marked a direct assault on the ideals of 1864, and the antithesis of that overarching juridical framework within which Jews were to enjoy Russian citizenship.

Another ardent nationalist and member of the bar, Vladimir Ptitsyn, came

---

66. *Zamechaniia prisiazhnykh poverennykh okruga S.-Peterburgskoi Sudebnoi Palaty po proektu novoi redaktsii uchrezhdeniia sudebnykh ustanovlenii: Razdel desiatyi—o prisiazhnykh poverennykh, stat´i 394–478* (St. Petersburg, 1901), pp. 10–22.

67. *Vysochaishe uchrezhdennaia komissiia dlia peresmotra zakonopolozhenii po sudebnoi chasti*, vol. 3, app. 3, pp. 4–5: emphasis in original. Plevako's professional encounters with Alexander Passover may have helped to foster (as they did for Spasovich) an enduring and ambivalent impression of Jewish lawyers. Commenting on Passover's manner, Plevako wrote, "A remarkable mind, perhaps non-Russian—he doesn't squander his energies in the least, he doesn't glance off to the side. A mind as sharp as a razor, mercilessly piercing precisely what it seeks to pierce." See *Severnyi Vestnik*, no. 3 (1897), p. 323, quoted in Kucherov, "Evrei v russkoi advokature," p. 411.

Figure 33. Fedor Nikiforovich Plevako (1842–1908).

to similar conclusions in his 1905 pamphlet *The Russian Legal Profession and the Jews.* This work is particularly striking for the way it combines bold calls for greater professional authority for lawyers—including equality with state prosecutors, freedom of speech in court, the right to address juries concerning sentencing, and to be informed of the results of investigations of one's clients—with attacks on Jewish members of the bar. Even after fifteen years of highly restricted admissions, Ptitsyn claimed, Jewish lawyers enjoyed a "dominant position" in the legal profession, owing to an entire inventory of ingrained qualities: "Shrewdness, formal logic, pushiness, stubbornness, obsequiousness, zeal, slyness, servility, limitless patience, massive love of money, sobriety, restraint, kahal solidarity, and many other similar talents—priceless when it comes to securing material benefits and success, but repugnant to and uncharacteristic of Russians." Even Russian lawyers, according to Ptitsyn, preferred Jewish apprentices:

The Jewish apprentice lawyer . . . will stop at nothing. He will visit the bailiff five times and make inexpensive arrangements with him; not a single item of an inventory will escape his penetrating eye. If in the meantime a hostile interlocutor . . . calls him a "scab," he will pay him no attention. Whereas a Russian apprentice lawyer in such circumstances will begin to fume, protest, or spit at everyone and leave, thereby taking a loss.[68]

The future survival of Russian lawyers thus depended on creating two separate sets of functions within the legal profession, one for Jews, the other for Russians. This Ptitsyn proposed to accomplish by banning all members of the bar from performing certain lucrative and morally dubious procedures (e.g., court orders and seizures of property). Jews, ever in search of big profits and finding it difficult to gain admission to the bar, would naturally gravitate to these areas, thereby leaving the rest of the field to Russians.[69]

Neither Ptitsyn's proposals nor those of the Murav'ev Commission were translated into reality, and admission of Jews to the bar continued as before to depend on case-by-case review by the minister of justice. To be sure, the upheavals surrounding the 1905 Revolution temporarily unlocked the gates that had previously barred Jews from full status in the profession. The newly formed Union of Lawyers, representing that part of the profession sympathetic to the liberation movement (Maksim Vinaver was one of the union's founders), publicly demanded an end to all discrimination against minorities.[70] In 1904, 45 Jews across the empire gained admission to the bar, after only 15 had done so during the preceding decade and a half. In 1905, 189 Jews were accepted. Then, in 1906, the number fell precipitously to 109, in 1907 to 62, in 1908 to 55, and in 1909 to 45.[71] Thereafter admission was again suspended. In 1912, moreover, the Senate—responding to renewed complaints from regional bar associations—reversed its earlier (1895) decision and ruled that the November 1889 decree required permission from the minister of justice not only for Jews seeking membership in the bar but for those applying to become apprentice lawyers as well.[72]

68. Vladimir Ptitsyn, *Russkaia advokatura i evrei: Ocherk s prilozheniem* (St. Petersburg, 1905), pp. 4, 11, 14, 15.
69. Ibid., pp. 18–21.
70. GARF, f. 518 (Union of Unions), op. 1, d. 28, l. 19. A gathering of the Petersburg bar in March 1905 also formally demanded the abolition of all restrictions against non-Christian lawyers. See P. S. Tsypkin, ed., *Svod zakonopolozhenii o prisiazhnoi i chastnoi advokature* (Petrograd, 1916), p. 199.
71. "Evrei v russkoi advokature," *Vestnik Prava*, no. 6 (1916), p. 163, cited in Pomeranz, "Emergence and Development of the Russian *Advokatura*," pp. 79–80.
72. Protests against this ruling followed quickly from representatives of the Petersburg bar and, in 1916, from the first All-Russian Congress of Lawyers (which condemned the 1889 decree and its 1912 reinterpretation as an attack on a "self-governing corporation"), but to no avail. See Tsypkin, *Svod zakonopolozhenii o prisiazhnoi i chastnoi advokature*, pp. 197–99, and *Materialy k sozyvu Vserossiiskogo Advokatskogo S˝ezda*, p. 122.

Thus within a half-century of the creation of an open, semi-independent legal profession in Russia, Jews were entirely barred from admission to its ranks.

In his carefully balanced assessment of attitudes toward the "Jewish Question" among Russia's ruling circles, Hans Rogger has shown how the regime's "patriarchal, conservative populism" led it to pursue, however confusedly, a policy of protecting the lower classes of the population, especially peasants, from alleged Jewish exploitation. "The perceived need to keep Jews away from peasants and the land," Rogger concludes, "appears to have been a key element" driving official policy.[73] The fate of Jews in the legal profession suggests that a similar paternalism and a similar rhetoric of Russian vulnerability in the face of alleged Jewish competition and solidarity extended to Russian social elites as well. In tsarist Russia one could hardly find a more highly educated, urban, Westernized, and independent-minded group than lawyers, and yet even here the need to combat Jewish influence took on an irresistible logic.

Moreover, as our examination of the genesis of restrictions on Jews in the bar has shown, the impetus for state protection came not only from ruling circles but from elements within the legal profession itself. When liberal journals such as *Russkaia Mysl'* argued that the hidden motivation behind lawyers' call for quotas was fear of competition, they missed the point: this motive was anything but hidden.[74] In contrast to the received view of the professions in Russia as struggling for autonomy against an overbearing state, when it came to the "Jewish Question" there was ample support within the bar for state regulation of fundamental mechanisms of professional life, namely, admission to the profession and election to its regional councils.[75]

73. Rogger, *Jewish Policies*, pp. 111, 175.

74. "The real reason for all restrictions," asserted *Russkaia Mysl'*, "is competition. But the lawyers carefully disguise this motive, taking cover under the [supposed] dubious moral qualities of the Jews." See no. 3 (1888), p. 198. For a similar interpretation, see Gessen, *Istoriia russkoi advokatury*, 1: 298.

75. On the professions see Harley Balzer, ed., *Russia's Missing Middle Class: The Professions in Russian History* (Armonk, N.Y., 1996); idem., "The Problem of Professions in Imperial Russia," in Edith Clowes et al., eds., *Between Tsar and People: Educated Society and the Quest for Public Identity in Late Imperial Russia* (Princeton, 1991), pp. 183–98; and Charles Timberlake, "Higher Learning, the State, and the Professions in Russia," in Konrad Jarausch, ed., *The Transformation of Higher Learning, 1860–1930: Expansion, Diversification, Social Opening, and Professionalization in England, Germany, Russia, and the United States* (Chicago, 1983), pp. 321–44. For views of the legal profession that are less beholden to the narrative of struggle for autonomy from the tsarist regime, see Pomeranz, "Emergence and Development of the Russian *Advokatura*"; Baberowski, *Autokratie und Justiz;* and esp. Laura Engelstein, "Combined Underdevelopment: Discipline and the Law in Imperial and Soviet Russia," *American Historical Review* 98, no. 2 (April 1993): 338–53 and the responses that follow.

To be sure, a significant minority of lawyers—their precise proportion (not to mention religious affiliation) is impossible to determine—opposed state discrimination against their Jewish colleagues and invoked the privileges of corporate autonomy. It was also possible for lawyers like Spasovich and Ptit-syn to *support* restrictions against Jews precisely in the hope of salvaging some form of professional autonomy and dignity.

There was something especially troubling in the introduction of discriminatory practices, as *Russkaia Mysl´* put it, "even in the midst of that part of the intelligentsia which officially supports the unshakable pillar of law—the consciousness that law represents something above partisan passions."[76] To the editors of *Vestnik Evropy* it seemed a sad case of "arbitrariness" rearing its ugly head "in one of our few self-governing corporations."[77] Indeed, lawyers enjoyed a higher degree of self-regulation and empire-wide coordination than did any other professional group in tsarist Russia.[78] Because its high level of professionalization was largely the creation of the autocracy as part of the judicial reform, however, rather than evolving independently out of self-regulating guilds, the legal profession in Russia remained vulnerable to state interference. The same regulatory mechanisms that defined the bar's elite status—educational requirements, apprenticeships, licensure—paradoxically created convenient sites for artificial and discriminatory interventions by the tsarist government.

With striking consistency, in fact, debates about Jews in the legal profession extended to other professions as well, and by implication to the entire nascent public sphere. The St. Petersburg Juridical Society insisted, for example, that "Jews should not be allowed to predominate in any corporation [*korporatsiia*] whatsoever," while the Murav´ev Commission warned of the dangers resulting from the subordination of "public institutions" to "points of view alien to Christian morality."[79] A liberal newspaper observed, with regret, that "there is no estate from which one does not hear calls for new restrictions against the Jews."[80]

Behind many of the calls for restrictions on Jewish lawyers was a traumatic conviction that unregulated social mobility according to educational and other ethnically neutral criteria would put Russians at a decisive disadvantage in their own empire. Those who insisted, despite the absence of any evidence, that Jewish lawyers were lowering the standards of the profession had

---

76. *Russkaia Mysl´*, no. 4 (1890), p. 215.

77. *Vestnik Evropy*, no. 5 (1888), p. 418.

78. Timberlake, "Higher Learning, the State, and the Professions in Russia," p. 322.

79. *Zhurnal grazhdanskogo i ugolovnogo prava*, no. 6 (1889), p. 147; see also the passage on p. 154, quoted above; *Vysochaishe uchrezhdennaia komissiia dlia peresmotra zakonopolozhenii po sudebnoi chasti*, 3: 33.

80. *Russkaia Mysl´*, no. 3 (1888), p. 197.

virtually no confidence that satisfactory mechanisms for screening applicants and disciplining wayward lawyers could ever be devised. A profound ethno-cultural pessimism, not to say despair, seems to have insinuated itself into fin-de-siècle Russian elites, both within and outside the government.

This pessimism, moreover, was a response to a perceived Jewish threat that had nothing to do with the revolutionary movement, but rather arose from the rapid influx of Jews into new, highly skilled urban professions. "They have undermined everything," wrote Konstantin Pobedonostsev, adviser to the last two tsars, in a letter to Dostoevsky, "but the spirit of the century supports them."[81] Spasovich's loss of faith in liberalism's answers to the ethnic divisions within his profession was only a milder form of such pessimism. Somewhere in between the two was the fear demonstrated by many of Spasovich's colleagues. When one considers the remarkable loyalty expressed by Jewish lawyers toward their profession, their high level of general acculturation, and the utter lack of evidence linking unethical behavior specifically to Jewish lawyers; when one considers that by 1887 admission of Jews not only to universities but to secondary schools throughout the empire was already subject to quotas; and when one considers that on top of all this the Murav´ev Commission felt compelled to recommend that, in order to contain their influence, Jewish lawyers should be allowed to constitute not a minority but merely one-tenth of the profession—then one begins to appreciate the loss of confidence at work.

Debates about Jews in the legal profession after 1889 severely compromise the received image of Russification and discrimination against minorities as driven primarily by the state.[82] Without denying the state's readiness to discriminate against Jews and other minorities, I would argue that the decisive impetus for such action increasingly came from within the Russian public itself. Before 1889, it was the conservative press and groups within the legal profession that first raised and substantiated demands for restrictions on admission of Jews. To be sure, the government hardly needed to have its arm twisted in order to act on such demands. But it is worth noting that when it did act, as in the 1889 decree, the government operated within certain limits. It did not target Jewish lawyers who converted to Christianity. It did not, until 1912, target Jews who worked as apprentice lawyers. It did not retroactively revoke membership in the bar. By contrast, debates among lawyers after 1889 show that substantial portions of the profession, includ-

---

81. Quoted in Rogger, *Jewish Policies,* p. 67.

82. One can certainly appreciate how this misleading image fitted the self-understanding of the prerevolutionary intelligentsia, who regarded themselves as fighting for liberation and progress against a despotic regime. Even in recent research on the professions and the middle class in Russia, however, the liberal mythology retains a certain influence. See, e.g., Clowes et al., *Between Tsar and People,* and Balzer, *Russia's Missing Middle Class.*

ing many of its most respected representatives, wanted to go much further than the government. As a case study, the legal profession illustrates with maximum clarity the dilemma confronting what one might call Russia's imperial civil society, whose development was profoundly complicated by ethnic and religious fault lines and not solely by the resistance of the autocracy.

Against the background of gloom and bitterness regarding the presence of Jews within the bar, the glowing testimonies to their profession by Jewish lawyers presented at the outset of this chapter begin to take on a rather more complex hue. Can the post-1889 bar really have seemed to Teitel "an oasis in the midst of a desert"? Can Gruzenberg, in 1916, have felt unsullied "pride and joy" in the traditions of his profession? In autobiographical and other accounts of their profession by Russian-Jewish lawyers, one finds a strange silence regarding the role their colleagues played in the genesis of restrictions on the admission of Jews. "The question of Jews in the legal profession," Maksim Vinaver insisted, "is a question about Jews, and not about the legal profession."[83] This terse pronouncement was written at a time when Vinaver had been involuntarily kept in the status of apprentice lawyer for over a decade. Though hardly reluctant to write about the plight of Russian Jewry in general, Jewish lawyers preferred to explain discrimination in the bar, if they mentioned it at all, as yet another example of the tyranny of the tsarist state.[84]

When the Senate delivered its ruling in 1912 allowing restrictions on Jews in the legal profession to be extended down to the level of apprentice lawyers, it justified the move in part by arguing that the earlier practice of allowing Jews to advance as far as apprenticeships but then denying them full admission to the bar was counterproductive. The resulting perpetual apprentices, according to the Senate, "constitute a cadre that is to a considerable degree hostile to the judicial system and the courts, which they are supposed to serve in the search for truth." This is in fact what one might expect of people denied equal status in the profession for which they had long trained and were eminently qualified. And yet such seems rarely to have been the case. As representatives of the Petersburg bar insisted in their response to the Senate

83. Vinaver, *Ocherki ob advokature*, p. 29.

84. In his account of restrictions against Jews in the bar, Grigorii Rubinshtein, another lawyer from the prerevolutionary period, mentions only the November 1889 decree, glossing over debates within the bar that preceded it. See Rubinshtein, *Vospominaniia starogo advokata*, p. vi. A notable exception is Sliozberg, who recorded in his consistently clear-eyed memoirs that "there was no order from the Ministry of Justice for the council to compile statistics on religious affiliation [in its annual report of 1889]. Thus the appearance [of these statistics] bears witness to the initiative of the council itself." Sliozberg goes on to argue that "the initiative to restrict and reduce the rights of the privileged classes of Jews very often came from their Christian competitors": *Dela minuvshikh dnei*, 1: 208, 2: 253.

ruling, "As regards the reference to the hostile influence of 'old' apprentices on their milieu and their hostile attitudes toward the judicial system—such a claim is not only completely unfounded, but is utterly contradicted by experience."[85] The undiminished loyalty of Jewish lawyers and apprentice lawyers to the Russian legal system, in their careers as in their memoirs, is perhaps the most eloquent testimony of all to the power of the ideals of integration, professionalism, and the rule of law that were the legacy of the Reform era.

85. Tsypkin, *Svod zakonopolozhenii o prisiazhnoi i chastnoi advokature,* p. 199.

Conclusion

The Russian–Jewish Encounter
in Comparative Perspective

In all the European states, the so-called Jewish Question, in its general meaning, has long since been resolved and filed away in the archives.
ADOLF LANDAU, *The Jewish Library* (1873)

Every country has the Jews it deserves.
V. D. SPASOVICH, *After-dinner Speech* (1889)

The tragic Jewish love for Russia corresponds to our equally tragic love . . . for Europe. After all, we ourselves are the Jews of Europe, our border marks the same Pale of Settlement, that strange imperial Russian ghetto.
LEONID ANDREEV, *"First Step"* (1916)

Were history a closed book, sealed after each epoch, we would not be much interested in the story of the privileged Jews.
HANNAH ARENDT, *"Privileged Jews"* (1946)

Russia! If my faith in you were any less great
I might have said something different.
I might have complained: You have led us astray,
And seduced us young wandering gypsies.
SHMUEL HALKIN, *"Rusland"* (1923)

When Rabbi Max Lilienthal arrived in Russia's western borderlands from Germany in 1840, he had the distinct sensation of entering not just a different country but another historical era. "Transport yourself fifty years back in Germany," he wrote to his father, "when there were five hundred *bakhorim* [yeshiva students] in Fürth, and as many in Frankfurt and Mainz, when the Jew was bearded and wore a mantle and a broad cap, and even then you would have a very weak facsimile of conditions here." In the main synagogue of what he called the "Jewish metropolis" of Vilna, the time warp drew Lilienthal back further still: "It was as if the past centuries of Jewish history were greeting me. It was as if they themselves, used to seeing only the costume and dress of the fourteenth century, were astonished to perceive a modern Jewish stranger in their midst."[1]

Lilienthal was of course not alone among nineteenth-century European visitors to Russia in his sensation of having stepped back in time. Tomáš Masaryk, the great historian and future president of Czechoslovakia, spoke for many when he related his impression that "Russia has preserved the childhood of Europe," in particular its "Christian medievalism."[2] Conversely, over the course of the nineteenth century, educated Russians—whether they had seen Berlin or Paris with their own eyes or just read about them—developed a permanent obsession with Europe as the model of what they hoped, or feared, would be Russia's future. Among Slavophiles and Westernizers, reactionaries and revolutionaries, European civilization provided the touchstone for virtually all schools of thought concerning Russia's autocracy, society, and empire.

The question of what to do with the empire's recently acquired Jewish population, how to bring it within the orbit of state control and reduce the allegedly harmful features of its relationship with the surrounding population, lent itself perfectly to such an obsession. European states had faced the same issues with regard to their own Jews, and by the opening of the nineteenth century they had begun to transform their status with notable results. During the period in which Russia's policy of selective integration was planned and implemented, invoking the lessons of Europe's experience became a commonplace of official as well as public discussion of the "Jewish Question" in Russia. In fact, the Russian government commissioned several studies of Jewish policies in various European countries, and occasionally sent fact-finding missions abroad for the same purpose. After surveying the Jewish policies of Austria, Baden, Bavaria, Prussia, and France, for example, Nicholas I's minister of state domains, Pavel Kiselev, concluded that Russia should follow the example set by its western neighbors and dismantle Jewish communal autonomy while fostering a modernized rabbinate to free Jewish education from the harmful influence of the Talmud.[3] By contrast, when N. P. Giliarov-Platonov, a professor of Orthodox theology at the Spiritual Academy in Moscow, was sent to Western Europe in 1857 with the assignment to study how governments there had managed to integrate their Jewish populations, he concluded that the European model was less successful

---

1. Philipson, *Max Lilienthal*, pp. 140, 264, 271. The latter passages are from Lilienthal's diaries.

2. Thomas Masaryk, *The Spirit of Russia: Studies in History, Literature, and Philosophy* (London, 1955), p. 5. Masaryk's work was originally published in 1913 in German and was based on years of research and travel in Slavic lands.

3. "Ob ustroistve evreiskogo naroda v Rossii (1840)," reprinted in *Voskhod*, no. 4 (1901), pp. 37–40.

than it appeared and could not be duplicated in Russia without disturbing fundamental aspects of Russia's state structure. Citing contemporary German opponents of Jewish emancipation, Giliarov-Platonov argued that even emancipated Jews had failed to "merge" into the surrounding population. From the experience of Belgium and the Netherlands, moreover, he concluded that multinational states could not afford to unleash the ambitions of their subject peoples (Jewish or otherwise), or to toy with "artificial" notions of voluntary, contractual citizenship, without risking imperial breakup.[4]

Among Russian observers of the "Jewish Question" in Europe, however, Giliarov-Platonov's alarming assessment was, for the time being, an exception. Far more common was the argument that Russia should selectively adapt European strategies to increase the Jews' utility to the state, by dismantling their separate communal institutions, recasting their occupational profile, and "merging" them with the surrounding population. Indeed, in 1860 St. Petersburg's ambassador to Belgium, a certain Rikhter, submitted a lengthy memorandum urging that Russia jump ahead of the Europeans by creating a central authority for Jewish communities all over the world. Given world Jewry's "incalculable influence on financial and political relations," he wrote, the creation of such an authority "under the protection and influence of the Russian government" would doubtless redound to Russia's benefit while preempting the recently established Alliance Israélite Universelle in Paris. To be sure, the Jewish Committee dismissed Rikhter's idea with the sober observation that "the establishment of a central authority to lead the Jewish population of the entire earth in the very state where the Jews' rights are most restricted would be unnatural." But the committee endorsed Rikhter's observation that Jews had successfully "merged" with surrounding populations in England, France, and other countries where they had been granted equal rights, and that there was every reason to expect that similar results could be obtained in Russia. Tsar Alexander II wrote that he "fully shared" the committee's assessment.[5] So widespread was the urge to duplicate the apparent success of European states in managing Jewish integration that the Slavophile Ivan Aksakov was led to complain, "The French, the Ger-

---

4. On Giliarov-Platonov's mission, see RGIA, f. 1269, op. 1, d. 3b, l. 91. His findings are summarized in N. P. Giliarov-Platonov, *Evreiskii vopros v Rossii: Sostavleno na osnovanii statei i pisem Giliarova-Platonova* (St. Petersburg, 1906), pp. 3–26, which notes (p. 10) that publication of his report on his mission abroad was barred in Russia at the time on the grounds that it could "arouse public opinion among Christians against the broadening of rights for Jews." Giliarov-Platonov was especially influenced by the German Protestant theologian Heinrich Eberhard Gottlob Paulus, whose anti-emancipation pamphlet, *Die jüdische Nationalabsonderung nach Ursprung, Folgen, und Besserungsmitteln, oder über Pflichten, Rechte und Verordnungen zur Verbesserung der jüdischen Schutzbürgerschaft in Deutschland* (Heidelberg, 1831), had received wide attention in Germany, inspiring Giliarov-Platonov to prepare a Russian translation with commentary.

5. GARF, f. 109, Sekretnyi Arkhiv, op. 3, d. 2319, ll. 3–10.

mans, the British have solved [the Jewish Question] in the most liberal manner; what is left to doubt? Who would dare go against such an authority? On the contrary . . . here one can play the liberal without risk, gain the attention of foreign journalists, and feel oneself a progressive human being!"[6]

New Jewish elites, whether merchants or members of the diploma intelligentsia, were also enthusiastic observers of the European example. "It has been the fate of Russian Jewry," concluded Adolf Landau in 1873, "to lag behind their co-religionists in Germany on the field of historical development by more than half a century. Russian Jews must now undergo virtually the same process of self-transformation so brilliantly marked out by German Jews." Although Russian Jewry had not yet produced a Moses Mendelssohn or Russia a Lessing, Landau urged his readers to take comfort in having "a ready example and model," so that the Jews' civil and social transformation in Russia could be completed "in a much shorter period, and without repeating the mistakes that retarded this process in Western Europe."[7]

Until the 1880s, the tsarist regime too regarded European states' handling of their Jewish populations as a model. But it hardly shared Landau's sense of urgency. As we have seen, Russia's rulers sought to ensure that any changes in the status of the empire's Jews proceed as gradually as possible. Those who sought to justify the slow pace of Jewish integration (and some who opposed it altogether) typically invoked the idea that Russia's Jews, mired in a fanatical separatism and hostility toward Christian society, were not (or not yet) like those of France or Germany. As Minister of Enlightenment Sergei Uvarov once remarked to Max Lilienthal, "Believe me, if we had such Jews as I met in the different capitals of Germany, we would treat them with the utmost distinction, but our Jews are entirely different."[8]

Historians, seeking not to justify but to explain why Russian Jewry entered the twentieth century still subject to a dense labyrinth of legal disabilities, have tended to shift the focus to another form of difference. Rather than emphasizing the contrast between Eastern and Western Jewries, they point to Russia's backwardness, the persistence there of a corporative social structure, the absence of a liberal middle class, and a certain insecurity vis-à-vis the modern world. Taken together, these factors deprived the state of the necessary confidence, despite several promising starts, to lift the burden of disabilities it had placed on the Jews.

The comparative perspective implicit in both forms of exceptionalism—one concerning Russia's Jews, the other concerning Russia itself—brings me to the central task of my conclusion, which is to place the Russian–Jewish

6. I. S. Aksakov, "Otchego Evreiam v Rossii imet´ tu ravnopravnost´, kotoroi ne daetsia nashim raskol´nikam?" *Den´* (Moscow), May 26, 1862.

7. *Evreiskaia Biblioteka*, vol. 3 (1873): 237–38.

8. Philipson, *Max Lilienthal*, p. 194.

encounter in a broader historical context in order to highlight both its distinctive traits and its similarities to other analogous encounters. Was the path of Jewish integration in Russia essentially a variation on a European theme, distinguished only in its timing? Or does it constitute a distinct trajectory, a *Sonderweg* in modern European as well as modern Jewish history? Was that trajectory characteristic of other minority groups in the tsarist empire? What was the significance of European examples for the fate of Jewish emancipation in Russia? What roles did Jews, non-Jews, and the state play in Russia as compared to their counterparts in other countries? And how did the late imperial Russian–Jewish encounter shape the subsequent path of Russian Jews and of Russia itself?

Viewed diachronically and from a certain distance, the path of Jewish emancipation in Russia conforms to a remarkable degree to the European pattern, or at least has close parallels in the prior experience of individual European states. Like Prussia and Austria, Russia acquired the vast majority of its Jewish population unintentionally, as a result of the partitions of Poland. The same was true of France (with the conquest of Alsace and Lorraine in the sixteenth and seventeenth centuries) and Bavaria (as a result of the redrawing of political boundaries at the Congress of Vienna in 1815). Late imperial Russia employed many of the same techniques to control its Jewish population as did early modern European states, including restrictions on residence, occupation, marriage, and property ownership, as well as collective taxation and payment for privileges. Only Nicholas I's introduction of compulsory military service for Jews independent of any movement toward either emancipation or universal conscription departed significantly from the European pattern.[9]

The oft-noted contradictions and inertia of tsarist policy toward Russia's Jews were hardly unique in the European context.[10] Like Russia in the Re-

9. Stanislawski, *Tsar Nicholas I*, p. 13.

10. The strongest case for the fundamental incoherence of tsarist policy toward the Jews has been made by Michael Stanislawski: "Policy on the Jews—and thus the legal and political status of the Jews—was never addressed rationally or coherently by the Russian state; sporadic measures were taken to confront individual and isolated problems, with no articulation of a clear goal or end to these policies." See Stanislawski, "Russian Jewry and Jewish Emancipation," in Birnbaum and Katznelson, *Paths of Emancipation*, pp. 264–65. For surprisingly similar judgments regarding pre-1848 Germany and the vaunted Prussian bureaucracy, see Michael A. Meyer, *German-Jewish History in Modern Times: Emancipation and Acculturation, 1780–1871* (New York, 1996), 2: 20; and Reinhard Rürup, *Emanzipation und Antisemitismus: Studien zur "Judenfrage" der bürgerlichen Gesellschaft* (Göttingen, 1975), pp. 29, 40. It is not clear what standard of coherence and rationality is being used in any of these judgments. My own view, which this study has attempted to elaborate, is that there were recognizable means and ends to tsarist

form era, most European states (with the exception of France) had dismantled legal disabilities against Jews not in a single grand gesture but in fits and starts, a nearly century-long zigzag that produced countless varieties of partial emancipation. The role played by the Gintsburgs and other wealthy Jewish intercessors in Russia before 1881 echoes the career of Central Europe's court Jews, whose financial services to early modern absolutist states secured them a privileged legal status and occasional influence over Jewish policies—and at times the resentment of Jewish communities on the receiving end of those policies.[11] The various arguments elaborated in the course of decades of debate over Jewish emancipation, moreover, while varying in strength, were not qualitatively different in late imperial Russia from their predecessors elsewhere in Europe.

Nearly everywhere on the European continent, revolutions, wars (especially lost wars), and the redrawing of political boundaries were necessary catalysts in the process of lifting legal disabilities against Jews, and here too Russia was no exception. This was the case in France in 1791, in the German and Italian states during the Napoleonic invasions, across Central and Western Europe during the revolutionary year of 1848, in Austria-Hungary after its defeat by Prussia in 1866, and in Germany and Italy after their respective unifications. In Russia, key shifts in the Jews' legal status were ushered in by the 1855 Crimean defeat (selective integration) and the revolutions of 1905 (political rights) and 1917 (full civil emancipation). In this respect, Jewish emancipation came late to the tsarist empire only in the sense that the necessary seismic shocks came relatively late to Russia's Old Regime.

Within these broad parallels to its earlier European counterparts, however, the Russian–Jewish encounter displayed a number of distinctive qualities. First, it unfolded in an era when Russia's hereditary corporate estates were still key sources of social identity and the grid through which the tsarist state perceived and managed its population. Unprepared to dismantle the various "civil societies," as Russia's disparate corporative groups were sometimes called, the tsarist autocracy instead attempted to use them as conduits for Jewish integration. This approach all but ensured that, whatever form integration took in imperial Russia, the Jewish population would be fragmented by widely differing privileges and obligations. Nowhere else in Europe was the internal stratification of the Jewish population so integral and so consequential a part of state policy. To be sure, other states distinguished

---

policy vis-à-vis the Jews, especially during the Reform era, and that, while in many respects selective integration did not achieve the goals envisioned by its architects, it remained a cornerstone of official policy across the entire late imperial period.

11. Selma Stern, *The Court Jew: A Contribution to the History of the Period of Absolutism in Central Europe* (Philadelphia, 1950), esp. pp. 177–207. See also the judicous remarks of Jacob Katz in *Out of the Ghetto*, pp. 28–31.

among Jews according to wealth and occasionally education, but rarely in a way meant to select and disperse entire groups into corresponding (Gentile) corporative units. A brief glance at such policies in various European countries illustrates the point.

Across early modern Europe, small numbers of individual Jews and their families were granted special privileges by princes and monarchs, usually as a reward for financial services. Thus a bill passed by the British Parliament in 1753 (and later repealed under pressure of popular unrest) opened up the possibility of naturalization for Jews, but only on an individual basis and with approval by Parliament in each case. Many rulers also differentiated among Jews residing in various territories under their control; the Edicts of Tolerance (1781–82) issued by Joseph II of Austria, for example, offered different privileges to the Jews of Vienna, Bohemia, Hungary, and elsewhere.[12] In Old Regime France, acculturated Sephardic communities of the southwest explicitly requested such differential treatment, petitioning the monarchy for greater privileges while distancing themselves from the more insular (and far more numerous) Ashkenazim of Alsace and Lorraine. Indeed, despite their opposition to particularism of any kind, the French revolutionaries initially (in 1790) bestowed "active citizenship" on the Sephardim alone, rather than on all of France's Jews. Stung by the argument that this amounted to the "consecration among the Jews of a sort of aristocracy," however, they extended equal terms to the Ashkenazim the following year.[13] The Jews of France thus experienced for scarcely a year the kind of internal legal stratification that governed Russian Jewry for over half a century.

Prussia offered the closest precedent to Russia's practice of imposing different legal statuses within the Jewish population over a long period of time. As was the case in many states, Prussia's treatment of its Jews varied geographically, such as between Brandenburg, where Jews had lived continuously since 1671, and Posen (Poznan), where most of the Jewish population had been acquired during the Polish partitions. In Brandenburg the monarchy established in 1750 an elaborate hierarchy of categories, including "generally privileged Jews" (those entitled to settle freely, to purchase real estate, and to pass these rights on to their heirs), "unprivileged protected Jews" (those whose residence rights were conditional on their practicing a "useful" profession), and "tolerated Jews," whose residence required the sponsorship of a "protected" Jew and who were subject to a host of other restrictions. These and other distinctions, which were in effect until 1812,

12. Katz, *Out of the Ghetto,* pp. 40, 162; Dubin, *Port Jews of Habsburg Trieste,* 198–99.

13. Paula Hyman, *The Jews of Modern France* (Berkeley, 1998), pp. 5–32 (quotation on p. 30).

unquestionably heightened tensions within the Jewish community.[14] But here too it is important to note the contrasts to the Russian case. Jewish elites in Prussia had virtually no role in shaping the 1750 legislation, which aimed at increasing the Jews' economic utility but not at integrating them. Indeed, the hierarchical grid imposed on the Jewish population bore little resemblance to the larger Prussian system of estates. And outside Brandenburg-Prussia, German Jews continued to depend on letters of protection or toleration granted to individuals rather than to categories, at least until the Napoleonic invasion.

A second factor distinctive to the Russian–Jewish encounter has to do with the nature of Russian Jewry itself. Contrary to the mythology of shtetl solidarity, nineteenth-century Russian Jewry was far more deeply divided internally than its counterparts elsewhere in Europe had been a century before. Beyond the ubiquitous divides of wealth and learning that characterized European Jewry as a whole, the Hasidic schism (a genuinely mass phenomenon) and the various outposts of the Haskalah (a tiny vanguard eager to ally itself with the state) in Eastern Europe had given rise to bitter rivalries and mutual denunciations. Together with the enormous pressures of enforced military conscription and the tsarist regime's withdrawal of its recognition of the kahal, intramural rivalries formed an unprecedentedly powerful solvent of traditional forms of communal solidarity. The petitions from Jewish merchants, students, and other elements that helped launch the policy of selective integration bear witness to the profound fault lines within Jewish society by the middle of the nineteenth century. The process of Jewish integration thus began in Russia at a time when the dissolution of the Jews' internal communal structures was far more advanced than it had been in Europe a century before. The centrifugal effect of state-imposed stratification on Russian Jewry was therefore considerably greater.[15]

Third, across the long nineteenth century, Russia's size and external

14. See the summary of the 1750 legislation in Meyer, *German-Jewish History*, 1: 148–49, 266.

15. Just how strong the centrifugal pressures were in the Russian-Jewish world is suggested by two marginal but telling examples. The tiny sect of Karaites, Tatar-speaking Jews acquired by Russia in the course of Catherine the Great's conquests against the Ottoman Empire, consistently sought to distinguish themselves from the Jews of the Pale in an effort to retain their legal privileges. In 1863 they achieved their long hoped-for recognition by the tsarist government as a separate, non-Jewish nationality—a form of separatism unparalleled among Karaites in other countries. See Miller, *Karaite Separatism in Nineteenth-Century Russia*. pp. xv–xix. Similarly, during the late imperial period two sects that attempted to blend Christianity and Judaism (one led by Jacob Priluker, the other by Jacob Gordon) also attempted to secure emancipation apart from, and ahead of, the rest of Russian Jewry. See Steven Zipperstein, "Heresy, Apostasy, and the Transformation of Joseph Rabinovich," in Todd Endelman, ed. *Jewish Apostasy in the Modern World* (New York, 1987), p. 222.

strength allowed its rulers to elaborate policies toward the Jews in an environment almost entirely free of foreign interference. Napoleon did not attempt to import Jewish emancipation during his conquest of Russia in 1812, in contrast to his practice in the German and Italian territories he occupied. The Peace of Paris (1856) after the Crimean war likewise left Russia's internal policies wholly undisturbed, in stark contrast to the Congress of Berlin (1878), which forced Romania, Bulgaria, Serbia, and Montenegro to grant their Jewish subjects legal equality, at least on paper.[16] There was nothing in Russia's experience to compare with that of the crumbling Ottoman Empire, where Western powers freely intervened to protect the rights of non-Muslim subjects, and where the modernizing educational mission of the Alliance Israélite Universelle transformed Ottoman Jewry's status within the surrounding society.[17] At best, outsiders attempted to change Russia's treatment of its Jews by organizing public protests in response to pogroms and blood libels, a strategy whose impact on events in Russia does not appear to have been significant. As late as the Paris Peace Conference in 1919, the Entente powers felt free to dictate treaties to the newly independent states of Eastern Europe, in which the rights of minorities (including Jews) were guaranteed. Russia, however—now Bolshevik Russia—remained as before beyond their grasp. The European model of Jewish emancipation thus presented itself to Russians and Russian Jews not from behind the barrel of a gun or in the text of an international treaty but by example, through the force of ideas and opinions.

Fourth—and here the limits of a diachronic analysis come most clearly to the fore—the Russian experiment with selective integration began just as Jews in contemporary Europe were concluding their long march toward full legal emancipation. However compelling the analogies between Jews in late imperial Russia and their counterparts elsewhere in Europe fifty or one hundred years earlier may have been for Lilienthal, Landau, and others, in practice the "real existing" Jewish emancipation that swept from west to east across the European continent greatly accelerated expectations among Russia's reform-minded Jews. By the 1870s—not to mention by the dawn of the twentieth century—Russia's cautious and selective approach to Jewish integration already appeared far less enlightened than had analogous policies by European governments in a previous era. Only in the context of the Russian-Jewish intelligentsia's heightened expectations can we grasp the intensity of resentment against Evzel and Horace Gintsburg, Emanuel Levin, Genrikh Sliozberg, and others who for decades appeared ready to settle for

16. The requirement to protect Jewish rights was imposed on Balkan countries over the objection of the Russian delegate to Berlin. See Greenberg, *Jews in Russia*, 1: 98.

17. Aron Rodrigue, "From *Millet* to Minority: Turkish Jewry," in Birnbaum and Katznelson, *Paths of Emancipation*, p. 260.

less than full emancipation. By the 1890s, recalled Sliozberg, "we were forced to direct all our efforts toward preserving [those rights] that had previously been granted and preventing future restrictions," an approach that often cast the notables as de facto defenders of stark inequities among Jews long after freedom and equality had become the norm elsewhere in Europe.[18] Whether it was better to push for nothing less than full emancipation or to aim for piecemeal improvements and accountability along the lines pursued by the Petersburg elites remains a question of historical judgment. What is certain, though, is that this dilemma, faced by practically every liberation movement, pitting within its own ranks radicals against moderates, idealists against pragmatists, was greatly intensified by the living examples of Jewish emancipation to Russia's west.

Russian Jews typically assumed that the situation of their co-religionists elsewhere in Europe, rather than that of other non-Russian minorities in the tsarist empire, was the standard by which their own condition should be judged. The imperial framework nonetheless offers a useful context in which to reflect on the Russian–Jewish encounter. As scholars of Russia's empire have noted, at no time was there a consistent, overarching policy toward ethnic and religious minorities, or even a particular bureaucratic department responsible for imperial management. Whenever possible, however, the tsarist state managed its non-Russian subjects by absorbing them into the Russian estate system. Privileges and obligations were typically doled out not to entire nationalities or confessions or regions but to corporate units defined as closely as possible according to Russia's own social hierarchy.[19] Before the Reform era, this practice was most visible at the top of the social ladder, where non-Russian hereditary ruling elites (for example, among Poles, Baltic Germans, Georgians, and Tatars) were incorporated into the Russian nobility and turned into instruments of imperial management.

Many of the empire's minority groups, however, lacked hereditary ruling classes. In the Jewish case, as we have seen, the tsarist government at first attempted to fashion its own (nonhereditary) elite, an officially trained rabbinate loyal to and dependent on the state for its status. As this approach failed, policy toward the Jews followed the general postreform pattern of abandoning special privileges for indigenous elites, restricting their function as local proxies for the imperial government, and instead drawing economically "useful" elements of minority populations into the Russian estate

---

18. Sliozberg, *Baron G. O. Gintsburg,* p. 48.

19. S. Frederick Starr, "Tsarist Government: The Imperial Dimension," in Jeremy Azrael, ed., *Soviet Nationality Policies and Practices* (New York, 1978), pp. 5, 20.

hierarchy. What is distinctive in the Jewish case is the absence of typical al-liance-building strategies: neither intermarriage (impossible without con-version) nor state service ever played a substantial role in Jewish integration. Despite their eagerness for acculturation, new Jewish elites were kept at arm's length from Russia's ruling circles, and after 1881 were largely deprived of whatever influence proximity to power might have gained them in the eyes of the Jewish population.

In the end, selective integration was a highly uneven experiment. In some respects—the attempt to transform Jews into peasants, for example—it failed from the very start. In others—the entrance of Jews into the Russian edu-cational system, and from there into the professions and other white-collar arenas—it succeeded far beyond the government's intentions. The aston-ishing rise of Jews in late imperial Russia's embryonic civil society, as much as the specter of Jewish participation in the revolutionary movement, led the tsarist regime to lose confidence in its own policies. To be sure, demands that all Jews once again be confined to the Pale, or that they be expelled en masse from Russia, had little effect on state policies.[20] Like the Great Reforms, selective integration was not so much reversed as constricted. The channels through which Jews could legally gain access to the vast Russian interior, to higher education, and to modern careers were purposely narrowed, even as the size of the empire's Jewish population and its aspirations dramatically expanded.

For a slender but highly visible minority of Jews, however, selective inte-gration produced effects remarkably similar to those of European-style emancipation. It brought dramatic opportunities for social and geographic mobility in a country starved for entrepreneurship and professional services. It opened up the possibilities and perils of a strictly voluntary Jewish com-munity, of acculturation without the price of apostasy. By the 1880s there were in effect two Russian Jewries: the mass of legally and culturally segre-gated Jews confined to the Pale and a small but growing number in and be-yond the Pale whose integration into the upper reaches of the surrounding society (though certainly not into the ruling elites) was proceeding far more rapidly than anyone had expected. In this telescoping of phases, more or less medieval modes of Jewish separatism flourished side by side with char-acteristically modern forms of mobility.

By sanctioning new forms of hierarchy in the Jewish world, selective in-tegration in effect helped advance what the French revolutionaries had sought to avoid, namely, the "consecration among the Jews of a sort of aris-tocracy." This was not, to be sure, an aristocracy in the sense of a hereditary ruling elite, although many contemporaries regarded the three-generation

---

20. On such demands, see Rogger, *Jewish Policies and Right-Wing Politics*, pp. 60, 227.

Gintsburg dynasty as a close approximation of one. Nor did the new forces fostered by selective integration ever fully eclipse the authority of the traditional rabbinic elite. Nonetheless, the movement of Jewish wealth and learning literally and figuratively beyond the Pale profoundly reoriented Jewish society. Most strikingly, the privileges attached by the state to higher education, combined with the subsidies provided by wealthy notables to Jewish students, helped give rise for the first time to a Jewish intelligentsia whose aspirations for authority lay outside inherited communal institutions and forms of legitimacy.

As it entered the twentieth century, Russian-Jewish society was thus the site of extraordinary fractiousness—a quality often missed by contemporary Russian observers but painfully apparent to Jews—as well as extraordinary ferment. Like their Russian counterparts, the Jewish intelligentsia found their calling in various forms of service to "the people" as a kind of compensation for their growing remoteness from the Jewish masses of the Pale. What the historian Fritz Ringer once called the "psychic costs of mobility" may have been a prerequisite for the remarkable birth of historical and ethnographic interest in Russian Jewry on the part of fin-de-siècle Jewish elites.[21] It was while living in St. Petersburg that Simon Dubnov conceived his lifelong project of gathering primary sources for the history of Russian Jewry, a task he likened to the expeditions of Burton and Stanley in Central Africa.[22] With financial support from the Gintsburgs, Dubnov's work eventually took institutional form as the Jewish Historical-Ethnographic Society, headquartered in the Russian capital.[23] There, too, Shaul Ginzburg and Pavel Marek compiled the first collection of Yiddish folksongs, while the folklorist and writer Ansky planned his celebrated ethnographic expeditions to the Pale and the resulting Jewish Museum (which briefly opened its doors in Petrograd during the First World War), again with financial backing from the Gintsburgs.[24]

While Petersburg continued to function as the front line of Jewish integration in Russia, many members of the city's Jewish intelligentsia cast their gaze back at the Pale as the living, human reservoir of Jewish civilization, or,

21. Fritz Ringer, *Education and Society in Modern Europe* (Bloomington, 1979), p. 11.

22. S. M. Dubnov, *Ob izuchenii istorii russkikh evreev i ob uchrezhdenii russko-evreiskogo istorich-eskogo obshchestva* (St. Petersburg, 1891), p. 36. For more on the background of this work, see Nathans, "On Russian-Jewish Historiography." The first but far less well known ethnographic study of Russian Jewry was also written in Petersburg by Moisei Iosifovich Berlin, an "expert Jew" in the Ministry of Internal Affairs: *Ocherki etnografii evreiskogo narodonaseleniia Rossii* (St. Petersburg, 1861).

23. In his 1908 speech inaugurating the society's activities, Dubnov described the Pale of Settlement as the "dark continent" of Jewish historiography. See *Evreiskaia Starina*, 1, no. 1 (1909): 154.

24. On Ansky's Petersburg period and the Historical-Ethnographic Society, see Beizer, *Jews of St. Petersburg*, pp. 92–94, 115–24; Sliozberg, *Dela minuvshikh dnei*, 3: 331–33.

in Dubnov's words, "the greatest [Jewish] center, following Babylon and Spain, in the historical diaspora."[25] Acculturated Russian Jews, even those in the imperial capital, were not sufficiently removed from traditional Jewish society to indulge in the nostalgia for the shtetl that would arise among their descendants in the New World. But they might well be seen as forerunners of their Central European counterparts in the early twentieth century, figures such as Martin Buber, Alfred Döblin, Franz Kafka, and Franz Rosenzweig, in whose eyes the *Ostjuden* became bearers of a vibrant Jewish authenticity. In this sense, Petersburg was the first in a series of increasingly distant vantage points from which secularized Jews were able to conceive of the Pale and the shtetl as historical entities.

As one might expect, expanded social intercourse between Russians and Jews in the Reform era heightened rather than reduced anxieties on both sides, as new sites of friction emerged and formerly unquestioned boundaries of identity began to blur. What had once been the "Jewish enigma" (*evreiskaia zagadka*), a minor species of Orientalism that grouped the Jews with gypsies and other exotic "Eastern" peoples, gave birth to the "Jewish Question" (*evreiskii vopros*), a point of intense public contention that, as the term itself implies, demanded an answer.[26] During the last half-century of tsarist rule, the Russian search for answers to the "Jewish Question" revealed its own telescoping of phases, as archaic forms of discrimination, from territorial confinement to accusations of ritual murder, coexisted with the deliberate integration of select categories of Jews into various arenas of Russian society. It would be difficult indeed to find another country in which, as happened to Shmarya Levin in 1906, a Jew could be democratically elected to a national legislative assembly (the first state duma) but barred by law from setting foot in the city where that assembly convened. "I have no right to be living in St. Petersburg at all," Levin quipped to his fellow representatives, "and I am only here for the purpose of helping to make the country's laws."[27]

If late imperial Russia stood out for the stark inequalities it imposed within the Jewish population, elsewhere in Europe the most important contradictions were now between state policies of full legal emancipation and emerging antimodernist movements in which anti-Semitism served as the principal ideological glue. Like the wave of Jewish emancipation that preceded it, the resurgence of anti-Semitism in Europe beginning in the 1880s, which cast Jews as hidden manipulators of the economy, the press, culture, and on and on, found a powerful echo in late imperial Russia. Several historians, in

25. See the text of Dubnov's 1908 speech to the Jewish Historical-Ethnographic Society in *Evreiskaia Starina* 1, no. 1 (1909): 154.

26. G. B. Sliozberg, "Baron G. O. Gintsburg i pravovoe polozhenie evreev," *Perezhitoe* 2 (1910): 96.

27. Shmarya Levin, *The Arena* (New York, 1932), p. 291.

fact, have invoked the idea of anticipatory anti-Semitism to explain the introduction in Russia of anti-Jewish quotas in institutions of higher education and the professions, as well as various other forms of discrimination.[28] This argument draws on the larger paradigm of late imperial Russia's precocious dissatisfaction with modernity, that is, the fact that in Russia a critique of capitalism, liberalism, and bourgeois culture emerged before any of them had taken root in Russian soil.[29]

In my view, there is no need to interpret Russian anxieties concerning the presence of Jews in institutions of civil society as a precocious or preemptive response to contemporary trends elsewhere in Europe. As the case of Russia's legal profession suggests, by the end of the nineteenth century, after three decades of accelerated, state-driven reform, the consequences of even a highly selective form of Jewish integration were becoming fully apparent. The tsarist regime's program of reform fostered dramatic mobility among Jews (and several other minorities as well), who on the whole were more urbanized, more literate, and better positioned than Russians to enter new, modern occupations. In the context of an ethnic shatter zone—the dense conglomeration of many nationalities within a single polity—Russia's relatively late but accelerated transition to modernity took its revenge on aspirations for professional autonomy, and more broadly on the formation of a stable and independent civil society.

The introduction in tsarist Russia of quotas on admission of Jews to public institutions was in fact anticipatory in an entirely different and unexpected manner: it prefigured developments after World War I in right-wing states in Central and Eastern Europe. In interwar Poland and Hungary, and in the most extreme form in Nazi Germany, state-sanctioned ethnic or racial restrictions became the norm in universities and professional associations. In all these cases, whether the result was a quota system, separate professional associations for ethnic minorities, or outright expulsion of minority members, the initiative began within the professions themselves, coinciding with a loss of confidence in the efficacy of laissez-faire development and a willingness on the part of professional elites to allow direct intervention by the state.[30]

---

28. Rogger, *Jewish Policies and Right-Wing Politics*, p. 110; Vital, *Origins of Zionism*, p. 203. Löwe, *Tsars and the Jews*, links this argument to his larger thesis of anticipatory anticapitalism on the part of late imperial Russian elites, a point challenged by Rogger (p. 236n55).

29. The paradigm of Russia's precocious dissatisfaction with bourgeois liberalism is especially well articulated in Laura Engelstein, *The Keys to Happiness: Sex and the Search for Modernity in Fin-de-Siècle Russia* (Ithaca, 1992), pp. 3–4.

30. See Konrad Jarausch, *The Unfree Professions: German Lawyers, Teachers, and Engineers, 1900–1950* (New York, 1990), and idem., "Jewish Lawyers in Germany, 1848–1938: The Disintegration of a Profession," *Leo Baeck Institute Year Book* 36 (1991): 71–90; and Maria Kovacs, *Liberal Professions and Illiberal Politics: Hungary from the Habsburgs to the Holocaust* (New York, 1995).

In interwar Russia, of course, the Bolshevik Revolution and the building of a socialist society created a radically transformed context for Jewish integration. Nonetheless, the forces unleashed during the era of selective integration continued to shape the Russian–Jewish encounter. The Jewish exodus from the Pale to the urban centers of the Russian interior, especially to Moscow and St. Petersburg (Leningrad), grew exponentially, reaching rates of in-migration even higher than those of the population as a whole, and thereby placing the majority of the Jewish population in the USSR's largest cities. Soviet Jews continued to shun state efforts to promote agricultural labor among them, preferring white-collar occupations as before. In the 1920s, the proportion of Jews in Soviet universities and technical institutes approached and possibly surpassed the high levels achieved before the imposition of quotas in the 1880s.[31] And once again, despite the Bolsheviks' conviction that national differences would quickly wither away under socialism, the specter of a disproportionate Jewish presence in elite sectors of society led to the reintroduction of quotas, part of a larger effort to manipulate the privileges doled out to the USSR's many ethnic minorities. Whereas before the Revolution the concern had been over the ethnic composition of public institutions that made up a burgeoning civil society, by the 1930s attention focused most sharply on the ethnic composition of the Communist Party itself, which in both theory and practice had all but replaced civil society.[32] To be sure, Jewish quotas in the Soviet empire, in contrast to those in tsarist Russia, were never officially acknowledged. But they too were a response to the intersection of empire and modernity that had begun under tsarist rule.

31. And this despite the slightly lower proportion of Jews in the Soviet population as compared to that of late imperial Russia, due to the secession of Poland, Lithuania, and Bessarabia. See Halevy, *Jewish University Students*, p. 5.

32. Benjamin Pinkus, *The Jews of the Soviet Union: The History of a National Minority* (Cambridge, 1988), pp. 89–98, 266–68.

BIBLIOGRAPHY

Only works mentioned in the text or notes are listed here. Articles in the contemporary press, with a few exceptions, are not included.

ARCHIVAL SOURCES

Gosudarstvennyi arkhiv rossiiskoi federatsii (GARF, formerly TsGAOR), Moscow

Fond 102	MVD, Departament politsii
Fond 109	Tret´e otdelenie
Fond 518	Soiuz soiuzov
Fond 579	Pavel Nikolaevich Miliukov
Fond 730	Nikolai Pavlovich Ignat´ev

Rossiiskaia natsional´naia biblioteka (RNB, formerly GPB), otdel rukopisei, St. Petersburg

Fond 183	David Goratsievich Gintsburg
Fond 211	Arkadii Georgievich Gornfel´d

Rossiiskii gosudarstvennyi istoricheskii arkhiv (RGIA, formerly TsGIA SSSR), St. Petersburg

Fond 733	MNP, Departament narodnogo prosveshcheniia
Fond 821	MVD, Departament dukhovnykh del inostrannykh ispovedanii
Fond 846	Aleksandr Ivanovich Georgievskii
Fond 1269	Evreiskii komitet
Fond 1284	MVD, Departament obshchikh del
Fond 1287	MVD, Khoziaistvennyi departament

Fond 1532   Obshchestvo dlia rasprostraneniia prosveshcheniia mezhdu
             evreiami v Rossii

Tsentral´nyi gosudarstvennyi istoricheskii arkhiv
goroda Sankt-Peterburga (TsGIA-SPb, formerly TsGIAL), St. Petersburg

Fond 14   Peterburgskii universitet
Fond 113   Petrogradskie vysshie zhenskie Bestuzhevskie kursy
Fond 139   Kantseliaria popechitelia Petrogradskogo uchebnogo okruga
Fond 184   Institut grazhdanskikh inzhenerov
Fond 223   Petrogradskaia remeslennaia uprava
Fond 422   Sankt-Peterburgskaia khoral´naia sinagoga
Fond 542   Mariinsko-Sergievskii priiut dlia kreshchaemykh i kreshchennykh
             v pravoslavnuiu veru evreiskikh detei
Fond 2049   Mikhail Isaakovich Sheftel´

Sankt-Peterburgskii filial Instituta vostokovedeniia
Rossiiskoi Akademii Nauk (formerly LOIV AN-SSSR), St. Petersburg

Fond 85   David Gillarionovich Maggid
Fond 86   Sergei (Israel) Lazarovich Tsinberg

YIVO Institute for Jewish Research, New York

Tcherikover Archive, Horace Guenzburg [Gintsburg] Papers, Record Group 89

Hoover Institution, Stanford

Boris Nikolaevskii Collection, box 215

UNPUBLISHED DOCTORAL DISSERTATIONS

Bartal, Israel. "Ha-lo-yehudim ve-hevratam be-sifrut ivrit ve-yidish be-mizrah eropah ben ha-shanim 1856–1914." Hebrew University of Jerusalem, 1980.

Freeze, ChaeRan. "Making and Unmaking the Jewish Family: Marriage and Divorce in Imperial Russia, 1850–1914." Brandeis University, 1997.

Litvak, Olga. "The Literary Response to Conscription: Individuality and Authority in the Russian-Jewish Enlightenment." Columbia University, 1999.

Ochs, Michael Jerry. "St. Petersburg and the Jews of Russian Poland, 1862–1905." Harvard University, 1986.

Petrovsky-Shtern, Yohanan. "Jews in the Russian Army: Through the Military to Modernity." Brandeis University, 2001.

Pomeranz, William. "The Emergence and Development of the Russian *Advokatura:* 1864–1905." University of London, 1990.

Seltzer, Robert M. "Simon Dubnow: A Critical Biography of His Early Years." Columbia University, 1970.

OTHER UNPUBLISHED SOURCES

Ginsburg, Michael. "The Ginsburg Family: 1864–1947. A Memoir of Their Life and Times in Russia, Paris and the U.S."

Gunzburg, Alexandre de. "Mémoire du Baron Alexandre de Gunzburg."

Khiterer, Victoria. "Evreiskie dokumenty v arkhivakh Kieva, XVI–XX vv."

Kreiz, Semyon. "Toldot ha-yehudim be-eizorim she-mihuts le-tehum ha-moshav." M.A. thesis, University of Haifa, 1984.

Contemporary Periodicals

Biblioteka dlia Chteniia
Den´
Evreiskaia Biblioteka
Evreiskaia Letopis´
Evreiskii Mir
Evreiskaia Nedelia
Evreiskaia Starina
Evreiskaia Zhizn´
Evreiskii Student
Golos
Ha-Magid
Ha-Melits
Nakanune: Sotsial´no-Revoliutsionnoe Obozrenie
Nedel´naia Khronika Voskhoda
Novoe Vremia
Novorossiiskii Telegraf
Novosti i Birzhevaia Gazeta
Novyi Voskhod
Odesskii Listok
Odesskii Vestnik
Osvobozhdenie
Perezhitoe
Peterburgskaia Gazeta
Peterburgskii Listok
Razsvet (Odessa)
Razsvet (St. Petersburg)
Rossiia
Russkaia Mysl´
Russkii Arkhiv
Russkii Evrei
Russkii Pedagogicheskii Vestnik
Sankt-Peterburgskie Vedomosti
Severnyi Kur´er
Severnyi Vestnik
Sion
Sudebnaia Gazeta

Vestnik Evropy
Vestnik Obshchestva prosveshcheniia evreev
Vilenskii Vestnik
Voskhod
Vpered
Vseobshchaia Gazeta
Zhizn´
Zhurnal grazhdanskogo i ugolovnogo prava
Zhurnal Ministerstva narodnogo prosveshcheniia
Zeitschrift für Demographie und Statistik der Juden

OTHER PUBLISHED SOURCES

Abramovich, Rafael. *In tsvey revolutsiyes: Di geshikhte fun a dor.* New York, 1944.

Agursky, Mikhail. "Conversions of Jews to Christianity in Russia." *Soviet Jewish Affairs* 20, no. 2–3 (1990): 69–84.

Aizenshtat, Iakov I. "Ze'ev Zhabotinskii—iurist." In Mikhail Parkhomovskii, ed., *Evrei v kul´ture russkogo zarubezh´ia: Sbornik statei, publikatsii, memuarov i esse 1919–1939.* Vol. 1. Jerusalem, 1992.

Akselrod, Pavel. "Pogromen un di revolutsionere bavegung mit 43 yor tsurik." *Di tsukunft,* no. 29 (1924).

Aleichem, Sholem. *Ale verk fun Sholem Aleichem.* 7 vols. New York, 1944.

———. *The Bloody Hoax.* Trans. Aliza Shevrin. Bloomington, 1991.

———. *In the Storm.* Trans. Aliza Shevrin. New York, 1984.

———. *Tevye the Dairyman and the Railroad Stories.* Trans. Hillel Halkin. New York, 1987.

Alston, Patrick. *Education and the State in Tsarist Russia.* Stanford, 1969.

Anan´ich, B. V. *Bankirskie doma v Rossii, 1860–1914 gg.: Ocherki istorii chastnogo predprinimatel´stva.* Leningrad, 1991.

Andreev, Leonid, Maksim Gor´kii, and Fedor Sologub, eds. *Shchit: Literaturnyi sbornik.* 3d ed. Moscow, 1915.

Antin, Mary. *The Promised Land.* New York, 1997

Arendt, Hannah. *The Origins of Totalitarianism.* Cleveland, 1969.

Armstrong, John. "Mobilized Diaspora in Tsarist Russia: The Case of the Baltic Germans." In Jeremy Azrael, ed., *Soviet Nationality Policies and Practices,* pp. 63–104. New York, 1978.

Aronson, Chaim. *A Jewish Life under the Tsars: The Autobiography of Chaim Aronson, 1825–1888.* Trans. Norman Marsden. Totowa, N.J., 1983.

Aronson, I. M. "Russian Commissions on the Jewish Question in the 1880s." *East European Quarterly* 14, no. 1 (1980): 59–74.

———. *Troubled Waters: The Origins of the 1881 Anti-Jewish Pogroms in Russia.* Pittsburgh, 1990.

Asch, Sholem. *Peterburg.* Warsaw, 1929.

Baberowski, Jörg. *Autokratie und Justiz: Zum Verhältnis von Rechtsstaatlichkeit und Rückständigkeit im ausgehenden Zarenreich, 1864–1914.* Frankfurt a. M., 1996.

Badrakh, Iu., ed. *Pol´skie professora i studenty v universitetakh Rossii, XIX–nachalo XX v.* Warsaw, 1995.

Balzer, Harley. "The Problem of Professions in Imperial Russia." In Edith Clowes et al., eds., *Between Tsar and People: Educated Society and the Quest for Public Identity in Late Imperial Russia*, pp. 183–98. Princeton, 1991.

———, ed. *Russia's Missing Middle Class: The Professions in Russian History.* Armonk, N.Y., 1996.

Barnavi, Eli. *A Historical Atlas of the Jewish People.* New York, 1992.

Baron, Salo W. "Ghetto and Emancipation." *Menorah Journal* 14 (June 1928).

———. "The Impact of the Revolution of 1848 on Jewish Emancipation." In Abraham Duker, ed., *Emancipation and Counter-Emancipation.* New York, 1974.

———. *The Russian Jew under Tsars and Soviets.* New York, 1987.

Bater, James H. "Between Old and New: St. Petersburg in the Late Imperial Era." In Michael Hamm, ed., *The City in Late Imperial Russia*, pp. 43–78. Bloomington, 1986.

———. *St. Petersburg: Industrialization and Change.* London, 1976.

Bauer, Henning, Andreas Kappeler, and Brigitte Roth, eds. *Die Nationalitäten des Russischen Reiches in der Volkszählung von 1897.* 2 vols. Stuttgart, 1991.

Bazylow, Ludwik. *Polacy w Petersburgu.* Wroclaw, 1984.

Beauvois, Daniel. *Lumières et société en Europe de l'Est: L'Université de Vilna et les écoles polonaises de l'Empire russe, 1803–1832.* 2 vols. Paris, 1977.

Becker, Christopher. *"Raznochintsy:* The Development of the Word and of the Concept," *American Slavic and East European Review* 18, no. 1 (1959).

Bein, Alex. "Notes on the Semantics of the Jewish Problem with Special Reference to Germany." *Leo Baeck Institute Year Book* 9 (1964): 3–40.

Beizer, Mikhail. *Evrei Leningrada, 1917–1939: Natsional'naia zhizn' i sovetizatsiia.* Jerusalem, 1999.

———. *Evrei v Peterburge.* Jerusalem, 1989.

———. *The Jews of St. Petersburg: Excursions through a Noble Past.* Trans. Michael Sherbourne. Ed. Martin Gilbert. Philadelphia, 1989.

Beletskii, A. *Vopros ob obrazovanii russkikh evreev v tsarstvovanii Imperatora Nikolaia I.* St. Petersburg, 1894.

Benasik, M., comp. *Studenchestvo v tsifrakh po dannym perepisi 1907 goda v Iur'eve.* St. Petersburg, 1909.

Berk, Stephen. *Year of Crisis, Year of Hope: Russian Jews and the Pogroms of 1881–82.* Westport, Conn., 1985.

Berlin, M. I. *Ocherki etnografii evreiskogo narodonaseleniia Rossii.* St. Petersburg, 1861.

Berman, L. S.-Peterburgskiia evreiskiia uchilishcha: Otchet za pervyia piatnadtsat' let ikh sushchestvovaniia 1865–1880, s prilozheniem 1880–1884.* St. Petersburg, 1885.

Berman, Marshal. *All That Is Solid Melts into Air: The Experience of Modernity.* New York, 1988.

Bernstein, Laurie. *Sonia's Daughters: Prostitutes and Their Regulation in Imperial Russia.* Berkeley, 1995.

Besançon, Alain. *Éducation et société en Russie dans le second tiers du XIXᵉ siècle.* Paris, 1974.

Bickerman, I. M. *Cherta evreiskoi osedlosti.* St. Petersburg, 1911.

Binshtok, B. I., and S. A. Novosel'skii. "Evrei v Leningrade, 1900–1924 gg." In Binshtok et al., eds., *Voprosy biologii i patologii evreev,* 2 vols. Leningrad, 1926.

Birnbaum, Pierre, and Ira Katznelson, eds. *Paths of Emancipation: Jews, States, and Citizenship.* Princeton, 1995.

Brafman, Iakov. *Kniga Kagala: Materialy dlia izucheniia evreiskogo byta.* Vilna, 1869.

Broido, Eva. *Memoirs of a Revolutionary.* Trans. and ed. Vera Broido. London, 1967.

Brower, Daniel R. *The Russian City between Tradition and Modernity, 1850–1900.* Berkeley, 1990.

————. *Training the Nihilists: Education and Radicalism in Tsarist Russia.* Ithaca, 1975.

Brubaker, Rogers. *Citizenship and Nationhood in France and Germany.* Cambridge, Mass., 1992.

Brusilovskii, S. M., ed. *Za cherty osedlosti: Protsess dantistov v moskovskoi sudebnoi palate.* Moscow, 1913.

Brutskus, Boris. *Statistika evreiskogo naseleniia: Raspredelenie po territorii, demograficheskie i kul'turnye priznaki evreiskogo naseleniia po dannym perepisi 1897 g.* St. Petersburg, 1909.

Brutskus, I. "Ha-studentim ha-yehudim ba-universitah ha-moskva'it." *He'Avar,* no. 18 (1971): 63–65.

Bukhbinder, N. A. *Literaturnye etiudy: Russko-evreiskie pisateli.* Leningrad, 1927.

Byrnes, Robert. *V. O. Kliuchevskii, Historian of Russia.* Bloomington, 1995.

Cahan, Abraham. *The Education of Abraham Cahan.* Trans. Leon Stein, Abraham P. Conan, and Lynn Davison. Philadelphia, 1969.

Chicherin, Boris. *Pol'skii i evreiskii voprosy.* Berlin, 1901.

Christian, David. *'Living Water': Vodka and Russian Society on the Eve of Emancipation.* Oxford, 1990.

Clowes, Edith, et al., eds. *Between Tsar and People: Educated Society and the Quest for Public Identity in Late Imperial Russia.* Princeton, 1991.

Cohen, Israel. *Vilna.* Philadelphia, 1943.

Conze, Werner, et al., eds. *Geschichtliche Grundbegriffe.* 8 vols. Stuttgart, 1975.

Corrsin, Stephen D. "Language Use in Cultural and Political Change in Pre-1914 Warsaw: Poles, Jews, and Russification." *Slavic and East European Review* 68, no. 1 (1990): 69–90.

————. *Warsaw before the First World War: Poles and Jews in the Third City of the Russian Empire, 1880–1914.* Boulder, Colo., 1989.

Creuzberger, Stefan, et al., eds. *St. Petersburg—Leningrad—St. Petersburg: Eine Stadt im Spiegel der Zeit.* Stuttgart, 2000.

D. [A. Diakonov]. *1905 i 1906 god v Peterburgskom Universitete.* St. Petersburg, 1907.

Dal', Vladimir, comp. *Tolkovyi slovar' zhivogo velikorusskogo iazyka.* 2d ed. 4 vols. St. Petersburg, 1880–82.

Dawidowicz, Lucy, ed. *The Golden Tradition: Jewish Life and Thought in Eastern Europe.* New York, 1967.

————. *What Is the Use of Jewish History?* New York, 1992.

Deych [Deich], G. M., comp. *Arkhivnye dokumenty po istorii evreev v Rossii v XIX–nachale XX vv.: Putevoditel'.* Ed. Benjamin Nathans. Moscow, 1994.

————, ed. *Tsarskoe pravitel'stvo i khasidskoe dvizhenie v Rossii: Arkhivnye dokumenty.* N.p., 1994.

Dinur, Ben-Tsiyon. "Tokhniyotav shel Ignatev le-fitron 'she'elat ha-yehudim' u-veidat netsige ha-kehilot be-peterburg bi-shnot 1881–82." *He-'Avar* 10 (1963): 5–82.

Dnevnik gosudarstvennogo sekretaria A. A. Polovtsova. 2 vols. Moscow, 1966.

Dostoevskii, F. M. *Dnevnik pisatelia.* In Dostoevskii, *Polnoe sobranie sochinenii v tridtsati tomakh,* vol. 25. Leningrad, 1983.

Dreizin, Felix. *The Russian Soul and the Jew: Essays in Ethno-Literary Criticism.* Philadelphia, 1990.

Druyanov, Alter, and Shulamit Laskov, eds. *Ketavim le-toldot hibat-tsiyon ve-yishuv Erets-Yisrael.* 7 vols. Tel Aviv, 1982.

Dubin, Lois C. *The Port Jews of Habsburg Trieste: Absolutist Politics and Enlightenment Culture.* Stanford, 1999.

Dubnov [Dubnow], S. M. *History of the Jews in Russia and Poland from the Earliest Times until the Present Day.* Trans. I. Friedlander. 3 vols. Philadelphia, 1916.

———. *Kniga zhizni.* 3 vols. Riga, 1934–35 (vols. 1 and 2); New York, 1957 (vol. 3).

———. *Ob izuchenii istorii russkikh evreev i ob uchrezhdenii russko-evreiskogo istoricheskogo obshchestva.* St. Petersburg, 1891.

———. *Pis´ma o starom i novom evreistve.* St. Petersburg, 1907.

Dubnova-Erlikh, Sofiia. *Khleb i matsa.* St. Petersburg, 1996.

Dudgeon, Ruth. "The Forgotten Minority: Women Students in Imperial Russia, 1872–1917." *Russian History/Histoire Russe,* no. 9 (1982): 1–26.

Eckardt, Julius [presumed author]. *Aus der Petersburger Gesellschaft.* Leipzig, 1881.

Ehrlich, Adolf. *Entwickelungsgeschichte der israelitischen Gemeindeschule zu Riga.* St. Petersburg, 1894.

Eisenbach, Artur. *The Emancipation of the Jews in Poland, 1780–1870.* London, 1991.

Eklof, Ben, et al., eds. *Russia's Great Reforms, 1855–1881.* Bloomington, 1994.

El´iashevich, D. A. ed. *Dokumental´nye materialy po istorii evreev v arkhivakh SNG i stran Baltii.* St. Petersburg, 1994.

Emmons, Terence. *The Russian Landed Gentry and the Peasant Emancipation of 1861.* Cambridge, 1968.

Encyclopedia Judaica. 16 vols. Jerusalem, 1972.

Endelman, Todd. *The Jews of Georgian England, 1714–1830: Tradition and Change in a Liberal Society.* Philadelphia, 1979.

Engel, Barbara Alpern. "Russian Peasant Views of City Life." *Slavic Review* 52, no. 3 (Fall 1993): 446–59.

Engel´, G., and V. Gorokhov. *Iz istorii studencheskogo dvizheniia, 1899–1906.* St. Petersburg, n.d.

Engelstein, Laura. "Combined Underdevelopment: Discipline and the Law in Imperial and Soviet Russia." *American Historical Review* 98, no. 2 (April 1993): 338–53.

———. *The Keys to Happiness: Sex and the Search for Modernity in Fin-de-Siècle Russia.* Ithaca, 1992.

Engman, Max. "The Finns in St. Petersburg." In Engman, ed., *Ethnic Identity in Urban Europe.* New York, 1992.

Entsiklopedicheskii slovar´ Brokgaus-Efrona. 41 vols. St. Petersburg, 1890–1904.

Etkes, Imanuel. "Parashat ha-haskalah mi-ta‘am ve-hatemurah be-ma‘amad tenuat ha-haskalah be-rusiyah." *Tsiyon,* no. 43 (1978): 264–313.

Evreiskaia entsiklopediia: Svod znanii o evreistve i ego kul´ture v proshlom i nastoiashchem. 16 vols. St. Petersburg, 1906–13.

Evreiskii vopros v kartinkakh. Kiev, 1885.

Evreiskoe Statisticheskoe Obshchestvo. *Evreiskoe naselenie Rossii po dannym perepisi 1897 g. i po noveishim istochnikam.* Petrograd, 1917.

Field, Daniel. *The End of Serfdom: Nobility and Bureaucracy in Russia, 1855–1861.* Cambridge, Mass., 1976.

Fishman, David. *Russia's First Modern Jews: The Jews of Shklov.* New York, 1995.

Flynn, James. *The University Reform of Alexander I, 1802–1835.* Washington, D.C., 1988.

Frankel, Jonathan. "The Crisis of 1881–82 as a Turning Point in Modern Jewish History." In David Berger, ed., *The Legacy of Jewish Migration: 1881 and Its Impact.* New York, 1983.

———. *The Damascus Affair: "Ritual Murder," Politics, and the Jews in 1840.* Cambridge, 1997.

———. *Prophecy and Politics: Socialism, Nationalism, and the Russian Jews, 1862–1917.* Cambridge, 1981.

Frankel, Jonathan, and Steven Zipperstein, eds. *Assimilation and Community: The Jews in Nineteenth-Century Europe.* Cambridge, 1992.

Freeze, ChaeRan. "The Litigious Gerusha: Jewish Women and Divorce in Imperial Russia." *Nationalities Papers* 25, no. 1 (1997).

Freeze, Gregory. *The Parish Clergy in Nineteenth-Century Russia: Crisis, Reform, Counter-Reform.* Princeton, 1983.

———. "The *Soslovie* (Estate) Paradigm and Russian Social History." *American Historical Review* 91, no. 1 (February 1986): 11–36.

Furet, François. *Interpreting the French Revolution.* Cambridge, 1981.

Garkavi [Harkavi], Vladimir Osipovich. *Otryvki vospominaniia.* St. Petersburg, 1913.

Gassenschmidt, Christoph. *Jewish Liberal Politics in Tsarist Russia, 1900–1914.* New York, 1995.

Gegidze, Boris. *V universitete: Nabroski studencheskoi zhizni.* 6th ed. St. Petersburg, n.d.

Georgievskii, A. *Doklad po voprosu o merakh otnositel´no obrazovaniia evreev.* St. Petersburg, 1886.

Gernet, M. N. *Istoriia russkoi advokatury.* Vol. 2: *Soslovnaia organizatsiia advokatury, 1864–1914.* Moscow, 1916.

Gertsen [Herzen], Aleksandr. *Byloe i dumy.* 3 vols. Moscow, 1982. Published in English as *My Past and Thoughts: The Memoirs of Alexander Herzen,* trans. Constance Garnett. New York, 1968.

Gessen, Iu. I. *Istoriia evreiskogo naroda v Rossii.* 2 vols. Leningrad, 1925–27.

———. "Popytka emansipatsii evreev v Rossii (po neizdannym materialam)." *Perezhitoe* 1 (1909): 144–63.

Gessen, I. V. *Istoriia russkoi advokatury.* Vol. 1: *Advokatura, obshchestvo i gosudarstvo, 1864–1914.* Moscow, 1914.

———. *V dvukh vekakh: zhiznennyi otchet.* Berlin, 1937.

Gessen, I. V., and V. Fridshtein, eds. *Sbornik zakonov o evreiakh s ras˝iasneniiami po opredeleniiam Pravitel´stvuiushchago Senata i tsirkuliaram Ministerstv.* St. Petersburg, 1904.

Gessen, V. Iu. *K istorii Sankt-Peterburgskoi evreiskoi religioznoi obshchiny: Ot pervykh evreev do XX veka.* St. Petersburg, 2000.

Gilman, Sander. *Smart Jews: The Construction of the Image of Jewish Superior Intelligence.* Lincoln, Neb., 1996.

Gimpel´son, Ia. I., comp. *Zakony o evreiakh: Sistematicheskii obzor deistvuiushchikh zakonopolozhenii o evreiakh.* Ed. L. M. Bramson. 2 vols. St. Petersburg, 1914–15.

Gintsburg, E[vzel]. "Zapiska, predstavlennaia pochetnym grazhdaninom Ginzburgom [*sic*], po voprosu o postepennoi emansipatsii russkogo Evreiskogo naseleniia." In *Materialy Komissii po ustroistvu byta evreev*, item 15. St. Petersburg, 1879.

Gintsburg, Sophie. "David avi." *He-ʿAvar*, no. 6 (1958): 152–65.

Ginzburg, S. M. *Amolike Peterburg: Forshungn un zikhroynes vegn yidishn lebn in der rezidents-shtot fun tsarishn rusland*. New York, 1944.

——. *Historishe verk*. 3 vols. New York, 1937.

——. *Otechestvennaia voina 1812 goda i russkie evrei*. St. Petersburg, 1912.

Ginzburg, S. M., and P. S. Marek. *Evreiskie narodnye pesni*. St. Petersburg, 1901.

Glubokovskii, N. N. *Po voprosu o "prave" evreev imenovatʹsia khristianskimi imenami: Traktat i istoricheskaia spravka*. St. Petersburg, 1911.

Golʹdberg, B. A. *L. O. Levanda kak publitsist: Po sluchaiu 40-letnego iubeleia vozniknoveniia russko-evreiskoi pechati*. Vilna, 1900.

Golʹdshtein, M. L. *Advokatskie portrety*. Paris, 1932.

——. *Rechi i statʹi*. Paris, 1929.

Goldstein, David. *Dostoevsky and the Jews*. New York, 1981.

Gordon, Y. L. *Kitve Yehudah Leib Gordon: Prozah*. Tel Aviv, 1960.

——. *Kitve Yehudah Leib Gordon: Shirah*. Tel Aviv, 1956.

Gradovskii, N. D. *Torgovye i drugie prava evreev v Rossii v istoricheskom khode zakonodatelʹnykh mer*. St. Petersburg, 1885.

Greenberg, Louis. *The Jews in Russia: The Struggle for Emancipation*. 2 vols. New York, 1976.

Greenfeld, Liah. *Nationalism: Five Roads to Modernity*. Cambridge, Mass., 1993.

Grinberg, S. *Jewish Life in St. Petersburg: A Paper Read before the Cambridge Branch of the Anglo-Jewish Association on Friday, February 13, 1914*. Cambridge, 1914.

Grossman, L. P. *Ispovedʹ odnogo evreia*. Moscow, 1924.

Grossman, Vladimir. *Amol un heynt*. Paris, 1955.

Gruzenberg, O. O. *Ocherki i rechi*. New York, 1944.

——. *O petrogradskoi advokatskoi gromade*. Petrograd, 1916.

Haberer, Erich. *Jews and Revolution in Nineteenth-Century Russia*. Cambridge, 1995.

Hagen, Mark L. von. "Writing the History of Russia as Empire: The Perspective of Federalism." In Catherine Evtuhov, Boris Gasparov, Alexander Ospovat, and Mark von Hagen, eds., *Kazan, Moscow, St. Petersburg: Multiple Faces of the Russian Empire*, pp. 393–410. Moscow, 1997.

Ha-Kohen, Mordechai ben Hillel. *Olami*. 4 vols. Jerusalem, 1927–29.

Halevy, Zvi. *Jewish University Students and Professionals in Tsarist and Soviet Russia*. Tel Aviv, 1976.

Hamburg, Gary. *Boris Chicherin and Early Russian Liberalism, 1828–1866*. Stanford, 1992.

Hamm, Michael. *Kiev: A Portrait, 1800–1917*. Princeton, 1993.

——. "Liberalism and the Jewish Question: The Progressive Bloc." *Russian Review* 31 (1972): 163–72.

Hammer-Schenk, Harold. *Synagogen in Deutschland: Geschichte einer Baugattung im 19. und 20. Jahrhundert*. 2 vols. Hamburg, 1981.

Hausmann, Guido. "Der Numerus clausus für jüdische Studenten im Zarenreich." *Jahrbücher für Geschichte Osteuropas* 41 (1993): 509–31.

Herzog, Elizabeth, and Mark Zborowski. *Life Is with People: The Culture of the Shtetl*. New York, 1952.

Hildermeier, Manfred. *Bürgertum und Stadt in Russland, 1760–1870: Rechtliche Lage und soziale Struktur*. Cologne, 1986.

———. "Die jüdische Frage im Zarenreich: Zum Problem der unterbliebenen Emanzipation." *Jahrbücher für Geschichte Osteuropas* 32, no. 3 (1989): 321–57.

Hirshbein, Peretz. *In gang fun lebn: Zikhroynes*. 2 vols. New York, 1948.

Hoberman, J. *Bridge of Light: Yiddish Film between Two Worlds*. New York, 1991.

Hoch, Steven. "The Banking Crisis, Peasant Reform, and Economic Development in Russia, 1857–1861." *American Historical Review* 96, no. 3 (June 1991): 795–820.

Hosking, Goeffrey. *Russia: People and Empire*. Cambridge, Mass., 1997.

Hunt, Lynn, ed. and trans. *The French Revolution and Human Rights: A Brief Documentary History*. Boston, 1996.

Hyman, Paula. *The Jews of Modern France*. Berkeley, 1998.

Israel, Jonathan. *European Jewry in the Age of Mercantilism, 1550–1750*. New York, 1989.

Iukhneva, N. V. *Etnicheskii sostav i etnosotsial′naia struktura naseleniia Peterburga, vtoraia polovina XIX–nachalo XX veka: Statisticheskii analiz*. Leningrad, 1984.

———. *Peterburg i guberniia: Istoriko-etnograficheskie issledovaniia*. Leningrad, 1989.

———. "Peterburg kak tsentr natsional′no-kul′turnykh dvizhenii narodov Rossii." In *Etnografiia Peterburga-Leningrada*, vol. 1. Leningrad, 1987.

Ivanov, A. E. *Studenchestvo Rossii kontsa XIX–nachalo XX veka: Sotsial′no-istoricheskaia sud′ba*. Moscow, 1999.

Izgoev, A. S. "Ob intelligentnoi molodezhi." In M. O. Gershenzon et al., eds., *Vekhi: Sbornik statei o russkoi intelligentsii*. 2d ed. 1909; rpt. St. Petersburg, 1990.

Janowsky, Oscar. *The Jews and Minority Rights, 1898–1919*. New York, 1933.

Jarausch, Konrad. "Jewish Lawyers in Germany, 1848–1938. The Disintegration of a Profession." *Leo Baeck Institute Year Book* 36 (1991): 71–90.

———. *Students, Society, and Politics in Imperial Germany: The Rise of Academic Illiberalism*. Princeton, 1982.

———. *The Unfree Professions: German Lawyers, Teachers, and Engineers, 1900–1950*. New York, 1990.

Johanson, Christine. *Women's Struggle for Higher Education in Russia, 1855–1900*. Montreal, 1987.

Judge, Edward. *Easter in Kishinev: Anatomy of a Pogrom*. New York, 1992.

Kahan, Arcadius. *Essays in Jewish Social and Economic History*. Chicago, 1986.

Kampe, Norbert. "Jews and Antisemites at Universities in Imperial Germany (I). Jewish Students: Social History and Social Conflict." *Leo Baeck Institute Year Book* 30 (1985): 357–94.

———. *Studenten und "Judenfrage" im deutschen Kaiserreich: Die Entstehung einer akademischen Tragerschicht des Antisemitismus*. Göttingen, 1988.

Kaniel, Y. *Hemshekh u-tmurah: Ha-yishuv ha-yashan ve-hayishuv he-hadash be-tkufat ha-ʿaliyah ha-shniyah*. Jerusalem, 1982.

Kaplan, Marion. *The Making of the Jewish Middle Class: Women, Family, and Identity in Imperial Germany*. New York, 1991.

Kappeler, Andreas. *Rußland als Vielvölkerreich: Entstehung, Geschichte, Zerfall*. Munich, 1992.

Kassow, Samuel. *Students, Professors, and the State in Tsarist Russia*. Berkeley, 1989.

Katz, Jacob. *Emancipation and Assimilation: Studies in Modern Jewish History*. Westmead, 1972.

————. *Out of the Ghetto: The Social Background of Jewish Emancipation, 1770–1870.* New York, 1978.

————. *Tradition and Crisis: Jewish Society at the End of the Middle Ages.* New York, 1961.

————, ed. *Toward Modernity: The European Jewish Model.* New Brunswick, 1987.

Kelly, Catriona, and David Shepherd, eds. *Constructing Russian Culture in the Age of Revolution, 1881–1940.* New York, 1998.

Kel´ner, Stanislav. "Soiuz dlia dostizheniia polnopraviia evreiskogo naroda v Rossii i ego lidery." *Iz glubiny vremen* 7 (1996): 3–14.

Kerensky, Alexander. *The Crucifixion of Liberty.* New York, 1934.

Khiterer, V. *Dokumenty sobrannye evreiskoi istoriko-arkheograficheskoi komissiei vseukrainskoi akademii nauk.* Kiev and Jerusalem, 1999.

Khodasevich, V. F., and L. B. Iaffe, eds. *Evreiskaia Antologiia: Sbornik molodoi evreiskoi poezii.* Moscow, n.d.

Kiselev, P. D. "Ob ustroistve evreiskogo naroda v Rossii." *Voskhod,* nos. 4–5 (1901): 25–40 and 3–21.

Kistiakovskii, B. A. "V zashchitu prava: Intelligentsiia i pravosoznanie." In *Vekhi: Sbornik statei o russkoi intelligentsii.* 2d ed. 1909; rpt. St. Petersburg, 1990.

K kharakteristike evreiskogo studenchestva (po dannym ankety sredi evreiskogo studenchestva g. Kieva v noiabre 1910 g.). Kiev, 1913.

K kharakteristike sovremennogo studenchestva (po dannym perepisi 1909–10 g. v SPb-skom Tekhnologicheskom Institute). St. Petersburg, 1910.

Klier, John D. "The Concept of 'Jewish Emancipation' in a Russian Context." In Olga Crisp and Linda Edmondson, eds., *Civil Rights in Imperial Russia,* pp. 121–44. Oxford, 1989.

————. *Imperial Russia's Jewish Question, 1855–1881.* Cambridge, 1995.

————. "The Jewish *Den´* and the Literary Mice, 1869–1871." *Russian History* 10, no. 1 (1983): 31–49.

————. "The Jewish Question in the Reform-Era Russian Press, 1855–1865." *Russian Review* 39, no. 3 (1980): 1–15.

————. "1855–1894 Censorship of the Press in Russia and the Jewish Question." *Jewish Social Studies* 48, no. 3–4 (1986): 257–68.

————. *Russia Gathers Her Jews: The Origins of the "Jewish Question" in Russia, 1772–1825.* De Kalb, Ill., 1986.

————. "The Russian Press and the Anti-Jewish Pogroms of 1881." *Canadian-American Slavic Studies* 17, no. 1 (1983): 199–221.

————. "Russification and the Polish Revolt of 1863: Bad for the Jews?" *Polin* 1 (1986): 91–106.

————. "Russkaia voina protiv 'Hevra kadisha.'" In D. A. El´iashevich, ed., *Istoriia evreev v Rossii: Problemy istochnikovedeniia i istoriografii.* St. Petersburg, 1993.

————. "*Zhid:* The Biography of a Russian Pejorative." *Slavonic and East European Review* 60, no. 1 (January 1982): 1–15.

Klier, John, and Shlomo Lambroza, eds. *Pogroms: Anti-Jewish Violence in Modern Russian History.* Cambridge, 1992.

Kohn, Hans. *The Idea of Nationalism: A Study in Its Origins and Background.* New York, 1944.

Kolonitskii, Boris Ivanovich. "'Democracy' in the Political Consciousness of the February Revolution." *Slavic Review* 57, no. 1 (Spring 1998): 95–107

Koprzhiva-Lur´e, B. Ia. *Istoriia odnoi zhizni.* Paris, 1987.

Kots, Elena Semenova. *"Kontrabandisty* (Vospominaniia)." *Byloe: Zhurnal, posviash-chennyi istorii osvoboditel´nogo dvizheniia* 3, no. 37 (1926): 42–50.

Kovacs, Maria. *Liberal Professions and Illiberal Politics: Hungary from the Habsburgs to the Holocaust.* New York, 1995.

Krestovskii, Vsevolod V. *Peterburgskie trushchoby.* Rpt. Moscow, 1990.

———. *Zhid idet!* St. Petersburg, 1899.

Krol´, Moisei Aronovich. *Stranitsy moei zhizni.* New York, 1944.

———. "Vospominaniia o L. Ia. Shternberge." *Katorga i ssylka* 27/28 (1929).

Krupnik, I. I., ed. *Etnicheskie gruppy v gorodakh evropeiskoi chasti SSSR (formirovanie, ras-selenie, dinamika kul´tury).* Moscow, 1987.

Krylov, V., and S. Litvin. *Syny Izrailia: Drama v 4-kh deistviiakh i 5-i kartinakh.* St. Peters-burg, 1899.

Kucherov, Samuel L. *Courts, Lawyers, and Trials under the Last Three Tsars.* New York, 1953.

———. "Evrei v russkoi advokature." In *Kniga o russkom evreistve.* New York, 1960.

Kupovetskii, Mark, et al., eds. *Dokumenty po istorii i kul´ture evreev v arkhivakh Moskvy.* Moscow, 1997.

Kuznets, Simon. "Immigration of Russian Jews to the United States: Background and Structure," *Perspectives in American History* 9 (1975): 35–124.

Lederhendler, Eli. *The Road to Modern Jewish Politics: Political Tradition and Political Re-construction in the Jewish Community of Tsarist Russia.* New York, 1989.

Levanda. L. O. *Goriachee vremia.* St. Petersburg, 1875.

———. *Ispoved´ del´tsa.* St. Petersburg, 1880.

[Levin, E. B.]. *Obzor nyne deistvuiushchikh iskliuchitel´nykh zakonov o evreiakh, sos-toiashchikh v poddanstve Rossii.* St. Petersburg, 1883.

———. *Svod uzakonenii o Evreiakh: S izmeneniiami, posledovavshimi po 15 oktiabria 1884 goda.* St. Petersburg, 1885.

———. "Zapiska ob emansipatsii evreev v Rossii." *Evreiskaia Starina* 8, no. 3 (1915): 300–308.

Levin, Shmarya. *The Arena.* New York, 1932.

———. *Youth in Revolt.* New York, 1930.

Levin, V. A. "Ocherk istorii evreiskogo shkol´nogo obrazovaniia v dorevoliutsionnom Peterburge." In *Evreiskaia Shkola,* pp. 74–86. St. Petersburg, 1993.

Levitats, Isaac. *The Jewish Community in Russia, 1844–1917.* Jerusalem, 1981.

Levitskii, Vladimir. *Za chertvert´ veka.* Moscow, 1926.

Liakhovetskii, L. L. *Mechta i deistvitel´nost´: Rasskaz iz zhizni evreiskoi molodezhi.* St. Peters-burg, 1884.

Lifshits, G. *Ispoved´ prestupnika: Iumoristicheskii rasskaz iz zhizni peterburgskikh evreev.* St. Petersburg, 1881.

Lifshitz, Yaʿakov Halevi. *Zikhron Yaʿakov.* 3 vols. Frankfurt a. M., 1924.

Lilienblum, Moshe Leib. *Ketavim otobiografiyim.* Ed. Shlomo Breiman. 3 vols. Jeru-salem, 1970.

Lincoln, W. Bruce. *The Great Reforms: Autocracy, Bureaucracy, and the Politics of Change in Imperial Russia.* De Kalb, Ill., 1990.

———. *In the Vanguard of Reform: Russia's Enlightened Bureaucrats, 1825–1861.* De Kalb, Ill., 1982.

Lindenmeyr, Adele. *Poverty Is Not a Vice: Charity, Society, and the State in Imperial Russia.* Princeton, 1996.

Lotman, Iurii, and Boris Uspensky. "The Role of Dual Models in the Dynamics of Russian Culture." In Lotman and Uspensky, *The Semiotics of Russian Culture,* pp. 3–35. Ann Arbor, 1984.

Löwe, Heinz-Dietrich. *Antisemitismus und reaktionäre Utopie: Russischer Konservatismus im Kampf gegen den Wandel von Staat und Gesellschaft, 1890–1917.* Hamburg, 1978.

———. *The Tsars and the Jews: Reform, Reaction, and Anti-Semitism in Imperial Russia.* New York, 1992.

Lur´e, Iosif. *Ukazaniia o prave zhitel´stva dlia pereseliaiushchikhsia vo vnutrennie gubernii.* St. Petersburg, 1908.

Maksim Moiseevich Vinaver i russkaia obshchestvennost´ nachala XX veka: Sbornik statei. Paris, 1937.

Malia, Martin. *Alexander Herzen and the Birth of Russian Socialism.* New York, 1971.

Malkin, Carole, ed. *The Journeys of David Toback.* New York, 1981.

Mandel´shtam, L. I. *V zashchitu evreev: Stat´i.* St. Petersburg, 1859.

Mandel´shtam, Osip E. *Sobranie sochineniia.* 3 vols. Moscow, 1991.

Maor, Yitshak. "Eliyahu Orshanski u-mekomo be-historiografiyah shel yehudei rusiyah." *He-ʿAvar* 20 (1973): 49–61.

———. *She'elat ha-yehudim ba-tenuah ha-liberalit ve-ha-mahapehanit be-rusiyah, 1890–1914.* Jerusalem, 1964.

Marchand, Suzanne. *Down from Olympus: Archeology and Philhellenism in Germany, 1750–1970.* Princeton, 1996.

Marek, Pavel. *Ocherki po istorii prosveshcheniia evreev v Rossii: Dva vospitaniia.* Moscow, 1909.

Margolin, Arnold D. *The Jews of Eastern Europe.* New York, 1926.

Markish, Shimon. "Stoit li perechityvat´ L´vu Levandu?" *Vestnik evreiskogo universiteta v Moskve,* no. 3 (10) (1995): 89–140, and no. 2 (12) (1996): 168–93.

Masaryk, Thomas. *The Spirit of Russia: Studies in History, Literature, and Philosophy.* London, 1955.

Materialy k sozyvu vserossiiskogo advokatskogo s˜ezda: Protokoly soveshchanii predstavitelei sovetov prisiazhnykh poverennykh v Petrograde i Moskve. Moscow, 1916.

Materialy po voprosu o prieme evreev v sredniia i vysshiia uchebnyia zavedeniia. St. Petersburg, 1908.

McClelland, Charles. *State, Society, and University in Germany, 1700–1914.* Cambridge, 1980.

McClelland, James C. *Autocrats and Academics: Education, Culture, and Society in Tsarist Russia.* Chicago, 1979.

McReynolds, Louise. *The News under Russia's Old Regime: The Development of a Mass-Circulation Press.* Princeton, 1991.

Medem, Vladimir. *The Life and Soul of a Legendary Jewish Socialist.* Trans. Samuel Portnoy. New York, 1979.

Meinecke, Friedrich. *Die deutsche Katastrophe.* Wiesbaden, 1965.

Mendelsohn, Ezra. *Class Struggle in the Pale: The Formative Years of the Jewish Workers' Movement in Tsarist Russia.* Cambridge, 1970.

Mendes-Flohr, Paul, and Jehuda Reinharz, comps. *The Jew in the Modern World: A Documentary History.* 2d ed. New York, 1995.

Meyer, Michael A. "The German Model of Religious Reform and Russian Jewry." In
  I. Twersky, ed. *Danzig, between East and West: Aspects of Modern Jewish History.* Har-
  vard Judaic Texts and Studies 4. Cambridge, 1985.
———, ed. *German-Jewish History in Modern Times.* Vol. 2: *Emancipation and Accultur-
  ation, 1780–1871.* New York, 1996.
Mill, John Stuart. *Mill on Bentham and Coleridge.* London, 1967.
Miller, Phillip E., ed. and trans. *Karaite Separatism in Nineteenth-Century Russia: Joseph
  Solomon Lutski's "Epistle of Israel's Deliverance."* Cincinatti, 1993.
Ministerstvo narodnogo prosveshcheniia. *Trudy vysochaishe uchrezhdennoi komissii po
  preobrazovanniiu vysshykh uchebnykh zavedenii.* St. Petersburg, 1903–.
Minor, Zalkind. *Glas radosti. Rech´ po sluchaiu Vysoch. Darovannykh, v 27 den´ noiabria
  1861 goda, preimushchestv evreiam, poluchivshim obrazovanie i sluzhashchim pri evreiskikh
  uchebnykh zavedeniiakh. Proiznesena 21-go ianvaria 1862 g. v Minskom bol´shom
  Molitvennom Dome.* Minsk, 1862.
———. *Posle pogromov, ili tri glavy o evreiskom voprose.* Moscow, 1882.
Montefiore, Sir Moses, and Lady Judith Cohen Montefiore. *The Diaries of Sir Moses
  and Lady Montefiore.* (1890.) Ed. Louis Loewe. Facs. ed. 2 vols. in 1. London, 1983.
Morgenstern, A. *Meshihiut ve-yishuv erets-yisrael be-mahatsit ha-rishonah shel ha-me'ah ha-
  19.* Jerusalem, 1985.
Morgulis, M. G. "Bezporiadki 1871 goda v Odesse po dokumentam i lichnym vospom-
  inaniiam." In *Teoreticheskie i prakticheskie voprosy evreiskoi zhizni: Prilozhenie k zhurnalu
  "Evreiskii Mir."* St. Petersburg, 1911.
———. *Voprosy evreiskoi zhizni: Sobranie statei.* St. Petersburg, 1903.
Morrissey, Susan. *Heralds of Revolution: Russian Students and the Mythologies of Radical-
  ism.* New York, 1998.
Mosse, George. "Jewish Emancipation between *Bildung* and Respectability." In Jehuda
  Reinharz and Walter Schatzberg, eds., *The Jewish Response to German Culture from
  the Enlightenment to the Second World War,* pp. 1–16. Hannover, 1985.
Mosse, W. E. *Alexander II and the Modernization of Russia.* New York, 1962.
Mysh, M. I., comp. *Rukovodstvo k russkim zakonam o evreiakh.* 3d ed. St. Petersburg, 1904.
[N. N.] "Iz vpechatlenii minuvshogo veka. Vospominaniia srednogo cheloveka."
  Evreiskaia Starina 6, no. 2–4 (1914): 234–46, 429–42; 7, no. 1–2 (1915): 85–99,
  186–200.
Nash Put´: Sbornik, posviashchennyi interesam evreiskogo studenchestva. Petrograd, 1916.
Nathans, Benjamin. "On Russian-Jewish Historiography." In Thomas Sanders, ed.,
  *Historiography of Imperial Russia: The Profession and Writing of History in a Multi-
  National State,* pp. 397–432. Armonk, N.Y., 1999.
———. "The Other Modern Jewish Politics: Integration and Modernity in Fin-de-
  Siècle Russia." In Zvi Gitelman, ed., *A Century of Modern Jewish Politics.* Pittsburgh,
  forthcoming.
Nekrasov, N. A. *Polnoe sobranie sochinenii i pisem.* Vol. 2. Leningrad, 1981.
Neuberger, Joan. " 'Shysters' or Public Servants? Uncertified Lawyers and Legal Aid
  for the Poor in Late Imperial Russia." *Russian History/Histoire Russe* 23, nos. 1–4
  (1996): 295–310.
Neumann, Daniela. *Studentinnen aus dem Russischen Reich in der Schweiz (1867–1914).*
  Zurich, 1987.

Nowinski, Franciszek. *Polacy na uniwersytecie petersburgskim w latach 1832–1884.* Wroclaw, 1986.

Obshchaia zapiska vysshei komissii dlia peresmotra deistvuiushchikh o evreiakh v imperii zakonov. St. Petersburg, 1888.

Odesskoe studenchestvo: itogi ankety sredi evreiskikh studentov, proizvedenoi v 1911–1912 gg. Odessa, 1913.

Orbach, Alexander. "The Jewish People's Group and Jewish Politics in Tsarist Russia, 1906–1914." *Modern Judaism* 10, no. 1 (1990): 1–16.

————. *New Voices of Russian Jewry: A Study of the Russian-Jewish Press of Odessa in the Era of the Great Reforms, 1860–1871.* Leiden, 1980.

————. "The Russian-Jewish Leadership and the Pogroms of 1881–82: The Response from St. Petersburg," *Carl Beck Papers in Russian and East European Studies,* no. 308 (Pittsburgh, 1984).

Orshanskii, I. G. *Evrei v Rossii: Ocherki ekonomicheskogo i obshchestvennogo byta russkikh evreev.* St. Petersburg, 1877.

————. *Russkoe zakonodatel´stvo o evreiakh: Ocherki i issledovaniie.* St. Petersburg, 1877.

Otchet obshchestva dlia rasprostraneniia prosveshcheniia mezhdu evreiami v Rossii. St. Petersburg, annually between 1864 and 1894.

Otchet pravleniia S.-Peterburgskoi evreiskoi obshchiny za vremia s 10 aprelia 1870 goda po 1 ianvaria 1873 goda. St. Petersburg, 1873.

Otchet pravleniia S.-Peterburgskoi evreiskoi obshchiny za 1881 god. St. Petersburg, 1882.

Otchet pravleniia S.-Peterburgskoi evreiskoi obshchiny za 1882 god. St. Petersburg, 1884.

Palen [Pahlen], K. I., and N. N. Golitsyn. *Osoboe mnenie po dokladu A. I. Georgievskogo.* St. Petersburg, 1887.

Panchulidzev, S. A. *Spravka k dokladu po evreiskomu voprosu.* 12 vols. St. Petersburg, 1908–12.

Patai, Raphael. *The Jewish Mind.* Detroit, 1977.

Perlmann, Moshe. "Notes on *Razsvet,* 1860–61." *Proceedings of the American Academy for Jewish Research* 33 (1965): 31–36.

Pervaia vseobshchaia perepis´ naseleniia Rossiiskoi imperii, 1897 goda. 89 vols. St. Petersburg, 1899–1905.

Petrograd po perepisi naseleniia 15 dekabria 1910 goda. Petrograd, n.d.

Philipson, David, ed. *Max Lilienthal, American Rabbi: Life and Writings.* New York, 1915.

Pickus, Keith. *Constructing Modern Identities: Jewish University Students in Germany, 1815–1914.* Detroit, 1999.

Pinkus, Benjamin. *The Jews of the Soviet Union: The History of a National Minority.* Cambridge, 1988.

Pinsker, Lev. *Autoemanzipation! Mahnruf an seine Stammesgenossen von einem russischen Juden.* 1882; rpt. Berlin, 1920.

Pipes, Richard. "Catherine II and the Jews: The Origins of the Pale of Settlement." *Soviet Jewish Affairs* 5 (1975): 3–20.

————. *Russia under the Old Regime.* New York, 1974.

Pistohlkors, Gert von, Toivo Raun, and Paul Kaegbein, eds. *Die Universitäten Dorpat/Tartu, Riga und Wilna/Vilnius, 1579–1979: Beiträge zu ihrer Geschichte und ihrer Wirkung im Grenzbereich zwischen West und Ost.* Cologne and Vienna, 1987.

Polnoe sobranie zakonov Rossiiskoi imperii: Sobranie tret´e. 33 vols. St. Petersburg, 1885–1916.

Polnoe sobranie zakonov Rossiiskoi imperii: Sobranie vtoroe. 62 vols. St. Petersburg, 1830–84.

Pomeranz, William. "Justice from Underground: The History of the Underground *Advokatura.*" *Russian Review* 52 (July 1993): 321–40.

Postel´s, F. [presumed author]. *Materialy, otnosiashchiesia k obrazovaniiu evreev v Rossii.* St. Petersburg, 1865.

——— *Otchet chlena soveta Ministerstva narodnogo prosveshcheniia Postel´sa po obozreniiu evreiskikh uchilishch.* St. Petersburg, 1865.

Pozner, S. V. *Evrei v obshchei shkole: K istorii zakonodatel´stva i pravitel´stvennoi politiki v oblasti evreiskogo voprosa.* St. Petersburg, 1914.

Pravitel´stvuiushchii Senat. *Sobranie uzakonenii i rasporiazhenii pravitel´stva.* St. Petersburg, 1884.

Protsess A. I. Gillersona. St. Petersburg, 1910.

Ptitsyn, Vladimir. *Russkaia advokatura i evrei: Ocherk s prilozheniem.* St. Petersburg, 1905.

Purishkevich, Vladimir M. *Materialy po voprosu o razlozhenii sovremennogo russkogo universiteta.* St. Petersburg, 1914.

Raeff, Marc. *Origins of the Russian Intelligentsia: The Eighteenth-Century Nobility.* New York, 1966.

Rainer, Mirjam. "The Awakening of Jewish National Art in Russia." *Jewish Art,* nos. 16–17 (1990–91): 98–121.

Raisin, Jacob. *The Haskalah Movement in Russia.* Philadelphia, 1913.

Rapaport, Shlomo [Ansky]. *Zikhroynes.* Warsaw, 1925.

Richarz, Monika. *Der Eintritt der Juden in die Akademischen Berufe: Jüdische Studenten und Akademiker in Deutschland, 1678–1848.* Tübingen, 1974.

Rieber, Alfred. "The Formation of 'La Grande Societé des Chemins de Fer Russes.'" *Jahrbücher für Geschichte Osteuropas* 21 (1973): 375–91.

———. *Merchants and Entrepreneurs in Imperial Russia.* Chapel Hill, 1982.

Ringer, Fritz. *Education and Society in Modern Europe.* Bloomington, 1979.

Robinson, Geroid Tanquary. *Rural Russia under the Old Regime: A History of the Landlord-Peasant World and a Prologue to the Peasant Revolution of 1917.* Berkeley, 1967.

Rogger, Hans. *Jewish Policies and Right-Wing Politics in Imperial Russia.* Berkeley, 1986.

Romish [sic]. *Kakoe obrazovanie nuzhno evreiam i gde poluchit´ ego? Blagorazumnyi sovet roditeliam evreiam.* Odessa, 1900.

Rosenthal, Y. L. *Toldot hevrat marbe haskalah be-'erets rusiyah.* 2 vols. St. Petersburg, 1885–1890.

Roskies, David. "S. Ansky and the Paradigm of Return." In Jack Wertheimer, ed., *The Uses of Tradition: Jewish Continuity in the Modern Era,* pp. 243–60. New York, 1992.

Rossiiskaia evreiskaia entsiklopediia. 4 vols. to date. Moscow, 1995–.

Roth, Cecil. "The Jews in the English Universities." *Jewish Historical Society of England: Miscellanies* 4 (1942): 102–15.

Rozenblit, Marsha. *The Jews of Vienna, 1867–1914: Assimilation and Identity.* Albany, 1983.

Rubinshtein, Grigorii. *Vospominaniia starogo advokata.* Riga, 1940.

Ruderman, David. *Jewish Thought and Scientific Discovery in Early Modern Europe.* New Haven, 1995.

Rürup, Reinhard. *Emanzipation und Antisemitismus: Studien zur "Judenfrage" der bürgerlichen Gesellschaft.* Göttingen, 1975.

Samoilovich, G. [Vol′tke, Grigorii Samoilovich]. *O pravakh remeslennikov-evreev.* St. Petersburg, 1894.

Sanktpeterburg po perepisi 10 dekabria 1869 goda. St. Petersburg, 1872.

Sanktpeterburg po perepisi 15 dekabria 1881 goda. St. Petersburg, 1883.

S.-Peterburg po perepisi 15 dekabria 1890 goda. St. Petersburg, 1891.

S.-Peterburg po perepisi 15 dekabria 1900 goda. St. Petersburg, 1903.

"S.-Peterburgskoe okhrannoe otdelenie v 1895–1901 gg.: 'Trud' chinovnika Otdeleniia P. Statkovskii." *Byloe: Zhurnal, posviashchennyi istorii osvoboditel′nogo dvizheniia,* no. 16 (1921).

Schorsch, Ismar. "Emancipation and the Crisis of Religious Authority: The Emergence of the Modern Rabbinate." In Werner Mosse, Arnold Paucker, and Reinhard Rürup, eds., *Revolution and Evolution: 1848 in German-Jewish History,* pp. 205–44. Tübingen, 1981.

Seder ha-ʿavodah le-hanukat bet ʾadonai le-ʿadat yisrael be-kiryat melekh rav s˜t peterburg. St. Petersburg, 1893.

Seltzer, Robert. "From Graetz to Dubnov: The Impact of the East European Milieu on the Writing of Jewish History." In David Berger, ed., *The Legacy of Jewish Migration: 1881 and Its Impact.* New York, 1983.

Serbyn, Roman. "The *Sion-Osnova* Controversy of 1861–1862." In Peter Potichnyi and Howard Aster, eds., *Ukrainian-Jewish Relations in Historical Perspective,* pp. 85–100. Edmonton, 1988.

Shazar, Zalman. *Morning Stars.* Philadelphia, 1967.

Sheinis, D. I. *Evreiskoe studenchestvo v Moskve po dannym ankety 1913 g.* Moscow, 1914.

———. *Evreiskoe studenchestvo v tsifrakh (po dannym perepisi 1909 g. v Kievskom universitete i politekhnicheskom institute).* Kiev, 1911.

Shimonovich, D. "Sfinsky." In V. F. Khodasevich and L. B. Iaffe, eds., *Evreiskaia Antologiia: Sbornik molodoi evreiskoi poezii.* Moscow, n.d.

Shochat, Azriel. "Ha-hanhaga be-kehilot rusiya im bitul ha-kahal." *Tsiyon* 42, nos. 3–4 (1977): 143–233.

———. "Hashkafotav ha-asimilatoriyot shel Zalkind Minor, ha-rav mi-taʿam shel kehillat moskvah." *Tsiyon* 44 (1979): 303–20.

———. *Mosad "ha-rabanut mi-taʿam" be-rusiyah.* Haifa, 1975.

Sistematicheskii ukazatel′ literatury o evreiakh na russkom iazyke s vremeni vvedeniia grazhdanskogo shrifta 1708 g. po dekabr′ 1889 goda. St. Petersburg, 1892.

Sliozberg, G. B. "Baron G. O. Gintsburg i pravovoe polozhenie evreev." *Perezhitoe* 2 (1910): 94–115.

———. *Baron G. O. Gintsburg, ego zhizn′ i deiatel′nost′.* Paris, 1933.

———. *Dela minuvshikh dnei: Zapiski russkogo evreia.* 3 vols. Paris, 1933.

———. "Dorevoliutsionnoe russkoe studenchestvo." In P. A. Bobrinskoi et al., eds., *Pamiati russkogo studenchestva: Sbornik vospominanii,* pp. 82–94. Paris, 1934.

Slovar′ akademii rossiiskoi. St. Petersburg, 1806–22.

Slovar′ tserkovno-slavianskogo i russkogo iazyka. St. Petersburg, 1847.

Slutskii, M. B. *Moi vospominaniia iz detstva, iunosti i poluvekovoi vrachebnoi i obshchestvennoi deiatel′nosti.* Kishinev, 1927.

Slutsky, Yehuda. *Ha-itonut ha-yehudit-rusit ba-meʾah ha-tesha-ʿesre.* Jerusalem, 1970.

Smith, Anthony. *The Ethnic Origins of Nations.* New York, 1987.

Smolenskin, P. *Gemul Yesharim.* Warsaw, 1905.

Soiuz Studentov S.-Peterburgskogo Universiteta i Akademicheskii Soiuz Slushatel´nits S.-Peterburgskikh Vysshikh Zhenskikh Kursov. *Universitet i politika.* St. Petersburg, 1906.

Spasovich, V. D. *Zastol´nyia rechi V. D. Spasovicha v sobraniiakh sosloviia prisiazhnykh poverennykh okruga S.-Peterburgskoi sudebnoi palaty, 1873–1901.* Leipzig, 1903.

Spravochnaia kniga po voprosam obrazovaniia evreev: Posobie dlia uchitelei i uchitel´nits evreiskikh shkol i deiatelei po narodnomu obrazovaniiu. St. Petersburg, 1901.

Stampfer, Shaul. "Gender Differentiation and Education of the Jewish Woman in Nineteenth-Century Eastern Europe." *Polin* 7 (1992): 63–87.

———. *Ha-yeshivah ha-lita'it be-hithavutah.* Jerusalem, 1995.

———. "Heder Study, Knowledge of Torah, and the Maintenance of Social Stratification in Traditional East European Jewish Society." *Studies in Jewish Education* 3 (1988): 271–89.

———. "Remarriage Among Jews and Christians in Nineteenth-Century Eastern Europe." *Jewish History* 3, no. 2 (Fall 1988): 85–114.

———. "Yedi'at kero ukhtov etsel yehude mizrah eropah ba-tekufah ha-hadashah." In Shmuel Elmog et al., eds., *Temurot ba-historiyah ha-yehudit ha-hadashah: Kovets ma'amarim: Shai li-Shmu'el Etinger,* pp. 459–83. Jerusalem, 1987.

Stanislawski, Michael. *For Whom Do I Toil? Judah Leib Gordon and the Crisis of Russian Jewry.* New York, 1988.

———. *Psalms for the Tsar.* New York, 1988.

———. *Tsar Nicholas I and the Jews: The Transformation of Jewish Society in Russia, 1825–1855.* Philadelphia, 1983.

Starn, Randolph. "Historians and Crisis." *Past and Present,* no. 52 (August 1971), pp. 3–22.

———. "Meaning-Levels in the Theme of Historical Decline." *History and Theory* 14, no. 1 (1975): 1–31.

Starr, S. Frederick. "Tsarist Government: The Imperial Dimension." In Jeremy Azrael, ed., *Soviet Nationality Policies and Practices,* pp. 3–31. New York, 1978.

Stasov, V. V. ed. *M. M. Antokol´skii: Ego zhizn´, tvoreniia, pis´ma, i stat´i.* St. Petersburg, 1905.

Statisticheskii ezhegodnik S.-Peterburga 1881 goda. St. Petersburg, 1882.

Statisticheskii ezhegodnik S.-Peterburga 1883 goda. St. Petersburg, 1884.

Statisticheskii ezhegodnik S.-Peterburga 1884 goda. St. Petersburg, 1885.

Statisticheskii ezhegodnik S.-Peterburga 1892 goda. St. Petersburg, 1893.

Statisticheskii ezhegodnik S.-Peterburga 1896–97 gg. St. Petersburg, 1899.

Stead, W. T. *The Truth about Russia.* London, 1888.

Stern, Selma. *The Court Jew: A Contribution to the History of the Period of Absolutism in Central Europe.* Philadelphia, 1950.

Stites, Richard. *Russian Popular Culture: Entertainment and Society since 1900.* Cambridge, 1992.

———. *The Women's Liberation Movement in Russia: Feminism, Nihilism, and Bolshevism, 1860–1930.* Princeton, 1978.

Tarnopol, I. *Opyt sovremennoi i osmotritel´noi reformy v oblasti iudaizma v Rossii.* Odessa, 1868.

Tazbir, Janusz. "Images of the Jew in the Polish Commonwealth." *Polin* 4 (1989): 18–29.

Tcherikover, E. [Cherikover, I.]. *Istoriia Obshchestva dlia rasprostraneniia prosveshcheniia mezhdu evreiami v Rossii, 1863–1913*. St. Petersburg, 1913.

———, ed. *Historishe Shriftn*. Vol. 1. Warsaw, 1929.

Teitel, Iakov. *Aus meiner Lebensarbeit: Erinnerungen eines jüdischen Richters im alten Rußland*. Frankfurt a. M., 1929.

———. *Iz moei zhizni*. Paris, 1925.

Timberlake, Charles. "Higher Learning, the State, and the Professions in Russia." In Konrad Jarausch, ed., *The Transformation of Higher Learning, 1860–1930: Expansion, Diversification, Social Opening, and Professionalization in England, Germany, Russia, and the United States*. Chicago, 1983.

Timoshenko, Stephen P. *As I Remember: The Autobiography of Stephen P. Timoshenko*. Trans. Robert Addis. Princeton, 1968.

Tobias, Henry. *The Jewish Bund in Russia from Its Origins to 1905*. Stanford, 1972.

Tönnies, Ferdinand. *Community and Society*. Trans. and ed. Charles P. Loomis. New York, 1963.

Toury, Jacob. " 'The Jewish Question': A Semantic Approach." *Leo Baeck Institute Year Book* 11 (1966): 85–106.

Trainin, A. N. "Ia zhil za chertoi." *Sovietskoe studenchestvo*, no. 8 (1937).

Trudy Chernigovskoi komissii po evreiskomu voprosu. Chernigov, 1881.

Trudy s˝ezdov po evreiskomu professional´nomu obrazovaniiu. St. Petersburg, 1911.

Tsinberg, Israel [S. L.]. *Istoriia evreiskoi pechati v Rossii v sviazi s obshchestvennymi techeniiami*. St. Petersburg, 1915.

Tsitron, S. L. *Shtadlonim: Interesante yidishe tipn fun noentn avar*. Warsaw, 1926.

Tsunzer, E. *Tsunzers biografiye, geshribn fun im aleyn*. New York, 1905.

Tsypkin, P. S., ed. *Svod zakonopolozhenii o prisiazhnoi i chastnoi advokature*. Petrograd, 1916.

Turner, Frank. *The Greek Heritage in Victorian Britain*. New Haven, 1981.

Tuve, Jeanette. *The First Russian Women Physicians*. Newtonville, Mass., 1984.

Ukaz ego imperatorskogo Velichestva kasatel´no togo, v kakom razstoianii ot pravoslavnykh tserkvei dolzhny byt´ ustraivaemy evreiskie sinagogi i molitvennyia shkoly. St. Petersburg, 1844.

Ukaz Ministru narodnogo prosveshcheniia: Polozhenie o evreiskikh nachal´nykh uchilishchakh. St. Petersburg, n.d.

Vartanov, Iu. P. "Nekotorye dannye o byte peterburgskikh evreev v 70-e gody na stranitsakh gazety 'ha-melits.' " In *Etnografiia Peterburga-Leningrada*, vol. 1. Leningrad, 1987.

Verner, Andrew M. "What's in a Name? Of Dog-killers, Jews, and Rasputin." *Slavic Review* 53, no. 4 (Winter 1994): 1046–70.

Vinaver, M. M. *Nedavnee (vospominaniia i kharakteristiki)*. Paris, 1926.

———. *Ocherki ob advokature*. St. Petersburg, 1902.

Vishniak, Mark Veniaminovich. *Dan´ proshlomu*. New York, 1954.

Vital, David. *The Origins of Zionism*. Oxford, 1975.

Vladimirskii-Budanov, M. F. *Istoriia imperatorskogo universiteta Sv. Vladimira*. Kiev, 1884.

Vol´tke, Grigorii. "Russkie liudi po voprosu ob obrazovanii evreev." *Sbornik v pol´zu evreiskikh shkol*, pp. 493–513. St. Petersburg, 1896.

Vydrin, Rafail. *Osnovnye momenty studencheskogo dvizheniia v Rossii*. Moscow, 1908.

Vysochaishe uchrezhdennaia komissiia dlia peresmotra zakonopolozhenii po sudebnoi chasti:

Ob˝iasnitel´naia zapiska k proektu novoi redaktsii uchrezhdeniia sudebnykh ustanovlenii. Vol. 3. St. Petersburg, 1900.

Vysochaishe uchrezhdennaia pri Ministerstve iustitsii komissiia. St. Petersburg, 1897.

Walicki, Andrzej. *Legal Philosophies of Russian Liberalism.* Oxford, 1987.

Weeks, Theodore. *Nation and State in Late Imperial Russia: Nationalism and Russification on the Western Frontier, 1863–1914.* De Kalb, Ill., 1996.

Weinberg, Robert. *The Revolution of 1905 in Odessa: Blood on the Steps.* Bloomington, 1993.

Weinreich, Max. *Fun bayde zaytn ployt: Dos shturemdike lebn fun Uri Kovner, dem nihilist.* Buenos Aires, 1955.

Weinryb, Bernard. *The Jews of Poland: A Social and Economic History of the Jewish Community in Poland from 1100 to 1800.* Philadelphia, 1973.

Weisser, Albert. *The Modern Renaissance of Jewish Music: Events and Figures, Eastern Europe and America.* New York, 1953.

Weizmann, Chaim. *Trial and Error: The Autobiography of Chaim Weizmann.* New York, 1949.

Wengeroff, Pauline. *Memoiren einer Grossmutter: Bilder aus der Kulturgeschichte der Juden Russlands im 19. Jahrhundert.* 2 vols. Berlin, 1922.

Wertheimer, Jack. "The Ausländerfrage at Institutions of Higher Learning—A Controversy over Russian-Jewish Students in Imperial Germany." *Leo Baeck Institute Year Book* 27 (1982): 187–215.

———. "Between Tsar and Kaiser: The Radicalization of Russian-Jewish University Students in Germany." *Leo Baeck Institute Year Book* 28 (1983): 329–49.

Wirtschafter, Elise Kimerling. *Social Identity in Imperial Russia.* De Kalb, Ill., 1997.

———. *Structures of Society: Imperial Russia's "People of Various Ranks."* De Kalb, Ill., 1994.

Wistrich, Robert. *The Jews of Vienna in the Age of Franz Joseph.* Oxford, 1989.

Wortman, Richard. *The Development of a Russian Legal Consciousness.* Chicago, 1976.

———. *Scenarios of Power: Myth and Ceremony in Russian Monarchy.* 2 vols. Princeton, 1995–2000.

Wynn, Charters. *Workers, Strikes, and Pogroms: The Donbass-Dnepr Bend in Late Imperial Russia, 1870–1905.* Princeton, 1992.

Yerushalmi, Yosef Hayim. *Zakhor: Jewish History and Jewish Memory.* New York, 1989.

Zamechaniia prisiazhnykh poverennykh okruga S.-Peterburgskoi Sudebnoi Palaty po proektu novoi redaktsii uchrezhdeniia sudebnykh ustanovlenii: Razdel desiatyi—o prisiazhnykh poverennykh, stat´i 394–478. St. Petersburg, 1901.

Zelnik, Reginald E. *Labor and Society in Tsarist Russia: The Factory Workers of St. Petersburg, 1855–1870.* Stanford, 1971.

Zernack, Klaus. "Im Sog der Ostseemetropole: St. Petersburg und seine Ausländer." *Jahrbücher für Geschichte Osteuropas* 35, no. 2 (1987): 232–40.

Zhurakovskii, K. S., and S. M. Rabinovich, eds. *Polnoe sobranie evreiskikh imen s napisaniem ikh na russkom i evreiskom iazykakh.* St. Petersburg, 1874.

Zipperstein, Steven. *Elusive Prophet: Ahad Ha'am and the Origins of Zionism.* Berkeley, 1993.

———. "Heresy, Apostasy, and the Transformation of Joseph Rabinovich." In Todd Endelman, ed., *Jewish Apostasy in the Modern World*, pp. 206–31. New York, 1987.

———. *Imagining Russian Jewry: Memory, History, Identity.* Seattle, 1999.

———. *The Jews of Odessa: A Cultural History, 1794–1881.* Stanford, 1986.

INDEX

Jewish Question and the Anti-Jewish Movement in Russia in 1881 and 1882, The (Levin), 194
Jewish socialists, 320, 332
Jewish students, 199–307; asking for rights to be extended to, 60–62; caricature of, *276*; complete segregation proposed for, 266; economics of higher education, 225–30; enrollment just prior to World War I, 307; and fraternities, 251–52; in German and Austrian universities, 252–53, 279n88, 280–81, 300; Gintsburg's alleged influence on, 136, 136n43, 265, 265n30; in incoming university classes, 1905 and 1906, *296*; increase in numbers, 1840–86, 217–19, *218*; as keeping their distance from local Jewish communities, 248; and Kishinev pogrom of 1903, 293; name changes by, 246–48; negative influence on Christian counterparts alleged, 259, 260–63; in non-Jewish educational system in 1886, 229, *229*; particularism emerging in, 284; and pogroms of 1881–82, 254–56; in pre-reform period, 207–14; quotas of 1887, 18, 257–307; reforms of November 1861 for, 62, 214–21; religious belief and observance of, 304, 304n173; as retreating from politics, 302–3; in revolutionary groups, 249, 264; in Revolution of 1905, 292–95; Russification and, 230–34; selective integration expanded to include, 170, 185; self-organized student groups, 248, 250–53, 282–85; and *The Smugglers,* 285–92; social background of, 303; statistical portrait of, 301–4; in the student subculture, 239–56; studying abroad, 279–81; unrest, 264, 284–85; women in higher education, 222–25; women students compared with, 306–7
Jewish women: as auditors at universities, 296; educational quotas for, 266–67; in employment in St. Petersburg, 109; in higher education, 222–25; literacy in, 112–13, *113*, 222; midwives, 108, 220; new state courts used by, 314; prostitutes, 103, 104, 104n62, 117; Russian language adopted in St. Petersburg, 110, *111*; school enrollment of girls in St. Petersburg, 112–13; selective integration affecting, 108–10; Society for the Spread

of Enlightenment funding elementary education for girls, 228; among students indicted in 1886, 264; studying abroad, 279
Jews: court Jews, 372; Gentile elites appealed to for protection by, 53–54; migration as fact of life for, 24–25; as "most literate people in Europe," 212; as pan-European minority, 4; on secular education, 202, 206–8, 221; sense of intellectual superiority of, 277; Western model of passage to modernity of, 6–7, 67, 75, 367–76. *See also* anti-Semitism; Eastern European Jews; Judaism; Western European Jews
Judaism: attempts to blend Christianity with, 374n15; in census data, 96–97; as foreign religion, 73; religious law (halakhah), 312; seen as incompatible with positive law, 208; Talmud, 33, 36, 60, 236; Torah, 206. *See also* Hasidism; Jews; Orthodoxy; Reform Judaism
judicial reform of 1864, 311–39; and historiography of Russian Jews, 315–20; and Jewish identity, 334–39; lawyers in struggle for emancipation, 320–34; proposals for scaling back, 346
juries, 313, 343, 343n12

Kafka, Franz, 379
kahal: Brafman on secret survival of, 175; compulsory military service and attacks on, 28; formal abolition of, 33–34, 154, 198, 374; loss of exclusive right to deal with the state, 38, 38n46; in Poland, 25; Russian state using, 26, 27, 34n28; Society for the Spread of Enlightenment compared with, 174
Kahan, Arcadius, 39, 67n69
Kamenets, 115n98, 116
Kaplanskaia, Elena, 250, 250n172
Karaites, 96n35, 374n15
Kasso, L. A., 298
kassy (mutual aid funds), 249–50
Katsenelenbogen, Shaul, 141, 142
Katz, Jacob, 338
Katzenelson, Berl, 199
Kavelin, Dmitrii, 240
Kazan: attacks on Jewish students in 1905, 293; Jewish lawyers and apprentice lawyers in judicial circuit, 1890 and 1895, *354*; postsecondary education for

STUDIES ON THE HISTORY OF SOCIETY AND CULTURE

Victoria E. Bonnell and Lynn Hunt, Editors

Compositor:	Integrated Composition Systems
Text:	Baskerville
Display:	Baskerville
Printer and binder:	Thomson-Shore